MISSOURI APPROVED JURY INSTRUCTIONS [MAI]

Prepared by the
MISSOURI SUPREME COURT COMMITTEE
ON
CIVIL JURY INSTRUCTIONS

Compiled and Edited by
STEPHEN H. RINGKAMP
St. Louis
Chair

RICHARD E. McLEOD
Kansas City
Reporter

SIXTH EDITION

WEST GROUP
A THOMSON COMPANY

Mat #40043962

CITE THIS BOOK

MAI ____ [20__

____]

West Group has created this publication to provide you with accurate and authoritative information concerning the subject matter covered. However, this publication was not necessarily prepared by persons licensed to practice law in a particular jurisdiction. West Group is not engaged in rendering legal or other professional advice, and this publication is not a substitute for the advice of an attorney. If you require legal or other expert advice, you should seek the services of a competent attorney or other professional.

MISSOURI SUPREME COURT COMMITTEE ON JURY INSTRUCTIONS

Stephen H. Ringkamp, Chair
The Hullverson Law Firm
1010 Market Street, Suite 1550
St. Louis, MO 63101–2091

Gary R. Cunningham
Cunningham, Harpool &
  Cordonnier, L.L.C.
3171 East Sunshine Street
P.O. Box 10306
Springfield, MO 65808

W. James Foland
Foland & Wickens P.C.
911 Main St., Suite 2900
Kansas City, MO 64105

Hamp Ford
Ford, Parshall & Baker L.L.C.
609 E. Walnut Street
Columbia, MO 65201

James P. Frickleton
Bartimus, Frickleton, Robertson &
  Obetz, P.C.
11150 Overbrook Rd., Suite 200
Zeawood, KS 66221

MISSOURI SUPREME COURT COMMITTEE ON JURY INSTRUCTIONS

Richard E. McLeod, Reporter
The McLeod Law Firm
1100 Main Street, Suite 2900
Kansas City, MO 64105

Gretchen Myers
Law Offices of Gretchen Myers, P.C.
1010 Market Street, Suite 650
St. Louis, MO 63101

Robert F. Ritter
Gray, Ritter & Graham, P.C.
701 Market Street, Suite 800
St. Louis, MO 63101

Stephen M. Schoenbeck
Lathrop & Gage, L.C.
1010 Market Sreet, Suite 1300
St. Louis, MO 63101

Dennis P. Wilson
Parson And Wilson, P.C.
7 North Elm Street
P.O. Box 428
Dexter, MO 63841

CURRENT AND PAST MAI
COMMITTEE MEMBERS

Name	City	Years of Service
Eugene E. Andereck	Trenton	1962–1976
Paul S. Brown	St. Louis	1981–1993
Judge James D. Clemens	St. Louis	1969–1983
John David Collins	Macon	1986–1987
Gary R. Cunningham	Springfield	1991–present
John S. Divilbiss	Columbia	1962–1967
William W. Evans	St. Louis	–1976
W. James Foland	Kansas City	1981–present
Hamp Ford	Columbia	1987–present
Max W. Foust	Kansas City	1983–1992
James P. Frickleton	Kansas City	1992–present
Reed O. Gentry	Kansas City	1962–1976
Horace S. Haseltine	Springfield	1962–1975
James W. Jeans	Kansas City	1962–1976
Judge William M. Kimberlin	Harrisonville	1962–1976
John H. Lashly	St. Louis	1962–
Nanette K. Laughrey	Columbia	1995–1997
Richard E. McLeod	Kansas City	1991–present
John C. Milholland	Harrisonville	1976–1995
John P. Montrey	St. Louis	1962–
Gretchen Godar Myers	St. Louis	1987–present
James E. Reeves	Caruthersville	1962–1975
Judge Eugene E. Reeves	Caruthersville	1986–1987
Kenneth H. Reid	Springfield	1976–1986
Stephen H. Ringkamp	St. Louis	1981–present
Robert F. Ritter	St. Louis	1988–present
Donald L. Schlapprizzi	St. Louis	1976–1988
Stephen M. Schoenbeck	St. Louis	1993–present
Jerome W. Seigfreid	Mexico	1978–1986
Judge Tom J. Stubbs	Kansas City	1962–1976
Elwood L. Thomas	Kansas City	1976–1991
Harry P. Thomson, Jr.	Kansas City	1962–1981
O. W. Watkins, Jr.	St. Joseph	1962–1976
Charles S. Wilcox	St. Joseph	–1976
Dennis P. Wilson	Dexter	1987–present

COORDINATED RESEARCH IN MISSOURI FROM WEST

MISSOURI PRACTICE SERIES™

Missouri Methods of Practice—Transaction Guide
Stinson, Mag & Fizzell, P.C.

Missouri Methods of Practice—Litigation Guide
Jeffrey A. Burns and Elwood L. Thomas

Missouri Probate Forms Manual
John A. Borron, Jr.

Missouri Probate Code Manual
Francis M. Hanna

Missouri Probate and Surrogate Laws Manual
John A. Borron, Jr.

Missouri Probate Law and Practice
John A. Borron, Jr.

Missouri Legal Forms
Eric Ziegenhorn and M. Elizabeth Fast

Missouri Procedural Forms
Thomas P. Dvorak and James D. Burlison

Missouri Jurisdiction, Venue, and Limitations
Steven A. Katz

Missouri Uniform Commercial Code Forms
William H. Henning

Missouri Civil Rules Practice
Mary Coffey, Steven A. Katz, Daniel P. Card II,
Thomas M. Blumenthal, and Richard L. Schnake

Missouri Real Estate Law—Transactions and Disputes
Theodore H. Hellmuth

Missouri Criminal Practice and Procedure
William A. Knox

Missouri Administrative Practice and Procedure
Alfred S. Neely IV

Missouri Family Law
Jack Cochran and Nancy A. Beardsley

Missouri Evidence
William A. Schroeder

VII

COORDINATED RESEARCH FROM WEST

Missouri Appellate Practice
Daniel P. Card II and Alan E. Freed

Missouri Business Organizations
Philip G. Louis, Jr.

Missouri Criminal Practice Forms
Donald L. Wolff and Susan Sherberg Kister

Missouri Criminal Practice Handbook
Robert H. Dierker

Missouri Workers' Compensation Law and Practice
B. Michael Korte

Missouri Insurance Law and Practice
Almon H. Maus

Missouri Civil Rules Handbook
Douglas R. Sprong and Jeffrey T. McPherson

Missouri Criminal Law
Robert H. Dierker

Courtroom Handbook on Missouri Evidence
William A. Schroeder

Missouri Personal Injury and Torts Handbook
Robert H. Dierker and Richard J. Mehan

Missouri Contracts, Equity, and Statutory Actions Handbook
Robert H. Dierker and Richard J. Mehan

Missouri Approved Jury Instructions—Civil (MAI)
Missouri Supreme Court Committee on Jury Instructions
[also available in computer disk]

Vernon's Annotated Missouri Statutes

Missouri Cases

Missouri Court Rules

Missouri Family Law

Vernon's Annotated Missouri Rules

Missouri Digest

Missouri Law Finder

Westlaw®

COORDINATED RESEARCH FROM WEST

WIN®

WESTCheck® and WESTMATE®

WESTfax®

WestDoc

West CD–ROM Libraries™

KeyCiteSM

To order any of these Missouri practice tools, call your West Representative or 1–800–344–5009 (FAX 1–800–213–2323).

If you have research questions concerning Westlaw or West Publications, call West's Reference Attorneys at 1–800–733–2889.

WESTLAW® ELECTRONIC RESEARCH GUIDE

Westlaw, Computer–Assisted Legal Research

Westlaw is part of the research system provided by West Group. With Westlaw, you find the same quality and integrity that you have come to expect from West Group's books. For the most current and comprehensive legal research, combine the strengths of West Group's books and Westlaw.

Westlaw Adds to Your Library

Whether you wish to expand or update your research, Westlaw can help. For instance, Westlaw is the most current source for case law, including slip opinions and unreported decisions. In addition to case law, the online availability of statutes, statutory indexes, legislation, court rules and orders, administrative materials, looseleaf publications, texts, periodicals, news and business information makes Westlaw an important asset to any library. Check the online Westlaw Directory or the print Westlaw Database Directory for a list of available databases and services. The following is a brief description of some of the capabilities that Westlaw offers.

Natural Language Searching

You can search most Westlaw databases using WIN®, the revolutionary Natural Language search method. As an alternative to formulating a query using terms and connectors, WIN allows you to simply enter a description of your research issue in plain English:

> What is the government's obligation to warn military personnel of the danger of past exposure to radiation?

Westlaw then retrieves the set of documents that have the highest statistical likelihood of matching your description.

Retrieving a Specific Document

When you know the citation to a case or statute that is not in your library, use the Find service to retrieve the document on Westlaw. Access Find and type a citation like the following:

> 181 ne2d 520
> in st 27–1–12–1

Updating Your Research

You can use Westlaw to update your research in many ways:

- Retrieve cases citing a particular statute.

- Update a state or federal statute by accessing the Update service from the displayed statute using the Jump marker.

- Retrieve newly enacted legislation by searching in the appropriate legislative service database.

- Retrieve cases not yet reported by searching in case law databases.

- Read the latest U.S. Supreme Court opinions within an hour of their release.

- Update West Digests by searching with topic and key numbers.

Determining Case History and Retrieving Cited Cases

KeyCite^{SM}, the new citation research service developed by West Group and made available through the Westlaw computer-assisted legal research service, integrates all the case law on Westlaw, giving you the power to

- trace the history of a case;

- retrieve a list of all cases that cite to a case; and

- track legal issues in a case.

Citing references from the extensive library of secondary sources on Westlaw, such as ALR® annotations and law review articles, are covered by KeyCite as well. You can use these citing references to find case discussions by legal experts.

Now, in this one service on Westlaw, you receive

- the case-verification functions of Insta–Cite®; and

- the currentness of QuickCite®.

In addition, KeyCite is completely integrated with West Group's Key Number System so that it provides the tools for navigating the case law databases on Westlaw. Only KeyCite combines the up-to-the-minute case-verification functions of an online citator service with the case-finding tools needed to find relevant case law.

Additional Information

For more detailed information or assistance, contact your Westlaw account representative or call 1–800–REF–ATTY (1–800–733–2889).

MISSOURI APPROVED JURY INSTRUCTIONS FORMS ON DISK™

The **Forms on Disk**™ which accompany the *Missouri Approved Jury Instructions, Sixth Edition,* provide instant access to Corel© WordPerfect© versions of most of the instructions included in this edition. These electronic forms will save you hours of time drafting jury instructions. Each electronic form includes text and punctuation identical to the forms in this volume. The electronic forms can be loaded into your word processing software and formatted to match the document style of your law firm. These electronic forms become templates for you to use over and over without having to retype them each time.

The **Forms on Disk**™ include textual forms displayed in both the main bound volume and its updating pocket part.

SUMMARY OF CONTENTS

SUMMARY OF CONTENTS

TABLE OF INSTRUCTIONS

TABLE OF INSTRUCTIONS

DAMAGES

4.00

DAMAGES—GENERAL

5.00

DAMAGES—WRONGFUL DEATH

TABLE OF INSTRUCTIONS

TABLE OF INSTRUCTIONS

DEFINITIONS

11.00

DEFINITIONS—NEGLIGENCE

12.00

DEFINITIONS—UNINSURED MOTOR VEHICLE

13.00

DEFINITIONS—AGENCY

TABLE OF INSTRUCTIONS

14.00

DEFINITIONS—YIELD THE RIGHT–OF–WAY

15.00

DEFINITIONS—WILL CONTEST

16.00

DEFINITIONS—MISCELLANEOUS

TABLE OF INSTRUCTIONS

PLAINTIFF VERDICT DIRECTING INSTRUCTIONS

17.00

VERDICT DIRECTING—MOTOR VEHICLES

TABLE OF INSTRUCTIONS

18.00

VERDICT DIRECTING—AGENCY IN ISSUE

19.00

VERDICT DIRECTING MODIFICATION

20.00

VERDICT DIRECTING—WRONGFUL DEATH

21.00

ACTIONS AGAINST HEALTH CARE PROVIDERS

TABLE OF INSTRUCTIONS

TABLE OF INSTRUCTIONS

Page

24.00

VERDICT DIRECTING—FEDERAL EMPLOYERS' LIABILITY ACT

25.00

VERDICT DIRECTING—BREACH OF WARRANTY
AND PRODUCT LIABILITY

TABLE OF INSTRUCTIONS

TABLE OF INSTRUCTIONS

TABLE OF INSTRUCTIONS

32.00

AFFIRMATIVE DEFENSES

TABLE OF INSTRUCTIONS

33.00

CONVERSE INSTRUCTIONS

TABLE OF INSTRUCTIONS

34.00

WITHDRAWAL INSTRUCTIONS

TABLE OF INSTRUCTIONS

TABLE OF INSTRUCTIONS

36.00

FORMS OF VERDICT

TABLE OF INSTRUCTIONS

37.00

COMPARATIVE FAULT

TABLE OF INSTRUCTIONS

TABLE OF EFFECTIVE DATES OF MISSOURI APPROVED JURY INSTRUCTIONS [p. 795]

SUPREME COURT OF MISSOURI

en banc

April 8, 2002

ORDER

The forms of Jury Instructions, Notes on Use, and Committee Comments, as finally submitted to the Court by the Committee on Jury Instructions as set forth on pages 1 through 794 of the attached volume entitled Missouri Approved Jury Instructions, (MAI), Sixth Edition, published by West Group, Eagan, Minnesota, copyright 2002, are approved and hereby adopted by the Court.

The aforesaid forms must be used on and after January 1, 2003, and may be used prior thereto without such use being presumed to be error.

Day – to – Day

STEPHEN N. LIMBAUGH, JR.
Chief Justice

*

IN THE SUPREME COURT OF MISSOURI
EN BANC

Tuesday, March 6, 1962

Re: Appointment of Supreme Court Committee on Jury Instructions

ORDER

Acting on a resolution adopted by the Board of Governors of the Missouri Bar and a resolution adopted at the 1961 annual meeting of the Missouri Bar, the Court hereby appoints a committee to study the problem of jury instructions and to advise the Court from time to time of the Committee's recommendations with respect thereto. The Committee is directed to consider means for simplification of instructions to juries including consideration of whether and to what extent standardized or pattern instructions might be used for this purpose.

The Committee is as follows:

JUDGE TOM J. STUBBS, Chairman, Kansas City
PROFESSOR JOHN S. DIVILBISS, Reporter
Columbia

JUDGE WILLIAM M. KIMBERLIN	—	Harrisonville
EUGENE E. ANDERECK	—	Trenton
REED O. GENTRY	—	Kansas City
HORACE S. HASELTINE	—	Springfield
JAMES W. JEANS	—	St. Louis
JOHN H. LASHLY	—	St. Louis
JOHN P. MONTREY	—	St. Louis
JAMES E. REEVES	—	Caruthersville
HARRY P. THOMSON, JR.	—	Kansas City
O.W. WATKINS, JR.	—	St. Joseph

The above are appointed to serve as the "Supreme Court Committee on Jury Instructions" until June 30, 1964 and until their successors are appointed.

The Committee may recommend to this Court the appointment of such number of Associate Members as the Committee deems desirable.

/s/ Henry J. Westhues
HENRY J. WESTHUES, Chief Justice

*

1963 REPORT TO MISSOURI SUPREME COURT

The Supreme Court Committee on Jury Instructions having completed a portion of its work submits this report of its activities and recommendations.

GENERAL APPROACH

The Court's order appointing this Committee directed what measures be considered for simplifying instructions. This has been a primary goal. These instructions were written with a view to what would be easily understood by the average juror. We also recognize that sheer volume of words may itself be confusing to a juror, so we departed from our prolix past and cut the instructions to bare essentials. This was done, we believe, without any sacrifice of meaning or clarity and without any change of substantive law.

Each pattern instruction was also subjected to these four tests:

(1) Is it a correct statement of law?

(2) Is it a complete statement?

(3) Is it concise?

(4) Is it stated in language the average juror can understand?

Instructions are intended to inform the jury of the law and what their decisions must be based on that law. Too often instructions have served more -as written arguments so that the jury reads a page of plaintiff's arguments and then a page of defendant's arguments. The instructions are the court's and the jury should so understand. The Committee has tried to write these instructions without the partisan flavor common in our present system.

MAJOR CHANGES

Method of Drafting

1. *Submitting Ultimate Issues*

Justice Cardozo once wrote that too much detail obscures rather than clarifies. His observation is demonstrated by a good many verdict directing instructions which, playing it safe, hypothesize every conceivable fact. A good many such hypothesizations are unnecessary, even under our existing system, but the lawyer's fears if not commendable are at least understandable. Lawyers are now required to chart a course between the Scylla of inadequate fact hypothesization and the Charybdis of commenting on the evidence. The legal coast is littered with the wreckage of cases navigated by those who could not find this elusive channel.

The origin of our present requirement is somewhat obscure. Instructions in early Missouri cases contained little recitation of evidentiary facts, but somehow the idea developed and gradually grew to its present proportions. Current decisions express the fear that unless evidentiary facts are hyphothesized the jury may reach a conclusion without having gone through the proper preliminary mental processes. For example, hypothesizing excessive speed, negligence, causation and damage is not now adequate. Particular evidentiary facts indicating excessive speed must now be hypothesized and found true. Only then can the jury go to the next plateau and decide whether these evidentiary facts demonstrate excessive speed. The Committee believes that if a jury is so confused as to find excessive speed while at the same time believing evidence of proper speed, that jury will not be helped by a long recitation of evidentiary facts.

The recommended change is not without precedent. The courts currently approve humanitarian instructions which submit ultimate issues without evidentiary detail. Hypothesizing failure to keep a lookout which would have averted a collision is also accepted as an adequate submission although barren of evidentiary detail. There is no indication that juries so instructed have been handicapped by the brevity. In these cases evidentiary detail has simply been left to argument, and this is where it belongs.

Verdict directing instructions reduced to ultimate issues are easier for the jury to read and understand and they can express the law as accurately as our current evidentiary submissions. The Committee recommends that the ultimate issue hypothesization now permitted in humanitarian and lookout cases be extended to other verdict directing instructions.

2. *Submitting Burden of Proof*

Every court in the country has labored over the problem of simply and accurately telling the jury what is meant by burden of proof. To begin with the word "proof" has a myriad of meanings to laymen. To the scientist or engineer it may mean something approaching universal certainty. To the housewife it may be something more akin to intuition. The relative nature of "proof" is perhaps best understood by the drinker.

The Committee first considered adopting the short form burden of proof currently approved by this Court. This met with three objections. First, the words "preponderance" and "greater weight" may, without some further explanation, be understood as requiring proof which removes all doubt. After studying the decisions of nearly every court in the country we concluded that attempts to explain universally add to the confusion. Second, an integral part of our present system is a kind of a "converse" burden of proof instruction given by the plaintiff telling the jury that if they believe "from the greater weight of the credible evidence the propositions and issues to be as submitted (in plaintiffs verdict directing instruction)" then the burden of proof has been carried. So on one hand the burden of proof is made to look formidable and on the next page comparatively easy. This probably confuses. Third, Missouri's existing explanation that the "preponderance" of the evidence means "evidence which you think is more worthy of belief than that offered in opposition thereto" is not accurate. A defendant may offer no evidence in opposition to plaintiff's case, thus making plaintiffs evidence more worthy of belief than that offered in opposition. But if the jury does not accept plaintiff's evidence, plaintiff has not carried his burden of proof. Even if defendant offers some evidence, plaintiff's case is not established by simply offering testimony which is more believable than defendant's. The jury may disbelieve both versions, and in such case plaintiff should lose.

Professor Wigmore said: "There is no measure of the weight of evidence (unless the witnesses on evidential facts are counted) other than the *feeling of probability* which it engenders."

With this view in mind the Committee considered an instruction telling the jury that plaintiff carried his burden if the jury believed his story was "more probably true than not true." Again we ran into the problem that these words might be misunderstood as implying a loose standard of proof not intended.

The Committee finally concluded that the word "believe" most accurately expresses that degree of conviction necessary to sustain the burden of proof. We think the term neither implies an unduly heavy burden nor an improperly loose standard. Each verdict directing instruction begins with a statement that the verdict shall be for a named party if the jury believes certain hypothesized facts. To meet the problem of correctly placing the risk of non-persuasion, the jury is instructed that if it is unable to form a belief on a proposition, that proposition fails.

3. *Submitting in the Conjunctive*

Plaintiffs and defendants, when in doubt as to whether their evidence supported each theory of recovery or defense, have often submitted all such theories in the conjunctive. This practice enabled them, in most cases, to avoid reversible error when it developed that one or more of their theories was not supported by the evidence.

The Committee believes that the jury should not be instructed on a theory of recovery or defense not supported by the evidence, and that any such submission, whether in the conjunctive or disjunctive, should be reversible error. A theory of recovery or defense should not be submitted unless it can stand alone. The present practice has been a crutch which has done little but confuse by presenting imaginary issues for the jury's determination.

The Committee recognizes that some instructions will still have several elements which must be submitted in the conjunctive, but these will be in support of a single theory of recovery or defense.

4. *Use of Affirmative Language*

The Committee believes that instructions should tell the jury what they should do rather than what they should not do. Negative language is generally argumentative and does little to educate the jury as to the law. The Committee has departed from this policy in only one case. Wrongful death damage instructions tell the jury that grief is not to be considered. Grief is the most obvious consequence of a loved one's death. It is the pain most easily understood. Plaintiffs grief is apt to be so vivid in the jurors' minds that the limiting words "measured in money" will be overlooked or misinterpreted. For this reason grief is expressly withdrawn as an element of damages in death actions.

Method of Submission

The Committee recommends that the jury be instructed before the trial begins about its duty to determine the facts solely from the evidence, how it shall determine the believability of evidence, and its obligation to give each party fair and impartial consideration without sympathy or prejudice. The Committee believes that it is better to draw the jury's attention to these matters before the trial rather than waiting until after the jurors may have reached a decision.

As each jury may have some neophytes, the recommended pretrial instruction will explain the trial sequence and the effect of objections, rulings and arguments.

The Committee recognizes that some cases may require additional cautionary instructions, but the instruction proposed should suffice in the majority of cases. Some judges decline to give any cautionary instructions, and since their use is discretionary, the refusal is not reversible error. Other judges have sometimes given a handful for each side and unduly complicated the jury's work. The instruction proposed should eliminate both evils.

Other Changes

1. *Unavoidable Accident Instructions*

About 34 years ago the Missouri Supreme Court said: "[t]he word 'accident' in popular acceptation and sometimes in law, may denote an occurrence arising without intent or design or even from the carelessness of man; but in the law of negligence it signifies an event resulting in damage or injury, proceeding from an unknown cause or from a known cause without human agency or without human fault."

Unfortunately the same decision suggested that an unavoidable accident instruction may on occasion be proper. This was all the encouragement needed. Bold counsel, enchanted with the patently misleading language of the unavoidable accident instruction, have periodically tried to make it fit their cases. Their success is best described by a recent Supreme Court decision which said "[O]ur research has disclosed no case [in the past 34 years] in which an accident instruction has been approved, and we find it difficult to conceive of a factual situation in which an accident instruction may properly be given under the rule there set out, notwithstanding the language indicating that such situations could exist."

The Committee heartily agrees with this. In cases where the evidence shows that the cause of the casualty is unknown, thus apparently authorizing an accident instruction, defendants will probably be entitled to directed verdicts.

Unless this instruction is given a formal burial, it will periodically stalk the courtroom contaminating every case it touches. The services should not be delayed.

2. *Sole Cause Instructions*

Sole cause instructions have been used primarily in the field of humanitarian negligence. They have often improperly injected plaintiff's contributory negligence into the case.

The Committee recommends that no verdict instruction be given on behalf of the defendant which hypothesizes that the conduct of one other than defendant was the sole cause of the occurrence. There are three reasons for this recommendation. These are: (1) The negligence of one other than defendant is of no consequence and reference thereto is confusing and misleading. (2) The prescribed converse instruction forms adequately present this defense. (3) Such instructions require the recitation of detailed evidentiary facts. As mentioned above, the Committee recommends that this practice no longer be permitted in any instruction.

MANDATORY USE OF APPROVED INSTRUCTIONS

The Committee proposes that the Supreme Court adopt the recommended rules requiring that when an approved instruction is applicable it must be given to the exclusion of any other instruction on the same subject.

There are hundreds of currently acceptable instructions which use language more favorable to one side or the other than the proposed instructions. If counsel are permitted to "improve" the approved instructions, even within the confines of specific precedents, the value of these instructions will be lost. Each such "improvement" by one counsel will prompt an offsetting "improvement" by his opponent and after a while the court will not be able to find the original with a divining rod.

CONCLUSION

The present system of instructing jurors has met with two major criticisms. First, the instructions are so complex, detailed and argumentative that jurors have trouble understanding them. Second, competent lawyers and judges have too much difficulty determining what instructions are free from error. The Committee believes that the proposed instructions will largely eliminate both criticisms without changing the substantive law, and the Committee unanimously recommends their adoption.

Respectfully, submitted,

SUPREME COURT COMMITTEE ON JURY INSTRUCTIONS

TOM J. STUBBS, Chairman
JOHN S. DIVILBISS, Reporter
EUGENE E. ANDERECK, Member
REED O. GENTRY, Member
HORACE S. HASELTINE, Member
JAMES W. JEANS, Member
WILLIAM M. KIMBERLIN, Member
JOHN H. LASHLY, Member
JOHN P. MONTREY, Member
JAMES E. REEVES, Member
HARRY P. THOMSON, JR., Member
O.W. WATKINS, JR., Member

RULE 70—INSTRUCTIONS

RULE 70. INSTRUCTIONS

70.01 APPROVAL OF INSTRUCTIONS—EFFECTIVE DATE—PUBLICATION PROCEDURE

Approval of instructions in civil actions will be made by order of this court. The caption of the approved instructions shall state the effective date. The Missouri Bar is directed to publish such approved instructions and notes on use or committee notes as this court authorizes, together with the date upon which the use thereof shall be required.

RULE 70.02 INSTRUCTIONS TO JURIES

(a) Requests for Instructions. Any party may, and a party with the burden of proof on an issue shall, submit written requests for instructions on the law applicable to the issues. Requests shall be submitted prior to an instruction conference or at such time as the court directs. A party need not request a converse instruction until the court has indicated the verdict directing instruction expected to be given. The court may give instructions without requests of counsel. All instructions shall be submitted in writing and shall be given or refused by the court according to the law and the evidence in the case. Each instruction shall be submitted with an original and one copy for the court and one copy for each party. Each copy shall indicate whether it was prepared at the court's direction or by which party it was tendered and shall contain a notation as follows:

"MAI No. ___" or "MAI No. ____ modified" or "Not in MAI" as the case may be.

(b) Form of Instructions. Whenever Missouri Approved Instructions contains an instruction applicable in a particular case that the appropriate party requests or the court decides to submit, such instruction shall be given to the exclusion of any other instructions on the same subject. Where an MAI must be modified to fairly submit the issues in a particular case, or where there is no applicable MAI so that an instruction not in MAI must be given, then such modifications or such instructions shall be simple, brief, impartial, free from argument, and shall not submit to the jury or require findings of detailed evidentiary facts.

(c) Violation of Rule—Effect. The giving of an instruction in violation of the provisions of this Rule 70.02 shall constitute error, its prejudicial effect to be judicially determined, provided that objection has been timely made pursuant to Rule 70.03.

(d) Converse Instruction—Effect of Requesting. The request of a converse instruction shall not be deemed to waive any objection to the instruction conversed.

(e) Instructions Conference and Record. The court shall hold an instructions conference with counsel to determine the instructions to be given. The court shall inform counsel as to the instructions that are to be given prior to the time they are delivered to the jury. All instructions refused and all instructions given, including a record of who tendered them, shall be kept as a part of a record in the case. An opportunity shall be given for counsel to make objections on the record, out of the hearing of the jury, before the jury retires to deliberate.

(f) Instructions—How and When Given. After a jury has been sworn to try a case but before opening statements, the court shall read to the jury Missouri Approved Instructions 2.01, which shall be marked and given to the jury along with the other instructions at the close of the case but shall not be reread by the court. With agreement of all parties, the court may give such other preliminary instructions during the trial as will assist the jury in understanding its role or the issues in the case. Agreement is not required for cautionary or withdrawal instructions during the trial. Final instructions in the case, submitting the law applicable to the case, ordinarily should be given prior to final arguments. Instructions that are to be given shall be consecutively numbered and all shall be given as instructions of the court. Except where otherwise provided in Missouri Approved Instructions, they shall be given in such order as the court shall deem advisable. The final instructions on the law governing the case shall be read to the jury by the court and provided to the jury in writing.

RULE 70.03 OBJECTIONS TO INSTRUCTIONS

Counsel shall make specific objections to instructions considered erroneous. No party may assign as error the giving or failure to give instructions unless that party objects thereto before the jury retires to consider its verdict, stating distinctly the matter objected to and the grounds of the objection. Counsel need not repeat objections already made on the record prior to delivery of the instructions. The objections must also be raised in the motion for new trial in accordance with Rule 78.07.

HOW TO USE THIS BOOK

Committee Comment (1996 Revision)

FIRST, KNOW RULES OF PROCEDURE 70 AND 71

Before you can use this book you must understand Civil Rule 70 which prescribes procedure for instructing civil juries and Rule 71 which limits the verdicts which may be returned by civil juries. The approved instructions and forms of verdict in this book are drafted according to and are extensions of that procedural law.

It should be obvious that if you don't know the procedural law which spawns the approved instructions, you will not use this book well and accurately.

After more than a decade of reversals for jury instruction errors at an intolerable rate and at the urging of the bar, the supreme court created this committee charged to study civil jury instructions and to report to and advise the court from time to time. The committee's 1963 report was adopted by the court and resulted in Rule 70 which requires the use of standardized civil jury instructions called MAI.

The committee's 1963 report is included in this book for its help in illustrating the more terse language of Rule 70. The report promulgated four practice standards for drafting an instruction in the mandatory form of an MAI. To those standards, two caveats have been added:

    (1) Is it a complete statement of law?

    (2) Is it a complete statement?

    (3) Is it concise?

    (4) Is it stated in language the average juror can understand?

CAVEATS:

    (5) Do not attempt to make your not-in-MAI instruction argue your position. Civil Rule 70.02(b).

    (6) Do not include abstract statements of law. Your verdict directing instruction must follow the form of MAI which directs the jury to make a certain finding required by unstated law if the propositions of fact are believed.

OLD PRINCIPLES OF JURY INSTRUCTION ARE STILL IN FORCE

MAI has changed only the method of instruction and not the principles. An instruction must be a correct statement of the law. That is an old principle which remains unchanged. The statement of law is made differently than it was before. For illustration, MAI 17.01 instructs on the law which requires traffic lights to be obeyed, "Your verdict must be for . . . if you believe: First defendant violated the traffic signal, and . . . ." Before MAI, the court would have said by instruction, "you are instructed that under the law the defendant had a duty to observe and obey the traffic control lights at the intersection of . . . ." The rule of law submitted remains the same; its submission is made differently.

All of the old principles of jury instruction (unless expressly changed by a case decision, rule of procedure or statute) remain the same. It remains error to submit a theory which is not pleaded or supported by substantial evidence. Each of the instructions remains as a part of the single charge. It is still error to assume a disputed fact. Principles relating to "invited error" and "common error" are still applicable. The principles of instruction have not been changed. It is the methods of applying those principles of instruction which have been changed by the adoption of MAI.

NOTES ON USE, COMMITTEE COMMENTS, AND ANNOTATIONS

The Notes on Use following each instruction in this book dictate the circumstances under which the instruction may be used. These must be followed.

The Committee Comments are intended to show the source of the approved instructions and to aid lawyers in finding some of the authorities relevant to the instruction.

The annotations are brief synopses of cases dealing with the specific instruction in question to assist your research. Inasmuch as many of the MAIs have been revised, be certain the case cited is applicable to the existing instruction.

KNOW THE APPLICABLE SUBSTANTIVE LAW

Verdict directing MAIs hypothesize propositions of fact to be found or rejected by the jury. They are the ultimate facts which support the submitted claim or defense. The theory of claim or defense is based on the applicable law.

Since the trial court will decide the law by its selection of instructions, it is essential for you, the lawyer, to research and be familiar with the law. It is your task to prepare the instructions correctly. If the correct instruction is not prepared, you have failed your task. You cannot prepare the correct instructions unless you know the applicable law.

SELECT THE APPROPRIATE INSTRUCTION

When you know the law which applies to your case or defense, you will find it relatively simple in most cases to select the appropriate verdict directing instruction. If your claim is for work and labor and you can prove no express contract, your theory may be quantum meruit. It is obvious that you should look for a quantum meruit form and bypass any express contract instruction.

When you are making your selections, you are applying the applicable law. When the trial judge decides to give or to refuse instructions, the court is deciding which is applicable law. Know your law.

MODIFICATIONS AND WHEN NO APPLICABLE INSTRUCTION IS IN THE BOOK

You may have the ability to improve an instruction in MAI but you do not have the authority to do it. Do not do it. The use of a provided MAI is mandatory. If you think the change of a word or phrase will make it a better instruction, do not do it. You are falling into error if you do.

Changes in the law may render an applicable MAI instruction a misstatement of then current law. If so, counsel and the trial judge should revise or rewrite the MAI instruction to make it consistent with then current law. A thorough record, including citations to the new law, should be included to alert appellate courts to the reason for the deviation from an apparently applicable MAI instruction.

A modification which is necessary to make a provided MAI fit the facts of your case, however, is not only permissible but is required.

If it is plain from the pleadings, trial or an express admission that an essential ultimate fact element is not in issue, the applicable MAI may be modified by deletion of that element.

By the same token, it may be necessary to modify an instruction to submit an issue which is in dispute in your case but which usually is not disputed and thus is not submitted by the approved MAI. For example, none of the motor vehicle verdict directors hypothesize that the defendant was driving the vehicle at the time of the collision because this matter usually is not in dispute. However, in a hit-and-run situation, where defendant denies he was driving the vehicle that hit plaintiff, the verdict director must be modified to include the fact issue.

When you are sure that an approved instruction does not fit your case precisely but one or more instructions are close to it, modifications must be made. Occasionally the modification will be made by incorporating part of another MAI. For instance, when the provided MAI hypothesizes that the defendant's negligence directly resulted in damage to the plaintiff, this would not be a sufficiently clear statement in a consortium case where the defendant's negligence caused injury to plaintiffs spouse, which in turn damaged plaintiff. A modification is required to clarify, to bridge the reasoning gap between defendant's negligence and the damage to plaintiff who might not even have been present at the casualty.

MAI 31.04 is the verdict directing instruction to use to submit this additional element of damage to the spouse of the injured plaintiff.

If you think an MAI should be modified to submit another issue of fact, be very careful to ascertain that the issue you propose to add is actually in issue and that it is an essential ultimate fact. If it is not, you run afoul of the Civil Rule 70.02 requirements for brevity and freedom from submission of detailed evidentiary fact.

When there is no MAI which is usable, even with modification, then you must undertake for yourself the task which is routinely performed by the MAI committee. You must research the law, determine the essential, ultimate facts which are in dispute and draft your own instruction, following the principles of the committee's 1963 original report to the supreme court and Civil Rule 70.02. Your not-in-MAI drafting is required to be in the form of the MAIs.

DEFINITIONS, MANDATORY OR PERMISSIBLE

In practice, some confusion has arisen concerning definitions. Included in this book are indications in the Notes on Use for each instruction when it contains a term or phrase which must be defined. The definitions are necessary to interpret a legal term for a lay jury and they are utilized in accord with standard No. 4 of the 1963 report to the Supreme Court:

(4) Is it stated in language the average juror can understand?

Thus, when it is indicated that a term or phrase must be defined, it is error to omit the provided definition.

If you use a term not having an MAI definition which you believe should be defined, prepare a definition and tender it to the trial judge. Whether the judge gives a definition instruction which is not mandatory is largely discretionary. Giving a definition of an MAI instruction term obtained from an approved instruction is a modification of the instruction and is subject to all of the standards of modification.

OTHER MANDATORY INSTRUCTIONS

There are mandatory instructions which must be given in every case. In addition each case will dictate on its own facts that there are additional mandatory instructions required in that particular case. Mandatory instructions are indicated throughout this book. A detailed discussion of mandatory instructions is included in the reprinted article included in this book, "Why and How To Instruct a Jury."

CONVERSE INSTRUCTIONS

In accord with Civil Rule 70.02(d), converse instructions are provided. Before you submit converse instructions you should read and understand MAI 33.01 CONVERSE INSTRUCTIONS—GENERAL COMMENT.

AFFIRMATIVE DEFENSES

If a complete affirmative defense, such as a release, is submitted, the verdict directing instruction must be modified by the addition of an affirmative defense "tail" which references the affirmative defense instruction. See the bracketed "tail" to MAI 17.01 and other verdict directing instructions. Such a "tail" should also be used if there is a defense to an affirmative defense. See MAI 32.21 and 32.22.

USE OF TERMS PLAINTIFF AND DEFENDANT; COUNTERCLAIMS, CROSSCLAIMS AND OTHER CLAIMS

To keep the Missouri Approved Instructions as simple as possible, some were prepared in terms of a single male plaintiff and a single male defendant. Obviously pronoun modifications will be needed for multiple parties, corporations and females. In addition, in cases which submit more than one claim [whether several claims by plaintiffs, counterclaims, crossclaims or third party claims] it may be necessary to use a short identifying term, "John Brown's claim for damages," "Mary Brown's claim for loss of services," and the like.

The first two editions of MAI used the formalistic identifying phrases, "for plaintiff on Count I," "for plaintiff on Count II." Those are discarded in favor of the more helpful, short descriptions of the nature of the claim being decided.

The Notes on Use and Committee's Comment to each instruction are instructive in this regard.

ROLE OF THE TRIAL JUDGE

The trial judge has the duty of deciding the issues of law in every case. In jury instruction, the decision to give or refuse any instruction is a decision of an issue of law. The importance of the decisional duty is made to appear, for example, in the rear end collision submissions.

Therefore, each instruction given or refused reflects the trial judge's performance and it is a judicial duty to give a complete charge to the jury. Civil Rule 70.02 reflects that nondelegable duty in its reference to identifying instructions prepared "at the court's direction." That is a very real and vital duty in the administration of justice and no trial judge can abdicate judicial responsibilities to the discretion of the trial lawyers who prepare the instructions. No judge should fail in this duty upon the premise that if the lawyers want to create error they are free to do so.

Some of the instructions and the substantive law they reflect impose important duties on the trial judge in writing the judgment after return and acceptance of the jury's verdicts. Notable in this regard are the apportionment of fault judgments. The trial judge may call freely upon the assistance of the trial lawyers but ultimately it is the duty of the judge and the judge may not escape it.

The tasks of the trial judge are eased somewhat in the verdict forms now employed. A great deal of the chance of scrivener error in the jury room is eliminated by having the verdict forms prepared in advance for the jury so that the jury now fills in the blanks. The requirement of a separate prepared verdict form for each packaged submission of a claim also helps eliminate the overlooked claim and the failure of the verdict of the jury to decide the whole case.

As is noted above, the method for giving the jury its instructions on the law is subtle. It is in the form of a direction of legal result from stated findings. The trial court does not tell the jury why such a result is dictated. In pre-MAI jury instructions, the legal explanations for the results were freely sprinkled throughout instructions by argumentative statements of rules of law and pure argument, "even though," "the mere fact," "you are instructed the defendant had a duty," and so on *ad infinitum*. Such statements of reasons being no longer permitted in instructions, the duty of advocacy has been returned to the argument of the trial lawyers.

Each trial judge should recognize the CHANGE and adjust his views and rulings on jury arguments accordingly. Lawyers must leave their argument of the reasons for actions and results in their place, in the jury arguments and not in the instructions. Thus, the lawyer's argumentative statements that under the law my client had a right to believe or a right to rely or a right to proceed or any of the multitude of rights or duties are entirely proper so long as he does not misstate the law. It now is in the jury arguments that the jury gets its only lucid insight into why it is given any particular instruction.

Because argument of law is eliminated from the instructions and is argued in summation, the trial judge is required to be alert and judgmental during the entire course of jury arguments for misstatements of the law. The catch-all observation that the jury will remember the instructions and evidence will not suffice if the argument includes a misstatement of law. The corollary is that an erroneous denial of the trial lawyer's right to argue an applicable rule of law may also be a denial of a fair trial.

HOW TO USE THIS BOOK

In short, MAI has taken advocacy out of the instructions and re-turned it to the trial lawyers. The case is no longer fully argued when the instructions are read. It is argued in the jury arguments and the trial judge's function of deciding the issues of law continues throughout the arguments.

No system of jury instruction will work without the active supervising control of the most important individual in a jury trial, an alert trial judge, and that is particularly true in the use of MAI.

WHY AND HOW TO INSTRUCT A JURY

By John C. Milholland[1]

All editions of MAI have included "How to Use This Book", a section written for trial judges and lawyers who are experienced in jury instructions. But, believing also that an "instruction book" should be as helpful as possible, committee assignment was made to draft "Why and How to Instruct a Jury", an article in the nature of a primer or guide for instructing civil juries, originally published both in the Journal of the Missouri Bar and in the Third Edition of the MAI. It was not intended to be legal authority to support adversary positions. It was intended to be a practical teaching tool, to be informative. This revision of that primer carries no committee stamp of approval and it does not carry the endorsement of the Supreme Court of Missouri.

Landmarks. Prior to 1930, circuit judges were not required to instruct civil juries in writing. That procedure was changed by the decision of *Dorman v. East St. Louis Ry. Co.,* 75 S.W.2d 854 (Mo.1934) which imposed the duty on trial lawyers to prepare and tender, in writing, all instructions they want the jury to be given.

In the practice which developed after 1934, when an appeal presented an issue of the validity of a questionable instruction, the instruction either was held to be error or came to carry the appellate court stamp of an "approved" instruction. A pernicious practice of drafting marginally correct argumentative instructions to act as "judicial advocates" for one side or the other but still be held to be "approved" by an appellate court led to the creation of the procedure of civil jury instructions by the MAI.

To coerce the bench and bar into using MAI to the exclusion of other instructions, the decision of *Brown v. St. Louis Public Service Co.,* 421 S.W.2d 255 (Mo.banc 1967) construed Rule 70.01 to mean that when a given instruction's language deviated from an applicable MAI, its error was presumed to be prejudicial.

Then came the next landmark, *Fowler v. Park Corp.,* 673 S.W.2d 749 (Mo.banc 1984) which, in apparent retreat from *Brown, supra,* emphasized the requirement that the prejudicial effect of instructional error shall be determined judicially. Fowler held that an instruction was not prejudicial which imposed on the defendant the duty to exercise the highest degree of care while defendant's burden under the law was only to exercise ordinary care.

Now there is an important change in Rule 70.03 which requires specific objections to instructions before submission of the case to the jury.

1. Revised and edited by Stephen H. Ringkamp, 1996, 2002.

WHY AND HOW TO INSTRUCT A JURY

Why Written Jury instructions? Instructions must be given to the jury to explain how its determination of the facts affects the outcome. The jury is not learned in the law. You, the trial lawyer, and the court, are. The jury must have help and direction in how the law affects the case. Simply to tell the jury abstractly "An automobile driver must exercise the highest degree of care" gives no guidance as to how the abstract rule of law applies to the facts of the case.

The jury instructions must be given in writing because jurors, even collectively, do not have total recall of an oral charge. Justice requires that the jury shall have exact reference to the court's charge available during deliberations. There is no advantage in testing jurors' memories for the instructions as well as for the evidence.

It is the trial court's responsibility to give the instructions. But, since the decision of Dorman, supra, it has been your job, the task of the trial lawyer, to aid the court by preparing and tendering to the judge all of the correct written instructions you desire the court to give. If the court doesn't give an instruction to which your client is entitled or you have not prepared it correctly, and *asked that it be given*, you are to blame, not the court.

Why Compulsory MAIs? The reason for compulsory MAIs is the need for simplicity.

Lawyers, left to their own devices, know no bounds to attempts to "improve" instructions by changing or adding a few more words here and there. Before the advent of MAI, a jury instruction on so simple a concept as the requirement that a plaintiff must prove facts entitling recovery, became verbose, redundant, and argumentative messages of a page and a half in length. Because their verbosity did not constitute *reversible* error, they became "court approved".

Increasing confusion of juries and reversals for other instructional error required that some standard of simple, understandable language and style be imposed. That standard is MAI. If a provided MAI is applicable it must be used. If there is no MAI precisely applicable to the case, the *form* of MAI must be used.

Innovation and improvement on MAI is prohibited in the interest of a standard for jury instruction. Doubtless you could improve on any of several of the MAI instructions, but, *you* channel the trial court into error if you do. Why take the chance that the error might be held, judicially, to be prejudicial?

Drafting a jury instruction is an exercise in precise translation.

It is commonly known that in Europe some proficiency in foreign language is taught in the schools, and that when a German and a Spaniard meet, they converse in German or Spanish, or, if neither is comfortable in the other's native tongue, they converse in a third common language, i.e., English, French or Russian.

Communicating the result of your own legal education to a lay jury by MAI is similar. Think of your task in that manner as you worry about MAI problems in instructing your juries.

You know your native tongue, "Legalese", but the jury does not. Both you and the jury can understand "MAIyan", the language of MAI. It is your task to translate your "Legalese" thoughts and principles into "MAIyan" so that the jury may understand clearly the factual issues of your claim or defense and act properly in deciding the case.

Lawyers pride themselves on accuracy of expression. But that precision is largely used for other lawyers. Contracts, deeds and statutes contain groups of words which seem to have the same meaning to a lay person. Lawyers recognize shades of differences and nuances according to law. Ordinarily, jurors do not.

It can not be stressed too heavily nor repeated too often: jury instructions are written to communicate with lay people. Thus, if there is no way to avoid using "Legalese" in an MAI instruction, i.e., "negligence" or "fair market value", you are required to translate the "Legalese" for the jury. Again, there are to be no flights of fancy or ingenuity employed, no free translations. Translation of legal terms must be made by one of the provided MAI definitions, or, if none is provided, then by a not-in-MAI instruction drawn in the form of the MAI examples of definitions.

The MAI definitions provided are mandatory if applicable. Other definitions *may* be required but you must protect your trial record if that is so. If the other lawyer uses a legal term for which there is no mandatory definition but which you think requires definitions, you must request the definition. Otherwise, *you* waive it.

Naturally there are bound to be differences of opinion over whether a term which is not defined in the MAI definitions *requires* definition. That is why disputes over requirements of definition are left, ordinarily, to the sound discretion of the judge. Someone must decide. It is the court, whose criteria are that the instructions shall be clear, correct, and not unnecessarily complex.

In summary, jury instructions translate complicated legal concepts into clear *written* lay language so that as the jury members deliberate, yes or no, on disputed evidence, they may know where the verdict goes.

But, on the chance that in your opinion even the best efforts at translation from "Legalese" into "MAIyan" need further clarification, you are given the chance at explanation of even what the "MAIyan" means by illustrations in "plainer" English (favorable to your client's position) by your jury arguments. See **Use,** *infra.*

Understanding. You must understand what pleadings and evidence mean.

Your task of jury instruction commences as the pleading is drawn no matter whether you are counsel for plaintiff or defendant. Some lawyers check their pleadings against MAI before ever filing the lawsuit. The single most important part of instructing a jury in the law is your own *understanding* of the law. The MAI is a valuable reference in that regard.

The lawyer *must* know the controlling law of the case.

Understanding a "cause of action", a "claim", a "denial", an "affirmative defense", all require an *understanding* of factual elements. You must *understand* the pleadings in order to use MAI accurately, whether you are claimant's counsel or defense counsel.

If you don't *understand the elements* of your own pleaded position you can not expect to select, consistently, the proper MAI instructions by chance, or by hit or miss. The MAI book can not do it for you. You are the lawyer. The same is true if you do not understand the elements of your opponent's position. You can not do combat if you do not understand.

The understanding which is true of the pleadings is true of the evidence. If you do not understand the legal and probative significance of *evidence* as it comes in at trial, you will be sorely pressed to accurately select the MAI instructions. Evidence admitted by consent of the parties can change the pleadings, whether the pleadings are mechanically amended to conform to the proof or are simply deemed in law to have been amended to conform with the proof. Unpleaded issues frequently are tried by consent.

You must understand what the *fact* issues are.

If the dispute is over the color of a shirt, you serve no purpose in having the jury waste its time deciding where the shirt was purchased.

Two basic causes of reversal for erroneous jury instruction, which occur frequently enough to cause worry, are twin, (1) the erroneous instruction submitted a claim (or defense) which was not pleaded nor tried by consent and (2) the erroneous instruction was not supported by substantial, probative evidence. In other words, you are not entitled to have the jury find facts which you have not proved.

Such errors may be laid at the door of not *understanding* what the pleading says in terms of legal claim or defense or to not *understanding* what the evidence means in terms of proof.

If your petition states plainly that the defendant who hit your client's car did not stop at the stop sign when your client was driving by, and the answer admits that the defendant failed to stop at the stop sign; it would seem that you have no worry about submitting an instruction under MAI 17.01. But, you may. Have you pleaded that the vehicles and the stop sign were upon public highways? Failure to stop at a stop sign on private property does not necessarily prove breach of a duty which is an element of a tort claim. Have you pleaded that the failure to stop at the stop sign was a direct cause of your client's injury? Causation is a necessary element of a tort claim.

Don't forget!! Your *failure to plead the ultimate facts* necessary to state a claim may be raised defensively for the first time on appeal. Rule 55.27(g)(2).

Instructions submitting unpleaded issues, even those actually tried over objection, are erroneous.

Such an error is not cured by the fact that the instruction is directly from your MAI book.

You must understand the elements of a submitted claim or defense and make the instructions conform. If you don't and the trial judge gives your instructions, it is judicial error but your loss.

The following sort of elemental reasoning is suggested as appropriate in approaching your task of jury instruction in a simple negligence tort case. The elements of the claim are three, (1) a duty, (2) a breach and (3) a harmful result (causation of damage).

Take the facts of a simple case of negligence as an illustration of thinking of how to instruct a jury. Plaintiff has the first burden and both sides may profit from the illustration of how a plaintiff might approach the task of preparing instructions.

Plaintiff, George White, drove east on a public street protected by stop signs. Crossing southbound, defendant, Joe Black, did not stop at the stop sign and collided with plaintiff's car in the intersection. Plaintiff claims injury. Defendant (1) denies and (2) claims excuse as a defense—a sudden, unanticipated brake failure.

The elements of the claimant's right to recover are in the conjunctive; *all* elements must be proved. Thus, your logic of the claimant's legal claim might be; "If the defendant had a duty to exercise care to avoid injury to the claimant and breached that duty *and* thereby caused resultant damage to the claimant, the claimant is entitled to recover money damages by judgment".

On the other hand, the defendant has a denial defense ("it didn't happen.") which is disjunctive all the way. Under the defense of denial if *any* element of the claimant's proof is missing or unbelievable, defendant wins. The defendant also has a positive "defense"—excuse—in which *all* of defendant's elements must be proved in order to prevail.

Thus, for the defense, the thinking is by progressive steps and is a little more complex, "If I had *no duty* to claimant, I win", or, "If I *had* a duty to claimant but did not breach it, I win", *or*, "If I had a duty to claimant and breached it but did *no harm* to claimant, I win". Defendant thinks further, "If I can prove my brakes failed suddenly and unforeseeably, I can win because I will have proved that I did not violate my duty to stop, my brakes did." (No negligence.)

That is the sort of legal analysis which must be used in approaching MAI, partly fact and partly law. The fact issues portion of it goes to the jury via MAI for decision. The law of it is employed in the selection, preparation, and tender of MAI instructions to the court and, very importantly, in your jury arguments. See: **Use,** *infra*.

For those who may wonder how the existence of a legal duty could ever be a question of fact rather than a matter of law, it is suggested that the *facts* comprising the legal condition of the agency of an active tortfeasor (which is a condition precedent to a *legal duty being imposed upon his principal*) would be such an occasion.

The plaintiff's attorney in approaching the MAI analysis in this simple factual case should think along these lines and if it is helpful, make a checklist:

    a. What duty did defendant Black owe to plaintiff?—(specifically, a duty to stop at the stop sign.) Defendant may have had other duties but that is the duty upon which reliance is placed in view of the anticipated evidence.

    b. How did defendant breach the duty?

Defendant failed to stop. Defendant says the brakes failed, but that's just what the defendant says. Under the evidence, can defendant prove it? It is up to defendant to show an excuse for violating a traffic regulation enacted for plaintiff's safety.

    c. How did defendant damage plaintiff?

Defendant hit plaintiff broadside in the intersection spraining plaintiff's back causing loss of wages, medical expense and impaired working ability.

On the probability that plaintiff will make a submissible case, defendant's counsel will think similarly:

    a. There is no doubt that defendant had a duty to stop.

Since duty is admitted, there will not be any dispute for the jury to decide.

b. There is an issue over whether defendant breached the duty.

Sudden brake failure can be believed by the jury, and, if it is, defendant will be excused for failing to stop. The defense wins because plaintiff will *fail to convince* that defendant breached the duty; the law excuses defendant for failure to stop.

c. There is a dispute over whether plaintiff was injured.

The impact was slight; the physical damage to the cars was almost insignificant and there is evidence that plaintiff made a claim for back injury once before. Even if defendant breached a duty, the defense wins if plaintiff can not prove injury caused by defendant's breach.

Selection. Your selection of instructions is a three part task.

First, there are instructions which must be given in every case. Those are the *mandatory* instructions. Omission is error.

Second, there are instructions which *must* be given *in your particular* case. According to what "Legalese" unavoidably must be used in the instructions (here, "*negligent*", "*highest degree of care*"), translation (definition) instructions must be given. Those are also mandatory instructions. Omission is error. If you have a damage suit, a damage instruction is mandatory. (*Exception.* In some claims the amount is not in dispute, e.g., an indemnity claim where the amount in dispute is an admitted figure. In those cases the damage instruction is included in the verdict director.)

Third, the format of MAI is mandatory for the instructions which counsel must draft. Thus, if you are for the plaintiff and you do not prepare a verdict directing instruction, that is, an instruction which instructs the jury to return a verdict for your client if it believes the elements of your claim, or if you do not prepare it in the form of MAI (using specific MAI, if applicable), then you have caused the trial judge to err in instructing the jury. It is the court's error but your loss.

It is mandatory in every case to tell the jury at the outset what it may expect in the trial (MAI 2.01) and at the close of the case to explain the jury's use of the instructions (MAI 2.03). It is mandatory to assign the burden of proof (MAI 3.01), to disclaim the court's assumption of any fact which may be mentioned in an instruction (MAI 2.02), and to instruct the jury in its powers to return a verdict by concurrence of nine or more jurors (MAI 2.04).

Because the case is a claim for damages as a result of negligent injury, it becomes mandatory to define negligence (Ch.11), to give a measure of damages instruction (See MAI 4.01 or 37.03), and to give the proper verdict form. (Ch.36).

Consequently, the mandatory instructions total nine in our sample case. Eight may be selected without the difficulty of tailoring them to fit our facts. Those may be taken right from the MAI book:

(1) MAI 2.01, mandatory pre-evidence outline of the trial procedure. It must be given as Instruction No. 1 in every case. It must be read at the commencement of the case.

(2) MAI 2.03, mandatory post-evidence explanation of jury's use of the instructions. It must be given as Instruction No. 2 in every case. It must be read as the first of the instructions given at the close of the case.

(3) MAI 2.02, mandatory caution that court does not assume facts in the instructions. It must be given in every case and may be numbered at the court's discretion.

(4) MAI 2.04, mandatory advice of the power of nine members of the jury to return its verdict. It must be given in every case.

(5) MAI 3.01, mandatory statement of the burden of proof. It must be given in every case.

(6) MAI 11.03, mandatory definition of negligence. Since our sample case must have instructional reference to negligence but will be limited to operators of motor vehicle on the public streets, MAI 11.03 becomes mandatory *in this case.*

(7) MAI 4.01, mandatory measure of damages. Because our case is confined to a claim for personal injury damage, MAI 4.01 comes mandatory *in this case.* (Assuming no comparative fault.)

(8) MAI 36.01, mandatory form of verdict. Our sample case is a single claim of the plaintiff against a single defendant. MAI 36.01 is applicable and thus is mandatory *in this case.*

Since the above eight instructions are mandatory in this case they may be selected at any free time during the pendency of the case, prepared for tender and placed in the file with one worry of trial eliminated in advance, long before final trial preparation.

(9) Selecting the proper verdict directing instruction calls into play your understanding of the law of your claim. In **Understanding,** plaintiff's claim was reduced to its lowest common denominators, (1) duty, (2) breach, and (3) resulting damage. You must have in mind each element of each part of the claim in order to sort out the uncontested ultimate fact issues from those which are contested and must be decided by the jury and to eliminate mere *evidentiary* fact issues which are addressed by jury arguments of counsel. **Use,** *infra.*

What fact raises defendant's duty to the plaintiff? It is the mere fact that defendant drove a motor vehicle on the public highway when plaintiff, also, was there. Is that fact, defendant's driving, contested? The answer is no. Thus, the fact of defendant's driving should not be hypothesized. Is the fact that the casualty occurred on the public highways contested? The answer is no. It should not be hypothesized. Either of those two, *if contested,* would be an ultimate (decisive) fact and would require hypothesis in the verdict directing instruction.

The preceding paragraph illustrates a most difficult concept for neophytes to jury instruction. By MAI 17.01, the judge never does say, expressly, that the defendant had a duty to stop and yield to plaintiff. Why not? Well, the trial judge has got to decide the issues of law. The court can not have the jury second guessing an application of the law to the facts of the case. By telling the jury nothing about defendant's legal duties but telling the jury what to do on its decision of the facts, the judge has instructed the jury in the *application of the law* to the facts. By using MAI 17.01, the judge instructs, legally, that if the defendant "violated the traffic signal" he has violated a legal duty imposed on those who (1) operate motor vehicles (2) on public streets and (3) approach traffic control signals which (4) are in place under authority of law. The judge does not instruct by stating abstract rules of law but by deciding, as a matter of law, which rules of law are applicable and telling the jury what to do on the jury's decision of the facts.

The frequently heard complaint, "The judge didn't tell the jury the defendant had a duty to stop" is invalid. The judge does tell the jury. This message is paraphrased as; "If you find the fact to be that defendant violated the traffic signal, then he violated his legal duty to plaintiff to stop and yield to plaintiff." Under MAI, the judge continues to decide and apply the law and, thus, instructs in the law; the jury decides the facts and does what the judge tells them to do (as a matter of applied law) with the facts.

Back to the instruction.

What was the breach? Well, there was a lawful traffic sign in a position which made it mandatory for defendant to stop before entering the intersection and defendant did not stop. Put another way, defendant breached the general duty not to collide with plaintiff's car, or, not to injure plaintiff. Is the fact that the stop sign was there contested? The answer is no. That fact should not be hypothesized. Is the fact that the stop sign was placed there by some person with authority contested? The answer is no and that fact should not be hypothesized.

Are the facts that plaintiff was driving east or that defendant was driving south or that there was a collision in the intersection contested? No. Those facts should not be hypothesized. They are examples of evidentiary facts. Not only are they not in dispute, even if they were in dispute they would not be hypothesized because they would *be only evidentiary facts.*

Is the fact that defendant disobeyed the stop sign contested? The answer is yes. Defendant admits that defendant did not manage to get the car stopped at the stop sign, but defendant contests the allegation that defendant disobeyed or violated the traffic signal because defendant claims that the car's brakes *unexpectedly* failed. If brake failure is true, the jury could find that defendant was helpless and could not avoid passing the sign without stopping and was not negligent in doing so. Because of the evidence tending to show unexpected brake failure, both the violation of the stop sign and the *ultimate fact* that the violation was negligent must be submitted to the jury as disputed *ultimate* facts. The evidentiary facts are the subject of jury argument. Only the *ultimate* disputed facts should be hypothesized in the instructions.

A discussion of this principle of evidentiary fact versus *ultimate* fact is important. One of the major faults with pre-MAI instructions lay in the unnecessary hypothesis of undisputed evidentiary facts with the result that instructions became so long, through caution of counsel to include all possible essential facts, that they became unmanageable.

In this sample case, whether or not defendant's brakes unexpectedly failed is a disputed fact, true enough. But, it is only evidentiary and bears upon the ultimate fact of whether defendant *negligently* violated the traffic signal. Defendant is not entitled to an instruction on brake failure. Defendant must argue it and is given full opportunity to do so. Defendant has the instructional definition of negligence to argue. Even with the highest degree of care, if the brakes went out unexpectantly, defendant may argue that there was nothing defendant could do about it and thus can not be found to have failed to exercise care in not stopping at the stop sign. That is the negative of plaintiff's burden to prove the ultimate fact of negligence in failing to stop at the stop sign. Whether or not hydraulic fluid was found on the street to the north of the stop sign at a position which would indicate brake failure at a point where defendant could have gotten stopped except for brake failure also is an evidentiary fact. Evidentiary facts should not be hypothesized. Plaintiff can argue the absence of brake fluid on the street from which the jury could find that if the brakes actually did fail to stop defendant's car, the brake failure was not unexpected. Plaintiff is not entitled to an instruction on the absence of brake fluid in the street.

The ultimate fact question is, "Did defendant *negligently* violate the traffic signal?" Plaintiff says: "Yes, defendant just came right on through the stop sign." The testimony is evidentiary. Defendant says: "No, my brakes unexpectedly failed." That testimony is evidentiary and an excuse for not stopping. Neither version of how the stop sign was violated should be hypothesized.

The third element of plaintiff's case is the question of resultant damage.

Is the fact that plaintiff was damaged in dispute? The answer is yes and that fact must be submitted for jury decision.

MAI 17.01 is the instruction form which fits plaintiff's need. The only further decision plaintiff need make is whether or not to include the bracketed "tail" reference to a complete affirmative defense and that depends upon defendant's success in proving a *submissible* affirmative defense, such as a release, and then in deciding *to submit* on it.

The plaintiff can not know for certain whether a complete affirmative defense will be submitted to the jury. It is error for a verdict directing instruction (MAI 17.01) to fail to refer to a complete affirmative defense. It behooves plaintiff to have MAI 17.01 typed up both ways, with and without the "tail" so that the instruction conference will not be extended while an instruction is retyped to meet the need. The plaintiff should take the same approach in preparing alternate instructions depending on whether or not comparative fault is submissible.

Understanding, Revisited. You must understand the pleadings *and* the evidence.

In this hypothetical, defendant may decide there is ground to plead that plaintiff is partly responsible for his own damage for failing to lookout and avoid the collision. Thus, we now assume defendant has pleaded that plaintiff's comparative negligence partly caused any damage plaintiff sustained. Although contributory negligence no longer is a complete bar to recovery of tort damages; under principles of comparative fault, plaintiff's negligence will reduce the amount of damages reflected in a plaintiff's verdict as total damages.

For the defense, the analysis has added a step. It now is, "If I had *no duty* to claimant, I win", or, "If I *had* a duty to claimant but did not breach it, I win", or "If I had a duty to claimant and breached it but did *no harm* to claimant, I win", or, "If I had a duty to claimant *and* breached it *and* caused him damage *and if* claimant also had a duty to himself and breached it and thereby contributed to cause his own damage, I *can still partly win.*"

MAI 17.01 does not provide for part-win cases. With plaintiff's required understanding of the petition as affected by defendant's answer, plaintiff realizes that if defendant makes a submissible case on comparative fault, plaintiff's use of MAI 17.01 must be as that instruction is changed under MAI 37.01. Rather than being entitled to an absolute verdict and judgment for all his damages against defendant, plaintiff is relegated to having a percentage of fault assessed against defendant and to having plaintiff's damages reduced by an assessment of fault against plaintiff.

It is imperative to understand the pleadings and the evidence.

Preparation. Prepare your instructions early. It is comparatively easy to sit in the quiet of an evening and look over this article on how to prepare and use instructions. It is quite another thing to try to read it, apply it, and prepare instructions in the limited time available during a trial. If instructions were the only thing to worry about during trial, mistakes of omission in the instructions seldom would occur. An accident of omission by a typist can require another trial. During trial the immediate pressing matters of trial crowd the problems of instructions for time. You have to worry about jury selection, opening statement, witnesses appearing at proper times, the order of witnesses, shuffling order to accommodate prima donna witnesses, elements of proof, foundations, unexpected rulings on evidence, and a multitude of problems which require your immediate attention. Trial time or lack of time is not conducive to the deliberation which you must give to the instructions which you prepare and tender.

Use of a separate folder to contain the instructions and any amendments to pleadings made during trial is advisable. A most helpful part of such a folder is a checklist which is attached so that it may be located immediately. For the plaintiff in our hypothetical case it could take this form:

<u>Offered Marked Ruling</u>

Petition amendment
Answer amendment
Motion, close of plaintiff's evidence
Motion, close of evidence

<u>Instructions:</u>
<u>Mandatory</u>
2.01   1 given
2.03   2
court does not assume facts (2.02)
return of verdict explanation (2.04)
burden of proof (3.01)
definition of negligence (11.03)
measure of damages (4.01 or 37.03)
form of verdict (36.01 or 37.07)

<u>Needed</u>
verdict director:
   without comparative fault modification (17.01)
   with comparative fault modification (37.01)
Defendant's offers:
   Comparative fault (37.02)
   Converse (Ch. 33)

You must prepare each instruction you intend to offer in a clean form to be sent to the jury and, for the court file, a copy of each instruction bearing a notation of its source and, for each opponent, a similar copy. (If one lawyer represents more than one party, one copy for each lawyer will suffice). For your own use you will need two copies of each instruction which you offer.

Why two?

When you tender an instruction the court may refuse to give it. If you think the refusal is erroneous, you should have it marked as a tendered and refused instruction for identification on appeal. If the court indicates that the refused instruction would be given with some editing, then you may use your extra copy to make the necessary changes by interlineation for retyping in clean form for tender and submission under a different instruction number or letter. For simplicity, a "given" instruction should be numbered and a "refused" instruction should be lettered.

Thus (except for the mandatory instructions which are straight out of MAI without any alteration made to fit the case), you should prepare an original (without any marking to show its source) and four copies (bearing MAI number, MAI number modified, not-in-MAI and prepared by plaintiff, or defendant) of each instruction: a copy for the court, a copy for your opponent, and two copies for you.

As you have seen, some instructions should be prepared in more than one form. It is too late to have the verdict director typed after the close of the evidence when the plaintiff ordinarily first will know for certain that a complete affirmative defense or comparative fault will or will not be submitted. You should have plaintiff's verdict directing instructions typed both ways, in advance.

When you are preparing your instructions you may believe that a particular essential element of your case or defense will be conceded or agreed to but you are not sure. Although it may be essential, if it is not an issue, your instruction need not hypothesize it as a controverted ultimate fact. However, if it is *not conceded,* the instruction must hypothesize it for the finding of the jury. An example would be the fact of who was driving a car in an automobile collision case. Ordinarily, no issue is made of who was driving. On occasion, particularly in catastrophic cases where all occupants are dead, the issue of who was driving is vital and might not be conceded.

Thus, if you have reason to believe that an essential element may be conceded but you are not sure, the instruction should be prepared both ways, with and without that hypothesized element.

Particularly in rural circuits, one day jury trials are not uncommon. It is obvious that there is a practical necessity to have your instructions prepared and typed in all forms for which you can anticipate need.

There may be no overnight recess to use for instruction preparation. Thus, although you may have a simple case, you may have in your possession for *possible* use an amazing number of alternative different instructions. Not all will be tendered to the court for use. You must have some order in your instruction folder.

One such plan is this. Assume that you are not decided at the time you draw your instructions whether you will submit on speed and failure to keep a lookout or only on speed. Often times you will not decide until the close of the evidence. That indecision will require two forms of your main verdict directing instruction. Then on top of that, you do not know whether the defendant will be permitted to submit on comparative fault. That additional indecision will require two versions of each of your two forms, with and without the comparative fault modification of MAI 37.01. Thus, you will have prepared four different forms of one instruction to take to court with you.

Prepare an instruction label for each form of the instruction on a separate piece of paper or card about the size of a business card and type on it a generic description of the instruction, i.e.,

"Verdict director, Speed only"

"Verdict director, Speed and lookout"

Those small labels can be slipped under the paper clip which hold the original and copies of each instruction together, and all four such versions of one instruction, being labeled for easy identification, can be clipped together in your instruction folder. In the instruction conference you readily can select your verdict director bundle of four versions and see, without reading and comparing them, which of the four you are handing for tender and distribution to the court and your opponent. The others can be left fastened together and laid aside as a bundle.

It may be helpful and advisable to label all instructions similarly and to clip them together in natural bunches of instructions. For instance, all mandatory instructions can be clipped together for easy access in the instruction conference and, similarly, all cautionary instructions which you prepare for possible tender.

If you do not settle upon some usable system to keep your prepared instructions readily available when called for in the instruction conference, you will find yourself involved in the distraction of an embarrassing paper shuffle instead of being able to devote your attention to the substance of the conference.

Tender. The actual tender of your instructions to the court will depend upon the trial judges. They are individuals and each may handle the instruction conferences according to differing experience and ideas.

If you do not know what the judge expects, ask!

In some circuits, MAI 2.01 is prepared by the court; in others the plaintiff is expected to prepare it. If you are plaintiff and in doubt, prepare it. (**Caution:** Judges' stenographers are not immune to typographical error. An error is an error regardless of who mistyped it. Read all prepared instructions. If a furnished instruction leaves something out, it is error.)

If the judge does not read Instruction No. 1 (MAI 2.01) to the jury at the commencement of trial, it is error. It is the court's error but your loss. See that the judge is reminded to read it if it should be overlooked. It is your responsibility to do it.

Ordinarily, a trial judge will ask for instructions during the instruction conference in the order they will be considered. The judge may even ask for your verdict directing instructions in advance of the conference or even in advance of trial. If the court does ask in advance and for some reason you have not yet drawn it, be ready to tell the judge what grounds you intend to submit, or from what grounds you yet intend to make your selection.

If the judge asks only for specific instructions during the jury instruction conference, give only the ones asked for. Do not drop a whole bundle on the desk and impose the task of paper shuffler upon the judge. There will be enough paper shuffling despite all efforts to keep it to a minimum.

If the trial judge does not make specific requests but leaves it to you to tender your instructions in the order you wish, make it plain what it is that you are handing to the court and your opponent. It costs you nothing to say, "Here is the cautionary against assuming facts", or, "This is the measure of damages", or, "This is the verdict director on speed." Of course, the judge and your opponent can read an instruction to see what it references but your identifying statement can save time. They will know what to expect when they commence to read it. That is the reason we put titles on books.

If you have followed the suggestions of this section on how to instruct juries, you will have prepared a checklist attached to your instruction folder. See, **Preparation,** above.

The judge will number the instructions to be given to the jury. Numbering on instructions is in large part discretionary but there are important exceptions. The number for MAI 2.01 is always No. 1. So, also, is the number 2 reserved for MAI 2.03. If your case requires submission of more than one claim to the jury, the order and numbering of instructions is governed more closely by the requirements of the "package" method of submission. You should pay attention to the sequence in which the instructions are numbered in order to help prevent error.

As you tender an instruction to the judge, make a check mark on your checklist, indicating that it has been tendered. Mark on your checklist in the column headed "Marked" the number and in the column headed "Ruling" a symbol indicating that it is given. If it is refused and the court does not mark it refused of its own volition, request that it be marked for identification as a refused instruction and check your list accordingly. You will find that your checklist is invaluable to you if there is an appeal.

Mark your own file copies of the instructions (both your own and the copies furnished to you of opponent's tendered instructions) with the numbers used by the court and note right on them, either "given" or "refused". Keep your own file in order. If you do, at the end of the instruction conference you will have an accurate record of the status of every instruction you prepared as either not tendered or tendered and, if tendered, either given or refused. You will also have a similar record of all instructions your opponent tendered.

It is possible to function without a checklist in a simple case, it is true. But, as you consider the complexities of jury instructions in a multiclaim, multiparty case, you will come to a quick realization that an adequate checklist is essential to your efficient operation.

During the instruction conference it may occur to you that there is an error in your opponent's instruction. What you do about this is for you to decide. You are the advocate. Beware however, Rule 70.03 requires ALL objections to instructions to be made BEFORE submission of the case to the jury. You are the advocate. If no objection is made BEFORE submission, an appellate court will not view kindly an effort at "sandbagging" on those objections.

Use. Your use of the instructions at trial commences when the trial judge reads them to the jury. Listen to the reading.

It is a great temptation to be thinking about your clever argument to the jury, but listen to the judge read the instructions. Few things are more discouraging than to realize immediately after the jury has decided in your opponent's favor, and has been discharged, that there is reversible but unpreserved error in the instructions.

More than one lawyer has been caught short by the realization that the judge read an erroneous instruction to the jury.

What should you do?

Call it to the attention of the court immediately.

The judge has control of the trial and can do what is necessary to eliminate error.

As the reading of that or the next instruction is completed, stand and politely interrupt and ask leave to approach the bench. The judge will realize something is wrong. Suggest that opposing counsel join you at the bench and point out the error. If it is a matter of mere typographical omission of a word or phrase, the judge may correct it by interlineation and read the correct instruction to the jury with no more than a simple explanation that a word was left out by mistake. If it is a more extensive correction, the judge may choose to tell the jury that it has come to the attention of the court that more work must be done, declare a recess, and cure the error.

The important thing is that the error should be corrected before the jury is permitted to taint its deliberation with that error.

From 1934 to 1962, jury instructions had come to contain argument. Argument should not be included in MAI instructions. Therefore, your use of MAI includes your supplemental jury summation, explanations of the underlying law, and reasons for the instructions the court has given in writing. In this way, the lawyers "flesh out" the instructions.

A frequent unjustified criticism heard of MAI is that the jury is not advised abstractly of the rights of a litigant by the instructions. The answer is that the jury is not supposed to be so advised in the instructions. Those are argued by counsel.

The instruction message is simply, "if you believe these propositions of fact to be true, plaintiff wins. If you fail to believe them, plaintiff loses."

In our exemplar case, failing to stop at the stop sign can be found to have been negligence. It need not be so found. It is up to the advocates to persuade the jury that it was or was not negligence under the circumstances. That must be done in argument. That is advocacy. The instructions support your argument and your argument illustrates the operation of the instructions on the case.

Many things can not be stated in the instructions. Those are the matters which are rules of law, presumptions, inferences and the like.

Every lawyer knows that a deceased accident victim is presumed to have exercised care for decedent's own safety until evidence of lack of care appears; that every person is presumed to know the law; that there is an arguable adverse inference that a civil litigant who fails to testify on that party's own behalf would not have helped a particular position, that an adverse presumption arises against the spoiler of evidence, ad infinitum. Nevertheless, none of those presumptions or inferences or abstract statements of law has any place in a jury instruction.

The exclusion of such matters from instructions has cast a relatively greater importance upon the content of closing argument. With the required disappearance of argument from the court's instructions, it is in the lawyers' arguments that the jury now must be "instructed" upon the effect of presumptions, inference, bits of evidence and the like if it will ever be so instructed. Your attention is called to some concrete illustrations of the importance of "fleshing out" the instructions by argument.

Lovelace v. Reed, 486 S.W.2d 417 (Mo. 1972) is a case of a child-pedestrian, wrongful-death by motor vehicle. The submission was on the ultimate fact of the defendant's failure to keep a lookout. From the written instructions, the jury had no way of knowing the legal effect of defendant's failure to swerve or sound a warning to the child as those failures would tend to demonstrate causation. The burden fell upon plaintiff's counsel to "instruct" the jury in those matters by argument. The trial court erroneously restricted plaintiff's argument of those matters and suffered reversal of its judgment for the defendant because of the court's unwarranted limitation on argument.

Cook v. Cox, 478 S.W.2d 678 (Mo. 1972) likewise held that although no sole cause instruction may be given, sole cause remains a viable and permissible jury argument if the evidence justifies its use. Thus, all of the intricacies of sole cause as a defense, if supported by evidence, may be developed and urged in argument.

For the proposition that jury arguments are not to be limited by the context of the jury instructions but by the scope of the trial, the interested may see, listed in chronological order: *Lewis v. Bucyrus-Erie, Inc.,* 622 S.W.2d 920 (Mo.banc 1981); *Lippard v. Houdaille Industries, Inc.,* 715 S.W.2d 491 (Mo.banc 1986); *Barnes v. Tool & Machinery Buildings, Inc.,* 715 S.W.2d 518 (Mo.banc 1986); *Moore v. Missouri Pacific Railroad Co.,* 825 S.W.2d 839 (Mo.banc 1992); *Callahan v. Cardinal Glennon Hospital,* 863 S.W.2d 852 (Mo.banc 1993).

Examination of MAI 4.01 reveals no listing of the elements of damage. The jury knows of those lawful elements only if counsel tells the jury in argument. If defense counsel thinks it is worthwhile that the jury know that its award for personal injury will not be taxed, it is up to counsel in cases other than FELA cases to tell the jury so *if permissible under the law.*

A non-lawyer who reads this monograph might wonder if there is any control over what a lawyer might choose to argue to the jury as controlling rules of law. There is. Each advocate controls the other. The moment an advocate leaves the boundary of the law it is the duty of his opponent to object to *misstatement of the law.*

Differing recollections of the testimony, flights of fancy based on evidence, and strained inferences all come normally in argument and may be accepted under the theory and ruling that the jury will remember and weigh the evidence.

There is no such panacea for misstatements of the law.

If plaintiff's advocate in a commercial case asks for damages for loss of future profits as an element of damage while the evidence is insufficient to take such calculations out of the realm of speculation, the defendant must preserve the issue with a proper objection. The trial court must rule on the objection and will do so. It is not simply a matter that the "jury will remember the evidence" in such a case of an erroneous request for damages which are not supported by evidence if the trial court is advised by the objection that the argument oversteps the boundary of the litigant's legal rights.

So it is if a claimant asks for damages for permanent injury when there is no evidence of permanency or argues an unfavorable inference from the absence of a witness when the witness is not under control of an adversary and so on.

Thus, when the complaint is made that the jury has not been told of the rights of the parties, you might be reasonably sure that counsel has failed in argument. Counsel's failure may well be deliberate and intentional and tactical, but, nevertheless, counsel has failed if the jury has not been advised of the rights of the litigants. The failure does not lie with MAI.

You may reread some, all, or none of the instructions in your argument. You may "flesh out" the instructions in argument by explanation and illustration. You may ignore the instructions in argument.

The decisions are yours.

*

MISSOURI APPROVED JURY INSTRUCTIONS

Civil (MAI)

Sixth Edition

1.00

EXCLUDED AREAS

Analysis of Instructions

Westlaw Electronic Research

See Westlaw Electronic Research Guide preceding the Table of Instructions.

Library References:

C.J.S. Negligence § 871–878, 880–905.
West's Key No. Digests, Negligence ☞1720–1747.

1

1.01   [1965 New] Unavoidable Accident Instructions

No unavoidable accident instructions may be given.

Committee Comment (1965 New)

The decisions on the subject point out that the word "accident" is apt to be misunderstood by the jury. As the Court said in the landmark case of *Hogan v. Kansas City Public Service Co.*, 322 Mo. 1103, 1115, 19 S.W.2d 707, 713 (banc 1929):

> The word "accident" in popular acceptation and sometimes in law, may denote an occurrence arising without intent or design or even from the carelessness of man; but in the law of negligence it signifies an event resulting in damage or injury, proceeding from an unknown cause or from a known cause without human agency or without human fault.

The *Hogan* case suggests that there are times when an accident instruction would be proper, but lawyers have had difficulty finding such cases. The Missouri Supreme Court in *Littlefield v. Laughlin*, 327 S.W.2d 863, 868 (Mo.1959) said:

> ... our research has disclosed no case subsequent to the Hogan case in which an accident instruction has been approved, and we find it difficult to conceive of a factual situation in which an accident instruction may properly be given under the rule there set out notwithstanding the language indicating that such situations could exist.

In cases where the evidence shows that the cause of the casualty is unknown, thus apparently authorizing an accident instruction, defendants will probably be entitled to directed verdicts. The accident instruction should not be missed.

Library References:

C.J.S. Negligence § 871–878, 880–905.
West's Key No. Digests, Negligence ☞1720–1747.

Notes of Decisions

In general   1
Skidding   2

———

1. In general

Prohibition against unavoidable accident instructions did not change right of defendants in wrongful death action to deny claim of negligence against them and to present evidence that they were free of such negligence, and defense counsel's argument that did not exceed those boundaries was not plain error. Chong Kee Min v. Wun Sik Hong, 802 S.W.2d 171 (Mo.App.1991).

Although emergency instructions are no longer permitted under MAI, defense of justification or excuse remains, and defendant may introduce any evidence which tends to establish he is not guilty of negligence. Cowell v. Thompson, 713 S.W.2d 52 (Mo.App. 1986).

MAI's 1.01, 1.03 and 1.04 do not preclude the defenses of unavoidable accident, sudden emergency or sole cause, which defenses negated defendant's negligence, but are sufficiently presented by evidence, a converse of plaintiff's verdict director and argument to the jury. Coffel v. Spradley, 495 S.W.2d 735[11–13] (Mo.App.1973).

Defendant's verdict director exonerating him if sudden brake failure was sole cause of rear end collision was condemned as a sole cause instruction (MAI 1.04), as a sudden emergency instruction (MAI 1.01) and as an unavoidable accident instruction (MAI 1.01). Johnson v. Harrington, 443 S.W.2d 1[1–3] (Mo.App.1969).

Rear-ended plaintiff submitted under MAI 17.16. Defendant's excuse was unexpected slide and brake failure. Defendant offered, but the court refused, an "if you believe" instruction hypothesizing the unexpected slide and brake failure. Refusal upheld because the instruction presented prohibited defense of unavoidable accident. Suchara v. St. Louis Public Service Co., 410 S.W.2d 93[1] (Mo.App.1966).

2. Skidding

Where plaintiff properly submitted MAI 17.13, driving on wrong side of the road, and defendant testified she skidded across the center line, it was error to give defendant's affirmative defense instruction exonerating her if she skidded. (This would have been error even had defendant further submitted that her skidding was not negligent.) Such an instruction is akin to an accident instruction condemned by MAI 1.01 and a sole-cause instruction condemned by MAI 1.03. Defendant should be limited to conversing negligence by MAI 33.02(2), and then arguing non-negligent skidding. Stover v. Patrick, 459 S.W.2d 393[1, 2] (Mo. banc 1970).

1.02 [1965 New] Conjunctive Submissions

The practice of submitting dual or multiple theories of recovery or defense in the conjunctive is prohibited.

Committee Comment (1996 Revision)

Plaintiffs and defendants, when in doubt as to whether their evidence supported each theory of recovery or defense, have often submitted all such theories in the conjunctive. This practice enabled them, in most cases, to avoid reversible error when it developed that one or more of their theories was not supported by the evidence.

The rule was expressed in *Corley v. Kroger Grocery & Baking Co.,* 355 Mo. 4, 11, 193 S.W.2d 897, 900 (1946), as follows:

> ... [w]here plaintiff's verdict-directing instruction submits several charges of negligence in the conjunctive and there is substantial evidence establishing one or more but not all of said charges, the giving of the instruction is not reversible error.

While conjunctive submissions were probably used more often by plaintiffs, defendants also made use of the technique by submitting multiple theories of defense. In approving the practice the Court said, "... the rule applicable to the plaintiff's instructions should also apply to the defendant's instructions." *Knox v. Weathers,* 363 Mo. 1167, 257 S.W.2d 912, 915 (1953).

The practice has not been free from criticism. In *Adams v. Thompson,* 178 S.W.2d 779, 785 (Mo.App.1944), the late Judge Cave said:

> We deem it unnecessary to decide whether the failure of proof of notice would prevent plaintiff from submitting that ground of negligence in his instruction, because, if so, it was submitted in conjunction with two other grounds of negligence of which there was substantial proof, either of which would entitle the plaintiff to recover. It has frequently been held that where a plaintiff submits several charges of negligence in the conjunctive in an instruction predicating a recovery and there is substantial evidence establishing one or more but not all of said charges, the giving of the instruction is not reversible error. Such submissions have not been approved as technically correct, but have been considered not reversible error and have been tolerated, on the theory that the plaintiff has assumed an unnecessary burden and hence defendant has not been prejudiced. Guthrie v. City of St. Charles, 347 Mo. 1175, 152 S.W.2d 91 (banc 1941); Lindquist v. Kansas City Public Service Co., 350 Mo. 905, 169 S.W.2d 366 (1943). The writer's personal opinion is that such a principle is questionable because it tends to lead to confusion instead of clarity, but it has been announced and followed so many times by the Supreme Court and the other appellate courts

of this state that we should and will follow the numerous prior decisions along that line.

Conjunctive submissions have not been a "cure all." The litigant whose conjunctive submission included an incorrect statement of statutory or case law committed reversible error though the balance of his submission was legally correct and supported by the evidence. *Miles v. Gaddy,* 357 S.W.2d 897, 901 (Mo. banc 1962); *Donaldson v. Manzella,* 338 S.W.2d 78 (Mo.1960).

The Committee believes that the jury should not be instructed on a theory of recovery or defense not supported by the evidence and that any such submission, whether in the conjunctive or disjunctive, should be reversible error. A theory of recovery or defense should not be submitted unless it can stand alone. It should be made clear that most verdict directing instructions have several *elements* which must be submitted in the conjunctive, but these are in support of a *single theory of recovery or defense.*

Library References:

C.J.S. Trial § 326, 339, 346.
West's Key No. Digests, Trial ☞228, 233, 243.

Notes of Decisions

In general 1
Dual elements 2
Evidentiary support 3

------

1. In general

Verdict directing instructions on fraud claim and on breach of warranty claim which contained multiple representations connected by conjunction "and" did not violate rule prohibiting submission of conjunctive theories of recovery; single theory of fraud and single theory of breach of warranty were supported by series of representations found in single brochure distributed by asbestos manufacturer in connection with fireproofing spray installed in city's airport. Kansas City v. Keene Corp., 855 S.W.2d 360 (Mo.1993).

Although MAI 1.02 proscribes the submission of dual or multiple theories of defense or recovery in the conjunctive, the court held that the instruction in this case did not submit two alternative independent hypotheses but rather permitted a recovery upon either of two alternative (disjunctive) findings, which is permissible if there is support in the

record for each disjunctive hypothesis. The court further held that no essential element of plaintiff's verdict director may be omitted, but an instruction is not erroneous when a finding of the essential element is necessarily implied from the other findings required. Reed v. Sale Memorial Hosp. and Clinic, 698 S.W.2d 931[11–15] (Mo.App.1985).

Since "a theory of recovery or defense should not be submitted unless it can stand alone" it was proper to refuse an instruction submitting two theories where one was incorrect as a matter of law. Commerford v. Kreitler, 462 S.W.2d 726[10] (Mo.1971).

Committee comment to MAI 1.02, conjunctive submissions, declares that every theory of recovery must be supported by evidence. Hounihan v. State Farm Mutual Auto. Ins., 441 S.W.2d 58[8, 9] (Mo.App.1969).

Error to submit excessive speed and wrong side of the road conjunctively. Strickland v. Barker, 436 S.W.2d 37[2] (Mo.1969).

Conjunctive submissions of negligence in maintaining defective screen door and defective porch railing erroneous absent evidence to support each submission. Woods v. Gould, 515 S.W.2d 592[8] (Mo.App.1968).

Error to submit MAI 23.05 hypothesizing two fraudulent submissions conjunctively when there was evidence of only one of them. Knepper v. Bollinger, 421 S.W.2d 796[5] (Mo.App.1967).

Where plaintiff submitted on (1) primary negligence and (2) humanitarian failure to stop or slacken, each of these elements must be supported by evidence. Johnson v. Bush, 418 S.W.2d 601[7–10] (Mo.App.1967).

Affirmative defenses, submitted disjunctively, must each be supported by evidence. Madison v. Dodson, 412 S.W.2d 552[7–11] (Mo.App.1967).

Where there are separate verdict directors on each of two theories, each must be supported by evidence. Toenjes v. L.J. McNeary Const. Co., 406 S.W.2d 101[7] (Mo.App.1966).

2. Dual elements

Submitting "slackened his speed, swerved and sounded a warning" was an erroneous conjunctive submission. Cassin v. Theodorow, 504 S.W.2d 203[6] (Mo.App.1973).

A modified MAI 17.04 submitting that defendant could have avoided the collision if he had "swerved, slackened his speed, swerved and sounded a warning" submitted three separate theories of recovery conjunctively and violated MAI 1.02. Cook v. Cox, 478 S.W.2d 678[5] (Mo.1972).

Submitting that defendant drove at less than normal speed and failed to drive in the right-hand lane (§ 304.015.5(3), V.A.M.S.) was a single theory of recovery composed of dual elements, not a conjunctive submission. Rooney v. Lloyd Metal Products Co., 458 S.W.2d 561[11] (Mo.1970).

3. Evidentiary support

Every verdict directing instruction, whether plaintiff's or defendant's, must be supported by evidence. Stotler v. Bollinger, 501 S.W.2d 558[1, 2] (Mo.App.1973).

1.03   [1965 New] Sole Cause Instructions

No instruction shall be given on behalf of the defendant which hypothesizes that the conduct of one other than defendant was the sole cause of the occurrence.

Committee Comment (1981 Revision)

There are three reasons for this restriction:

1. Such instructions require the recitation of detailed evidentiary facts and this practice is no longer permitted.

2. The negligence of one other than defendant is properly submitted in the causation element of the verdict director and reference thereto in an additional instruction is confusing and misleading.

3. The prescribed converse forms adequately present the same defense.

Library References:

C.J.S. Negligence § 871.
West's Key No. Digests, Negligence ☞1740.

Notes of Decisions

In general   1
Argument to jury   4
Intervening cause   3
Skidding   2

------

1. In general

Submission of instruction providing that verdict must be for railroad on former employee's Safety Appliances and Equipment Act claim if jury believed employee's negligence was sole cause of his injury was error, even though sole cause instruction was permissible under federal law, as instruction was confusing and misleading; Missouri law forbids sole cause instructions, instruction was duplicative, and negligence of employee was properly submitted in verdict director stating that verdict must be for employee if railroad's use of defective coupler mechanism resulted in whole or in part in employee's injury. Drury v. Missouri Pacific R. Co., 905 S.W.2d 138 (Mo.App.1995).

MAI's 1.01, 1.03 and 1.04 do not preclude the defenses of unavoidable accident, sudden emergency or sole cause, which defens-

es negated defendant's negligence, but are sufficiently presented by evidence, a converse of plaintiff's verdict director and argument to the jury. Coffel v. Spradley, 495 S.W.2d 735[11-13] (Mo.App.1973).

Defendant's verdict director exonerating him if sudden brake failure was sole cause of rear end collision was condemned as a sole cause instruction (MAI 1.03), as a sudden emergency instruction (MAI 1.04) and as an unavoidable accident instruction (MAI 1.01). Johnson v. Harrington, 443 S.W.2d 1[1-3] (Mo.App.1969).

Although a defendant may *argue* that the action of a third person was the proximate cause of plaintiff's injury, to submit that to a jury would violate MAI 1.03. Will v. Gilliam, 439 S.W.2d 498[1-3] (Mo.1969).

The defense of intervening cause is akin to sole cause, and may be submitted only by conversing plaintiff's element of proximate cause. Gathright v. Pendegraft, 433 S.W.2d 299[12] (Mo.1968).

Converse instruction adequately covers defense of sole cause. Birmingham v. Smith, 420 S.W.2d 514[3] (Mo.1967).

2. Skidding

Where plaintiff properly submitted MAI 17.13, driving on wrong side of the road, and defendant testified she skidded across the center line, it was error to give defendant's affirmative defense instruction exonerating her if she skidded. (This would have been error even had defendant further submitted that her skidding was not negligent.) Such an instruction is akin to an accident instruction condemned by MAI 1.01 and a sole cause instruction condemned by MAI 1.03. Defendant should be limited to conversing negligence by MAI 33.02(2), and then arguing non-negligent skidding. Stover v. Patrick, 459 S.W.2d 393[1, 2] (Mo. banc 1970).

3. Intervening cause

In humanitarian case a defendant may not present a sole cause defense, but if his evidence supports an intervening cause—as distinguished from a concurring cause—defendant may converse causation by MAI 33.05. Fowler v. Robinson, 465 S.W.2d 5[7–10] (Mo.App.1971).

4. Argument to Jury

MAI 1.03 does not prevent a defendant from introducing evidence and arguing that the acts of one other than the defendant were the sole cause of the accident. Simpson v. Smith, 771 S.W.2d 368, 372–73 (Mo.App.1989).

Although instructions on sole cause are impermissible, defense counsel may argue facts showing collision was solely caused by another's negligence. Cook v. Cox, 478 S.W.2d 678[10, 11] (Mo.1972).

MAI 1.03 does not prevent defendant from introducing evidence and arguing to jury that the acts of another were the sole cause of collision. Hoehn v. Hampton, 483 S.W.2d 403[7, 12] (Mo.App.1972).

1.04 [1965 New] Sudden Emergency Instructions

No "sudden emergency" instructions may be given.

Committee Comment (1965 New)

Sudden emergency instructions were often given at the request of a party who, prior to the accident, was confronted with an emergency not of his own making. These instructions told the jury that one acting during the emergency is not required to exercise the judgment of one who has time for calm deliberation. The Committee recommended that no such instructions be permitted. There were three reasons for this recommendation:

1. The language is argumentative.

2. The jury has already been instructed that the standard of care is measured by what would be done by others similarly situated.

3. The instruction may cause reversible error when submitted to cover antecedent negligence not in issue.

Library References:

C.J.S. Negligence § 871, 880–895.
West's Key No. Digests, Negligence ☞1726.

Notes of Decisions

1. In general

MAI's 1.01, 1.03 and 1.04 do not preclude the defenses of unavoidable accident, sudden emergency or sole cause, which defenses negated defendant's negligence, but are sufficiently presented by evidence, a converse of plaintiff's verdict director and argument to the jury. Coffel v. Spradley, 495 S.W.2d 735[11–13] (Mo.App.1973).

Defendant's verdict director exonerating him if sudden brake failure was sole cause of rear end collision was condemned as a sole cause instruction (MAI 1.03), as a sudden emergency instruction (MAI 1.04) and as an unavoidable accident instruction (MAI 1.01). Johnson v. Harrington, 443 S.W.2d 1[1–3] (Mo.App.1969).

1.05 [1965 New] Physical Facts Instructions

No instruction may be given the substance of which:

(a) informs the jury that they are to take into consideration the physical facts, or

(b) directs the jury to disregard testimony in conflict with the physical facts, or

(c) instructs the jury that any testimony contrary to physical facts shall be given such credit as the jury believes it is entitled to receive.

Committee Comment (1981 Revision)

The committee believes such instructions are pure argument not properly included in the court's instructions. The jurors are already told by MAI 2.01 that they will decide the facts and that the testimony of any witness shall be given such weight and value as they believe it is entitled to receive.

Library References:

C.J.S. Trial § 273, 306–307, 348.
West's Key No. Digests, Trial ⚷186, 204, 234.

1.06 [1983 New] Advance Payment or Partial Settlement Instructions

No instruction shall be given directing the jury to credit its verdict with the amount of any advance payment or partial settlement.

Committee Comment (1983 New)

Handling of any payment to be credited against plaintiff's claim is a matter of procedure. At the time of the adoption of MAI, the procedure was to advise the jury with respect to any prior settlement payments and to require the jury to deduct that amount from the damages it assessed and return a defendant's verdict if the settlement payment exceeded the plaintiff's damages. MAI 7.01 and 7.02 accommodated that procedure whether payment was admitted or disputed.

In 1972, the legislature adopted a procedure for handling advance payments made under § 490.710, RSMo. This was considered in *Taylor v. Yellow Cab Co.,* 548 S.W.2d 528 (Mo. banc 1977), wherein the Court pointed to the logic of making all deductions, whether advance payments or partial settlement payments by joint tort-feasors, a court function:

> If the only purpose in putting the payment in advance on the record was to allow for the reduction of the verdict by that amount, then that result is reached by *simply advising the court of the prior payment* and the court will reduce the payment accordingly. (Emphasis added).

Id. at 533, n. 1.

In considering a settlement payment by a joint tort-feasor in *Taylor,* the Court commented:

> In some states this is handled by the court reducing the judgment by the amount of the previous partial settlement rather than the jury doing so. *This may be a better way to handle this situation ....* (Emphasis added).

Id. at 532 n. 1.

Missouri Pacific Railroad Co. v. Whitehead & Kales Co., 566 S.W.2d 466 (Mo. banc 1978), raised further questions about the use of MAI 7.01 and 7.02. In apportionment of fault cases, a settling defendant may have paid more than the total amount of compensable damages; instructing the jury to return a verdict for the nonsettling defendant foreclosed the jury from apportioning fault between the settling and nonsettling tort-feasors even though apportionment of fault may have been applicable in that situation.

The former procedure also caused problems in cases in which the nonsettling tortfeasor would have been liable for punitive damages. If plaintiff is seeking punitive damages against the remaining defendant, he should be entitled to have the jury consider punitive damages if he has sustained some actual damages even though his actual damage may have been covered by the partial settlement already entered. MAI 7.01 and MAI 7.02 foreclose this consideration.

Requiring the jury to make the subtraction has led to mistakes. The trial court is better equipped to compute the credit. Accordingly, MAI 7.01 and its Notes on Use have been withdrawn.

Under the new procedure, the parties should make a record out of the hearing of the jury regarding undisputed prior settlement payments made either as an advancement by the defendant or as a partial settlement payment by a joint tort-feasor. The trial judge, as a matter of law, then will take any prior payments into consideration and will credit them on the damages assessed by the jury's verdict as required by law.

If there is a disputed issue as to whether there was a settlement payment, as to whether a certain payment was attributable to a settlement or as to the amount of a settlement payment, this issue is submitted to the jury by modifying the damage instruction as required by MAI 7.02 and using Form of Verdict MAI 36.19. If evidence of the fact or amount of a settlement is admitted for any other purpose, modify the damage instruction to include the Withdrawal Instruction in MAI 34.05.

Library References:

C.J.S. Damages § 177.
West's Key No. Digests, Damages ⚖210.

Notes of Decisions

1. In general

Defendants did not waive their right to seek setoff of amount received by plaintiffs in Illinois settlement against Missouri death claim on basis that they failed to offer jury instruction on issue; defendants took position that amount attributable to Missouri death claim from Illinois settlement was not in dispute, and in such a situation it was function of trial court to reduce amount re-covered by amount of settlement and no instruction is given to jury. Walihan v. St. Louis–Clayton Orthopedic Group, Inc., 849 S.W.2d 177 (Mo.App.1993).

It is a function of the court to reduce the amount recovered if there has been an advance payment which should be credited to a claim or counterclaim. Allen v. Foster, 668 S.W.2d 277[4] (Mo.App.1984).

12

2.00

EXPLANATORY

Analysis of Instructions

Westlaw Electronic Research

See Westlaw Electronic Research Guide preceding the Table of Instructions.

Library References:

C.J.S. Trial § 326.
West's Key No. Digests, Trial ⚖228.

13

2.00   [1996 Revision] Submissions in Multi–Party or in Multi–Claim Litigation—General Comment

A.   The Need for Better Organized Instructions in Complex Litigation

The former MAI system worked well in a simple case where one plaintiff brings one claim against one defendant. As litigation has become more complex, it is not unusual for several plaintiffs and several defendants to be combined in the same lawsuit with the various plaintiffs often making claims for different losses based on differing theories of liability and with the various defendants counterclaiming or maintaining cross-claims or filing third-party petitions for apportionment of fault or asserting other theories of recovery. The former MAI system has been modified and supplemented to meet the needs of such multi-claim litigation.

B.   Packaging

Much of the complexity in instructions in such a case results from the large number of instructions necessary to properly submit the case. To aid the jury in understanding and organizing this large number of instructions, the Court has adopted a method of arranging and organizing the various instructions in such a case by grouping together the general instructions which apply generally to the overall litigation and placing in separate packages the specific instructions which apply to a particular claim. This system, called "packaging," is to be used as described herein in all cases having more than one verdict form. Such a case (one having more than one verdict form) is referred to herein as a "complex case." The primary purpose of "packaging" is to aid the jury in complex litigation in moving through the instructions and thus through their deliberations from one claim to another in an organized and understandable manner. One could describe the concept of "packaging" as a series of mini-sets of instructions, each of which is a subdivision of the overall set of instructions in the case. Once the general instructions which apply to the entire case have been given, each "package" will constitute a complete package of the remaining instructions applicable to a particular claim followed at the end of the package by the verdict form on which the jury will return its verdict as to that claim.

After the close of the evidence, MAI 2.03, an introductory instruction, is to be given in every case. This is to be followed by all of the instructions which apply generally to more than one claim in the case. This will include the burden of proof instruction, definition instructions of terms used in more than one claim, MAI 2.02 Facts Not Assumed, which is no longer required to be given immediately before the Form of Verdict instruction, and MAI 2.04, which designates the number of claims in a multi-claim case and instructs that nine or more jurors may return a verdict.

The remaining instructions which apply to a particular claim will then be "packaged" by claim. Each of these packages will begin with MAI 2.05, which specifies the particular instructions which apply to the particular claim described therein and refers the jury to the appropriate verdict form. MAI 2.05 will be followed by all of the instructions which apply only to that particular claim. These would include one or more verdict directors, one or more converse instructions if they are used, the appropriate affirmative defense instruction, the damage instruction, and any definitions which are applicable only to this claim. The last page of the package will be the verdict form, which will be designated alphabetically (A, B, C, etc.) rather than numerically. Further packages consisting of MAI 2.05, the other instructions applying to a particular claim, and a further verdict form will make up such other packages as are necessary to submit the case fully in an organized and understandable manner.

The set of general instructions and each package is to be stapled separately or similarly fastened so as not to be readily separated. These packages should then be stacked together in the appropriate order and the entire set of instructions secured together with a removable fastener such as a paper clip or other appropriate binder clip. The arrangement should be such that the jury can separate the packages if they wish and each package, except the package of general instructions, will begin with MAI 2.05 and end with a verdict form which the jury will complete.

C.   Packaging Not Applicable To "Simple" Cases

"Packaging" is designed to simplify the submission of complex cases. In a simple case, where only one claim is involved, "packaging" is not necessary and to require its use in such a case would only serve to complicate the system. At the same time, the Court does not wish to create a trap for the unwary by drawing technical distinctions as to when "packaging" is or is not required. As discussed in Section E hereof, the basis for "packaging" (by claim or otherwise) is for the determination of the trial judge based on what will present the case to the jury in a manner which will best allow them to consider all the issues in the case in an organized, understandable, and comprehensible manner. If the basis for "packaging" decided upon by the trial court results in two or more packages in addition to the package of general instructions, then the general "packaging" rules for multi-claim cases will apply. A simple and effective way to recognize and describe such a case is that it will be any case in which two or more verdict forms are used (since each package other than the package of general instructions ends with a verdict form).

In a case in which there is only one verdict form, there will be only one package containing both the general instructions and all other instructions. In such a case, referred to herein as a "simple" case, the Court will give the same general instructions in the same order as is described in Paragraph B above for multi-claim cases. These general instructions will be followed by the other instructions which would otherwise be separately packaged in a multi-claim case except that MAI 2.05 will not be given in a "simple" case. Thus, the single package of instructions in a simple case will begin with MAI 2.01 and end with the verdict form.

In summary, the packaging rules to be followed in multi-claim cases will be modified as follows for the submission of a "simple" case (one containing only one verdict form):

1.   MAI 2.04 is to be modified by omitting the first sentence (see bracketed sentence footnoted number 1 in MAI 2.04).

2.   MAI 2.05 is not to be given in the "simple" case.

3.   All instructions will be contained in a single package.

D.   Numbering

Verdict forms will carry a letter designation rather than a number, i.e., A, B, C, etc. All other instructions will be numbered sequentially beginning with MAI 2.01 which will be Instruction No. 1 and followed by MAI 2.03 numbered Instruction No. 2 and the other general instructions. The numbering will then continue sequentially through the instructions in the various packages so that, for example, in a complex case one package may consist of instructions Nos. 8 through 14 and Verdict Form A and the next package of instructions Nos. 15 through 21 and verdict form B, etc.

E.   The Basis for Packaging

Subject to the specific directions set out herein, the trial judge has discretion to determine the order in which the instructions will be given. It will be up to the trial judge to determine the basis for "packaging" of a complex case so that the overall instructions will present the case to the jury in a manner which will best allow them to consider all of the issues in the case in an organized, understandable, and comprehensible manner. In most instances, the case should be packaged so that the claim for damages of each party asserting a claim for damages will be covered by a separate package.

For example, if plaintiff A is claiming damages for personal injuries, all of the instructions applicable to this claim would be included in one package. If plaintiff A is proceeding on alternative theories of negligence and strict liability, the verdict directors for both such theories would be included in the same package. If plaintiff A is making his claim against both defendant X and defendant Y, the verdict directors against both defendants would be included in the

17

package.   If these defendants claim that plaintiff A was contributorily negligent, the contributory negligence instruction would also be included in the package.   Any other instructions necessary to this claim such as plaintiff A's damage instruction would likewise be included in the package.

If defendant X is asserting a counterclaim against plaintiff A for property damage, this would constitute a second claim and would be submitted in a second package.   If defendant Y was claiming Apportionment of Fault from defendant X, this would be a third claim and would be submitted in a third package.

While "packaging" based on the claim asserted will be the most common basis upon which most cases will be packaged, there is no rigid requirement as to the criteria for "packaging."   It should be done in any manner which will submit the case to the jury in a well-organized, understandable, and comprehensible manner.

F.   Describing the Claim Covered by the Package

MAI 2.05, the introductory instruction for each individual package, and the verdict form should include a descriptive phrase which describes and identifies the claim which is being submitted in that package.   Since MAI 2.05 limits the intervening instructions to the claim described in MAI 2.05 and submitted in that package, it is not necessary that each instruction in the package contain this descriptive phrase. However, certain instructions in the package may require further identification if they do not apply to the entire claim covered by the package.   For example, if the package submits a claim against more than one defendant requiring separate verdict directors for each defendant, the verdict directors must be modified to identify the defendant to which each applies.   In such a situation, the first line of the instruction would be changed to read, "Your Verdict must be for plaintiff Jones against defendant Smith if you believe:".

Identifying phrases should be as non-inflammatory and as neutral as possible and should avoid the assumption of disputed facts.   The following are examples of the types of identifying phrases which are appropriate to describe the claim in the first (MAI 2.05) and last (verdict form) instruction of each package:

... on the claim of plaintiff Joe Smith for personal injuries ...

... on the claim of plaintiff Susie Smith for damages as a result of any injury to her husband ...

... on the claim of plaintiff Joe Smith and Susie Smith for property damage ...

... on the claim of defendant John Jones for personal injuries ...

... on the claim of plaintiff Mary Adams for the death of her husband....

If plaintiff claims damages for more than one type of injury in the same package (such as for his own personal injuries and for loss of consortium for injuries to his wife) under circumstances where he may be entitled to recover one type of damage even if he does not recover on the other, a description of both claims in the verdict form may be misleading because it may suggest he cannot recover on either unless he recovers on both. For example, the verdict form would state, "On the claim of plaintiff for personal injuries and for damages for any injury to his wife, against defendant, we, the undersigned jurors, find in favor of:...." This ambiguity can be avoided by omitting the specific reference to both types of damages so that the verdict form will read, "On the claim of plaintiff against defendant, we, the undersigned jurors, find in favor of:...." The same problem arises when plaintiff seeks damages for both personal injury and property damage.

G. Multiple Theories—Overlapping Damages

In complex litigation with multiple theories of liability (e.g.—commercial litigation), elements of damages under various theories may be identical in some respects, distinct in others, and overlapping in still others. The issue will then arise as to whether multiple theories should be submitted in a single package (with a single damage instruction and a single verdict form) or in separate packages (with a separate damage instruction and a separate verdict form for each theory). The Committee takes no position requiring a particular approach in all such cases. The facts and law applicable to each case will determine the best approach in a given case. The problems to be considered in making the selection of a single package or multiple package approach include the issues of duplicate or overlapping damages, the judgment to be entered if a jury returns damages on more than one theory submitted as separate packages, and the effect of a reversal on appeal on one theory but an affirmance on another. Care should be taken to thoroughly consider the impact of duplicate or overlapping damages under separate theories so that the jury is given adequate guidance on the elements of damages and an appropriate means to express the jury's intent without confusion as to the total judgment to be entered by the trial court. See: Illustration 35.15 for a method of submitting multiple theories in a single package; and MAI 36.02, 36.10, and 36.22 for methods of fashioning a verdict form with categories of damages.

H. Conclusion

The unique virtue of the MAI system is the recognition that the primary purpose of the instructions in a case is to convey to the jury the law applicable to the case in an understandable, non-argumentative and non-technical manner. "Packaging" is designed to help meet this goal. No rigid set of specific rules can insure understanding and comprehension for every juror and every type of complex case. "Packaging" is not intended to be a rigid set of rules; it is a tool for lawyers and judges to use with judgment and with consideration for all the facts and circumstances involved in the particular case. If "packaging" is misused as a tool of advocacy to benefit one party and to the detriment of another, it will not serve the purpose for which it is designed. When lawyers and judges use "packaging" in a bona fide effort to present the jury with an organized, understandable and comprehensible set of instructions, it will serve as a major step forward in improving and perfecting the MAI system to meet the demands of modern litigation.

Notes of Decisions

1. In general

Fraudulent misrepresentation jury instruction package should have included actual damage instruction; fact that actual damage instruction was contained in breach of contract package did not cure error, since jury was instructed that damage instruction applied only to breach of contract claim; damage instruction is mandatory in damage suit unless amount of damage is not in dispute. Dierker Associates, D.C., P.C. v. Gillis, 859 S.W.2d 737 (Mo.App.1993).

Trial court's decision on whether and how to package jury instructions will not be disturbed without a showing of prejudice; trial court properly refused to submit contractor's default under three surety bonds in separate packages where all claims and defenses were interrelated. Howard Const. Co. v. Teddy Woods Const. Co., 817 S.W.2d 556 (Mo.App.1991).

Giving the same converse instruction in both packages of instructions in action by automobile passenger and her parents was not error. Such duplication of instructions is necessary so that each claim will contain all of the instructions, except for general instructions, which are necessary for the complete submission of that particular claim. Seithel v. Clifford, 689 S.W.2d 91[1] (Mo.App.1985).

As noted in the general comments, packaging is not a rigid set of rules; it is a tool for lawyers and judges to use with judgment and with consideration for all the facts and circumstances involved in a particular case. The burden of showing prejudice by use of the verdict forms in MAI 2.00 rests upon the appellant. Affiliated Foods Inc. v. Strautman, 656 S.W.2d 753[5–6] (Mo.App.1983).

2.01   [2002 Revision] Explanatory Instruction for All Cases

(1) GENERAL—JURY INSTRUCTIONS

This instruction and other instructions that I will read to you near the end of the trial are in writing. All of the written instructions will be handed to you for guidance in your deliberation when you retire to the jury room. They will direct you concerning the legal rights and duties of the parties and how the law applies to the facts that you will be called upon to decide.

(2) OPENING STATEMENTS

The trial may begin with opening statements by the lawyers as to what they expect the evidence to be. What is said in opening statements is not to be considered as proof of a fact. However, if a lawyer admits some fact on behalf of his client, the other party is relieved of the responsibility of proving that fact.

(3) EVIDENCE

After the opening statements, the plaintiff(s) will introduce evidence.[1] The defendant(s) may then introduce evidence. There may be rebuttal evidence after that. The evidence may include the testimony of witnesses who appear personally in court, the testimony of witnesses who may not appear personally but whose testimony may be read or shown to you, and exhibits such as pictures, documents, and other objects.

(4) OBJECTIONS

There may be some questions asked or evidence offered by the parties to which objection may be made. If I overrule an objection, you may consider that evidence when you deliberate on the case. If I sustain an objection, then that matter and any matter I order to be stricken is excluded as evidence and must not be considered by you in your deliberations.

(5) RULINGS OF LAW AND BENCH CONFERENCES

While the trial is in progress, I may be called upon to determine questions of law and to decide whether certain matters may be considered by you under the law. No ruling or remark that I make at any time during the trial will be intended or should be considered by you to indicate my opinion as to the facts. There may be times when the lawyers come up to talk to me out of your hearing. This will be done in order to permit me to decide questions of law. These conversations will be out of your hearing to prevent issues of law, which I must decide, from becoming mixed with issues of fact, which you must decide. We will not be trying to keep secrets from you.

(6) OPEN MINDS AND NO PRELIMINARY DISCUSSIONS

Justice requires that you keep an open mind about the case until the parties have had the opportunity to present their cases to you. You must not make up your mind about the case until all evidence, and the closing arguments of the parties, have been seen or heard. You must not comment on or discuss with anyone, not even among yourselves, what you hear or learn in trial until the case is concluded and then only when all of you are present in the jury room for deliberation of the case under the final instructions I give to you.

(7) OUTSIDE INFLUENCES

During the trial, you should not remain in the presence of anyone who is discussing the case when the court is not in session. Otherwise, some outside influence or comment might influence a juror to make up his or her mind prematurely and be the cause of a possible injustice. For this reason, the lawyers and their clients are not permitted to talk with you until the trial is completed. Your decision must be based only on the evidence presented to you in the proceedings in this courtroom; and you may not conduct your own research or investigation into any of the issues in this case.

(8) FINAL INSTRUCTIONS

After all of the evidence has been presented, you will receive my final instructions. They will guide your deliberation of the issues of fact you are to decide in arriving at your verdict.

(9) CLOSING ARGUMENTS

After you have received my final instructions, the lawyers may make closing arguments. In closing arguments, the lawyers have the opportunity to direct your attention to the significance of the evidence and to suggest the conclusions that may be drawn from the evidence.

(10) DELIBERATIONS

You will then retire to the jury room for your deliberations. It will be your duty to select a foreperson, to decide the facts, and to arrive at a verdict. When you enter into your deliberations, you will be considering the testimony of witnesses as well as other evidence. In considering the weight and value of the testimony of any witness, you may take into consideration the appearance, attitude, and behavior of the witness, the interest of the witness in the outcome of the case, the relation of the witness to any of the parties, the inclination of the witness to speak truthfully or untruthfully, and the probability or improbability of the witness' statements. You may give any evidence or the testimony of any witness such weight and value as you believe that evidence or testimony is entitled to receive.

[(11) NOTETAKING

Each of you may take notes in this case, but you are not required to do so. I will give you notebooks. Any notes you take must be in those notebooks only. You may not take any notes out of the courtroom before the case is submitted to you for your deliberations. No one will read your notes while you are out of the courtroom. If you choose to take notes, remember that notetaking may interfere with your ability to observe the evidence and witnesses as they are presented.

Do not discuss or share your notes with anyone until you begin your deliberations. During your deliberations, if you choose to do so, you may use your notes and discuss them with other jurors. Notes taken during trial are not evidence. You should not assume that your notes, or those of other jurors, are more accurate than your own recollection or the recollection of other jurors.

After you reach your verdict, your notes will be collected and destroyed. No one will be allowed to read them.][2]

Notes on Use (1996 Revision)

1. When the facts of the case indicate a reversal of the parties in the order of proof, the instruction reference to plaintiff(s) and defendant(s) must be changed to show the actual order to be followed; i.e., in a case of a claim and counterclaim wherein the claim has been dismissed and the trial proceeds on the counterclaim, the defendant proceeds with evidence ahead of the plaintiff; in condemnation cases, the defendant is first in the order of proof; the trial court has discretion in some cases to vary the order. In will contests where the validity of the entire will or codicil is contested under § 473.083, RSMo, substitute for the first sentence of the third paragraph the sentence, "After the opening statements, the defendant-proponent(s) of the disputed document will present their evidence consisting of the formal proof of the document, first." In will contests challenging only a portion of a will or codicil under § 473.081, RSMo, no such change is necessary.

This instruction shall be read by the trial judge immediately after the jury is sworn and before opening statements of counsel. It is not to be reread by the judge at the conclusion of all the evidence, but it is to be given to the jury with the other written instructions. The attorney for either side may read all or portions of the instruction during closing arguments.

2. If the court allows notetaking by jurors, these bracketed paragraphs should be added.

Committee Comment (2002 Revision)

Directions or admonitions given by a trial judge to a jury during the course of trial are technically not instructions. Examples of such directions or admonitions include a direction not to visit the scene of an accident or an oral repetition of the admonition to refrain from discussing the case during a recess. Considerable discretion is afforded to the trial judge, subject to appropriate requests or objections of counsel, to determine the scope and frequency of such directions or admonitions. An appropriate admonition may be in the following form, and may be given orally:

> Justice requires that you not make up your mind about the case until all of the evidence has been seen and heard. You must not discuss this case among yourselves or with anyone else or comment

on anything you hear or learn in this trial until the case is concluded and you retire to the jury room for your deliberations. Also, you must not remain in the presence of anyone who is discussing the case when the court is not in session.

Other appropriate oral admonitions or directions to the jury may be formulated and given by the trial judge as determined in light of the particular facts or circumstances of a given case.

Supreme Court Rule 69.03 provides:

Juror Note-taking

Upon the court's own motion or upon the request of any party, the court shall permit jurors to take notes. If jurors are permitted to take notes, the court shall supply each juror with suitable materials.

Jurors shall not take their notes out of the courtroom except to use their notes during deliberations.

The court shall collect all juror notes immediately before discharge of the jury.

After the jury is discharged, the court shall destroy the notes promptly without permitting their review by the court or any other person.

Juror notes shall not be used to impeach a verdict.

Rule 70.02(f) requires that the final instructions of the court be given to the jury in writing. While Rule 70.02 does not explicitly require that each juror be provided with a copy of the final instructions, such approach is implicitly permitted. In its report to the Supreme Court of October 2000, the Civil Jury Study Committee recommended "that each juror be given a copy of the instructions before instruction reading, final argument, and deliberation." (Emphasis supplied.) That committee also noted that juror "understanding increased significantly when each juror received his or her own copy of the instructions." The MAI Committee encourages compliance with this recommendation whenever feasible.

Library References:

C.J.S. Trial § 297–298, 320, 322.
West's Key No. Digests, Trial ⚏201, 217.

Notes of Decisions

In general   1
Criminal cases   3
Deviation   5
Exhibits   7
Hammer instruction   4
Modification   6
Omissions   2

———

1.   In general

Medical malpractice and wrongful death plaintiffs' objections to argument of defendant medical center, which argument could

have been allegedly construed as stating that jury could only consider particular evidence and not other evidence, were properly overruled; trial court admonished jurors that they heard evidence and ruling on objections and were instructed to consider only those facts still alive at trial, and trial court gave jury general instruction that jurors could consider all evidence except what had been withdrawn because trial court had sustained objections. Vititoe v. Lester E. Cox Medical Centers, 27 S.W.3d 812 (Mo.App. 2000).

The effect of MAI 2.01 is to put jurors on notice that their duty under law is not defined by argument of counsel except to extent counsel admits fact in evidence; instruction undergirds general rule that verdicts should not be set aside on appeal for erroneous argument absent clear abuse of discretion by trial judge. Tune v. Synergy Gas Corp., 883 S.W.2d 10 (Mo.1994).

2. Omissions

Omitting clause from Par. 8 of MAI 2.01 was presumptively prejudicial. Chapman v. Bradley, 478 S.W.2d 873 (Mo.App.1972).

Omission of "reasonable inference" and "relationship of the witness" clauses from MAI 2.01 is prejudicial error. McCory v. Knowles, 478 S.W.2d 682[5] (Mo.App.1972).

Omitting the reasonable-inference clause and the relationship-of-witness-to-party clause was presumptively prejudicial. City of Jackson v. Barks, 476 S.W.2d 162[1] (Mo. App.1972).

3. Criminal cases

MAI 2.01 properly refused in criminal case since MAI applies only to civil cases. State v. Bohlen, 487 S.W.2d 543[1, 2] (Mo.1972).

4. Hammer instruction

Error to give "hammer" instruction requiring jury to reach verdict by agreement of the whole jury is error, but harmless where there was 9–to–3 verdict. Garner v. Jones, 589 S.W.2d 66[5–7] (Mo.App.1979).

Hammer instruction may be given after submission of case to jury, but MAI–CR 1.10 is inappropriate in a civil trial where the verdict need not be unanimous. Cowan v. McElroy, 549 S.W.2d 543 (Mo.App.1977).

5. Deviation

Trial court's interpretative embellishment of MAI 2.01 reversible error by violating Rule 72.02(b) excluding other instructions. Washington v. Sears, Roebuck, 585 S.W.2d 137[1] (Mo.App.1979).

6. Modification

Modification not required to have defendant proceed first. Truck Insurance Exchange v. Hunt, 590 S.W.2d 425[10] (Mo. App.1979).

7. Exhibits

Error in permitting deliberating jury to view damage chart with inadmissible calculations of damages for past and future pain and suffering by child pedestrian required reversal of verdict in favor of pedestrian, but not her mother, in action arising out of collision with truck, even though jury properly viewed chart during closing arguments immediately before deliberations, and even though judge instructed jurors that nothing said in opening statements or closing arguments could be considered as proof of fact; jury set damages in exact amount listed on chart as high award. Lester v. Sayles, 850 S.W.2d 858 (Mo.1993).

2.02 [1980 Revision] Facts Not Assumed

In returning your verdict[s] you will form beliefs as to the facts. The court does not mean to assume as true any fact referred to in these instructions but leaves it to you to determine what the facts are.

Notes on Use (1980 Revision)

This instruction must be given once and only once in every case.

It may be given in such order as the trial court shall deem advisable. However, in multi-claim submission cases, it should be given along with the other explanatory instructions early in the sequence of instructions as part of the package of general instructions. See MAI 2.00 General Comment.

Committee Comment (1980 Revision)

This instruction reduces the chances of a jury improperly concluding that a controverted fact has been assumed by the court to be true. See *Ogilvie v. Kansas City Public Service Co.,* 27 S.W.2d 733, 735 (Mo.App. 1930), and *Allen v. Purvis,* 30 S.W.2d 196, 201 (Mo.App.1930).

Similar instructions have been approved in *Greenwood v. Wiseman,* 305 S.W.2d 474, 476 (Mo.1957), and in *Potter v. Sac–Osage Electric Cooperative, Inc.,* 335 S.W.2d 192, 199 (Mo.1960).

The first sentence is intended to clarify the function of this instruction.

Library References:

C.J.S. Trial § 279.
West's Key No. Digests, Trial ☞191.

Notes of Decisions

1. In general

Whether contributory negligence instruction confused jury by improperly assuming controverted fact is tested by principle of "reasonable men" construction. Kewanee Oil Co. v. Remmert–Werner, 508 S.W.2d 23[2–4] (Mo.App.1974).

Where issue was whether roadway was public or had become private by non-use, it was error for instruction to refer to it as a public road. Terhune v. Caton, 487 S.W.2d 19[2, 3] (Mo.1972).

2.03 [1980 New] Explanatory—Order of Instructions

As you remember, the court gave you a general instruction before the presentation of any evidence in this case. The court will not repeat that instruction at this time. However, that instruction and the additional instructions, to be given to you now, constitute the law of this case and each such instruction is equally binding upon you. You should consider each instruction in light of and in harmony with the other instructions, and you should apply the instructions as a whole to the evidence. The order in which the instructions are given is no indication of their relative importance. All of the instructions are in writing and will be available to you in the jury room.

Notes on Use (1980 New)

This instruction is to be given in every case as the first instruction after the close of the evidence. It should be numbered Instruction Number 2 following MAI 2.01 which is Instruction Number 1.

Library References:

C.J.S. Trial § 298, 320, 322.
West's Key No. Digests, Trial ☞217.

2.04   [1981 Revision] Explanatory—Return of Verdict

[There are _____ claims submitted to you and each of them contains a separate verdict form.] [1] The verdict form[s] included in these instructions contain[s] directions for completion and will allow you to return the permissible verdict[s] in this case. Nine or more of you must agree in order to return any verdict. A verdict must be signed by each juror who agrees to it.

Notes on Use (1980 New)

1. The bracketed sentence should be used only in multi-claim cases (those having two or more verdict forms). See MAI 2.00 General Comment.

This instruction must be given in every case. In multi-claim cases, it should be given along with the other explanatory instructions as part of the package of general instructions.

Library References:

C.J.S. Trial § 298, 317, 320, 322.
West's Key No. Digests, Trial ☞215, 217.

Notes of Decisions

1. In general

Verdict form providing for one set of jurors' signatures, as well as jury instructions that "nine or more of you [jurors] must agree in order to return any verdict", adequately advised jury in wrongful death action that same nine jurors should have agreed on same element, act of negligence, causation, and amount of damages. Stacy v. Truman Medical Center, 836 S.W.2d 911 (Mo.1992).

2.05 [1980 New] Multi–Claim Submissions—Designation of Applicable Instructions

Instructions _____ [1] through _____ [2] and general instructions 1 through _____ [3] apply to the claim of (*here insert party and designation of claim such as "plaintiff Joe Smith for personal injury"*).[4] Use Verdict _____ to return your verdict on this claim.

Notes on Use (1980 New)

1. Insert the number of the present instruction which will be the first instruction in this package.

2. Insert the number of the instruction immediately preceding the verdict form in this package.

3. Insert the number of the last instruction in the first package which is the package containing general instructions.

4. This instruction should contain a descriptive phrase which describes and identifies the claim submitted by this particular package. The identifying phrase should be non-inflammatory and as neutral as possible and should avoid the assumption of disputed facts. See MAI 2.00 General Comment for a discussion and for examples of the appropriate identifying phrase.

In multi-claim cases the instructions will be "packaged." See MAI 2.00 General Comment and Illustrations in Chapter 35 in this regard. MAI 2.05 is to be used as the first instruction for each such "package" after the package of general instructions and will be used as many times as there are such "packages" in the complete set of instructions. MAI 2.05 is not to be given in cases using only one verdict form. In such a case only one package will be used; it will contain both general and other instructions. See MAI 2.00 General Comment, Section C.

Library References:

C.J.S. Trial § 317.
West's Key No. Digests, Trial ☞215.

Notes of Decisions

1. In general

Trial court correctly included fire insurer's affirmative defense instruction in each package of claims by insureds, even though insureds claimed that doing so resulted in improper multiple submission of affirmative defense of arson. Joiner v. Auto–Owners Mut. Ins. Co., 891 S.W.2d 479 (Mo.App. W.D.,1994).

2.06 [1983 New] Explanatory—Inconsistent or Erroneous Verdict

The court cannot accept your verdict[s] as written. [Verdict _____ and Verdict _____ are inconsistent.][1] You should examine your verdict[s] in light of all of the instructions. [A] [N]ew verdict form[s] are [is] attached for your use, if needed. Do not destroy any of the verdict forms.

Notes on Use (1989 Revision)

1. Insert sentence describing the problem in the verdict or verdicts proposed, for example, "Your findings in Verdict _____ are inconsistent." or "Verdict _____ is not complete." or "The meaning of Verdict _____ is not clear."

This instruction may be given only if the jury attempts to return an inconsistent, incomplete, ambiguous or otherwise erroneous verdict. The court should identify each of the new verdict forms submitted with this instruction with an appropriate designation such as "Second Set."

Library References:

C.J.S. Trial § 511, 562–563, 567.
West's Key No. Digests, Trial ☞339, 358, 359, 362.

Notes of Decisions

1. In general

When a trial court sends a jury back for further deliberations because it has returned inconsistent verdicts, instruction on deliberations following inconsistent verdicts is mandatory. Franklin v. Allstate Ins. Co., 985 S.W.2d 893 (Mo.App.1999).

In suit by injured union members against union local and its former president arising out of former president's assault of them following union election, trial court's error in refusing local union's request that jury be returned to their deliberations for correction of its verdict warranted reversal and remand for new trial on issue of compensatory damages only; though former president's acts of willfulness and local union's negligence were separate and independent, they were joint tortfeasors insofar as injuries caused were single and indivisible, and jury should have been given other forms of verdicts patterned after MAI Form of Verdict 36.05, which would have allowed single verdict and single amount of compensatory damages for each plaintiff. Fincher v. Murphy, 825 S.W.2d 890 (Mo.App.1992).

Seller of computer and software system waived any error based on inconsistency of verdict in favor of seller on its claim for payment of balance of purchase price and in favor of buyer on its claims for breach of warranty and conversion, where seller did not ask for, and in fact objected to, any possibility that jury be instructed to deliberate further. Clayton X–Ray Co. v. Professional Systems Corp., 812 S.W.2d 565 (Mo. App.1991).

MAI 2.06 was properly utilized to re-submit the case to the jury after the return of an ambiguous verdict with regard to the amount of damages where the jury used the words "One Million Eight Hundred Eighty." A verdict is not final unless it is submitted to the court, accepted by the court, assented to by the jury, and recorded by the court. An ambiguous, inconsistent, or otherwise defective verdict may be re-submitted to the jury to give an opportunity to correct it or render a new verdict. On re-submission, the jury returned a verdict for $1,880,000.00. Parker v. Midwestern Distribution, Inc., 797 S.W.2d 721 (Mo.App.1990).

3.00

BURDEN OF PROOF

Analysis of Instructions

Westlaw Electronic Research

See Westlaw Electronic Research Guide preceding the Table of Instructions.

Library References:

C.J.S. Trial § 308, 354, 382.
West's Key No. Digests, Trial ⚖️205, 234(7), 252(6, 18).

35

3.01 [1998 Revision] Burden of Proof—General

In these instructions, you are told that your verdict depends on whether or not you believe certain propositions of fact submitted to you. [The burden is upon plaintiff to cause you to believe that the evidence has clearly and convincingly established the propositions of fact required for the recovery of punitive damages[1] as submitted in Instruction Number ___ (*insert the number of the punitive damage instruction*). However, on all other propositions of fact,][2] (T)he burden is upon the party who relies upon any such proposition to cause you to believe that such proposition is more likely to be true than not true. In determining whether or not you believe any proposition, you must consider only the evidence and the reasonable inferences derived from the evidence. If the evidence in the case does not cause you to believe a particular proposition submitted, then you cannot return a verdict requiring belief of that proposition.

Notes on Use (1998 Revision)

1. Substitute the phrase "damages for aggravating circumstances" for the phrase "punitive damages" if aggravating circumstances are submitted under MAI 6.02 in a wrongful death case.

2. Add bracketed material if punitive damages or damages for aggravating circumstances are submitted. See *Rodriguez v. Suzuki Motor Corp.*, 936 S.W.2d 104 (Mo. banc 1996).

A burden of proof instruction must be given in every case. MAI 3.01 is to be used except where another burden of proof instruction has been provided.

Committee Comment (1981 Revision)

It is no longer necessary to modify the instruction to specifically refer to the burden of proof on an affirmative defense or a counterclaim because the second sentence of the instruction covers each party's burden of proof.

Library References:

C.J.S. Trial § 308, 354.
West's Key No. Digests, Trial ☞205, 234(7).

Notes of Decisions

---

1. Deviation

Inadvertent use of prior approved burden of proof instruction after effective date of 1998 Revision, did not misstate the law, was not prejudicial to plaintiff, and, thus, did not justify award of new trial to plaintiff. Jury was told both in voir dire and closing argument that plaintiff had burden of causing jury to believe that a proposition was more likely true than not true, there was no indication that jury was confused or misunderstood plaintiff's burden of proof, plaintiff did not consider error sufficiently prejudicial at time of discovery to request proper instruction, and case was argued at all times as though proper instruction had in fact been given. Hill v. Hyde, 14 S.W.3d 294 (Mo.App.2000).

Defendant driver's closing argument, that MAI 3.01 did not mention anything about 51%, was a proper clarifying response to plaintiff driver's closing argument that she only had to tip the scales in her favor by 51% to be entitled to judgment, and did not constitute plain error. Williams v. Jacobs, 972 S.W.2d 334 (Mo.App.1998).

When reviewing cases for instructional error resulting from deviation from Missouri Approved Instructions (MAI) format, it is role of court to determine whether erroneous instruction caused prejudicial effect, and no judgment will be reversed on account of instructional error unless error materially affected merits of case. Porta–Fab Corp. v. Young Sales Corp., 943 S.W.2d 686 (Mo. App.1997).

Burden is on party who offered erroneous instruction which deviated from Missouri Approved Instruction (MAI) format to show on appeal that erroneous instruction created no substantial potential for prejudicial effect.

Porta–Fab Corp. v. Young Sales Corp., 943 S.W.2d 686 (Mo.App.1997).

While deviation from the use of MAI constitutes error, it falls to the courts to judicially determine the prejudicial effect, if any, thereof, the burden of proving that there was no prejudice falling upon the proponent of the instruction. Where defendants suffered no prejudice as a result of adding the term "or defense" to the burden of proof instruction where there was no affirmative defense issue submitted to the jury, there was no prejudicial error. Affiliated Foods, Inc. v. Strautman, 656 S.W.2d 753[11–12] (Mo.App. 1983).

Use of singular instead of plural forms held harmless error in view of other proper instructions. Penn v. Columbia Asphalt Co., 513 S.W.2d 679[18] (Mo.App.1974).

Improper use of "his" instead of "her" was error but not prejudicial where identity of female plaintiff was apparent to the jury; instruction was "substantially correct." Gormly v. Johnson, 451 S.W.2d 45[3] (Mo. 1970).

Slight error in burden-of-proof instruction harmless when clarified by verdict director, to which it referred by number. Bauser v. Denoble, 412 S.W.2d 409[4, 5] (Mo.1967).

Error to depart from MAI 3.01 (burden of proof) by using pre–MAI language. Pasternak v. Mashak, 428 S.W.2d 565[11] (Mo. 1967).

2. Affirmative defense

Insurer bears burden of proof on affirmative defense that insured failed to comply with policy condition. Nichols v. Preferred Risk Group, 44 S.W.3d 886 (Mo.App.2001).

Inclusion of phrase "or defense" in MAI 3.01 was error where no affirmative defense was raised, but the error was harmless since the instruction viewed in light of totality of instructions indicated that plaintiff still had the burden of proof. Wilson v. Lockwood, 711 S.W.2d 545[9, 10] (Mo.App.1986).

Trial court committed prejudicial error in giving a separate burden of proof instruction as to an affirmative defense where MAI 3.01 already had been submitted. Begley v. Werremeyer Associates, Inc., 638 S.W.2d 817[1–3] (Mo.App.1982).

Defendant has burden of proving affirmative defenses of release or payment. Winter v. Elder, 492 S.W.2d 146[2] (Mo.App.1973).

3. Invited error

Plaintiff may not complain of omission in his own burden-of-proof instruction. Blankenship v. Kansas City Terminal Ry. Co., 462 S.W.2d 650[1] (Mo.1971).

4. Fraud

Burden of proof in a fraud case tried to a jury is no greater than in any other case tried to a jury, and the proper burden of proof instruction is MAI 3.01; thus, bankruptcy order could have collateral estoppel effect on subsequent common law fraud action, which had same burden of proof. Hartsfield v. Barkley, 856 S.W.2d 342 (Mo.App.1993).

Burden of proof in fraud case is no greater than other cases, and defendant was not entitled to an instruction requiring clear, cogent and convincing evidence. Crawford v. Smith, 470 S.W.2d 529[1] (Mo. banc 1971).

5. Third-method converse

Instructions accurately portrayed burden of proof in action brought by creditor to recover business debt, where jury was instructed that burden of causing jury to believe proposition of fact was upon party who relied on proposition, and defendant's converse verdict director, as modified by trial judge, instructed jury to find for defendant if plaintiff was unsuccessful in proving that defendant had any ownership interest in business. Petry Roofing Supply, Inc. v. Sutton, 839 S.W.2d 337 (Mo.App.1992).

MAI 3.01 need not be modified to meet defendant's burden of proof or affirmative converse instruction. Restaurant Industries, Inc. v. Lum's Inc., 495 S.W.2d 668[5] (Mo. App.1973).

6. Modification

Where defendant's claim to an inter vivos gift was made after alleged donor's death, the burden of proof instruction should be modified to require that evidence of gift must be by clear, cogent and convincing proof. Matter of Passman's Estate, 537 S.W.2d 380[2] (Mo. banc 1976).

7. Mandatory

MAI 3.01 mandatory. Sears, Roebuck & Co. v. Peerless Products, Inc., 539 S.W.2d 768[3] (Mo.App.1976).

8. Malicious prosecution

MAI 3.01 is proper burden of proof instruction in civil malicious prosecution case. Proctor v. Stevens Employment Services, Inc., 712 S.W.2d 684[1] (Mo. banc 1986).

9. Wrongful death

Wrongful death defendant's closing argument reference to conviction for murder did not warrant setting aside of verdict in favor of defendant on ground that jury might have been misled into applying burden of proof in criminal case, which was greater than burden applied in civil cases; objection to comment was sustained, no comment about burden of proof imposed in criminal case was made to jury, and court properly instructed jury on burden of proof in civil cases. McPherson v. David, 805 S.W.2d 260 (Mo. App.1991).

10. Directed verdict

Trial court should not withdraw case from jury unless all of evidence is so strongly against plaintiffs as to leave no room for reasonable minds to differ; if it is determined that reasonable minds could differ, it is incumbent upon judge to let case go to jury, who will then be instructed as to party bearing burden of proof and persuasion. Friend v. Holman, 888 S.W.2d 369 (Mo.App. W.D.,1994).

11. New Trial

Adoption of approved pattern instruction, requiring jury to 'believe' hypothesis necessary to warrant verdict for plaintiff, has not changed rule as to sufficiency of evidence in connection with granting motion for new trial. Clark v. Quality Dairy Co., 400 S.W.2d 78 (Mo.1966).

3.02 [1981 Revision] Burden of Proof—Eminent Domain

The burden is on the defendant to cause you to believe that he has sustained damage and the amount thereof. In determining the amount of your verdict, you must consider only the evidence and the reasonable inferences derived from the evidence. If you do not believe certain evidence, then you cannot consider that evidence in arriving at the amount of your verdict.

Notes on Use (1977 Revision)

A burden of proof instruction must be given in every case. MAI 3.02 is to be used in all eminent domain cases.

Committee Comment (1969 New)

The Committee felt that the issues in eminent domain cases are sufficiently distinctive as to require a special burden of proof instruction.

Library References:

C.J.S. Eminent Domain § 308.
West's Key No. Digests, Eminent Domain ⊗222.

Notes of Decisions

In general 1
Amendment 3
Mandatory instruction 2

1. In general

Absence of burden-of-proof clause compels reevaluation of MAI 3.02, but giving in original form not error. State ex rel. State Highway Commission v. Sams, 484 S.W.2d 276[1] (Mo.1972).

Giving MAI 3.01 in condemnation case, tried prior to adoption of MAI 3.02, was not error. State ex rel. State Highway Commission v. Delisle, 462 S.W.2d 641[1] (Mo. 1971).

2. Mandatory instruction

Giving MAI 3.02 in condemnation case is mandatory. State ex rel. Highway Commission v. Nickerson & Nickerson, Inc., 494 S.W.2d 344[5] (Mo.1973).

3. Amendment

In a condemnation action remanded for retrial to be held after July 1, 1973 the revised version of MAI 3.02 must be used. State ex rel. Hwy. Commission v. Baker, 505 S.W.2d 433[9] (Mo.App.1974).

3.03   [1981 Revision] Burden of Proof—Will Contest

The burden is upon defendant, proponent, to cause you to believe that the document dated _____ is the last will and testament [codicil] of _____ (*name of testator*).

The burden is upon plaintiff, contestant, to cause you to believe (*here insert the affirmative defense raised such as "his claim of undue influence as submitted in Instruction Number* _____ ").[1]

In determining whether or not you believe any proposition, you must consider only the evidence and the reasonable inferences derived from the evidence.

If the evidence in the case does not cause you to believe a particular proposition submitted, then you cannot return a verdict requiring belief of that proposition.

Notes on Use (1995 Revision)

1.   Omit this paragraph if no affirmative defense is submitted.

A burden of proof instruction must be given in every case. MAI 3.03 is to be used in a will contest. When only part of a will is contested under § 473.081, RSMo, the first paragraph should be omitted and the second paragraph modified as follows: "The burden is upon plaintiff to cause you to believe the claim of (*insert claimed basis of partial invalidity such as 'undue influence'*) as submitted in Instruction Number _____ ."

Committee Comment (1995 New)

Will contests are somewhat unique and, in the Committee's judgment, require a burden of proof instruction tailored to fit the issue raised. Section 473.081, RSMo, permits a challenge to only a portion of a will. In a case in which only a portion of a will is challenged, the remainder of the will is unchallenged, and no issue would exist as to those matters covered by MAI 31.06; therefore, the proponent of the will would have no burden of proof.

Library References:

C.J.S. Wills § 478.
West's Key No. Digests, Wills ⟡329(3).

Notes of Decisions

1. In general

Burden of proof instruction submitted by contestants placing upon contestants the burden of showing that decedent was of unsound mind which cast upon them a greater burden of proof than they were required to meet was harmless error. Keifer v. St. Jude's Children's Research Hosp., 654 S.W.2d 236[5] (Mo.App.1983).

In a will contest it was error to put burden of proof on contestant to show decedent was of unsound mind; that burden rests on proponents throughout the trial. Brug v. Manufacturers Bank & Trust Co., 461 S.W.2d 269[8] (Mo. banc 1970).

3.04 [1981 Revision] Burden of Proof—Clear and Convincing—Gift

The burden is upon (*insert name of alleged donee*) to cause you to believe by clear and convincing evidence that the (*describe the property such as "bonds"*) were a gift to [him, her] by the decedent. In determining whether or not you believe any proposition, you must consider only the evidence and the reasonable inferences derived from the evidence. If the evidence in the case does not cause you to believe a particular proposition submitted, then you cannot return a verdict requiring belief of that proposition.

Committee Comment (1977 New)

This instruction is to be used in those cases where the proof must be "clear and convincing" or "clear, cogent and convincing." See *In re Passman's Estate*, 537 S.W.2d 380 (Mo. banc 1976). These cases usually involve the issue of whether a gift was made (*inter vivos or causa mortis*). Some of the gift cases before *Passman* called for "clear, cogent and convincing proof to convince the jury beyond a reasonable doubt." In *Passman* the court held that a special burden of proof instruction is required but it rejected the argument that the modification must include "reasonable doubt" language.

If the proposition to be established is other than a gift, the language of the first sentence of the instruction should be modified accordingly.

Library References:

C.J.S. Gifts § 121.
West's Key No. Digests, Gifts ☞84.

Notes of Decisions

1. In general

In action for fraud and undue influence in connection with transfer of bank account, court properly instructed jury that plaintiff's burden of proof was "clear and convincing evidence." McMullin v. Borgers, 806 S.W.2d 724 (Mo.App.1991).

3.05 [1998 Revision] Burden of Proof—Libel or Slander—Plaintiff a Public Official or Public Figure

In these instructions, you are told that your verdict depends on whether or not you believe certain propositions of fact submitted to you. The burden is upon plaintiff to cause you to believe that the evidence has clearly and convincingly established that the (*describe the alleged libelous or slanderous statement, such as "newspaper article", "statement", etc.*) referred to in the evidence was false and that defendant (*describe the act of publication, such as "published the newspaper article", "wrote the letter", etc.*) with knowledge that it was false or with reckless disregard for whether it was true or false at a time when defendant had serious doubt as to whether it was true. However, on all other propositions of fact, the burden is upon the party who relies upon any such proposition to cause you to believe that such proposition is more likely to be true than not true. In determining whether or not you believe any proposition, you must consider only the evidence and the reasonable inferences derived from the evidence. If the evidence in the case does not cause you to believe a particular proposition submitted, then you cannot return a verdict requiring belief of that proposition.

Notes on Use (1989 Revision)

A burden of proof instruction must be given in every case.

Committee Comment (1980 New)

The Missouri courts recognize that the federal cases require that the actual malice standard set forth in *New York Times Company v. Sullivan*, 376 U.S. 254, 84 S.Ct. 710, 11 L.Ed.2d 686 (1964), must be proved by clear and convincing evidence. *Whitmore v. Kansas City Star Co.*, 499 S.W.2d 45 (Mo.App.1973), discussing *New York Times v. Sullivan*, supra, *Curtis Publishing Company v. Butts*, 388 U.S. 130, 87 S.Ct. 1975, 18 L.Ed.2d 1094 (1967), and *Rosenbloom v. Metromedia, Inc.*, 403 U.S. 29, 91 S.Ct. 1811, 29 L.Ed.2d 296 (1971). See also *Gertz v. Robert Welch,*

Inc., 418 U.S. 323, 94 S.Ct. 2997, 41 L.Ed.2d 789 (1974), appeal after remand 680 F.2d 527 (7th Cir.1982).

Library References:

> C.J.S. Libel and Slander; Injurious Falsehood § 181.
> West's Key No. Digests, Libel and Slander ⚡124(2).

Notes of Decisions

1. In general

Verdict directing instruction should have been submitted in action by employee against former employer for allegedly defamatory communication to other employees and customer that employee was terminated for stealing company money; employer's communications to other employees and customer were protected by qualified privilege, but employee made submissible case of actual malice to defeat that privilege. Deckard v. O'Reilly Automotive, Inc., 31 S.W.3d 6 (Mo.App.2000).

3.06 [1998 Revision] Burden of Proof—Libel or Slander—Punitive Damages Sought by a Plaintiff Not a Public Official or Public Figure

In these instructions, you are told that your verdict depends on whether or not you believe certain propositions of fact submitted to you. The burden is upon plaintiff to cause you to believe that the evidence has clearly and convincingly established the propositions of fact required for the recovery of punitive damages as submitted in the second paragraph of Instruction Number ___ (*insert the number of the damage instruction, which will be MAI 4.15*). However, on all other propositions of fact, the burden is upon the party who relies upon such proposition to cause you to believe that any such proposition is more likely to be true than not true. In determining whether or not you believe any proposition, you must consider only the evidence and the reasonable inferences derived from the evidence. If the evidence in the case does not cause you to believe a particular proposition submitted, then you cannot return a verdict requiring belief of that proposition.

Notes on Use (1989 Revision)

This burden of proof instruction is for use where a private plaintiff (not a public official or public figure) seeks both actual and punitive damages. If a private plaintiff does not seek punitive damages, use MAI 3.01 as the burden of proof instruction.

Committee Comment (1980 New)

Gertz v. Robert Welch, Inc., 418 U.S. 323, 94 S.Ct. 2997, 41 L.Ed.2d 789 (1974), holds that the *New York Times* standard of actual malice must be met for the recovery of punitive damages. The Missouri courts recognize that the federal cases require that the actual malice standard of *New York Times* be proved by clear and convincing evidence. *Whitmore v. Kansas City Star Co.*, 499 S.W.2d 45 (Mo.App.1973).

Library References:

C.J.S. Libel and Slander; Injurious Falsehood § 181.
West's Key No. Digests, Libel and Slander ⚷124(2).

3.07 [1983 New] Burden of Proof—Clear and Convincing—Commitment for Mental Illness

In these instructions, you are told that your finding depends on whether or not you believe certain propositions of fact submitted to you. The burden is upon petitioner to cause you to believe by clear and convincing evidence that respondent is mentally ill and, as a result, presents a likelihood of serious physical harm to himself or others. In determining whether or not you believe any such proposition, you must consider only the evidence and the reasonable inferences derived from the evidence. If the evidence in the case does not cause you to believe a particular proposition submitted, then you cannot return a finding requiring belief of that proposition.

Committee Comment (1983 New)

This instruction is meant for use in a hearing governed by the civil detention procedures for a person suffering from a mental illness. A finding must be based upon clear and convincing evidence. §§ 632.300–632.475, RSMo.

Library References:

C.J.S. Insane Persons § 49, 54, 59–64, 66–70.
West's Key No. Digests, Mental Health ☞41.

3.08 [1998 Revision] Burden of Proof—Paternity Actions

In these instructions, you are told that your verdict depends on whether or not you believe certain propositions of fact submitted to you. The burden is upon plaintiff to cause you to believe that the propositions necessary to support the claim(s) as submitted in Instruction(s) Number ___ [and Number ___ (*here insert number(s) of plaintiff's verdict director(s)*)] are more likely to be true than not true. [The burden is upon the defendant to cause you to believe that the evidence has clearly and convincingly established those propositions necessary to support his claim as submitted in Instruction Number ___ (*here insert number of defendant's MAI 31.20 submission*)].[1] In determining whether or not you believe any proposition, you must consider only the evidence and the reasonable inferences derived from the evidence. If the evidence in the case does not cause you to believe a particular proposition submitted, then you cannot return a verdict requiring belief of that proposition.

Notes on Use (1994 New)

1. Add this bracketed sentence only if the case is submitted under MAI 31.19 and the putative father submits a rebuttal of the statutory presumption under MAI 31.20.

Committee Comment (1998 Revision)

The bracketed sentence submits the appropriate burden of proof in accordance with section 210.822.2, RSMo, in a case where the defendant submits evidence and an instruction to rebut the statutory presumption. It should be used only if the defendant submits MAI 31.20 to rebut a statutory presumption. The burden of proof to support the presumption or to otherwise support the plaintiff's claim remains on the plaintiff. Section 210.822.2, RSMo, does not shift the burden of proof, rather it places a separate and different burden on the defendant if he or she submits a rebuttal to the presumption.

MAI 3.08, MAI 31.18, MAI 31.19, MAI 31.20, and MAI 36.28 were drafted for civil paternity actions under sections 210.817 et seq., RSMo. Effective July 1, 1997, section 210.839.4 was amended to provide that no party in such a paternity action has a right to trial by jury. The Committee has chosen not to withdraw these instructions and the related verdict form in the event that they are instructive or perhaps useful in the future since the Supreme Court has held that the Parentage Act (sections 210.817 et seq.) is not the exclusive means to determine paternity. *Matter of Nocita*, 914 S.W.2d 358 (Mo. banc 1996).

Library References:

C.J.S. Children Out-of-Wedlock § 116.
West's Key No. Digests, Children Out-of-Wedlock ⟳60.

DAMAGES

4.00

DAMAGES—GENERAL

Analysis of Instructions

Westlaw Electronic Research

See Westlaw Electronic Research Guide preceding the Table of Instructions.

Library References:

C.J.S. Damages § 177.
West's Key No. Digests, Damages ☞209.

49

4.01 [2002 Revision] Damages—Personal and Property

If you find in favor of plaintiff,[1] then you must award plaintiff such sum as you believe will fairly and justly compensate plaintiff for any damages you believe plaintiff sustained [and is reasonably certain to sustain in the future][2] as a direct result of the occurrence[3] mentioned in the evidence. [If you find that plaintiff failed to mitigate damages as submitted in Instruction Number ___, in determining plaintiff's total damages you must not include those damages that would not have occurred without such failure.][4]

Notes on Use (2002 Revision)

1. If there is a counterclaim, add the words "on plaintiff's claim for damages".

2. This may be added if supported by the evidence.

3. When the evidence discloses a compensable event and a non-compensable event, both of which are claimed to have caused damage, the term "occurrence" may need to be modified. See *Vest v. City National Bank & Trust Co.*, 470 S.W.2d 518 (Mo.1971). When the term "occurrence" is modified, substitute some descriptive phrase that specifically describes the compensable event or conduct. As an example, if the plaintiff claims plaintiff sustained damages as a direct result of negligent medical care while being treated for a non-compensable fall or illness, the instruction may be modified to read, "... as a direct result of the conduct of defendant as submitted in Instruction Number ___ (*here insert number of verdict directing instruction*)." As another example, if plaintiff sustained damages in an automobile collision but also had a non-compensable illness, the instruction may be modified to read "... as a direct result of the automobile collision."

In a case such as *Carlson v. K–Mart*, 979 S.W.2d 145 (Mo. banc 1998), where MAI 19.01 is used in the verdict director, delete the entire phrase "as a direct result of the occurrence mentioned in the evidence" from MAI 4.01 and substitute the phrase "that (*describe the compensable event or conduct*) directly caused or directly contributed to cause."

Other modifications also may be appropriate.

4. If failure to mitigate damages is submitted, this instruction must be modified by adding this bracketed sentence. See MAI 32.29 for the appropriate method of submission of failure to mitigate damages in cases other than FELA. For FELA cases, use MAI 32.07(A) and MAI 8.02.

This instruction should not be used in a comparative fault case. See MAI 37.03 for the damage instruction in a comparative fault case, and MAI 21.04 for the damage instruction in a comparative fault case involving health care providers.

See MAI 21.03 for the damage instruction in a case involving health care providers without comparative fault.

Committee Comment (2002 Revision)

This instruction is short, simple, and easily understood. Since no particular items of damage are set out, there is no risk of the jury being improperly instructed on damages not supported by the record.

During the instruction conference, the parties and the court should discuss (on the record) just what damages are supported by the evidence and can properly be argued to the jury. In this way, jury arguments can proceed without undue interruptions.

Rule 71.06 requires the jury verdict to separately state the amounts awarded for personal injuries and property damage.

In the past, varied approaches have been suggested for the manner of instructing on the issue of mitigation of damages. For example, the plurality opinion in *Love v. Park Lane Medical Center*, 737 S.W.2d 720 (Mo. banc 1987), suggested using a comparative fault approach. The product liability statute, section 537.765, RSMo, also could be read to suggest a comparative fault approach. *Tillman v. Supreme Exp. & Transfer, Inc.*, 920 S.W.2d 552 (Mo.App.1996), seemed to indicate that MAI 6.01 is the correct approach, although it also observed that MAI 6.01 is limited to wrongful death cases.

In fact, rather than the doctrine of avoidable consequences, MAI 6.01 submits a completely different type of mitigation (mitigating circumstances attendant upon the fatal injury in a wrongful death case pursuant to section 537.090, RSMo). *Tillman* also rejected the comparative fault approach to mitigation of damages. In order to avoid potential inconsistencies in alternative methods of submission (comparative fault approach in some cases, the FELA approach in other cases, and yet other possible approaches in other cases), the Committee has concluded that it is best to adopt a uniform approach to the submission of the doctrine of mitigation of damages in all cases as reflected in MAI 32.29 and the revision of MAI 4.01. This approach is both legally and logically correct and consistent with the approach already taken in FELA cases (See MAI 32.07(A) and MAI 8.02). It is also in compliance with the mandate of section 537.765 that failure to mitigate damages "shall diminish proportionately the amount awarded as compensatory damages ...."; thus, the method of submission of mitigation of damages in a product liability case should utilize the approach taken in MAI 32.29 and MAI 4.01.

Library References:

C.J.S. Damages § 185–186.
West's Key No. Digests, Damages ☞216, 217.

Notes of Decisions

------

1. In general

Property damage only instruction, rather than instruction relating to personal and property damage, was proper instruction for submitting question of damages in contract and warranty suit against elevator installation and service company for improper maintenance and repair of elevators in trustee's building, given highlighted titles of two instructions and notes on use for property damage only instruction. Dubinsky v. U.S. Elevator Corp., 22 S.W.3d 747 (Mo.App. 2000).

Use of modified version of approved instruction used in cases involving personal and property damage was proper in breach of warranty action by bank against company that improperly installed uninterruptible power supply system for bank's computers, inasmuch as bank sought recovery and provided evidence of expenses proximately related to property damage, including costs for employee to work through weekend to enable repairs to computers by next business day, and modification to instruction properly encompassed damages reasonably expected by installer when it performed its services.

St. John's Bank & Trust Co. v. Intag, Inc., 938 S.W.2d 627 (Mo.App.1997).

Jury instruction on personal and property damages should only be given where there has been damage to both the person and property. John Kelley, Denise Kelley v. Kelly Residential Group, Inc. (Two Cases), 945 S.W.2d 544 (Mo.App.1997)

Trial court erred in giving MAI 4.01, applicable when both personal injury and property damages are claimed, in insurance contract action alleging coverage for collapse of retaining wall in which only property damage was claimed; MAI 4.02 should have been given instead. Pace Properties, Inc. v. American Mfrs. Mut. Ins. Co., 918 S.W.2d 883 (Mo.App.1996).

In absence of more narrowly applicable instruction, MAI 4.01 is correct damage instruction in breach of contract actions. Metro Waste Systems, Inc. v. A.L.D. Services, Inc., 924 S.W.2d 335 (Mo.App.1996).

Deficiency in damage instruction of failure to advise jury that judge would reduce plaintiff's recovery by percentage of plaintiff's fault was not prejudicial error where verdict form disclosed to the jury the court's role in determining the actual damages awarded to plaintiff. Wheeler v. Evans, 708 S.W.2d 677[3] (Mo.App.1986).

In an action by a discharged employee against his union for failing to fairly represent him in his complaint for wrongful discharge against his employer, MAI 4.01 was the proper instruction to use and the court properly excluded from the instruction such matters as the apportionment between union and employer, such being matters left to jury argument. Osborne v. Warehouse, Mail Order, Inc., 666 S.W.2d 822[3] (Mo.App.1984).

The giving of MAI 4.01 twice, following the verdict directors on both contract and tort claims arising out of a singular act, constituted prejudicial error. Ross v. Holton, 640 S.W.2d 166[7] (Mo.App.1982).

MAI 4.02 is not applicable where the damages sought include items not measurable by before and after value or by cost of repair. Thus reasonable expenses proximately resulting from damage to property, although usually recoverable, do not fall within MAI 4.02, and were properly charged under MAI 4.01. Stegan v. H.W. Freeman Const. Co., Inc., 637 S.W.2d 794[7, 8] (Mo.App.1982).

Giving MAI 4.01 in property damage-only case is prejudicial error warranting a new trial. Wright v. Edison, 619 S.W.2d 797, 800 (Mo.App.1981).

In bailment action, where property was returned but in damaged condition, proper damage instruction was MAI 4.02 based on before-and-after values, not MAI 4.01. Emcasco Ins. Co. v. Auto Driveaway Co., 586 S.W.2d 780[2] (Mo.App.1979).

Where plaintiff's recovery was based only on diminution of property value, giving MAI 4.01 instead of MAI 4.02 was error. Sands v. R.G. McKelvey Bldg. Co., 571 S.W.2d 726[1–5] (Mo.App.1978).

Alternative damage instructions discussed in buyers' suit against seller for cost of repairing latent defects. Matulunas v. Baker, 569 S.W.2d 791[9, 10] (Mo.App.1978).

Different elements of damage, including offset, need not be particularized in damage instruction; explanation to be made in oral argument. Morgan v. Wartenbee, 569 S.W.2d 391[1] (Mo.App.1978).

Where evidence showed an earlier similar injury, it was error to give MAI 4.01 without modifying it to limit damages to the injury in dispute. Wagoner v. Hurt, 554 S.W.2d 587[5, 6] (Mo.App.1977).

Where plaintiff sought damages for a November 9, 1966 back injury and his evidence showed two earlier back injuries, MAI should have been modified by deleting the words "mentioned in evidence" and substituting therefor the words "of November 9, 1966." Plaintiff's verdict director should have been similarly modified. Russell v. Terminal R.R. Ass'n, 501 S.W.2d 843[2, 6] (Mo. banc 1973).

Giving defendant's pre-MAI instruction that an award to plaintiff was not subject to income tax was an impermissible "improvement" on MAI and prejudicial error. Senter v. Ferguson, 486 S.W.2d 644[1] (Mo.App. 1972).

Generality of plaintiff's MAI 4.01 cannot be raised by defendant who fails to offer a more specific instruction. Epperson v. Nolan, 452 S.W.2d 263[15] (Mo.App.1970).

In using MAI 4.01 it is contemplated that closing arguments will properly advise the jury as to the elements of and proper measure of damages. Arguments are subject to objections made at instruction conference and during course of argument. Boten v. Brecklein, 452 S.W.2d 86[9, 10] (Mo.1970).

Defendant was not entitled to an instruction detailing the elements of damage the jury should not consider. Jurgeson v. Romine, 442 S.W.2d 176[2] (Mo.App.1969).

Even though plaintiff's physician improperly diagnosed her condition, her MAI 4.01 was adequate and she was not entitled to another instruction that defendant was liable for damages flowing from misdiagnosis. Aubuschon v. Witt, 412 S.W.2d 136[1, c. 137 & (3)] (Mo.1967).

Generality in plaintiff's MAI 4.01 cured by defendant's failure to offer a more specific damage instruction. Miller v. Ranson & Co., 407 S.W.2d 48[11] (Mo.App.1966).

Where defendant admits liability, but not injuries, it is error to instruct jury to return verdict in favor of plaintiff. Watts v. Handley, 427 S.W.2d 272[4] (Mo.App.1968).

2. Deviation

Where there is a counter-claim plaintiff's damage instruction must add the words "on plaintiff's claim for damages", and failure to do so is presumptively reversible error. Duren v. Dougherty, 585 S.W.2d 527[1–3] (Mo. App.1979).

Where there was no issue as to the amount of plaintiff's damages, the error in omitting the last clause of MAI 4.01 "as a direct result of the occurrence mentioned in evidence," was harmless. Nu–Way Services, Inc. v. Mercantile Trust Co., 530 S.W.2d 743[4, 5] (Mo.App.1975).

Omission of "as the direct result of the occurrence mentioned in evidence" in MAI 4.01 was reversible error. Not corrected by the damage requirement in plaintiff's verdict director since the two instructions conflicted. Chappell v. City of Springfield, 423 S.W.2d 810[2, 3] (Mo.1968).

Omitting the word "direct" in MAI 4.01 is presumptively prejudicial. Brown v. St. Louis Public Service Co., 421 S.W.2d 255[1–3] (Mo. banc 1967).

3. Modification

Even if damage instruction was improperly modified by modifying the word "occurrence" in MAI 4.01, no prejudice was shown, particularly where no special objection to instruction on that ground was presented. Ray v. Upjohn Co., 851 S.W.2d 646 (Mo. App.1993).

Because MAI 4.01 does not provide for damages that were reasonably contemplated by defendant at the time it warranted its work, the court remanded for retrial on issue of damages and recommended that MAI 4.01 be modified to properly state the law for recovery in action based on breach of warranty of workmanlike performance. Crank v. Firestone Tire & Rubber Co., 692 S.W.2d 397[11] (Mo.App.1985).

Modification of MAI 4.01 is required where the evidence discloses more than one event which is claimed to have caused plaintiff's injuries. Even though an instruction deviates from the MAI, there is a trend away from reversal unless there is a substantial indication of prejudice. Grady v. American Optical Corp., 702 S.W.2d 911[9] (Mo.App.1985).

Modification of MAI 4.01 to describe an obligation sued on as a "debt" instead of "damages" was not prejudicial, nor was the substitution of the description of the unpaid debt for the word "occurrence," the court finding that such substitution could not have

been injurious to plaintiff. Owen v. Owen, 642 S.W.2d 410[24, 27] (Mo.App.1982).

Where there was no evidence that two or more occurrences contributed proportionately to the plaintiff's injury but rather that plaintiff was injured either by the occurrence of a negligently administered hip spinal as contended by plaintiff or by a faulty embolism as contended by defendant, only one event or occurrence is claimed to have caused plaintiff's injury and an unmodified MAI 4.01 damage instruction was proper. However, verdict director was found to be reversible error because it assumed facts in dispute. Yoos v. Jewish Hosp. of St. Louis, 645 S.W.2d 177 (Mo.App.1982).

Where one of three defendants settled with plaintiff, MAI 4.01, as mandated by MAI 7.01, note 2, was properly modified by changing "award" to "determine," so as to show deduction of plaintiff's partial settlement. Smith v. Courter, 575 S.W.2d 199[3] (Mo.App.1978). (MAI 7.01 was withdrawn in 1983. Now see MAI 7.02).

Where plaintiff was injured in collision with defendant, and due to that injury he was further injured in a second collision, MAI 4.01 was properly modified to allow damages for both injuries. Ponciroli v. Wyrick, 573 S.W.2d 731[5–7] (Mo.App.1978).

Where there is evidence of damage caused by extraneous acts, MAI 4.01 should be modified to limit recovery to damage caused by defendant. North County School Dist. R–1 v. Fidelity & Deposit Co., 539 S.W.2d 469[13] (Mo.App.1976).

Giving defendant's pre-MAI instruction that an award to plaintiff was not subject to income tax was an impermissible "improvement" on MAI 4.01 and prejudicial error. Senter v. Ferguson, 486 S.W.2d 644[1] (Mo. App.1972).

Where plaintiff's medical evidence showed treatment for another similar injury just three weeks previous to injury on trial, it was error to give MAI 4.01 without modifying the phrase "occurrence mentioned in evidence"; this in accordance with Notes on Use, which must be followed. Homm v. Oakes, 453 S.W.2d 679 (Mo.App.1970).

Where new trial was had on issue of damages only and liability and causation were no longer in issue, MAI 4.01 was inapplicable and was properly modified by deleting the opening words "If you find the issues in favor of the plaintiff, then. . . ." Reynolds v. Arnold, 443 S.W.2d 793[3, 4] (Mo.1969).

Prior to MAI 4.04 on damages in quantum meruit, in action for services rendered it was not error to give a not-in-MAI damage instruction allowing a sum that would "fairly, reasonably and justly compensate plaintiff". McAtee v. Greenspon, 439 S.W.2d 187[3, 4] (Mo.App.1969).

"Reasonable men" construction applied to modified MAI 4.01. Stewart v. Sioux City & New Orleans Barge Lines, Inc. 431 S.W.2d 205[10] (Mo.1968).

Modified damage instruction on suit for fixed commission. Bomson v. Electra Mfg. Co., 402 S.W.2d 7[3] (Mo.App.1966).

4. "Occurrence"

MAI 4.01, which included reference to damages sustained as result of "occurrence mentioned in the evidence," was appropriate, even though self-insured employer sought damages for only property damage, and not personal injury, in action against insurance brokers for obtaining stop-loss medical policy with active-at-work provision. A.G. Edwards & Sons, Inc. v. Drew, 978 S.W.2d 386 (Mo.App.1998).

MAI 4.01, instructing jury to award such sum as it believes will fairly and justly compensate plaintiff for damages which plaintiff sustained and is reasonably certain to sustain in future as direct result of occurrence, rather than MAI 9.02, addressing eminent domain damages for taking of part of property, is appropriate when damage goes beyond mere property loss. Shady Valley Park & Pool, Inc. v. Fred Weber, Inc., 913 S.W.2d 28 (Mo.App.1995).

Second collision case involving enhanced leg injuries to a motorcyclist as a result of a defective fairing bracket following a motor vehicle collision. The damage instruction was properly submitted without modification of the word "occurrence" even though the manufacturer claimed that there were separate occurrences involving the original collision and then the enhanced leg injury caused by the fairing bracket. Plaintiff was only required to show that fairing bracket was a substantial factor in producing leg injuries and was not required to show that lesser injuries would have resulted from saf-

er design. McDowell v. Kawasaki Motors Corporation USA, 799 S.W.2d 854 (Mo.App. 1990).

In an action to recover damages for a sprained ankle, modification of the damage instruction to include a reference to a prior ankle injury suffered by the customer was not necessary where the store owner failed to prove that the past injury had not healed prior to the accident in the store. Burns v. Schnuck Mkts., Inc., 719 S.W.2d 499[6] (Mo. App.1986).

Failure to modify instruction on damages under MAI 4.01, which submitted only "the occurrence mentioned in the evidence," was not prejudicial, where plaintiff pleaded only the collapse of surface of parking lot as the cause of her injuries and where her verdict directing instruction submitted only that event as a basis for recovery, even though plaintiff testified that she also sustained injuries in incidents which occurred after the collapse of the parking lot. However, it would have been better practice to modify the instruction. Asher v. Broadway–Valentine Center, Inc., 691 S.W.2d 478[6] (Mo. App.1985).

Where evidence shows but a single indivisible injury which may be the result of a combination of tortious acts of a defendant and others, it is not reversible error to fail to modify the word "occurrence" in MAI 4.01. Koenig v. Babka, 682 S.W.2d 96, 99 (Mo. App.1984).

The jury having been supplied a separate set of instructions for each claim, each instruction format serving to segregate each "occurrence" with the set of instructions including the verdict director applicable to it, a jury of normal intelligence could not have entertained any confusion as to what occurrence was involved and therefore explicit definition of "occurrence" was not required. Essex v. Getty Oil Co., 661 S.W.2d 544[26] (Mo.App.1983).

Plaintiff sued for neck injuries received in a collision and testified to later injuries to her arm and ankle. Error to give unmodified MAI 4.01. Thweatt v. Haefner, 539 S.W.2d 734 (Mo.App.1976).

Two defendant motorists were jointly and severally liable for plaintiff's injuries received in separate collisions. Separate MAI 4.01's each referred to "the occurrence" mentioned in evidence. In view of their joint liability, neither defendant was prejudiced by each instruction referring to "occurrence" in the singular. Barlow v. Thornhill, 537 S.W.2d 412[5] (Mo. banc 1976).

Where plaintiffs submitted one count for conversion and another for wrongful ejectment, both on the same date, plaintiffs' MAI 4.01's were erroneous by each referring to "the occurrence of October 29." Defendant invited the error by agreeing to the trial court's oral explanation of the two instructions. Fletcher v. Cummings, 532 S.W.2d 890 (Mo.App.1976).

Where plaintiff had an earlier back injury not attributable to defendant it was error to give MAI 4.01 without modification of "occurrence." Clark v. McCloskey, 531 S.W.2d 36[4] (Mo.App.1975).

Where both verdict directors were based on damages *after* January 5 it was necessary to modify damage instruction MAI 4.02 to include evidence of *prior damage* since instructions are read together. Goodwin v. S.J. Groves & Sons Co., 525 S.W.2d 577[2] (Mo.App.1975).

Where plaintiff sought damages for a November 9, 1966 back injury and his evidence showed two earlier back injuries, MAI should have been modified by deleting the words "mentioned in evidence" and substituting therefor the words "of November 9, 1966." Plaintiff's verdict director should have been similarly modified. Russell v. Terminal R.R. Ass'n, 501 S.W.2d 843[2, 6] (Mo. banc 1973).

Where defendant doctors in malpractice action could be liable for only part of plaintiff's injuries, MAI 4.01 should have been modified by substituting some descriptive term for the word "occurrence;" this to comply with Notes on Use. Vest v. City Nat. Bank & Trust Co., 470 S.W.2d 518[1, 2] (Mo.1971).

Where plaintiff's medical evidence showed treatment for another similar injury just three weeks previous to injury on trial, it was error to give MAI 4.01 without modifying the phrase "occurrence mentioned in evidence"; this in accordance with Notes on Use, which must be followed. Homm v. Oakes, 453 S.W.2d 679 (Mo.App.1970).

Where water damage to plaintiff's crops was caused by defendant's obstructing a creek and also by natural flooding, MAI 4.01 should have been modified by omitting the word "occurrence" and using instead the phrase "the obstruction across the creek." Jurgeson v. Romine, 442 S.W.2d 176[4, 5] (Mo.App.1969).

Where rain damage to plaintiff's house was only partly caused by the defendant, plaintiff's MAI 4.01 should have been modified by changing the word "occurrence" to a more descriptive term that would limit recovery to damages for which the defendant was liable. This, in accord with the Notes on Use of MAI 4.01. Miller v. American Ins. Co., 439 S.W.2d 238[1] (Mo.App.1969).

In MAI 4.01 the word "occurrence" refers to the defendant's wrongful act, and that act need not be further described. Nelson v. R.H. Macy & Co., 434 S.W.2d 767[7] (Mo. App.1968).

The word "occurrence" in MAI 4.01 should be used in the singular unless the injury was produced by more than one occurrence. Gant v. Scott, 419 S.W.2d 262[3–4] (Mo.App. 1967).

5. Conversing damages

Where court gave defendant's instruction 33.02(5) (withdrawn 1980) conversing damages, it was error to give an additional converse on the same subject. McBee v. Schlupbach, 529 S.W.2d 435 (Mo.App. 1975).

A measure of damage instruction as distinguished from the damage element of plaintiff's verdict director may not be conversed. City of Gladstone v. Hamilton, 463 S.W.2d 622 (Mo.App.1971).

6. Future damage

Trial court erred by excluding future damages clause from MAI 4.01 while allowing future damages to be argued to jury by former employee in wrongful discharge action; if future damages were supported by record, then they should have been both instructed on and argued. Brenneke v. Department of Missouri, Veterans of Foreign Wars of U.S. of America, 984 S.W.2d 134 (Mo.App.1998).

Future damages may not be submitted if they are not supported by the evidence. Fincher v. Murphy, 825 S.W.2d 890 (Mo.App. 1992).

Where plaintiff testified that after recovery from injury she was *unable to find work* it was proper to give an instruction withdrawing that evidence. Abraham v. Johnson, 579 S.W.2d 734[5] (Mo.App.1979).

In FELA case, where defendant contended plaintiff's correct future damage instruction should be limited to "present value," defendant must offer such a limiting instruction. Chaussard v. Kansas City Southern Ry. Co., 536 S.W.2d 822[5] (Mo.App.1976). (Now see MAI 8.02).

Future pain and suffering must be supported by evidence but that evidence need not show *permanent* injury. Chaussard v. Kansas City Southern Ry. Co., 536 S.W.2d 822[9] (Mo.App.1976).

Evidence that pains began at time of accident and persisted until trial time warranted inclusion of future damage clause. Pryor v. American Oil Co., 471 S.W.2d 492[2] (Mo. App.1971).

To warrant future damage clause it is sufficient to show the sudden onset of pain and its continuation to time of trial; no need for corroborating medical evidence. Jones v. Allen, 473 S.W.2d 763[2, 3] (Mo.App.1971).

Plaintiff need not show permanency of injuries to be entitled to submit future damages clause. Gaynor v. Horwltz, 464 S.W.2d 537[6–7] (Mo.App.1971).

Evidence supported future damage clause. Young v. Frozen Foods Express, Inc., 444 S.W.2d 35[7, 8] (Mo.App.1969).

Future damage clause in MAI 4.01 must have evidentiary support. Kramer v. May Lumber Co., 432 S.W.2d 617[4] (Mo.App. 1968).

Insertion of future damage clause in MAI 4.01 is error absent medical opinion or evidence of sudden onset of defect continuing to time of trial. Harrison v. Weller, 423 S.W.2d 226[6, 13] (Mo.App.1967).

Future damage clause in MAI 4.01 must be supported by substantial evidence. Zoeller v. Terminal R.R. Assn. of St. Louis, 407 S.W.2d 73[2–4] (Mo.App.1966).

7. Diminution of value

Plaintiff's verdict of $4,500 damages to its building was adequately supported by evidence of $2,400 for repairs and $5,000 diminution of value. Yellow Service Co. Inc. v. Human Development Corp. of St. Louis, 539 S.W.2d 713[5] (Mo.App.1976).

Where plaintiffs sought damages for flooding their property, MAI 4.02 was the proper damage instruction, and giving MAI 4.01 was error warranting the new trial granted. Ogle v. Terminal R.R. Ass'n, 534 S.W.2d 809[4] (Mo.App.1976).

Not-in-MAI damage instruction approved although based on before-and-after values of damaged truck. Cameron v. Virginia Surety Co., 423 S.W.2d 219[3, 7] (Mo.App.1967).

In action for damage to building MAI 4.02, not MAI 4.01 was the proper damage instruction. DeArmon v. City of St. Louis, 525 S.W.2d 795[5] (Mo.App.1975).

Where plaintiff's damage was only to property it was prejudicial error to give MAI 4.01 instead of MAI 4.02. State ex rel. Hwy. Commission v. Beaty, 505 S.W.2d 147[4–7] (Mo.App.1974).

In suit to recover damages for permanent nuisance the correct measure of damages is based on before-and-after values and is improperly submitted by MAI 4.01. Bower v. Hog Builders, Inc., 461 S.W.2d 784[5] (Mo. 1970).

In damage suit for breach of house repair contract where evidence showed both (1) the diminution of value and (2) the cost of repairs, MAI 4.01 was proper, and it was not error to refuse a specific measure of damage instruction calling for the lesser of (1) and (2). Stamm v. Reuter, 432 S.W.2d 784[1, 2] (Mo.App.1968).

In permanent nuisance case, sole damage issue was diminution of value, like condemnation cases; MAI 9.02 was proper and MAI 4.01 improper. Stewart v. Marshfield, 431 S.W.2d 819[1, 2] (Mo.App.1968).

Property damage was properly submitted by MAI 4.01, and a not-in-MAI, before-and-after value instruction was properly refused since MAI 4.01 is adequate in view of evidence and argument on before-and-after values. Jack L. Baker Co. v. Pasley Mfg. & Dist. Co., 413 S.W.2d 268[5, 6] (Mo.1967).

Points to need for separate MAI 4.01 on property value before and after. Dettler v. Santa Cruz, 403 S.W.2d 651[8] (Mo.App. 1966).

MAI 4.01 properly submits issues of diminution in value or cost of replacement whichever is less. Hounihan v. State Farm Mutual Auto. Ins., 441 S.W.2d 58[7] (Mo.App.1969).

8. Breach of contract

Buyers, in action for breach of contract to sell chiropractic practice, were not prejudiced by inclusion of elective language pertaining to future damages in approved jury instruction, since jury did not award future damages. Dierker Associates, D.C., P.C. v. Gillis, 859 S.W.2d 737 (Mo.App.1993).

Jury instruction in action alleging that majority shareholder breached contractual obligation to register minority shares as expeditiously as possible so as to permit public sale improperly allowed jury to award damages for plaintiff minority shareholder's unexercised warrants and options, and error was prejudicial; range of evidence as to value of shares and date by when registration as "expeditiously as possible" could have been reasonably accomplished confounded post-hoc surmise of amount of award allocated as damages to shares. Wulfing v. Kansas City Southern Industries, Inc., 842 S.W.2d 133 (Mo.App.1992).

In an action brought for breach of contract, the giving of MAI 4.01 rather than MAI 4.02 was error. Steffens v. Paramount Properties, Inc., 667 S.W.2d 725, 728 (Mo.App. 1984).

In actions for breach of special types of contracts, a not-in-MAI instruction correctly specifying the measure of damages is preferable to modifying an MAI. Leh v. Dyer, 643 S.W.2d 65[1, 2] (Mo.App.1982).

Breach of contract. Damage allowed is contract price less cost of completing contract. Ark Const. Co., Inc. v. City of Florissant, 558 S.W.2d 418[8–11] (Mo.App.1977).

Where liability is no longer an issue and the amount of damages is the only issue, MAI 4.01 must be amended accordingly. Sears, Roebuck & Co. v. Peerless Products, Inc., 539 S.W.2d 768[4] (Mo.App.1976).

MAI 4.01 is proper in actions for breach of contract. North County School Dist. R–1 v. Fidelity & Deposit Co., 539 S.W.2d 469[12] (Mo.App.1976).

MAI's 4.01 and 4.05 are appropriate in a breach of contract action. S.P. Personnel Associates, Inc. v. Hospital, etc., 525 S.W.2d 345[8–10] (Mo.App.1975).

MAI 4.01 properly used in breach of contract case, subject to defendants' right to offer a more specific instruction. Boten v. Brecklein, 452 S.W.2d 86[11–12] (Mo.1970).

MAI 4.01 properly used in a breach of contract action. Gottlieb v. Hyken, 448 S.W.2d 617[4] (Mo.1970).

9. Multiple plaintiffs

Where multiple plaintiffs had separate verdict-directors, each was entitled to a separate damage instruction. Kennedy v. Tallent, 492 S.W.2d 33[5] (Mo.App.1973). (Now compare MAI 4.18).

10. Multiple defendants

Two defendant motorists were jointly and severally liable for plaintiff's injuries received in separate collisions. Separate MAI 4.01's each referred to "the occurrence" mentioned in evidence. In view of their joint liability, neither defendant was prejudiced by each instruction referring to "occurrence" in the singular. Barlow v. Thornhill, 537 S.W.2d 412[5] (Mo. banc 1976).

11. Multiple injuries

Where plaintiff was injured in collision with defendant, and due to that injury he was further injured in a second collision, MAI 4.01 was properly modified to allow damages for both injuries. Ponciroli v. Wyrick, 573 S.W.2d 731[5–7] (Mo.App.1978).

12. Quantum meruit

Damage instruction, before adoption of MAI 4.04, was properly modified to cover value of work and labor. Kaiser v. Lyon Metal Products, Inc., 461 S.W.2d 893[4] (Mo. App.1970).

13. Fraud

Missouri permits the use of instructions based on MAI 4.01 where the peculiar circumstances of the fraud makes the benefit of the bargain rule an inadequate measure of damages. Kerr v. First Commodity Corp. of Boston, 735 F.2d 281, 285 (8th Cir.1984).

Giving MAI 4.01 in fraud case held proper, particularly when neither party offered a modification nor contended later that the verdict was either inadequate or excessive. Crawford v. Smith, 470 S.W.2d 529[6–9] (Mo. banc 1971).

14. Conversion

Court found prejudicial the damages instruction given in counterclaim for conversion by secured party because it allowed the jury to speculate on the debtor's damages for loss of profits. Southern Missouri Bank v. Fogle, 738 S.W.2d 153[7, 13] (Mo.App. 1987).

In action for conversion, value must be determined as of time of conversion, to be submitted by a not-in-MAI damage instruction. Breece v. Jett, 556 S.W.2d 696[10–12] (Mo.App.1977).

15. Nuisance

The appropriate damages instruction in an action for damages for a temporary nuisance is MAI 4.01. Scantlin v. City of Pevely, 741 S.W.2d 48[7] (Mo.App.1987).

MAI 4.01 is the approved submission for a temporary nuisance. Fletcher v. City of Independence, 708 S.W.2d 158[28] (Mo.App. 1986).

When plaintiff's damages are temporary rather than permanent it was error to submit on MAI 4.02. Mondelli v. Saline Sewer Co., 628 S.W.2d 697[4] (Mo.App.1982).

MAI 4.01 is proper for damages for temporary nuisance and MAI 9.02 is proper for damages for permanent nuisance. Spain v. City of Cape Girardeau, 484 S.W.2d 498[5] (Mo.App.1972).

16. Waste

MAI 4.01 is not the proper measure of damages in an action for waste. Lustig v. U.M.C. Industries, Inc., 637 S.W.2d 55, 58 (Mo.App.1982).

17. Direct result

Damage instruction based on MAI 4.01, providing that injured customer's damages were only those that "directly resulted" from store owner's conduct, should have been modified to track verdict director based on MAI 19.01, providing that store owner was liable if its failure to use ordinary care "directly caused or directly contributed to cause" damage to customer; confusion engendered by conflict between these instructions prejudiced customer, entitling her to a new trial. Carlson v. K–Mart Corp., 979 S.W.2d 145 (Mo. banc 1998).

4.02 [1980 Revision] Damages—Property Only

If you find in favor of plaintiff, then you must award plaintiff such sum as you may find from the evidence to be the difference between the fair market value [1] (*here identify property*) before it was damaged and its fair market value [1] after it was damaged, [plus such sum as you may find from the evidence will fairly and justly compensate plaintiff for the loss of use thereof during the time reasonably necessary for the property to be repaired or replaced.] [2]

Notes on Use (2002 Revision)

1. The phrase "fair market value" must be defined. Use the first paragraph of MAI 16.02.

2. The bracketed portion of the above instruction should be used only where loss of use is pleaded and supported by the evidence.

This instruction should be used in cases involving property damage only.

In those rare cases in which the cost of repair is the appropriate measure of damages (as recited in the Committee Comment), the instruction should read:

If you find in favor of plaintiff, then you must award the plaintiff such sum as you may find from the evidence to be the reasonable cost of repair of any damage to (*here identify property*), [plus such sum as you may find from the evidence will fairly and justly compensate plaintiff for the loss of use thereof until such property could be reasonably repaired].

Where comparative fault is submitted in a case involving property damage only, this instruction should be modified in the format of MAI 37.03.

In a case in which mitigation of damages is properly submitted under MAI 32.29, this damage instruction should be modified with the bracketed sentence required by Note 4 of the Notes on Use to MAI 4.01.

Committee Comment (1969 New)

This instruction was added to meet the special case of property damage only when MAI 4.01 might not provide the precise guidelines available. Where *both* personal and property damages are involved 4.01 must still be used.

In *Randall v. Steelman*, 294 S.W.2d 588, 594 (Mo.App.1956) the court said: "The damage allowable for personal property is the difference between the reasonable market value before it was damaged and the reasonable market value after it was damaged."

In *Brunk v. Hamilton–Brown Shoe Co.*, 334 Mo. 517, 533, 66 S.W.2d 903, 910 (1933) the Supreme Court said: "As to personal property damage, however, there is a definite rule for calculation, to wit: The difference between the reasonable market value before and after injury; and the jury should be so informed."

In *Hayes v. Dalton*, 257 S.W.2d 198, 201 (Mo.App.1953) the court said:

> Fundamentally the measure of damages for injury to an article of personal property such as an automobile is the difference in the reasonable market value of the automobile before and after the injury, which may be shown by proof of the reasonable and necessary cost of repairing and restoring the automobile to its condition prior to the injury. If the cost of repairs results in causing the automobile to be more valuable than it was before the injury, such excess must be deducted from the cost of repairs, while if the automobile, after the repairs are made upon it, is still not as valuable as it was before the injury, the owner may then recover, in addition to the cost of repairs, such amount as will equal the difference between the value of the automobile after the repairs are made upon it and immediately prior to the injury. General Exchange Ins. Corporation v. Young, 206 S.W.2d 683; Conner v. Aalco Moving & Storage Co., 218 S.W.2d 830; Blanke v. United Rys. Co., 213 S.W. 174.

In some rare cases the cost of repair is the appropriate measure of damages. In *Gulf, M. & O. R. Co. v. Smith–Brennan Pile Co.*, 223 S.W.2d 100 (Mo.App.1949), the plaintiff was suing for damage to one of its bridges. The court said:

> The general rule as heretofore stated, is that the measure of damage is the difference between the reasonable value of the property before and the reasonable value thereof after the accident. We are aware that in cases where the amount of damage is insignificant, as compared to the value of the property as a whole and involves only a small part thereof, there is an exception to the above general rule. However, before allowing plaintiff to rely solely on evidence of the costs of repair, there should be a showing of the comparative insignificance of the damage to bring the case within such exception to the general rule.

> If an exception to the market value theory of the measure of damages were to be allowed in this kind of case because of the absence of a 'market' value of a bridge, the exception should most certainly go no farther than to permit plaintiff to show what the actual reasonable costs of repair would be on the open market if made by competent persons engaged in such business.

See also *Curtis v. Fruin–Colnon Contracting Co.*, 363 Mo. 676, 253 S.W.2d 158 (1952).

Library References:

C.J.S. Damages § 186.
West's Key No. Digests, Damages ⊕217.

Notes of Decisions

_____

1. In general

Property damage only instruction, rather than instruction relating to personal and property damage, was proper instruction for submitting question of damages in contract and warranty suit against elevator installation and service company for improper maintenance and repair of elevators in trustee's building, given highlighted titles of two instructions and notes on use for property damage only instruction. Dubinsky v. U.S. Elevator Corp., 22 S.W.3d 747 (Mo.App. 2000).

Fire insurer was not prejudiced by jury instruction on damages telling jury to consider uses to which "property may be applied or for which it is best adapted, under existing conditions and under conditions to be reasonably expected in the near future," as evidence revealed nothing of significance with respect to other uses for insured's house and lot other than residential use. Sharaga v. Auto Owners Mut. Ins. Co., 831 S.W.2d 248 (Mo.App.1992).

In action for permanent nuisance the correct damages instruction is MAI 9.02, not MAI 4.02. Scantlin v. City of Pevely, 741 S.W.2d 48[7] (Mo.App.1987).

While pattern instruction on property damages should have been modified to account for issue of multiple causation, reversal was not required, where damages for which city could be held liable was explained to jury in other instructions. Larabee v. City of Kansas City, 697 S.W.2d 177 (Mo.App.1985).

MAI 4.02 was not proper damage instruction where plaintiff sought to recover consequential damages caused by defendant's breach of warranty of workmanlike performance of vehicle maintenance, since MAI 4.02 would limit plaintiff's recovery to only the damage to his car. Crank v. Firestone Tire & Rubber Co., 692 S.W.2d 397[8–10] (Mo.App.1985).

Where case involved a total fire loss of both real and personal property, MAI 4.02 was not applicable since "fair market value" is not relevant to recovery for damages to a house and its contents, and the other damages claimed did not relate to fair market value. Travelers Indem. Co. v. Woods, 663 S.W.2d 392[2] (Mo.App.1983).

When plaintiff's damages are temporary rather than permanent it was error to submit on MAI 4.02. Mondelli v. Saline Sewer Co., 628 S.W.2d 697[4] (Mo.App.1982).

MAI 4.02 is not applicable where the damages sought include items not measurable by before and after value or by cost of repair. Thus reasonable expenses proximately resulting from damage to property, although usually recoverable, do not fall within MAI 4.02, and were properly charged under MAI 4.01. Stegan v. H.W. Freeman Const. Co., Inc., 637 S.W.2d 794[7, 8] (Mo. App.1982).

In bailment action, where property was returned but in damaged condition, proper damage instruction was MAI 4.02 based on before-and-after values, not MAI 4.01. Emcasco Ins. Co. v. Auto Driveaway Co., 586 S.W.2d 780[2] (Mo.App.1979).

A party may not complain of lack of evidence to support his own instruction. Smith v. Norman, 586 S.W.2d 84[4] (Mo.App. 1979).

Alternative damage instructions discussed in buyers' suit against seller for cost of repairing latent defects. Matulunas v. Baker, 569 S.W.2d 791[9, 10] (Mo.App.1978).

Damage to automobile is determined by before and after values except where cost of repair is comparably insignificant. Groves v. State Farm Mutual Auto. Ins. Co., 540 S.W.2d 39 (Mo. banc 1976).

In action for damage to building MAI 4.02, not MAI 4.01 was the proper damage instruction. DeArmon v. City of St. Louis, 525 S.W.2d 795[5] (Mo.App.1975).

MAI 4.02 permits plaintiff to recover for diminution in value existing after repair. Winter v. Elder, 492 S.W.2d 146[3, 4] (Mo. App.1973).

Where plaintiffs granted powerline easement for defendant's promise to pay stated amount for each pole installed it was error to give plaintiffs' not-in-MAI instructions authorizing recovery for difference between before and after values, since plaintiffs' recovery was limited to breach of defendant's promise to pay agreed amount. Shelton v. M & A Elec. Power Co-op., 451 S.W.2d 375[1, 6] (Mo.App.1970).

In suit to recover damages for permanent nuisance the correct measure of damages is based on before-and-after values and is improperly submitted by MAI 4.01. Bower v. Hog Builders, Inc., 461 S.W.2d 784[5] (Mo. 1970).

2. Modification

Where damage is the result of multiple causation, the damage instruction should require the jury by its findings to separate or apportion the damages directly resulting from the negligence of the defendant. Moore v. Woolbright, 670 S.W.2d 190[1–3] (Mo.App.1984).

Where both verdict directors were based on damages *after* January 5 it was necessary to modify damage instruction MAI 4.02 to include evidence of *prior damage* since instructions are read together. Goodwin v. S.J. Groves & Sons Co., 525 S.W.2d 577[2] (Mo.App.1975).

Where plaintiff's damage was only to property it was prejudicial error to give MAI 4.01 instead of MAI 4.02. State ex rel. Hwy. Commission v. Beaty, 505 S.W.2d 147[4–7] (Mo.App.1974).

Where there was no open market for condemned school property MAI 9.02 was properly modified by deleting the words "fair market." Reorganized School District v. Missouri Pac. R.R. Co., 503 S.W.2d 153[1–2] (Mo.App.1973).

Where statutory measure of damages was difference between contract price and value of goods in damaged condition, MAI 4.02 was properly modified to so state. National Beef Packing Co. v. Missouri Pac. R. Co., 479 S.W.2d 155[4] (Mo.App.1972).

3. Permanent damages

Where plaintiffs sought damages for flooding their property, MAI 4.02 was the proper damage instruction, and giving MAI 4.01 was error warranting the new trial granted. Ogle v. Terminal R.R. Ass'n, 534 S.W.2d 809[4] (Mo.App.1976).

MAI 4.02 proper in action for permanent, major damage by negligently flooding land. Kelso v. C.B.K. Agronomics, Inc., 510 S.W.2d 709 (Mo.App.1974).

4. Definition

Giving a modified MAI 4.02 without definition of fair market value (MAI 16.02) was a roving commission and plain error. Floyd v. Brenner, 542 S.W.2d 325[6, 7] (Mo.App. 1976).

5. Conversion

In action for conversion, value must be determined as of time of conversion, to be submitted by a not-in-MAI damage instruction. Breece v. Jett, 556 S.W.2d 696[10–12] (Mo.App.1977).

6. Loss of use

MAI 4.02 and notes on use for that instruction do not require or provide for a definition of "loss of use"; therefore, the court did not err in failing to define it. Kaiser v. Kadean Const. Co., 719 S.W.2d 892, 895 (Mo.App. 1986).

In cause of action seeking damages, whereby plaintiff as seller of house had lent house key to defendant as purchaser of house before actual closing of the deal, and defendant used the key to radically alter the interior of the house in plaintiff's absence, compensation for loss of use may be a proper item and certainly the expenses attendant upon living elsewhere until the house could be restored to a condition that would be suitable for habitation would be an item of expense that could be included in damage. Wright v. Edison, 619 S.W.2d 797, 801 (Mo.App.1981).

7. Consequential damages

When plaintiff seeks consequential damages caused by defendant's breach of warranty, approved instruction used in cases involving property damage only, which measures damages as difference between fair market value before and after occurrence, plus compensation for loss of use, is inapplicable, in that it does not correctly state rule for recovery of consequential damages. St. John's Bank & Trust Co. v. Intag, Inc., 938 S.W.2d 627 (Mo.App.1997).

4.03 [1969 New] Damages—Property—Misrepresentation

If you find in favor of the plaintiff, then you must award plaintiff such sum as you believe was the difference between the actual value of the (*describe property, such as "the furnace"*) on the date it was sold to plaintiff and what its value would have been on that date had (*describe property*) been as represented by defendant.

Notes on Use (1981 Revision)

This damage instruction is to be used where plaintiff is suing for misrepresentation. Where plaintiff has evidence of other damages (such as personal injuries suffered because the property was not as represented), MAI 4.01 should be used.

Committee Comment (1969 New)

This additional damage instruction was prepared to meet a special situation in which MAI 4.01 might not give adequate guidance.

In *Reynolds v. Davis*, 303 Mo. 418, 432, 260 S.W. 994, 997 (1924), the Missouri Supreme Court said:

> In a case of this sort and under proper pleading, a defrauded plaintiff may be awarded such damages as will enable him to receive not only the difference between the actual market value of the property and the price which he paid therefor, but something over and above such damages, if any represented by the difference between the price actually paid by him for such property and what its value would have been if it had been as represented. Such damages enable a defrauded party to obtain "the benefit of his bargain." Recovery of such damages is authorized in Missouri, as is clearly shown by the following cases, which we find in respondent's brief: Kendrick v. Ryus, 225 Mo. 150, l.c. 165, 123 S.W. 937; Morrow v. Franklin, 289 Mo. 549, 233 S.W. 224, l.c. 232; Ryan v. Miller, 236 Mo. 496, l.c. 508, 139 S.W. 128; Addis v. Swofford, 180 S.W. 548, l.c. 555; Bank v. Byers, 139 Mo. 627, 41 S.W. 325; Boyce v. Gingrich, 154 Mo.App. 198, l.c. 204, 134 S.W. 79; Boyd v. Wahl, 175 Mo.App. 181, 157 S.W. 833.

Library References:

West's Key No. Digests, Fraud ☞59(2), 65.

Notes of Decisions

1. In general

Error, if any, by trial court in submitting instruction on actual damages in fraud action brought by purchasers against real estate sales company was not prejudicial and did not require reversal; company did not object to instruction, failure of instruction to identify "property" which was referenced did not present real possibility of prejudice, and actual damages awarded did not evidence realization of whatever possibility of prejudice existed. Haberstick v. Gordon A. Gundaker Real Estate Co., 921 S.W.2d 104 (Mo. App.1996).

MAI 4.03 is ordinarily the correct measure of damages in a case of fraud. However, Missouri permits the use of other measures of damages where the peculiar circumstances of the fraud make the benefit of the bargain rule an inadequate measure of damages. Kerr v. First Commodity Corp. of Boston, 735 F.2d 281, 285 (8th Cir.1984).

In action for misrepresentation by buyer of boat against seller, trial court committed reversible error by instructing jury on personal and property measure of damages instead of misrepresentation measure of damages. Strebler v. Rixman, 616 S.W.2d 876[6] (Mo. App.1981).

4.04 [1981 Revision] Damages—Quantum Meruit

If you find in favor of plaintiff, then you must award plaintiff the reasonable value of the goods furnished [with ___% interest thereon from _____].[1]

Notes on Use (1981 Revision)

1. If claiming interest, use bracketed phrase and insert appropriate interest rate and date.

Committee Comment (1980 Revision)

§ 408.020 RSMo, states:

Creditors shall be allowed to receive interest at the rate of nine percent per annum, when no other rate is agreed upon, for all moneys after they become due and payable, on written contracts, and on accounts after they become due and demand for payment is made; for money recovered for the use of another, and retained without the owner's knowledge of the receipt, and for all other money due or to become due for the forbearance of payment whereof an express promise to pay interest has been made.

In *Weekley v. Wallace,* 314 S.W.2d 256, 257 (Mo.App.1958) the court said:

But a demand is essential to the right to recover interest on such accounts. [Citing cases.] The demand need be in no certain form, but must be definite as to amount and time. [Citing cases.] In the absence of such a demand for payment of an unwritten account, the filing of the suit substitutes for the previous demand, and starts the interest-bearing period, to be computed as of the date of the verdict.

If plaintiff elects to sue in quantum meruit even though he has an express contract, he may not recover a sum in excess of his contract price. *Cross v. Robinson,* 281 S.W.2d 22, 26 (Mo.App.1955).

Library References:

West's Key No. Digests, Implied and Constructive Contracts ⊙122.

Notes of Decisions

In general 1
Modification 2

_____

1. In general

Submission of a quantum meruit theory by a bilateral contract verdict directing instruc-

tion was error, and such error was compounded by the use of a bilateral contract verdict director in conjunction with a quantum meruit damages instruction. Instructions which intermingle inconsistent guides for recovery are prejudicially erroneous. Hall v. Cooper, 691 S.W.2d 507[1, 7] (Mo. App.1985).

In home builder's action for balance of price of house, MAI 4.04 was proper damage instruction with MAI 26.03. Wehrend v. Roknick, 664 S.W.2d 247[4] (Mo.App.1983).

Error to give second damage instruction, modified MAI 4.01, in action on account in which MAI 4.04, the appropriate damage instruction, properly modified to include "material and labor" instead of "goods," was given, but such error was not prejudicial where jury awarded amount alleged as due on account. Kunkle Water and Elec. Inc. v. Nehai Tonkayea Lake Association, Inc., 639 S.W.2d 177[1] (Mo.App.1982).

Plaintiff contracted and was paid for specific work at stated price, but sued for "extras" done on estimated basis. Plaintiff properly submitted on quantum meruit; not error to submit without reference to contract price. Bodde v. Burnham, 588 S.W.2d 516[2–5] (Mo.App.1979).

Where plaintiff submitted on MAI 26.03— Action on Account, its proper damage instruction was MAI 4.04. Hereford Concrete Products v. Aerobic Services, 565 S.W.2d 176[4–5] (Mo.App.1978).

Modified MAI 26.05 to submit plaintiff's claim for services rendered beyond agreed salary, and modified damages instruction for same. Austin v. Kansas City General Hospital, 570 S.W.2d 752[3, 4] (Mo.App.1978).

Damage instruction, before adoption of MAI 4.04, was properly modified to cover value of work and labor. Kaiser v. Lyon Metal Products, Inc., 461 S.W.2d 893[4] (Mo.App.1970).

Prior to MAI 4.04 on damages in quantum meruit, in action for services rendered it was not error to give a not-in-MAI damage instruction allowing a sum that would "fairly, reasonably and justly compensate plaintiff". McAtee v. Greenspon, 439 S.W.2d 187[3, 4] (Mo.App.1969).

2. Modification

Jury instructions were not erroneous, despite being taken from two separate approved instructions, where suit asserted claims of both quantum meruit and breach of warranty, core language from each approved instruction was given, and instructions stated that if jury found for plaintiff, amount awarded would be lower of the two theories. Executone of St. Louis, Inc. v. Normandy Osteopathic Hosp., et al., 735 S.W.2d 772[2] (Mo.App.1987).

4.05 [1996 Revision] Damages—Broker's Commission—Agreed Percentage

If you find in favor of plaintiff, then you must award him such sum as you believe he and defendant agreed upon as a commission [with __% interest thereon from _____, 19__].[1]

Notes on Use (1996 New)

1. If claiming interest, use bracketed phrase and insert appropriate interest rate and date.

Library References:

C.J.S. Brokers § 228.
West's Key No. Digests, Brokers ⟂88(13).

Notes of Decisions

1. In general

In action by investment banking firm for breach of contract for it to provide underwriting services, there was no prejudice in instruction that damages were to be in such sum as jury believed that parties agreed upon as a commission where the discrepancy between amount of agreed underwriter's discount and the substantially lower amount awarded made it evident that jury took into consideration the costs firm did not incur because it did not have to buy and resell bonds. Smith Moore & Co. v. J.L. Mason Realty & Investment, Inc., 817 S.W.2d 530 (Mo.App.1991).

Error to modify MAI 4.05 to direct allowance of specific amount where the amount was in dispute. Shurtz v. Jost, 597 S.W.2d 652[1] (Mo.App.1979).

MAI's 4.01 and 4.05 are appropriate in a breach of contract action. S.P. Personnel Associates, Inc. v. Hospital, etc., 525 S.W.2d 345[8–10] (Mo.App.1975).

4.06 [1996 Revision] Damages—Broker's Commission—No Amount Agreed

If you find in favor of plaintiff, you must award him such sum as you believe is a fair and just commission [with ___% interest thereon from _____, 19__].[1]

Notes on Use (1996 New)

1. If claiming interest, use bracketed phrase and insert appropriate interest rate and date.

Library References:

C.J.S. Brokers § 228.
West's Key No. Digests, Brokers ☞88(13).

Notes of Decisions

1. In general

Prior to MAI 4.04 on damages in quantum meruit, in action for services rendered it was not error to give a not–in–MAI damage instruction allowing a sum that would "fairly, reasonably and justly compensate plaintiff". McAtee v. Greenspon, 439 S.W.2d 187[3, 4] (Mo.App.1969).

4.07 [1996 Revision] Damages—Action to Recover for Services Furnished Decedent

If you find in favor of plaintiff, then you must award him the reasonable value of the services furnished [with ___% interest thereon from _____, 19__].[1]

Notes on Use (1996 New)

1. If claiming interest, use bracketed phrase and insert appropriate interest rate and date.

Committee Comment (1980 Revision)

Section 408.020 RSMo states:

Creditors shall be allowed to receive interest at the rate of nine percent per annum, when no other rate is agreed upon, for all moneys after they become due and payable, on written contracts, and on accounts after they become due and demand for payment is made; for money recovered for the use of another, and retained without the owner's knowledge of the receipt, and for all other money due or to become due for the forbearance of payment whereof an express promise to pay interest has been made.

In *Weekley v. Wallace,* 314 S.W.2d 256, 257 (Mo.App.1958) the Court said:

But a demand is essential to the right to recover interest on such accounts. [Citing cases.] The demand need be in no certain form, but must be definite as to amount and time. [Citing cases.] In the absence of such a demand for payment of an unwritten account, the filing of the suit substitutes for the previous demand, and starts the interest-bearing period, to be computed as of the date of the verdict.

Library References:

West's Key No. Digests, Executors and Administrators ☞451(3).

4.08 [1980 New] Damages—Contract—When Substantial Performance Submitted

If you find in favor of plaintiff, then you must award plaintiff such sum as you believe is the balance due plaintiff under the contract less any sum necessary to correct any variations.

Notes on Use (1980 New)

This instruction is to be used only in cases involving contracts in which substantial performance is sufficient. See the verdict directing instruction MAI 26.07.

Library References:

C.J.S. Architects § 45, 48, 50; Contracts § 795; Damages § 187.
West's Key No. Digests, Contracts ⟨⟩353; Damages ⟨⟩218.

4.09 [1980 Revision] Damages—Amount Not in Dispute

If you find in favor of plaintiff, then you must award plaintiff $_____. (*insert amount*)

Notes on Use (1980 Revision)

This instruction is to be used where there is no dispute as to the amount of damages.

Library References:

C.J.S. Damages § 177.
West's Key No. Digests, Damages ☞210.

Notes of Decisions

1. In general

Use of approved damage instruction designed for cases where damages were undisputed would have been inappropriate, where liquidated damage sum provided for under contract was but one of the damage elements sought and proper amount of attorney fees was disputed. Metro Waste Systems, Inc. v. A.L.D. Services, Inc., 924 S.W.2d 335 (Mo.App.1996).

Use of MAI 4.09 is mandatory when the only element of damage sought is a liquidated damage amount (use of MAI 4.09 would have been inappropriate in instant case because dispute over proper amount of attorney fees called for a factual evaluation; MAI 4.01 would have been correct damage instruction in this breach of contract action).

Metro Waste Systems, Inc. v. A.L.D. Services, Inc., 924 S.W.2d 335 (Mo.App.1996).

In case involving breach of home improvement contract containing a liquidated damages clause, MAI 4.09 was properly submitted instead of MAI 4.01. Standard Imp. Co. v. DiGiovanni, 768 S.W.2d 190, 192 (Mo. App.1989).

Court's instruction which did not allow jury to assess lesser amount of damages on third-party claim than consent judgment against third-party plaintiff was proper where there was no issue of amount of consent judgment or contention that amount of such judgment was excessive. O'Neil Lumber Co. v. Allied Builders Corp., 663 S.W.2d 326[9, 10] (Mo.App.1983).

4.10   [1980 Revision] Damages—Ejectment

If you find in favor of plaintiff, then you must award plaintiff such sum as you may find from the evidence [to be the difference between the fair market value [1] of the property before it was damaged and its fair market value [1] after it was damaged] [2, 3] [(*plus such sum as you may find from the evidence*) [4] will fairly and justly compensate plaintiff for the loss of rents and profits from the date defendant received notice of plaintiff's right to possession to the date of your verdict] [5, 3] [will fairly and justly compensate plaintiff for deprivation of possession of the property from the date defendant had notice of plaintiff's claim to possession to the date of your verdict]. [6, 3] [You must also state separately in your verdict such sum as you reasonably find to be the monthly value of the rents and profits from the property at the time of your verdict.] [7]

Notes on Use (2002 Revision)

1.   The phrase "fair market value" must be defined. Use the first paragraph of MAI 16.02.

2.   Use only if there is evidence of waste committed by the defendant after notice of plaintiff's claim of possession.

3.   If the notice of plaintiff's claim to possession was received by defendant more than five years prior to commencement of the action, the bracketed material must be modified to limit the period of damage to five years next preceding the filing of the action.

4.   Use the parenthetical material if damage assessments for both waste and loss of rents and profits are supported by the evidence.

5.   Use if there is evidence of the loss of rents and profits.

6.   Use only if there is no evidence of either waste or loss of rents and profits. The jury's verdict supporting a writ of ejectment justifies the award of nominal damages without evidence of substantial damages.

7.   The plaintiff is entitled to damages for loss of rents and profits between the date of the verdict and the date of restoration of possession; the monthly rate is determined by the jury; the multiplication is performed and the judgment for such post-verdict damages is entered by the judge. Use bracketed material only when defendant holds possession on date of verdict, plaintiff's right of possession has not expired and there is evidence to support the jury's finding of the monthly rate.

In a case in which mitigation of damages is properly submitted under MAI 32.29, this damage instruction should be modified with the bracketed sentence required by Note 4 of the Notes on Use to MAI 4.01.

Library References:

C.J.S. Ejectment § 118.
West's Key No. Digests, Ejectment ⚷110.

4.11   [1980 Revision] Damages—Uninsured Motor Vehicle—Suit Against Insurer Only

If you find in favor of plaintiff, then you must find plaintiff's damages in such sum as you believe will fairly and justly compensate plaintiff for any damages you believe he sustained [and is reasonably certain to sustain in the future] [1] as a direct result of the collision [2] mentioned in the evidence.

Notes on Use (2002 Revision)

1.   This may be added if supported by the evidence.

2.   In a non-hit-and-run case, in which there is no collision, an appropriate term such as "occurrence" must be substituted for the term "collision."

In a case such as *Carlson v. K–Mart*, 979 S.W.2d 145 (Mo. banc 1998), where MAI 19.01 is used in the verdict director, delete the entire phrase "as a direct result of the collision mentioned in the evidence" from this instruction and substitute the phrase "that (*describe the compensable event or conduct*) directly caused or directly contributed to cause."

Other modifications also may be appropriate. For further discussion, see MAI 4.01.

In a case in which mitigation of damages is properly submitted under MAI 32.29, this damage instruction should be modified with the bracketed sentence required by Note 4 of the Notes on Use to MAI 4.01.

This instruction should be used only where a suit on uninsured motor vehicle coverage names the insurer as the single defendant and the operator of the uninsured motor vehicle is not joined. This instruction should be used only where form of verdict MAI 36.14 is used.

This instruction requires the jury to define the amount of the plaintiff's damages but does not determine the amount of the judgment against the insurer. That amount is determined as a matter of law by the court.

The effect of the adoption of the doctrine of comparative fault upon a contractual right of recovery under uninsured motor vehicle coverage is unclear. If the law and the insurance policy permit the application of comparative fault in such a case, modify this instruction in accordance with the format of MAI 37.03.

Library References:

C.J.S. Insurance § 56, 1647–1648, 1650–1653, 1657, 1659–1671, 1675–1684, 1703, 1706–1708.
West's Key No. Digests, Insurance ⟨⟩2772–2816, 3579.

Notes of Decisions

1. In general

The omission of the qualifying terms "fairly and justly" did not change the essential sense of MAI 4.11 and, therefore, this omission did not require a reversal. Stuart v. State Farm Mut. Automobile Ins. Co., 699 S.W.2d 450, 457 (Mo.App.1985).

4.12   [1979 New] Apportionment of Fault—Plaintiff Claiming Against All From Whom Apportionment Is Sought—Plaintiff's Claim and Apportionment Decided in Same Trial

If Verdict _____ [1] is in favor of plaintiff and against *(here use descriptive phrase designation, i.e., both defendants; more than one defendant; etc.)*, you must assess the proportion of the fault which each party listed in Verdict _____ [2] has for plaintiff's damage [assessed in Verdict _____ [1]]. [3]

Notes on Use (1979 New)

1. Insert the letter designation of the form of verdict deciding plaintiff's claim for damages.

2. Insert the letter designation of the form of verdict assessing the proportions of fault (MAI 36.15).

3. Use when necessary to limit the apportionment to damages assessed in Verdict _____ [1].

The MAI Committee recommends this instruction for use where plaintiff's claim and the apportionment of fault issues are tried in the same trial. It can be used either where all issues are submitted simultaneously or in a "split-submission", i.e., a "bifurcated trial" procedure.

Add the following paragraph when a master's liability is submitted only on vicarious liability for the servant's conduct and both master and servant are defendants:

> If Verdict _____ is against both *(insert names of master and servant)* because of the conduct of *(insert name of servant)* only, then in deciding proportions of fault you must consider them both as one party and assess only the fault of *(insert name of servant)* as the fault of both *(insert names of master and servant)*.

In preparing the verdict form for apportionment in such a case wherein the master's liability is submitted only on his servant's conduct, insert the names of both master and servant on the same line in accordance with the direction to the jury to assess only the fault of the servant as the fault of both.

Committee Comment (1996 Revision)

Missouri Pacific R. Co. v. Whitehead & Kales Co., 566 S.W.2d 466 (Mo.banc 1978), authorizes a defendant to request apportionment of the relative fault for plaintiff's damage. The case recognizes the right of the plaintiff either to file a claim against a third party defendant or to refuse to do so. It also recognizes that the apportionment issue may be severed for a separate trial. This instruction is intended for use in a case where plaintiff claims and submits against all parties against whom apportionment of fault is sought and in which the apportionment issues are submitted in the same trial with plaintiff's claims.

If apportionment of fault is sought against one or more parties against whom plaintiff asserts no claim, use MAI 4.13; if the apportionment issues are not submitted in the same trial with plaintiff's claims, MAI 4.14 should be used.

This instruction, Notes on Use, and Committee Comment were originally promulgated as recommended by the Committee, but were neither approved nor disapproved by the Supreme Court. The Supreme Court, with the publication of the Fifth Edition of MAI, approved the approach to "apportionment of fault" contemplated by MAI 4.12, 4.13, 4.14 and verdict forms 36.15 and 36.16.

Library References:

C.J.S. Negligence § 871, 891, 900–901.
West's Key No. Digests, Negligence ⚷1746.

4.13   [1979 New] Apportionment of Fault—Plaintiff Not Claiming Against All From Whom Apportionment of Fault Is Sought—Plaintiff's Claim and Apportionment Decided in Same Trial

If Verdict _____[1] is in favor of plaintiff and against (*insert name of party or parties seeking apportionment*)[2] and if Verdict _____[3] is in favor of (*insert name of party or parties seeking apportionment*),[2] you must assess the proportion of the fault which each party listed in Verdict _____[4] has for plaintiff's damage [assessed in Verdict _____[1]].[5]

Notes on Use (1979 New)

1. Insert the letter designation of the form of verdict deciding plaintiff's claim for damages.

2. If more than one party is seeking apportionment insert [either or both] [one or more of] before the name of the parties seeking apportionment.

3. Insert the letter of the form of verdict requiring apportionment of fault (MAI 36.16).

4. Insert the letter designation of the form of verdict assessing the proportions of fault (MAI 36.15).

5. Use when necessary to limit the apportionment to damages assessed in Verdict _____[1].

The MAI Committee recommends this instruction for use where plaintiff's claim and the apportionment of fault issues are tried in the same trial. It can be used either where all issues are submitted simultaneously or in a "split-submission", i.e., a "bifurcated trial" procedure.

Add the following paragraph when a master's liability is submitted only on vicarious liability for the servant's conduct and both master and servant are defendants:

> If Verdict _____ is against both (*insert names of master and servant*) because of the conduct of (*insert name of servant*) only, then in deciding proportions of fault you must consider them both as one party and assess only the fault of (*insert name of servant*) as the fault of both (*insert names of master and servant*).

In preparing the verdict form for apportionment in such a case wherein the master's liability is submitted only on his servant's conduct, insert the names of both master and servant on the same line in accordance with the direction to the jury to assess only the fault of the servant as the fault of both.

Committee Comment (1996 Revision)

Missouri Pacific R. Co. v. Whitehead & Kales Co., 566 S.W.2d 466 (Mo.banc 1978), authorizes a judgment apportioning fault of a third party defendant against whom the plaintiff does not claim or submit. This instruction is intended for use in such a case wherein the apportionment issues are submitted in the same trial with plaintiff's claim.

Since the plaintiff will not submit the issue of the third party defendant's liability (fault) for plaintiff's damage, the party seeking apportionment will need to submit the issue of third party's fault for plaintiff's damage by an appropriate verdict directing instruction.

This instruction, Notes on Use, and Committee Comment were originally promulgated as recommended by the Committee, but were neither approved nor disapproved by the Supreme Court. The Supreme Court, with the publication of the Fifth Edition of MAI, approved the approach to "apportionment of fault" contemplated by MAI 4.12, 4.13, 4.14 and verdict forms 36.15 and 36.16.

Library References:

C.J.S. Negligence § 871, 891, 900–901.
West's Key No. Digests, Negligence ⊗1746.

4.14 [1979 New] Apportionment of Fault—Separate Trial

If your verdict is in favor of (*insert name of party or parties seeking apportionment*) [1] and against (*here use descriptive phrase designation, i.e., the defendant, one or more of the defendants, both defendant Doe and third-party defendant Roe, defendant Doe and one or more of the third-party defendants, etc.*) on the claim[s] for apportionment of fault for the (*state the amount*) damages awarded (*state name of successful claimant*) in the other trial mentioned in evidence, you must assess the proportion of the fault which each party listed in Verdict _____ [2] has for such damage.

Notes on Use (1979 New)

1. If more than one party is seeking apportionment insert [either or both] [one or more of] before the name of the parties seeking apportionment.

2. Insert the letter designation of the form of verdict apportioning fault.

Add the following paragraph when a master and servant are parties and the master's liability is submitted only on vicarious liability for the servant's conduct:

In deciding proportions of fault you must consider both (*insert names of master and servant*) as one party and assess only the fault of (*insert name of servant*) as the fault of both (*insert names of master and servant*).

In preparing the Verdict form for apportionment in such a case wherein the master's liability is based only on his servant's conduct, insert the names of both master and servant on the same line in accordance with the direction to the jury to assess only the fault of the servant as the fault of both.

Committee Comment (1996 Revision)

A claim for indemnity does not arise, technically, until the claimant's own liability to the original plaintiff is fixed. Civil Rule 55.06(b) specifically permits such a claim to be joined in the action which seeks to establish the liability of the claimant for which he seeks indemnity. *Missouri Pacific R. Co. v. Whitehead & Kales Co.*, 566 S.W.2d 466 (Mo.banc 1978) and Rule 66.02, recognize that simultaneous trial of both claims may be had or that the claims may be tried in separate trials.

This instruction is intended for use in an apportionment of damage case tried after trial of the claimant's damage suit. Thus, the claimant for apportionment may carry the party designation of defendant or plaintiff or third-party plaintiff, etc. The damage which is the basis for apportionment of fault will have been previously adjudicated. The instructions will need to submit the issue of the claimed fault of the party or parties against whom apportionment is sought.

This instruction, Notes on Use, and Committee Comment were originally promulgated as recommended by the Committee, but were neither approved nor disapproved by the Supreme Court. The Supreme Court, with the publication of the Fifth Edition of MAI, approved the approach to "apportionment of fault" contemplated by MAI 4.12, 4.13, 4.14 and verdict forms 36.15 and 36.16.

Library References:

C.J.S. Negligence § 871, 891, 900–901.
West's Key No. Digests, Negligence ☞1746.

4.15 [1980 New] Damages—Libel or Slander—Plaintiff Not a Public Official or Public Figure

If you find the issues in favor of plaintiff, then you must award plaintiff such sum as you believe will fairly and justly compensate plaintiff for any damages you believe he sustained [and is reasonably certain to sustain in the future] [1] as a direct result of the (*describe the publication such as "publishing of the newspaper article", "making of the statement", etc.*) mentioned in the evidence.

[If you find the issues in favor of plaintiff, and if you believe that defendant (*describe the act of publication such as "published the newspaper article", "wrote the letter", "made the statement", etc.*) with knowledge that it was false or with reckless disregard for whether it was true or false at a time when defendant had serious doubt as to whether it was true, then in addition to any damages to which you find plaintiff entitled under the foregoing paragraph, you may award plaintiff an additional amount as punitive damages in such sum as you believe will serve to punish defendant and to deter him and others from like conduct.] [2]

Notes on Use (1980 New)

1. This may be added if supported by the evidence.

2. Use the bracketed second paragraph if plaintiff's evidence supports the submission of punitive damages under the requirements of *Gertz v. Robert Welch, Inc.,* 418 U.S. 323, 94 S.Ct. 2997, 41 L.Ed.2d 789 (1974), which requires that for punitive damages, actual malice must be shown under the test set forth in *New York Times Company v. Sullivan,* 376 U.S. 254, 84 S.Ct. 710, 11 L.Ed.2d 686 (1964).

This damage instruction is for use in a case where MAI 23.06(1) or 23.10(1) is used as the verdict director. Use MAI 3.06 as the burden of proof instruction if punitive damages are submitted. If punitive damages are not sought, use MAI 3.01.

Committee Comment (1980 New)

See *Time, Inc. v. Firestone,* 424 U.S. 448, 96 S.Ct. 958, 47 L.Ed.2d 154 (1976), for a discussion of the type of damage instruction required to meet the actual damage test of *Gertz v. Robert Welch, Inc.,* supra.

Library References:

C.J.S. Libel and Slander; Injurious Falsehood § 181.
West's Key No. Digests, Libel and Slander ⬦124(8).

Notes of Decisions

1. In general

Plaintiff need only to plead and prove unified defamation elements set out in applicable model jury instructions to establish defamation. Boyd v. Schwan's Sales Enterprises, Inc., 23 S.W.3d 261 (Mo.App.2000).

No prejudicial error resulted from instruction on actual damages which failed to also include instruction on punitive damages, as required by Notes on Use, where punitive damages were struck by trial court pursuant to defendant's motion for new trial. Joseph v. Elam, 709 S.W.2d 517[13] (Mo.App.1986).

4.16 [1980 New] Damages—Libel or Slander—Plaintiff a Public Official or Public Figure

If you find the issues in favor of plaintiff, then you must award plaintiff such sum as you believe will fairly and justly compensate plaintiff for any damages you believe he sustained [and is reasonably certain to sustain in the future] [1] as a direct result of the (*describe the publication such as "publishing of the newspaper article", "making of the statement", etc.*) mentioned in the evidence.

In addition to any damages to which you find plaintiff entitled under the foregoing paragraph, you may award plaintiff an additional amount as punitive damages in such sum as you believe will serve to punish defendant and to deter him and others from like conduct.

Notes on Use (1996 Revision)

1. This may be added if supported by the evidence.

This damage instruction is for use in a case where MAI 23.06(2) or 23.10(2) is used as the verdict director. Use MAI 3.05 as the burden of proof instruction.

Library References:

C.J.S. Libel and Slander; Injurious Falsehood § 181.
West's Key No. Digests, Libel and Slander ⟨⟩124(8).

Notes of Decisions

1. In general

Plaintiff need only to plead and prove unified defamation elements set out in applicable model jury instructions to establish defamation. Boyd v. Schwan's Sales Enterprises, Inc., 23 S.W.3d 261 (Mo.App.2000).

4.17   [1980 New] Damages—Breach of Warranty Under Uniform Commercial Code—Accepted Goods

If you find in favor of plaintiff, then you must award plaintiff such sum as you believe was the difference between the fair market value [1] of (*describe the article or product*) when plaintiff discovered or should have discovered [it did not conform] [2] [it was unfit] [3] and its fair market value [1] had it been as represented by defendant [plus such sum as you believe will fairly and justly compensate plaintiff for any other damage plaintiff sustained as a direct result of (*describe the article or product*) [failing to conform] [2] [being unfit].[3]] [4]

Notes on Use (1996 Revision)

1.   The phrase "fair market value" must be defined. Use the first paragraph of MAI 16.02.

2.   Use these bracketed phrases for an express warranty.

3.   Use these bracketed phrases for an implied warranty.

4.   Use the bracketed phrase where the evidence supports the submission of incidental and consequential damages described § 400.2–715, RSMo.

This instruction is applicable in situations which involve a breach of warranty under §§ 400.2–313 and 400.2–314 RSMo and the goods have been accepted. The measure of damages is set forth in § 400.2–714 RSMo.

Where the goods have been rejected or acceptance has been revoked, see §§ 400.2–711 through 400.2–713.

Committee Comment (1980 New)

See MAI 4.01 Committee Comment for procedure to be followed in closing argument in the use of a short, simple damage instruction.

Library References:

C.J.S. Sales § 307.
West's Key No. Digests, Sales ⬡446(9).

Notes of Decisions

1. In general

Testimony by expert of 20% reduction in automobile's value due to its unknown mileage, along with evidence of numerous repairs, was sufficient to establish automobile's fair market value when purchasers discovered problems with automobile, for purposes of purchasers' damages for breach of warranty against automobile manufacturer; damage instruction for breach of warranty was not required to elaborate on what aspect of product did not conform. Carpenter v. Chrysler Corporation, 853 S.W.2d 346 (Mo.App.1993).

MAI 4.17 does not require that a damage instruction for breach of warranty elaborate on what aspect of the product did not conform. Carpenter v. Chrysler Corporation, 853 S.W.2d 346 (Mo.App.1993).

4.18 [1991 New] Damages—Personal Injury and Loss of Consortium, Loss of Services or Medical Expenses—Spouse or Child Injured—Non–Comparative Fault Only

If you find in favor of plaintiff (*name of plaintiff with the primary claim*), then you must award plaintiff (*name of plaintiff with primary claim*) such sum as you believe will fairly and justly compensate plaintiff (*name of plaintiff with primary claim*) for any damages you believe [he] [she][1] sustained [and is reasonably certain to sustain in the future][2] as a direct result of the occurrence[3] mentioned in the evidence.

If you further find that plaintiff (*name of plaintiff with derivative claim*) did sustain damage as a direct result of injury to [his] [her] [husband] [wife] [child][1], you must award plaintiff (*name of plaintiff with derivative claim*) such sum as you believe will fairly and justly compensate plaintiff (*name of plaintiff with derivative claim*) for any damages due to injury to [his] [her] [husband] [wife] [child][1] which you believe [he] [she][1] sustained [and is reasonably certain to sustain in the future][2] as a direct result of the occurrence[3] mentioned in the evidence.

Notes on Use (2002 Revision)

1. Select appropriate word(s).

2. This may be added if supported by the evidence.

3. When the evidence discloses a compensable event and a non-compensable event, both of which are claimed to have caused damage, the term "occurrence" may need to be modified. See *Vest v. City National Bank and Trust Company*, 470 S.W.2d 518 (Mo.1971). When the term "occurrence" is modified, substitute some descriptive phrase that specifically describes the compensable event or conduct. As an example, if the plaintiff claims plaintiff sustained damages as a direct result of negligent medical care while being treated for a non-compensable fall or illness, the instruction may be modified to read, "... as a direct result of the conduct of defendant as submitted in Instruction Number ___ (*here insert number of verdict directing instruction*)." As another example, if plaintiff sustained damages in an automobile collision but also had a non-compensable illness, the instruction may be modified to read "... as a direct result of the automobile collision."

In a case such as *Carlson v. K–Mart*, 979 S.W.2d 145 (Mo. banc 1998), where MAI 19.01 is used in the verdict director, delete the entire phrase "as a direct result of the occurrence mentioned in the evidence" from this instruction and substitute the phrase "that (*describe the compensable event or conduct*) directly caused or directly contributed to cause."

Other modifications also may be appropriate.

In a case in which mitigation of damages is properly submitted under MAI 32.29, this damage instruction should be modified with the bracketed sentence required by Note 4 of the Notes on Use to MAI 4.01. In a case involving combined primary and derivative claims, the law of Missouri has not yet developed to indicate whether mitigation of damages instructions may be given on both claims or only on the primary injury claim. The Committee takes no position on this issue.

Committee Comment (1991 New)

This is a damage instruction for both the primary and the derivative claim in a non-comparative fault personal injury case with a derivative loss of consortium, loss of services or medical expense claim. See MAI 31.04 for the appropriate verdict directing instruction for the derivative claim and MAI 36.23 for the appropriate verdict form. See also Illustration 35.17.

This instruction should not be used in a comparative fault case. See MAI 37.08 for the damage instruction in a comparative fault case submitting both a primary claim and a derivative claim. See also Illustration 35.16.

Library References:

C.J.S. Damages § 177.
West's Key No. Digests, Damages ☞209.

Notes of Decisions

1. In general

Spouse is not entitled to judgment on claim for loss of consortium merely because injured spouse was found entitled to recover. Consortium claimant is not entitled to nominal damages. Lear v. Norfolk & Western Ry. Co., 815 S.W.2d 12 (Mo.App.1991).

The Missouri Supreme Court refused to recognize a cause of action for loss of parental consortium (consortium action by child due to injury to parent) or filial consortium (consortium action by sibling due to injury to another sibling). Powell v. American Motors Corp., 834 S.W.2d 184 (Mo. banc 1992).

5.00

DAMAGES—WRONGFUL DEATH

Analysis of Instructions

Westlaw Electronic Research

See Westlaw Electronic Research Guide preceding the Table of Instructions.

Library References:

C.J.S. Death § 90.
West's Key No. Digests, Death ⚷104.

5.01 [1996 Revision] Damages—Wrongful Death

If you find in favor of plaintiff, then you must award plaintiff such sum as you believe will fairly and justly compensate plaintiff[1] for any damages you believe plaintiff[2] [and decedent][3] sustained [and plaintiff[4] is reasonably certain to sustain in the future][5] as a direct result of the fatal injury to (*insert name of decedent*).

You must not consider grief or bereavement suffered by reason of the death.

Notes on Use (1996 Revision)

1. In the case where not all beneficiaries are joined as plaintiffs in the claim for wrongful death or the plaintiff is a plaintiff ad litem, substitute for the word "plaintiff[s]" the phrase "the survivor[s] of (*insert name of decedent*)".

2. Make an appropriate substitution if Note 1 is applicable, i.e., "they," "he," "she".

3. Use bracketed phrase where the evidence supports the submission of damages to decedent between the time of injury and time of death, i.e. pain and suffering.

4. If Note 1 is applicable, substitute for the phrase "plaintiff is" the phrase "the survivor[s] of (*insert name of decedent*) [is] [are]".

5. This may be added if supported by the evidence.

Where aggravating or mitigating circumstances are submitted in a wrongful death case, see Chapter 6.00.

Committee Comment (2002 Revision)

Section 537.090, RSMo, lists elements of compensable damage that were a part of the damage law before its enactment as well as permitting recovery for decedent's damages between injury and death. The separate elements of damage are properly a matter for argument and are not and should not be listed in this damage instruction.

During the instruction conference, the parties and the court should discuss (on the record) just what damages are supported by the evidence and properly can be argued to the jury. In this way, jury arguments can proceed without undue interruptions.

In *Bennett v. Owens–Corning Fiberglas Corporation*, 896 S.W.2d 464 (Mo. banc 1995), the Court held that aggravating circumstance damages of section 537.090, RSMo, are the equivalent of punitive damages and may be awarded only if accompanied by due process safeguards articulated in *Pacific Mutual Life Insurance Co. v. Haslip*, 499 U.S. 1, 111 S.Ct. 1032, 113 L.Ed.2d 1(1991). See Chapter 6.00 for the submission of aggravating and mitigating circumstances.

The Committee is unable to determine under existing Missouri law whether the doctrine of mitigation of damages/avoidable consequences (see MAI 32.29 and MAI 4.01) is applicable to wrongful death cases in addition to the statutory "mitigating circumstances attending the death" under section 537.090, RSMo (see MAI 6.01). Thus, the Committee takes no position on such issue.

Library References:

C.J.S. Death § 90.
West's Key No. Digests, Death ☞104.

Notes of Decisions

In general   **1**
Aggravating circumstances   **2**

------

1. In general

In wrongful death suit, instruction that jury should award sum to compensate "survivors of" decedent, rather than to "plaintiff," who was decedent's mother, was proper. O'Neal v. Pipes Enterprises, Inc., 930 S.W.2d 416 (Mo.App. W.D.1995).

MAI 5.01 is designed for use in a one-stage trial and is not appropriate for use in two-stage trial; any error in instructions and verdict forms in wrongful death action against pharmacy which supplied improperly compounded cardioplegic solution for use during patient's open-heart surgery was invited by pharmacy, by its motion to use bifurcated trial procedure which created unnecessary instruction problems and which prevented use of proper damage instruction. Schroeder v. Lester E. Cox Medical Center, Inc., 833 S.W.2d 411 (Mo.App.1992).

Parents of minor child are no longer limited to pecuniary loss *during child's minority.* But, defendant is entitled to bracketed clause excluding parents' grief. Mitchell v. Buchheit, 559 S.W.2d 528[6–7] (Mo. banc 1977).

In parents' action for wrongful death of minor child plaintiffs properly submitted their measure of damages by "the broad pecuniary loss standard" of MAI 5.03, and the court properly refused defendant's modified MAI

5.03 telling the jury the value of the child's services should be reduced by the parents' prospective cost of supporting her. MAI 5.03 is both a correct and a complete statement of the law. Mudd v. Quinn, 462 S.W.2d 757[1] (Mo.1971).

2. Aggravating circumstances

Jury instruction on "aggravating circumstance" damages in wrongful death action was inadequate to guide jury's award of such punitive damages; while court correctly refused to give approved aggravating circumstance instruction due to its failure to give adequate guidance, and required aggravating circumstance damages to be set out separately from actual damages, modified approved instruction actually given lacked language informing jury to award "such sum as you believe will serve to punish defendant and to deter defendant and others from like conduct," and standard for awarding such damages remained unconstitutionally vague. Bennett v. Owens–Corning Fiberglas Corp., 896 S.W.2d 464 (Mo.1995).

In wrongful death action against asbestos manufacturers, manufacturers were not precluded from requesting instruction on mitigation of damages simply because plaintiffs exercised their option of not requesting instruction on aggravating circumstances. Hagen v. Celotex Corporation, 816 S.W.2d 667 (Mo. banc 1991).

Aggravating circumstances may be submitted in uninsured motorist case; trial court in wrongful death case abused its discretion when it refused to include issue of aggravating circumstances in damage instruction; policy exclusions for punitive and exemplary damages do not preclude coverage for aggravating circumstances. Moreland v. Columbia Mut. Ins. Co., 842 S.W.2d 215 (Mo. App.1992).

Aggravating circumstances in a wrongful death action may be submitted where the defendant knew or had reason to know that there was a high degree of probability that the negligent action would result in injury. No definition of "aggravating circumstances," MAI 5.01, should be given. Elliot v. Kesler, 799 S.W.2d 97 (Mo.App.1990).

Damages instruction MAI 5.01, modified in accordance with MAI 37.03 to submit comparative fault, that permitted the jury to consider aggravating circumstances in assessing damages in wrongful death action is proper when the defendant could have reasonably been charged with knowledge of potentially dangerous situation but failed to act to prevent or reduce danger. Blum v. Airport Term. Serv. Inc., 762 S.W.2d 67, 72–73 (Mo.App.1988).

In order for the issue of aggravating circumstances to be submitted to the jury, there must be a showing of "willful misconduct, wantonness, recklessness, or a want of care indicative of indifference to consequences." Weast v. Festus Flying Service, Inc., 680 S.W.2d 262[5] (Mo.App.1984).

Aggravating circumstances where brakeman saw pedestrian approaching close to crossing but took no action to apply emergency brake. Wiseman v. Missouri Pacific R. Co., 575 S.W.2d 742[5] (Mo.App.1978).

Evidence that defendant overtook another car while approaching a crest which hid approaching cars warranted the paragraph on aggravating circumstances. Dougherty v. Smith, 480 S.W.2d 519[3] (Mo.App.1972).

Driving heavy truck down exit ramp with brakes constructively known to be inadequate warranted aggravating circumstances clause in wrongful death damage instruction. Mudd v. Quinn, 462 S.W.2d 757[2] (Mo. 1971).

Evidence that busy crossing was without effective warning warranted submission of aggravating circumstances clause. Grothe v. St. L.–S.F. Ry. Co., 460 S.W.2d 711[5] (Mo.1970).

6.00

DAMAGES—MITIGATING AND AGGRAVATING CIRCUMSTANCES—WRONGFUL DEATH

Analysis of Instructions

Westlaw Electronic Research

See Westlaw Electronic Research Guide preceding the Table of Instructions.

Library References:

C.J.S. Damages § 184.
West's Key No. Digests, Damages ⚖213, 214.

6.01 [1996 Revision] Wrongful Death—Mitigating Circumstances

If your verdict is for plaintiff, then in assessing damages you may take into consideration any mitigating circumstances attendant upon the fatal injury.

Notes on Use (1965 New)

This instruction may be given by defendant where the evidence supports the submission.

Committee Comment (2002 New)

The Committee is unable to determine under existing Missouri law whether the doctrine of mitigation of damages/avoidable consequences (See MAI 32.29 and MAI 4.01) is applicable to wrongful death cases in addition to the statutory "mitigating circumstances attending the death" under section 537.090, RSMo (See MAI 6.01). Thus, the Committee takes no position on such issue.

Library References:

C.J.S. Damages § 184.
West's Key No. Digests, Damages ⟳214.

Notes of Decisions

1. In general

Trial court committed reversible error, in vehicle collision case in which only damages were at issue, by submitting non-Missouri Approved Instruction (MAI) which included elements of both comparative fault and mitigation of damages and allowed jury to assess percentage of fault to passenger for failing to mitigate damages; MAI instruction 6.01 was available, instruction used was not supported by either facts or evidence, and instruction allowed jury to confuse issues of fault with issue of mitigation. Tillman v. Supreme Exp. & Transfer, Inc., 920 S.W.2d 552 (Mo.App.1996).

In wrongful death action against asbestos manufacturers, manufacturers were not precluded from requesting instruction on mitigation of damages simply because plaintiffs exercised their option of not requesting instruction on aggravating circumstances. Hagen v. Celotex Corporation, 816 S.W.2d 667 (Mo. banc 1991).

6.02 [1998 Revision] Wrongful Death—Aggravating Circumstances

Where aggravating circumstances are submitted in a wrongful death case, select an exemplary damage instruction from Chapter 10.00 that fits the theory of the case (e.g., intentional tort, negligence, strict liability, etc.) and substitute the phrase "damages for aggravating circumstances" for the phrase "punitive damages" in the Chapter 10.00 instruction selected.

For example, if a wrongful death case is submitted on a negligence theory, MAI 10.02 would be selected to submit aggravating circumstances in the following, modified form:

If you find in favor of plaintiff under Instruction Number ___ (*here insert number of plaintiff's verdict directing instruction based on negligence*), and if you believe the conduct of defendant as submitted in Instruction Number ___ (*here insert number of plaintiff's verdict directing instruction based on negligence*) showed complete indifference to or conscious disregard for the safety of others, then in addition to any damages to which you may find plaintiff entitled under Instruction Number ___ (*here insert number of plaintiff's damage instruction*) you may award plaintiff an additional amount as damages for aggravating circumstances in such sum as you believe will serve to punish defendant and to deter defendant and others from like conduct.

The burden of proof instruction (MAI 3.01) and the verdict form from Chapter 36.00 (MAI 36.11) would be modified similarly by substituting the phrase "damages for aggravating circumstances" for the phrase "punitive damages."

Committee Comment (1996 New)

See *Bennett v. Owens-Corning Fiberglas Corporation*, 896 S.W.2d 464 (Mo.banc 1995).

Library References:

C.J.S. Damages § 184.
West's Key No. Digests, Damages ☞213.

Notes of Decisions

1. In general

Instruction should inform jury that award for aggravating circumstances should be in such sum as is believed will serve to punish defendant and deter defendant and others from like conduct. Bennett v. Owens–Corning Fiberglas Corp., 896 S.W.2d 464 (Mo. 1995).

Aggravating circumstance damages must be set out separately from actual damages in verdict form, but form should not set forth separate line for reduction by mitigating circumstances; once punitive damages become issue in wrongful death action, mitigating evidence may be adduced. Bennett v. Owens–Corning Fiberglas Corp., 896 S.W.2d 464 (Mo.1995).

7.00

DAMAGES—JOINT TORT–FEASORS

Analysis of Instructions

Westlaw Electronic Research

See Westlaw Electronic Research Guide preceding the Table of Instructions.

Library References:

7.01 [Withdrawn 1983] Damages—Deduction for Admitted Settlement With Joint Tort–Feasor

Notes on Use (Withdrawn 1983)
Committee Comment (1983 Revision)

See Committee Comment to MAI 1.06 for a discussion of the reasons for the withdrawal of MAI 7.01 and for the procedure now to be followed.

Notes of Decisions

1. In general

Where one of three defendants settled with plaintiff, MAI 4.01, as mandated by MAI 7.01, note 2, was properly modified by changing "award" to "determine," so as to show deduction of plaintiff's partial settlement. Smith v. Courter, 575 S.W.2d 199[3] (Mo.App.1978).

MAI 7.01 is for use where plaintiff has *settled* with one defendant and goes to trial against the other; it is not to be followed when one defendant has made partial payments to plaintiff under § 490.710 and case goes to trial against that defendant. Taylor v. Yellow Cab Co., 548 S.W.2d 528[1–12] (Mo. banc 1977).

Where plaintiff has settled with a joint tortfeasor, his *verdict director* must include the "deduction clause" specified by MAI 7.01, Notes on Use. Hunter v. Norton, 412 S.W.2d 163[10] (Mo.1967).

7.02 [1983 Revision] Damages—Disputed Partial Settlement

The following addendum must be added to the appropriate damage instruction (MAI 4.01–5.01) when there is a disputed issue as to whether there has been a settlement payment, as to whether a certain payment was attributable to a settlement or if the amount of the settlement payment is disputed:

In determining the amount of plaintiff's damages you are not to consider any evidence of prior payment made [to] [on behalf of] [1] plaintiff. The judge will consider any such payment and adjust your award as required by law.

If you believe (*state the name*) previously paid plaintiff some amount on plaintiff's claim, then you must find the amount which you believe (*state the name*) paid on plaintiff's claim.

Notes on Use (1983 Revision)

1. Select the appropriate bracketed phrase; if both are appropriate, use both in the disjunctive.

Use verdict form 36.19 with this addendum. When the verdict is returned, the trial judge will take any finding of settlement payments into consideration and will give credit for any amount allowable as a credit.

Neither MAI 7.02 nor MAI 34.05 is to be used to submit the affirmative defense of complete release. Use an appropriate affirmative defense instruction, such as MAI 32.21, to submit this issue.

Committee Comment (1983 Revision)

For advance payments under § 490.710, RSMo or undisputed settlement payments, see MAI 1.06.

Library References:
C.J.S. Damages § 184.
West's Key No. Digests, Damages ☞214.

8.00

DAMAGES—FEDERAL EMPLOYERS' LIABILITY ACT

Analysis of Instructions

	Instruction Number
Death of Employee Under F.E.L.A.	8.01
F.E.L.A.—Injury to Employee	8.02

Westlaw Electronic Research

See Westlaw Electronic Research Guide preceding the Table of Instructions.

Library References:

C.J.S. Employers' Liability for Injuries to Employees § 341, 343, 346.
West's Key No. Digests, Employers' Liability ⚖261–266.

8.01 [1996 Revision] Damages—Death of Employee under F.E.L.A.

If you find in favor of the plaintiff, then you must award plaintiff such sum as you believe will fairly and justly compensate (*here identify the beneficiaries*) for any damages you believe (*he, she, they*) [and decedent][1] sustained [and (*here identify the beneficiaries*) are reasonably certain to sustain in the future][2] as a direct result of the fatal injury to (*name of decedent*). Any award of future pecuniary damages must be included at present value. [Any award you may make is not subject to income tax.][3] [If you find decedent contributorily negligent as submitted in Instruction Number _____, then your award must be determined by diminishing total damages in proportion to the amount of negligence attributable to decedent.][4]

You must not consider grief or bereavement suffered by reason of the death.

Notes On Use (1996 Revision)

1. Use bracketed phrase where the evidence supports the submission of damages to decedent between the time of injury and the time of death, i.e. pain and suffering.

2. This may be added if supported by the evidence.

3. If requested this bracketed sentence must be given. See: *Norfolk & Western Ry. Co. v. Liepelt*, 444 U.S. 490, 100 S.Ct. 755, 62 L.Ed.2d 689 (1980).

4. If contributory negligence is submitted the damage instruction must be modified by adding this bracketed sentence. See MAI 32.07(B) for the appropriate contributory negligence instruction in an F.E.L.A. case.

If the law and facts permit a mitigation of damages submission in an F.E.L.A. death case, see MAI 8.02 and 32.07(A) for the appropriate method of submission of failure to mitigate damages.

Committee Comment (1991 Revision)

This instruction is used only in an F.E.L.A. case wherein the employee was fatally injured. The reference to present value is used in F.E.L.A. cases in compliance with *St. Louis Southwestern Ry. Co. v. Dickerson*, 470 U.S. 409, 105 S.Ct. 1347, 84 L.Ed.2d 303 (1985). *Dickerson* clearly requires inclusion of the sentence relating to present value if requested. It is not clear under *Dickerson* whether it is error to omit the present value sentence if inclusion is not requested.

The submission of comparative fault in an F.E.L.A. case differs from the method in Chapter 37.00 for use in cases based on Missouri law. F.E.L.A. cases are governed by federal law. Under 45 U.S.C.A. § 53, the *jury* diminishes damages in proportion to the employee's negligence. Under Chapter 37.00, the jury determines *total damages* and plaintiff's percentage of fault but the *judge* makes the actual computation diminishing total damages to the amount recoverable by plaintiff.

Library References:

C.J.S. Employers' Liability for Injuries to Employees § 341, 343.
West's Key No. Digests, Employers' Liability ⊗261, 262.

8.02 [1996 Revision] Damages—F.E.L.A.—Injury to Employee

If you find in favor of plaintiff, then you must award plaintiff such sum as you believe will fairly and justly compensate plaintiff for any damages you believe plaintiff sustained [and is reasonably certain to sustain in the future][1] as a result of the occurrence[2] mentioned in the evidence. Any award of future pecuniary damages must be included at present value. [Any award you make is not subject to income tax.][3] [If you find that plaintiff failed to mitigate damages as submitted in Instruction Number _____, in determining plaintiff's total damages you must not include those damages which would not have occurred without such failure.][4] [If you find plaintiff contributorily negligent as submitted in Instruction Number _____, then your award must be determined by diminishing plaintiff's total damages in proportion to the amount of negligence attributable to plaintiff.][5]

Notes on Use (1996 Revision)

1. This bracketed phrase may be added if supported by the evidence.

2. When the term "occurrence" must be modified, substitute some descriptive term which specifically describes the compensable event or conduct. For example, if the plaintiff claims that he was injured in a fall which occurred at work but the defendant claims that the injury did not result from the fall but rather resulted from a non-compensable automobile accident, the instruction may be modified to read "as a result of the fall on (the date of the compensable event)."

3. If requested, this bracketed sentence must be given. See: *Norfolk & Western Ry. Co. v. Liepelt*, 444 U.S. 490, 100 S.Ct. 755, 62 L.Ed.2d 689 (1980).

4. If failure to mitigate damages is submitted, the damages instruction must be modified by adding this bracketed sentence. See MAI 32.07(A) for the appropriate method of submission of failure to mitigate damages in an F.E.L.A. case. *Kauzlarich v. Atchison, Topeka, and Santa Fe Ry. Co.*, 910 S.W.2d 254 (Mo.banc 1995).

5. If contributory negligence is submitted, the damages instruction must be modified by adding this bracketed sentence. See MAI 32.07(B) for the appropriate contributory negligence instruction in an F.E.L.A. case.

Committee Comment (1996 Revision)

The reference to present value is used in F.E.L.A. cases in compliance with *St. Louis Southwestern Ry. Co. v. Dickerson*, 470 U.S. 409, 105 S.Ct. 1347, 84 L.Ed.2d 303 (1985). *Dickerson* clearly requires inclusion of the sentence relating to present value if requested. It is not clear under *Dickerson* whether it is error to omit the present value sentence if inclusion is not requested.

The submission of comparative fault in an F.E.L.A. case differs from the method in Chapter 37.00 for use in cases based on Missouri law. F.E.L.A. cases are governed by federal law. Under 45 U.S.C. § 53, the *jury* diminishes damages in proportion to the employee's negligence. Under Chapter 37.00, the jury determines *total damages* and plaintiff's percentage of fault but the *judge* makes the actual computation diminishing total damages to the amount recoverable by plaintiff.

This instruction is used only in F.E.L.A. cases where the employee sustained injury. Other than the references to taxation, present value, and mitigation of damages, it is essentially the same as MAI 4.01 with the exception that the word "direct" is deleted from the fifth line of MAI 4.01. This is required in an F.E.L.A. case so that the instruction complies with the substantive law set forth in *Wilmoth v. Chicago, Rock Island & P.R. Co.*, 486 S.W.2d 631 (Mo.1972); *Crane v. Cedar Rapids & Iowa City Ry. Co.*, 395 U.S. 164, 89 S.Ct. 1706, 23 L.Ed.2d 176 (1969); and *Rogers v. Missouri Pac. R. Co.*, 352 U.S. 500, 77 S.Ct. 443, 1 L.Ed.2d 493 (1957).

Library References:

C.J.S. Employers' Liability for Injuries to Employees § 341, 343.
West's Key No. Digests, Employers' Liability ⚭261, 262.

Notes of Decisions

---

1.   Multiple events

Where there is a dispute in the evidence as to which of more than one event caused plaintiff's injury, MAI 8.02 should be modified to confine the jury's consideration of damages to the event asserted by the plaintiff as the basis for the defendant's liability. Furthermore, Notes on Use require the specification of the date of the incident for which the railroad is responsible in all cases where more than one event is claimed to be the cause of the claimant's injury. Dickerson v. St. Louis Southwestern Ry. Co., 674 S.W.2d 165[6–7] (Mo.App.1984), reversed on other grounds 470 U.S. 409, 105 S.Ct. 1347, 84 L.Ed.2d 303 (1985).

Trial court was not required to modify MAI 8.02, even though there was some evidence at trial that the claimant had sustained multiple injuries prior to the date of the accident. Bair v. St. Louis–San Francisco Ry. Co., 647 S.W.2d 507, 510 (Mo. banc 1983).

2.   Present value

Either plaintiff or defendant in FELA case may offer present value evidence, but regardless of whether such evidence is offered, subject is open to jury instruction if requested and to jury argument; absent contrary indication, Supreme Court could assume that each juror complied with instruction and determined present value of future wage loss when returning general verdict in FELA suit. Anglim v. Missouri Pacific Railroad Co., 832 S.W.2d 298 (Mo.1992).

3. Comparative fault

In a case arising under FELA, where comparative fault was in issue, MAI 8.02 was applicable and was therefore required to be given. Gilliam v. Chicago & North Western Transp. Co., 859 S.W.2d 155 (Mo.App.1993).

4. Constitutionality

Railroad waived appellate review of claim that manner in which trial court instructed jury to diminish total damages by comparative fault in FELA case pursuant to MAI 8.02 violated Missouri constitution's due process, equal protection, and supremacy clauses; railroad did not cite to provisions of Missouri constitution that were allegedly violated and did not argue how those provisions were violated, but limited argument portion of brief to discussion of alleged violation of federal law and federal constitution. Giddens v. Kansas City Southern Railway Company, 29 S.W.3d 813 (Mo.banc 2000).

Railroad failed to preserve for appellate review its claim that federal due process clause was violated without means of determining whether jury correctly diminished employee's total damages by amount of his negligence, pursuant to MAI 8.02, where same argument was not made to trial court below in FELA proceeding. Giddens v. Kansas City Southern Railway Company, 29 S.W.3d 813 (Mo.banc 2000).

9.00

DAMAGES—EMINENT DOMAIN

Analysis of Instructions

Westlaw Electronic Research

See Westlaw Electronic Research Guide preceding the Table of Instructions.

Library References:

C.J.S. Eminent Domain § 311.
West's Key No. Digests, Eminent Domain ⚖222(5).

9.01 [1965 New] Damages—Eminent Domain—All Property Taken

You must award defendant such sum as you believe [was] [1] is the fair market value [2] of defendant's property [immediately before the taking (*insert date of appropriation*)].[1]

Notes on Use (1981 Revision)

1. The bracketed terms shall be used where the appropriation takes place before trial. Where the appropriation does not take place until after trial, as in some condemnations by cities, the bracketed words should be omitted.

2. The phrase "fair market value" must be defined. See definition in MAI 16.02.

This instruction shall be used where defendant's total property is taken so there is no issue of damages or special benefits to his remaining property.

Committee Comment (1965 New)

See *Union Electric Co. v. Stahlschmidt,* 365 S.W.2d 493 (Mo.1963) and Rule 86.06.

Library References:

C.J.S. Eminent Domain § 311.
West's Key No. Digests, Eminent Domain ⚷222(5).

9.02 [1965 New] Damages—Eminent Domain—Part of Property Taken

You must award defendant such sum as you believe is [was] [1] the difference between the fair market value [2] of defendant's whole property immediately before the taking [on (*insert date of appropriation*)] [1] and the value of defendant's remaining property immediately after such taking, which difference in value is the direct result of the taking and of the uses which plaintiff has the right to make of the property taken.

Notes on Use (1981 Revision)

1. The bracketed terms shall be used where the appropriation takes place before trial. Where the appropriation does not take place until after the trial, as in some condemnations by cities, the bracketed words should be omitted.

2. The phrase "fair market value" must be defined. See definition in MAI 16.02.

See MAI 34.03 for withdrawal of general benefits.

Where the condemning authority offers evidence that the property owner sustained no damage from the taking, MAI 31.05 must also be given.

Committee Comment (1983 Revision)

This instruction shall be used where only part of defendant's property is taken. It authorizes damages for the value of the property condemned and the resulting damage to the remaining property. This instruction is appropriate whether or not special benefits to defendant's remaining property are in issue.

Library References:

C.J.S. Eminent Domain § 311.
West's Key No. Digests, Eminent Domain ⊶222(5).

Notes of Decisions

Anticipated damage 6
Capitalization method 4
Conversing damages 5
Inverse condemnation 8
Modification 1
Multiple verdicts 7
Permanent nuisance 3

Special benefits 2
Valuation 9

---

1. Modification

Modification of MAI 9.02 by changing the words "taking" to read "after the line was laid" (as in Instruction No. 2, Illustration 35.10) is for defendant's benefit, not plaintiff's, and plaintiff is not prejudiced by failure to modify. Southwestern Bell Tel. Co. v. Roussin, 534 S.W.2d 273[10] (Mo.App. 1976).

Where there was no open market for condemned school property MAI 9.02 was properly modified by deleting the words "fair market." Reorganized School District v. Missouri Pac. R.R. Co., 503 S.W.2d 153[1–2] (Mo.App.1973).

Condemnation by constitutional charter cities is subject to rules of civil procedure, and the use of MAI 9.02 is mandatory. Bueche v. Kansas City, 492 S.W.2d 835[4–7] (Mo. banc 1973).

MAI 9.02 is mandatory in case where plaintiff condemns easement across defendant's land, and may not be modified by changing "*property* taken" to "*rights* taken." State ex rel. Kansas City Power & Light Co. v. Campbell, 433 S.W.2d 606[1] (Mo.App. 1968).

2. Special benefits

Permissible but not mandatory. Where condemnee objected to court's erroneous admission of evidence of general benefits, condemnee did not waive the error by failing to offer a withdrawal instruction. State ex rel. State Hwy. Comm. v. Johnson, 544 S.W.2d 276[2] (Mo.App.1976).

Instruction on presumption of special benefits properly refused where court gave MAI 9.02 which allows the question to be considered only by argument, as indicated in Committee's Comment. Kansas City v. Cone, 433 S.W.2d 88[5–7] (Mo.App.1968).

3. Permanent nuisance

In action for permanent nuisance the correct damages instruction is MAI 9.02, not MAI 4.02. Scantlin v. City of Pevely, 741 S.W.2d 48[7] (Mo.App.1987).

MAI 4.01 is proper for damages for temporary nuisance and MAI 9.02 is proper for damages for permanent nuisance. Spain v. City of Cape Girardeau, 484 S.W.2d 498[5] (Mo.App.1972).

In suit to recover damages for permanent nuisance the correct measure of damages is based on before-and-after values and is improperly submitted by MAI 4.01. Bower v. Hog Builders, Inc., 461 S.W.2d 784[5] (Mo. 1970).

In permanent nuisance case, sole damage issue was diminution of value, as in condemnation cases; MAI 9.02 was proper and MAI 4.01 improper. Stewart v. Marshfield, 431 S.W.2d 819[1, 2] (Mo.App.1968).

4. Capitalization method

MAI 9.02 and its fair market value definition (MAI 16.02) are not designed for cases in which valuation is based on capitalization method. State ex rel. Missouri Highway and Transportation Comm. v. McDonald's Corp., 896 S.W.2d 652 (Mo.App.1995).

Where there was no open market for condemned school property MAI 9.02 was properly modified by deleting the words "fair market." Reorganized School District v. Missouri Pac. R.R. Co., 503 S.W.2d 153[1–2] (Mo.App.1973).

Where there was no evidence of reasonable market value of cemetery, court erred in giving MAI 9.02 and 15.01 [Now 16.02], and should have submitted a not-in-MAI damage instruction drafted on the capitalization method. State ex rel. State Hwy. Commission v. Mount Moriah Cemetery Ass'n, 434 S.W.2d 470[2] (Mo.1968).

5. Conversing damages

In condemnation suit where there was no evidence of special benefits, some damage is presumed, and it was error to give plaintiff's MAI 33.03(3) conversing damages since that converse is designed to converse the damage element of a plaintiff's verdict director in a suit for damages, not the plaintiff's measure of damage instruction which cannot be conversed. City of Gladstone v. Hamilton, 463 S.W.2d 622 (Mo.App.1971).

6. Anticipated damage

MAI 4.01, instructing jury to award such sum as it believes will fairly and justly compensate plaintiff for damages which plaintiff sustained and is reasonably certain to sustain in future as direct result of occurrence, rather than MAI 9.02, addressing eminent domain damages for taking of part of property, is appropriate when damage goes beyond mere property loss. Shady Valley Park & Pool, Inc. v. Fred Weber, Inc., 913 S.W.2d 28 (Mo.App.1995).

In condemnation case court properly refused to withdraw evidence of construction damage which could have been anticipated at time of taking. Northeast Missouri Elec. Power Co-op v. Cary, 485 S.W.2d 862[4] (Mo.App.1972).

7. Multiple verdicts

Where two condemnation exceptions were consolidated for trial and separate verdicts were required, it was not error to give two separate MAI 9.02 damage instructions each referring to a separate tract. M & A Electric Power Co-op. v. True, 480 S.W.2d 310[10, 12] (Mo.App.1972).

8. Inverse condemnation

Owners sued utility for actual and punitive damages for unlawful entry onto their land, and utility counterclaimed for condemnation. Owners submitted MAI 9.02 for actual and MAI 10.01 for punitive damages, but erroneously offered no instruction on the basic, essential element of trespass. Keeven v. St. Charles County Utilities Co., Inc., 542 S.W.2d 349[1] (Mo.App.1976).

9. Valuation

Trial court properly gave MAI instructions 16.02 and 9.02 on market value in eminent domain proceeding and properly refused landowner's proffered instruction that jurors were to assume that the condemnor would make the fullest use of its right-of-way and use it in a manner as injurious to landowner's remaining rights as would be permitted. City of Kansas City v. Habelitz, 857 S.W.2d 299 (Mo.App.1993).

Damages in a condemnation case are temporally restricted in that they are to be determined with reference to the time of taking or appropriation rather than with reference to the time of trial or to the time of construction. State of Missouri, ex. rel. Missouri Highway and Transp. Com'n v. McNary et al., 664 S.W.2d 589, 592–3 (Mo.App. 1984).

10.00

DAMAGES—EXEMPLARY

Analysis of Instructions

Westlaw Electronic Research

See Westlaw Electronic Research Guide preceding the Table of Instructions.

Library References:

C.J.S. Damages § 188.
West's Key No. Digests, Damages ⊗215.

117

10.01 [1990 Revision] Damages—Exemplary—Outrageous Conduct—Intentional Torts

If you find the issues in favor of plaintiff, and if you believe the conduct of defendant as submitted in Instruction Number _____ (*here insert number of plaintiff's verdict directing instruction*) was outrageous because of defendant's evil motive or reckless indifference to the rights of others, then in addition to any damages to which you find plaintiff entitled under Instruction Number _____ (*here insert number of plaintiff's damages instruction*), you may award plaintiff an additional amount as punitive damages in such sum as you believe will serve to punish defendant and to deter defendant and others from like conduct.

Notes on Use (1998 Revision)

Rule 71.06 provides in part:

"When exemplary or punitive damages are allowed by the jury, the amount thereof shall be separately stated in the verdict."

Where the claim for actual damages is submitted on negligence as opposed to an intentional tort, MAI 10.01 is not applicable; use MAI 10.02 or MAI 10.07, whichever is appropriate. *Sharp v. Robberson*, 495 S.W.2d 394 (Mo. banc 1973). Where the claim for actual damages is submitted on strict liability as opposed to intentional tort or negligence, use MAI 10.04 or MAI 10.05, whichever is appropriate. *Racer v. Utterman*, 629 S.W.2d 387 (Mo.App.1981). Where the claim for actual damages is submitted on negligence and strict liability, use MAI 10.06.

Under *Menaugh v. Resler Optometry, Inc.*, 799 S.W.2d 71 (Mo. banc 1990), the defendant is entitled to a converse of a punitive damage instruction. See MAI 33.16.

The "clear and convincing" standard of proof for punitive damages adopted by *Rodriguez v. Suzuki Motor Corporation*, 936 S.W.2d 104 (Mo. banc 1996), has been incorporated into the burden of proof instruction, MAI 3.01.

Committee Comment (1996 Revision)

In *Burnett v. Griffith*, 769 S.W.2d 780 (Mo. banc 1989); the Missouri Supreme Court adopted this instruction for the submission of punitive damages in intentional tort cases and held that the definition of "legal malice" in MAI 16.01 should no longer be used.

See MAI 4.15 and 4.16 for submission of punitive damages in libel and slander cases.

See Illustration 35.19 for an example of a submission of punitive damages in a bifurcated trial pursuant to R.S.Mo. § 510.263.

Library References:

C.J.S. Damages § 188.
West's Key No. Digests, Damages ☞215.

Notes of Decisions

---

1. In general

Counsel's attempt at questioning prospective jurors, in bifurcated trial, regarding their willingness to award punitive damage, by reading language from MAI 10.01, then asking venire whether they would be able to follow the law as instructed by the trial court, was proper; counsel was not attempting to declare what the law would be but, rather, whether venire would follow an instruction on punitive damages if given by the court. Ashcroft v. TAD Resources Intern., 972 S.W.2d 502 (Mo.App.1998).

Pattern jury instruction on punitive damages did not violate due process clause; instruction gave jury sufficient guidance in determining imposition and amount of damages, punitive damage submissions did not require clear and convincing evidence, and instruction required jury to reasonably relate award to degree and character of wrongdoing. Moore v. Missouri–Nebraska Exp., Inc., 892 S.W.2d 696 (Mo.App. W.D.,1994).

MAI 10.01 does not overrule cases which have held that punitive damages require wilful, wanton or malicious culpable mental state; rather, word "outrageous" in instruction focuses on matter of moral culpability so that jury will not impose punitive sanction on defendant for mere commission of intentional tort. Ryburn v. General Heating & Cooling, Co., 887 S.W.2d 604 (Mo.App.1994).

Instruction offered by doctor regarding punitive damages, in false imprisonment suit by doctor against hospital and security guards, was not erroneous where instruction was patterned after model jury instructions and only variation was substitution of "a defendant" or "any defendant" in place of "defendant" because suit involved multiple defendants. Desai v. SSM Health Care, 865 S.W.2d 833 (Mo.App.1993).

MAI 10.01 does not improperly lack limits on the amount of a punitive damage award, and it does not fail to require a relationship between actual damages sustained and the amount of punitive damages award; even though a jury has great discretion in fixing the amount of punitive damages, the review by the trial or appellate courts provides a reasonable constraint on the amount of the punitive damage award. Carpenter v. Chrysler Corporation, 853 S.W.2d 346 (Mo. App.1993).

In an intentional tort action, punitive damages may be awarded if defendant's conduct is shown to be outrageous because of defendant's evil motive or reckless indifference to the rights of others. Northland Ins. Co. v. Chet's Tow Service, Inc., 804 S.W.2d 54 (Mo.App.1991).

MAI 10.01 [1978 Revision] does not clearly articulate the circumstances justifying punitive damages in a case of intentional tort, and hereafter should not be used. Burnett v. Griffith, 769 S.W.2d 780, 789 (Mo. banc 1989).

Punitive damages award was not appropriate in false arrest case absent any evidence in record that defendant's conduct was outrageous or indication that it had an evil motive or displayed reckless indifference to the rights of others. Signorino v. National Super Markets, 782 S.W.2d 100 (Mo.App. 1989).

Where evidence for both of plaintiff's tortious interference claims concerned defendant franchisers' course of conduct relating to operation of franchise and effect of their activities on plaintiff's interest, separate instructions on punitive damages were not required. Honigmann v. Hunter Group, Inc., 733 S.W.2d 799[22] (Mo.App.1987).

Error to submit only *one* punitive damage instruction covering *two* verdict directors. Breece v. Jett, 556 S.W.2d 696[13] (Mo.App. 1977).

Error to give both MAI 4.01 for actual damages arising from negligence and MAI 10.01 for punitive damages arising from wilfulness since the theories of recovery are incompatible. Ervin v. Coleman, 454 S.W.2d 289[9–10] (Mo.App.1970).

2. Actual damages

Although ordinary negligence is inconsistent with "willful, wanton or malicious" conduct (MAI 10.01) it is not inconsistent with "complete indifference to or conscious disregard for the safety of others" (MAI 10.02). Hence, plaintiff may submit both actual damages, by MAI 4.01, and punitive damages, by MAI 10.02, but not by MAI 10.01. Sharp v. Robberson, 495 S.W.2d 394[3] (Mo. banc 1973).

To entitle plaintiff to punitive damages under MAI 10.01 there must be evidence of actual damages. Ervin v. Coleman, 454 S.W.2d 289[9–10] (Mo.App.1970).

3. Pleading

Pleading warranted submission of punitive damages although not in precise words of MAI 10.01. Bower v. Hog Builders, Inc., 461 S.W.2d 784[6] (Mo.1970).

4. Evidentiary support

Doctor was entitled to punitive damages instruction, in false imprisonment suit against hospital and security guards, where doctor testified that one guard called doctor a derogatory name and that guards pushed doctor's head against trunk of car, and guards detained doctor because he accused one guard of assault, not because guards believed doctor had trespassed. Desai v. SSM Health Care, 865 S.W.2d 833 (Mo.App.1993).

Evidence that automobile manufacturer, which sold damaged car as new, had offered to replace it was admissible to mitigate punitive damages sought by buyers; buyers would also be allowed to present evidence regarding timing and prompting of offer, with ultimate weight given to fact that replacement offer was made being determined by jury. Maugh v. Chrysler Corp., 818 S.W.2d 658 (Mo.App.1991).

In false imprisonment claim, evidence was sufficient to support that the conduct of defendant was prompted by ill will, spite, or grudge. Wilton v. Cates, 774 S.W.2d 570, 572 (Mo.App.1989).

In fraud case evidence warranted instruction on exemplary damages. Throckmorton v. M.F.A. Central Co-op., 462 S.W.2d 138[2] (Mo.App.1970).

5. Trespass

Defendant's conduct following its initial trespass of inadvertently digging trench across plaintiff's property, in allowing trench to remain open for several days with sink water present therein while parties negotiated over purchase of easement, was not sufficiently "outrageous" and did not manifest the "reckless indifference" required for award of punitive damages. White v. James, 848 S.W.2d 577 (Mo.App.1993).

Evidence that landlord's agents told tenant that they could do anything they wanted to when tenant complained about agents' intrusions upon leased agricultural property was sufficient to show that landlord had evil motive or was recklessly indifferent to tenant's rights, as required to support submission of punitive damages issue to jury in action based on alleged trespass. Davis v. Jefferson Sav. & Loan Ass'n, 820 S.W.2d 549 (Mo.App.1991).

Approved punitive damage instruction in trespass case. Hawkins v. Burlington Northern, Inc., 514 S.W.2d 593[12–14] (Mo. banc 1974).

6. Modification

Modifying MAI 10.01 by substituting "defendants" for "defendant" is not a proper instruction for submission of punitive damages against multiple defendants since it does not include provisions of MAI 10.03, the appropriate punitive damage charge for multiple defendants, whereby defendants are accorded their right to have their conduct considered separately and that the amounts assessed as punitive damages, if any, may be different or the same. Saunders v. Flippo, 639 S.W.2d 411[1, 2] (Mo.App.1982).

7. Malice

To recover punitive damages in a case of false arrest, plaintiff must prove malice; that proof must entail showing of ill will, spite, or grudge, either toward injured person or toward all persons in the group of which injured person is a member. Hollingsworth v. Quick, 770 S.W.2d 291, 296 (Mo.App.1989).

In case of false arrest, court improperly instructed jury on legal definition of malice, MAI 16.01, because a definition of actual malice is required. Stewart v. K–Mart Corp., 747 S.W.2d 205[5, 6] (Mo.App.1988).

Where defendant's instruction defining legal but not actual malice was submitted to jury on issue of punitive damages for both assault and malicious prosecution claims, it was error because proper standard for awarding punitive damages in a malicious prosecution case arising out of a criminal proceeding is actual malice. Schoor v. Wilson, 731 S.W.2d 308[9] (Mo.App.1987).

MAI 16.01, a definition of malice in law, does not adequately express degree of culpability required for an award of punitive damages in a malicious prosecution case arising from a civil proceeding. Instead, the jury must be instructed that in order to award punitive damages, "the proceedings must have been initiated or continued primarily for a purpose other than that of securing the proper adjudication of the claim on which they are based." Proctor v. Stevens Employment Services, Inc., 712 S.W.2d 684[6, 7] (Mo. banc 1986).

MAI 16.01 does not adequately express the degree of culpability required for punitive damages in malicious prosecution cases. Sanders v. Daniel Intern. Corp., 682 S.W.2d 803[6–11] (Mo. banc 1984).

8. Slander

MAI 10.01 is not the instruction to be given to the jury in an action brought for slander. Joseph v. Elam, 709 S.W.2d 517, 525 (Mo. App.1986).

9. Conversion

Purported prospective buyers of automobile failed to present evidence sufficient to support submission of punitive damages to jury on conversion claim against credit corporation which took possession of automobile; although corporation's order of delivery was void because of absence of particular fact allegations in supporting affidavit, and while order was no defense to conversion claim, it tended to negate evil motive and reckless indifference on part of corporation. Ross v. Ford Motor Credit Co., 867 S.W.2d 546 (Mo.App.1993).

Evidence supported award of punitive damages in amount of $5,000 against towing company for conversion of trailer when it refused owner's cashier's check for more than amount owing for towing and storage, where towing company lied about its charges, changed amount due without valid explanation when owner sought to take possession of trailer, refused cashier's check because competitor had been sent to take delivery of the trailer, and attempted to double bill for towing service. Northland Ins. Co. v. Chet's Tow Service, Inc., 804 S.W.2d 54 (Mo.App.1991).

10. Due process

Award of punitive damages did not violate due process clause where trial court gave MAI 10.01; this instruction provides a sufficient standard to guide jurors in their determination of what conduct supports an award of punitive damages; the standards for imposition of punitive damages under MAI 10.01 are not unconstitutionally vague. Carpenter v. Chrysler Corporation, 853 S.W.2d 346 (Mo.App.1993).

10.02 [1983 Revision] Damages—Exemplary—Negligence Constituting Conscious Disregard for Others

If you find in favor of plaintiff under Instruction Number _____ (*here insert number of plaintiff's verdict directing instruction based on negligence*), and if you believe the conduct of defendant as submitted in Instruction Number _____ (*here insert number of plaintiff's verdict directing instruction based on negligence*) showed complete indifference to or conscious disregard for the safety of others, then in addition to any damages to which you may find plaintiff entitled under Instruction Number _____ (*here insert number of plaintiff's damage instruction*) you may award plaintiff an additional amount as punitive damages in such sum as you believe will serve to punish defendant and to deter defendant and others from like conduct.

Notes on Use (1998 Revision)

This is the appropriate instruction in a case where exemplary damages are submissible in connection with a claim for actual damages based on negligence as opposed to intentional tort or strict liability. *Sharp v. Robberson*, 495 S.W.2d 394 (Mo. banc 1973).

Caution: Under *Menaugh v. Resler Optometry, Inc.*, 799 S.W.2d 71 (Mo. banc 1990), MAI 10.02 will not be adequate to submit punitive damages under the following circumstances:

1. *Where the verdict directing instruction contains alternative submissions of negligence but fewer than all submissions will support a punitive damage instruction.* Under these circumstances, *Menaugh* suggests that the punitive damage instruction be limited to that portion of the verdict director that requires the jury to find the essential mental element. Id. at 74, 75.

2. *Where the verdict directing instruction contains a single submission of negligence but the evidence demonstrates alternate sets of facts, both of which support the submission, but only one of which will support punitive damages.* Under these circumstances, *Menaugh* suggests the addition of such additional facts to MAI 10.02 as are necessary to justify a punitive damage submission. Id. at 74, 75.

3. *Where the verdict directing instruction does not contain a submission on the issue of defendant's "knowledge".* Under these circumstances, *Menaugh* states that MAI 10.02 is inadequate

because it does not require the jury to find the essential mental element. Id. at 74. *Menaugh* recognizes that those verdict directing instructions such as the "premises liability" instruction in *Sharp* will be sufficient to submit the issue of defendant's "knowledge" and may then be followed by MAI 10.02 without modification. Id. at 74. For further discussion of the "knowledge" issue, see *Hoover's Dairy, Inc. v. Mid–America Dairymen,* 700 S.W.2d 426 (Mo. banc 1985).

The problems addressed in *Menaugh* should be resolved by utilization of MAI 10.07.

Such problems should not arise when using MAI 10.04 [Strict Liability—Either Product Defect or Failure to Warn Submitted] or MAI 10.05 [Strict Liability—Both Product Defect and Failure to Warn Submitted] but may arise when using MAI 10.06 [Both Negligence and Strict Liability Submitted] in the context of the negligence submission. If such a problem arises in using MAI 10.06, counsel should adapt that portion of MAI 10.06 relating to negligence with the method of submission demonstrated by MAI 10.07.

See MAI 10.01 for submission of punitive damages in connection with an intentional tort.

Under *Menaugh,* the defendant is entitled to a converse of a punitive damage instruction. See MAI 33.16.

Where punitive damages are submitted in a case involving only pecuniary harm, without bodily injury, this instruction may be modified by substituting the phrase "rights of others" for the phrase "safety of others". *Haynam v. Laclede Elec. Co-op., Inc.,* 889 S.W.2d 148 (Mo.App. 1994).

The "clear and convincing" standard of proof for punitive damages adopted by *Rodriguez v. Suzuki Motor Corporation,* 936 S.W.2d 104 (Mo. banc 1996), has been incorporated into the burden of proof instruction, MAI 3.01.

Committee Comment (1996 Revision)

Existing MAI 10.01 fits some cases but does not fit the drunken driver case.

In *Nichols v. Bresnahan,* 357 Mo. 1126, 212 S.W.2d 570, 573 (1948) the Court cited with approval Restatement of Torts, Sec. 500 (1935) as follows:

"The actor's conduct is in reckless disregard of the safety of another if he intentionally does an act or fails to do an act which it is his duty to the other to do, knowing or having reason to know of facts which would lead a reasonable man to realize that the actor's conduct not only creates an unreasonable risk of bodily harm to the other, but also involves a high degree of probability that substantial harm will result to him."

The Court approved an instruction requiring a finding that defendant's conduct exhibited "a conscious disregard or indifference to the ... consequences." *Id.*

In *Evans v. Illinois Central R. Co.,* 289 Mo. 493, 233 S.W. 397, 400 (banc 1921) the Court said:

"A wanton act is a wrongful act done on purpose, or in malicious disregard of the rights of others. Recklessness is an indifference to the rights of others and an indifference whether wrong or injury is done or not. As we understand the words 'conscious disregard of the life and bodily safety', they add nothing to the words 'willful, wanton and reckless', and are included within the meaning of those words. As applied to an act, they necessarily mean that such act was intentionally done without regard to the rights of others, and in full realization of the probable results thereof."

See also, *Stojkovic v. Weller,* 802 S.W.2d 152 (Mo. banc 1991) regarding the submissibility of punitive damages in a case involving an intoxicated driver.

See Illustration 35.19 for an example of a submission of punitive damages in a bifurcated trial pursuant to R.S.Mo. § 510.263.

Library References:

C.J.S. Damages § 188.
West's Key No. Digests, Damages ⟜215.

Notes of Decisions

1. Actual damages

Although ordinary negligence is inconsistent with "willful, wanton or malicious" conduct (MAI 10.01) it is not inconsistent with "complete indifference to or conscious disregard for the safety of others" (MAI 10.02). Hence, plaintiff may submit both actual damages, by MAI 4.01, and punitive damages, by MAI 10.02, but not by MAI 10.01. Sharp v. Robberson, 495 S.W.2d 394[3] (Mo. banc 1973).

2. Res ipsa loquitur

Error to submit instruction on punitive damages, where plaintiff's general negligence claim was based upon res ipsa loquitur, which did not require jury to find any specific negligent conduct. Johnson v. National Super Markets, Inc., 710 S.W.2d 455[2] (Mo.App.1986).

3. Burden of proof

Punitive damages issue submitted by MAI 3.01 conjointly with MAI 10.02 which requires only a simple belief by the jury that the defendant acted with complete indifference to or conscious disregard for the safety of the plaintiffs rather than requiring beyond a reasonable doubt was proper and did not deprive defendant of equal protection of the laws. Elam v. Alcolac, Inc., 765 S.W.2d 42, 219–20, 224–25 (Mo.App.1988).

4. Evidentiary support

Evidence of driver's intoxication, leaving scene of accident, and erratic driving would have supported submission of issue of punitive damages to jury in automobile accident case arising when driver's car collided with that of another motorist after running red light. Stojkovic v. Weller, 802 S.W.2d 152 (Mo.1991).

Evidence of prior similar occurrence two days before was insufficient to show that store owner knew, or had reason to know, that its conduct was substantially likely to cause physical harm, as required to support award of punitive damages to child injured when display furniture fell on him; furthermore, store owner had policy for addressing safety problems posed by display furniture, and it was clear that defendant attempted to follow that policy, performing periodic inspections, ordering displays be secured both as general rule and specifically in response to incidents. Litchfield By and Through Litchfield v. May Department Stores Co., 845 S.W.2d 596 (Mo.App.1992).

Evidence was insufficient to support punitive damages award against gas company which converted truck so that it could be operated on propane gas in negligence action arising out of explosion which occurred when hose connected to propane tank on truck became entangled in overhead brush inside car wash; reasonable juror could not properly find that conduct of company in failing to install solid steel plug in tank was outrageous and posed immediate threat to safety of others. May v. AOG Holding Corp., 810 S.W.2d 655 (Mo.App.1991).

5. Punitive damages

Punitive damage instruction submitted by plaintiff in negligence action was properly rejected, as it failed to include necessary element of defendant's knowledge. Alack v. Vic Tanny Intern. Of Missouri, Inc., 923 S.W.2d 330 (Mo.1996).

10.03 [1983 Revision] Damages—Exemplary—Multiple Defendants

When submitting against more than one defendant for punitive damages, use an appropriate instruction from Chapter 10 as a separate paragraph for each such defendant. Use the following sentence as the concluding paragraph of the punitive damage instruction:

If punitive damages are assessed against more than one defendant, the amounts assessed against such defendants may be the same or they may be different.

Library References:

C.J.S. Damages § 188.
West's Key No. Digests, Damages ⟞215.

Notes of Decisions

1. In general

Instruction offered by doctor regarding punitive damages, in false imprisonment suit by doctor against hospital and security guards, was not erroneous where instruction was patterned after model jury instructions and only variation was substitution of "a defendant" or "any defendant" in place of "defendant" because suit involved multiple defendants. Desai v. SSM Health Care, 865 S.W.2d 833 (Mo.App.1993).

Doctor was entitled to punitive damages instruction, in false imprisonment suit against hospital and security guards, where doctor testified that one guard called doctor a derogatory name and that guards pushed doctor's head against trunk of car, and guards detained doctor because he accused one guard of assault, not because guards believed doctor had trespassed. Desai v. SSM Health Care, 865 S.W.2d 833 (Mo.App.1993).

Modifying MAI 10.01 by substituting "defendants" for "defendant" is not proper instruction for submission of punitive damages against multiple defendants since it does not include provisions of MAI 10.03, the appropriate punitive damage charge for multiple defendants, whereby defendants are accorded their right to have their conduct considered separately and that the amounts assessed as punitive damages, if any, may be different or the same. Saunders v. Flippo, 639 S.W.2d 411[1, 2] (Mo.App.1982).

Damages for "outrageous conduct." Golston v. Lincoln Cemetery, 573 S.W.2d 700[2] (Mo.App.1978).

Error to substitute "conduct of the defendants" for "conduct of one or more of the defendants." Annbar Associates v. American Express Company, 565 S.W.2d 701[6] (Mo.App.1978).

10.04 [1983 New] Damages—Exemplary—Strict Liability—Either Product Defect or Failure to Warn Submitted

If you find in favor of plaintiff under Instruction Number _____ (*here insert number of plaintiff's strict liability verdict directing instruction*) and if you believe:

First, at the time defendant sold the (*describe product*), defendant knew of the [defective condition and danger][1] [danger][2] submitted in Instruction Number _____ (*here insert number of plaintiff's strict liability verdict directing instruction*), and

Second, defendant thereby showed complete indifference to or conscious disregard for the safety of others,

then in addition to any damages to which you may find plaintiff entitled under Instruction Number _____ (*here insert number of plaintiff's damage instruction*) you may award plaintiff an additional amount as punitive damages in such sum as you believe will serve to punish defendant and to deter defendant and others from like conduct.

Notes on Use (1998 Revision)

1. When plaintiff's only strict liability submission is based on MAI 25.04, use this bracketed phrase.

2. When plaintiff's only strict liability submission is MAI 25.05, use this bracketed term.

This is the appropriate instruction in a case where exemplary damages are submissible in connection with a claim for actual damages based on strict liability under either MAI 25.04 or MAI 25.05, as opposed to negligence or intentional tort. If plaintiff submits under both MAI 25.04 and MAI 25.05, use MAI 10.05. If plaintiff submits on both negligence and strict liability, use MAI 10.06.

Under *Menaugh v. Resler Optometry, Inc.,* 799 S.W.2d 71 (Mo. banc 1990), the defendant is entitled to a converse of a punitive damage instruction. See MAI 33.16.

The "clear and convincing" standard of proof for punitive damages adopted by *Rodriguez v. Suzuki Motor Corporation,* 936 S.W.2d 104 (Mo. banc 1996), has been incorporated into the burden of proof instruction, MAI 3.01.

Committee Comment (1996 Revision)

It was held in *Racer v. Utterman*, 629 S.W.2d 387 (Mo.App.1981), that MAI 10.02 is inappropriate for submission of punitive damages in a case wherein compensatory damages are awarded against a strict liability defendant but that:

> If plaintiff, in addition to proving the conduct necessary to support such a strict liability claim, can also establish a degree of fault in such conduct sufficient to justify punitive damages, those damages may also be recovered.

Id. at 396.

MAI 10.04 is drafted to submit the issue of punitive damages under the evidence detailed in the *Racer* opinion. If the substantive law and evidence support a submission on a theory other than actual knowledge of the product defect, then there should be an appropriate modification of paragraph First.

See Illustration 35.19 for an example of a submission of punitive damages in a bifurcated trial pursuant to R.S.Mo. § 510.263.

Library References:

C.J.S. Damages § 188.
West's Key No. Digests, Damages ⊙215.

Notes of Decisions

In general 1
Knowledge 2

_____

1. In general

Products liability plaintiff whose hand was severed by allegedly defective power miter saw was not entitled to award of punitive damages where there was no indication of complete indifference or conscious disregard for safety of others on part of saw's manufacturer. Bilderback v. Skil Corp., 856 S.W.2d 73 (Mo.App.1993).

The difference between MAI 10.02 and MAI 10.04 is the additional element of knowledge required in the latter. The reason for including knowledge directly in the punitive damage instruction for strict liability is that knowledge is not submitted as an element to establish liability. Hoover's Dairy, Inc. v. Mid–America Dairymen, Inc., et al., 700 S.W.2d 426, 436 (Mo. banc 1985).

2. Knowledge

Actual knowledge on part of manufacturer is required to submit punitive damages issue to jury in products liability action; punitive damages claim may not be submitted in products liability action on theory of constructive knowledge of product defect. Angotti v. Celotex Corp., 812 S.W.2d 742 (Mo. App.1991).

Punitive damages issue was not submissible to jury in products liability action brought against successor to manufacturer of asbestos products by retired insulator who was suffering from asbestosis where evidence merely showed that information regarding harmful effect of asbestos was still developing and did not show that manufacturer's finished products were actually known to present health hazard to insulators. Angotti v. Celotex Corp., 812 S.W.2d 742 (Mo.App. 1991).

10.05 [1983 New] Damages—Exemplary—Strict Liability—Both Product Defect and Failure to Warn Submitted

First, if you find in favor of plaintiff under Instruction Number _____ (*here insert number of plaintiff's verdict directing instruction MAI 25.04*) and if you believe that at the time defendant sold the (*describe product*) defendant knew of the defective condition and danger submitted in Instruction Number _____ (*here insert number of plaintiff's verdict directing instruction MAI 25.04*), or

if you find in favor of plaintiff under Instruction Number _____ (*here insert number of plaintiff's verdict directing instruction MAI 25.05*) and if you believe that at the time defendant sold the (*describe product*) defendant knew of the danger submitted in Instruction Number _____ (*here insert number of plaintiff's verdict directing instruction MAI 25.05*), and

Second, if you believe that defendant, in one or more of the respects submitted in paragraph First, thereby showed complete indifference to or conscious disregard for the safety of others,

then in addition to any damages to which you may find plaintiff entitled under Instruction Number _____ (*here insert number of plaintiff's damage instruction*) you may award plaintiff an additional amount as punitive damages in such sum as you believe will serve to punish defendant and to deter defendant and others from like conduct.

Notes on Use (1998 Revision)

This is the appropriate instruction where exemplary damages are submissible in connection with a claim for actual damages based on both MAI 25.04 and MAI 25.05 and the evidence would permit an award of punitive damages under either theory.

Under *Menaugh v. Resler Optometry, Inc.*, 799 S.W.2d 71 (Mo. banc 1990), the defendant is entitled to a converse of a punitive damage instruction. See MAI 33.16.

The "clear and convincing" standard of proof for punitive damages adopted by *Rodriguez v. Suzuki Motor Corporation*, 936 S.W.2d 104 (Mo.

banc 1996), has been incorporated into the burden of proof instruction, MAI 3.01.

Committee Comment (1996 New)

See Illustration 35.19 for an example of a submission of punitive damages in a bifurcated trial pursuant to R.S.Mo. § 510.263.

Library References:

C.J.S. Damages § 188.
West's Key No. Digests, Damages ⚖︎215.

10.06 [1983 New] Damages—Exemplary—Both Negligence and Strict Liability Submitted

If you find in favor of plaintiff under Instruction Number _____ (*here insert number of plaintiff's verdict directing instruction based on negligence*), and if you believe the conduct of defendant as submitted in Instruction Number _____ (*here insert number of plaintiff's verdict directing instruction based on negligence*) showed complete indifference to or conscious disregard for the safety of others, or

If you find in favor of plaintiff under Instruction Number _____ (*here insert number of plaintiff's strict liability verdict directing instruction*) and if you believe:

First, at the time defendant sold the (*describe product*), defendant knew of the [defective condition and danger][1] [danger][2] submitted in Instruction Number _____ (*here insert number of plaintiff's strict liability verdict directing instruction*), and

Second, defendant thereby showed complete indifference to or conscious disregard for the safety of others,

then in addition to any damages to which you may find plaintiff entitled under Instruction Number _____ (*here insert number of plaintiff's damage instruction*) you may award plaintiff an additional amount as punitive damages in such sum as you believe will serve to punish defendant and to deter defendant and others from like conduct.

Notes on Use (1998 Revision)

1. When plaintiff's only strict liability submission is MAI 25.04, use this bracketed phrase.

2. When plaintiff's only strict liability submission is MAI 25.05, use this bracketed term.

This is the appropriate instruction in a case where exemplary damages are submissible in connection with a claim for actual damages based on both negligence and strict liability under either MAI 25.04 or MAI 25.05 and the evidence would permit an award of punitive damages under either theory. If plaintiff submits a claim for actual damages based on some other combination of theories that supports the submission of punitive damages, this instruction should be modified to combine the appropriate instructions for Chapter 10 in the manner of MAI 10.06.

Under *Menaugh v. Resler Optometry, Inc.,* 799 S.W.2d 71 (Mo. banc 1990), the defendant is entitled to a converse of a punitive damage instruction. See MAI 33.16.

The "clear and convincing" standard of proof for punitive damages adopted by *Rodriguez v. Suzuki Motor Corporation,* 936 S.W.2d 104 (Mo. banc 1996), has been incorporated into the burden of proof instruction, MAI 3.01.

See the **Caution** in the Notes on Use to MAI 10.02 for further discussion of potential problems in the submission of punitive damages based on negligence addressed in *Menaugh.* See also MAI 10.07.

Committee Comment (1996 New)

See Illustration 35.19 for an example of a submission of punitive damages in a bifurcated trial pursuant to R.S.Mo. § 510.263.

Library References:

C.J.S. Damages § 188.
West's Key No. Digests, Damages ☞215.

10.07 [1991 New] Damages—Exemplary—Modification of MAI 10.02—Submission of Specific Acts and Knowledge

If you find in favor of plaintiff under Instruction Number _____ (*here insert number of plaintiff's verdict directing instruction based on negligence*), and if you believe that:

First, (*here describe the act or omission which justifies the submission of punitive damages*), and

Second, defendant knew or had information from which defendant, in the exercise of ordinary care,[1] should have known that such conduct created a high degree of probability of injury, and

Third, defendant thereby showed complete indifference to or conscious disregard for the safety of others,

then in addition to any damages to which you find plaintiff entitled under Instruction Number _____ (*here insert number of plaintiff's damage instruction*) you may award plaintiff an additional amount as punitive damages in such sum as you believe will serve to punish defendant and to deter defendant and others from like conduct.

Notes on Use (1998 Revision)

1. The phrase "ordinary care" must be defined. See Chapter 11.

This instruction is MAI 10.02 modified to resolve the problems addressed in *Menaugh v. Resler Optometry, Inc.*, 799 S.W.2d 71 (Mo. banc 1990). See the **Caution** in the Notes on Use to MAI 10.02 for further discussion.

The use of the phrase "had information from which defendant, in the exercise of ordinary care, should have known" is the equivalent of the phrase "had reason to know" as defined in Restatement (First) and (Second) of Torts, § 12, and as used in *Stojkovic v. Weller*, 802 S.W.2d 152 (Mo. banc 1991), and *Hoover's Dairy, Inc. v. Mid–America Dairymen*, 700 S.W.2d 426 (Mo. banc 1985). The Committee has opted to use this equivalent phrase rather than "had reason to know" because it is thought that the phrase "had reason to know" may be confusing or misleading to the jury.

Under *Menaugh,* the defendant is entitled to a converse of a punitive damage instruction. See MAI 33.16.

Where punitive damages are submitted in a case involving only pecuniary harm, without bodily injury, this instruction may be modified by substituting the phrase "rights of others" for the phrase "safety of others". *Haynam v. Laclede Elec. Co-op., Inc.*, 889 S.W.2d 148 (Mo.App. 1994).

The "clear and convincing" standard of proof for punitive damages adopted by *Rodriguez v. Suzuki Motor Corporation*, 936 S.W.2d 104 (Mo. banc 1996), has been incorporated into the burden of proof instruction, MAI 3.01.

Committee Comment (1996 New)

See Illustration 35.19 for an example of a submission of punitive damages in a bifurcated trial pursuant to R.S.Mo. § 510.263.

Library References:

C.J.S. Damages § 188.
West's Key No. Digests, Damages ⊂⇒215.

Notes of Decisions

1. In general

Survivors of individuals killed in helicopter crash that followed collision with unmarked power line did not show knowing violation of duty or conscious disregard of safety by electrical cooperative and, thus, did not support submission of aggravating circumstances instruction; cooperative obtained advice of counsel that no regulation or statute required any markings, cooperative had knowledge of only one accident and one near accident over 20 years prior, prior accident involved negligence by pilot, which had been complete defense at time, there was no evidence that either accident or prior accident involved violation of statute or regulation designed to prevent injury that occurred, and questionaire aimed at establishing violation of industry standard was neither clear nor specific enough to support claim for punitive damages. Lopez v. Three Rivers Elec. Co-op., Inc., 26 S.W.3d 151 (Mo.2000).

There must be clear and convincing evidence in support of claim for damages for aggravating circumstances in negligence case. Lopez v. Three Rivers Elec. Co-op., Inc., 26 S.W.3d 151 (Mo.2000).

For negligence plaintiff to recover aggravating circumstances damages, evidence must show that defendant either knew or had reason to know that there was high degree of probability that defendant's conduct would result in injury. Lopez v. Three Rivers Elec. Co-op., Inc., 26 S.W.3d 151 (Mo.2000).

Defendant's conduct must be tantamount to intentional wrongdoing, where natural and probable consequence of conduct is injury, in order for negligence plaintiff to recover for aggravating circumstances based upon defendant's complete indifference to or conscious disregard for safety of others. Lopez v. Three Rivers Elec. Co-op., Inc., 26 S.W.3d 151 (Mo.2000).

Weighing against submission of punitive or aggravating circumstances damages instruction in negligence cases are circumstances in which prior similar occurrences known to defendant have been infrequent, injurious event was unlikely to have occurred absent negligence on part of someone other than defendant, and defendant did not knowingly violate statute, regulation, or clear industry standard designed to prevent type of injury that occurred. Lopez v. Three Rivers Elec. Co-op., Inc., 26 S.W.3d 151 (Mo.2000).

10.08 [1992 New] Damages—Penalty and Attorney's Fees—Vexatious Refusal to Pay by Insurance Company

If you find in favor of plaintiff on the claim on the insurance policy, and if you believe that defendant insurance company [refused to pay] [1] [failed or refused to pay for a period of thirty days after demand] [2] without reasonable cause or excuse, then, in addition to any amount you may award on the insurance policy under Instruction No. _____, you may award plaintiff an additional amount as a penalty not to exceed [twenty percent of the first $1,500.00 of the award on the policy not including interest and ten percent of the remainder of such award] [3] and you may award plaintiff a reasonable sum for attorney's fees.

Notes on Use (1992 New)

1. This bracketed phrase applies to actions under § 375.420 RSMo.

2. This bracketed phrase applies to actions under § 375.296, RSMo.

1. and 2.   Select appropriate bracketed phrase.

3. This bracketed phrase applies to actions under § 375.296 and § 375.420, RSMo. If there is no dispute as to the amount due, if any, under the policy, a calculation may be made of the maximum amount of the penalty and inserted in lieu of the formula.

Committee Comment (1992 New)

See the verdict form at MAI 36.10.

Library References:

C.J.S. Insurance § 1585.
West's Key No. Digests, Insurance ☞3376.

DEFINITIONS

11.00

DEFINITIONS—NEGLIGENCE

Analysis of Instructions

Westlaw Electronic Research

See Westlaw Electronic Research Guide preceding the Table of Instructions.

Library References:

C.J.S. Negligence § 871–878, 880–905.
West's Key No. Digests, Negligence ⚎1720–1747.

11.01 [1996 Revision] Definition—Highest Degree of Care

The phrase "highest degree of care" as used in this [these] instruction[s] means that degree of care that a very careful person would use under the same or similar circumstances.

Notes on Use (1978 Revision)

When the phrase "highest degree of care" is used, it must be defined.

Where the phrase is used in only one instruction, this definition may be added to the instruction using the phrase. If it is used in more than one instruction, the definition should be given as a separate instruction.

Library References:

C.J.S. Negligence § 871–878, 880–905.
West's Key No. Digests, Negligence ☞1720–1747.

Notes of Decisions

1. In general

Jury instruction term "highest degree of care" appropriately defined degree of care driver was mandated to exercise during operation of his motor vehicle. Hansen v. James, 847 S.W.2d 476 (Mo.App.1992).

Plaintiff could not be charged with a standard of "highest degree of care" in operation of a motor vehicle on a bridge which was under construction and not yet open to the public. McTeer v. Clarkson Construction Co., Inc., 807 S.W.2d 174 (Mo.App.1991).

Giving both MAI's 11.01 and 11.03 criticized as repetitive, but not prejudicial. Knowles v. Goswick, 476 S.W.2d 563[4] (Mo. 1972).

Where term "negligence" is used it must be defined; failure to do so creates a roving commission. Brewer v. Swift & Co., 451 S.W.2d 131[2] (Mo. banc 1970).

Where defendant's duty was to use ordinary care it was error for plaintiff to define highest degree of care. Schneider v. Bi-State Development Agency, 447 S.W.2d 788[1, 6–7] (Mo.App.1969). But see, Fowler v. Park Corp., 673 S.W.2d 749 (Mo. banc 1984).

Where a definable term is used in two or more instructions, the term may be defined in a separate definition instruction, as per Notes on Use. Epps v. Ragsdale, 429 S.W.2d 798[11] (Mo.App.1968).

11.02 [1996 Revision] Definition—Negligence of Adult

I

The term "negligent" or "negligence" as used in this [these] instruction[s] means the failure to use that degree of care that an ordinarily careful person would use under the same or similar circumstances.

II

The term "negligent" or "negligence" as used in this [these] instruction[s] means the failure to use that degree of care that a very careful person would use under the same or similar circumstances.

Notes on Use (1996 Revision)

Definition No. I is appropriate where only ordinary care is required. Definition No. II is appropriate where the law requires the highest degree of care.

When the term "negligent" or "negligence" is used, it must be defined.

Where either or both terms are used in only one instruction, this definition may be added to the instruction using the term. If they are used in more than one instruction, the definition should be given as a separate instruction.

Caution: The same definition may not properly apply to all the negligence submitted. For example if a driver is sued by a passenger and the driver asserts comparative negligence of the passenger, Definition No. I would apply to the passenger's negligence and Definition No. II would apply to the driver's negligence. See MAI 11.08 for one method of instructing on two standards of care in the same case.

Library References:

C.J.S. Negligence § 871–878, 880–905.
West's Key No. Digests, Negligence ⊶1720–1747.

Notes of Decisions

In general   1
Separating definition   2

1. In general

MAI 11.02, subd. II—defining negligence as failure to use "degree of care that a very careful person would use under the same or similar circumstances," but not including phrase "highest degree of care" set forth in MAI 11.03 that incorporates statutory duty of care for operation of motor vehicles—nevertheless properly conveyed requisite degree of care applicable to personal injury case involving automobiles; both instructions ultimately define requisite degree of care in terms of that exercised by very careful person under same or similar circumstances. Williams v. Jacobs, 972 S.W.2d 334 (Mo. App.1998).

Trial court's error in instructing the jury that negligence means care that a "very careful and prudent person" would use, instead of properly instructing jury that negligence is care that an "ordinary careful and prudent person" would use, had no substantial prejudicial effect on jury. Fowler v. Park Corp., 673 S.W.2d 749[10] (Mo. banc 1984).

The phrase "highest degree of care" need not and should not be defined twice, but the terms "negligence" and "highest degree of care" are not synonymous and must be separately defined. Kindle v. Keene, 676 S.W.2d 82[3] (Mo.App.1984).

Where plaintiff failed to define the term "negligently" used in his humanitarian verdict-director, and defendant did not request the definition, held not necessarily reversible error. Carter v. Consolidated Cabs, 490 S.W.2d 39[3] (Mo.1973).

Failure to define "ordinary care" used in contributory negligence instruction was not necessarily erroneous. Robinett v. Kansas City Power & Light Co., 484 S.W.2d 506[2, 3] (Mo.App.1972).

Defining the term "negligence" used in a res ipsa verdict director was mandatory. Cunningham v. Hayes, 463 S.W.2d 555[13–15] (Mo.App.1971).

Inclusion of additional words which do not alter the meaning of the definition of "negligence" held not prejudicial error. Newsom v. Crockett, 453 S.W.2d 674[2] (Mo.App. 1970).

Where term "negligence" is used it must be defined; failure to do so creates a roving commission. Brewer v. Swift & Co., 451 S.W.2d 131[2] (Mo. banc 1970).

Where verdict director hypothesizes "negligence" it is error to define "ordinary care." Zipp v. Gasen's Drug Stores, Inc., 449 S.W.2d 612[5] (Mo.1970).

Where defendant's duty was to use ordinary care it was error for plaintiff to define highest degree of care. Schneider v. Bi-State Development Agency, 447 S.W.2d 788[1, 6–7] (Mo.App.1969).

Driver's not-in-MAI submission of passenger's contributory negligence in failing to request driver to reduce speed properly defined passenger's negligence as failure to use ordinary care. Underwood v. Crosby, 447 S.W.2d 566[5] (Mo. banc 1969).

Adding an MAI 19.01 joint tortfeasor clause to an MAI 22.02–22.05 type verdict director without definition of negligence "would raise a serious question" since the former uses the word "negligence" and the latter is based on failure to use "ordinary care." Chambers v. Kansas City, 446 S.W.2d 833[5–7] (Mo.1969).

Where a verdict director uses the term "negligence" a definition of that term is mandatory. Helfrick v. Taylor, 440 S.W.2d 940[5] (Mo.1969).

Where verdict director submitted defendant's "negligence" it was error to give MAI 11.05 defining "ordinary care" instead of MAI 11.02(I) defining "negligence". Epps v. Ragsdale, 429 S.W.2d 798[6] (Mo.App. 1968).

2. Separating definition

Giving MAI 11.05 separately from verdict director was not error. Friend v. Gem International, Inc., 476 S.W.2d 134[18] (Mo.App. 1971).

Where a definable term is used in two or more instructions, the term may be defined in a separate definition instruction, as per Notes on Use. Epps v. Ragsdale, 429 S.W.2d 798[11] (Mo.App.1968).

11.03 [1996 Revision] Definitions—Negligence and Highest Degree of Care Combined

The term "negligent" or "negligence" as used in this [these] instruction[s] means the failure to use the highest degree of care. The phrase "highest degree of care" means that degree of care that a very careful person would use under the same or similar circumstances.

Notes on Use (1978 New)

When the term "negligent" or "negligence" is used, it must be defined. When the phrase "highest degree of care" is used, it must be defined.

Where these terms are used in only one instruction, this definition may be added to the instruction using the term. If they are used in more than one instruction, the definition should be given as a separate instruction.

Committee Comment (1978 New)

This instruction may be used instead of MAI 11.01, and MAI 11.02II, in a proper case. For example, it may be used to define the term "negligent" or "negligence" only or it may be used to define these terms as well as the phrase "highest degree of care."

Library References:

C.J.S. Negligence § 871–878, 880–905.
West's Key No. Digests, Negligence ⚲1720–1747.

Notes of Decisions

1. In general

An instruction imposing upon a defendant a standard of care greater than that required by law is prejudicially erroneous. Lee v. Terminal Railroad Ass'n, 669 S.W.2d 564[2] (Mo.App.1984). But see, Fowler v. Park Corp., 673 S.W.2d 749 (Mo. banc 1984).

The phrase "highest degree of care" need not and should not be defined twice, but the terms "negligence" and "highest degree of care" are not synonymous and must be separately defined. Kindle v. Keene, 676 S.W.2d 82[3] (Mo.App.1984).

Giving both MAI 11.01 and 11.03 criticized as repetitive, but not prejudicial. Knowles v. Goswick, 476 S.W.2d 563[4] (Mo.1972).

11.04 [1996 Revision] Definition—Negligence of Minor

The term "negligent" or "negligence" as used in this [these] instruction[s] with respect to (*here describe minor such as plaintiff or decedent*) means the failure to use that degree of care which an ordinarily careful [boy] [girl] of the same age, capacity and experience would use under the same or similar circumstances.

Notes on Use (1996 Revision)

This instruction should be given when a minor's negligence is in issue.

When the term "negligent" or "negligence" is used, it must be defined.

Where either or both terms are used with reference to a minor in only one instruction, this definition may be added to the instruction using the term. If they are used in more than one instruction with reference to a minor, the definition should be given as a separate instruction.

See MAI 11.08 for one method of instructing on two standards of care in the same case.

Committee Comment (1996 Revision)

In *Anderson v. Woodward Implement Co.,* 256 S.W.2d 819, 824 (Mo.1953), the court approved an instruction which said in part: "Negligence, within the meaning of this instruction, means the failure to exercise that degree of care which would be exercised by an ordinarily prudent boy of plaintiff's age, capacity and experience under the same or similar circumstances."

In *Lester v. Sayles,* 850 S.W.2d 858 (Mo. banc), the court held:

"The fault of a child should be determined by the fact finder in each case, based upon that degree of care exercised by children of the same or similar age, judgment, and experience. Only if the child is so young or the evidence is so overwhelming that reasonable minds could not differ on the issue, should the trial courts rule as a matter of law, usually pursuant to a motion for directed verdict, that the child cannot be capable of fault."

Caution: This definition is not applicable to minors who are operating motor vehicles. *Wilson v. Shumate,* 296 S.W.2d 72, 77 (Mo. 1956).

Library References:

C.J.S. Negligence § 871–878, 880–905.
West's Key No. Digests, Negligence ⊙1720–1747.

11.05 [1996 Revision] Definition—Ordinary Care

The phrase "ordinary care" as used in this [these] instruction[s] means that degree of care that an ordinarily careful person would use under the same or similar circumstances.

Notes on Use (1996 Revision)

When the phrase "ordinary care" is used, it must be defined.

Where the phrase is used in only one instruction, this definition may be added to the instruction using the phrase. If it is used in more than one instruction, the definition should be given as a separate instruction.

This definition of "ordinary care" should not be used in fraudulent misrepresentation cases. In such cases, see MAI 11.09.

Library References:

C.J.S. Negligence § 871–878, 880–905.
West's Key No. Digests, Negligence ☞1720–1747.

Notes of Decisions

In general   1
Modification   2
Separating definition   3

———

1. In general

Even though jury was instructed as to ordinary care regarding conduct of helicopter pilot and passenger prior to accident, and survivors did not focus on highest degree of care standard in argument, electrical cooperative was prejudiced by jury instructions that confined cooperative to argument that very careful person in exercising highest degree of care would not have placed warnings on power lines into which victims of helicopter crash flew and, thus, erroneously indicated that highest degree of care standard applied to cooperative's decision not to place warnings on power lines; proper instruction would have informed jury that ordinary care standard required cooperative to exercise degree of care ordinarily careful person would use under same or similar circumstances. Lopez v. Three Rivers Elec. Co-op., Inc., 26 S.W.3d 151 (Mo.2000).

Failure to define "ordinary care" used in contributory negligence instruction was not necessarily erroneous. Robinett v. Kansas City Power & Light Co., 484 S.W.2d 506[2, 3] (Mo.App.1972).

Where verdict director hypothesizes "negligence" it is error to define "ordinary care." Zipp v. Gasen's Drug Stores, Inc., 449 S.W.2d 612[5] (Mo.1970).

Adding an MAI 19.01 joint tortfeasor clause to an MAI 22.02–22.05 type verdict director without definition of negligence "would raise a serious question" since the former uses the word "negligence" and the latter is based on failure to use "ordinary care." Chambers v. Kansas City, 446 S.W.2d 833[5–7] (Mo.1969).

Where verdict director submitted defendant's "negligence" it was error to give MAI 11.05 defining "ordinary care" instead of MAI 11.02(I) defining "negligence". Epps v. Ragsdale, 429 S.W.2d 798[6] (Mo.App. 1968).

2. Modification

Defendants in wrongful death case involving fall of workman through unprotected sky-

144

light on roof of building were not entitled to instruction that standard of care applicable to workman was that exercised by ordinary careful and prudent experienced workman under like or similar circumstances; appropriate standard was that of "ordinarily careful and prudent person." Pyle v. Prairie Farms Dairy, Inc., 777 S.W.2d 286, 294 (Mo.App. 1989).

MAI 11.05 is not applicable to a fraud case and "ordinary care" may be defined as " . . .

that degree of care that would be reasonable in view of plaintiff's situation." Throckmorton v. MFA Central Co-op., 462 S.W.2d 138[2] (Mo.App.1970).

3. Separating definition

Giving MAI 11.05 separately from verdict director was not error. Friend v. Gem International, Inc., 476 S.W.2d 134[18] (Mo.App. 1971).

11.06 [1990 Revision] Definitions—Negligence— Health Care Providers

The term "negligent" or "negligence" as used in this [these] instruction[s] means the failure to use that degree of skill and learning ordinarily used under the same or similar circumstances by the members of defendant's profession.

Notes on Use (1990 Revision)

This instruction should be used when a health care provider's negligence is in issue.

When the term "negligent" or "negligence" is used, it must be defined.

Where either or both terms are used in only one instruction, this definition may be added to the instruction using the term. If they are used in more than one instruction, the definition should be given as a separate instruction.

Committee Comment (1978 Revision)

This instruction conforms to the court's holding in *Gridley v. Johnson,* 476 S.W.2d 475 (Mo.1972), where the court approved of the deletion from the former instruction of the words "in good standing" and did away with the locality rule in medical malpractice cases.

Library References:

> C.J.S. Hospitals § 20–31; Physicians, Surgeons, and other Health-Care Providers § 62–64, 70, 73–74, 79, 92, 97–100, 124.
> West's Key No. Digests, Hospitals ☞7, 8; Physicians and Surgeons ☞14, 15, 18.100.

Notes of Decisions

In general   1
Amendment of instruction   2
Hospitals   3
Modification   4

---

1. In general

Jury in medical malpractice action brought by patient who had undergone hysterectomy after being told that she had tumor in uterus which she did not in fact have was properly instructed that term negligent or negligence meant failure to use that degree of skill and learning ordinarily used under same or simi-lar circumstances by members of physician's profession; evidence was sufficient to establish physician-patient relationship, and give rise duty of care stated in instruction. Smith v. Kovac, 927 S.W.2d 493 (Mo.App.1996).

Verdict directors in medical malpractice action arising out of arthroscopy in which patient's radial nerve was partially severed did not permit jury to infer negligence from fact of injury; if jury had believed defendants' evidence, challenged instructions permitted finding that regardless of fact that nerve was partially severed, defendants were not negligent. Spain v. Brown, 811 S.W.2d 417 (Mo.App.1991).

The phrase "in good standing" should be omitted, and the phrase "practicing in similar localities" criticized. Gridley v. Johnson, 476 S.W.2d 475[5] (Mo.1972).

2. Amendment of instruction

Modifying MAI 11.06 to read, "by the members of defendant's employees' profession," does not constitute error since there is no specific MAI for hospital corporations. Eichelberger v. Barnes Hosp., 655 S.W.2d 699[19] (Mo.App.1983).

3. Hospitals

Where allegations of negligence against hospital were that it failed to observe or medicate psychiatric patients or provide locks or limit stops on windows in a psychiatric ward, MAI 11.07 was not applicable because a hospital clearly has specialized knowledge with respect to the care and treatment of psychiatric patients. MAI 11.06 also was not precisely applicable because the parents' cause of action for wrongful death was not, strictly speaking, medical malpractice. Under these circumstances it was necessary to modify MAI 11.06 to accurately submit parents' case. Honey v. Barnes Hosp., 708 S.W.2d 686[1] (Mo.App. 1986).

4. Modification

Where decedent's comparative negligence injected more than one standard of care into the case, MAI 11.06 was properly modified by MAI 11.08. Additionally, the phrase "health-care provider" was unambiguous and needed no further definition. The modified instruction began "The term negligent or negligence as applied to a health care provider ..." Schiles v. Schaefer, 710 S.W.2d 254[10] (Mo.App.1986).

11.07 [1996 Revision] Definitions—Negligence and Ordinary Care Combined

The term "negligent" or "negligence" as used in this [these] instruction[s] means the failure to use ordinary care. The phrase "ordinary care" means that degree of care that an ordinarily careful person would use under the same or similar circumstances.

Notes on Use (1978 New)

When the term "negligent" or "negligence" is used, it must be defined. When the phrase "ordinary care" is used, it must be defined.

Where these terms are used in only one instruction, this definition may be added to the instruction using the term. If they are used in more than one instruction, the definition should be given as a separate instruction.

Committee Comment (1978 New)

This instruction may be used instead of MAI 11.05, and MAI 11.02I, in a proper case. For example, it may be used to define the term "negligent" or "negligence" only or it may be used to define these terms as well as the phrase "ordinary care."

Library References:

C.J.S. Negligence § 871–878, 880–905.
West's Key No. Digests, Negligence ⟨⟩1720–1747.

Notes of Decisions

1. In general

Submitting MAI 11.07 when an instruction on res ipsa loquitur was appropriate was not prejudicial error. The standard of care and definition of negligence used in MAI 11.07 is in harmony with cases and statutory law applicable to a warehouseman bailee. Royster v. Pittman, 691 S.W.2d 305[10] (Mo. App.1985).

Where allegations of negligence against hospital were that it failed to observe or medicate psychiatric patients or provide locks or limit stops on windows in a psychiatric ward, MAI 11.07 was not applicable because a hospital clearly has specialized knowledge with respect to the care and treatment of psychiatric patients. MAI 11.06

also was not precisely applicable because the parents' cause of action for wrongful death was not, strictly speaking, medical malpractice. Under these circumstances it was necessary to modify MAI 11.06 to accurately submit parents' case. Honey v. Barnes Hosp., 708 S.W.2d 686[1] (Mo.App. 1986).

Where plaintiff's verdict-directing instruction used "ordinary care," converse instruction used "negligent" and "negligence," and instructions gave identical definitions for all three terms, jury could not have been confused or misled and there was no error in submitting those instructions. Brown v. National Super Markets, Inc., 731 S.W.2d 291[4] (Mo.App.1987).

11.08 [1996 Revision] Definitions—Negligence—Different Standards of Care

The term "negligent" or "negligence" as applied to the driver of a motor vehicle means the failure to use that degree of care that a very careful person would use under the same or similar circumstances. The term "negligent" or "negligence" as applied to a [passenger in a motor vehicle] [pedestrian][1] means the failure to use that degree of care that an ordinarily careful person would use under the same or similar circumstances.

Notes on Use (1978 New)

1. Select the appropriate term or phrase.

In a case which involves two different standards of care such as when the plaintiff is a pedestrian or a passenger in a motor vehicle and the defendant is the driver of a motor vehicle, this instruction may be used to define the terms "negligent" and "negligence" as they apply to the respective parties.

Library References:

C.J.S. Motor Vehicles § 530.
West's Key No. Digests, Automobiles ⚷246.

Notes of Decisions

1. In general

In automobile accident litigation, jury instruction defining negligence in terms of highest degree of care as "failure to use that degree of care that a very careful and prudent person would use under the same or similar circumstances," which instruction was in accordance with MAI 11.08, was proper. Hagedorn v. Adams, 854 S.W.2d 470 (Mo.App.1993).

Trial court could conclude that erroneous instruction stating that driver was required to be very careful and prudent person prejudiced driver and warranted new trial in action arising out of driver's collision with bridge floor approximately seven and one-half inches above bed of road under construction; driver was not required to exercise highest degree of care and to act as very careful and prudent person, where there was no evidence of public's premature use of new highway, where driver had not previously used the highway, and where highway had never been opened. McTeer v. Clarkson Const. Co., Inc., 807 S.W.2d 174 (Mo. App.1991).

Where decedent's comparative negligence injected more than one standard of care in the case, MAI 11.06 was properly modified by MAI 11.08. Schiles v. Schaefer, 710 S.W.2d 254[10] (Mo.App.1986).

11.09 [1996 Withdrawn] Definition—Ordinary Care— Fraudulent Misrepresentation

(This instruction, its Notes on Use and Committee Comment are withdrawn. Since this definition of "ordinary care" was used only in MAI 23.05, its meaning has been incorporated directly in that verdict directing instruction.)

Library References:

C.J.S. Fraud § 132.
West's Key No. Digests, Fraud ⚬=65(1).

11.10 [1996 Revision] Definitions—Negligence—Ordinary Care—Manufacturers of Certain Products

I

The term "negligent" or "negligence" as used in this [these] instruction[s] means the failure to use that degree of skill and learning ordinarily used under the same or similar circumstances by an expert in defendant's business.

II

The phrase "ordinary care" as used in this [these] instruction[s] means that degree of care, skill and learning that an ordinarily careful expert in defendant's business would use under the same or similar circumstances.

Notes on Use (1988 New)

Where the term "negligent" or "negligence" is used, it must be defined.

Where the phrase "ordinary care" is used, it must be defined.

Select the appropriate definition according to the term or phrase used in the instruction. Where the appropriately selected term or phrase is used in only one instruction, the appropriate definition may be added to the instruction using the term or phrase. If used in more than one instruction, the definition should be given as a separate instruction.

Caution: The above definition may not properly apply to all the negligence submitted. See MAI 11.08 for one method of instruction on two standards of care in the same case.

Committee Comment (1988 New)

Manufacturers of certain products are held to the standard of care of an expert in that defendant's field. See *Krug v. Sterling Drug, Inc.*, 416 S.W.2d 143 (Mo.1967) (prescription drug); *Braun v. Roux Distributing Company, Inc.*, 312 S.W.2d 758 (Mo.1958) (hair dye); and *La Plant v. E.I. Du Pont De Nemours and Company, Inc.*, 346 S.W.2d 231 (Mo.App. 1961) (weed killer). Where such a standard is applicable, select one of the above definitions, whichever is appropriate.

Some other manufacturers have a duty of ordinary care. See *Stevens v. Durbin–Durco, Inc.*, 377 S.W.2d 343 (Mo.1964).

Library References:

C.J.S. Products Liability § 93.
West's Key No. Digests, Products Liability ⚲96.

12.00

DEFINITIONS—UNINSURED MOTOR VEHICLE

Analysis of Instructions

Westlaw Electronic Research

See Westlaw Electronic Research Guide preceding the Table of Instructions.

Library References:

C.J.S. Insurance § 56, 1647–1648, 1650–1653, 1657, 1659–1671, 1675–1684, 1703, 1706–1708.
West's Key No. Digests, Insurance ☞2772–2816, 3579.

12.01 [1988 Revision] Definitions—Uninsured Motor Vehicle

I

The phrase "uninsured motor vehicle" as used in this [these] instruction[s] means a motor vehicle which has no bodily injury liability insurance applicable at the time of the collision.

II

The phrase "uninsured motor vehicle" as used in this [these] instruction[s] means a motor vehicle with respect to which the company writing insurance on said vehicle has denied coverage.

III

The phrase "uninsured motor vehicle" as used in this [these] instruction[s] means a motor vehicle with respect to which there was a bodily injury liability insurance policy applicable at the time of the collision but the company writing said policy became insolvent [within two years after the collision].[1]

IV

The phrase "uninsured motor vehicle" as used in this [these] instruction[s] means a motor vehicle with respect to which the identity of the owner or operator cannot be established because the motor vehicle departed the scene of the occurrence with or without physical contact between such vehicle and the plaintiff or the plaintiff's vehicle.

Notes on Use (1988 Revision)

1. Revise if policy contains more favorable terms. See section 379.203.3, RSMo.

When the phrase "uninsured motor vehicle" is used, it must be defined. Select the appropriate definition.

Where the phrase is used in only one instruction, this definition may be added to the instruction using the phrase. If it is used in more than one instruction, the definition should be given as a separate instruction.

Library References:

C.J.S. Insurance § 56, 1647–1648, 1650–1653, 1657, 1659–1671, 1675–1684, 1703, 1706–1708.

West's Key No. Digests, Insurance ⬦2772–2816, 3579.

12.02   [1978 New] Definition—Uninsured Motor Vehicle—Hit-and-Run Vehicle

The phrase "hit-and-run vehicle" as used in this [these] instruction[s] refers to a motor vehicle which causes bodily injury arising from physical contact with (*select appropriate term, i.e. "plaintiff" or "the vehicle occupied by plaintiff"*) where the identity of neither the operator nor owner of such vehicle can be determined.

Notes on Use (1978 New)

This instruction is mandatory when MAI 31.13 is submitted.

Where the phrase is used in only one instruction, this paragraph may be added to the instruction using the phrase. If it is used in more than one instruction, the definition should be given as a separate instruction.

Library References:

C.J.S. Insurance § 56, 1647–1648, 1650–1653, 1657, 1659–1671, 1675–1684, 1703, 1706–1708.
West's Key No. Digests, Insurance ⟜2772–2816, 3579.

13.00

DEFINITIONS—AGENCY

Analysis of Instructions

Westlaw Electronic Research

See Westlaw Electronic Research Guide preceding the Table of Instructions.

Library References:

C.J.S. Agency § 553.
West's Key No. Digests, Principal and Agent ⚷194.

157

13.01 [1996 Revision] Definitions—Agency—General Comment

As the pattern instructions submit only ultimate issues, a question of respondeat superior liability might be submitted simply "The driver Jones was operating the (*defendant's*) motor vehicle within the scope and course of his agency for (*defendant*)." But these words alone are not apt to mean much to lay jurors, so some clarification is needed. The definitions following are intended to supply this clarification.

Agency questions arise in a variety of cases. Typical are:

1. Tort actions by third persons against an alleged principal who raises the defense that the tort-feasor was an independent contractor.

2. Tort actions by third persons against master who raises the defense that the servant was not engaged in master's business at time of tort. These include route deviations, dual purpose trips and independent frolics of the servant.

3. Tort actions by third persons against the master for battery by a servant where the master raises the defense that the servant acted beyond the scope of his authority.

A universally applicable definition of scope of agency is not practicable. For this reason the Committee has prepared definitions to fit the most common cases. Other definitions may be needed for other problems, but these patterns should serve as a guide in those areas not specifically covered. The purpose of these definitions is to call to the jury's attention the fact issues which determine liability in a particular case.

The difference between an agent and a servant is sometimes misunderstood and this causes confusion when instructing. The Restatement (Second) of Agency § 200, Comment e (1957), says:

It is important to distinguish between a servant and an agent who is not a servant, since ordinarily a principal is not liable for the incidental physical acts of negligence in the performance of duties committed by an agent who is not a servant. See § 250. One who is employed to make contracts may, however, be a servant. Thus, a shop girl is, and a traveling salesman may be, a servant and cause the employer to be liable for negligent injuries to a customer or for negligent driving while traveling to visit prospective customers. The important distinction is between service in which the actor's physical activities and his time are surrendered to the control of the master, and service under an agreement to accomplish results or to use care and skill in accomplishing results. Those rendering service but retaining control over the manner of doing it are not servants. They may be agents, agreeing to use care and skill to accomplish a result and subject to the fiduciary duties of loyalty and obedience to the wishes of the principal; or they may be persons employed to accomplish or to use care to accomplish physical results, without fiduciary obligations, as where a contractor is paid to build a house. An agent who is not subject to control as to the manner in which he performs the acts that constitute the execution of his agency is in a similar relation to the principal as to such conduct as one who agrees only to accomplish mere physical results. For the purpose of determining liability, they are both "independent contractors" and do not cause the person for whom the enterprise is undertaken to be responsible, under the rule stated in Section 219.

See MAI 37.05(1) and (2) for submission of vicarious liability issues in comparative fault cases.

Library References:

C.J.S. Agency § 553.
West's Key No. Digests, Principal and Agent ⏀194.

Notes of Decisions

1. In general

Medical center was liable for patient's death caused by fire in room despite jury verdict in favor of medical center's employee where center's liability was not predicated solely upon conduct of employee. Plaintiff also submitted primary negligence of medical center consisting of allowing smoking without approved ashtray, absence of smoke detector, inadequate fire training, etc. Stacy

v. Truman Medical Center, 836 S.W.2d 911 (Mo.1992).

Although agency is denied by answer, where defendants' evidence showed agency, that issue was properly omitted from plaintiff's verdict director. Hulahan v. Sheehan, 522 S.W.2d 134[9, 10] (Mo.App.1975).

Where undisputed evidence showed defendant's employee created a dangerous condition plaintiff's verdict director need not hypothesize that element. Cline v. Carthage Crushed Limestone Co., 504 S.W.2d 102[4] (Mo.1973).

Where agency of defendant's negotiators was conceded it was not necessary to define "scope and course of employment." Kaiser v. Lyon Metal Products, Inc., 461 S.W.2d 893[5] (Mo.App.1970).

Where defendant denied its employee was acting within the scope of his employment plaintiff's verdict director must hypothesize that element and the term must be defined. Ratterree v. General Motors Corp., 460 S.W.2d 309[2] (Mo.App.1970).

In action against truck owner for his driver's negligence it was error to give a converse instruction exonerating the owner unless the jury believed the owner was negligent; it should have submitted the driver's lack of negligence. Denny v. Mathieu, 452 S.W.2d 114[6] (Mo. banc 1970).

Not error to omit definition of "scope of employment" where agency was not in issue. Terry v. Sweeney, 420 S.W.2d 368[9] (Mo.App.1967).

13.02 [1978 Revision] Definition—Agency—Battery Committed by Servant

Acts were within the "scope and course of employment" as that phrase is used in this [these] instruction[s] even though not specifically authorized by (*name of master*) if:

1. they were done by (*name of servant*) to further the [business] [interests] [1] of (*name of master*) under the general authority and direction of (*name of master*), and

2. they naturally arose from the performance of (*name of servant's*) work.

Notes on Use (1978 Revision)

1. Select the appropriate term.

When the phrase "scope and course of employment" or the phrase "scope and course of agency" is used, it must be defined. See MAI 18.01.

Where the phrase is used in only one instruction this definition may be added to the instruction using the phrase. If it is used in more than one instruction, the definition should be given as a separate instruction.

Committee Comment (1965 New)

The leading Missouri case on this subject is *Haehl v. Wabash R. Co.,* 119 Mo. 325, 24 S.W. 737 (1893). There the court said: "The principle of respondeat superior applies only when what is complained of was done in the course of the employment. The principal is responsible, not because the servant has acted in his name or under color of his employment, but because the servant was actually engaged in and about his business, and carrying out his purposes. He is then responsible, because the thing complained of, although done through the agency of another, was done by himself; and it matters not in such case whether the injury with which it is sought to charge him is the result of negligence, unskillfulness or of wrongful conduct, for he must choose fit agents for the transaction of his business. But if his business is done, or is taking care of itself, and his servant, not being engaged in it, not concerned about it, but impelled by motives that are wholly personal to himself, and simply to gratify his own feeling of resentment, whether provoked or unprovoked, commits an assault upon another, when that has and can have no tendency to promote any purpose in which the principal is interested, and to promote that for which the servant was employed, then the wrong is the purely personal wrong of the servant, for which he, and he alone, is responsible."

The same language was quoted with approval in *Bova v. St. Louis Public Service Co.*, 316 S.W.2d 140 (Mo.App.1958), where a bus driver intentionally struck plaintiff. Plaintiff's verdict directing instruction hypothesized that "the bus driver was acting in the course and scope of his employment" and defendant's instruction hypothesized that "the fight had no connection with the duties of [driver] ... and was not intended to promote or further [defendant's] business and was personal between [driver and plaintiff]."

The court held that together the instructions "... contain a complete exposition of the law...."

The *Bova* case also quoted from an earlier Missouri Supreme Court decision which said: "... in general terms, it may be said that an act is within the course of the employment if (1) it be something fairly and naturally incident to the business, and if (2) it be done while the servant was engaged upon the master's business and be done, although mistakenly or ill advisedly with a view to further the master's interests, or from some impulse or emotion which naturally grew out of or was incident to the attempt to perform the master's business, and did not arise wholly from some external, independent, and personal motive on the part of the servant to do the act upon his own account."

Compare *Noland v. Morris & Co.*, 212 Mo.App. 1, 248 S.W. 627 (Mo.App.1922), where defendant's foreman apparently ordered the battery committed. See also *Adler v. Ewing*, 347 S.W.2d 396 (Mo.App. 1961).

For cases where servant was held as a matter of law to be acting outside the scope of his employment see *Porter v. Thompson*, 357 Mo. 31, 206 S.W.2d 509 (1947); *State ex rel. Gosselin v. Trimble*, 328 Mo. 760, 41 S.W.2d 801 (1931); *Milazzo v. Kansas City Gas Co.*, 180 S.W.2d 1 (Mo.1944); *Rohrmoser v. Household Finance Corp.*, 231 Mo.App. 1188, 86 S.W.2d 103 (Mo.App.1935); *Tockstein v. P.J. Hamill Transfer Co.*, 291 S.W.2d 624 (Mo.App.1956).

See also 4 Mo.L.Rev. 190 (1939).

Restatement (Second) of Agency § 245 (1957) states: "A master is subject to liability for the intended tortious harm by a servant to the person or things of another by an act done in connection with the servant's employment, although the act was unauthorized, if the act was not unexpectable in view of the duties of the servant."

There appear to be no Missouri cases where the jury has been instructed that "expectability" of servant's act is an issue.

"To assault and beat a creditor is not a recognized or usual means resorted to for the collection of a debt...." *Collette v. Rebori,* 107 Mo.App. 711, 720, 82 S.W. 552, 555 (1904).

Library References:

C.J.S. Agency § 553.
West's Key No. Digests, Principal and Agent ⇒194.

Notes of Decisions

In general 1
Other servants 2

_____

1. In general

MAI 13.02 is designed to submit the issue of whether one admittedly employed was acting within the scope of his employment, while MAI 13.06 is designed to submit the issue of whether the wrongdoer is an agent (or employee) or is an independent contractor. Jefferson County Bank & Trust Co. v. Dennis, 523 S.W.2d 165[5–6] (Mo.App. 1975).

MAI 13.02 is proper to define agency in other kinds of cases, such as fraud by agent.

Tietjens v. General Motors Corp., 418 S.W.2d 75[15] (Mo.1967).

Verdict director for false arrest based on agency (MAI 18.01–23.04) requires definition of scope of employment. Peak v. W.T. Grant Co., 409 S.W.2d 58[1] (Mo. banc 1966).

2. Other servants

MAI 13.02 is proper to submit other wrongful or tortious conduct of an agent. Jefferson County Bank & Trust Co. v. Dennis, 523 S.W.2d 165[5, 6] (Mo.App.1975).

13.03   [1990 Revision] Definition—Agency—Scope of Employment—Dual Purpose Acts

Acts[1] were within the "scope and course of employment" as that phrase is used in this [these] instruction[s] if:

1. they were done by (*name of servant*) partially to serve the [business] [interests][2] of (*name of master*) and partially to carry out the [business] [interests][2] of (*here insert name of servant or such other party as is appropriate*), and

2. (*master's*) business created the necessity for the trip, and

3. (*name of master*) either controlled or had the right to control the physical conduct of (*name of servant*).

Notes on Use (1990 Revision)

1. A phrase describing the general conduct which is the subject of the alleged employment or agency, such as "operation of the motor vehicle", may be substituted for the word "acts". Grammatical changes to the rest of this instruction then may be appropriate.

2. Select the appropriate term.

When the phrase "scope and course of employment" or the phrase "scope and course of agency" is used, it must be defined. See MAI 18.01.

Where the phrase is used in only one instruction, this definition may be added to the instruction using the phrase. If it is used in more than one instruction, the definition should be given as a separate instruction.

Committee Comment (1965 New)

The dual purpose doctrine has arisen most frequently in workmen's compensation cases. In *Gingell v. Walters Contracting Corp.,* 303 S.W.2d 683, 688 (Mo.App.1957), the court quoted with approval from Judge Cardozo's decision in *Marks' Dependents v. Gray,* 251 N.Y. 90, 167 N.E. 181 (1929) which said: "We do not say that service to the employer must be the sole cause of the journey, but at least it must be a concurrent cause. To establish liability, the inference must be permissible that the trip would have been made though the private errand had been cancelled. * * * The test in brief is this: If the work of the employee creates the necessity for travel, he is in the course of his employment, though he is serving at the same time some purpose of his own. * * * If, however, the work has had no part in creating the necessity for travel, if the journey would have gone forward though the business errand had been dropped, and would have been cancelled upon failure of the private purpose, though the business errand was undone, the travel is then personal, and personal the risk."

The court then concluded that the employer's needs were sufficiently pressing that had the employee not consented to perform them, some other person would have been required to make the trip. That being true the employee was within the scope of his employment.

See also *Corp v. Joplin Cement Co.,* 337 S.W.2d 252 (Mo. banc 1960), approving the Cardozo decision and the language in *Gingell v. Walters Contracting Corp.*

The dual purpose doctrine was applied in a respondeat superior liability case in *Foster v. Campbell,* 355 Mo. 349, 196 S.W.2d 147 (1946). The court said "If the trip was for the mixed or double purpose of her business and the business of her husband as well, and there was no material deviation from those purposes, it may not be said that she was not engaged upon her husband's business when she was returning home, after having sold her produce and purchased feed, with the gasoline which she had procured at his request.... 'An act may be within the scope of employment, although done in part to serve the purposes of the servant or a third person.... The fact that the predominant motive of the servant is to benefit himself or a third person does not prevent the act from being within the scope of employment'. 1 Restatement, Agency, Sec. 236 and comment pp. 530, 531."

Compare *Stokes v. Four States Broadcasters,* 300 S.W.2d 426 (Mo. 1957).

See also *Massey v. Berlo Vending Co.,* 329 S.W.2d 772 (Mo.1959), where the dual purpose question was said to be a jury issue.

See also Restatement (Second) of Agency § 236 (1957).

Library References:

C.J.S. Agency § 553.
West's Key No. Digests, Principal and Agent ⊕194.

13.04 [1990 Revision] Definition—Agency—Scope of Employment—Route Deviation

Acts[1] were within the "scope and course of employment" as that phrase is used in this [these] instruction[s] if they were done to serve the [business] [interests][2] of (*name of master*) while (*name of servant*) was at a place where the performance of his work required him to be.

Notes on Use (1990 Revision)

1. A phrase describing the general conduct which is the subject of the alleged employment or agency, such as "operation of the motor vehicle", may be substituted for the word "acts". Grammatical changes to the remainder of this instruction then may be appropriate.

2. Select the appropriate term.

This definition assumes that there is no controversy about the existence of a master-servant relationship. See MAI 13.06 in case master-servant relationship is disputed.

When the phrase "scope and course of employment" or the phrase "scope and course of agency" is used, it must be defined. See MAI 18.01.

Where the phrase is used in only one instruction, this definition may be added to the instruction using the phrase. If it is used in more than one instruction, the definition should be given as a separate instruction.

Committee Comment (1965 New)

In *Thomas v. McBride Express Co.*, 266 S.W.2d 11, 13 (Mo.App. 1954), the court said: "An act of a servant is not within the scope of employment if it is done with no intention to perform it as a part of or incident to a service on account of which the servant is employed.... A servant may in certain instances deviate from the most direct or authorized route and still be in the master's service. Thus it may be that one turns aside to avoid heavy traffic or to seek a smoother route. There may be parallel routes leading in the direction of his ultimate destination, either of which could be said to be within his sphere of service, on the theory that it might be reasonably expected that he would, in the exercise of his best judgment, choose either while in the pursuit of his master's business; or he might turn aside to attend to necessary personal wants which are considered incidental to his employment. But any turning aside from the designated or customary route, where the sole motive is self-interest, unmixed with any intent to serve the master, separates the servant from the master's service, regardless of the extent

166

of the deviation. Any other rule would lead to inconsistencies and ultimate confusion in the law."

In *Cable v. Johnson,* 63 S.W.2d 433, 437 (Mo.App.1933), the court said: "... where a servant, who takes the automobile of his master in performing some service for this master at a distant point, deviates temporarily from the path of duty by using the master's car for his own purpose, he may be considered as having returned to his master's service when he reaches a point on his return trip where his original mission might reasonably have required him to be...."

In *Kinkead v. Management & Engineering Corp.,* 103 S.W.2d 545, 547 (Mo.App.1937), the court said: "It is the law that where the servant deviates from the scope of his employment for his own purposes, he is still upon his own trip, even though engaged in returning to his employment, until he has returned either to the point of his departure from the path of duty, or to a point where, in the performance of his duty, he is required to be."

The Missouri view is somewhat different from that adopted by Restatement (Second) of Agency § 237 (1957) which places the deviating servant within the scope of employment so long as he is "reasonably near the authorized space" limit authorized by the master.

Library References:

C.J.S. Agency § 553.
West's Key No. Digests, Principal and Agent ☞194.

13.05   [1990 Revision] Definition—Agency—Scope of Employment

Acts[1] were within the "scope and course of employment" as that phrase is used in this [these] instruction[s] if:

1. they were a part of the work (*name of servant*) was employed to perform, and

2. they were done by (*name of servant*) to serve the [business] [interests][2] of (*name of master*).

Notes on Use (1990 Revision)

1. A phrase describing the general conduct which is the subject of the alleged employment or agency, such as "operation of the motor vehicle", may be substituted for the word "acts". Grammatical changes to the remainder of this instruction then may be appropriate.

2. Select the appropriate term.

This definition may be used where the master-servant relationship is admitted but the master alleges that the servant was not on the master's business. See MAI 13.06 in case master-servant relationship is disputed.

When the phrase "scope and course of employment" or the phrase "scope and course of agency" is used, it must be defined. See MAI 18.01.

Where the phrase is used in only one instruction, this definition may be added to the instruction using the phrase. If it is used in more than one instruction, the definition should be given as a separate instruction.

Committee Comment (1965 New)

See Restatement (Second) of Agency § 228 (1957).

In *Wolf v. Terminal R.R. Ass'n of St. L.*, 282 Mo. 559, 222 S.W. 114 (1920), the court said: "The fact that the act was done during the time of servant's employment is not conclusive, nor is the motive of servant so. The question is, Was the act done by virtue of the employment and in furtherance of the master's business?"

See also 10 Mo.L.Rev. 169 (1951).

Library References:

C.J.S. Agency § 553.
West's Key No. Digests, Principal and Agent ⊕194.

Notes of Decisions

1. In general

Jury instruction that attempted to find an agency relationship between two wrecking companies was prejudicial because it failed to require a finding that any representations made by one company were authorized in some fashion by the other company. It also was prejudicial in defining acts within the scope of employment because there was no evidence to show that the subcontractor was an employee of the wrecking company. Snyder Bros. Co. v. Library Landholders, Inc., 718 S.W.2d 633[1–6] (Mo.App.1986).

In suit on accidental death policy, the term "course of employment" as used in instruction defining "non-occupational injury" was plain and unambiguous and the jury needed no instruction to define it. Brock v. Firemens Fund of America Ins. Co., 637 S.W.2d 824[5] (Mo.App.1982).

Where plaintiffs' recovery depends on agency of defendant's employee, that disputed fact must be submitted not only by definition of agency but also by inclusion in plaintiffs' verdict director. Galemore Motor Co., Inc. v. State Farm Ins. Co., 513 S.W.2d 161[11] (Mo.App.1974).

Where as a matter of law evidence showed employee was acting within the scope of his employment it was unnecessary to hypothesize that element in his verdict director. Elliott v. St. Louis S.W. Ry. Co., 487 S.W.2d 7[11] (Mo.1972).

Error for plaintiff to omit MAI 13.05 when verdict director used MAI 18.01 requiring a finding that driver was "within the scope and course of his employment." Chandler v. New Moon Homes, Inc., 418 S.W.2d 130[11] (Mo. banc 1967).

13.06 [1990 Revision] Definition—Agency—Scope of Agency—Servant or Independent Contractor

Acts [1] were within the "scope and course of agency" as that phrase is used in this [these] instruction[s] if:

1. they were performed by (*name of alleged servant*) to serve the [business] [interests] [2] of (*name of alleged master*) according to an express or implied agreement with (*name of alleged master*), and

2. (*name of alleged master*) either controlled or had the right to control the physical conduct of (*name of alleged servant*).

Notes on Use (1990 Revision)

1. A phrase describing the general conduct which is the subject of the alleged employment or agency, such as "operation of the motor vehicle", may be substituted for the word "acts". Grammatical changes to the remainder of this instruction then may be appropriate.

2. Select the appropriate term.

This definition is to be used only when defendant is charged with *respondeat superior* liability and there is a dispute that the alleged tort-feasor was not his servant. See MAI 13.04 and MAI 13.05 where there is no dispute as to the master-servant relationship.

When the phrase "scope and course of employment" or the phrase "scope and course of agency" is used, it must be defined. See MAI 18.01.

Where the phrase is used in only one instruction, this definition may be added to the instruction using the phrase. If it is used in more than one instruction, the definition should be given as a separate instruction.

The phrase "scope and course of agency" is to be used where the issue is whether the tort-feasor was a servant rather than an independent contractor. Liability is imposed on the principal even though he engages another for only one task. See *Leidy v. Taliaferro*, 260 S.W.2d 504 (Mo.1953). To use the phrase "scope and course of employment" in such a case might be misleading to lay jurors who probably think of employees as those who receive regular weekly paychecks. The phrase "scope and course of agency" is less apt to mislead and is therefore preferable although technically "scope and course of employment" would be more appropriate.

Committee Comment (1965 New)

In *Leidy v. Taliaferro,* 260 S.W.2d 504, 505 (Mo.1953), the court said: " 'Agency is the relationship which results from the manifestation of consent by one person to another that the other shall act on his behalf, and subject to his control, and consent by the other so to act.' Restatement (First) of Agency § 1. The parties may not have intended to create the legal relationship or to have subjected themselves to the liabilities which the law imposes as a result of it, nevertheless, the relationship exists 'if there has been a manifestation by the principal to the agent that the agent may act on his account, and consent by the agent so to act.' "

On page 507 the court said: " . . . compensation to the agent is not essential to the relationship . . . ."

See also *Talley v. Bowen Construction Co.,* 340 S.W.2d 701, 704 (Mo.1960). Compare also Restatement (Second) of Agency § 220 (1957).

See also *Foster v. Campbell,* 355 Mo. 349, 196 S.W.2d 147 (1946), where wife was held to be servant of husband while running an errand for him.

In *Wigger v. Consumers Cooperative Ass'n,* 301 S.W.2d 56 (Mo.App. 1957) the court said:

> The courts have many times held that in determining whether the relationship of master and servant or employer and employee exists, one of the essential or primary elements is the right to control the means and manner of the service as distinguished from controlling the ultimate results of the service. McFarland v. St. Louis Car Co., 262 S.W.2d 344; O'Brien v. Rindskopf, 334 Mo. 1233, 70 S.W.2d 1085; McFarland v. Dixie Machinery & Equipment Co., 348 Mo. 341, 153 S.W.2d 67, 136 A.L.R. 516; Hackler v. Swisher Mower & Machine Co., 284 S.W.2d 55, 58. However, it is equally well established that "every case has been decided on its particular facts, and while the element of control is of the greatest significance in determining the existence of the required relationship, *the fact of control standing alone is not conclusive.*"

By way of contrast, *Williamson v. Southwestern Bell Tel. Co.,* 265 S.W.2d 354 (Mo.1954), defines an independent contractor as a person who " 'contracts with another to do something for him but who is not controlled by the other nor subject to the other's right to control with respect to his physical conduct in the performance of the undertaking.' " This definition is the general rule of and definition of independent contractor. See Restatement (First) of Agency § 2(3) (1934).

In *Madsen v. Lawrence,* 366 S.W.2d 413, 415 (Mo.1963), the court said:

A master is a principal who employs another to perform service in his affairs and who controls or has the right to control the physical conduct of the other in the performance of the service.

A servant is a person employed by a master to perform service in his affairs whose physical conduct in the performance of the service is controlled or subject to the right of control by the master.

An independent contractor is a person who contracts with another to do something for him, but who is not controlled by the other nor subject to the other's right to control with respect to his physical conduct in the performance of the undertaking.

See also *Gardner v. Simmons,* 370 S.W.2d 359, 362 (Mo.1963).

Library References:

C.J.S. Agency § 553.
West's Key No. Digests, Principal and Agent ⊕194.

Notes of Decisions

In general   1
Employees   2

———

1. In General

Automobile case. Plaintiff submitted agency as to driver of trucking company. Defendant attempted to converse the definitional instruction relating to "scope and course of agency" rather than conversing the verdict directing instruction. Held that such a converse was prejudicially erroneous, particularly where the converse of the definitional instruction in MAI 13.06 limited the right to control the conduct of the alleged agent to "the performance of the undertaking of hauling asphalt" rather than the "operation of the truck" as submitted by the verdict director. Gaynor v. Circle B Trucking, Inc., 801 S.W.2d 369 (Mo.App.1990).

Doctor, who was one of two stockholder employees of professional corporation, who shared responsibility for treatment of kidney patient and who was out of town when other stockholder employee negligently treated patient, could not give directions and had no right of control over other stockholder employee concerning patient's treatment; therefore, agency instruction given in wrongful death action arising out of patient's death warranted reversal of judgment against doc-

tor and remand for further proceedings. Goff v. St. Luke's Hosp. of Kansas City, 753 S.W.2d 557, 561 (Mo. banc 1988).

In defining "scope and course of agency" the instruction should use names rather than "principal" and "agent." Parker v. Stern Bros. & Co., 499 S.W.2d 397[3] (Mo.1973).

Where evidence did not show plaintiff's driver was her agent it was error to give a contributory negligence instruction. McAuliffe v. Vondera, 494 S.W.2d 692[1, 2] (Mo. App.1973).

Defendant contending tort-feasor was not his agent but was "employee" of "independent contractor" must define those terms by MAI 13.06. Barkley v. Mitchell, 411 S.W.2d 817[1–8] (Mo.App.1967).

2. Employees

MAI 13.02 is designed to submit the issue of whether one admittedly employed was acting within the scope of his employment, while MAI 13.06 is designed to submit the issue of whether the wrongdoer is an agent (or employee) or is an independent contractor. Jefferson County Bank & Trust Co. v. Dennis, 523 S.W.2d 165[5–6] (Mo.App. 1975).

13.07(1) [1996 Revision] Definition—Contract—Apparent Authority—Conduct of Principal

Acts of (*name of apparent agent*) were within the "scope and course of agency" as that phrase is used in this [these] instruction[s] if:

First, the conduct of (*name of apparent principal*) was such that an ordinarily careful person would believe that (*name of apparent agent*) had authority to perform such acts on behalf of (*name of apparent principal*), and

Second, (*name of relying person*) reasonably relied on such conduct of (*name of apparent principal*) at the time of the transaction mentioned in the evidence.

Notes on Use (1986 New)

When the phrase "scope and course of employment" or the phrase "scope and course of agency" is used, it must be defined. See MAI 18.01.

Where the phrase is used in only one instruction, this definition may be added to the instruction using the phrase. If it is used in more than one instruction, the definition should be given as a separate instruction.

Committee Comment (1986 New)

This instruction is not based upon an agreement between principal and agent (although they may have an agreement). It is based on an estoppel of the principal to deny the apparent authority of the actor to act for the principal.

MAI 13.07(1) defines acts "within the scope and course" of apparent "agency" when the person relying on appearances of authority is led by the conduct of the principal to believe that the actor has actual authority from the principal to act for the principal.

MAI 13.07(2) defines acts "within the scope and course" of apparent "agency" when the person relying on apparent authority is led solely by the conduct of the actor (in the circumstances) to believe the actor has actual authority from the principal to act for the principal. Although the relying person may not know of the principal's knowledge of the conduct of the actor at the time of reliance, his proof must show both that the principal knew or had reason to know of the actor's misleading conduct and failed to act to prevent reliance on such misleading conduct of the actor.

For case law discussions of apparent authority in conventional contractual settings, see: *Martin v. First National Bank in St. Louis,* 358 Mo. 1199, 219 S.W.2d 312 (1949); *Koewing v. Greene County Building and Loan Ass'n of Springfield,* 327 Mo. 680, 38 S.W.2d 40 (1931). In *Dierks & Sons Lumber Co. v. Morris,* 404 S.W.2d 229, 232 (Mo.App.1966), the Court set out the requirements:

In order for one to sanction another as his agent by holding him out as such, two essentials must concur: the purported agent must conduct himself in a manner consistent with some pretense of authority, and knowledge of his conduct in that particular, or some reasonable basis for the suspicion of it, must be brought home to the alleged principal.

See also, *Springfield Television, Inc. v. Gary,* 628 S.W.2d 398 (Mo.App. 1982); *Sturgeon v. State Bank of Fisk,* 616 S.W.2d 578 (Mo.App.1981); *Molasky Enterprises, Inc. v. Carps, Inc.,* 615 S.W.2d 83 (Mo.App.1981).

For a discussion of apparent authority in a tort setting, see *State ex rel. Massman v. Bland,* 355 Mo. 17, 194 S.W.2d 42 (en banc 1946).

Library References:

C.J.S. Agency § 553.
West's Key No. Digests, Principal and Agent ⚷194.

Notes of Decisions

1. In general

In appropriate cases, MAI 13.07(1) applies to tort cases; evidence supported instruction on apparent agency of person who was in electricity supplier's warehouse and gave transformer fuse to customer who injured himself in attempt to install it. Mobley v. Webster Elec. Co-op., 859 S.W.2d 923 (Mo. App.1993).

Jury instruction that attempted to find an agency relationship between two wrecking companies was prejudicial because it failed to require a finding that any representations made by one company were authorized in some fashion by the other company. It also was prejudicial in defining acts within the scope of employment because there was no evidence to show that the subcontractor was an employee of the wrecking company. Snyder Bros. Co. v. Library Landholders, Inc., 718 S.W.2d 633[1–6] (Mo.App.1986).

13.07(2) [1996 Revision] Definition—Contract—Apparent Authority—Acts of Agent With Principal's Knowledge

Acts of (*name of apparent agent*) were within the "scope and course of agency" as that phrase is used in this [these] instruction[s] if:

First, the conduct of (*name of apparent agent*) was such that an ordinarily careful person would believe that (name of apparent agent) had authority to perform such acts on behalf of (*name of apparent principal*), and

Second, (*name of apparent principal*) knew or had reason to know of such conduct and allowed such conduct, and

Third, (*name of relying person*) reasonably relied on such conduct of (*name of apparent agent*) at the time of the transaction mentioned in the evidence.

Notes on Use (1986 New)

When the phrase "scope and course of employment" or the phrase "scope and course of agency" is used, it must be defined. See MAI 18.01.

Where the phrase is used in only one instruction, this definition may be added to the instruction using the phrase. If it is used in more than one instruction, the definition should be given as a separate instruction.

Committee Comment (1986 New)

This instruction is not based upon an agreement between principal and agent (although they may have an agreement). It is based on an estoppel of the principal to deny the apparent authority of the actor to act for the principal.

MAI 13.07(1) defines acts "within the scope and course" of apparent "agency" when the person relying on appearances of authority is led by the conduct of the principal to believe that the actor has actual authority from the principal to act for the principal.

MAI 13.07(2) defines acts "within the scope and course" of apparent "agency" when the person relying on apparent authority is led solely by the conduct of the actor (in the circumstances) to believe the actor has actual authority from the principal to act for the principal. Although the relying person may not know of the principal's knowledge of the conduct of the actor at the time of reliance, his proof must show both that the principal knew or had reason to know of the actor's misleading conduct and failed to act to prevent reliance on such misleading conduct of the actor.

For case law discussions of apparent authority in conventional contractual settings, see: *Martin v. First National Bank in St. Louis,* 358 Mo. 1199, 219 S.W.2d 312 (1949); *Koewing v. Greene County Building and Loan Ass'n of Springfield,* 327 Mo. 680, 38 S.W.2d 40 (1931). In *Dierks & Sons Lumber Co. v. Morris,* 404 S.W.2d 229, 232 (Mo.App.1966), the Court set out the requirements:

> In order for one to sanction another as his agent by holding him out as such, two essentials must concur: the purported agent must conduct himself in a manner consistent with some pretense of authority, and knowledge of his conduct in that particular, or some reasonable basis for the suspicion of it, must be brought home to the alleged principal.

See also, *Springfield Television, Inc. v. Gary,* 628 S.W.2d 398 (Mo.App. 1982); *Sturgeon v. State Bank of Fisk,* 616 S.W.2d 578 (Mo.App.1981); *Molasky Enterprises, Inc. v. Carps, Inc.,* 615 S.W.2d 83 (Mo.App.1981).

For a discussion of apparent authority in a tort setting, see *State ex rel. Massman v. Bland,* 355 Mo. 17, 194 S.W.2d 42 (en banc 1946).

Library References:

C.J.S. Agency § 553.
West's Key No. Digests, Principal and Agent ⚷194.

14.00

DEFINITIONS—YIELD THE RIGHT–OF–WAY

Analysis of Instructions

Westlaw Electronic Research

See Westlaw Electronic Research Guide preceding the Table of Instructions.

Library References:

C.J.S. Motor Vehicles § 530.
West's Key No. Digests, Automobiles ⚫246.

177

14.01 [1978 Revision] Definitions—Yield the Right-of–Way—General Comment

In its report to the Supreme Court, the Committee recommended that instructions submit only "ultimate issues" without evidentiary detail. Failure to yield the right-of-way is such an issue, but submitting this issue without explanation might be inadequate. When such issues as following too closely or failing to signal are submitted, the jurors know what is meant and a further explanation would be superfluous. But jurors are not apt to understand which party has the duty to yield in every situation. In addition to the common law duty to yield the right-of-way, the statutes dictate which party must yield in a variety of situations. For this reason a number of definitions have been prepared which explain to the jury the circumstances under which the duty to yield exists.

These definitions are to be used when and only when there is evidence to show that the defined duty to yield existed and the failure to yield caused damage.

Failure to yield the statutory right-of-way may be negligence per se if there is no evidence of valid excuse for the violations. *Lay v. McGrane,* 331 S.W.2d 592 (Mo.1960); *MacArthur v. Gendron,* 312 S.W.2d 146 (Mo.App.1958).

These instructions define the phrase "failure to yield the right-of-way." As such, the instruction which submits "failure to yield the right-of-way" (verdict director or contributory negligence instruction) and the definition instruction, which supplements that instruction, speak of the same party, i.e., the party who is in the less favored position at the intersection. Any negligence of the party asserting the right-of-way should be submitted in the instruction directed to the conduct of that party. This would usually be submitted as failure to keep a careful lookout (MAI 17.05), failure to act after danger of collision apparent (MAI 17.04) or the like. The failure of the favored party to exercise the highest degree of care in asserting the right-of-way does not relieve the less favored party from his duty to yield the right-of-way. In *Haymes v. Swan,* 413 S.W.2d 319, 325 (Mo.App.1967) the court said:

Whether or not plaintiff [the favored party] was contributorily negligent in entering the intersection at a time when it appeared or should have appeared to a reasonably prudent person that to do so would probably result in an accident would not obviate the primary duty of defendant to permit plaintiff, first into the intersection, to pass in safety.

Library References:

C.J.S. Motor Vehicles § 530.
West's Key No. Digests, Automobiles ⟜246.

Notes of Decisions

In general   1
Affirmative defense   2
Definition mandatory   3
Proximate cause   4

_____

1.   In general

Where plaintiff's verdict director submitted defendant's failure to keep a lookout it was error to give MAI 14.02 defining right-of-way, an element not applicable to the issues. Corbin v. Wennerberg, 459 S.W.2d 505[1, 8] (Mo.App.1970).

MAI 14.02 properly modified to define right-of-way according to Maritime Law. Wiesemann v. Pavlat, 413 S.W.2d 23[2, 10] (Mo.App.1967).

Where evidence differed about which vehicle first reached intersection, both MAI 14.02 and 14.03 were properly used for defining right-of-way at uncontrolled intersection, as declared by Notes on Use. Kratzer v. King, 401 S.W.2d 405[2] (Mo.1966).

2.   Affirmative defense

Pedestrian v. Motorist, contributory negligence instruction need not define "place of safety" or "immediate path." Frantz v. State Farm Mut. Auto. Ins. Co., 526 S.W.2d 345[3, 5] (Mo.App.1975).

3.   Definition mandatory

Giving verdict-directing instruction on failure to yield right-of-way without an MAI definition was reversible error. Jensen v. Walker, 496 S.W.2d 317[1] (Mo.App.1973).

4.   Proximate cause

Verdict director erroneously submitted that driver failed to yield the right-of-way when entering highway from private roadway when evidence failed to show other car was then so close as to create an immediate hazard. (§ 304.351(5)). Cope v. Thompson, 534 S.W.2d 641[6] (Mo.App.1976).

14.02 [1978 Revision] Definition—Yield the Right-of-Way—Vehicle Entering Intersection After Another Vehicle

The phrase "yield the right-of-way" as used in this [these] instruction[s] means a driver is required to yield to another vehicle which enters the intersection first.

Notes on Use (1978 Revision)

This definition is intended for use where there is a collision at intersecting highways and there are no traffic controls at the intersection. The definition does not apply where the accident occurs at the intersection of a highway with a private road, alley, or driveway. For such a case use Yield the Right-of-Way Definition MAI 14.06.

This definition will also be appropriate where city ordinances establish a duty to yield the right-of-way at intersecting streets or to define the common law duty to yield the right-of-way.

Committee Comment (1990 Revision)

This definition is based on § 304.351.1, RSMo. This section of the statute specifically covers the duty to yield the right-of-way to a vehicle which has already entered the intersection. The common law establishes a similar duty to yield the right-of-way. See *Wilson v. Toliver*, 365 Mo. 640, 285 S.W.2d 575 (1955).

See General Comment at MAI 14.01.

Library References:

C.J.S. Motor Vehicles § 530.
West's Key No. Digests, Automobiles ⇒246.

Notes of Decisions

In general   1
Modification   2

_____

1. In general

Trial court properly gave MAI 14.02 in action arising out of motor vehicle accident at uncontrolled intersection in which stalled motor vehicle was struck by truck, whether or not the stalled vehicle was planning to make a left turn; truck had absolute duty to yield right-of-way because motor vehicle had already entered intersection, duty was not obviated by truck driver's antecedent negligence in approaching at too high of speed, and neither of streets which formed intersection was a through highway. Krenski v. Aubuchon, 841 S.W.2d 721 (Mo.App.1992).

MAI 14.02 is for the statutory right-of-way on public roads, not a private parking lot; in that latter case common law right-of-way is based on duty of reasonable care, not the highest degree of care. Doolin v. Swain, 524 S.W.2d 877[3–5] (Mo. banc 1975).

Error to give MAI 14.02 in case where plaintiff was struck at intersection controlled by a flashing red light. Riley v. Bi–State Transit System, 459 S.W.2d 753[3, 4] (Mo. App.1970).

Where plaintiff's verdict director submitted defendant's failure to keep a lookout it was error to give MAI 14.02 defining right-of-way, an element not applicable to the issues. Corbin v. Wennerberg, 459 S.W.2d 505[1, 8] (Mo.App.1970).

Modified MAI 28.01 [Now 32.01]–14.02 proper as a defensive failure to yield right-of-way instruction against MAI 17.01 (violation of traffic signal) where there was evidence

traffic signals were not working. Jefferson v. Biggar, 416 S.W.2d 933[4–6] (Mo.1967).

Where evidence differed about which vehicle first reached intersection, both MAI 14.02 and 14.03 were properly used for defining right-of-way at uncontrolled intersection, as declared by Notes on Use. Kratzer v. King, 401 S.W.2d 405[2] (Mo.1966).

2. Modification

MAI 14.02 properly modified to define right-of-way according to Maritime Law. Wiesemann v. Pavlat, 413 S.W.2d 23[2, 10] (Mo.App.1967).

14.03 [1978 Revision] Definition—Yield the Right-of-Way—Vehicle on the Left

The phrase "yield the right-of-way" as used in this [these] instruction[s] means the driver on the left is required to yield if both vehicles reach the intersection at approximately the same time.

Notes on Use (1978 Revision)

This definition is intended for use where there is a collision at intersecting highways and there are no traffic controls at the intersection. The definition does not apply where the accident occurs at the intersection of a highway with a private road, alley, or driveway. For such a case use Yield the Right-of-Way Definition MAI 14.06.

This definition will also be appropriate where city ordinances establish the same duty to yield the right-of-way at intersecting streets.

Committee Comment (1990 Revision)

The definition is based on § 304.351.2, RSMo. See *Klee v. Bryan,* 346 S.W.2d 695 (Mo.App.1961), where the right-of-way was established by ordinance. The court instructed that a violation was negligence per se. See also *Knight v. Richey,* 363 Mo. 293, 250 S.W.2d 972 (1952), where plaintiff instructed on defendant's failure to yield to plaintiff's vehicle which was on the right as required by statute. Plaintiff also instructed on defendant's failure to yield the common law right-of-way to plaintiff who had entered the intersection first.

See also General Comment at MAI 14.01.

Library References:

C.J.S. Motor Vehicles § 530.
West's Key No. Digests, Automobiles ⊚246.

Notes of Decisions

1. In general

Instruction was inappropriate where defendant collided with rear of plaintiff's vehicle after plaintiff had already completed left turn. McLeod v. Beloate, 891 S.W.2d 476 (Mo. App. W.D.,1994).

MAI 14.03 is the proper instruction for collision occurring in a four-way stop intersection. McCarthy v. Cullom, 634 S.W.2d 494[2] (Mo.App.1982).

Where evidence differed about which vehicle first reached intersection, both MAI 14.02 and 14.03 were properly used for defining right-of-way at uncontrolled intersection, as declared by Notes on Use. Kratzer v. King, 401 S.W.2d 405[2] (Mo.1966).

14.04 [1978 Revision] Definition—Yield the Right-of-Way—Vehicle Making Left Turn at Intersection

The phrase "yield the right-of-way" as used in this [these] instruction[s] means a driver attempting to make a left turn is required to yield when another vehicle is approaching from the opposite direction and is within the intersection or is so close to the intersection that it is an immediate hazard.

Notes on Use (1978 Revision)

Making a left turn into an alley, private road or driveway is covered by Yield the Right-of-Way definition, MAI 14.07.

Committee Comment (1996 Revision)

This definition is based on § 304.351.3, RSMo. This section was the basis of an instruction in *MacArthur v. Gendron,* 312 S.W.2d 146 (Mo.App.1958), involving a collision at the intersection of Clemens Avenue and Skinker Boulevard in St. Louis. As there was no evidence of any circumstances excusing the violation of the statute, the court held proper an instruction making such violation negligence per se.

See also *Anthony v. Jennings,* 368 S.W.2d 533 (Mo.App.1963).

See also General Comment at MAI 14.01.

Library References:

C.J.S. Motor Vehicles § 530.
West's Key No. Digests, Automobiles ⛛246.

Notes of Decisions

In general   1
Harmless error   2

_____

1. In general

Error to give defensive right-of-way instruction where that is not an issue in the case. Will v. Gilliam, 439 S.W.2d 498[1–3] (Mo. 1969).

2. Harmless error

Where collision occurred at a driveway—rather than at a street intersection—the proper right-of-way definition was MAI 14.07 and it was error to give MAI 14.04. The error however, was beneficial to defendant and harmless. Griggs v. Riley, 489 S.W.2d 469[6, 7] (Mo.App.1972).

14.05 [1978 Revision] Definition—Yield the Right-of-Way—Vehicle Entering at Stop Sign or Yield Sign

The phrase "yield the right-of-way" as used in this [these] instruction[s] means a driver is required to yield at the [stop sign] [yield sign] [1] if the other vehicle is within the intersection or is so close to the intersection that it is an immediate hazard.

Notes on Use (1978 Revision)

1. Select the appropriate term.

The duty to yield the right-of-way at a stop sign or yield sign is to be distinguished from the duty to yield the right-of-way when entering a highway from an alley, private road, or driveway. The latter is covered by Yield the Right-of-Way definition, MAI 14.06.

Committee Comment (1996 Revision)

This definition is based on § 304.351.4, RSMo. The definition does not make reference to a through highway because the present statute establishes the duty to yield the right-of-way at a stop sign or a yield sign. The definition does not include the statutory reference to stopping because the duty is to yield, and a reference to stopping is unnecessary.

This definition is also appropriate where ordinances impose the same duty to yield the right-of-way.

See also General Comment at MAI 14.01.

Library References:

C.J.S. Motor Vehicles § 530.
West's Key No. Digests, Automobiles ⬦246.

Notes of Decisions

1. In general

In negligence action arising from two-vehicle collision, instruction on failure to yield right-of-way at stop sign was supported by evidence that defendant was still stopped at stop sign when other vehicle was only 20 feet from intersection, that other vehicle was traveling with flow of traffic in 35 mile-per-hour zone, and that defendant had unobstructed view of 1,125 feet in direction from which other vehicle approached. Hudson v. Whiteside, 34 S.W.3d 420 (Mo.App.2000).

MAI 14.02 is for the statutory right-of-way on public roads, not a private parking lot; in that latter case common law right-of-way is based on duty of reasonable care, not the highest degree of care. Doolin v. Swain, 524 S.W.2d 877[3–5] (Mo. banc 1975).

Right-of-way MAI 14.06, rather than MAI 14.05, should be used to define right-of-way when entering highway from a private road, but evidence must show it was in fact a private road. McDowell v. Mohn, 426 S.W.2d 95[2] (Mo.1968).

Contributory negligence instruction defining right-of-way by MAI 14.05 was proper where plaintiff drove into through highway, creating an immediate hazard. Todd v. Presley, 413 S.W.2d 173[5] (Mo.1967).

14.06 [1978 Revision] Definition—Yield the Right-of-Way—Vehicle Entering From an Alley or Driveway

The phrase "yield the right-of-way" as used in this [these] instruction[s] means a driver entering the roadway from an [alley] [private road] [driveway] [1] is required to yield to another vehicle approaching on the highway.

Notes on Use (1978 Revision)

1. Select the appropriate term.

Committee Comment (1996 Revision)

This definition is based on § 304.351.5, RSMo.

Failure to yield the right-of-way was offered in a contributory negligence (now comparative fault) instruction in *Hulse v. Herren,* 357 S.W.2d 154 (Mo.1962).

A city ordinance with similar provisions was held applicable and admissible in *Kenney v. J.A. Folger & Company,* 192 S.W.2d 73 (Mo.App. 1946).

See also General Comment at MAI 14.01.

Library References:

C.J.S. Motor Vehicles § 530.
West's Key No. Digests, Automobiles ⟜246.

Notes of Decisions

In general   1
Proximate cause   2

_____

1. In general

Right-of-way MAI 14.06, rather than MAI 14.05, should be used to define right-of-way when entering highway from a private road, but evidence must show it was in fact a private road. McDowell v. Mohn, 426 S.W.2d 95[2] (Mo.1968).

2. Proximate cause

Absence of "immediate hazard" language in MAI 14.06 requiring that a driver of a vehicle entering a highway from a private road yield right-of-way to a vehicle on a highway to be entered was clearly intended by the legislature. Karashin v. Haggard Hauling & Rigging, Inc., 653 S.W.2d 203 (Mo. banc 1983); overruling Cope v. Thompson, 534 S.W.2d 641 (Mo.App.1976); and Taylor v. Schneider, 370 S.W.2d 725 (Mo. App.1963).

14.07 [1978 Revision] Definition—Yield the Right-of-Way—Making Left Turn Into Alley or Driveway

The phrase "yield the right-of-way" as used in this [these] instruction[s] means a driver attempting to make a left turn into an [alley] [private road] [driveway] [1] is required to yield when another vehicle is approaching from the opposite direction and the making of the left turn would create a traffic hazard.

Notes on Use (1978 Revision)

1. Select the appropriate term.

Committee Comment (1996 Revision)

This definition is based on § 304.351.6, RSMo 1986.

See *Bowman v. Ryan,* 343 S.W.2d 613 (Mo.App.1961); *Steele v. Goosen,* 329 S.W.2d 703 (Mo.1959). Compare *Wilkins v. Stuecken,* 359 Mo. 1047, 225 S.W.2d 131 (1949), where such a turn made defendant negligent as a matter of law.

See also General Comment at MAI 14.01.

Library References:

C.J.S. Motor Vehicles § 530.
West's Key No. Digests, Automobiles ⚷246.

Notes of Decisions

1. Harmless error

Where collision occurred at a driveway—rather than at a street intersection—the proper right-of-way definition was MAI 14.07 and it was error to give MAI 14.04. The error, however, was beneficial to defendant and harmless. Griggs v. Riley, 489 S.W.2d 469[6, 7] (Mo.App.1972).

14.08 [1978 New] Definition—Yield the Right-of-Way—Vehicle on the Left Combined With Vehicle Entering Intersection After Another Vehicle

The phrase "yield the right-of-way" as used in these instructions means that if both vehicles reach the intersection at approximately the same time, the driver on the left is required to yield but if both vehicles do not reach the intersection at approximately the same time, then a driver is required to yield to another vehicle which enters the intersection first.

Notes on Use (1978 New)

This definition is intended for use where both parties claim the other party failed to yield the right-of-way. This instruction covers the situation where the evidence supports the claim of the vehicle on the left that he reached the intersection first and the evidence also supports the claim of the vehicle on the right that both vehicles reached the intersection at approximately the same time. If both parties claim the other party failed to yield the right-of-way under some other combination of definitions contained in Chapter 14.00, the appropriate definitions should be combined in a single definition instruction in a manner similar to this instruction.

Library References:

C.J.S. Motor Vehicles § 530.
West's Key No. Digests, Automobiles ⚷246.

14.09 (1990 New) Definition—Yield the Right-of-Way—Special Pedestrian Control Signals

The phrase "yield the right-of-way" as used in this [these] instruction[s] means a driver is required to yield to a pedestrian crossing the roadway facing a special pedestrian control signal exhibiting the word "walk" at the time the pedestrian entered the roadway.

Notes on Use (1990 New)

This definition is intended for use only when there is a collision with a pedestrian where there are pedestrian-control signals.

Committee Comment (1990 New)

This definition is based on § 304.291 RSMo.

Where an intersection or other location is not controlled by special pedestrian-control signals, other statutes or ordinances governing pedestrian right-of-way may be applicable. For example, see § 304.281 RSMo. An appropriate Not-in-MAI instruction may be drafted and used in accordance with another applicable statute or ordinance governing "right-of-way" in other situations.

See also General Comment at MAI 14.01.

Library References:

C.J.S. Motor Vehicles § 530.
West's Key No. Digests, Automobiles ⬫246.

15.00

DEFINITIONS—WILL CONTEST

Analysis of Instructions

Westlaw Electronic Research

See Westlaw Electronic Research Guide preceding the Table of Instructions.

Library References:

C.J.S. Wills § 468.
West's Key No. Digests, Wills ⚖➤328.

191

15.01   [1969 New] Definition—Will Contest—Sound and Disposing Mind and Memory

The phrase "sound and disposing mind and memory" as used in this [these] instruction[s] means that when a person signed his [will] [codicil] [1] he:

First, was able to understand the ordinary affairs of life, and

Second, was able to understand the nature and extent of his property, and

Third, was able to know the persons who were the natural objects of his bounty, and

Fourth, could intelligently weigh and appreciate his natural obligations to those persons.

Notes on Use (1978 New)

1. Select the appropriate term.

When the phrase "sound and disposing mind and memory" is used, it must be defined. See MAI 31.06.

Where the phrase is used in only one instruction, this definition may be added to the instruction using the phrase. If it is used in more than one instruction, the definition should be given as a separate instruction.

Committee Comment (1969 New)

In *Strahl v. Turner,* 310 S.W.2d 833, 838 (Mo.1958), the court quoted *Hardy v. Barbour,* 304 S.W.2d 21, 34 (Mo.1957), which stated:

... This court recently restated the time honored general rule as to testamentary capacity in this way: "A testator with mind enough to understand the ordinary affairs of life, the kind and extent of his property, who are the natural objects of his bounty and that he is giving property to persons mentioned in the will in the manner therein stated, is capable of making a will under the law of this state."

In *Sturm v. Routh,* 373 S.W.2d 922, 928 (Mo.1964) the court said:

It has long been the rule in this state that "[t]o have a mind and memory enough to make a will, testator should be able at the time to understand the ordinary affairs of life, the value and extent of his property, the number and names of the persons who were the natural objects of his bounty, their deserts with reference to their conduct and treatment of him, their capacity and necessities. He should have active memory enough to retain all these facts in his mind, without the aid of others, long enough to have his will made . . . ."

Library References:

C.J.S. Wills § 471.
West's Key No. Digests, Wills ⊜330.

Notes of Decisions

In general 1
Burden of proof 2

_____

1. In general

Since the purpose of MAI is to submit fact issues accurately and concisely, a rambling, argumentative pre-MAI-type defense instruction in a will contest was properly refused. Barnes v. Marshall, 467 S.W.2d 70[10–11] (Mo.1971).

In a will contest it was error to put burden of proof on contestant to show decedent was of unsound mind; that burden rests on proponents throughout the trial. Brug v. Manufacturers Bank & Trust Co., 461 S.W.2d 269[8] (Mo. banc 1970).

Use of a pre-MAI definition of "sound and disposing memory" which used the name of the testatrix instead of "a person" in the first paragraph was not prejudicial error. Arterburn v. Meadows, 451 S.W.2d 85[1] (Mo. 1970).

2. Burden of proof

Contestants' wordy instruction on testamentary capacity which failed to submit ultimate issue was properly refused. Earney v. Clay, 462 S.W.2d 672[2] (Mo.1971).

15.02 [Withdrawn 1995] Definition—Will Contest—Fraud Affecting Validity of Will

(This instruction, Notes on Use, and Committee Comment thereto are withdrawn. The substance of this instruction has been incorporated directly into MAI 31.21 Verdict Directing—Partial Invalidity of Will Due to Fraud and MAI 32.17 Affirmative Defenses—Will Contest—Fraud Invalidating Will without use of the term "fraud". Definition of the term "fraud" is no longer necessary in will contest cases.)

Library References:

C.J.S. Wills § 473.
West's Key No. Digests, Wills ⟳332.

15.03 [1995 Revision] Definition—Will Contest—Undue Influence

The phrase "undue influence" as used in this [these] instruction[s] means such influence as destroys the free choice of the person making the [will] [codicil][1] [contested part of the will] [2].

Notes on Use (1995 Revision)

1. Select the appropriate term.

2. This alternative is for use where only a part of the will is contested under § 473.081. See MAI 31.21, 31.22 and verdict form 36.17(B).

When the phrase "undue influence" is used, it must be defined. For example, see MAI 31.22 and 32.18.

Where the phrase is used in only one instruction, this definition may be added to the instruction using the phrase. If it is used in more than one instruction, the definition should be given as a separate instruction.

Library References:

C.J.S. Wills § 473.
West's Key No. Digests, Wills ⊕332.

Notes of Decisions

1. In general

MAI 15.03 is a will contest instruction and does not mandatorily apply to a case for discovery of assets. Estate of Gross v. Gross, 840 S.W.2d 253 (Mo.App.1992).

16.00

DEFINITIONS—MISCELLANEOUS

Analysis of Instructions

Westlaw Electronic Research

See Westlaw Electronic Research Guide preceding the Table of Instructions.

Library References:

C.J.S. Damages § 186; Ejectment § 118; Insane Persons § 49, 54, 59–64, 66–70; Malicious Prosecution or Wrongful Litigation § 90.

West's Key No. Digests, Damages ☞217; Ejectment ☞110; Malicious Prosecution ☞72; Mental Health ☞41.

16.01 [1996 Withdrawn] Definition—Legal Malice

(This instruction, its Notes on Use and Committee Comment are withdrawn. See MAI 16.01(1) for the definition of "malice in law" and MAI 16.01(2) for the definition of "legal malice".)

Library References:

C.J.S. Malicious Prosecution or Wrongful Litigation § 92.
West's Key No. Digests, Malicious Prosecution ⬤⧤72(4).

Notes of Decisions

In general 1
Malicious prosecution 2

1. In general

Jury instruction that malice does not mean hatred, spite or ill-will, as commonly understood, but means the doing of a wrongful act intentionally without just cause or excuse, did not correctly state the law with regard to the submission of punitive damages in intentional tort case; bad motive or reckless disregard for rights of others is required. Burnett v. Griffith, 769 S.W.2d 780, 788–89 (Mo. banc 1989).

The submission of two different definitions of malice in punitive damages instructions, one for battery and one for malicious prosecution, did not mislead or confuse the jury; the instructions were packaged and it was clear from them that different definitions applied. Chapman v. Duraski, 721 S.W.2d 184[5] (Mo.App.1986).

Where court gave MAI 16.01 defining malice, defendant was not entitled to a converse definition. Duensing v. Huscher, 431 S.W.2d 169[5] (Mo.1968).

2. Malicious prosecution

Where defendant's instruction defining legal but not actual malice was submitted to jury to be used in awarding punitive damages for both assault and malicious prosecution claims, it was error because proper standard for awarding punitive damages in a malicious prosecution case arising out of a criminal proceeding is actual malice. Schoor v. Wilson, 731 S.W.2d 308[9] (Mo. App.1987).

MAI 16.01, a definition of malice in law, is proper definition of malice in a civil malicious prosecution action. Proctor v. Stevens Employment Services, Inc., 712 S.W.2d 684[5] (Mo. banc 1986).

MAI 16.01, a definition of malice in law, does not adequately express degree of culpability required for an award of punitive damages in a malicious prosecution case arising from a civil proceeding. Instead, the jury must be instructed that in order to award punitive damages, "the proceedings must have been initiated or continued primarily for a purpose other than that of securing the proper adjudication of the claim on which they are based." Proctor v. Stevens Employment Services, Inc., 712 S.W.2d 684[6, 7] (Mo. banc 1986).

MAI 16.01 improperly defines the element of malice in a malicious prosecution action arising from criminal proceedings and does not adequately express the degree of culpability required for punitive damages. Sanders v. Daniel Intern. Corp., 682 S.W.2d 803[6–11] (Mo. banc 1984).

16.01(1) [1996 New] Definition—Malice in Law—Liability for Actual Damages in Malicious Prosecution Cases Arising Out of Civil Actions

The term "maliciously" as used in this [these] instruction[s] means intentionally doing a wrongful act without just cause or excuse. It does not necessarily mean hatred, spite or ill will.

Notes on Use (1996 New)

This instruction is for use only in defining "maliciously" as used in MAI 23.07 when submitting the requisite elements for liability for actual damages for malicious prosecution based on the filing of a civil action. See MAI 16.01(2) for the definition of "maliciously" in determining liability for actual damages for malicious prosecution for the instigation of a criminal proceeding. See MAI 10.01 and *Burnett v. Griffith*, 769 S.W.2d 780 (Mo.banc 1989) for submitting punitive damages in a malicious prosecution case.

Where the term is used in only one instruction, this definition may be added to the instruction using the term. If it is used in more than one instruction, the definition may be given as a separate instruction.

Committee Comment (1996 New)

Sanders v. Daniel International Corp., 682 S.W.2d 803 (Mo.banc 1984), held that "malice in law" is insufficient to support either actual or punitive damages in a malicious prosecution case arising out of a criminal prosecution. See also, *Proctor v. Stevens Employment Services, Inc.*, 712 S.W.2d 684 (Mo.banc 1986), which held that "malice in law" is sufficient to support liability for actual damages in a malicious prosecution case arising out of a civil action.

16.01(2)   [1996 New] Definition—Legal Malice—Liability for Actual Damages in Malicious Prosecution Cases Arising Out of Criminal Actions

The term "maliciously" as used in this [these] instruction[s] means [acting intentionally with an evil motive], [or acting with reckless indifference to the rights of others], [or acting primarily for a purpose other than bringing an offender to justice].[1]

Notes on Use (1996 New)

1.   Select the appropriate bracketed phrase or phrases. *Sanders v. Daniel International Corp.*, 682 S.W.2d 803 (Mo.banc 1984) requires this definition for submitting liability for actual damages in a malicious prosecution case arising out of a criminal prosecution.

This instruction is for use only in defining "maliciously" as used in MAI 23.07 when submitting the requisite elements for liability for actual damages for malicious prosecution for the instigation of a criminal judicial proceeding. See MAI 16.01(1) for the definition of "maliciously" in determining liability for actual damages for malicious prosecution based on the filing of a civil action. See MAI 10.01 and *Burnett v. Griffith*, 769 S.W.2d 780 (Mo.banc 1989) for submitting punitive damages in a malicious prosecution case.

Where the term is used in only one instruction, this definition may be added to the instruction using the term. If it is used in more than one instruction, the definition may be given as a separate instruction.

Committee Comment (1996 New)

Sanders v. Daniel International Corp., 682 S.W.2d 803 (Mo.banc 1984), held that "malice in law" is insufficient to support either actual or punitive damages in a malicious prosecution case arising out of a criminal prosecution. See also, *Proctor v. Stevens Employment Services, Inc.*, 712 S.W.2d 684 (Mo.banc 1986), which held that "malice in law" is sufficient to support liability for actual damages in a malicious prosecution case arising out of a civil action.

Library References:

C.J.S. Malicious Prosecution or Wrongful Litigation § 92.
West's Key No. Digests, Malicious Prosecution ☞72(4).

16.02 [1978 Revision] Definition—Fair Market Value

The phrase "fair market value" as used in this [these] instruction[s] means the price which the property in question would bring when offered for sale by one willing but not obliged to sell it, and when bought by one willing or desirous to purchase it but who is not compelled to do so.

In determining fair market value you should take into consideration all the uses to which the property may best be applied or for which it is best adapted, under existing conditions and under conditions to be reasonably expected in the near future.

Notes on Use (1978 New)

When the phrase "fair market value" is used, it must be defined. In an eminent domain case use both paragraphs of the above definition. See MAI 9.01 and 9.02. In other types of cases involving the fair market value of personal property, use only the first paragraph of the above definition. See MAI 4.02, 4.10 and 4.17.

Where the phrase is used in only one instruction, this definition may be added to the instruction using the phrase. If it is used in more than one instruction, the definition should be given as a separate instruction.

Committee Comment (1969 New)

See *City of St. Louis v. Vasquez,* 341 S.W.2d 839, 843 (Mo.1960) and *State ex rel. Board of Regents v. Moriarty,* 361 S.W.2d 133 (Mo.App. 1962).

See also MAI 9.02 and 31.05.

Library References:
C.J.S. Damages § 186; Eminent Domain § 273(6), 310; Evidence § 227, 235, 238.
West's Key No. Digests, Damages ☞217; Eminent Domain ☞222(4); Evidence ☞113.

Notes of Decisions

In general 1
Eminent domain 3
Mandatory 2

_____

1. In general

Testimony by expert of 20% reduction in automobile's value due to its unknown mileage, along with evidence of numerous repairs, was sufficient to establish automobile's fair market value when purchasers discovered problems with automobile, for purposes of purchasers' damages for breach of warranty against automobile manufacturer; damage instruction for breach of warranty was not required to elaborate on what aspect of product did not conform. Carpenter v. Chrysler Corporation, 853 S.W.2d 346 (Mo.App.1993).

Definition of "Fair Market Value" approved. Peterson v. Continental Boiler Works, Inc., 783 S.W.2d 896 (Mo. banc 1990).

MAI 16.02 does not give jury "a roving commission." DeArmon v. City of St. Louis, 525 S.W.2d 795[6] (Mo.App.1975).

Where plaintiffs granted powerline easement for defendant's promise to pay stated amount for each pole installed it was error to give plaintiffs' not-in-MAI instructions authorizing recovery for difference between before and after values, since plaintiffs' recovery was limited to breach of defendant's promise to pay agreed amount. Shelton v. M & A Elec. Power Co-op., 451 S.W.2d 375[1, 6] (Mo.App.1970).

Where there was no evidence of reasonable market value of cemetery, court erred in giving MAI 9.02 and 15.02 [Now 16.02], and should have submitted a not-in-MAI damage instruction drafted on the capitalization method. State ex rel. State Hwy. Com'n v. Mount Moriah Cemetery Ass'n, 434 S.W.2d 470[2] (Mo.1968).

2. Mandatory

Property damage instruction based on MAI 4.02, which did not define "fair market value", did not prejudice defendant and, thus, was harmless error; damage award showed that jury based its award on the cost of repairing or restoring the property plus the compensation for the lack of use, rather than any decrease in the fair market value, of plaintiffs' property. Farley v. Wappapello Foods, Inc., 959 S.W.2d 888, 1997 WL 806538 (Mo.App. S.D.1997).

Giving a modified MAI 4.02 without definition of fair market value (MAI 16.02) was a roving commission and plain error. Floyd v. Brenner, 542 S.W.2d 325[6, 7] (Mo.App. 1976).

3. Eminent domain

Trial court properly gave MAI instructions 16.02 and 9.02 on market value in eminent domain proceeding and properly refused landowner's proffered instruction that jurors were to assume that the condemnor would make the fullest use of its right-of-way and use it in a manner as injurious to landowner's remaining rights as would be permitted. City of Kansas City v. Habelitz, 857 S.W.2d 299 (Mo.App.1993).

16.03 [1978 New] Definition—Good Faith in Ejectment

The phrase "good faith" as used in this [these] instruction[s] means the absence of any intention to defraud or take unfair advantage of anyone else who might have a better right than defendant to possession of the premises.

Notes on Use (1978 New)

When the phrase "good faith" is used in MAI 27.04 in an ejectment case, it must be defined. Where the phrase is used in only one instruction, this definition may be added to the instruction using the term. If it is used in more than one instruction, the definition should be given as a separate instruction.

Committee Comment (1978 New)

This definition of the phrase "good faith" conforms to the statutory requirement of good faith in constructing improvements for which a defendant may recover in an ejectment case. Before using this definition in other than an ejectment case, the substantive law should be checked to determine its accuracy in the contemplated use.

Library References:

C.J.S. Ejectment § 118.
West's Key No. Digests, Ejectment ⚯110.

16.04 [1980 New] Definition—Substantial Performance

The phrase "substantially performed" as used in this [these] instruction[s] means performance of all important parts of the contract with only slight variations.

Notes on Use (1996 Revision)

Where the phrase "substantially performed" is used, it must be defined. For example, see MAI 26.07.

Where the phrase is used in only one instruction, this definition may be added to the instruction using the term. If it is used in more than one instruction, the definition should be given as a separate instruction.

Committee Comment (1980 New)

See *Boteler v. Roy*, 40 Mo.App. 234 (1890); *Cross v. Robinson*, 281 S.W.2d 22 (Mo.App.1955); and *McAlpine Co. v. Graham*, 320 S.W.2d 951 (Mo.App.1959).

Library References:

C.J.S. Contracts § 589, 800.
West's Key No. Digests, Contracts ⟺293, 353(8).

Notes of Decisions

1. In general

In compliance with Notes on Use, the phrase "substantially performed" must be defined, but in suit based on bank's unauthorized payment on checking account proceeds, trial court's omission of the definition did not mislead the jury. Smith v. American Bank & Trust Co., 639 S.W.2d 169[11–13] (Mo.App.1982).

16.05 [1996 Revision] Definition—Malicious Prosecution—Reasonable Grounds—Criminal Action

The phrase "reasonable grounds" as used in this [these] instruction[s] means the existence of facts which would cause an ordinarily careful person to believe plaintiff (*state the name*) was guilty of the offense charged.

Committee Comment (1996 Revision)

The six elements necessary to make a submissible case for malicious prosecution have been: (1) the commencement of a prosecution against plaintiff; (2) its legal causation by defendant; (3) its termination in favor of plaintiff; (4) the absence of probable cause therefor; (5) the presence of malice; and (6) damage to plaintiff therefrom. *Hoene v. Associated Dry Goods Corp.*, 487 S.W.2d 479, 483 (Mo.1972).

Probable cause for the initiation of a criminal prosecution "is reasonable cause and may be defined as the existence of such a state of facts as would warrant an ordinarily cautious and prudent man in the belief that the accused was guilty of the offense charged." *Higgins v. Knickmeyer–Fleer Realty & Inv. Co.*, 335 Mo. 1010, 1026, 74 S.W.2d 805, 813 (1934); *Haswell v. Liberty Mut. Ins. Co.*, 557 S.W.2d 628, 633 (Mo. banc 1977).

See MAI 23.07 and 16.01(2).

Library References:

C.J.S. Malicious Prosecution or Wrongful Litigation § 90.
West's Key No. Digests, Malicious Prosecution ☞72.

Notes of Decisions

1. In general

Instruction that submits affirmative defense of justification for arrest with less certainty than belief misstates premise of defense; instruction that dilutes that belief by "may have committed" or justifies arrest by suspicion of guilt does not satisfy requirement of probable cause. Palcher v. J.C. Nichols Co., 783 S.W.2d 166 (Mo.App.1990).

16.06 [1996 Revision] Definition—Malicious Prosecution—Reasonable Grounds—Civil Action

The phrase "reasonable grounds" as used in this [these] instruction[s] means that under the circumstances an ordinarily careful person after having made a reasonable inquiry would have believed the facts alleged and that the judicial proceeding was valid.

Committee Comment (1996 Revision)

In *Haswell v. Liberty Mutual Ins. Co.*, 557 S.W.2d 628, 633 (Mo. banc 1977), the Court stated:

> However, guilt or innocence of a criminal offense is not involved in a civil case and for that reason the test of probable cause for initiation of a civil action has been stated somewhat differently.... Thus, it can be said that probable cause for initiating a civil action consists of a belief in the facts alleged, based on sufficient circumstances to reasonably induce such belief by a person of ordinary prudence in the same situation, plus a reasonable belief by such person that under such facts the claim may be valid under the applicable law.

See Hughes v. Aetna Ins. Co., 261 S.W.2d 942 (Mo.1953); *Woods v. Standard Personal Loan Plan, Inc.*, 420 S.W.2d 380 (Mo.App.1967); *Young v. Jack Boring's, Inc.*, 540 S.W.2d 887 (Mo.App.1976); *Restatement (Second) of Torts* § 675 (1977).

See MAI 23.07 and 16.01(1).

Library References:

C.J.S. Malicious Prosecution or Wrongful Litigation § 90.
West's Key No. Digests, Malicious Prosecution ⟶72.

Notes of Decisions

1. In general

"Probable cause" to initiate criminal proceeding sufficient to rebut a claim of malicious prosecution is reasonable grounds for suspicion, supported by circumstances and evidence sufficiently strong to warrant a cautious man in his belief that the person accused is guilty of offense charged. Thompson v. Wal–Mart Stores, Inc., 890 S.W.2d 780 (Mo.App. W.D.,1995).

Employer had probable cause to initiate criminal proceedings against employee for stealing and, thus, was not liable for malicious prosecution where videotape showed employee removing currency from cash register, hiding it and surreptitiously placing it in his pocket, and there was no indication that employee returned the money, or change for the money, to the register. Thompson v. Wal–Mart Stores, Inc., 890 S.W.2d 780 (Mo. App. W.D.,1995).

16.07 [1983 New] Definition—Mental Illness—Commitment for Mental Illness

The phrase "mentally ill" or "mental illness" as used in this [these] instruction[s] means a state of impaired mental processes which distorts the respondent's capacity to recognize reality and interferes with his ability to reason, understand or exercise conscious control over his actions. [(State the condition excluded by § 630.005 RSMo. such as "mental retardation" or "simple intoxication") by itself is not mental illness.] [1]

Notes on Use (1983 New)

1. If there is evidence of both "a mental illness" and one or more of the statutory conditions which are not mental illness standing alone, the bracketed sentence must be added.

When the phrase "mentally ill" or "mental illness" is used, it must be defined.

Where the phrase is used in only one instruction, this definition may be added to the instruction using the phrase. If it is used in more than one instruction, the definition should be given as a separate instruction.

This definition is based on § 630.005, RSMo. The statute also provides that certain conditions, such as mental retardation, simple intoxication or senility, not of an actively psychotic nature, are not mental illness "unless they are accompanied by a mental illness as otherwise defined" in the instruction. If there is evidence of only one of those conditions without evidence of "a mental illness" as defined, there is no submissible case.

Library References:

C.J.S. Insane Persons § 49, 54, 59–64, 66–70.
West's Key No. Digests, Mental Health ⚷41.

16.08   [1992 New] Definition—Inherently Dangerous Activity

The term "inherently dangerous activity" as used in this [these] instructions means an activity that necessarily presents a substantial risk of harm unless adequate precautions are taken. [, but does not include a risk of harm that is not inherent in or a normal part of the work to be performed and that is negligently [1] created solely as a result of the improper manner in which the work under the contract is performed.] [2]

Notes on Use (1992 New)

1. The term "negligent" or "negligence" must be defined. See MAI 11.00.

2. This bracketed phrase may have some application in some situations. If the law and the evidence support the addition of this bracketed phrase, it should be added to the definition at the request of the defendant. See: *Ballinger v. Gascosage Elec. Co-op.*, 788 S.W.2d 506, 511 (Mo. banc 1990); and Restatement (Second) of Torts, § 426.

Committee Comment (1996 New)

See Committee Comment to MAI 31.15.

Library References:

C.J.S. Negligence § 871–878, 880–905.
West's Key No. Digests, Negligence ⟺1720–1747.

PLAINTIFF VERDICT DIRECTING INSTRUCTIONS

17.00

VERDICT DIRECTING—MOTOR VEHICLES

Analysis of Instructions

Westlaw Electronic Research

See Westlaw Electronic Research Guide preceding the Table of Instructions.

Library References:

> C.J.S. Motor Vehicles § 530; Trial § 348.
> West's Key No. Digests, Automobiles ⊙246; Trial ⊙234.

17.01   [1980 Revision] Verdict Directing—Single Negligent Act Submitted

Your verdict must be for plaintiff[1] if you believe:

First, defendant violated the traffic signal, and

Second, defendant was thereby negligent,[2] and

Third, as a direct result of such negligence[2] plaintiff sustained damage.

* [unless you believe plaintiff is not entitled to recover by reason of Instruction Number _____ (*here insert number of affirmative defense instruction*)].

Notes on Use (1996 Revision)

1. In any case involving more than one plaintiff or defendant, any reference to a particular party should include the name of that party, or other descriptive term. Where plaintiff submits against more than one defendant in separate verdict directors, the first line of the verdict director should be modified to indicate the particular defendant covered by this verdict director, i.e.:

Your verdict must be for plaintiff against defendant John Jones if you believe:

If the verdict director is applicable to the plaintiff's claim against more than one defendant, it can be described as follows:

Your verdict must be for plaintiff [against both defendants] [against defendant John Jones and defendant Ace Trucking Lines] if you believe:

2. The terms "negligent" and "negligence" must be defined. See definitions in Chapter 11.00.

* Add if affirmative defense is submitted. This bracketed material should not be used to submit comparative fault.

For modification of verdict directing instructions to submit comparative fault, see MAI 37.01.

Committee Comment (1996 Revision)

Where agency is in issue, see MAI 18.01.

Where suit involves multiple causes of damages, see MAI 19.01.

Where suit is for wrongful death, see MAI 20.01 and 20.02.

Where suit is for loss of services or medical expenses of dependent, see MAI 31.04.

This instruction submits the single act of violating a traffic signal. For other wrongful acts or omissions which may be hypothesized, see MAI 17.03 to 17.21. For submitting multiple negligent acts, see MAI 17.02.

In addition to hypothesizing violation of the signal, the instruction also requires that the jury find that in violating the signal defendant was negligent. Although the violation of a traffic statute or ordinance may be negligence per se (*Rowe v. Kansas City Public Service Co.*, 241 Mo.App. 1225, 1231, 248 S.W.2d 445, 448 (1952)), it is safer to further hypothesize negligence for "Under the circumstances of a particular case there may be a valid excuse for failing to comply with a statutory rule of the road, as where nonobservance of the statute is induced by considerations of safety ... or where compliance is impossible...." *MacArthur v. Gendron*, 312 S.W.2d 146, 150 (Mo.App.1958). See also *Lincoln v. Railway Express Agency, Inc.*, 359 S.W.2d 759, 763 (Mo.1962), where the court approved an instruction telling the jury that if it found a hypothesized traffic violation, such a violation was negligence. See MAI 33.05(2) regarding legal justification for negligence per se, and the Committee Comment to 33.05(2).

Library References:

C.J.S. Motor Vehicles § 530.
West's Key No. Digests, Automobiles ⚖246.

Notes of Decisions

In general 1
Carrier's negligence 11
Changing lanes 6
Defining negligence 2
Deviation 7
Intentional tort 8
Multiple plaintiffs 5
Negating defense 3
Negligence per se 9
Plaintiff's status 4
Rule of the road 10

---

1. In general

Verdict director against mortician and cemetery for negligent burial. Golston v. Lincoln Cemetery, 573 S.W.2d 700[1] (Mo. App.1978).

Where there was evidence that flasher light was not working it was error to submit a finding that plaintiff failed to heed the flasher light; the word "operating" should have been added. Silvey v. Missouri Pac. Ry. Co., 445 S.W.2d 354[12] (Mo.1969).

Where defendant motorist's duty to take evasive action did not arise until danger was apparent, plaintiff should have modified MAI 17.04 instead of using MAI 17.01 which omits elements of apparent danger and defendant's ability to safely avoid collision thereafter. Thompson v. Gray, 415 S.W.2d 299[2–6] (Mo.App.1967).

2. Defining negligence

Where term "negligence" is used it must be defined; failure to do so creates a roving commission. Brewer v. Swift & Co., 451 S.W.2d 131[2] (Mo. banc 1970).

3. Negating defense

Unnecessary inclusion of bracketed clause in MAI 17.01 was a minor deviation and harmless. State Farm Mutual Auto. Ins. Co. v. Jessee, 523 S.W.2d 832[7] (Mo.App. 1975).

Failure of plaintiff's verdict director submitting multiple acts to negate defense of contributory negligence is reversibly erroneous. Trimble v. Sipes, 506 S.W.2d 353[4] (Mo. 1974).

Plaintiff's failure to negate defendant's erroneous affirmative defense instruction was not error. Clark v. Campbell, 492 S.W.2d 7[3] (Mo.App.1973).

Plaintiff's failure to negate defendant's contributory negligence instruction is harmless error where the contributory negligence instruction was not supported by evidence and should not have been given. Corbin v. Wennerberg, 459 S.W.2d 505[2] (Mo.App. 1970).

4. Plaintiff's status

Where passenger's recovery against driver depends on his being a "discovered trespasser", that element must be included in his verdict director. Day v. Mayberry, 421 S.W.2d 34[13] (Mo.App.1967).

5. Multiple plaintiffs

Separate plaintiffs are entitled to give separate verdict directors. Kennedy v. Tallent, 492 S.W.2d 33[5] (Mo.App.1973).

6. Changing lanes

Rule of the road § 304.015(5)(1) concerning 3–lane roads prohibits a change of lanes "until the driver has first ascertained that such movement can be made with safety." Plaintiff properly submitted this by hypothesizing that defendant negligently "moved his cab from his lane of traffic when it was not safe to do so." Furlow v. Laclede Cab Co., 502 S.W.2d 373[5, 6] (Mo.App.1973).

7. Deviation

Modifying plaintiff's verdict-directing stop-sign instruction by substituting "failed to stop" for the prescribed words, "violated the stop-sign" held harmless error. Phelps v. Parker, 569 S.W.2d 22[1–3] (Mo.App.1978).

Omission of "and" between numbered paragraphs was presumptively prejudicial.

Kirkendall v. Townsend, 559 S.W.2d 561 (Mo.App.1977).

Plaintiffs' verdict director, MAI 17.15, omitted the word "negligently" from paragraph Fifth, thereby being a prejudicially erroneous deviation. Epple v. Western Auto Supply Co., 548 S.W.2d 535[15, 16] (Mo. banc 1977).

Omission of "and" between paragraphs of verdict director is error. Wilkerson v. State Farm Ins. Co., 510 S.W.2d 50[8–9] (Mo.App. 1974).

Submitting claims of co-plaintiffs, motorist and passengers, by a single verdict director was error but held harmless where each plaintiff submitted a separate damage instruction and a separate form of verdict instruction. All instructions are read together. Hampton v. Cantrell, 464 S.W.2d 744[2–4] (Mo.App.1971).

MAI 17.02 was not erroneously modified in changing "violated the traffic signal" to read "failed to stop at the stop sign," but it was error to add a detailed description of the stop sign's location. Brittain v. Clark, 462 S.W.2d 153[1, 3] (Mo.App.1970).

Use of "or" between First and Second paragraphs of verdict director is error since that allows the jury to find for plaintiff if it believes either rather than both paragraphs. Quality Dairy Co. v. Openlander, 456 S.W.2d 608[3] (Mo.App.1970).

8. Intentional tort

Where plaintiff's substantive right arose from defendant's deliberately shooting him, it was error to refuse MAI 23.02 (battery, an intentional act) and to give instead modified MAI 17.01 (negligent act). Martin v. Yeoham, 419 S.W.2d 937[6] (Mo.App.1967).

9. Negligence per se

Where plaintiff's verdict director submitted facts constituting negligence per se and did not require a finding defendant was negligent, it was error to give defendant's converse to find for defendant if he was not negligent as submitted in plaintiff's verdict director. Oventrop v. Bi–State Dev. Agency, 521 S.W.2d 488[10] (Mo.App.1975).

Where not-in-MAI verdict-director hypothesized facts constituting violation of fire ordinance it was not necessary to hypothesize negligence. Derboven v. Stockton, 490 S.W.2d 301[18] (Mo.App.1972).

Plaintiff's verdict-directing instruction properly omitted submission of negligence where evidence showed defendant failed to drive as close as practical to right-hand edge of the highway. (§ 304.018.1(1)) Condos v. Associated Transports, Inc., 453 S.W.2d 682[1–5] (Mo.App.1970).

10. Rule of the road

Plaintiff properly submitted that defendant negligently failed to drive in the right-hand lane at less than normal speed (§ 304.015, 5(3)) without negating statutory exceptions. Rooney v. Lloyd Metal Products Co., 458 S.W.2d 561[5–10] (Mo.1970).

Plaintiff properly submitted that defendant negligently drove at less than 40 miles per hour minimum speed (§ 304.010(4)) without negating statutory exception that safety required a slower speed. Rooney v. Lloyd Metal Products Co., 458 S.W.2d 561[12] (Mo.1970).

11. Carrier's negligence

MAI 17.01 modified to submit carrier's negligence in failing to move cargo with reasonable dispatch. Bunge Corp. v. Valley Line Supply & Equip. Co., 480 S.W.2d 859[10] (Mo.1972).

Plaintiff bus passenger properly submitted defendant negligently violated a railroad crossing signal under modified MAI 17.01; that did not submit an illegal act. Myers v. Bi–State Dev. Agency, 567 S.W.2d 638[1–2] (Mo. banc 1978).

17.02 [1980 Revision] Verdict Directing—Multiple Negligent Acts Submitted

Your verdict must be for plaintiff[1] if you believe:

First, either:

    defendant failed to keep a careful lookout, or

    defendant drove at an excessive speed, or

    defendant's automobile was on the wrong side of the road, and

Second, defendant, in any one or more of the respects submitted in paragraph First, was thereby negligent,[2] and

Third, as a direct result of such negligence,[2] plaintiff sustained damage.

* [unless you believe plaintiff is not entitled to recover by reason of Instruction Number _____ (*here insert number of affirmative defense instruction*)].

Notes on Use (1996 Revision)

1. In any case involving more than one plaintiff or defendant, any reference to a particular party should include the name of that party, or other descriptive term. Where plaintiff submits against more than one defendant in separate verdict directors, the first line of the verdict director should be modified to indicate the particular defendant covered by this verdict director, i.e.:

    Your verdict must be for plaintiff against defendant John Jones if you believe:

If the verdict director is applicable to the plaintiff's claim against more than one defendant, it can be described as follows:

    Your verdict must be for plaintiff [against both defendants] [against defendant John Jones and defendant Ace Trucking Lines] if you believe:

2. The terms "negligent" and "negligence" must be defined. See definitions in Chapter 11.00.

This instruction submits three improper acts in the disjunctive. This instruction should be used as the format for any of the specifications of negligence shown separately throughout Chapter 17.00 except where the full verdict directing instruction is shown as in MAI 17.14 through MAI 17.18.

As is the case with all disjunctive submissions, there must be sufficient evidence to support all of the improper acts or the instruction will be erroneous.

* Add if affirmative defense is submitted. This bracketed material should not be used to submit comparative fault.

For modification of verdict directing instructions to submit comparative fault, see MAI 37.01.

Committee Comment (1996 Revision)

Where agency is in issue, see MAI 18.01.

Where suit involves multiple causes of damage, see MAI 19.01.

Where suit is for wrongful death, see MAI 20.01 and 20.02.

Where suit is for loss of services or medical expenses of dependent, see MAI 31.04.

For other acts or omissions which may be hypothesized, see MAI 17.03 through MAI 17.21. For submitting a single negligent act, see MAI 17.01.

See the last paragraph of the Committee Comment following MAI 17.01.

Library References:

C.J.S. Motor Vehicles § 530.
West's Key No. Digests, Automobiles ⊱246.

Notes of Decisions

In general   1
Apparent danger   4
Defining negligence   5
Deviation   3
Modification   2

---

1. In general

Submission of disjunctive charges of general negligence (failure to maintain control) and specific negligence (excessive speed) was error, in that instruction did not confine jury to factual issues but permitted jury to speculate on other omissions in the nature of a roving commission. Hicks v. Graves Truck Lines, Inc., 707 S.W.2d 439[10] (Mo. App.1986).

Verdict director submitting three assignments of negligence erroneous where evidence supported only two submissions. Bunch v. McMillian, 568 S.W.2d 809[1–2] (Mo.App.1978).

Evidence supported each element of verdict director based on failure to yield right-of-way, lookout and excessive speed. Yust v. Link, 569 S.W.2d 236[11] (Mo.App.1978).

Defendant not in error in submitting her counterclaim on MAI 32.01 (drove on the wrong side of the road) since it had not been amended to conform to MAI 17.13, amended (was on the wrong side of the road). Pittock v. Gardner, 530 S.W.2d 217[4–6] (Mo. banc 1975).

Contributory negligence instruction submitting defendant's multiple disjunctive acts must have evidentiary support for each. Saupe v. Kertz, 523 S.W.2d 826[4–5] (Mo. banc 1975).

Each alternative submission must have evidentiary support. Rakestraw v. Norris, 478 S.W.2d 409[4] (Mo.App.1972).

Each of two multiple submissions of negligence must be supported by evidence. Commerford v. Kreitler, 462 S.W.2d 726[1] (Mo.1971).

Error to submit driving on wrong side of the road or failure to keep a lookout where evidence failed to show causal connection between failure to keep a lookout and the collision. Shelton v. Bruner, 449 S.W.2d 673[1, 6] (Mo.App.1969).

Plaintiff bus passenger was injured in a right-angle collision between bus and motor vehicle at intersection controlled by stop lights. Each of plaintiff's verdict directors submitted the same negligence against bus company and motorist: failing to keep a lookout or violating the traffic light. Held erroneous as conflicting. Alfultis v. Bi–State Development Agency, 439 S.W.2d 206[6] (Mo.App.1969).

Error to combine general negligence (driving off road) with specific negligence (failure to keep a lookout). Skiles v. Schlake, 421 S.W.2d 244[4] (Mo.1967).

In disjunctive submissions each element must be supported by evidence. Wolfe v. Harms, 413 S.W.2d 204[1] (Mo.1967).

2. Modification

There is no MAI for the submission of toxic tort negligence. A modification of MAI 17.02 was appropriate for the submission of each of plaintiff's negligence causes of action. Elam v. Alcolac, Inc., 765 S.W.2d 42, 204 (Mo.App.1988).

Where plaintiff submitted failure to use the "highest degree of care" but did not submit that defendant was negligent, error to give defendant's converse based only on defendant's "negligence". Doyle v. Bi–State Dev. Agency, 628 S.W.2d 695[2] (Mo.App.1982).

Plaintiff bus passenger properly submitted defendant negligently violated a railroad crossing signal under modified MAI 17.01; that did not submit an illegal act. Myers v. Bi–State Dev. Agency, 567 S.W.2d 638[1–2] (Mo. banc 1978).

Failure of plaintiff's verdict director submitting multiple acts to negate defense of contributory negligence is reversibly erroneous. Trimble v. Sipes, 506 S.W.2d 353[4] (Mo. 1974).

A not-in-MAI contributory negligence instruction properly submitted, in the conjunctive, plaintiff's failure to keep a careful lookout and permitting his truck to contact an electric wire that was in plain view. Robinett v. Kansas City Power & Light Co., 484 S.W.2d 506[4, 5] (Mo.App.1972).

Court properly refused instruction which modified paragraph Third to read "... such negligence caused ... the collision...." since that relieved plaintiff of her burden of proving defendant's negligence caused plaintiff's damage. Daniels v. Smith, 471 S.W.2d 508[1] (Mo.App.1971).

Modified MAI 17.02 submitting violation of stop sign or driving with inadequate brakes was not erroneous for submitting inconsistent theories of recovery. Hampton v. Cantrell, 464 S.W.2d 744[1] (Mo.App.1971).

Modified MAI 17.02 verdict director submitting defendant's failure to obey rules of the road and have truck under control erroneous for submitting "a general hypothesis of negligence" rather than "an ultimate issue". McIntyre v. Whited, 440 S.W.2d 449[1–2] (Mo.1969).

MAI 17.02 modified as a not-in-MAI verdict director in plaintiff's action for injuries by uninsured motorist. Goodson v. MFA Ins. Co., 429 S.W.2d 294[1] (Mo.App.1968).

3. Deviation

Submitting "slackened his speed, swerved and sounded a warning" was an erroneous conjunctive submission. Cassin v. Theodorow, 504 S.W.2d 203[6] (Mo.App.1973).

Omission of word "either" in disjunctive submission not prejudicial error. Riley v. Bi–State Transit System, 459 S.W.2d 753[5] (Mo.App.1970).

Use of "or" between First and Second paragraphs of verdict director is error since that allows the jury to find for plaintiff if it believes either rather than both paragraphs. Quality Dairy Co. v. Openlander, 456 S.W.2d 608[3] (Mo.App.1970).

Although plaintiff's contributory negligence was not in issue on account of his infancy, adding "whether or not plaintiff was negligent" to MAI 17.02 is error. Slyman v. Grantello, 429 S.W.2d 282 (Mo.App.1968).

Connective words following multiple submissions should read "in one or more of the respects" not "thereby". Moore v. Huff, 429 S.W.2d 1[1] (Mo.App.1968).

Omission of word "either" in disjunctive submission, and using "on" instead of "in" in MAI 17.02, held not prejudicial. Absolute perfection not required; substantial compliance suffices. Johnson v. West, 416 S.W.2d 162[1, 2] (Mo.1967).

4. Apparent danger

Error to use MAI 17.02 in submitting failure to swerve without "apparent danger" clause of MAI 17.04. Sweatman v. McClure, 416 S.W.2d 665[2] (Mo.App.1967).

5. Defining negligence

Where term "negligence" is used it must be defined; failure to do so creates a roving commission. Brewer v. Swift & Co., 451 S.W.2d 131[2] (Mo. banc 1970).

17.03 [1965 New] Verdict Directing—Excessive Speed

Defendant drove at an excessive speed.

Notes on Use (1990 Revision)

This is an optional submission of negligence which may be used as paragraph First of Verdict Directing 17.01 or as one of the alternate submissions in paragraph First of Verdict Directing 17.02. It may also be used as a submission in wrongful death cases, see MAI 20.01 and 20.02; and in comparative fault submissions, see MAI 37.02.

Committee Comment (1965 New)

Excessive speed, negligence, causation and injury have been held to be the proper basis for a verdict directing instruction. *Knight v. Richey,* 363 Mo. 293, 301, 250 S.W.2d 972, 977 (1952). See also *Brooks v. Mock,* 330 S.W.2d 759, 765 (Mo.1959).

Library References:

C.J.S. Motor Vehicles § 530.
West's Key No. Digests, Automobiles ⊃246.

Notes of Decisions

In general 1
Evidentiary support 2
Modification 3

1. In general

Case may not be submitted on disjunctive charges of general and specific negligence because to do so leaves jury free to speculate, outside factual submission, on other omissions. Nakata by Nakata v. Platte County R–3 School Dist., 750 S.W.2d 669, 672 (Mo.App.1988).

2. Evidentiary support

Evidence supported each element of verdict director based on failure to yield right-of-way, lookout and excessive speed. Yust v. Link, 569 S.W.2d 236[11] (Mo.App.1978).

3. Modification

Error to modify MAI 17.03, Excessive Speed, by inserting "under the circumstances". Strickland v. Barker, 436 S.W.2d 37[1] (Mo.1969).

17.04 [1978 Revision] Verdict Directing—Failure to Act After Danger of Collision Apparent

Defendant knew or by the use of the highest degree of care [1] could have known that there was a reasonable likelihood of collision in time thereafter to have (*insert one or more of the following*)

stopped, or

swerved, or

slackened speed, or

sounded a warning, or

slackened speed and swerved, or

slackened speed and sounded a warning, or

swerved and sounded a warning

but defendant failed to do so.

Notes on Use (1990 Revision)

Caution. Do not omit the last phrase of this instruction: it is required whenever this instruction is used.

1. The phrase "highest degree of care" must be defined. See definitions at MAI 11.01 or MAI 11.03.

Use one or more of the specifications of conduct provided. If more than one are used, they must be submitted in the disjunctive.

The specifications of conduct listed in this instruction are not to be used alone as a complete specification of negligence; the portion of the instruction preceding the parenthetical phrase and the last phrase of the instruction must be used whenever this instruction is given.

This is an optional submission of negligence which may be used as paragraph First of Verdict Directing 17.01 or as one of the alternate submissions in paragraph First of Verdict Directing 17.02. It may be used as a submission in wrongful death cases, see MAI 20.01 and 20.02; and in comparative fault submissions, see MAI 37.02.

Committee Comment (1965 New)

In *Greenwood v. Bridgeways, Inc.*, 243 S.W.2d 111, 114 (Mo.App. 1951) the court, quoting *Stakelback v. Neff*, 13 S.W.2d 575, 577 (Mo.App. 1929), said:

Even though it is true that this instruction counts upon primary negligence, and not the humanitarian doctrine, there was nevertheless no duty upon defendant to take any of the precautions hypothesized therein, unless there was apparent danger of a collision.... It cannot be said that the law imposes the duty upon the driver of an automobile, upon approaching and entering an intersecting street, to stop, decrease the speed of, or change the course of, his car, merely because he sees another automobile in the street ahead of him. To the contrary, such duty to act would clearly not arise, unless the exercise of due care upon the part of the driver would lead him to believe that otherwise a collision would result.

See also *Chailland v. Smiley,* 363 S.W.2d 619 (Mo.banc 1963); *Anderson v. Bell,* 303 S.W.2d 93 (Mo.1957); *Alwood v. St. Louis Public Service Co.,* 238 S.W.2d 868 (Mo.App.1951); *Nydegger v. Mason,* 315 S.W.2d 816 (Mo.1958).

Library References:

C.J.S. Motor Vehicles § 530.
West's Key No. Digests, Automobiles ☞246.

Notes of Decisions

Apparent danger   3
Conjunctive submission   2
Contributory negligence   10
Degree of care   6
Deviation   5
Evidentiary support   1
Modification   4
Proximate cause   7
Slackening speed and lookout   9
Swerving   8
Warning   11

_____

1. Evidentiary support

Giving of instruction, patterned on approved jury instruction regarding failure of injured party to stop or swerve to avoid collision, is appropriate only where evidence shows party had sufficient time, distance means and ability, considering movement and speeds of vehicles, to stop or swerve to avoid collision but failed to do so. Frazier v. Emerson Electric Co., 867 S.W.2d 700 (Mo. App.1993).

In negligence action arising from driver's collision with tractor trailer, sufficient evidence existed to show that driver could have stopped or swerved to warrant submitting comparative fault instruction to jury; no evidence was present to indicate that driver attempted to stop or swerve, and driver had eight seconds of reaction time after head-lights of jack-knifing tractor trailer would have been visible bumping up and down and sweeping at angles. Frazier v. Emerson Electric Co., 867 S.W.2d 700 (Mo.App.1993).

To warrant submission of verdict directing instruction for failure to act after danger of collision is apparent, evidence must be presented that plaintiff had means and ability to avoid collision by doing each act described in the instruction. Gardner v. Reynolds, 775 S.W.2d 173 (Mo.App.1989).

"Failure to swerve" instruction was properly refused where plaintiff failed to show that defendant had the means and ability to avoid the collision by swerving. Kilgore v. Linville, 733 S.W.2d 62[2] (Mo.App.1987).

To submit either "failure to swerve" or "lookout" instructions, plaintiff in an automobile negligence case had to show when defendant knew or should have known about the potential danger, and that defendant had sufficient time to take effective precautionary action. Morgan v. Toomey, 719 S.W.2d 129 [2–5] (Mo.App.1986).

Having ability to avoid a collision means not only necessary mechanical appliances but also sufficient time and distance to take effective action. Saupe v. Kertz, 523 S.W.2d 826 [4–5] (Mo. banc 1975).

On issue of negligent failure to avoid a collision, evidence must show defendant had the time and distance within which to take effective evasive action. Cook v. Cox, 478 S.W.2d 678 [3–4] (Mo.1972).

2. Conjunctive submission

Submitting "slackened his speed, swerved and sounded a warning" was an erroneous conjunctive submission. Cassin v. Theodorow, 504 S.W.2d 203[6] (Mo.App.1973).

A modified MAI 17.04 submitting that defendant could have avoided the collision if he had "swerved, slackened his speed, swerved and sounded a warning." Submitted three separate theories of recovery conjunctively and violated MAI 1.02. Cook v. Cox, 478 S.W.2d 678[5] (Mo.1972).

3. Apparent danger

Instruction, in case in which plaintiff was hit by a pickup truck backing out of alley, on whether plaintiff could have moved to place of safety, but failed to do so, did not give jury roving commission since jury could have found that plaintiff should have known of impending danger and had ample room to move to avoid further contact with pickup. Miller v. Hanna, 757 S.W.2d 301, 302–03 (Mo.App.1988).

Verdict director—entering narrow bridge with bulldozer. State ex rel. Hwy. Com'n v. Beaty, 505 S.W.2d 147[1] (Mo.App.1974).

Plaintiff entitled to submit defendant's failure to stop at intersection when there was "a reasonable likelihood of collision" even though there was no evidence of precise speeds and stopping distances. Jefferies v. Saalberg, 448 S.W.2d 288[3] (Mo.App.1969).

Submission of contributory negligence in overtaking defendant's car as it made a sudden left-hand turn was erroneous for failure to include element of apparent danger (as in MAI 17.04). Schlegel v. Knoll, 427 S.W.2d 480[10] (Mo.1968).

Failing to slacken speed or to swerve must be submitted under MAI 17.04 (Failure to Act After Danger Apparent). Hecker v. Schwartz, 426 S.W.2d 22[5] (Mo.1968).

Error to use MAI 17.02 in submitting failure to swerve without "apparent danger" clause of MAI 17.04. Sweatman v. McClure, 416 S.W.2d 665[2] (Mo.App.1967).

Error to submit failure to swerve without submitting danger of collision required by MAI 17.04. Hunter v. Norton, 412 S.W.2d 163[7] (Mo.1967).

4. Modification

Where defendant motorist's duty to take evasive action did not arise until danger was apparent, plaintiff should have modified MAI 17.04 instead of using MAI 17.01 which omits elements of apparent danger and defendant's ability to safely avoid collision thereafter. Thompson v. Gray, 415 S.W.2d 299[2–6] (Mo.App.1967).

5. Deviation

Jury instruction prescribing precise action that plaintiff could have taken to have moved to a place of safety would violate concept of pattern instruction by submitting evidentiary details to jury rather than ultimate issues. Miller v. Hanna, 757 S.W.2d 301, 303 (Mo.App.1988).

In action in which motorcyclist sought to recover for injuries he sustained in avoiding highway collision with driver of pickup truck, substitution of "accident" for "collision" in contributory negligence instruction did not adequately direct jury's deliberation to acts defendant claimed amounted to contributory negligence. Large v. Carr, 670 S.W.2d 71[5] (Mo.App.1984).

Omission of "the use of" from instruction not harmless error. Jenkins v. Keller, 579 S.W.2d 166[1–4] (Mo.App.1979).

Substituting "to have stopped" for "to stop" in MAI 17.04 was harmless error. Offenbacker v. Sodowsky, 499 S.W.2d 421[2, 3] (Mo.1973).

Error to submit the element of causation in MAI 17.04 by adding the phrase "and thereby have avoided the accident," after the submitted act. Brittain v. Clark, 462 S.W.2d 153[4] (Mo.App.1970).

Substituting "exercise" for "use" concerning degree of care not prejudicial. Joly v. Wippler, 449 S.W.2d 565[3] (Mo.1970).

Substituting "applied his brakes" for "slackened her speed" in MAI 17.04 was prejudicial error. Motsinger v. Queen City Casket Co., 408 S.W.2d 857[1] (Mo.1966).

6. Degree of care

Error to submit failure to sound a horn where only evidence was answer of witness that she did not recall hearing a horn. Baker v. Brinker, 585 S.W.2d 256[1–4] (Mo.App. 1979).

Contributory negligence instruction, MAI 28.01 [Now 32.01]–17.04, imposing "highest" degree of care on bicyclist was error. Van Brunt v. Meyer, 422 S.W.2d 364[2] (Mo. App.1967).

7. Proximate cause

Having ability to avoid a collision means not only necessary mechanical appliances but also sufficient time and distance to take effective action. Saupe v. Kertz, 523 S.W.2d 826[4–5] (Mo. banc 1975).

Giving MAI 17.04 is proper only where evidence shows defendant could have taken effective evasive action after collision became actually or constructively apparent. Bolhofner v. Jones, 482 S.W.2d 80[2, 3] (Mo.App.1972).

8. Swerving

Giving of pattern instruction on motorist's duty to swerve to avoid collision is proper only where there is evidence that driver had sufficient time, distance, means, and ability, considering movement and speeds of vehicles, to stop or swerve to avoid collision but failed to do so. To submit instruction on failure of defendant to swerve to avoid collision, plaintiff has to show when potential danger of collision should have become actually or constructively apparent to defendant, and also that defendant had sufficient time thereafter to swerve or to take other effective precautionary action. Hollis v. Blevins, 927 S.W.2d 558 (Mo.App.1996).

Error to modify MAI 17.15 by submitting failure to swerve "to the right." Ritter v. Lindberg Acoustics, Inc., 501 S.W.2d 207[3, 4] (Mo.App.1973).

Intersectional collision. Where evidence was that defendant swerved to the left it was error for plaintiff to modify MAI 17.15 by hypothesizing defendant's negligence in failing to swerve "to the right." Bougeno v. Thompson, 499 S.W.2d 506[3, 4] (Mo. banc 1973).

Submission of failure to swerve properly refused absent showing of available time and space. Middleman v. Complete Auto Transit, Inc., 486 S.W.2d 456[3] (Mo. banc 1972).

9. Slackening speed and lookout

Error to submit MAI 17.04 (slackening speed) without requiring finding of apparent danger, even when combined with MAI 17.05 (failure to keep a lookout) which does not require that element. Hawkeye–Security Ins. Co. v. Thomas Grain Fumigant Co., 407 S.W.2d 622[7] (Mo.App.1966).

10. Contributory negligence

The Notes of Use to MAI 17.04 indicate that one or more of the specifications provided therein may be submitted as an act of contributory negligence as well, but they also provide that the phrase "highest degree of care" must be defined. The language is mandatory, not permissive, and failure to follow is presumed to be error. Kindle v. Keene, 676 S.W.2d 82[2] (Mo.App.1984).

Plaintiff's contributory negligence properly submitted by incorporating MAI 17.04—Failure to Act After Danger Apparent—in MAI 32.01. Creager v. Chilson, 453 S.W.2d 941[12] (Mo.1970).

11. Warning

Instruction submitting plaintiff-passenger's contributory negligence in failing to warn defendant-driver of impending danger. Worley v. Tucker Nevils, Inc., 503 S.W.2d 417[3] (Mo. banc 1973).

17.05 [1965 New] Verdict Directing—Failure to Keep a Lookout

Defendant failed to keep a careful lookout.

Notes on Use (1990 Revision)

This is an optional submission of negligence which may be used as paragraph First of Verdict Directing 17.01 or as one of the alternate submissions in paragraph First of Verdict Directing 17.02. It may also be used as a submission in wrongful death cases, see MAI 20.01 and 20.02; and in comparative fault submissions, see MAI 37.02.

Committee Comment (1965 New)

Negligently failing to keep a careful lookout with a resulting injury has been held to be a proper basis of recovery. *Anderson v. Bell*, 303 S.W.2d 93 (Mo.1957). In *Jenkins v. Wabash Railroad Co.*, 322 S.W.2d 788, 798 (Mo.1959), the Missouri Supreme Court quoted *Fortner v. St. Louis Public Service Co.*, 244 S.W.2d 10, 14 (Mo.1951), with approval the following statement: "In a primary negligence case it should be sufficient if a jury is authorized to find that a defendant was negligent specifically in failing to keep a proper lookout, ... and that such negligence directly caused plaintiff's injuries."

"It is 'unnecessary to submit the further hypothesis that by keeping a proper lookout defendant could have seen plaintiff' or could have averted the collisions." *Lincoln v. Railway Express Agency, Inc.*, 359 S.W.2d 759, 768 (Mo.1962).

It is error to submit failure to keep a lookout unless there is evidence from which the jury could find that the defendant could have seen the object in question sooner than he did. *Levin v. Caldwell*, 285 S.W.2d 655, 659 (Mo.1956); *O'Neill v. Claypool*, 341 S.W.2d 129, 135 (Mo.1960).

In *Harris v. Mound City Yellow Cab Co.*, 367 S.W.2d 43, 50 (Mo.App. 1963), the court said: "Since Instruction No. 8 in the instant case required the jury to find affirmatively that the driver of the cab failed to keep a proper lookout for other vehicles, including that of defendant Simms, and that such failure was negligence and caused or contributed to cause the collision, such charge is equivalent to a requirement that the jury find the cab driver could have seen the other vehicle if he had looked."

See also: *Whaley v. Zervas*, 367 S.W.2d 611 (Mo.1963); *Fortner v. St. Louis Public Serv. Co.*, 244 S.W.2d 10 (Mo.1951); see also *Boehm v. St. Louis Public Serv. Co.*, 368 S.W.2d 361, 366 (Mo.1963); *Dial v. Seven–Up Bottling Co.*, 373 S.W.2d 53 (Mo.1963).

The case of *Chandler v. Mueller,* 377 S.W.2d 288 (Mo.1964), held that the evidence did not justify this submission where the offending party testified that he did keep a lookout although his conduct was more consistent with failing to keep a lookout.

Compare *Zalle v. Underwood,* 372 S.W.2d 98 (Mo.1963), where the court held an instruction submitting failure to keep a lookout was error because the evidence did not show that such failure caused the accident.

Library References:

C.J.S. Motor Vehicles § 530.
West's Key No. Digests, Automobiles ⚿246.

Notes of Decisions

---

1. In general

Where plaintiff's verdict director submitted defendant's failure to keep a lookout it was error to give MAI 14.02 defining right-of-way, an element not applicable to the issues. Corbin v. Wennerberg, 459 S.W.2d 505[1, 8] (Mo.App.1970).

Adding words "for an approaching train" to failure-to-keep-a-lookout submission was unjustified. Silvey v. Missouri Pac. Ry. Co., 445 S.W.2d 354[9] (Mo.1969).

Where passenger's case was tried on theory that bus driver negligently failed to keep a lookout for a depression, MAI 17.05 was appropriate, and it was error to submit plaintiff's case on a modified MAI 17.01–26.02(1) [Now 31.02(1)] hypothesizing that driver negligently drove into the depression. The instruction given would unduly extend the res ipsa doctrine. Routt v. Bi–State Transit Development Agency, 423 S.W.2d 202[1, 2] (Mo.App.1967).

2. Evidentiary support

Failure-to-keep-careful-lookout instruction was supported by evidence that defendant, who had been stopped at stop sign before proceeding into intersection, had unobstructed view of 1,125 feet in direction from which car in which plaintiff was riding was approaching, and that defendant's car was still stopped when other car was only 20 feet from intersection, in middle of line of cars, and traveling with flow of traffic in 35 mile-per-hour zone. Hudson v. Whiteside, 34 S.W.3d 420 (Mo.App.2000).

Instructions submitting "failure to keep a careful lookout" must be supported by evidence that operator of vehicle could have avoided collision if careful lookout had been maintained, although instruction need not hypothesize means of avoidance; "lookout" disjunctive submission was erroneous where defendant driver stopped vehicle in a lane reserved for moving traffic and did not see plaintiff's approaching vehicle prior to collision; evidence was insufficient to support "lookout" submission where plaintiff introduced no evidence as to when defendant saw or could have seen plaintiff's vehicle or what defendant could have done to have avoided accident if he had seen approach of vehicle. Pringle v. State Highway Commission, 831 S.W.2d 735 (Mo.App.1992).

Evidence that school bus driver failed to see child walking along side of street after dropping her off, and struck her while travelling at speed of 5 miles per hour, was sufficient to establish submissible case of negligence based on failure to keep careful lookout. Countryman v. Seymour R–II School Dist., 823 S.W.2d 515 (Mo.App. 1992).

Submission on a failure to keep a lookout contains two inherent components—the ability to see and the ability, including the time and the means, to avoid, and it is plaintiff's burden to supply substantial evidence on both components. Bell v. United Parcel Serv., 724 S.W.2d 682[4] (Mo.App.1987).

Submission of jury instruction on failure to keep careful lookout must be supported by substantial evidence from which a jury could find that the allegedly negligent party could have seen the other vehicle or person in time to have taken effective precautionary action if the party had exercised the highest degree of care in keeping a lookout. Lewis v. State Sec. Ins. Co., 718 S.W.2d 539[1] (Mo.App. 1986).

To submit either "failure to swerve" or "lookout" instructions, plaintiff in an automobile negligence case had to show when defendant knew or should have known about the potential danger, and that defendant had sufficient time to take effective precautionary action. Morgan v. Toomey, 719 S.W.2d 129[2–5] (Mo.App.1986).

Trial court committed reversible error in its submission of instruction on contributory negligence of westbound driver, where driver had no duty to look for westbound traffic in eastbound lanes and driver of car which injured her provided no direct evidence that he had seen her in time to avoid collision, nor did he prove it circumstantially, providing nothing more than speculative deductions. Finninger v. Johnson, 692 S.W.2d 390[13] (Mo.App.1985).

Evidence warranted plaintiff's submission of defendant's driver's failure to keep a lookout. Williams v. M.C. Slater, Inc., 590 S.W.2d 357[1–5] (Mo.App.1979).

Circumstantial evidence may suffice to submit failure to keep a careful lookout. Watterson v. Portas, 466 S.W.2d 129[3] (Mo. App.1971).

Evidence supported lookout submission against driver who drove on wrong side of the road. Leonard v. Gordon's Transport, 575 S.W.2d 244[2] (Mo.App.1978).

Verdict director submitting three assignments of negligence erroneous where evidence supported only two submissions. Bunch v. McMillian, 568 S.W.2d 809[1–2] (Mo.App.1978).

Evidence supported defendant's contributory negligence instruction on (a) rearend collision, (b) failure to keep a lookout, and (c) following too closely. Pitezel v. Danielson, 571 S.W.2d 694[1–4] (Mo.App.1978).

Evidence supported each element of verdict director based on failure to yield right-of-way, lookout and excessive speed. Yust v. Link, 569 S.W.2d 236[11] (Mo.App.1978).

Failure to see that which is visible, standing alone, is insufficient to warrant MAI 17.05; there must be evidence driver could have taken timely evasive action. Butler v. Hicks, 554 S.W.2d 449[1] (Mo.App.1977).

Plaintiff pedestrian testified he was standing near the highway's edge when defendant motorist struck him; defendant testified she did not see plaintiff until he ran onto the highway into her path. Trial court erred in refusing plaintiff's lookout instruction. Plaintiff was not required to negate defendant's version which defendant could have submitted that by a third-method converse. Williams v. Christian, 520 S.W.2d 139[5–7] (Mo.App.1974).

Defendant's failure to see stop light at intersection warranted giving instruction on failure to keep a careful lookout. Rakestraw v. Norris, 478 S.W.2d 409[22–24] (Mo.App. 1972).

Lookout submission must be supported by evidence that driver could have seen the object in time to have taken effective preventive action. Corbin v. Wennerberg, 459 S.W.2d 505[3, 4] (Mo.App.1970).

Fact that plaintiff walked into the path of a clearly visible automobile is sufficient to support an instruction on failing to keep a careful lookout. Young v. Grotsky, 459 S.W.2d 306[5] (Mo.1970).

In an intersection collision case plaintiff's lookout submission was adequately supported by evidence that by keeping a careful lookout the left-turning defendant could have seen plaintiff in the intersection before striking him; this despite defendant's testimony that he was watching plaintiff at all times. Rickard v. Pratt, 459 S.W.2d 13[1, 2] (Mo. App.1970).

Circumstantial evidence may suffice to support submission of failure to keep a lookout. Commerford v. Kreitler, 462 S.W.2d 726[2] (Mo.1971).

Evidence that driver "did not watch ahead with sufficient diligence to permit timely action" was enough evidentiary support to give MAI on failure to keep a careful lookout. Welch v. Sheley, 443 S.W.2d 110[6–8] (Mo. 1969).

Proper to refuse lookout instruction absent evidence showing failure to keep a lookout. McDowell v. Mohn, 426 S.W.2d 95[4] (Mo. 1968).

Error to submit MAI 17.05 (failure to keep a lookout) without evidence that driver in the exercise of the highest degree of care could have seen the object sooner than he did. Hawkeye–Security Ins. Co. v. Thomas Grain Fumigant Co., 407 S.W.2d 622[2, 3] (Mo. App.1966).

3. Proximate cause

Failure to see that which is visible, standing alone, is insufficient to warrant MAI 17.05; there must be evidence driver could have taken timely evasive action. Butler v. Hicks, 554 S.W.2d 449[1] (Mo.App.1977).

Plaintiff pedestrian testified he was standing near the highway's edge when defendant motorist struck him; defendant testified she did not see plaintiff until he ran onto the highway into her path. Trial court erred in refusing plaintiff's lookout instruction. Plaintiff was not required to negate defendant's version which defendant could have submitted that by a third-method converse. Williams v. Christian, 520 S.W.2d 139[5–7] (Mo.App.1974).

A lookout submission actually submits failure to see and failure to avoid injury by any means supported by the evidence. Thus, plaintiff may argue defendant's failure to look and his failure to swerve and sound a horn even when those elements are not submitted by plaintiff's verdict director. Lovelace v. Reed, 486 S.W.2d 417[1–4] (Mo.1972).

Failure to keep a proper lookout may be shown circumstantially but MAI 17.05 proper only when failure to keep lookout is shown to be proximate cause of collision. Bolhofner v. Jones, 482 S.W.2d 80[1] (Mo.App. 1972).

Even where evidence showed driver failed to look before entering blind intersection it was error to give MAI 17.05 absent evidence that had driver kept a lookout he could have taken effective action to avoid the collision. Heberer v. Duncan, 449 S.W.2d 561[3] (Mo. banc 1970).

Error to submit driving on wrong side of the road or failure to keep a lookout where evidence failed to show causal connection between failure to keep a lookout and the collision. Shelton v. Bruner, 449 S.W.2d 673[1, 6] (Mo.App.1969).

Submission on failure to keep a lookout was erroneous absent evidence of proximate cause that looking could have prevented collision. Stegall v. Wilson, 416 S.W.2d 658[8] (Mo.App.1967).

To support an MAI 17.05 lookout submission, evidence must show failure to keep a lookout was proximate cause of plaintiff's injury. Janicke v. Hough, 400 S.W.2d 645[5] (Mo.App.1966).

4. Lookout and slackening

Error to submit MAI 17.04 (slackening speed) without requiring finding of apparent danger, even when combined with MAI 17.05 (failure to keep a lookout) which does not require that element. Hawkeye–Security Ins. Co. v. Thomas Grain Fumigant Co., 407 S.W.2d 622[7] (Mo.App.1966).

5. Negligence defined

Failure to define "negligence" in lookout submission was reversible error. Rakestraw v. Norris, 478 S.W.2d 409[25–27] (Mo.App. 1972).

17.06 [1965 New] Verdict Directing—Failure to Signal Intention to Turn

Defendant failed to signal an intention to turn.

Notes on Use (1990 Revision)

This is an optional submission of negligence which may be used as paragraph First of Verdict Directing 17.01 or as one of the alternate submissions in paragraph First of Verdict Directing 17.02. It may also be used as a submission in wrongful death cases, see MAI 20.01 and 20.02; and in comparative fault submissions, see MAI 37.02.

Committee Comment (1965 New)

Section 304.019, RSMo provides in part:

No person shall stop or suddenly decrease the speed of or turn a vehicle from a direct course or move right or left upon a roadway unless and until such movement can be made with reasonable safety and then only after the giving of an appropriate signal in the manner provided herein.

Of related significance is § 304.016.4(2), RSMo which provides in substance that vehicles shall not be driven to the left side of the highway when approaching within one hundred feet of or at any intersection or railroad grade crossing.

In *Ilgenfritz v. Quinn,* 318 S.W.2d 186 (Mo.1958), defendant failed to signal his intent to turn right into a private driveway. He defended on the basis that the hand signal would not have been visible as it was dark. The court held the duty to signal remained. See also *Highfill v. Brown,* 320 S.W.2d 493 (Mo.1959), where defendant failed to signal his intent to turn left from the highway into a private driveway. The court held that the point where the driveway intersected the highway was not an "intersection" within the meaning of § 304.016.4(2), RSMo.

Failing to signal was asserted as contributory negligence in *Grantham v. Herod,* 320 S.W.2d 536 (Mo.1959).

Library References:

C.J.S. Motor Vehicles § 530.
West's Key No. Digests, Automobiles ☞246.

Notes of Decisions

1. In general

In rear-end case defendant's evidence that plaintiff slowed and swerved slightly to his left warranted defendant's contributory negligence instruction that plaintiff "failed to signal his intention to turn left." Welch v. Hyatt, 578 S.W.2d 905[7] (Mo. banc 1979).

227

When turning is disputed MAI 17.06 should [be amended to] require submission that there *was a turn*. Welch v. Hyatt, 578 S.W.2d 905[8] (Mo. banc 1979).

Defendant's contributory negligence instruction (MAI 28.01, modified by 32.01) sub-mitting plaintiff's failure to keep a lookout or failure to signal. Lands v. Boyster, 417 S.W.2d 942, 944 (Mo.1967).

17.07 [2000 Withdrawn] Verdict Directing—Failure to Sound Horn

17.08   [1965 New] Verdict Directing—Failure to Yield Right-of-Way

Defendant failed to yield the right-of-way.

Notes on Use (1965 New)

This is an optional submission of negligence which may be used as paragraph First of Verdict Directing 17.01 or as one of the alternate submissions in paragraph First of Verdict Directing 17.02. It may also be used as a submission in comparative fault (MAI 37.02) and wrongful death cases (MAI 20.01 and 20.02).

The appropriate right-of-way definition must be used in conjunction with this submission.

Committee Comment (1996 Revision)

See General Comment at MAI 14.01 and Definitions MAI 14.02–14.09.

Library References:

C.J.S. Motor Vehicles § 530.
West's Key No. Digests, Automobiles ⚷246.

Notes of Decisions

In general   1
Definition   2
Evidentiary support   3

------

1.   In general

Comparative fault instruction concerning driver's failure to yield right of way was erroneously given, in action by estate of deceased driver whose vehicle had struck tow truck parked on highway; driver could not fail to yield right of way to parked vehicle. Austin v. Kruse, 874 S.W.2d 454 (Mo.App. W.D., 1994).

Plaintiff submitting failure to yield right-of-way must submit proper definition and may not complain of court's or defendant's failure to do so. Howe v. Bowman, 429 S.W.2d 339[3] (Mo.App.1968).

2.   Definition

MAI 14.02 is for the statutory right-of-way on public roads, not a private parking lot; in that latter case common law right-of-way is based on duty of reasonable care, not the highest degree of care. Doolin v. Swain, 524 S.W.2d 877[3–5] (Mo. banc 1975).

Error to give MAI 14.02 in case where plaintiff was struck at intersection controlled by a flashing red light. Riley v. Bi–State Transit System, 459 S.W.2d 753[3, 4] (Mo. App.1970).

3.   Evidentiary support

Evidence supported each element of verdict director based on failure to yield right-of-way, lookout and excessive speed. Yust v. Link, 569 S.W.2d 236[11] (Mo.App.1978).

17.09 [1965 New] Verdict Directing—Following Too Closely

Defendant was following the (*insert brief description of car followed*) car too closely.

Notes on Use (1990 Revision)

This is an optional submission of negligence which may be used as paragraph First of Verdict Directing 17.01 or as one of the alternate submissions in paragraph First of Verdict Directing 17.02. It may also be used as a submission in comparative fault cases (MAI 37.02) and wrongful death cases (MAI 20.01 and 20.02).

Committee Comment (1996 Revision)

Section 304.044, RSMo provides that trucks and buses shall not follow within 300 feet of other trucks or buses.

Hypothesizing failure of defendant to maintain this distance, negligence, causation and injury, is the proper basis for a verdict directing instruction. See *Thebeau v. Thebeau*, 324 S.W.2d 674, 678 (Mo. banc 1959). There the court said that "the main purpose of section 304.044 was, ..., to provide sufficient space between trucks and busses to permit lighter vehicles to pass, but we are not persuaded that this was its only purpose. We think it obvious that as a traffic safety regulation it was also intended for protection of forward trucks and those trucks following, as well as the drivers and passengers therein."

Section 304.017, RSMo provides in part:

The driver of a vehicle shall not follow another vehicle more closely than is reasonably safe and prudent, having due regard for the speed of such vehicle and the traffic upon and the condition of the roadway.

In *Binion v. Armentrout*, 333 S.W.2d 87 (Mo.1960), plaintiff was injured while changing a tire along a highway. The car ahead of defendant's car saw plaintiff, swerved, and missed him. Plaintiff argued that defendant was unable to do the same as he was following the front car too closely. Defendant contended that the statute was not designed to protect against this kind of injury and thus plaintiff could not recover simply because defendant violated the statute. The court said:

We see no reasonable basis for that position. Could it be reasonably said that the statute was designed for the sole protection of the forward vehicle or vehicles following, or parked vehicles, or a passing vehicle (and occupants of said vehicles), or pedestrians? We have concluded that said section was enacted for the protection of every person or vehicle which would reasonably be afforded a measure of protection by the enforcement of the terms thereof.

Where the facts bring plaintiff's case within the "rear end collision" doctrine, plaintiff may prefer to use MAI 17.16.

Following too closely was submitted as contributory negligence in *Terrell v. McKnight,* 360 Mo. 19, 26, 226 S.W.2d 714, 717 (1950). See MAI 37.02 for submission of comparative fault.

Library References:

C.J.S. Motor Vehicles § 530.
West's Key No. Digests, Automobiles ⊕246.

Notes of Decisions

In general   1
Evidentiary support   2

1. In general

Error to submit MAI 17.09 when evidence did not show a causal connection between the act of following too closely and the collision. Pyles v. Roth, 421 S.W.2d 261[3] (Mo. 1967).

2. Evidentiary support

Evidence supported defendant's contributory negligence instruction on (a) rear end collision, (b) failure to keep a lookout, and (c) following too closely. Pitezel v. Danielson, 571 S.W.2d 694[1–4] (Mo.App.1978).

17.10 [1965 New] Verdict Directing—Passing on the Right

Defendant passed the (*insert brief description of car passed*) car on the right.

Notes on Use (1990 Revision)

This is an optional submission of negligence which may be used as paragraph First of Verdict Directing 17.01 or as one of the alternate submissions in paragraph First of Verdict Directing 17.02. It may also be used as a submission in comparative fault cases (MAI 37.02) and wrongful death cases (MAI 20.01 and 20.02).

Committee Comment (1996 Revision)

Section 304.016.1(1), RSMo provides in part:

The driver of a vehicle overtaking another vehicle proceeding in the same direction shall pass to the left thereof at a safe distance and shall not again drive to the right side of the roadway until safely clear of the overtaken vehicle.

Section 304.016.2, RSMo provides in part these exceptions:

The driver of a motor vehicle may overtake and pass to the right of another vehicle only under the following conditions:

(1) When the vehicle overtaken is making or about to make a left turn.

(2) Upon a city street with unobstructed pavement of sufficient width for two or more lines of vehicles in each direction.

(3) Upon a one-way street.

(4) Upon any highway outside of a city with unobstructed pavement of sufficient width and clearly marked for four or more lines of traffic.

In *Willhite v. City of St. Louis,* 359 Mo. 933, 936, 224 S.W.2d 956, 957 (1949), the court said: "... we cannot hold that it is always negligence as a matter of law, under all circumstances, to pass another vehicle on the right, although usually it is."

The statute has been modified slightly since this decision.

See also *Sisk v. Driggers,* 364 S.W.2d 76 (Mo.App.1962), where the jury was instructed that passing on the right was negligent.

Library References:

C.J.S. Motor Vehicles § 530.
West's Key No. Digests, Automobiles ⚖246.

Notes of Decisions

1. In general

Comparative fault instruction charging plaintiff with negligence in passing on the right was erroneous since such action was permitted on four lane highway in question. Varner v. Weiss, 887 S.W.2d 659 (Mo.App. E.D., 1994).

17.11 [1965 New] Verdict Directing—Slowing Without Adequate Warning

Defendant suddenly slowed his automobile on the highway without first giving an adequate and timely warning of his intention to slow.

Notes on Use (1965 New)

This is an optional submission of negligence which may be used as paragraph First of MAI 17.01 or as one of the alternate submissions in paragraph First of MAI 17.02. It may also be used as a submission in comparative fault cases (MAI 37.02) and wrongful death cases (MAI 20.01 and 20.02).

Committee Comment (1965 New)

See Committee Comment following MAI 17.12.

Library References:

C.J.S. Motor Vehicles § 530.
West's Key No. Digests, Automobiles ⊷246.

Notes of Decisions

Deviation 2
Evidentiary support 3
Pleading 1

_____

1. Pleading

MAI 17.11 submitting "suddenly slowed his automobile" was not beyond pleadings alleging driver made a "sudden and abrupt stop." Boland v. Jando, 414 S.W.2d 560[6] (Mo.1967).

2. Deviation

When there was no evidence plaintiffs failed to give a warning signal defendant's contributory negligence instruction, combining MAI 32.01 with modifications of MAI 17.11 (slowing without adequate warning) and MAI 17.12 (stopping without adequate warning), was erroneous for substituting the words "at a time when it was not reasonably safe to do so." Burton v. Bi–State Dev. Agency, 468 S.W.2d 4 (Mo.1971).

Omission of "suddenly" in MAI 17.11 is error. Koehler v. Schott, 426 S.W.2d 677[1] (Mo.App.1968).

3. Evidentiary support

Evidence in negligence suit against preceding driver arising from rear-end collision was sufficient to go to jury on question of whether there was causal connection between preceding driver's alleged failure to signal intention to stop or slow down and damages sustained by passenger in following vehicle; evidence included proof that preceding driver observed stopped vehicle one quarter of a mile ahead, permitting jury to find that his failure to negotiate more gradual and controlled stop, thereby earlier activating the brake lights on his vehicle, proximately caused passenger's injury. Hawthorne v. Hills, 861 S.W.2d 337 (Mo.App. 1993).

Error to give MAI 28.01 [Now 32.01]–17.11 as contributory negligence instruction where (1) defendant was vague about whether plaintiff's brake lights did go on, and (2) defendant was not looking and would not

have seen the lights if they were on. Brassfield v. Sears, 421 S.W.2d 321[2, 4] (Mo.
1967).

17.12 [1965 New] Verdict Directing—Stopping Without Adequate Warning

Defendant suddenly stopped his automobile on the highway without first giving an adequate and timely warning of his intention to stop.

Notes on Use (1990 Revision)

This is an optional submission of negligence which may be used as paragraph First of Verdict Directing 17.01 or as one of the alternate submissions in paragraph First of Verdict Directing 17.02. It may also be used as a submission in comparative fault cases (MAI 37.02) and wrongful death cases (MAI 20.01 and 20.02).

Committee Comment (1996 Revision)

Section 304.019, RSMo, provides in part:

> No person shall stop or suddenly decrease the speed of or turn a vehicle from a direct course or move right or left upon a roadway unless and until such movement can be made with reasonable safety and then only after the giving of an appropriate signal in the manner provided herein.

In *Matthews v. Mound City Cab Co.*, 205 S.W.2d 243, 247 (Mo.App.1947), the court said (in construing the predecessor of the present statute):

> The defendant is in one sense correct when it says that a signal given by the electrical signaling device at the rear of the cab was all that was required by law.... But while a signal given by a statutory electrical signaling device is sufficient as regards the manner or form which the signaling shall take, the circumstances under which such a signal is given may nevertheless be such as to preclude the particular signal from constituting reasonable or adequate warning. For example, in the case of a sudden and abrupt stop, the flash of a signal during the fleeting moment of time within which a front vehicle is brought to a stop may well be insufficient.... This is not to imply that every sudden and abrupt stop of an automobile is in and of itself proof of negligence, but only that such a stop will constitute negligence if there is no emergency shown to justify it, and it is made in disregard of the presence of vehicles following so closely behind that they may be unable to avoid a collision.

See also *White v. Rohrer*, 267 S.W.2d 31 (Mo.1954), holding that no further definition of "timely" or "adequate" is required.

In *Terrell v. McKnight*, 360 Mo. 19, 24, 226 S.W.2d 714, 716 (1950), the court held that failing to signal a stop is not negligence if "considering the distance between (defendant's) vehicle and that of plaintiff, the speed at which plaintiff was driving and the condition of the highway as to other traffic, he could reasonably believe he could stop without colliding with plaintiff's car."

See also *Lafferty v. Wattle,* 349 S.W.2d 519 (Mo.App.1961). In *Pilkenton v. Fegley,* 321 S.W.2d 435, 438 (Mo.1959), the court cited two earlier cases which said: " 'There is nothing in this statute to justify a *sudden stopping,* that is one without timely warning. It is well settled that the driver of a forward car in making a sudden stop of this kind must give a warning to a car closely following [*Ritz v. Cousins Lumber Co.,* 227 Mo.App. 1167, 59 S.W.2d 1072, 1075 (1933)].... The test of sufficiency of the warning by a motorist is whether the warning is adequate and timely.' " [*Thaller v. Skinner & Kennedy Co.,* 315 S.W.2d 124, 130 (Mo. banc 1958)].

"... the sudden slowing of an automobile is not negligence unless the driver shall fail to give a reasonably adequate and timely warning of his intention to do so." *Tucker v. Blankenmeier,* 315 S.W.2d 724, 727 (Mo.1958).

Library References:

C.J.S. Motor Vehicles § 530.
West's Key No. Digests, Automobiles ⚿246.

Notes of Decisions

---

1. In general

Verdict director submitting negligent application of brakes causing skid (pre Friederich v. Chamberlain, 458 S.W.2d 360 (Mo. banc 1970)). Middleman v. Complete Auto Transit Inc., 486 S.W.2d 456[1, 2] (Mo. banc 1972).

Error to submit that defendant motorist stopped on the traveled portion of the highway since it omitted the elements of suddenly stopping without warning. (Given before adoption of MAI 17.20). Joly v. Wippler, 449 S.W.2d 565[1] (Mo.1970).

Defendant's MAI 28.01 [Now 32.01]–17.05–17.12 (contributory negligence involving lookout and sudden stop) proper in form, but erroneous where there was no evidence that plaintiff's stop was sudden. Markle v. Fallek, 424 S.W.2d 756[1] (Mo.App.1968).

2. Evidentiary support

Evidence in rear-end automobile collision suit against preceding driver was sufficient to submit to jury issue of whether preceding driver suddenly stopped vehicle or suddenly slowed vehicle without first giving adequate and timely warning, even if preceding driver proved that brake lights on his vehicle worked properly when activated. Hawthorne v. Hills, 861 S.W.2d 337 (Mo.App. 1993).

When there was no evidence plaintiffs failed to give a warning signal, defendant's contributory negligence instruction, combining MAI 32.01 with modifications of MAI 17.11 (slowing without adequate warning) and MAI 17.12 (stopping without adequate warning), was erroneous for substituting the words "at a time when it was not reasonably safe to do so." Burton v. Bi–State Dev. Agency, 468 S.W.2d 4 (Mo.1971).

Evidence must show a causal connection between negligent act and injury; where plaintiff-driver knew approaching school bus was going to stop, driver improperly submitted negligence of approaching bus driver in thereafter giving another belated signal to stop. Pruneau v. Cain, 458 S.W.2d 265[1] (Mo.1970).

3. Adequate warning

Where plaintiffs' evidence supported both MAI 17.20, defendant stopping on highway, and MAI 17.12, defendant stopping without adequate warning, plaintiffs are entitled to choose their own theory of recovery and the court did not err in giving MAI 17.20 rather than MAI 17.12 as contended by defendant. Certa v. Associated Bldg. Center, Inc., 560 S.W.2d 593[1–10] (Mo.App.1977).

Where rear-ended plaintiff had adequate warning that preceding car was going to slow down and turn but suddenly braked and stopped without signalling, her contributory negligence was properly submitted by MAI 32.01–17.12. Schoessel v. Robertson, 480 S.W.2d 95[1, 2] (Mo.App.1972).

17.13 [1978 Revision] Verdict Directing—Wrong Side of the Road

Defendant's automobile was on the wrong side of the road.

Notes on Use (1990 Revision)

This is an optional submission of negligence which may be used as paragraph First of Verdict Directing 17.01 or as one of the alternate submissions in paragraph First of Verdict Directing 17.02. It may also be used as a submission in comparative negligence and wrongful death cases.

This instruction is applicable both where the collision occurs on the wrong side of the road and where the collision occurs with the defendant on the correct side of the road but is caused by the defendant having driven on the wrong side of the road. This is the applicable instruction in both skidding and non-skidding cases.

Committee Comment (1978 Revision)

The law regarding the effect of skidding evidence in a case involving a motor vehicle accident on the wrong side of the road has been substantially revised by Friederich v. Chamberlain, 458 S.W.2d 360 (Mo. banc 1970). If the evidence shows that defendant is on the wrong side of the road, plaintiff is entitled to go to the jury. Skidding is a circumstance which the jury can consider in connection with all other facts and circumstances in deciding whether defendant was negligent.

Library References:

C.J.S. Motor Vehicles § 530.
West's Key No. Digests, Automobiles ⚷246.

Notes of Decisions

In general 1
Backing 6
Negating defense 3
Negligence per se 2
Skidding 4
Wrong side of road 5

---

1. In general

Evidence supported lookout submission against driver who drove on wrong side of the road. Leonard v. Gordon's Transport, 575 S.W.2d 244[2] (Mo.App.1978).

Rule of the road (§ 304.015(2)) regarding driving on the right side of the road makes exceptions, such as overtaking, but without evidence thereof verdict director need not negate the exceptions. Leonard v. Gordon's Transport, 575 S.W.2d 244[2] (Mo.App. 1978).

MAI 17.13 proper where defendant crossed center-line and then returned to right side into collision with plaintiff. Cryts v. Ford Motor Co., 571 S.W.2d 683[16] (Mo. App.1978).

Old MAI 17.13 is still proper, as a not-in-MAI verdict director, for northbound motorist who drove into southbound lane to avoid a weaving southbound motorist. New MAI 17.13 would not have been proper since southbound motorist was not on the wrong side of the road *at the time of the collision*. McCroskey v. Marshall, 519 S.W.2d 717 (Mo. App.1975).

In a head-on collision case where the only evidence defendant skidded across the center line came in defendant's case, the plaintiff's verdict director properly based defendant's liability on driving on the wrong side of the road, without reference to defendant's skidding since that was merely defensive evidence of no negligence. Turner v. Cowart, 450 S.W.2d 441[1, 2] (Mo.1969).

Where driver is lawfully making a left turn it is error to give a verdict director against him for driving on the wrong side of the road. Ellison v. Simmons, 447 S.W.2d 66[1] (Mo. 1969).

Where plaintiff's evidence showed defendant *skidded* onto wrong side of road, error to submit defendant *drove* onto wrong side of road. McIntyre v. Whited, 440 S.W.2d 449[4] (Mo.1969).

MAI 17.13 submitting that defendant *drove* on wrong side of the road was not supported by evidence that he *skidded* across center line. Strickland v. Barker, 436 S.W.2d 37[3–9] (Mo.1969).

When evidence showed the sole factual cause of collision was defendant's skidding across the center line, it was error for plaintiff to submit MAI 17.13 (*Driving* on the Wrong Side of the Road). Jokisch v. Life & Casualty Ins. Co. of Tenn., 424 S.W.2d 111[10] (Mo.App.1967).

2. Negligence per se

In personal injury action involving wrong side of the road case, it was reversible error to submit verdict directing instruction that withheld element of negligence from consideration where negligence per se theory of liability was not tried by consent; even though driver's guilty plea to traffic violation was admissible, submission of instruction based on negligence per se was improper where driver did not plead a statutory violation or negligence per se theory of liability. Myers v. Morrison, 822 S.W.2d 906 (Mo.App. 1991).

Driving on wrong side of road is negligence per se and "negligence" need not be hypothesized. Bentley v. Crews, 630 S.W.2d 99[4, 5] (Mo.App.1981).

Where defendant's car *skidded* off the wrong side of the highway plaintiff was entitled to a res ipsa verdict director. Silver v. Curtis, 490 S.W.2d 412[1–2] (Mo.App.1972).

Plaintiff's verdict-directing instruction properly omitted submission of *negligence* where evidence showed defendant failed to drive as close *as practical* to right-hand edge of the highway. Condos v. Associated Transports, Inc., 453 S.W.2d 682[1–5] (Mo.App. 1970).

3. Negating defense

MAI 17.13 proper and need not negate purely defensive evidence that there was no collision. State Farm Mut. Auto. Ins. Co. v. Jessee, 523 S.W.2d 832[4–5] (Mo.App. 1975).

4. Skidding

Where defendant's car *skidded* off the wrong side of the highway plaintiff was entitled to a res ipsa verdict director. Silver v. Curtis, 490 S.W.2d 412[1–2] (Mo.App.1972).

Verdict director submitting negligent application of brakes causing skid. (Friederich v. Chamberlain, 458 S.W.2d 360 (Mo.1970)). Middleman v. Complete Auto Transit, Inc., 486 S.W.2d 456[1, 2] (Mo. banc 1972).

Where defendant drove off the roadway, struck a culvert and then veered back onto the roadway, and struck plaintiff on wrong side of the road, plaintiff's case should have been submitted by MAI 17.13, wrong side of the road, rather than by MAI 31.02(1), res ipsa loquitur. Dwyer v. Moss, 462 S.W.2d 645 (Mo. banc 1971).

Where plaintiff properly submitted MAI 17.13, driving on wrong side of the road, and defendant testified she skidded across the center line, it was error to give defendant's affirmative defense instruction exonerating her if she skidded. (This would have been error even had defendant further submitted

241

that her skidding was not negligent.) Such an instruction is akin to an accident instruction condemned by MAI 1.01 and a sole-cause instruction condemned by MAI 1.03. Defendant should be limited to conversing negligence by MAI 33.02(2), and then arguing non-negligent skidding. Stover v. Patrick, 459 S.W.2d 393[1, 2] (Mo. banc 1970).

Where the evidence, either plaintiff's or defendant's, shows that defendant's car skidded onto the wrong side of the road into collision with plaintiff's car the plaintiff has made a submissible case of defendant's negligence in driving onto the wrong side of the road; thereupon the burden of evidence is upon the defendant to excuse the presence of his vehicle on the wrong side of the road. Friederich v. Chamberlain, 458 S.W.2d 360[4, 5] (Mo. banc 1970).

5. Wrong side of road

Driving on wrong side of road is negligence per se and "negligence" need not be hypothesized. Bentley v. Crews, 630 S.W.2d 99[4, 5] (Mo.App.1981).

Revised MAI 17.13 is to be used in all appropriate wrong-side-of-the-road cases. But where defendant was initially driving on the wrong side of the road and thereby forced plaintiff to move onto plaintiff's wrong side of the road and the collision occurred there, new MAI 17.13 was inappropriate since defendant was not on the wrong side of the road at the time of the collision, and plaintiff properly submitted that defendant negligently drove on the wrong side of the road. Pittock v. Gardner, 530 S.W.2d 217[1, 2] (Mo. banc 1975).

MAI 17.13 proper where defendant crossed center line and then returned to right side into collision with plaintiff. Cryts v. Ford Motor Co., 571 S.W.2d 683[16] (Mo. App.1978).

6. Backing

Where defendant's grader was being backed on the right-hand side of the road it was improper for plaintiff to submit driving on the wrong side of the road. Bounds v. Scott Const. Co., 498 S.W.2d 765[2] (Mo. 1973).

17.14   [Withdrawn 1990] Verdict Directing—Humanitarian Negligence, Compound

17.15   [Withdrawn 1990] Verdict Directing—Humanitarian Negligence, Disjunctive

17.16 [1973 Revision] Verdict Directing—Rear End Collision

Your verdict must be for plaintiff if you believe:

First, defendant's automobile came into collision with the rear of plaintiff's automobile, and

Second, defendant was thereby negligent,[1] and

Third, as a direct result of such negligence[1], plaintiff sustained damage.

*[unless you believe plaintiff is not entitled to recover by reason of Instruction Number _____ (*here insert number of affirmative defense instruction*)].

Notes on Use (1990 Revision)

1. The terms "negligent" and "negligence" must be defined. See definitions in Chapter 11.00.

The rear end doctrine is limited in scope and this instruction should not be used except where the facts show the doctrine is clearly applicable.

* Add if affirmative defense is submitted. This bracketed phrase should not be used to submit comparative fault.

For modification of verdict directing instructions to submit comparative fault, see MAI 37.01.

Committee Comment (1990 Revision)

This is the instruction to use in rear-end cases such as *Jones v. Central States Oil Co.*, 350 Mo. 91, 164 S.W.2d 914 (1942), and other such cases.

Paragraph Second must be included.

Where agency is in issue see MAI 18.01.

Where suit involves multiple cause of damage see MAI 19.01.

Where suit is for wrongful death see MAI 20.01 and 20.02.

Where suit is for loss of services or medical expenses of dependent see MAI 31.04.

Library References:

C.J.S. Motor Vehicles § 530.
West's Key No. Digests, Automobiles ⚷246.

Notes of Decisions

---

1. In general

It was error to submit an instruction based on the rearend collision doctrine in a case in which the defendant slid down an icy hill where defendant had neither time nor distance to stop after observing the vehicles ahead of her. Kaufmann v. Nagle, 807 S.W.2d 91 (Mo. banc 1991).

Jury question existed on crossclaim by driver against construction company as to whether construction company flagger, inappropriately dressed, negligently stopped vehicles suddenly and without adequate warning and was a partial cause of rear end collision. Trial court erroneously directed verdict on crossclaim in favor of construction company. Trial court properly submitted rear end doctrine against offending truck driver despite the fact that the accident took place in a construction zone. Donham v. Samo, 838 S.W.2d 174 (Mo.App.1992).

Jury instruction submitting as ground of negligence that driver of rear-ended car had "failed to keep proper control of her vehicle" was prejudicially erroneous in driver's action against driver of car that rear ended her. Havel v. Diebler, 836 S.W.2d 501 (Mo.App. 1992).

In an action brought by passenger in lead automobile against driver of following automobile to recover injuries sustained in rear-end collision, negligence on the part of the driver of the lead automobile did not preclude passenger from obtaining rear-end collision doctrine instruction. Wegeng v. Flowers, 753 S.W.2d 306, 309 (Mo.App. 1988).

Submission of rear-end instruction was reversible error where testimony was that truck's taillight was out and the other light was very dim and the truck was improperly parked. Jensen v. Pappas, 684 S.W.2d 524[3] (Mo.App.1984).

Rear-end submission proper where defendant rear-ended plaintiff's car while parked off the paved portion of the highway. Bar-

low v. Thornhill, 537 S.W.2d 412[7–9] (Mo. banc 1976).

Where Kansas law of the rear-end doctrine was substantively akin to Missouri law, MAI 17.16, not Kansas pattern instruction, should be given. Warriner v. Eblovi, 485 S.W.2d 700[3, 4] (Mo.App.1972).

Error to submit plaintiff's verdict director under rear-end doctrine absent substantial evidence that defendant struck plaintiff's car in *rear*. Neil v. Mayer, 426 S.W.2d 711[3–11] (Mo.App.1968).

Where plaintiff was struck from behind by moving hand truck, her not-in-MAI verdict director was akin to MAI 17.16 (rear-end collision). Scheele v. American Bakeries Co., 427 S.W.2d 361, 362 (Mo.1968).

2. Evidentiary support

Jury verdict for motorist who struck second motorist from behind was supported by probative evidence where evidence existed from which jury could have found following motorist was using highest degree of care and second motorist's sudden complete stop in fast lane was not reasonably foreseeable to driver exercising highest degree of care. Nishwitz v. Blosser, 850 S.W.2d 119 (Mo.App.1993).

Evidence that defendant turned into plaintiff's lane, drove 100 feet and then struck plaintiff's stopped car warranted submission of rear-end instruction. Becker v. Finke, 567 S.W.2d 136[1–3] (Mo.App.1978).

Evidence supported defendant's contributory negligence instruction on (a) rearend collision, (b) failure to keep a lookout, and (c) following too closely. Pitezel v. Danielson, 571 S.W.2d 694[1–4] (Mo.App.1978).

Plaintiff and defendant drivers were halted in tandem for a left turn when a third car rear-ended defendant shoving defendant's car into plaintiff's; since defendant did not "permit" his car to strike plaintiff's the rear-end doctrine did not apply. Cosens v. Smith, 528 S.W.2d 772[2] (Mo.App.1975).

Where leading car turned sharply into path of overtaking car, which had only 60 feet in distance and three seconds in time to avoid collision, the rear-end doctrine did not apply since adequate time and distance available to overtaking driver are essential elements of his liability. Lichtenberg v. Hug, 481 S.W.2d 527[1, 2] (Mo.App.1972).

Evidence that plaintiff was traveling in proper lane when struck by defendant from the rear was sufficient to warrant submission under rear-end doctrine. Gaynor v. Horwitz, 464 S.W.2d 537[1–3] (Mo.App.1971).

3. Harmless error

Giving old version of MAI 17.16 after new MAI 17.16 became effective was error but harmless because it required higher proof of negligence. Coffer v. Paris, 550 S.W.2d 915[1, 2] (Mo.App.1977).

4. Contributory negligence

Rear-end instruction may be used by defendant driver to submit *contributory negligence* of plaintiff-driver of following car. Mueller v. Storbakken, 583 S.W.2d 179[1–4, 7] (Mo. banc 1979).

17.17 [1978 Revision] Verdict Directing—Per se Negligence—Improper Turn

Your verdict must be for plaintiff if you believe:

First, defendant in approaching the intersection intending to turn left failed to drive his automobile in the portion of the right half of the roadway nearest the center line, and

Second, as a direct result of such conduct, plaintiff sustained damage.

* [unless you believe plaintiff is not entitled to recover by reason of Instruction Number _____ (*here insert number of affirmative defense instruction*)].

Notes on Use (1990 Revision)

Although the violation of a traffic statute or ordinance may be negligence per se (*Rowe v. Kansas City Public Service Co.*, 241 Mo.App. 1225, 1231, 248 S.W.2d 445, 448 (1952)), "[u]nder the circumstances of a particular case there may be a valid excuse for failing to comply with a statutory rule of the road, as where nonobservance of the statute is induced by considerations of safety—or where compliance is impossible. . . ." *MacArthur v. Gendron*, 312 S.W.2d 146, 150 (Mo.App.1958).

* Add if affirmative defense is submitted. This bracketed phrase should not be used to submit comparative fault.

For modifications of verdict directing instructions to submit comparative fault, see MAI 37.01.

See MAI 33.05(2) to submit legal justification or "excuse" for negligence per se.

Library References:

C.J.S. Motor Vehicles § 530.
West's Key No. Digests, Automobiles ⚷246.

Notes of Decisions

In general 1
Conversing 2

———

1. In General

In personal injury action involving wrong side of the road case, it was reversible error to submit verdict directing instruction that withheld element of negligence from consideration where negligence per se theory of liability was not tried by consent; even though driver's guilty plea to traffic violation was admissible, submission of instruction based on negligence per se was improper where driver did not plead a statutory violation or negligence per se theory of liability. Myers v. Morrison, 822 S.W.2d 906 (Mo.App. 1991).

Although emergency instructions are no longer permitted under MAI, defense of justification or excuse remains, and defendant may introduce any evidence which tends to establish he is not guilty of negligence. Cowell v. Thompson, 713 S.W.2d 52[3] (Mo. App.1986).

Plaintiff's verdict-directing instruction properly omitted submission of *negligence* where evidence showed defendant failed to drive as close *as practical* to right-hand edge of the highway. Condos v. Associated Transports, Inc., 453 S.W.2d 682[1–5] (Mo.App. 1970).

2. Conversing

Where plaintiff's verdict director does not require finding defendant negligent, it is error to give a converse which directs a finding for defendant if he was not negligent since a converse instruction must be in substantially the same language as the verdict director. The court, however, noted that defendant was entitled to an instruction on justification or excuse, and indicated that the error in defendant's converse instruction would have been avoided if it had been reworded, making it an affirmative converse. Cowell v. Thompson, 713 S.W.2d 52[1, 5, 6] (Mo.App. 1986).

Where plaintiff's verdict director submitted facts constituting negligence per se and did not require a finding defendant was negligent, it was error to give defendant's converse to find for defendant if he was not negligent as submitted in plaintiff's verdict director. Oventrop v. Bi–State Dev. Agency, 521 S.W.2d 488[10] (Mo.App.1975).

17.18 [1978 Revision] Per se Negligence—Violating Speed Limit

Your verdict must be for plaintiff if you believe:

First, defendant drove at a speed in excess of (*insert legal maximum*) miles per hour, and

Second, as a direct result of such conduct, plaintiff sustained damage.

* [unless you believe plaintiff is not entitled to recover by reason of Instruction Number _____ (*here insert number of affirmative defense instruction*)].

Notes on Use (1990 Revision)

Although the violation of a traffic statute or ordinance may be negligence per se (*Rowe v. Kansas City Public Service Co.*, 241 Mo.App. 1225, 1231, 248 S.W.2d 445, 448 (1952)), "[u]nder the circumstances of a particular case there may be a valid excuse for failing to comply with a statutory rule of the road, as where nonobservance of the statute is induced by considerations of safety—or where compliance is impossible...." *MacArthur v. Gendron,* 312 S.W.2d 146, 150 (Mo.App.1958).

* Add if affirmative defense is submitted. This bracketed phrase should not be used to submit comparative fault.

For modifications of verdict directing instructions to submit comparative fault, see MAI 37.01.

See MAI 33.05(2) for submission of legal justification or "excuse" for negligence per se.

Library References:

C.J.S. Motor Vehicles § 530.
West's Key No. Digests, Automobiles ⚖246.

Notes of Decisions

In general   1
Conversing   2

_____

1. In general

In personal injury action involving wrong side of the road case, it was reversible error to submit verdict directing instruction that withheld element of negligence from consideration where negligence per se theory of liability was not tried by consent; even though driver's guilty plea to traffic violation was admissible, submission of instruction based on negligence per se was improper where driver did not plead a statutory violation or negligence per se theory of liability. Myers v. Morrison, 822 S.W.2d 906 (Mo.App. 1991).

Although emergency instructions are no longer permitted under MAI, defense of justification or excuse remains, and defendant may introduce any evidence which tends to establish he is not guilty of negligence. Cowell v. Thompson, 713 S.W.2d 52[3] (Mo.App.1986).

2. Conversing

Where plaintiff's verdict director does not require finding defendant negligent, it is error to give a converse which directs a finding for defendant if he was not negligent since a converse instruction must be in substantially the same language as the verdict director. The court, however, noted that defendant was entitled to an instruction on justification or excuse, and indicated that the error in defendant's converse instruction would have been avoided if it had been reworded, making it an affirmative converse. Cowell v. Thompson, 713 S.W.2d 52[1, 5, 6] (Mo.App. 1986).

Where plaintiff submitted failure to use the "highest degree of care", error to give defendant's converse based only on defendant's "negligence". Doyle v. Bi–State Dev. Agency, 628 S.W.2d 695[2] (Mo.App.1982).

Where plaintiff's verdict director submitted facts constituting negligence per se and did not require a finding defendant was negligent, it was error to give defendant's converse to find for defendant if he was not negligent as submitted in plaintiff's verdict director. Oventrop v. Bi–State Dev. Agency, 521 S.W.2d 488[10] (Mo.App.1975).

17.19   [1969 New] Verdict Directing—Unable to Stop Within Range of Vision

Defendant drove at a speed which made it impossible for him to stop within the range of his visibility.

Notes on Use (1990 Revision)

This provision is to be used in lieu of paragraph First of 17.01 or as one of the alternate submissions in paragraph First of 17.02. It may also be used as a submission in comparative fault (MAI 37.02) and wrongful death cases (MAI 20.01 and 20.02).

Committee Comment (1969 New)

While Missouri does not have the assured clear distance rule, it does allow jurors to find driving beyond the range of vision to be negligent. The existing instruction on excessive speed does not adequately cover this particular kind of misconduct.

In *Johnson v. Lee Way Motor Freight, Inc.*, 261 S.W.2d 95 (Mo.1953) the plaintiff collided with the rear end of a stationary tractor-trailer owned by defendant which was stopped on the highway.

There were patches of fog along the highway but between the patches there was no limitation of visibility. Plaintiff had just emerged from a patch of fog at a speed of about 30 miles an hour when he saw defendant's truck 30 to 35 feet ahead of him. According to plaintiff, the truck had no lights on.

The Court said: "Defendants' contention that plaintiff was guilty of contributory negligence as a matter of law is based on the asserted proposition that it is always negligence as a matter of law to drive at such a speed that it is impossible to stop within the range of visibility." The Court then quotes plaintiff's own testimony as showing that he was driving at such a speed.

The Court said: "We continue to adhere to the view that one is not necessarily negligent as a matter of law solely because he drives at a speed which prevents his stopping within the distance his headlights reveal objects ahead of him; and that whether he is contributorily negligent as a matter of law depends upon all the circumstances in a particular case...."

"We are of the opinion that it was for the jury to decide in this case whether plaintiff was contributorily negligent in failing to so reduce his speed either before entering the fog patch or upon entering the fog patch to have assured himself that he could stop his automobile within his range of vision."

See also: *Thompson v. Byers Transportation Co., Inc.*, 362 Mo. 42, 239 S.W.2d 498 (1951) and *Haley v. Edwards*, 276 S.W.2d 153 (Mo.1955).

Library References:

C.J.S. Motor Vehicles § 530.
West's Key No. Digests, Automobiles ⊗246.

Notes of Decisions

1. In general

Gravamen of liability is excessive speed. Robertson v. Grotheer, 521 S.W.2d 452[2, 3, 8, 9] (Mo.App.1975).

17.20 [1969 New] Verdict Directing—Stopping in Lane Reserved for Moving Traffic

Defendant stopped his automobile in a lane reserved for moving traffic.

Notes on Use (1969 New)

Caution. Not every such stop is submissible as being a negligent act. The circumstances must be such that a jury could reasonably find the stop was negligent. This provision is to be used in lieu of paragraph First of 17.01 or as one of the alternate submissions in paragraph First of 17.02. This submission may be employed in comparative fault cases (MAI 37.02) and wrongful death cases (MAI 20.01 and 20.02) when applicable.

Committee Comment (1996 Revision)

There are occasions when the stop is neither sudden nor unsignaled but still negligent. Failure to pull onto the shoulder in cases of motor or tire trouble or when picking up passengers are typical, particularly when the stop is just past the crest of a hill or at night. Such a submission would, of course, have to be coupled with a finding that the act was negligent. See for example *Lane v. Supreme Cab Co.,* 374 S.W.2d 527 (Mo.App.1964) and *Lotshaw v. Vaughn,* 381 S.W.2d 43 (Mo.App.1964).

Library References:

C.J.S. Motor Vehicles § 530.
West's Key No. Digests, Automobiles ⟜246.

Notes of Decisions

In general 1
Parking on shoulder 2

_____

1. In general

Comparative fault instruction in negligence suit by motorist injured in rear-end collision was supported by evidence that motorist stopped vehicle on highway to allow oncoming truck to pass through bridge, bridge was as wide as paved portion of highway, motorist did not pull off onto shoulder of road, did not engage emergency flashing lights, and road conditions were dark and wet. Tennison v. State Farm Mut. Auto Ins. Co., 834 S.W.2d 846 (Mo.App.1992).

Where initial stopping was for red light, and any negligence that occurred was the result of remaining stopped, MAI 17.20 was inappropriate. Paxton v. American Family Mut. Ins. Co., 682 S.W.2d 896[1] (Mo.App. 1984).

Where plaintiffs' evidence supported both MAI 17.20, defendant stopping on highway, and MAI 17.12, defendant stopping without adequate warning, plaintiffs are entitled to choose their own theory of recovery and the court did not err in giving MAI 17.20 rather than MAI 17.12 as contended by defendant.

Certa v. Associated Bldg. Center, Inc., 560 S.W.2d 593[1–10] (Mo.App.1977).

Where plaintiff-motorist ran into rear of defendant's motor grader moving backward in her lane of traffic, it was error to give her modified MAI 17.20 submitting only that defendant negligently *operated* its grader in plaintiff's lane of traffic. Without the submission of a negligent act, such as failure to warn, that was a roving commission. Dick v. Scott Const. Co., 539 S.W.2d 688[1] (Mo.App.1976).

Verdict director on allowing stalled truck to remain on the highway. Hofstra v. Schriber, 475 S.W.2d 44 (Mo.1972).

Modified verdict director approved. Hofstra v. Schriber, 475 S.W.2d 44 (Mo.1972).

When there was no evidence plaintiffs failed to give a warning signal, defendant's contributory negligence instruction, combining MAI 32.01 with modifications of MAI 17.11 (slowing without adequate warning) and MAI 17.12 (stopping without adequate warning), was erroneous for substituting the words "at a time when it was not reasonably safe to do so." Burton v. Bi–State Dev. Agency, 468 S.W.2d 4 (Mo.1971).

Error to submit that defendant motorist stopped on the traveled portion of the highway since it omitted the elements of suddenly stopping without warning. (Given before adoption of MAI 17.20). Joly v. Wippler, 449 S.W.2d 565[1] (Mo.1970).

2. Parking on shoulder

Plaintiffs' verdict director against defendant for parking unlighted repair vehicle on shoulder of highway. Penn v. Columbia Asphalt Co., 513 S.W.2d 679[14] (Mo.App. 1974).

17.21 [1993 New] Verdict Directing—Driving While Intoxicated

Defendant drove while intoxicated [1] to the extent that defendant's driving ability was impaired.

Notes on Use (1996 Revision)

1. Intoxication may include being under the influence of alcohol, controlled substances, or drugs. See § 577.001(2) and § 577.010, RSMo. This term may be modified to identify whether intoxication was caused by alcohol, a controlled substance, a drug, or a combination, if that fact is in issue; e.g., "was intoxicated by cocaine".

This is an optional submission of negligence that may be used as paragraph First of MAI 17.01 or as one of the alternate submissions in paragraph First of MAI 17.02. It may also be used as a submission in wrongful death cases, see MAI 20.01 and 20.02, and in comparative fault submissions, see MAI 37.02.

Committee Comment (1993 New)

Driving while intoxicated can be the basis of recovery and may be negligence per se. See: *Bentley v. Crews,* 630 S.W.2d 99, 107 (Mo.App. 1981). There must be evidence to support a finding of proximate cause between defendant's intoxication and plaintiff's damages. See also: *Bowman v. Heffron,* 318 S.W.2d 269, 273 (Mo.1958). See MAI 17.17 and 17.18 for guidance when intoxication is submissible as negligence per se.

Library References:

C.J.S. Motor Vehicles § 530.
West's Key No. Digests, Automobiles ⚷246.

18.00

VERDICT DIRECTING—AGENCY IN ISSUE

Analysis of Instructions

Westlaw Electronic Research

See Westlaw Electronic Research Guide preceding the Table of Instructions.

Library References:

C.J.S. Agency § 553; Trial § 348.
West's Key No. Digests, Principal and Agent ⟨⟩194; Trial ⟨⟩234.

257

18.01 [1991 Revision] Verdict Directing—Agency in Issue—Modification Required

Servant Not Joined

Where defendant master or principal is being sued and he has denied agency of the alleged servant or agent, paragraph First in the verdict directing instruction shall be in the following form:

First, the driver Jones [was an employee of Ajax and] [1] was operating the (defendant's) motor vehicle within the scope and course of his [employment by] [agency for] [2] (defendant's name) [at the time of the collision].[1]

The remaining paragraphs of the verdict directing instruction will then be renumbered. The name of the servant or some other identification will be substituted for the word "defendant" in the remainder of the instruction. Thus if Verdict Directing Instruction 17.01 were to include the issue of agency it would read as follows:

Your verdict must be for plaintiff if you believe:

First, the driver Jones [was an employee of Ajax and] [1] was operating the Ajax Company motor vehicle within the scope and course of his employment by Ajax [at the time of the collision],[1] and

Second, Jones violated the traffic signal, and

Third, Jones was thereby negligent, and

Fourth, as a direct result of such negligence plaintiff sustained damage.

Both Master and Servant Joined

Where the master and servant are both joined as parties and agency is in issue, the verdict directing instruction against the servant will be a typical verdict directing instruction such as MAI 17.01. Since the verdict directing instruction contains those elements relevant to the liability of the servant, the only remaining issue relating to the master will be the agency issue. Under these circumstances it is not necessary to repeat the elements relating to the servant's negligence in the verdict directing instruction against the master. Thus, the verdict directing instruction against the master would read as follows:

> In your verdict you must find defendant Ajax responsible for any negligence of defendant Jones if you believe driver Jones was operating the Ajax Company motor vehicle within the scope and course of his employment by Ajax.

In preparing the verdict form where the master's liability is submitted only on the servant's conduct, the servant is also joined, and agency is in issue, MAI 36.01 should be modified by adding the following:

> Note: Complete the following paragraph by writing the word(s) required by your verdict.

> On the claim of plaintiff for personal injury against defendant (name of master), we, the undersigned jurors,

> _____ find (name of master) responsible for

> ("do" or "do not")

> any negligence of (name of servant).

Notes on Use (1990 Revision)

1. Use bracketed terms if in issue.

2. Select appropriate term.

When the issue of agency is submitted, the appropriate definition must also be submitted. See MAI 13.02 to MAI 13.07(2).

See MAI 37.05(1) and 37.05(2) for discussion of agency issues in comparative fault cases and alternative methods of submission of those issues depending on the nature of the dispute.

See Illustration 35.04.

Committee Comment (1965 New)

See General Comment at MAI 13.01.

Library References:

C.J.S. Agency § 553.

West's Key No. Digests, Master and Servant ⟜332(4); Principal and Agent ⟜194.

Notes of Decisions

In general 1
Agency in issue 2
Agency not in issue 3

------

1. In general

Trial court's error in substituting phrase "was agent of" for "was employee of" in jury instruction on issue of agency did not result in manifest injustice or miscarriage of justice as required for error to be plain error and warrant reversal of judgment that hospital was vicariously liable for negligence of physician, since closing argument of defendant equated concepts of agency and employment and so removed any potential confusion amongst jury over whether term "agent" meant something different from the term "employee." V.A.M.R. 84.13(c). Glidewell v. S.C. Management, Inc., 923 S.W.2d 940 (Mo.App.1996).

MAI 23.05–18.01 submitting fraudulent representations by agent. Tietjens v. General Motors Corp., 418 S.W.2d 75[1] (Mo. 1967).

2. Agency in issue

Where plaintiffs' recovery depends on agency of defendant's employee, that disputed fact must be submitted not only by definition of agency but also by inclusion in plaintiffs' verdict director. Galemore Motor Co. v. State Farm Mut. Auto. Ins. Co., 513 S.W.2d 161[11] (Mo.App.1974).

Where agency of defendant's driver was in issue, verdict-directing instruction must be modified by substituting the name of the driver for that of defendant. Failure prejudicially erroneous. Wills v. Townes Cadillac–Oldsmobile, Inc., 490 S.W.2d 257[6] (Mo. 1973).

Although defendant's answer denied salesman was its agent, where plaintiff's evidence of agency was not refuted by other evidence, agency was a question of law and need not be hypothesized in plaintiff's verdict director. Bowers v. S–H–S Motor Sales Corp., 481 S.W.2d 584[2] (Mo.App.1972).

Verdict director which assumes agency is erroneous. Dickey v. Nations, 479 S.W.2d 208[3–5] (Mo.App.1972).

Where defendant denied its employee was acting within the scope of his employment plaintiff's verdict director must hypothesize that element and the term must be defined. Ratterree v. General Motors Corp., 460 S.W.2d 309[2] (Mo.App.1970).

When defense of contributory negligence depends on driver's being plaintiff's agent, it is error to submit a contributory negligence instruction without hypothesizing and defining agency. Sanfilippo v. Bolle, 432 S.W.2d 232[2] (Mo.1968).

Error for plaintiff to omit MAI 13.05 (Definition–Agency–Scope of Employment) when verdict director used MAI 18.01 requiring a finding that driver was "within the scope and course of his employment." Chandler v. New Moon Homes, Inc., 418 S.W.2d 130[11] (Mo. banc 1967).

Verdict director for false arrest based on agency (MAI 18.01–23.04) requires definition of scope of employment (MAI 13.02). Peak v. W.T. Grant Co., 409 S.W.2d 58[1] (Mo. banc 1966).

3. Agency not in issue

Although plaintiff has the burden of proving agency, where collection manager's authority was uncontroverted, plaintiffs' verdict director properly omitted a finding on scope of authority. Price v. Ford Motor Credit Co., 530 S.W.2d 249[15, 16] (Mo.App.1975).

Where undisputed evidence showed defendant's employee created a dangerous condition plaintiff's verdict director need not hypothesize that element. Cline v. Carthage, etc., Co., 504 S.W.2d 102[4] (Mo. 1973).

Where undisputed evidence showed a partnership transaction there was no need to define acts within the scope of the partnership. Restaurant Industries, Inc. v. Lum's, Inc., 495 S.W.2d 668[4] (Mo.App.1973).

Where as a matter of law evidence showed employee was acting within the scope of his employment it was unnecessary to hypothesize that element in his verdict director. Elliott v. St. Louis S.W. Ry. Co., 487 S.W.2d 7[11] (Mo.1972).

Conceded facts need not be submitted, so where agency of defendant's driver was established by defendant's evidence plaintiff's verdict director properly omitted an MAI 18.01 submission of agency. Young v. Frozen Foods Express, Inc., 444 S.W.2d 35[5, 6] (Mo.App.1969).

Agency need not be submitted by MAI 18.01 nor scope of employment defined where agency is established as a matter of law by documentary evidence such as a policy of insurance. Baker v. St. Paul Fire & Marine Ins. Co., 427 S.W.2d 281[14–17] (Mo. App.1968).

Not error to omit definition of "scope of employment" where agency was not in issue. Terry v. Sweeney, 420 S.W.2d 368[9] (Mo.App.1967).

19.00

VERDICT DIRECTING MODIFICATION

Analysis of Instructions

Westlaw Electronic Research

See Westlaw Electronic Research Guide preceding the Table of Instructions.

Library References:

C.J.S. Trial § 350–351.
West's Key No. Digests, Trial ☞234(3, 4).

19.01 [1986 Revision] Verdict Directing Modification—Multiple Causes of Damage

In a case involving two or more causes of damage, the "direct result" language of paragraph Third of verdict directing instructions such as 17.01 and 17.02 might be misleading. In such cases plaintiff, at his option, may substitute one of the following:

Third, such negligence directly caused or directly contributed to cause damage to plaintiff.[1]

Third, such negligence either directly caused damage to plaintiff or combined with the [acts of (*here describe another causing damage*)] [condition of the (*here describe product*)][2] to directly cause damage to plaintiff.

Notes on Use (1999 Revision)

1. There is no longer a prohibition against using the first alternate where plaintiff is at fault in light of adoption of pure comparative fault in *Gustafson v. Benda*, 661 S.W.2d 11 (Mo. banc 1983).

2. Select the appropriate bracketed phrase.

These modifications may be used whether or not another causing damage is a party.

Caution: Where the verdict directing instruction is modified with one of the alternates in MAI 19.01 or an appropriate modification to submit "multiple causes" of damage in a case such as a death case, a products case, a premises case, or a medical malpractice case, care must be used in drafting a converse instruction by using substantially the same causation language as used in the verdict directing instruction. See *Hiers v. Lemley*, 834 S.W.2d 729 (Mo. banc 1992).

In a case such as *Carlson v. K–Mart*, 979 S.W.2d 145 (Mo. banc 1998), where MAI 19.01 is used in the verdict director, delete the entire phrase "as a direct result of the occurrence mentioned in the evidence" from MAI 4.01 and substitute the phrase "which (*describe the compensable event or conduct*) directly caused or directly contributed to cause."

Committee Comment (1995 New)

In 1986, the title of this instruction was changed from "Verdict Directing Modification—Joint Tortfeasors" to "Verdict Directing Modification—Multiple Causes of Damage" in order to avoid confusion and allow this modification in cases in which there are multiple causes of damage but which may not involve another party or tortfeasor. In *Gaines v. Property Servicing Company*, 276 S.W.2d 169 (Mo.1955), it was held:

> The general rule is "that if a defendant is negligent and his negligence combines with that of another, or with any other independent, intervening cause, he is liable, although his negligence was not the sole negligence or the sole proximate cause, and although his negligence, without such other independent, intervening cause, would not have produced the injury." Id. at 173, 174. (Citations omitted.)

This modification is intended to employ these principles.

See the discussion of causation in *Callahan v. Cardinal Glennon Hosp.*, 863 S.W.2d 852 (Mo. banc 1993), in which the Supreme Court cited the language of this instruction favorably as an expression of the "but for" test of "causation in fact" and also discussed the classic law school example of the "thin skulled" plaintiff in the context of causation by defendant's negligence.

Library References:

C.J.S. Negligence § 193–194.
West's Key No. Digests, Negligence ☞379.

Notes of Decisions

In general   1
Wrongful death   2

1. In general

Multiple-cause instruction was warranted upon request as to whether any negligence of defendant driver in motor vehicle accident directly caused "or directly contributed to cause" damage to plaintiff driver's right shoulder that was additional to her pre-existing right shoulder injury; medical records reflected that in six weeks before accident plaintiff was treated by chiropractor more than ten times for neck and shoulder problems, but chiropractor opined that condition of right shoulder was worse after accident. Higby v. Wein, 996 S.W.2d 95 (Mo.App. 1999).

Damage instruction based on MAI 4.01, providing that injured customer's damages were only those that "directly resulted" from store owner's conduct, should have been modified to track verdict director based on MAI 19.01, providing that store owner was liable if its failure to use ordinary care "directly caused or directly contributed to cause" damage to customer; confusion engendered by conflict between these instructions prejudiced customer, entitling her to a new trial. Carlson v. K–Mart Corp., 979 S.W.2d 145 (Mo. banc 1998).

If instruction was erroneous by failing to find that worker's damage was caused by defect which existed when chemical was sold by defendant, instruction did not prejudice defendant, where it was clear from both instruction and the evidence that if worker was injured due to chemical, it was caused by defect which existed when chemical was sold. Ray v. Upjohn Co., 851 S.W.2d 646 (Mo.App.1993).

Trial court properly instructed in automobile accident case that defendant's negligence must directly contribute to cause plaintiff's damage, while at same time instructing on plaintiff's comparative fault.

Krenski v. Aubuchon, 841 S.W.2d 721 (Mo. App.1992).

Appellate court approved modification of MAI 25.04 and 25.05 (strict liability) with MAI 19.01 (multiple causes of injury). Menschik v. Mid–America Pipeline Co., 812 S.W.2d 861 (Mo.App.1991).

Not-in-MAI definition of the term "product" in MAI 25.04, as a "ladder-type track," held to be permissible. Modification of MAI 25.04 with MAI 19.01 held to be proper in stating that the product "directly caused or directly contributed to cause" decedent's death. Eagleburger v. Emerson Electric Co., 794 S.W.2d 210 (Mo.App.1990).

MAI sanctions the 19.01 joint tort-feasor "directly caused or directly contributed to cause damage to plaintiff" modification whether or not the other tort-feasor is a party. Elam v. Alcolac, Inc., 765 S.W.2d 42, 205 (Mo.App.1988).

Verdict directors against physicians which hypothesized that negligence of physicians caused or directly contributed to cause death of decedent were proper even though contributory negligence of decedent was in issue and despite physician's contention that they were successive rather than joint tort feasors. Schiles v. Schaefer, 710 S.W.2d 254[12] (Mo.App.1986).

Omission of hospital which settled with wrongful death plaintiff at close of plaintiff's evidence from verdict directors and verdict forms for assessment of percentage of fault was not error. Schiles v. Schaefer, 710 S.W.2d 254[19] (Mo.App.1986).

Joint tort-feasors, whether or not both are sued, may have a determination of their *relative fault*. Missouri Pacific R.R. Co. v. Whitehead & Kales Co., 566 S.W.2d 466[1–7] (Mo. banc 1978).

In action against joint tort feasors the plaintiff may but need not use MAI 19.01. Failure to do so merely increases plaintiff's burden. Joly v. Wippler, 449 S.W.2d 565[4] (Mo.1970).

Adding an MAI 19.01 joint tortfeasor clause to an MAI 22.02–22.05 type verdict director without definition of negligence "would raise a serious question" since the former uses the word "negligence" and the latter is based on failure to use "ordinary care." (See now MAI 33.15). Chambers v.

Kansas City, 446 S.W.2d 833[5–7] (Mo. 1969).

Plaintiff bus passenger was injured in a right-angle collision between bus and motor vehicle at intersection controlled by stop lights. Each of plaintiff's verdict directors submitted the same negligence against bus company and motorist: failing to keep a lookout or violating the traffic light. Held erroneous as conflicting. Alfultis v. Bi–State Development Agency, 439 S.W.2d 206[2] (Mo.App.1969).

In action for gas explosion and unodorized gas against joint tort-feasors, joint negligence was properly submitted by including first clause of MAI 19.01 as third paragraph of verdict director. Gathright v. Pendegraft, 433 S.W.2d 299[19] (Mo.1968).

Where plaintiff sued drivers A and B his verdict director hypothesizing B's negligence was erroneous in not limiting recovery to driver B, as per MAI 31.03 [Now 35.03] (Illustration: Instructions No. 4, No. 6 and No. 8). Cash v. Bolle, 423 S.W.2d 743[1] (Mo. banc 1968).

2. Wrongful death

It was proper to apply modification of verdict directing instruction for multiple causes of damage to a verdict director in a wrongful death action. Bass v. National Super Markets, Inc., 1995 WL 95000 (Mo.App. E.D.,1995).

In wrongful death action arising out of accident on defendant's loading dock which allegedly led to truck driver's death by stroke, truck driver's preexisting arteriosclerosis condition, which may have made him more susceptible to stroke, was not additional cause of damage requiring use of MAI 19.01, since susceptibility was not equivalent of causation. Wailand v. Anheuser Busch, Inc., 861 S.W.2d 710 (Mo.App.1993). (But see 1995 Revisions to Notes on Use and Committee Comment to MAI 19.01.)

MAI 19.01 can apply to wrongful death cases if words "the death of" are substituted for "damage to" in third paragraph; in wrongful death action against asbestos manufacturers, trial court properly refused defendant's tendered instruction relating to "substantial contributing factor," since additional formulation of causation requirements would only have confused jury. Hagen v. Celotex

266

Corporation, 816 S.W.2d 667 (Mo. banc 1991).

The modification suggested by 19.01 applies to the applicable wrongful death verdict director, MAI 20.02. Where the only difference between MAI 19.01 and fourth paragraph of plaintiff's verdict director was that "the death of" was substituted for "damage to," there was no error. Honey v. Barnes Hosp., 708 S.W.2d 686[2] (Mo.App.1986).

20.00

VERDICT DIRECTING—WRONGFUL DEATH

Analysis of Instructions

Westlaw Electronic Research

See Westlaw Electronic Research Guide preceding the Table of Instructions.

Library References:

C.J.S. Trial §§ 350–351.
West's Key No. Digests, Trial ⚖234(3, 4).

269

20.01 [1981 Revision] Verdict Directing—Wrongful Death—Single Negligent Act Submitted

Your verdict must be for plaintiff[1] if you believe:

First, plaintiff was (*here insert statutory qualification required to bring the action*), and

Second, defendant violated the traffic signal, and

Third, defendant was thereby negligent,[2] and

Fourth, as a direct result of such negligence,[2] (*insert name of decedent*) died.

* [unless you believe plaintiff is not entitled to recover by reason of Instruction Number _____ (*here insert number of affirmative defense instruction*)].

Notes on Use (1996 Revision)

1. In any case involving more than one plaintiff or defendant, any reference to a particular party should include the name of that party, or other descriptive term. Where plaintiff submits against more than one defendant in separate verdict directors, the first line of the verdict director should be modified to indicate the particular defendant covered by this verdict director, i.e.:

Your verdict must be for plaintiff against defendant John Jones if you believe:

If the verdict director is applicable to the plaintiff's claim against more than one defendant, it can be described as follows:

Your verdict must be for plaintiff [against both defendants] [against defendant John Jones and defendant Ace Trucking Lines] if you believe:

2. The terms "negligent" and "negligence" must be defined. See definitions in Chapter 11.00.

This instruction submits the single act of violating a traffic signal. For other wrongful acts or omissions which may be hypothesized see MAI 17.03 and following. For submitting multiple acts of negligence see MAI 20.02.

In the event suit is brought by a plaintiff ad litem for the benefit of collateral heirs, see § 537.090, RSMo, and *Acton v. Shields,* 386 S.W.2d 363 (Mo.1965) on the question of whether pecuniary loss must be submitted in the verdict directing instruction.

* Add if affirmative defense is submitted. This bracketed material should not be used to submit comparative fault.

For modification of verdict directing instructions to submit comparative fault, see MAI 37.01.

Committee Comment (1981 Revision)

Pecuniary loss has not been hypothesized as an element of plaintiff's case because:

"where it appears in a statutory action for death that the death was caused by defendant's negligence, nominal damages may be recovered, although no actual pecuniary damage has been shown...." 25 C.J.S. Death § 96, *quoted in Stroud v. Masek,* 262 S.W.2d 47, 51 (Mo.1953).

"Judgment for nominal damages is a substantial right since such a judgment decides the incident of costs." *Stroud,* supra, at 51.

See §§ 537.080–537.095, RSMo.

Library References:

C.J.S. Negligence § 188, 191–192, 197.
West's Key No. Digests, Negligence ☞370.

Notes of Decisions

Aggravating circumstances   2
Causation   3
Conversing damages   1

_____

1.   Conversing damages

In wrongful death case it is error to give separate converse instructions, one conversing negligence and the other conversing damages. Higgins v. Gosney, 435 S.W.2d 653[8–9] (Mo.1968).

Where plaintiff mother gave MAI 20.01 in action for wrongful death of son omitting finding that plaintiff suffered damages (because nominal damages are presumed), and MAI 5.01 on her measure of damages, it was error for defendant to separately converse the element of damages. Aubuchon v. La-Plant, 435 S.W.2d 648[5–8] (Mo.1968).

2.   Aggravating circumstances

Evidence that busy crossing was without effective warning warranted submission of aggravating circumstances clause. Grothe v. St. L.–S.F. Ry. Co., 460 S.W.2d 711[5] (Mo.1970).

3.   Causation

A lookout submission actually submits failure to see and failure to avoid injury by any means supported by the evidence. Thus, plaintiff may argue defendant's failure to look and his failure to swerve and sound a horn even when those elements are not submitted by plaintiff's verdict director. Lovelace v. Reed, 486 S.W.2d 417[1–4] (Mo.1972).

20.02 [1983 Revision] Verdict Directing—Wrongful Death—Multiple Negligent Acts Submitted

Your verdict must be for plaintiff[1] if you believe:

First, plaintiff was (*here insert statutory qualification required to bring the action*), and

Second, either:

defendant failed to keep a careful lookout, or
defendant drove at an excessive speed, or
defendant's automobile was on the wrong side of the road, and

Third, defendant, in any one or more of the respects submitted in paragraph Second was thereby negligent,[2] and

Fourth, as a direct result of such negligence[2] (*insert name of decedent*) died.

* [unless you believe plaintiff is not entitled to recover by reason of Instruction Number _____ (*here insert number of affirmative defense instruction*)].

Notes on Use (1996 Revision)

1. In any case involving more than one plaintiff or defendant, any reference to a particular party should include the name of that party, or other descriptive term. Where plaintiff submits against more than one defendant in separate verdict directors, the first line of the verdict director should be modified to indicate the particular defendant covered by this verdict director, i.e.:

Your verdict must be for plaintiff against defendant John Jones if you believe:

If the verdict director is applicable to the plaintiff's claim against more than one defendant, it can be described as follows:

Your verdict must be for plaintiff [against both defendants] [against defendant John Jones and defendant Ace Trucking Lines] if you believe:

2. The terms "negligent" and "negligence" must be defined. See definitions in Chapter 11.00.

In the event suit is brought by a plaintiff ad litem for the benefit of collateral heirs, see: § 537.090, RSMo and *Acton v. Shields,* 386 S.W.2d 363 (Mo.1965), on the question of whether pecuniary loss must be submitted in the verdict directing instruction.

272

* Add if affirmative defense is submitted. This bracketed material should not be used to submit comparative fault.

For modification of verdict directing instructions to submit comparative fault, see MAI 37.01.

Committee Comment (1965 New)

See Committee Comment following MAI 20.01.

Library References:

C.J.S. Negligence § 199.
West's Key No. Digests, Negligence ☞422.

Notes of Decisions

1. In general

Verdict form providing for one set of jurors' signatures, as well as jury instructions that "nine or more of you [jurors] must agree in order to return any verdict", adequately advised jury in wrongful death action that same nine jurors should have agreed on same element, act of negligence, causation, and amount of damages; even though negligent acts were submitted to jury in multiple disjunctive form, verdict directors were properly used where each submission of negligence was supported by evidence. Stacy v. Truman Medical Center, 836 S.W.2d 911 (Mo. 1992).

The modification suggested by 19.01 applies to the applicable wrongful death verdict director, MAI 20.02. Where the only difference between MAI 19.01 and fourth paragraph of plaintiff's verdict director was that "the death of" was substituted for "damage to," there was no error. Honey v. Barnes Hosp., 708 S.W.2d 686[2] (Mo.App.1986).

21.00

ACTIONS AGAINST HEALTH CARE PROVIDERS

Analysis of Instructions

Westlaw Electronic Research

See Westlaw Electronic Research Guide preceding the Table of Instructions.

Library References:

C.J.S. Trial § 350–351.
West's Key No. Digests, Trial ☞234(3, 4).

275

21.01 [1988 Revision] Verdict Directing—Actions Against Health Care Providers—No Comparative Fault

Your verdict must be for the plaintiff if you believe:

First, defendant (*here set out act or omission complained of; e.g., "failed to set plaintiff's broken leg bones in natural alignment," or "left a sponge in plaintiff's chest after performing an operation," or "failed to administer tetanus antitoxin "*), and

Second, defendant was thereby negligent,[1] and

Third, as a direct result of such negligence[1] plaintiff sustained damage.

* [unless you believe plaintiff is not entitled to recover by reason of Instruction Number _____ (*here insert number of affirmative defense instruction*)].

Notes on Use (1990 Revision)

1. The terms "negligent" and "negligence" must be defined. See definition at MAI 11.06.

If physician-patient relationship is in issue, add: "First, defendant undertook to treat plaintiff as a physician or surgeon," and then renumber the other paragraphs.

* Add if complete affirmative defense is submitted. This bracketed material should not be used to submit comparative fault. See MAI 21.02.

Committee Comment (2002 Revision)

Where suit is for wrongful death, see MAI 20.01 and 20.02.

Where suit is for loss of services or medical expenses of dependent, see MAI 31.04.

Where there are multiple causes of damage, see MAI 19.01.

A doctor may be liable for failing to inform the patient of dangers incident to treatment. *Mitchell v. Robinson*, 334 S.W.2d 11 (Mo.1960). See also *Steele v. Woods*, 327 S.W.2d 187 (Mo.1959); and *Kinser v. Elkadi*, 674 S.W.2d 226 (Mo.App.1984); *Harrell v. Witt*, 755 S.W.2d 296 (Mo.App.1988); and *Baltzell v. Van Buskirk*, 752 S.W.2d 902 (Mo.App. 1988).

Where comparative fault of the patient is in issue, see MAI 32.06, MAI Chapter 37.00, and MAI 21.02.

If fault is to be apportioned between two or more defendants in a case where no comparative fault is sought against the plaintiff, see Illustration 35.22 (and Committee Comment) which may be adapted for a case in which there are multiple defendants but no settling tortfeasor.

Library References:

C.J.S. Physicians, Surgeons, and other Health-Care Providers § 97–100, 124.
West's Key No. Digests, Physicians and Surgeons ⟋18.100.

Notes of Decisions

----

1. In general

Jury instruction in medical malpractice case, which submitted one issue four times and another issue twice, was improperly duplicative, argumentative, complex, and long. Rogers v. Bond, 839 S.W.2d 292 (Mo.1992).

2. Modification

Malpractice case, arthroscopic surgery on elbow. Verdict directing instruction approved as to the following alternative submissions: "Placed the lateral incision at the wrong location in relation to the anatomical landmarks of the elbow," "failed to advise plaintiff of the risk of permanent loss of function * * *," and "failed to supervise placement of the lateral incision. * * *" Discussion of "ultimate facts." Use of the word "wrong" held to be appropriate. Not a roving commission and not argumentative. Spain v. Brown, 811 S.W.2d 417 (Mo.App. 1991).

In malpractice action against hospital premised on negligence of nurse anesthetist, plaintiffs' verdict-directing instruction was necessary modification of MAI 21.01 to submit plaintiffs' theory that administration of high spinal by nurse combined with other drugs to cause plaintiff's injury. Yoos v. Jewish Hosp. of St. Louis, 645 S.W.2d 177[14, 15] (Mo.App.1982).

3. Standard of negligence

Instruction defining informed consent should not be given in medical negligence cases based on failure of physicians to make full disclosure to patient before obtaining consent to treatment. Theory of negligence is the same in medical malpractice case regardless of the claim. Baltzell v. Van Buskirk, 752 S.W.2d 902, 908 (Mo.App.1988).

Instructions concerning negligent performance of surgery and informed consent, when read together, were prejudicially erroneous in medical malpractice action; one instruction defined informed consent as consent based upon not only requisite elements of professional standard, but also upon disclosure of information which would lead reasonable person to withhold consent to surgery. Harrell v. Witt, 755 S.W.2d 296, 298–99 (Mo.App.1988).

Where decedent's comparative negligence injected more than one standard of care into the case, MAI 11.06 was properly modified by MAI 11.08. Additionally, the phrase, "health care provider" was unambiguous and needed no further definition. Schiles v. Schaefer, 710 S.W.2d 254[10] (Mo.App. 1986).

MAI 11.06 (now revised) states the standard of medical negligence under Missouri law. Swope v. Printz, 468 S.W.2d 34[12] (Mo.1971).

4. Ultimate facts

The phrase "not medically proper" did not submit the ultimate facts which define for the jury plaintiffs' specific theory of negligence and gave the jury a "roving commission" to speculate and determine on its own and in what manner the procedure was "not medically proper." Grindstaff v. Tygett, 655 S.W.2d 70[1–4] (Mo.App.1983).

Jury instruction, in malpractice case, which tracked plaintiffs' expert's testimony as to possible causes for injury was proper. Wilson v. Lockwood, 711 S.W.2d 545[11] (Mo.App.1986).

5. Joint tort-feasors

Verdict directors against physicians which hypothesized that negligence of physicians caused or directly contributed to cause death of decedent were proper even though contributory negligence of decedent was in issue and despite physician's contention that they were successive rather than joint tort-feasors. Schiles v. Schaefer, 710 S.W.2d 254[12] (Mo.App.1986).

21.02   [1988 New] Verdict Directing—Actions Against Health Care Providers—Single or Multiple Defendants With Comparative Fault—Multiple Negligent Acts

In your verdict you must assess a percentage of fault to defendant (*state the name*) [whether or not plaintiff was partly at fault] [1] if you believe:

First, defendant (*state the name*) either:

(*here set out act or omission complained of*), or
(*here set out alternative act or omission complained of*), and

Second, defendant (*state the name*), in any one or more of the respects submitted in paragraph First, was thereby negligent,[2] and

Third, such negligence [2] directly caused or directly contributed to cause damage to plaintiff.[3]

* [unless you believe plaintiff is not entitled to recover by reason of Instruction Number _____ (*here insert number of complete affirmative defense instruction*)].

Notes on Use (1988 New)

1. This bracketed phrase may be used at plaintiff's option in a comparative fault case.

2. The terms "negligent" and "negligence" must be defined. See MAI 11.06.

3. Paragraph Third is shown here in accordance with the first alternate of MAI 19.01.

* Add if complete affirmative defense is submitted. This bracketed material should not be used to submit comparative fault.

Committee Comment (1988 New)

See Committee Comment to MAI 21.01.

Library References:

C.J.S. Physicians, Surgeons, and other Health-Care Providers § 97–100, 124.
West's Key No. Digests, Physicians and Surgeons ☞18.100.

Notes of Decisions

In general   1
Roving commission   2

1. In general

Verdict directors in medical malpractice action arising out of arthroscopy in which patient's radial nerve was partially severed did not permit jury to infer negligence from fact of injury; if jury had believed defendants' evidence, challenged instructions permitted finding that regardless of fact that nerve was partially severed, defendants were not negligent. Spain v. Brown, 811 S.W.2d 417 (Mo.App.1991).

2. Roving commission

Instruction, which directed verdict upon finding of "detectable sign of cancer," rather than "microcalcifications," did not create roving commission, and was not misleading, confusing, or prejudicial, in action in which husband of deceased patient alleged that radiologist's misdiagnosis of cancer caused patient's death; one doctor testified that microcalcifications could be suggestive of cancer, suspicious for cancer, and sometimes virtually diagnostic, another doctor testified that most calcifications are benign, and instruction with word "microcalcifications" would have allowed jury to find radiologist liable if he failed to report even benign microcalcifications. Portis v. Greenhaw, 38 S.W.3d 436 (Mo.App.2001).

21.03 [1988 New] Damages—Actions Against Health Care Providers—No Comparative Fault

If you find in favor of plaintiff, then you must award plaintiff such sum as you believe will fairly and justly compensate plaintiff for any damages you believe he sustained [and is reasonably certain to sustain in the future] [1] as a direct result of the occurrence [2] mentioned in the evidence.

Any damages you award must be itemized by the categories set forth in [the] verdict form [_____ (*insert letter of verdict form if multiple packages are submitted*)].

Notes on Use (2002 Revision)

1. This may be added if supported by the evidence.

2. When the term "occurrence" must be modified, substitute some descriptive phrase that specifically describes the compensable event or conduct. The term "occurrence" may be modified in any case where the evidence discloses more than one event or health care provider that is claimed to have caused injury or damage. See Note 3 of the Notes on Use to MAI 4.01.

In a case such as *Carlson v. K–Mart*, 979 S.W.2d 145 (Mo. banc 1998), where MAI 19.01 is used in the verdict director, delete the entire phrase "as a direct result of the occurrence mentioned in the evidence" from this instruction and substitute the phrase "that (*describe the compensable event or conduct*) directly caused or directly contributed to cause."

Other modifications also may be appropriate.

In a case in which mitigation of damages is properly submitted under MAI 32.29, this damage instruction should be modified with the bracketed sentence required by Note 4 of the Notes on Use to MAI 4.01.

This is the damage instruction to be used in cases against health care providers for personal injury where no issue of plaintiff's comparative fault is submitted. See verdict form MAI 36.20 and MAI 36.21.

Committee Comment (1996 Revision)

MAI 21.03 through MAI 21.07 and verdict forms 36.20 through 36.22 and 36.24 through 36.27 are applicable only to causes of action against health care providers accruing on or after February 3, 1986, and subject to the provisions of §§ 538.205 through 538.230, RSMo.

Library References:

C.J.S. Physicians, Surgeons, and other Health-Care Providers § 97–100, 124.
West's Key No. Digests, Physicians and Surgeons ⟝18.100.

Notes of Decisions

1. In general

MAI 21.03 and 36.20, which require itemization of damages in actions against "health care" providers, did not apply to amputee's professional negligence suit against orthot-ics and prosthetics laboratory, which was not licensed by any governmental body. Stalcup v. Orthotic & Prosthetic Lab, Inc., 989 S.W.2d 654 (Mo.App.1999).

21.04 [1988 New] Damages—Actions Against Health Care Providers—Comparative Fault

If you assess a percentage of fault to [any] [1] defendant, then, disregarding any fault on the part of plaintiff, you must determine the total amount of plaintiff's damages to be such sum as will fairly and justly compensate plaintiff for any damages you believe he sustained [and is reasonably certain to sustain in the future] [2] as a direct result of the occurrence [3] mentioned in the evidence. You must state such total amount of plaintiff's damages in your verdict, and you must itemize those total damages by the categories set forth in [the] verdict form [_____ (*insert letter of verdict form if multiple packages are submitted*)].

In determining the total amount of plaintiff's damages and in itemizing those total damages, you must not reduce such damages by any percentage of fault you may assess to plaintiff. The judge will compute plaintiff's recovery by reducing the amount you find as plaintiff's total damages by any percentage of fault you assess to plaintiff.

Notes on Use (2002 Revision)

1. Insert if more than one defendant.

2. This may be added if supported by the evidence.

3. When the term "occurrence" must be modified, substitute some descriptive phrase that completely describes the compensable event or conduct. The term "occurrence" may be modified in any case where the evidence discloses more than one event or health care provider claimed to have caused injury or damage. The first example in Note 3 of MAI 4.01, "... as a direct result of the conduct of defendant as submitted in Instruction Number _____", is not appropriate in a comparative fault case because the jury is instructed to determine "total damages," which are obviously the direct result of the conduct of *both* the defendant *and* the plaintiff. The above-quoted example would inappropriately restrict the jury's assessment of damages to those damages solely caused by defendant's conduct.

For further discussion see MAI 37.03 and MAI 4.01.

In a case such as *Carlson v. K–Mart*, 979 S.W.2d 145 (Mo. banc 1998), where MAI 19.01 is used in the verdict director, delete the entire phrase "as a direct result of the occurrence mentioned in the evidence" from this instruction and substitute the phrase "that (*describe the compensable event or conduct)* directly caused or directly contributed to cause."

In a case in which mitigation of damages is properly submitted under MAI 32.29, this damage instruction should be modified with the bracketed sentence required by Note 4 of the Notes on Use to MAI 4.01.

Committee Comment (1996 Revision)

MAI 21.03 through MAI 21.07 and verdict forms 36.20 through 36.22 and 36.24 through 36.27 are applicable only to causes of action against health care providers accruing on or after February 3, 1986, and subject to the provisions of §§ 538.205 through 538.230, RSMo.

Library References:

C.J.S. Physicians, Surgeons, and other Health-Care Providers § 97–100, 124.
West's Key No. Digests, Physicians and Surgeons ☜18.100.

21.05 [1988 New] Definitions—Categories of Damages—Actions Against Health Care Providers

In these instructions, you are told to itemize any damages you award by the categories set forth in [the] verdict form [_____ (*insert letter of verdict form if multiple packages are submitted*)].

The phrase "past economic damages" means those damages incurred in the past for pecuniary harm such as medical expenses for necessary drugs, therapy, and for medical, surgical, nursing, X-ray, dental, custodial, and other health and rehabilitative services and for past lost earnings and for past lost earning capacity.

The phrase "past non-economic damages" means those damages arising in the past from non-pecuniary harm such as pain, suffering, mental anguish, inconvenience, physical impairment, disfigurement, and loss of capacity to enjoy life.

The phrase "future medical damages" means those damages arising in the future for medical expenses such as necessary drugs, therapy, and medical, surgical, nursing, X-ray, dental, custodial, and other health and rehabilitative services.

The phrase "future economic damages" means those damages arising in the future from pecuniary harm such as lost earnings and lost earning capacity.

The phrase "future non-economic damages" means those damages arising in the future from non-pecuniary harm such as pain, suffering, mental anguish, inconvenience, physical impairment, disfigurement, and loss of capacity to enjoy life.

Notes on Use (1991 Revision)

The phrases in the verdict form describing the categories of damages to be itemized in a suit against a health care provider must be defined.

If a derivative claim such as loss of consortium, loss of services or medical expenses (spouse or minor injured) is also involved in an action against a health care provider, one or more definitions in this instruction may need to be modified depending on the elements of recoverable damages in the derivative claim. See MAI 21.07 and Illustration 35.18.

Committee Comment (1996 Revision)

MAI 21.03 through MAI 21.07 and verdict forms 36.20 through 36.22 and 36.24 through 36.27 are applicable only to causes of action against health care providers accruing on or after February 3, 1986, and subject to the provisions of §§ 538.205 through 538.230, RSMo.

By its terms, RSMo § 538.210.1 provides for applicability of Chapter 538 to both personal injury and wrongful death claims arising out of negligent health care. However, the definitions provided by § 538.205 only relate to actions for personal injury. Compare the elements of damage for which recovery is allowed under § 537.090 in wrongful death actions. Case law has not yet discussed or determined whether modification of MAI 21.05 is necessary in a wrongful death action against a health care provider.

Library References:

C.J.S. Physicians, Surgeons, and other Health-Care Providers § 97–100, 124.
West's Key No. Digests, Physicians and Surgeons ⚮18.100.

21.06 [1991 New] Limiting Instruction—Actions Against Health Care Providers—Settling Tortfeasor

If a released person is included in the verdict form, and the jury has knowledge from the evidence or a trial incident of a release or payment pursuant to a release, the following instruction should be given as a separate instruction:

Plaintiff's claim against (*name of released party*) has been settled. In determining the total amount of plaintiff's damages and in assessing percentages of fault, you are not to consider such settlement. The total damages assessed by you on plaintiff's claim against the defendant(s) (*or state the names of the defendant(s)*) will be reduced by the judge by any percentage of fault you assess to (*state the name or names of the released parties*).

Committee Comment (2002 Revision)

This instruction is to be used whenever the verdict form includes the name of a released person and the jury has knowledge that one or more persons have settled with the plaintiff. Case law will determine whether the jury is always entitled to know about the settlement or whether that fact will only be in evidence when it is relevant for some other purpose such as to show bias of a witness who has settled.

MAI 21.03 through MAI 21.07 and verdict forms 36.20 through 36.22 and 36.24 through 36.27 are applicable only to causes of action against health care providers accruing on or after February 3, 1986, and subject to the provisions of sections 538.205 through 538.230, RSMo.

Compare the law regarding settlements and settling tortfeasors in comparative fault cases other than those involving actions against health care providers under sections 538.205 through 538.230, RSMo. See section 537.060, RSMo; *Jensen v. ARA Services, Inc.*, 736 S.W.2d 374 (Mo.banc 1987); *Allen v. Perry*, 722 S.W.2d 98 (Mo.App.1986); and *Schiles v. Schaefer*, 710 S.W.2d 254 (Mo.App.1986).

See Illustrations 35.21 and 35.22 and Committee Comments.

Library References:

C.J.S. Physicians, Surgeons, and other Health-Care Providers § 97–100, 124.
West's Key No. Digests, Physicians and Surgeons ⚲18.100.

21.07   [1991 New] Derivative Claims—Loss of Consortium, Loss of Services or Medical Expenses—Actions Against Health Care Providers

In actions against health care providers involving a personal injury claim and a derivative claim for loss of consortium, services or medical expenses (spouse or minor injured), it will be necessary to modify some instructions from Chapter 21 and the verdict form (from MAI 36.20, 36.21, or 36.22) applicable to health care providers by incorporating aspects of those instructions applicable to derivative claims.

See MAI 4.18 for the damage instruction in a non-comparative fault case with both injury and derivative claims.   MAI 21.03 should be modified with MAI 4.18 to submit damages in such a case involving a health care provider.

Similarly, MAI 37.08 would be used to modify MAI 21.04 to submit damages for injury and derivative claims in a case against a health care provider involving comparative fault.

MAI 31.04 would be used as the verdict directing instruction to submit the derivative claim in any action against a health care provider.

MAI 21.05, defining the categories of damages in actions against health care providers, should be modified appropriately in a case involving both primary and derivative claims by including the phrase "loss of consortium" in the "non-economic damages" categories and by including a descriptive term identifying other recoverable damages in appropriate categories.

MAI 36.20 and MAI 36.21, the verdict forms for use in actions against health care providers (*without* comparative fault), will require modification with MAI 36.23 to allow the jury to itemize categories of damages on both the injury claim and the derivative claim in the non-comparative fault case against a health care provider.

MAI 36.22, the verdict form for use in actions against health care providers (*with* comparative fault), will require modification with MAI 37.09 to allow the jury to itemize damages on both claims in the comparative fault case against a health care provider.

See Illustration 35.18.

Library References:

C.J.S. Physicians, Surgeons, and other Health-Care Providers § 97–100, 124.
West's Key No. Digests, Physicians and Surgeons ⊕18.100.

21.08 [1995 Revision] Verdict Directing—Actions Against Health Care Providers—Lost Chance of Survival—No Comparative Fault—Multiple Negligent Acts

Your verdict must be for plaintiff (*state name of plaintiff ad litem or personal representative*), if you believe:

First, defendant (*state the name*) either:

> (*here set out act or omission complained of*), or

> (*here set out alternative act or omission complained of*), and

Second, (*state name of decedent*) then had a material chance of [survival] [recovery] [1], and

Third, defendant, in any one or more of the respects submitted in paragraph First, was thereby negligent [2], and

Fourth, as a direct result of such negligence[2], (*state name of decedent*) lost [all] [or] [a material part of] [3] such chance of [survival] [recovery] [1].

* [unless you believe plaintiff is not entitled to recover by reason of Instruction Number _____ (*here insert number of affirmative defense instruction*)].

Notes on Use (1993 New)

1. Select a term. The term "recovery" has reference to that recovery which could have been obtained if the negligently omitted or improper medical diagnosis or treatment had been properly rendered and had been successful. It does not necessarily mean a complete recovery. The term "recovery", under appropriate circumstances, may be modified to expand or clarify this concept.

2. The terms "negligent" and "negligence" must be defined. See definition at MAI 11.06.

3. Select applicable phrase or phrases.

If the physician-patient relationship is in issue, add an appropriate paragraph, such as: "First, defendant undertook to treat decedent as a physician or surgeon," and then renumber the other paragraphs.

* Add if complete affirmative defense is submitted. This bracketed material should not be used to submit comparative fault.

Committee Comment (2002 Revision)

Where there are multiple causes of lost chance of survival, see MAI 19.01.

Where this verdict directing instruction, MAI 21.08, is used to submit a "lost chance of recovery (survival)", see MAI 21.09 for the damage instruction and MAI 36.24 for the verdict form.

Where comparative fault of the patient is in issue, see MAI 32.06, MAI Chapter 37.00, MAI 21.10, and MAI 36.25.

If fault is to be apportioned between two or more defendants in a case where no comparative fault is sought against the decedent, see Illustration 35.22 (and Committee Comment) which may be adapted for a case in which there are multiple defendants but no settling tortfeasor.

This instruction applies to the cause of action for "lost chance of recovery (survival)" established in *Wollen v. DePaul Health Center*, 828 S.W.2d 681 (Mo.banc 1992). *Wollen* discussed the "lost chance of recovery" theory in the context of a survival action under section 537.020, RSMo, brought by a personal representative of the estate of an individual who died after losing a material chance of recovery from cancer. *Wollen* also discussed the "lost chance of recovery" theory in the context of "loss of a limb".

See the provisions affecting "lost chance" in section 537.021, RSMo, which provides that a person in the class entitled to recover for wrongful death under section 537.080, RSMo, may request the appointment of a plaintiff ad litem to maintain the "loss of a chance" action instead of a personal representative. The proceeds of the "loss of a chance" action are for the benefit of those class members delineated under section 537.080, and the "lost chance" theory may be maintained as an alternative theory in a wrongful death case.

Library References:

C.J.S. Physicians, Surgeons, and other Health-Care Providers § 97–100, 124.
West's Key No. Digests, Physicians and Surgeons ⚖18.100.

21.09 [1996 Revision] Damages—Actions Against Health Care Providers—Lost Chance of Survival—No Comparative Fault

If you find in favor of plaintiff (*state name of plaintiff ad litem or personal representative*), then you must determine the total amount that you believe will fairly and justly value any damages (*state name of decedent*) sustained before death as a direct result of the absence of recovery [1], and any damages (*state name of decedent*) survivors sustained after the death [and are reasonably certain to sustain in the future] [2] as a direct result of the death of (*state name of decedent*). You must state such total amount in your verdict, and you must itemize that total amount by the categories of damages set forth in the verdict form.

In your verdict, you must also state, as a percentage, the chance of [recovery] [survival] [3] that you find (*state name of decedent*) lost. In determining the total amount of damages, you must not reduce such damages by the percentage you assess as the lost chance of [recovery] [survival]. [3] The judge will compute the final award by multiplying the total amount you find as damages by the percentage you assess as the lost chance of [recovery] [survival] [3].

You must not consider grief or bereavement suffered by reason of the death.

Notes on Use (1996 Revision)

1. The term "recovery" has reference to that recovery which could have been obtained if the negligently omitted or improper medical diagnosis or treatment had been properly rendered and had been successful. It does not necessarily mean a complete recovery. The phrase "absence of recovery," under appropriate circumstances, may be modified to expand or clarify this concept.

2. This may be added if supported by the evidence.

3. Select a term.

This is the damage instruction to be used in actions against health care providers for lost chance of recovery (survival) where no issue of plaintiff's comparative fault is submitted. See verdict form MAI 36.24.

While a case in which the "lost chance of recovery" resulting in death is brought in the name of the plaintiff ad litem or personal representative of the decedent, damages are to be determined in accordance with elements of damages in a wrongful death case and set forth in § 537.090, RSMo. Likewise, the "survivors" of decedent referred to in this instruction, and from whose perspective damages due to the death are to be determined, are those persons allowed to recover in a wrongful death case as set forth in § 537.080, RSMo.

Committee Comment (2002 Revision)

In lost chance of recovery (survival) actions, damages are determined in accordance with the method mandated by *Wollen v. DePaul Health Center*, 828 S.W.2d 681, 684, n. 2 (Mo. banc 1992). See also section 538.205, RSMo, et seq., for actions against health care providers accruing on or after February 3, 1986.

During the instruction conference, the parties and the court should discuss (on the record) just what damages are supported and allowed by the law and the evidence and can be properly argued to the jury. In this way, jury arguments can proceed without undue interruption.

See Committee Comment to MAI 21.08.

The Committee is unable to determine under existing Missouri law whether the doctrine of mitigation of damages/avoidable consequences (See MAI 32.29 and MAI 4.01) is applicable to wrongful death cases in addition to the statutory "mitigating circumstances attending the death" under section 537.090, RSMo, (See MAI 6.01). Thus, the Committee takes no position on such issue.

Library References:

C.J.S. Physicians, Surgeons, and other Health-Care Providers § 97–100, 124.
West's Key No. Digests, Physicians and Surgeons ☞18.100.

21.10 [1993 New] Verdict Directing—Actions Against Health Care Providers—Lost Chance of Survival—Comparative Fault—Multiple Negligent Acts

In your verdict you must assess a percentage of fault to defendant (*state the name*) [whether or not (*state name of decedent*) was partly at fault] [1] if you believe:

First, defendant (*state the name*) either:

(*here set out act or omission complained of*), or

(*here set out alternative act or omission complained of*), and

Second, (*state name of decedent*) then had a material chance of [survival] [recovery] [2], and

Third, defendant, in any one or more of the respects submitted in paragraph First, was thereby negligent [3], and

Fourth, such negligence [3] directly caused or directly contributed to cause (*state name of decedent*) to lose [all] [or] [a material part of] [4] such chance of [survival] [recovery] [2].

*[unless you believe you must not assess a percentage of fault to defendant by reason of Instruction Number _____ (*here insert number of complete affirmative defense instruction*)].

Notes on Use (1993 New)

1. This bracketed phrase may be used at plaintiff's option in a comparative fault case.

2. Select a term. The term "recovery" has reference to that recovery which could have been obtained if the negligently omitted or improper medical diagnosis or treatment had been properly rendered and had been successful. It does not necessarily mean a complete recovery. The term "recovery," under appropriate circumstances, may be modified to expand or clarify this concept.

3. The terms "negligent" and "negligence" must be defined. See MAI 11.06.

4. Select applicable phrase or phrases.

Paragraph Fourth is shown here modified in accordance with the first alternate of MAI 19.01.

* Add if complete affirmative defense is submitted. This bracketed material should not be used to submit comparative fault.

Committee Comment (1993 New)

Where this verdict directing instruction, MAI 21.10, is used to submit a "lost chance of recovery (survival)" with comparative fault in issue, see MAI 21.11 for the damage instruction and verdict form MAI 36.25.

See Notes on Use and Committee Comment to MAI 21.08.

Library References:

C.J.S. Physicians, Surgeons, and other Health-Care Providers § 97–100, 124.
West's Key No. Digests, Physicians and Surgeons ⟲18.100.

21.11 [1996 Revision] Damages—Actions Against Health Care Providers—Lost Chance of Survival—Comparative Fault

If you assess a percentage of fault to [any] [1] defendant, then, disregarding any fault on the part of (*state name of decedent*), you must determine the total amount that you believe will fairly and justly value any damages (*state name of decedent*) sustained before death as a direct result of the absence of recovery [2], and any damages (*state the name of decedent*) survivors sustained after the death [and are reasonably certain to sustain in the future] [3] as a direct result of the death of (*state name of decedent*). You must state such total amount in your verdict, and you must itemize that total amount by the categories of damages set forth in the verdict form.

In your verdict, you must also state, as a percentage, the chance of [recovery] [survival] [4] that you find (*state the name of decedent*) lost. In determining the total amount of damages, you must not reduce such damages by the percentage you assess as the lost chance of [recovery] [survival].[4]

In determining the total amount of damages, you must not reduce such amount by any percentage of fault you may assess to (*state name of decedent*).

The judge will compute the final award by:

First, multiplying the amount you find as total damages by the percentage you assess as the lost chance of [recovery] [survival] [4]; and

Second, making a reduction by any percentage of fault you assess to (*decedent's name*).

You must not consider grief or bereavement suffered by reason of the death.

Notes on Use (1996 Revision)

1. Insert if more than one defendant.

2. The term "recovery" has reference to that recovery which could have been obtained if the negligently omitted or improper medical diagnosis or treatment had been properly rendered and had been successful. It does not necessarily mean a complete recovery. The phrase

"absence of recovery," under appropriate circumstances, may be modified to expand or clarify this concept.

3. This may be added if supported by the evidence.

4. Select a term.

This is the damage instruction to be used in actions against health care providers for lost chance of recovery (survival) where plaintiff's comparative fault is submitted. See verdict form MAI 36.25.

Committee Comment (2002 Revision)

See Committee Comment to MAI 21.08 and MAI 21.09.

The Committee is unable to determine under existing Missouri law whether the doctrine of mitigation of damages/avoidable consequences (See MAI 32.29 and MAI 4.01) is applicable to wrongful death cases in addition to the statutory "mitigating circumstances attending the death" under section 537.090, RSMo. (See MAI 6.01). Thus, the Committee takes no position on such issue.

Library References:

C.J.S. Physicians, Surgeons, and other Health-Care Providers § 97–100, 124.
West's Key No. Digests, Physicians and Surgeons ☞18.100.

21.12 [1994 New] Verdict Directing—Actions Against Health Care Providers—Lost Chance of Recovery (Non–Death) Cases—No Comparative Fault—Multiple Negligent Acts

Your verdict must be for plaintiff if you believe:

First, defendant (*state the name*) either:

(*here set out act or omission complained of*), or

(*here set out alternative act or omission complained of*), and

Second, plaintiff then had a material chance of [survival] [recovery] [1], and

Third, defendant, in any one or more of the respects submitted in paragraph First, was thereby negligent [2], and

Fourth, as a direct result of such negligence [2], plaintiff lost [all] [or] [a material part of] [3] such chance of [survival] [recovery] [1].

* [unless you believe plaintiff is not entitled to recover by reason of Instruction Number _____ (*here insert number of affirmative defense instruction*)].

Notes on Use (2002 Revision)

1. This may be added if supported by the evidence.

2. The term "recovery" has reference to the recovery that could have been obtained if the negligently omitted or improper medical diagnosis or treatment had been properly rendered and had been successful. It does not necessarily mean a complete recovery. The phrase "absence of recovery," under appropriate circumstances, may be modified to expand or clarify this concept.

3. Select a term.

This is the damage instruction to be used in actions against health care providers for lost chance of recovery ("lost limb") cases where *no* issue of plaintiff's comparative fault is submitted. See verdict form MAI 36.26.

In a case in which mitigation of damages is properly submitted under MAI 32.29, this damage instruction should be modified with the bracketed sentence required by Note 4 of the Notes on Use to MAI 4.01.

* Add if complete affirmative defense is submitted. This bracketed material should not be used to submit comparative fault.

Committee Comment (2002 Revision)

Where there are multiple causes of a loss of a chance, see MAI 19.01.

Where this verdict directing instruction, MAI 21.12, is used to submit a "loss of a chance" in "lost limb" cases, see MAI 21.13 for the damage instruction and MAI 36.26 for the verdict form.

Where comparative fault of the patient is in issue, see MAI 32.06, MAI Chapter 37.00, MAI 21.14, and MAI 36.27.

If fault is to be apportioned between two or more defendants in a case where no comparative fault is sought against the decedent, see Illustration 35.22 (and Committee Comment) which may be adapted for a case in which there are multiple defendants but no settling tortfeasor.

Wollen v. DePaul Health Center, 828 S.W.2d 681 (Mo.banc 1992), discussed the "lost chance of recovery" theory in the context of a survival action under section 537.020, RSMo, brought by a personal representative of the estate of an individual who died after losing a material chance of recovery from cancer. *Wollen* also discussed the "lost chance of recovery" theory in the context of "loss of a limb". This instruction applies to the "loss of a limb" lost chance theory, which is not necessarily limited to the loss of an arm or leg but may also apply to a lost chance of recovery from cancer or spinal injury and the like.

Library References:

C.J.S. Physicians, Surgeons, and other Health-Care Providers § 97–100, 124.
West's Key No. Digests, Physicians and Surgeons ⚍18.100.

21.13   [1994 New] Damages—Actions Against Health Care Providers—Lost Chance of Recovery (Non–Death) Cases—No Comparative Fault

If you find in favor of plaintiff, then you must determine the total amount which you believe will fairly and justly value any damages plaintiff sustained [and is reasonably certain to sustain in the future] [1] as a direct result of the absence of recovery [2]. You must state such total amount in your verdict, and you must itemize that total amount by the categories of damages set forth in the verdict form.

In your verdict, you must also state, as a percentage, the chance of [recovery] [survival] [3] which you find plaintiff lost. In determining the total amount of damages you must not reduce such damages by the percentage you assess as the lost chance of [recovery] [survival] [3]. The judge will compute the final award by multiplying the total amount you find as damages by the percentage you assess as the lost chance of [recovery] [survival] [3].

Notes on Use (1994 New)

1.   This may be added if supported by the evidence.

2.   The term "recovery" has reference to that recovery which could have been obtained if the negligently omitted or improper medial diagnosis or treatment had been properly rendered and had been successful. It does not necessarily mean a complete recovery. The phrase "absence of recovery," under appropriate circumstances, may be modified to expand or clarify this concept.

3.   Select a term.

This is the damage instruction to be used in actions against health care providers for "loss of a limb" where no issue of plaintiff's comparative fault is submitted. See verdict form MAI 36.26.

Committee Comment (1994 New)

In lost chance of recovery (survival) actions, damages are determined in accordance with the method mandated by *Wollen v. DePaul Health Center*, 828 S.W.2d 681, 684, n. 2 (Mo. banc 1992). See also §§ 538.205, et seq., RSMo, for actions against health care providers accruing on or after February 3, 1986.

During the instruction conference the parties and the court should discuss (on the record) just what damages are supported and allowed by the law and the evidence and properly can be argued to the jury. In this way arguments can proceed without undue interruption.

Library References:

C.J.S. Physicians, Surgeons, and other Health-Care Providers § 97–100, 124.
West's Key No. Digests, Physicians and Surgeons ⟰18.100.

21.14 [1994 New] Verdict Directing—Actions Against Health Care Providers—Lost Chance of Recovery (Non–Death) Cases—Comparative Fault—Multiple Negligent Acts

In your verdict you must assess a percentage of fault to defendant (*state the name*) [whether or not (*state name of plaintiff*) was partly at fault][1] if you believe:

First, defendant (*state the name*) either:

(*here set out act or omission complained of*), or

(*here set out alternate act or omission complained of*), and

Second, (*state name of plaintiff*) then had a material chance of [survival] [recovery][2], and

Third, defendant, in any one or more of the respects submitted in paragraph First, was thereby negligent[3], and

Fourth, such negligence[3] directly caused or directly contributed to cause (*state name of plaintiff*) to lose [all] [or] [a material part of][4] such chance of [survival] [recovery][2].

*[unless you believe you must not assess a percentage of fault to defendant by reason of Instruction Number _____ (*here insert number of complete affirmative defense instruction.*)].

Notes on Use (1994 New)

1. This bracketed phrase may be used at plaintiff's option in a comparative fault case.

2. Select a term. The term "recovery" has reference to that recovery which could have been obtained if the negligently omitted or improper medical diagnosis or treatment had been properly rendered and had been successful. It does not necessarily mean a complete recovery. The term "recovery," under appropriate circumstances, may be modified to expand or clarify this concept.

3. The terms "negligent" and "negligence" must be defined. See MAI 11.06.

4. Select applicable phrase or phrases.

Paragraph Fourth is shown here modified in accordance with the first alternate of MAI 19.01.

* Add if complete affirmative defense is submitted. This bracketed material should not be used to submit comparative fault.

Committee Comment (1994 New)

Where this verdict directing instruction, MAI 21.14, is used to submit a "lost chance of recovery (survival)" with comparative fault in issue, see MAI 21.15 for the damage instruction and MAI 36.27 for the verdict form.

See Notes on Use and Committee Comment to MAI 21.12.

Library References:

C.J.S. Physicians, Surgeons, and other Health-Care Providers § 97–100, 124.
West's Key No. Digests, Physicians and Surgeons ⚖18.100.

21.15 [1994 New] Damages—Actions Against Health Care Providers—Lost Chance of Recovery (Non–Death) Cases—Comparative Fault

If you assess a percentage of fault to [any] [1] defendant, then, disregarding any fault on the part of plaintiff, you must determine the total amount which you believe will fairly and justly value any damages plaintiff sustained [and is reasonably certain to sustain in the future] [2] as a direct result of the absence of recovery [3]. You must state such total amount in your verdict, and you must itemize that total amount by the categories of damages set forth in the verdict form.

In your verdict, you must also state, as a percentage, the chance of [recovery] [survival] [4] which you find (*state the name of plaintiff*) lost. In determining the total amount of damages you must not reduce such damages by the percentage you assess as the lost chance of [recovery] [survival] [4].

In determining the total amount of damages, you must not reduce such amount by any percentage of fault you may assess to (*state name of plaintiff*).

The judge will compute the final award by:

First, multiplying the amount you find as total damages by the percentage you assess as the lost chance of [recovery] [survival] [4]; and

Second, making a reduction by any percentage of fault you assess to plaintiff.

Notes on Use (2002 Revision)

1.   Insert if more than one defendant.

2.   This may be added if supported by the evidence.

3.   The term "recovery" has reference to the recovery that could have been obtained if the negligently omitted or improper medical diagnosis or treatment had been properly rendered and had been successful. It does not necessarily mean a complete recovery. The phrase "absence of recovery," under appropriate circumstances, may be modified to expand or clarify this concept.

4.   Select a term.

This is the damage instruction to be used in actions against health care providers for lost chance of recovery ("lost limb") cases where plaintiff's comparative fault *is* submitted. See verdict form MAI 36.27.

In a case in which mitigation of damages is properly submitted under MAI 32.29, this damage instruction should be modified with the bracketed sentence required by Note 4 of the Notes on Use to MAI 4.01.

Committee Comment (1994 New)

See Committee Comment to MAI 21.13.

Library References:

C.J.S. Physicians, Surgeons, and other Health-Care Providers § 97–100, 124.
West's Key No. Digests, Physicians and Surgeons ⬿18.100.

22.00

VERDICT DIRECTING—OWNERS
AND OCCUPIERS OF LAND

Analysis of Instructions

Westlaw Electronic Research

See Westlaw Electronic Research Guide preceding the Table of Instructions.

Library References:

C.J.S. Trial § 350–351.
West's Key No. Digests, Trial ☞234(3, 4).

22.01 [1996 Revision] Verdict Directing—Trespassing Children

Your verdict must be for plaintiff if you believe:

First, defendant maintained (*here describe the condition that caused the injury*), and

Second, defendant knew or had information from which defendant, in the exercise of ordinary care [1], should have known that children would be exposed to such condition, and

Third, defendant knew or by using ordinary care [1] could have known such condition presented an unreasonable risk of harm to children exposed to it, and

Fourth, children such as plaintiff, because of their youth, would not appreciate the risk of harm associated with such condition, and

Fifth, defendant failed to prevent plaintiff from being exposed to such harm, and

Sixth, defendant was thereby negligent [1], and

Seventh, as a direct result of such negligence [1], plaintiff sustained damage.

* [unless you believe plaintiff is not entitled to recover by reason of Instruction Number _____ (*here insert number of affirmative defense instruction*)].

Notes on Use (1991 Revision)

1. The terms "ordinary care", "negligent" and "negligence" must be defined. See definitions in Chapter 11.00.

Where comparative fault is submissible, modify this instruction in accordance with MAI 37.01.

* Add if affirmative defense is submitted. This bracketed material should not be used to submit comparative fault.

Committee Comment (1995 Revision)

The law on liability for injury to trespassing children is set forth in Restatement (First) of Torts § 339 (1934); *Anderson v. Cahill,* 485 S.W.2d 76 (Mo.1972). In such cases, the law requires a finding that the possessor of land knew or had reason to know children were likely to trespass. Restatement (Second) of Torts § 339(a) (1965); *Glastris v. Union Elec. Co.*, 542 S.W.2d 65 (Mo.App.1976).

Paragraph Second uses the phrase "had information from which defendant, in the exercise of ordinary care, should have known" as the equivalent of the phrase "had reason to know" as defined in Restatement (First) and (Second) of Torts § 12. The Committee has opted to use this equivalent phrase rather than "had reason to know" because it is thought that the phrase "had reason to know" may be confusing or misleading to the jury.

The 1995 Revision to this instruction changed the phrase "should have known" to "could have known" on the issue of constructive notice in Paragraph Third. Some MAI instructions had used one of the phrases and other instructions had used the other phrase. Questions had arisen as to whether "should have known" imposed a higher burden than "could have known". See *Benton v. City of Rolla*, 872 S.W.2d 882 (Mo.App.1994), and *Burrell v. Mayfair–Lennox Hotels, Inc.*, 442 S.W.2d 47 (Mo.1969). For consistency, the Committee has opted to use the phrase "could have known" to the extent possible in the context of constructive notice. Other instructions, such as MAI 10.07, paragraph Second of MAI 22.01, MAI 22.07, and MAI 25.10(A), continue to use the phrase "should have known" because that phrase is part of a "knew or had reason to know" standard as explained in the Committee Comments to those instructions.

Library References:

C.J.S. Negligence § 871, 881–882, 885 905.
West's Key No. Digests, Negligence ⊗1734.

Notes of Decisions

Description of condition   2
Restatement   1

---

1. Restatement

Attractive nuisance submission against electric utility erred in submitting failure to *insulate* wire, ignoring defense of isolating wire. Glastris v. Union Elec. Co., 542 S.W.2d 65[7, 8] (Mo.App.1976).

2. Description of condition

Description of a metal ladder as a "metal device in the form of a ladder" in a jury instruction regarding attractive nuisance doctrine was not prejudicially argumentative, in as much as jury was given ample opportunity to formulate a description of the ladder in their own minds and could not have been misled by the phraseology. Wiegers v. Fitzpatrick, 766 S.W.2d 126, 130 (Mo.App.1989).

22.02 [1995 Revision] Verdict Directing—Dangerous Condition Near Public Thoroughfare

Your verdict must be for plaintiff if you believe:

First, defendant [created] [maintained] [1] an [excavation] [*or describe other artificial condition such as "a junk yard where broken glass, bottles, jars, and jugs were kept"*] [1], close to a public [sidewalk] [alley] [street] [1], and

Second, that such [excavation] [(*or other artificial condition described*)] [1] was so close to a public [sidewalk] [alley] [street] [1] that persons using the [sidewalk] [alley] [street] [1] would be exposed to an unreasonable risk of falling [into] [onto] [1] the [excavation] [(*or other artificial condition described*)] [1], and

Third, defendant knew or by using ordinary care [2] could have known of such danger, and

Fourth, defendant failed to use ordinary care [2] to [barricade it] [warn of it] [remove it] [3], and

Fifth, as a direct result of such failure plaintiff sustained damage.

* [unless you believe plaintiff is not entitled to recover by reason of Instruction Number _____ (*here insert number of affirmative defense instruction*)].

Notes on Use (1991 Revision)

1. Select appropriate term.

2. The phrase "ordinary care" must be defined. See definition at MAI 11.05.

3. Select one or more of these phrases. If more than one phrase is used, they must be submitted in the disjunctive and each must be supported by the evidence. A modified submission of negligence may be used if supported by the evidence.

* Add if affirmative defense is in issue. This bracketed material should not be used to submit comparative fault. Where comparative fault is submissible, modify this instruction in accordance with MAI 37.01.

Committee Comment (1996 Revision)

Where suit is for wrongful death, see MAI 20.01 and 20.02.

Where suit is for loss of services or medical expenses of dependent, see MAI 31.04.

In *Wells v. Henry W. Kuhs Realty Co.*, 269 S.W.2d 761 (Mo.1954), plaintiff alleged that defendant maintained a "private dump" with broken bottles, jugs, etc., near a public alley; that plaintiff's child while chasing June bugs inadvertently strayed onto this dump and cut himself on the debris collected there; and that this injury caused the child's death. The trial judge sustained defendant's motion to dismiss for failure of the petition to state a claim for relief. The Supreme Court of Missouri reversed, saying:

> In these circumstances as pleaded we do not say, as a matter of law, that defendant should not be held responsible. It seems to us that facts may develop within the purview of the averments of the amended petition from which a jury could reasonably find that defendant should have realized there was a likelihood that some person, especially a child, in passing along the alley might inadvertently pass over onto defendant's land and dump, and become injured. Supra at 768.

See also: Restatement (Second) of Torts §§ 368, 369 and 370 (1965). For natural conditions, see Restatement (Second) of Torts, § 840.

The 1995 Revision to this instruction changed the phrase "should have known" to "could have known" on the issue of constructive notice. Some MAI instructions had used one of the phrases and other instructions had used the other phrase. Questions had arisen as to whether "should have known" imposed a higher burden than "could have known". See *Benton v. City of Rolla*, 872 S.W.2d 882 (Mo.App.1994), and *Burrell v. Mayfair–Lennox Hotels, Inc.*, 442 S.W.2d 47 (Mo.1969). For consistency, the Committee has opted to use the phrase "could have known" to the extent possible in the context of constructive notice. Other instructions, such as MAI 10.07, paragraph Second of MAI 22.01, MAI 22.07, and MAI 25.10(A), continue to use the phrase "should have known" because that phrase is part of a "knew or had reason to know" standard as explained in the Committee Comments to those instructions.

Library References:

C.J.S. Negligence § 871, 881–882, 885–905.
West's Key No. Digests, Negligence ☞1734.

Notes of Decisions

Evidentiary support 2
Modification 1
Negligence per se 3

1.　Modification

Failure to modify MAI 22.02, relating to obstruction on a public sidewalk, by adding a paragraph requiring the jury to find agency of an individual who supposedly created the debris in the course of his employment for defendant, was prejudicial error where that was a contested issue. DeLaporte v. Robey Building Supply, Inc., 812 S.W.2d 526 (Mo. App.1991).

MAI 22.02 properly modified to submit negligence in obstructing highway. Fowler v. Laclede Gas Co., 488 S.W.2d 934[8–10] (Mo.App.1972).

Adding an MAI 19.01 joint tortfeasor clause to an MAI 22.02–22.05 type verdict director without definition of negligence "would raise a serious question" since the former uses the word "negligence" and the latter is based on failure to use "ordinary care." (See now MAI 33.15). Chambers v. Kansas City, 446 S.W.2d 833[5–7] (Mo. 1969).

In suit for injuries from running into a metal post in a park, plaintiff submitted a modified MAI 22.02 or 22.03 but used "exposed to danger" instead of "not reasonably safe." Not error, since "danger" and "not reasonably safe" are equivalent. Jackson v. St. Louis, 422 S.W.2d 45[3, 4] (Mo.1967).

2.　Evidentiary support

Where defendant dug and later filled a hole, but it settled and caused collision, the evidence supported instruction on maintaining an *excavation*. Stenson v. Laclede Gas Co., 553 S.W.2d 309[1, 2] (Mo.App.1977).

Modified MAI 22.02 properly submitted defendant's liability for failing to turn off the power to a fallen transmission line. Calderone v. St. Joseph Light & Power Co., 557 S.W.2d 658[9–14] (Mo.App.1977).

3.　Negligence per se

Where defendant's submitted conduct was negligent per se, plaintiff's verdict director need not require a finding of negligence. Calderone v. St. Joseph Light & Power Co., 557 S.W.2d 658[15] (Mo.App.1977).

4."Roving commission"

Modified pattern jury instruction did not give jury "roving commission" to find railroad liable, in negligence action against railroad that owned crossing where collision with train occurred; instruction required verdict for automobile passenger if crossing was unusually hazardous because it did not afford southbound motorists adequate sight distance to observe trains approaching from west, if railroad knew or by using ordinary care should have known of condition, if it failed to use ordinary care to warn of condition, and if such failure directly caused or contributed to cause damage to passenger. Alcorn v. Union Pacific R.R. Co., 50 S.W.3d 226, 2001 WL 569104 (Mo.2001).

22.03 [1995 Revision] Verdict Directing—Invitee Injured

Your verdict must be for plaintiff if you believe [1]:

First, there was (*here describe substance on floor that caused the fall*) on the floor of defendant's store and as a result the floor was not reasonably safe, and

Second, defendant knew or by using ordinary care [2] could have known of this condition, and

Third, defendant failed to use ordinary care [2] to [remove it] [barricade it] [warn of it] [3], and

Fourth, as a direct result of such failure, plaintiff sustained damage.

* [unless you believe plaintiff is not entitled to recover by reason of Instruction Number _____ (*here insert number of affirmative defense instruction*)].

Notes on Use (1989 Revision)

1. Where comparative fault is submissible, modify this instruction in accordance with MAI 37.01. For submission of plaintiff's comparative fault for failure to keep a careful lookout, see MAI 32.28.

2. The phrase "ordinary care" must be defined. See definition at MAI 11.05.

3. Select one or more of these phrases. If more than one phrase is used, they must be submitted in the disjunctive and each must be supported by the evidence.

* Add if affirmative defense is submitted. This bracketed material should not be used to submit comparative fault. See MAI 37.01.

Committee Comment (1996 Revision)

Where suit is for loss of services or medical expenses of dependent see MAI 31.04.

See *Carter v. Kinney,* 896 S.W.2d 926 (Mo.banc 1995); *Harris v. Niehaus,* 857 S.W.2d 222 (Mo. banc 1993); *Patton v. May Dept. Stores Co.,* 762 S.W.2d 38 (Mo. banc 1988); *Cox v. J.C. Penney Co., Inc.,* 741 S.W.2d 28 (Mo. banc 1987); *Hefele v. National Super Markets, Inc.,* 748 S.W.2d 800 (Mo.App.1988); and §§ 343 and 343A(1), Restatement (Second) of Torts (1965).

The 1995 Revision to this instruction changed the phrase "should have known" to "could have known" on the issue of constructive notice. Some MAI instructions had used one of the phrases and other instructions had used the other phrase. Questions had arisen as to whether "should have known" imposed a higher burden than "could have known". See *Benton v. City of Rolla*, 872 S.W.2d 882 (Mo.App.1994), and *Burrell v. Mayfair–Lennox Hotels, Inc.*, 442 S.W.2d 47 (Mo.1969). For consistency, the Committee has opted to use the phrase "could have known" to the extent possible in the context of constructive notice. Other instructions, such as MAI 10.07, paragraph Second of MAI 22.01, MAI 22.07, and MAI 25.10(A), continue to use the phrase "should have known" because that phrase is part of a "knew or had reason to know" standard as explained in the Committee Comments to those instructions.

Library References:

C.J.S. Negligence § 452–453, 457, 463–541, 871, 881–882, 885–905.
West's Key No. Digests, Negligence ⊸1037(1), 1734.

Notes of Decisions

———

1. In general

The precise language used in jury instructions in a negligence action to define the defendant's duty or breach is not critical as long as the jury is required to find that the condition complained of presented a foreseeable risk of injury, that the defendant had actual or constructive knowledge of the risk, and that the defendant failed to remedy it. Pierce v. Platte–Clay Elec. Co–op., Inc., 769 S.W.2d 769, 777 (Mo. banc 1989).

Duration of existence of defect on business premises not important with respect to self-service type store. Self-service store owner must anticipate and exercise due care to guard against dangers from articles left in the aisle, even by customers. Sheil v. T.G. & Y. Stores Co., 781 S.W.2d 778, 780–82 (Mo. banc 1989).

The victim of a slip and fall may make a submissible case against the store owner upon a showing that store employees were regularly in the area in which the accident occurred. Moss v. National Super Markets, Inc., 781 S.W.2d 784, 785–86 (Mo. banc 1989).

A modified MAI 22.04, rather than 22.03, was proper verdict director where plaintiff fell on snow-covered parking lot, and need not submit plaintiff's lack of knowledge of danger. Carden v. Lester E. Cox Med. Center, 519 S.W.2d 338[4–7] (Mo.App.1975).

Where plaintiff's verdict director submits defendant's failure to use "ordinary care," such as MAI 22.03, Invitee Injured, defendant's converse must be in substantially the same language, and it is error to converse "negligence" since that word was not used in plaintiff's verdict director. Brewer v. Swift & Co., 451 S.W.2d 131[1] (Mo. banc 1970).

Omission of any essential element in plaintiff's verdict director is not cured by submission of that element in another instruction.

Brozovich v. Brozovich, 429 S.W.2d 330[4] (Mo.App.1968).

Under MAI 22.03 (Invitee Injured) plaintiff's verdict director must specify both the ultimate facts creating a dangerous condition and that such dangerous condition made the premises not reasonably safe. Enloe v. Pittsburgh Plate Glass Co., 427 S.W.2d 519[9–10] (Mo.1968).

2. Deviation

Where plaintiff's (Invitee Injured) verdict director required a finding that defendant "should" have known of defect instead of "could" have known, the deviation cast a greater burden on plaintiff than required, and was harmless error. Burrell v. Mayfair–Lennox Hotels, 442 S.W.2d 47[6, 7] (Mo.1969).

In drawing a not-in-MAI instruction to cover a slip and fall by a servant against a master, it was error to use the formerly approved phrase "caused or permitted" since the phrase "knew . . . or could have known" is approved for slip-and-fall cases by invitees. This, because where there is no approved MAI to fit a submission, counsel shall submit the issues "in the same manner as issues are submitted in MAI." Leathem v. Longenecker, 405 S.W.2d 873[5, 6] (Mo. 1966).

3. Modification

In premises liability case, verdict directing instruction that was patterned after MAI 22.03 was properly modified by describing the dangerous condition as a "defect in the pipe crossing on defendant's property" and by describing the negligence of defendant as the "failure to use ordinary care to make the pipe crossing reasonably safe"; such modifications used terms and language approved in other MAI instructions. Taylor v. Associated Elec. Co-op., Inc., 818 S.W.2d 669 (Mo.App.1991).

Verdict directing instruction against public entity under premises liability provisions of V.A.M.S. § 537.600 was properly patterned after MAI 22.03 which utilizes the term "not reasonably safe" rather than the term "dangerous condition" as used in the statute. Court declined to address the issue of how a verdict directing instruction should properly submit the statutory elements of § 537.600. Dennis v. St. Louis Board of Education, 809 S.W.2d 20 (Mo.App.1991).

In slip and fall case verdict director was properly modified to describe obstacle causing fall. Gipson v. Target Stores, Inc., 630 S.W.2d 107[3, 4] (Mo.App.1981).

Under circumstances of slip-and-fall case, it was necessary that instruction concerning store customer's knowledge and use of ordinary care be modified by inserting the words "in time to have avoided injury". Robinson v. Safeway Stores, Inc., 655 S.W.2d 617[8] (Mo.App.1983).

Modification to submit failure to warn of dangerous intersecting aisles in retail store. Blackburn v. Katz Drug Co., 520 S.W.2d 668[1] (Mo.App.1975).

Hypothesizing evidentiary facts not error where necessary to submission of ultimate facts. O'Connell v. Roper Elec. Co., 498 S.W.2d 847[10] (Mo.App.1973).

Where plaintiff slipped on icy step while alighting from defendant's bus and submitted the defect, defendant's knowledge thereof and negligent failure to remedy the defect, it was not necessary further to submit that defendant had time to remedy the defect since that evidentiary fact was embraced in the element of negligence. Swiastyn v. St. Joseph Light & Power Co., 459 S.W.2d 24[8] (Mo.App.1970).

Adding an MAI 19.01 joint tortfeasor clause to an MAI 22.02–22.05 type verdict director without definition of negligence "would raise a serious question" since the former uses the word "negligence" and the latter is based on failure to use "ordinary care." (See now MAI 33.15). Chambers v. Kansas City, 446 S.W.2d 833[5–7] (Mo. 1969).

MAI 22.03 modified to submit "inadequately secured tar paper on the roof" instead of "substance on the floor". Weber v. Hinds, 440 S.W.2d 129[1, 2] (Mo.App.1969).

MAI 22.03 properly modified to submit wet-slick pavement instead of "substance on the floor." Vinyard v. Vinyard Funeral Home, 435 S.W.2d 392[6] (Mo.App.1968).

MAI 22.03 properly submitted that door check was not reasonably safe (the ultimate fact) and need not submit that it was defective because of lack of fluid (an evidentiary fact). Jackson v. Cherokee Drug, 434 S.W.2d 257[4–5] (Mo.App.1968).

In suit for injuries from running into a metal post in a park, plaintiff submitted a modified MAI 22.02 or 22.03 but used "exposed to danger" instead of "not reasonably safe." No error, because "danger" and "not reasonably safe" are equivalent. Jackson v. St. Louis, 422 S.W.2d 45[3, 4] (Mo.1967).

4. Plaintiff's status

Where issue of plaintiff's status as tenant or invitee depended on undisputed facts, her status was one of law for the court and not one of fact for the jury. Friend v. Gem International, Inc., 476 S.W.2d 134[17] (Mo. App.1971).

Where status of plaintiff while visiting defendant church presented a critical factual issue of her status as an invitee or a licensee the trial court defined "invitee" and also gave an affirmative converse instruction for defendant submitting the elements of plaintiff's status as a "licensee". Claridge v. Watson Terrace Christian Church of St. Louis, 457 S.W.2d 785[1] (Mo. banc 1970).

MAI 22.03 properly modified by adding clause requiring finding of plaintiff's denied status as invitee. Bollman v. Kark Rendering Plant, 418 S.W.2d 39[22] (Mo.1967).

5. Knowledge of danger

Store was negligent with respect to customer's slip and fall on dog food; evidence revealed that dog food had spilled in aisle earlier that evening, that dog food remained in aisle due to improper cleanup, more spilling from same source, or new spill when employee climbed bags to put away broom and dust pan, and that, due to nature of spills and their frequency, store could have taken other or additional precautions to warn or protect customers but failed to do so. Emery v. Wal–Mart Stores, Inc., 976 S.W.2d 439 (Mo.1998).

Instruction in case involving death of worker who fell through unprotected skylight was not deficient for failure to set forth element of superior knowledge on the part of defendants of condition created by worker. Pyle v. Prairie Farms Dairy, Inc., 777 S.W.2d 286, 293–94 (Mo.App.1989).

Invitee's knowledge of obvious danger was to be considered in determining invitee's comparative negligence, rather than duty of owner. Luthy v. Denny's, Inc., 782 S.W.2d 661 (Mo.App.1989).

Injured customer in trip and fall case does not bear the burden to demonstrate she was without knowledge of the dangerous condition. Plaintiff's knowledge should no longer be submitted in the verdict directing instruction, but should be submitted by defendant under principles of comparative fault. Patton v. May Dept. Stores Co., 762 S.W.2d 38, 39–40 (Mo. banc 1988).

Where deliveryman brought action for injuries sustained in slip and fall on icy sidewalk in front of supermarket, MAI 22.04 was proper instruction, because MAI 22.03 contains language concerning plaintiff's knowledge of the danger, which has been held incompatible with comparative fault. Hefele v. National Super Markets, Inc., 748 S.W.2d 800[3] (Mo.App.1988).

In a suit by an invitee against a business for injuries sustained in a fall on the business premises, court erred in submitting verdict-directing instruction based on MAI 22.03, in that the second paragraph of the instruction submits issue of plaintiff's ordinary care in discovering an unsafe condition and thus is inimical to the concept of comparative fault. Cox v. J.C. Penney Co., 741 S.W.2d 28[3] (Mo. banc 1987).

In slip-and-fall case defendant was entitled to its own modified contributory negligence instruction on plaintiff's contributory negligence in failing to keep a careful lookout. Refusal was error, not waived by the requirement in plaintiff's verdict director that he had neither actual nor constructive knowledge of the dangerous condition. Wyatt v. Southwestern Bell Tel. Co., 573 S.W.2d 386[8, 9] (Mo.App.1978).

Plaintiff-invitee's verdict director basing recovery on defendant's failure to warn erroneously omitted plaintiff's lack of knowledge. Crain v. Webster Electric Co-op., 568 S.W.2d 781[16–18] (Mo.App.1978).

Hotel guest injured in common area need not show lack of knowledge of defect (MAI 22.05, Tenant Injured, etc.,), and court erred in requiring plaintiff to so show (MAI 22.03, Invitee Injured, etc.). Defendant could have submitted guest's contributory negligence under guest submission. Wilder v. Chase Resorts, Inc., 543 S.W.2d 527[1] (Mo.App. 1976).

Where undisputed evidence showed defendant's employee created a dangerous condition plaintiff's verdict director need not hypothesize that element. Cline v. Carthage, etc., Co., 504 S.W.2d 102[4] (Mo. 1973).

Where plaintiff was injured by cave-in of ditch where he was working, defendants' contributory negligence instruction properly hypothesized that ditch was dangerous and plaintiff had actual or constructive knowledge of danger, and plaintiff was negligent. Koirtyohann v. Washington Plumbing & Heating Co., 494 S.W.2d 665[1–3] (Mo.App. 1973).

Verdict-director basing liability on defendant's negligent failure to warn plaintiff was erroneous in omitting element of plaintiff's lack of knowledge of danger. Cover v. Phillips Pipe Line Co., 454 S.W.2d 507[11] (Mo. 1970).

Plaintiff-invitee's actual or constructive knowledge of danger properly submitted by a not-in-MAI contributory negligence instruction. Cover v. Phillips Pipe Line Co., 454 S.W.2d 507[1–3] (Mo.1970).

Owner liable to social guest for slip and fall only if owner has knowledge of the dangerous condition causing the fall. [2 Restatement, Law of Torts, § 342 (1934)]. Wells v. Goforth, 443 S.W.2d 155[2, 3] (Mo. banc 1969).

Where plaintiff was injured by shotgun while removing tools from defendant's car, plaintiff's not-in-MAI verdict director was erroneous for failure to require finding that plaintiff did not have actual or constructive knowledge of the danger. Brozovich v. Brozovich, 429 S.W.2d 330[4] (Mo.App.1968).

6. Conversing

Where plaintiffs' verdict-director MAI 22.03 submitted defendant's failure to use ordinary care it was error to give defendant's MAI 33.02(2) conversing *negligence* since the converse was not in substantially the same language as plaintiff's verdict director. Frogge v. Nyquist Plumbing & Ditching Co., 453 S.W.2d 913[6] (Mo. banc 1970).

7. Evidentiary support

Instruction requiring jury to assess percentage of fault to store if there was ice on sidewalk, store knew of condition, store failed to used ordinary care to remove it, and patron sustained damage as result, was properly given to jury; store attempted to remove ice from sidewalk before patron fell, but ice was apparently not removed well enough to make sidewalk safe, and there was no evidence that store took any alternative approach to treating sidewalk for safety. Gorman v. Walmart Stores, Inc., 19 S.W.3d 725 (Mo.App.2000).

Where plaintiff's evidence was only that she slipped on an icy step, it was error for her to hypothesize "ice and snow in the platform or steps". Swiastyn v. St. Joseph Light & Power Co., 459 S.W.2d 24[9, 10] (Mo.App.1970).

8. Contributory negligence

Where plaintiff was injured by cave-in of ditch where he was working, defendants' contributory negligence instruction properly hypothesized that ditch was dangerous and plaintiff had actual or constructive knowledge of danger, and plaintiff was negligent. Koirtyohann v. Washington Plumbing & Heating Co., 494 S.W.2d 665[1–3] (Mo.App. 1973).

22.04   [Withdrawn 1993] Verdict Directing—Sidewalk Defect

(This instruction, Notes on Use, and Committee Comment thereto are withdrawn. See MAI 31.16 and 31.17 for verdict directing instructions concerning the dangerous condition of a public entity's property. See MAI 22.09 for a verdict directing instruction against an adjoining landowner for creating or enhancing a dangerous condition on a public sidewalk.)

22.05 [1981 Revision] Verdict Directing—Tenant Injured on Premises Reserved for Common Use

Your verdict must be for plaintiff if you believe:

First, there was (*here describe condition which caused the injury, such as "a hole in the stairway"*) and as a result the stairway was not reasonably safe, and

Second, defendant knew, or by using ordinary care[1] could have known, of this condition, and

Third, defendant failed to use ordinary care[1] to make the stairway reasonably safe, and

Fourth, as a direct result of such failure, plaintiff sustained damage.

* [unless you believe plaintiff is not entitled to recover by reason of Instruction Number _____ (*here insert number of affirmative defense instruction*)].

Notes on Use (1996 Revision)

1. The phrase "ordinary care" must be defined. See the definition at MAI 11.05.

This instruction assumes that the landlord-tenant relationship is not in issue.

This instruction is to be used only where the injury occurred in an area where landlord has admittedly retained possession and where plaintiff has a right to be, such as a common stairway, hall, or yard.

If there is a dispute as to whether the site of the injury was an area in landlord's control, the additional issue should be hypothesized in the following form:

Second, the stairway was in the possession and control of defendant and was used by tenants of defendant with his consent.

Existing "Second" would then be renumbered "Third", etc.

* Add if affirmative defense is in issue. This bracketed material should not be used to submit comparative fault. See MAI 37.01.

Committee Comment (1981 Revision)

Where suit is for wrongful death see MAI 20.01 and 20.02.

Where suit is for loss of services or medical expenses of dependent see MAI 31.04.

See *Darlington v. Railway Exchange Building,* 353 Mo. 569, 183 S.W.2d 101 (1944), and *Peterson v. Brune,* 273 S.W.2d 278 (Mo.1954).

The instruction may be used where plaintiff is a tenant or an invitee of tenant. "... the general rule is not questioned that the rights of the respondent, as invitee of the tenant ... were co-extensive with those of the tenant.... In other words, if such duty was owing to the tenant, it was also owing to the respondent." *Darlington v. Railway Exchange Building,* 353 Mo. at 579, 183 S.W.2d at 105.

The rule is given in Restatement (Second) of Torts § 360 (1965) as follows: "A possessor of land, who leases a part thereof and retains in his own control any other part which the lessee is entitled to use as appurtenant to the part leased to him, is subject to liability to his lessee and others lawfully upon the land with the consent of the lessee or a sublessee for physical harm caused by a dangerous condition upon that part of the land retained in the lessor's control, if the lessor by the exercise of reasonable care could have discovered the condition and the unreasonable risk involved therein and could have made the condition safe."

In *Roman v. King,* 289 Mo. 641, 654, 233 S.W. 161, 165 (1921), the court quoted with approval, *Home Realty Co. v. Carius,* 189 Ky. 228, 224 S.W. 751 (1920):

It is urged that plaintiff's equal knowledge with defendant of the condition of the steps bars her right to recover herein. We cannot agree with this contention.... Mere continued use of a common passageway, after knowledge of its dangerous condition, is not of itself conclusive evidence of a lack of due care on the part of the tenant, since such knowledge does not require tenant to desist from using same in a careful manner, nor render the careful use of same contributory negligence.

In *Taylor v. Hitt,* 342 S.W.2d 489, 496 (Mo.App.1961), the court said: "... respondent's knowledge of this depression in the floor is not a defense but is of force only insofar as it bears on her contributory negligence.... The respondent may have had knowledge of this depression, but even so she was entitled to use this basement area provided she exercised due care in view of the hazard or unless the hazard was of such a dangerous character that no reasonable person in the exercise of due care would use the area."

"[P]laintiff must show that defendants had notice, actual or constructive, of the alleged defect in the common porch which was the proximate cause of plaintiff's injury." *Peterson v. Brune,* 273 S.W.2d 278, 282 (Mo.1954).

An instruction which failed to require a finding that landlord had reserved and controlled the area where tenant was injured was held to be reversible error when the matter was in issue. *Fitzpatrick v. Ford,* 372 S.W.2d 844 (Mo.1963).

Library References:

C.J.S. Landlord and Tenant § 417.
West's Key No. Digests, Landlord and Tenant ⚷164(1).

Notes of Decisions

In general   1
Evidentiary support   4
Modification   2
Plaintiff's status   3

———

1. In general

Error in dismissing claims against city was harmless, where verdict directing instruction under MAI 31.16 given on remaining claim was practically identical to instructions under MAI 22.05 and 25.10(B) from which plaintiff would have been required to choose if other claims had not been dismissed and jury returned verdict in city's favor; under circumstances, dismissal of those claims did not affect outcome of case. Benton v. City of Rolla, 872 S.W.2d 882 (Mo.App.1994).

Failure of verdict directing instructions to include the language "and as a result the stairway was not reasonably safe," as applied to each disjunctive, as required by MAI 22.05, did not prejudice defendant; only logical reading of instruction assumed required wording applied to each disjunctive. Venitz v. Creative Management, Inc., 854 S.W.2d 20 (Mo.App.1993).

Plaintiff, who had received workmen's liability benefits from General Motors, sued defendant for dangerous condition of freight car. Submitting defendant's duty and breach made submission of "negligence" unnecessary. MAI 31.01 inappropriate. Sampson v. Missouri Pacific R.R. Co., 560 S.W.2d 573[7, 8] (Mo. banc 1978).

Hotel guest injured in common area need not show lack of knowledge of defect (MAI 22.05, Tenant Injured etc.), and court erred in requiring plaintiff to so show (MAI 22.03, Invitee Injured, etc.). Defendant could have submitted guest's contributory negligence under guest submission. Wilder v. Chase Resorts, Inc., 543 S.W.2d 527[1] (Mo.App. 1976).

Submitting in paragraph First of MAI 22.05 that "the door closers allowed the doors to swing improperly" was proper as the ultimate fact, and the instruction properly admitted a finding that the door swung inwardly since that would be an evidentiary detail. Blond v. Overesch, 527 S.W.2d 663[1–5] (Mo.App.1975).

In suit by tenant's invitee against landlord the court properly gave MAI 32.01 to present the issue of plaintiff's contributory negligence in failing to keep a careful lookout; that phrase properly imposed a duty of ordinary care. Helfrick v. Taylor, 440 S.W.2d 940[4] (Mo.1969).

Where there was no dispute about plaintiff's status as tenant and defendant's status as landlord in control of premises where plaintiff was injured, the trial court properly submitted plaintiff's case under MAI 22.05; the issue of status was for the court, not the jury. Stoeppelman v. Hays–Fendler Const. Co., 437 S.W.2d 143[12–15] (Mo.App.1968).

In car loader's action for furnishing defective car, plaintiff's not-in-MAI verdict director properly omitted element of plaintiff's lack of knowledge of defect. (Akin to safe-place-to-work action or tenant against landlord for injury in common-use area [MAI 22.05].) Gorman v. St. Louis–San Francisco R.R. Co., 427 S.W.2d 390[4] (Mo.1968).

Where there was no dispute about plaintiff's status as tenant and defendant's status as landlord in control of premises where plaintiff was injured, the trial court properly submitted plaintiff's case under MAI 22.05; the issue of status was for the court, not the jury. Stoeppelman v. Hays–Fendler Const. Co., 437 S.W.2d 143[12–15] (Mo.App.1968).

In car loader's action for furnishing defective car, plaintiff's not-in-MAI verdict director properly omitted element of plaintiff's lack of knowledge of defect. (Akin to safe-place-to-work action or tenant against landlord for injury in common-use area [MAI 22.05].) Gorman v. St. Louis–San Francisco R.R. Co., 427 S.W.2d 390[4] (Mo.1968).

2. Modification

Plaintiff passenger sued for slip and fall injuries, hypothesizing accumulated water on floor of bus when it left yard. This submission was not supported by evidence of water on floor at time of fall. Blase v. Bi–State Dev. Agency, 503 S.W.2d 463[1] (Mo.App. 1973).

Adding an MAI 19.01 joint tortfeasor clause to an MAI 22.02–22.05 type verdict director without definition of negligence "would raise a serious question" since the former uses the word "negligence" and the latter is based on failure to use "ordinary care." (See now MAI 33.15). Chambers v. Kansas City, 446 S.W.2d 833[5–7] (Mo. 1969).

Modified MAI 22.05 (Injury to Tenant in Common–Use Area) submitting injury to child playing on abandoned automobile. Rawson v. Ellerbrake, 423 S.W.2d 14[1] (Mo. App.1967).

3. Plaintiff's status

Where issue of plaintiff's status as tenant or invitee depended on undisputed facts, her status was one of law for the court and not one of fact for the jury. Friend v. Gem International, Inc., 476 S.W.2d 134[17] (Mo. App.1971).

4. Evidentiary support

In employee's negligence suit against employer's landlord, evidence did not establish as matter of law that areas in which employee was injured were common areas subject to landlord's control, so that jury instruction on determination of common areas was properly given; both landlord's and employer's employees used same entrances, exits, and parking lot, and shared same restrooms and lunchroom, lease did not specify which areas were conveyed to employer, and all parts of building were available equally to landlord and employer. Caples v. Earthgrains Co., 43 S.W.3d 444 (Mo.App.2001).

Even though landlord had made repairs to premises before employee's injuries, employee injured on employer's leased premises failed to present sufficient evidence to make submissible jury issue regarding landlord's duty to repair in negligence action brought against landlord; lease allowed landlord limited access to premises to make repairs, and there was no evidence that landlord entered premises on its own initiative to make repairs. Caples v. Earthgrains Co., 43 S.W.3d 444 (Mo.App.2001).

Invitee's knowledge that steps between parking levels were dangerous did not absolve landlords from liability for fall as result of top step falling away when invitee stepped on it; danger was not so apparent or so great that it was unreasonable for invitee to encounter it, and invitee's actions appeared no less wary than caution of reasonable person under the same circumstances. Gregg v. Erb, 834 S.W.2d 253 (Mo.App. 1992).

Conjunctive submissions of negligence in maintaining defective screen door and defective porch railing erroneous absent evidence to support each submission. Woods v. Gould, 515 S.W.2d 592[7] (Mo.App.1968).

22.06 [1969 New] Verdict Directing—Private Nuisance

Your verdict must be for plaintiff if you believe:

First, plaintiff used his property as a residence, and

Second, (*here describe nuisance such as "defendant operated a slaughter house in close proximity to plaintiff's residence"*) and

Third, (*here describe the injury such as "ill-smelling odors escaped from defendant's premises onto plaintiff's property and this substantially impaired plaintiff's use of his property,"*) and

Fourth, such use by defendant of his property was unreasonable.

* [unless you believe that plaintiff is not entitled to recover by reason of Instruction Number _____ (*here insert number of affirmative defense instruction*)].

Notes on Use (1991 Revision)

* Add if affirmative defense is submitted.

This instruction has limited application. It should not be used except where the facts show the doctrine of private nuisance is applicable.

Committee Comment (1991 Revision)

"Private nuisance is a nontrespassory invasion of another's interest in the private use and enjoyment of land. Restatement (Second) of Torts, Sec. 821D (1977)." *Sofka v. Thal,* 662 S.W.2d 502, 508 (Mo. banc 1983).

This instruction is intended for use only when a nuisance is created after plaintiff has the right of enjoyment.

If the nuisance already exists when plaintiff acquires his possessory rights, then different doctrines variously called "priority of occupation" and "coming to the nuisance" may apply. For mention of "priority of occupation," *see, Fuchs v. Curran Carbonizing & Engineering Co.,* 279 S.W.2d 211, 218 (Mo.App.1955).

The common law private nuisance action, "an action for trespass on the case for nuisance," is discussed in *Smiths v. McConathy,* 11 Mo. 517 (1848). That case accords with the above instruction. The report speaks to the instruction's lack of a "directly damage" paragraph.

Damage from a private nuisance is presumed (not so in public nuisance) from the mere proof of the nuisance, *id.*, 522:

> In an action for a private nuisance it is not necessary to allege or prove any special damage. * * * But if a private nuisance be alleged and proved, the plaintiff is allowed to recover nominal damages at least, whatever amount of inconvenience or injury may have been occasioned by it.

In justification of the principle, *see, id.*, 523:

> When we look at the nature of most of the private nuisances spoken of in the books, we cannot fail to perceive the propriety of allowing a recovery upon the mere proof of the existence of the nuisance. Take the case of a smith's forge, a privy or a lime-kiln, (all of which are frequently spoken of as nuisance), erected so near a dwelling house as to render it unfit for habitation. How could the plaintiff establish any special damage resulting from the erection of such nuisance? If a pecuniary loss be the criterion of special damage, the most intolerable nuisances would be without redress.

For a more recent discussion where the facts failed, as a matter of law, to constitute a nuisance, *see, Sofka v. Thal, supra.*

Library References:

C.J.S. Nuisances § 144.
West's Key No. Digests, Nuisance ☞54.

Notes of Decisions

1. In general

In action for damages from increased flow of surface water from construction of store and parking lot on adjacent tract, verdict-directing instruction, based on MAI 22.06 and allegedly including evidentiary details rather than ultimate facts, was not erroneous; defendant did not argue that any fact hypothesized in the instruction lacked evidentiary support, and did not explain how the instruction was prejudicial. Farley v. Wappapello Foods, Inc., 959 S.W.2d 888 (Mo.App. S.D.1997).

Jury verdict assessing punitive damages in action for interference with easement did not cure erroneous jury instruction which omitted element that interference had to be unreasonable because willful and wanton is not the same as unreasonable. Gilbert v.

K.T.I., Inc., 765 S.W.2d 289, 296–97 (Mo. App.1988).

In action seeking damages for interference with easement, jury should not have been instructed based on ejectment damage instruction MAI 27.03. Liability for damages caused by interference or obstruction of easement is based upon nuisance instruction MAI 22.06. Gilbert v. K.T.I., Inc., 765 S.W.2d 289, 294, 297 (Mo.App.1988).

MAI 22.06 is the proper verdict director for all nuisances, intentional and nonintentional, temporary or permanent. Fletcher v. City of Independence, 708 S.W.2d 158[39] (Mo. App.1986).

Pre–MAI verdict director on private nuisance approved and compared with MAI 22.06. Bower v. Hog Builders, Inc., 461 S.W.2d 784[3] (Mo.1970).

22.07 [1991 Revision] Verdict Directing—Licensee

Your verdict must be for plaintiff if you believe [1]:

First, there was (*here describe the condition which caused the injury*) on defendant's premises and as a result the premises were not reasonably safe, and

Second, defendant knew of this condition and knew that such condition was not reasonably safe, and

Third, defendant knew or had information from which defendant, in the exercise of ordinary care [2], should have known that persons such as plaintiff would not discover such condition or realize the risk of harm, and

Fourth, defendant failed to use ordinary care [2] to [either] [make the condition reasonably safe] [or adequately warn of it],[3] and

Fifth, as a direct result of such failure, plaintiff sustained damage.

* [unless you believe plaintiff is not entitled to recover by reason of Instruction Number _____ (*here insert number of affirmative defense instruction*)].

Notes on Use (1991 Revision)

1. Where comparative fault is submissible, modify this instruction in accordance with MAI 37.01. For submission of plaintiff's comparative fault with respect to failure to keep a careful lookout, see MAI 32.28.

2. The phrase "ordinary care" must be defined. See definition at MAI 11.05.

3. Select one or both phrases. If both phrases are used, they must be submitted in the disjunctive and each must be supported by the evidence.

* Add if affirmative defense is submitted. This bracketed material should not be used to submit comparative fault.

Committee Comment (1996 Revision)

In *Wells v. Goforth,* 443 S.W.2d 155, 158 (Mo. banc 1969), the Court adopts the rule stated in Restatement (First) of Torts § 342 (1934) imposing liability upon a possessor of land toward a gratuitous licensee only upon proof of the defendant's actual knowledge of the offending condition.

See *Carter v. Kinney,* 896 S.W.2d 926 (Mo. banc 1995); *Harris v. Niehaus,* 857 S.W.2d 222 (Mo. banc 1993); *Cox v. J.C. Penney, Inc.,* 741 S.W.2d 28 (Mo. banc 1987); *Nichols v. Koch,* 741 S.W.2d 87 (Mo.App. 1987); and Restatement of Torts (Second) § 342 (1965).

Paragraph Third uses the phrase "had information from which defendant, in the exercise of ordinary care, should have known" as the equivalent of the phrase "had reason to know" as defined in Restatement (First) and (Second) of Torts § 12. The Committee has opted to use this equivalent phrase rather than "had reason to know" because it is thought that the phrase "had reason to know" may be confusing or misleading to the jury.

Library References:

C.J.S. Negligence § 432–541.
West's Key No. Digests, Negligence ⊗⇒1040(1).

Notes of Decisions

In general 1
Knowledge of danger 2
Status of plaintiff 3

———

1. In general

Evidence that road on which motorcyclist was injured was a private road rather than a public road supported jury instruction concerning landowner's liability arising from injuries occurring on his or her property, although motorcyclist's first amended petition alleged that road was a public street. Wilson v. Kaufmann, 847 S.W.2d 840 (Mo.App. 1992).

In motorcyclist's negligence action against landowner arising when motorcyclist struck earthen mound constructed by landowner at end of private road, it was error to omit the element of MAI 22.07 requiring a finding that the landowner knew or should have known that people using the road would not discover the dangerous condition; but this error was waived where landowner did not raise this omission either at trial or in motion for

new trial. Wilson v. Kaufmann, 847 S.W.2d 840 (Mo.App.1992).

2. Knowledge of danger

MAI 22.07 was properly modified in accordance with comparative fault principles by deleting the portion of the instruction which directed the jury to consider whether plaintiff, in the exercise of ordinary care, could have known of the condition which caused injury. Gillis v. Collins, 770 S.W.2d 503, 505 n. 1 (Mo.App.1989).

3. Status of plaintiff

In suit brought by guest against property owner for injuries she sustained when she fell on front porch of owner's residence, guest was entitled to duty of care owed to licensee, despite guest's contention that preparation of food in connection with picnic transformed her into invitee. Gillis v. Collins, 770 S.W.2d 503, 506 (Mo.App.1989).

22.08 [1978 New] Verdict Directing—Highway Danger Created by Highway Construction Contractor

Your verdict must be for plaintiff if you believe:

First, defendant (*describe the conduct creating the dangerous condition relied upon, such as, "removed the stop sign"*) and as a result the [sidewalk] [street] [highway] [1] was not reasonably safe for the public, and

Second, defendant failed to use ordinary care [2] to [remedy] [warn of] [3] such unsafe condition, and

Third, as a direct result of such failure, plaintiff sustained damage.

* [unless you believe plaintiff is not entitled to recover by reason of Instruction Number _____ (*here insert number of affirmative defense instruction*)].

Notes on Use (1990 New)

1. Select appropriate term.

2. The phrase "ordinary care" must be defined. See definitions in Chapter 11.00.

3. Select appropriate term or phrase.

* Add if affirmative defense is submitted. This bracketed material should not be used to submit comparative fault. See MAI 37.01.

Committee Comment (1996 Revision)

For elements of liability of a private contractor see *Morris v. Israel Brothers, Inc.,* 510 S.W.2d 437 (Mo.1974), and *Fowler v. Laclede Gas Co.,* 488 S.W.2d 934 (Mo.App.1972).

Library References:

C.J.S. Motor Vehicles § 228, 240.
West's Key No. Digests, Automobiles ☞309(2).

22.09   [1993 New] Verdict Directing—Sidewalk Defect—Dangerous Condition Created by Abutting Landowner

Your verdict must be for plaintiff if you believe [1]:

First, (*here describe condition that made the sidewalk dangerous, such as "there was oil on the sidewalk" or "there was a hole in the sidewalk"*), and as a result the sidewalk was not reasonably safe for the public, and

Second, [such condition was created by defendant] [defendant made a special use of the sidewalk which increased the danger of such condition][2], and

Third, defendant was thereby negligent[3], and

Fourth, as a direct result of such negligence[3], plaintiff sustained damage.

*[unless you believe plaintiff is not entitled to recover by reason of Instruction Number _____ (*here insert number of complete affirmative defense instruction*)].

Notes on Use (1993 New)

1.   Where comparative fault is submissible, modify this instruction in accordance with MAI 37.01.   For submission of plaintiff's comparative fault for failure to keep a careful lookout, see MAI 32.28.

2.   Select the appropriate alternative.

3.   The terms "negligent" and "negligence" must be defined.   See definitions in Chapter 11.00.

* Add if complete affirmative defense is submitted.   This bracketed material should not be used to submit comparative fault.

Committee Comment (1993 New)

Where suit is for wrongful death, see MAI 20.01 and 20.02.

Where suit is for loss of services or medical expenses of a dependent, see MAI 31.04.

The general rule in Missouri is that the affirmative duty to maintain public sidewalks rests on the municipality and does not require an abutting property owner to repair or maintain a public sidewalk.   See *Rauh v. Interco, Inc.,* 702 S.W.2d 497 (Mo.App.1985).   Two standard exceptions to this general rule exist where the abutting property owner:

1) enhanced the danger of the condition by making a special purpose use of the sidewalk or 2) has artificially created a condition which makes passage thereon unsafe. See *Martin v. Gilmore,* 358 S.W.2d 462 (Mo. App.1962).

Harris v. Woolworth, 824 S.W.2d 31 (Mo.App.1991), held that a verdict directing instruction against an adjoining landowner was deficient where the verdict director failed to hypothesize that the adjoining owner created a dangerous condition in an alley by spilling kitchen grease. See the *Harris* case for further discussion of an adjoining landowner's responsibility for creating a dangerous condition on a public way (street, sidewalk, alley) or enhancing a dangerous condition by making a special use of the public way.

Where suit is against a public entity for a dangerous condition of a public entity's property, see MAI 31.16 and 31.17.

Library References:

C.J.S. Negligence § 871, 881–882, 885–905.
West's Key No. Digests, Negligence ☞1734.

Notes of Decisions

---

1. In general

Modification of jury instruction regarding liability of landowner arising from injuries occurring on landowner's property to encompass theory that landowner constructed and knowingly maintained obstruction at end of private drive and failed to provide adequate lighting in such location did not improperly convert injured motorcyclist's theory from one of premises liability to one of abutting landowner's liability for dangerous condition on public roadway or sidewalks. Wilson v. Kaufmann, 847 S.W.2d 840 (Mo.App. 1992).

Verdict directing instruction in slip and fall action, based on MAI 22.04, was erroneous for failing to hypothesize that adjacent property owner was responsible for the presence of the dangerous condition in adjacent alley. Harris v. Woolworth (F.W.), 824 S.W.2d 31 (Mo.App.1991).

Using "was in an unsafe and dangerous condition for travel thereon by the public" not error since it was equivalent to "was not reasonably safe for the public." (See Jackson v. St. Louis, 422 S.W.2d 45[3–4].) Courtney v. City of Ferguson, 401 S.W.2d 172[1] (Mo.App.1966).

2. Modification

MAI modification which submits unnecessary evidentiary details creates error because undue emphasis of evidence, confusion and other unfairness which favor one litigant above the other can result. Modification of MAI 22.04 to submit case to recover for injuries sustained when plaintiff fell through bridge not error. Hall v. County of New Madrid, 645 S.W.2d 149[5] (Mo.App. 1982).

3. Knowledge of danger

Where deliveryman brought action for injuries sustained in slip and fall on icy sidewalk in front of supermarket, MAI 22.04 was proper instruction, because MAI 22.03 contains language concerning plaintiff's knowledge of the danger, which has been held incompatible with comparative fault. Hefele v. National Super Markets, Inc., 748 S.W.2d 800[3] (Mo.App.1988).

23.00

VERDICT DIRECTING—INTENTIONAL TORTS

Analysis of Instructions

Westlaw Electronic Research

See Westlaw Electronic Research Guide preceding the Table of Instructions.

Library References:

C.J.S. Trial § 350–351.
West's Key No. Digests, Trial ⚫═234(3, 4).

23.01   [1981 Revision] Verdict Directing—Assault

Your verdict must be for plaintiff if you believe:

First, defendant (*here describe act such as "pointed a gun at plaintiff"*) with the intent to cause plaintiff (*or if some other person here describe such person*) [offensive contact] [bodily harm] [apprehension of offensive contact] [apprehension of bodily harm],[1] and

Second, defendant thereby caused plaintiff to be in apprehension of [bodily harm] [offensive contact].[1]

* [unless you believe plaintiff is not entitled to recover by reason of Instruction Number _____ (*here insert number of affirmative defense instruction*)].

Notes on Use (1981 Revision)

1. Select the appropriate bracketed phrase or phrases. If more than one phrase is submitted, they should be submitted in the disjunctive.

* Add if affirmative defense is submitted.

Committee Comment (1981 Revision)

Where agency is in issue see MAI 18.01.

Cases of assault not accompanied with a battery are quite rare in Missouri. The elements of the offense were described in *Hickey v. Welch,* 91 Mo.App. 4, 14 (1901), as follows: "An assault is an inchoate battery. The wrong is putting a person in present fear of violence, so that any act fitted to have that effect on a reasonable man is an assault.... Witnesses swore defendant pointed a pistol at plaintiff and threatened to shoot her, and likewise raised a shotgun in a menacing way. Those acts were an assault."

See generally: Restatement (Second) of Torts §§ 21–34 (1965). It is there pointed out that words alone do not constitute an assault.

Provocation by plaintiff can serve to mitigate or defeat plaintiff's right to punitive damages. See: *Fordyce v. Montgomery,* 424 S.W.2d 746 (Mo.App.1968).

Library References:

C.J.S. Assault and Battery § 51.
West's Key No. Digests, Assault and Battery ⊱43(1).

23.02 [1990 Revision] Verdict Directing—Battery

Your verdict must be for plaintiff if you believe:

First, defendant intentionally (*here describe act such as "struck"*) plaintiff, and

Second, defendant thereby caused plaintiff bodily harm.[1,2]

*[unless you believe that plaintiff is not entitled to recover by reason of Instruction Number _____ (*here insert number of affirmative defense instruction*)].

Notes on Use (1990 Revision)

1. If the battery is an offensive touching, substitute the following for paragraph Second:

Second, defendant thereby caused a contact with plaintiff which was offensive to plaintiff, and

Third, such contact would be offensive to a reasonable person.

2. If the battery arises out of a claim that a public official, such as a police officer or jailer, used excessive force in his official duties, substitute the following for paragraph Second:

Second, defendant thereby used more force than was reasonably necessary, and

Third, defendant thereby caused plaintiff bodily harm.

* Add if affirmative defense is submitted.

Committee Comment (1996 Revision)

Where agency is in issue, see MAI 18.01.

Where suit involves multiple causes of damages, see MAI 19.01.

Where suit is for loss of services or medical expenses of dependents, see MAI 31.04.

See: Restatement (First) of Torts §§ 13–20 (1934); *Adler v. Ewing,* 347 S.W.2d 396, 402 (Mo.App.1961); *Carnes v. Thompson,* 48 S.W.2d 903 (Mo.1932).

For example of recovery for offensive touching, see *Edmisten v. Dousette,* 334 S.W.2d 746 (Mo.App.1960).

The Restatement takes no position on whether one is liable if he inflicts upon another a contact which he knows to be offensive to the other because of abnormal sensitivity.

Provocation by plaintiff can serve to mitigate or defeat plaintiff's right to punitive damages. See: *Fordyce v. Montgomery,* 424 S.W.2d 746 (Mo.App.1968).

If defendant is a public official possessing legal right to touch plaintiff, plaintiff must modify MAI 23.02 to accept burden of proving defendant used more force than was reasonably necessary. See: *Neal v. Helbling,* 726 S.W.2d 483 (Mo.App.1987).

Library References:

C.J.S. Assault and Battery § 51.
West's Key No. Digests, Assault and Battery ☞43(1).

Notes of Decisions

In general   1
Affirmative defense   2

------

1. In general

Where arresting police officers were defendants, fact of use of unreasonable force was an element of plaintiff's case and required modification of MAI 23.02. Neal v. Helbling, 726 S.W.2d 483 (Mo.App.1987).

Where plaintiff's substantive right arose from defendant's deliberately shooting him, it was error to refuse MAI 23.02 (battery, an intentional act) and to give instead modified MAI 17.01 (negligent act). Martin v. Yeoham, 419 S.W.2d 937[6] (Mo.App.1967).

2. Affirmative defense

Where defendant *shot* plaintiff, Paragraph First of his self-defense instruction should be modified to require a finding defendant believed he was in imminent danger of death or great bodily harm. Martin v. Yeoham, 419 S.W.2d 937[12] (Mo.App.1967).

23.03 [1965 New] Verdict Directing—Battery—Intent to Induce Apprehension

Your verdict must be for plaintiff if you believe:

First, defendant with the intent to place plaintiff (*or if intention was directed to some other person, substitute that person's name for plaintiff*) in apprehension of bodily harm (*here describe acts such as "struck plaintiff"*), and

Second, defendant thereby caused plaintiff bodily harm.[1]

* [unless you believe that plaintiff is not entitled to recover by reason of Instruction Number _____ (*here insert number of affirmative defense instruction*)].

Notes on Use (1990 Revision)

1. If the battery is an offensive touching, see the modification of paragraph Second in Note on Use 1 of MAI 23.02.

* Add if affirmative defense is submitted.

Committee Comment (1996 Revision)

Where agency is in issue, see MAI 18.01.

Where suit involves multiple causes of damages see MAI 19.01.

Where suit is for loss of services or medical expenses of dependent see MAI 31.04.

See Restatement (First) of Torts § 13, Comment (d) and § 18 (1934). See also, *Robbs v. Missouri Pac. Ry. Co.*, 210 Mo.App. 429, 242 S.W. 155 (1922).

Provocation by plaintiff can serve to mitigate or defeat plaintiff's right to punitive damages. See *Fordyce v. Montgomery*, 424 S.W.2d 746 (Mo.App.1968).

Library References:

C.J.S. Assault and Battery § 51.
West's Key No. Digests, Assault and Battery ⊙43(1).

23.04 [1983 Revision] Verdict Directing—False Imprisonment

Your verdict must be for plaintiff if you believe:

Defendant intentionally [restrained] [instigated the restraint of] [1] plaintiff against his will.

* [unless you believe plaintiff is not entitled to recover by reason of Instruction Number _____ (*here insert number of affirmative defense instruction*)].

Notes on Use (1980 Revision)

1. Select the appropriate phrase.

See affirmative defense MAI 32.13.

* Add if affirmative defense is submitted.

Committee Comment (1990 Revision)

Although similar in many respects, the elements of a claim for false imprisonment are different from those of a claim for malicious prosecution. This MAI 23.04 is for submission of a claim for false arrest. MAI 23.07 is provided for submission of a claim for malicious prosecution.

False imprisonment is an illegal act. Malicious prosecution is a legal act, done unsuccessfully, without cause and with malice. See, *Rustici v. Weidemeyer*, 673 S.W.2d 762 (Mo. banc 1984); 35 C.J.S. 625–627, quoted as authority in *Gray v. Wallace*, 319 S.W.2d 582, 585 (Mo.1958).

In cases involving detention by a merchant, see § 537.125, RSMo.

Library References:

C.J.S. False Imprisonment § 60.
West's Key No. Digests, False Imprisonment ⟳40.

Notes of Decisions

In general   1
Agency in issue   2

————

1. In general

Malice is not an element of false imprisonment. Wilton v. Cates, 774 S.W.2d 570, 573 (Mo.App.1989).

MAI 23.04 (verdict director) and MAI 28.10 [Now 32.13] (affirmative defense) properly submitted case of customer's arrest by off-duty policeman working as defendant's security officer. Nelson v. R.H. Macy & Co., 434 S.W.2d 767[5, 12] (Mo.App.1968).

2. Agency in issue

Verdict director for false arrest based on agency (MAI 18.01–23.04) required definition

of scope of employment (MAI 13.02).   Peak
v. W.T. Grant Co., 409 S.W.2d 58[1] (Mo.
banc 1966).

23.05   [1996 Revision] Verdict Directing—Fraudulent Misrepresentations

Your verdict must be for plaintiff if you believe:

First, defendant (*describe act such as "represented to plaintiff that the motor vehicle was new"*), intending that plaintiff rely upon such representation in (*purchasing the motor vehicle*), and

Second, the representation was false, and

Third, [defendant knew that it was false] [defendant knew that it was false at the time the representation was made] [defendant did not know whether the representation was true or false],[1] and

Fourth, the representation was material to the (*purchase by plaintiff of the motor vehicle*), and

Fifth, plaintiff relied on the representation in (*making the purchase*), and [in so relying plaintiff used that degree of care that would have been reasonable in plaintiff's situation, and][2]

Sixth, as a direct result of such representation the plaintiff was damaged.

*[unless you believe plaintiff is not entitled to recover by reason of Instruction Number _____ (*here insert number of affirmative defense instruction*)].

Notes on Use (1996 Revision)

1. Select the appropriate phrase. The second alternate for Paragraph Third is required to submit a misrepresentation of a future event. The third alternate is not appropriate for submission of a misrepresentation of a future event. See: *Klecker v. Sutton*, 523 S.W.2d 558 (Mo.App. 1975); and *Wolk v. Churchill*, 696 F.2d 621 (8th Cir.1982).

2. Omit when the right to rely is not in issue.

* Add if affirmative defense is submitted.

Committee Comment (1996 Revision)

Where agency is in issue see 18.01.

1. In *Wilson v. Murch*, 354 S.W.2d 332, 338 (Mo.App.1962) the court said:

To recover for fraudulent representations, it is not necessary that it be shown that defendant had actual knowledge of the falsity of the facts stated by him. It is sufficient that he made the representations with the consciousness that he was without knowledge as to their truth or falsity, when in fact, they were false.

In *John T. Brown, Inc. v. Weber Implement & Auto. Co.*, 260 S.W.2d 751, 755 (Mo.1953), the court said:

"It was essential to a recovery to establish a representation; its falsity; its materiality; the speaker's knowledge of its falsity; his intent that it be acted on by the hearer and in the manner reasonably contemplated; that hearer's ignorance of its falsity; his reliance on its truth; his right to rely thereon; and his consequent and proximate injury. A failure to establish any one of these elements is fatal to a recovery."

* * *

The same case at page 757 says:

"If it appears that there were facts and circumstances present at the time the false representations were made sufficient to put the injured party upon his guard or to cast suspicion upon their truth, and he neglected to avail himself of the warning thus given, he will not afterwards be heard to complain, for the reason that his own conduct contributed to his injury."

2. In *Orlann v. Laederich*, 338 Mo. 783, 791, 92 S.W.2d 190, 194 (1936), the court quotes from *McCaw v. O'Malley*, 298 Mo. 401, 249 S.W. 41, 44 (1923), which said: "... the burden is upon the plaintiff (defendant herein) to establish by proof that there was not only a false representation, but that he relied upon it, and that such reliance 'was an act of ordinary prudence,' and that such representations thus prudently relied upon influenced plaintiff to his damage."

This language has never been expressly overruled although it seems to have been tempered by later cases.

In *Meyer v. Brown*, 312 S.W.2d 158, 161 (Mo.App.1958), the court said: " 'However, the mere presence of opportunities for investigation will not of itself preclude the right of reliance; and this is especially true where the circumstances were such that a prudent man would not have been put on inquiry, as where positive statements were made in a manner not calculated to cause inquiry, where the relations between the parties were involuntary, where, although it was possible to ascertain the facts, an investigation would have been difficult, or where there was intentional fraud, as where the representations were made for the very purpose of preventing inquiry;' ...."

" 'The right to rely on representations is generally conceded where the hearer lacks equal facilities for ascertaining the truth, as where the facts are peculiarly within the knowledge of the speaker and are difficult for the hearer to ascertain....' "

Plaintiff's verdict directing instruction was not error although it did not hypothesize the right to rely. However, the court did note that defendant's instruction had required a specific finding of plaintiff's right to rely.

In *Shechter v. Brewer,* 344 S.W.2d 784, 788 (Mo.App.1961), the court said: "The tendency of modern decisions is not to extend, but to restrict the rule requiring diligence, and similar rules, such as *caveat emptor,* and the rule granting immunity for dealers talk; to condemn the falsehood of the fraud feasor rather than the credulity of his victim.... Since the very purpose of fraud is to cheat its victim by making him neglect the care essential to prevent injury, to deny relief because the victim was negligent would encourage the evil."

See also: *Monsanto Chemical Works v. American Zinc, Lead & Smelting Co.,* 253 S.W. 1006 (Mo.1923).

Restatement (First) of Torts § 541 (1934) expresses the rule as follows: "The recipient in a business transaction of a fraudulent misrepresentation is not justified in relying upon its truth if its falsity is obvious."

In *Emily v. Bayne,* 371 S.W.2d 663 (Mo.App.1963) plaintiff submitted in the alternative that (1) defendant knowingly made false representations and (2) that defendant made the representations without knowing whether they were true or false. Judgment for plaintiff was reversed because there was no evidence to support plaintiff's theory that defendant made the representations knowing them to be false.

See: *Schnuck v. Kriegshauser,* 371 S.W.2d 242 (Mo.1963) as to misrepresentations made in connection with the sale of a house.

For fraud in connection with failing to reveal limitations on use of property because of zoning ordinances, see *Gamel v. Lewis,* 373 S.W.2d 184 (Mo.App.1963).

Cases involving multiple misrepresentations.

Submission of multiple representations in a single verdict directing instruction may create a problem in determining whether all requisite elements (i.e. falsity, materiality, knowledge, etc.) have been found as to the same representation. A possible approach would be to submit a separate verdict directing instruction as to each alleged misrepresentation, all in a single package with a single damage instruction and a single verdict form.

Library References:

West's Key No. Digests, Fraud ⬥65(1).

Notes of Decisions

———

1. In general

Even if instruction based on MAI 23.05, standing alone, assumed disputed ultimate issue that agreement existed, no prejudicial error resulted since, under affirmative converse instruction requiring jury to return verdict for buyers if it believed parties did not make agreement, jury could not have returned verdict without first determining whether agreement existed. Dierker Associates, D.C., P.C. v. Gillis, 859 S.W.2d 737 (Mo.App.1993).

Even if buyers' representation regarding payment under contract to purchase chiropractic practice was made as to future event, no error occurred, even though third paragraph did not contain the alternate language that "[plaintiffs] knew that it was false at the time the representation was made," because trial court gave affirmative converse instruction providing that verdict must be for buyers if jury believed representation was false at time it was made. Dierker Associates, D.C., P.C. v. Gillis, 859 S.W.2d 737 (Mo.App. 1993).

Car manufacturer's practice of test driving cars with odometer unhooked, repairing any damage occurring during such use, and selling such cars as new constituted fraud. Maugh v. Chrysler Corp., 818 S.W.2d 658 (Mo.App.1991).

Failure to include the bracketed portion of Paragraph 5 "in so relying plaintiff was using ordinary care and . . ." constitutes error unless the right to rely is not in issue. Green Acres Enterprises, Inc. v. Nitsche, 636 S.W.2d 149[7] (Mo.App.1982).

Where a confidential relationship exists plaintiff had a right to rely on defendant's representation and need not submit the bracketed clause in paragraph Fifth requiring plaintiff to have used ordinary care in relying on defendant's representations. Vinyard v. Herman, 578 S.W.2d 938[1–5] (Mo.App. 1979).

Verdict director for fraud need not require finding of why statement was false. Dettler v. Santa Cruz, 403 S.W.2d 651[7] (Mo.App. 1966).

2. Burden of proof

Burden of proof in fraud case is no greater than other cases, and defendant was not entitled to an instruction requiring clear, cogent and convincing evidence. Crawford v. Smith, 470 S.W.2d 529[1] (Mo. banc 1971).

3. Intent

The phrase "defendant did not know whether the representation was true or false"—contained in instructions following the form of MAI 23.05—implied, without requiring a specific finding to that effect, that the defendant knew he did not know and, thus, did not misstate the element of scienter for the tort of fraudulent misrepresentation. Botanicals On The Park, Inc. v. Microcode Corp., 7 S.W.3d 465 (Mo.App.1999).

In instructing jury on elements necessary to prove insurance policy was void ab initio for fraudulent misrepresentation, trial court erred reversibly by adding to Missouri Approved Jury Instruction (MAI) language that intent to deceive would necessarily be implied if insured knew representation was false. Cova v. American Family Mut. Ins. Co., 880 S.W.2d 928[2] (Mo.App.1994).

Omission of element of fraud-feasor's *intent* that victim rely on the representation was error and prejudicial absent a clear showing of no prejudice. Jefferson County Bank & Trust Co. v. Dennis, 523 S.W.2d 165[2, 3] (Mo.App.1975).

4. Ordinary care clause

Although trial court failed to include, in fraudulent misrepresentation jury instruction, language from MAI 23.05 that seller was using "ordinary care" in relying on representations, no prejudice to buyers resulted; buyers did not object when instruction omitted language, instruction tendered by buyers omitted same language, and trial court instructed jury in next paragraph of its instruction that it must find that seller had right to rely on misrepresentations. Dierker Associates, D.C., P.C. v. Gillis, 859 S.W.2d 737 (Mo.App.1993).

Where customer acted on auto dealer's representation of facts peculiarly within dealer's knowledge there was no need to submit the clause "in so relying plaintiff was using ordinary care, and". Bowers v. S–H–S Motor Sales Corp., 481 S.W.2d 584[2] (Mo.App. 1972).

MAI 11.05 is not applicable to a fraud case and "ordinary care" may be defined as "... that degree of care that would be reasonable in view of plaintiff's situation." Throckmorton v. M.F.A. Central Co-op., 462 S.W.2d 138[2] (Mo.App.1970).

5. Conjunctive submission

Error to submit MAI 23.05 hypothesizing two fraudulent submissions conjunctively when there was evidence of only one of them. Knepper v. Bollinger, 421 S.W.2d 796[5] (Mo.App.1967).

6. Agency in issue

Although defendant's answer denied salesman was its agent, where plaintiff's evidence of agency was not refuted by other evidence, agency was a question of law and need not be hypothesized in plaintiff's verdict director. Bowers v. S–H–S Motor Sales Corp., 481 S.W.2d 584[2] (Mo.App.1972).

MAI 23.05–18.01 submitting fraudulent representations by agent. Tietjens v. General Motors Corp., 418 S.W.2d 75[1] (Mo. 1967).

7. Damages

Failure to give mandatory damage instruction on fraudulent misrepresentation claim required setting aside of damage award and ordering of new trial on issue of actual damages on such claim, even though proper actual damages may have been requested in closing argument and awarded. Dierker Associates, D.C., P.C. v. Gillis, 859 S.W.2d 737 (Mo.App.1993).

Giving MAI 4.01 in fraud case held proper, particularly when neither party offered a modification nor contended later that the verdict was either inadequate or excessive. Crawford v. Smith, 470 S.W.2d 529[6–9] (Mo. banc 1971).

8. Exemplary damages

MAI 11.05 is not applicable to a fraud case and "ordinary care" may be defined as "... that degree of care that would be reasonable in view of plaintiff's situation." Throckmorton v. MFA Central Co-op., 462 S.W.2d 138[2] (Mo.App.1970).

9. Negligence

"Negligent" was not required to be defined in fraudulent misrepresentation verdict director which inadvertently referred to "negligent misrepresentation," since it was not necessary for jury to decide whether party was negligent. Dierker Associates, D.C., P.C. v. Gillis, 859 S.W.2d 737 (Mo.App. 1993).

Use of term "negligent misrepresentation" instead of "fraudulent misrepresentation" in instruction based on MAI 23.05, was not prejudicial to buyers of chiropractic practice; body of instruction required jurors to find elements of fraudulent misrepresentation, and fact that buyers' counsel made same mistake in their proposed verdict director indicated that mistake would not be readily apparent to jury. Dierker Associates, D.C., P.C. v. Gillis, 859 S.W.2d 737 (Mo.App. 1993).

10. Future event

Log home kit manufacturer's statements of fact that homes' joints were designed to be weathertight, homes were to be long lasting and enduring, and that homes were chemically treated to minimize threat of rot were not representations of intention to perform or state of mind, but were present representations intended to induce buyers to purchase log homes, and thus did not warrant fraud verdict directing instruction pertaining to representations of future event. Judy v. Arkansas Log Homes, Inc., 923 S.W.2d 409 [1996 WL 131882] (Mo.App.1996).

23.06   [Withdrawn 1980] Verdict Directing—Libel

23.06(1)   [1980 New] Verdict Directing—Libel—Plaintiff Not a Public Official or Public Figure

Your verdict must be for plaintiff if you believe:

First, defendant (*describe act such as "published a newspaper article"*) containing the statement (*here insert the statement claimed to be libelous such as "plaintiff was a convicted felon"*), and [1]

Second, defendant was at fault in publishing such statement, and

Third, such statement tended to [expose plaintiff to (*select appropriate term or terms such as "hatred", "contempt" or "ridicule"*)] [or] [deprive the plaintiff of the benefit of public confidence and social associations],[2] and

Fourth, such statement was read by (*here insert name of person or persons other than plaintiff or the appropriate generic term such as "the public"*), and

Fifth, plaintiff's reputation was thereby damaged.

* [unless you believe plaintiff is not entitled to recover by reason of Instruction Number _____ (*here insert number of affirmative defense instruction*)].

Notes on Use (1980 New)

1. If the alleged libelous statement is a lengthy writing such as a newspaper or magazine article or a book, paragraph First may be modified to identify the writing by reference, for example:

First, defendant published the newspaper article identified as plaintiff's exhibit one, and

Also modify the other paragraphs of the instruction by changing the phrase "such statement" to "such article" or other appropriate generic term.

2. Select the appropriate phrase or phrases.

This instruction is intended for use in a case involving a private plaintiff, i.e., someone who is neither a public official nor a public figure. See Committee Comment to MAI 23.06(2) as to whether this instruction is applicable where the statement concerns a private plaintiff involved in a matter of public or general interest. Use MAI 23.06(2) if plaintiff is a public official or public figure.

It is a question of law for the court to decide whether qualified privilege applies. *Estes v. Lawton–Byrne–Bruner Insurance Agency Co.,* 437 S.W.2d 685 (Mo.App.1969). Use MAI 23.06(2) if the court determines that qualified privilege is applicable.

Use MAI 4.15 as the damage instruction with this verdict director. If punitive damages are submitted, use MAI 3.06 as the burden of proof instruction; if punitive damages are not submitted, use MAI 3.01.

* Add if affirmative defense is submitted.

Committee Comment (1980 New)

The federal decisions balancing the federal first amendment protections of free speech and freedom of the press against the states' interest in protecting citizens from defamation have produced standards of law which are imposed upon the states by the Federal Constitution. In *Gertz v. Robert Welch, Inc.,* 418 U.S. 323, 94 S.Ct. 2997, 41 L.Ed.2d 789 (1974), the Court held that so long as the states do not impose liability without fault, they may define for themselves the appropriate standard of liability for defamation to a private individual. Thus, the constitutional standard requires that liability must be based upon the fault of the defendant. This federal standard is submitted to the jury in paragraph Second; pursuant to Mo. Const. art. I, § 8 (1945) it is left to the jury to determine exactly what standard of fault shall be applied.

Gertz also prohibits liability without a finding of actual damages. Paragraph Fifth, which requires that the plaintiff's reputation be damaged, meets both this requirement and the requirement of the Missouri common law that the essence of defamation is injury to reputation.

See Committee Comment to MAI 23.06(2) regarding protected expressions of ideas versus actionable statements of "opinion" and assertions of "fact".

Library References:

C.J.S. Libel and Slander; Injurious Falsehood § 181.
West's Key No. Digests, Libel and Slander ☞124(1).

Notes of Decisions

In general 1
Actual malice 3
Damages 4
Defensive instructions 2

———

1. In general

Whether privilege exists to report on filing of court petition in circumstances proven is question of law and is not to be submitted to jury; newspaper story stating that defamation plaintiff was defendant in lawsuit was totally inaccurate report of petition filed with court and, thus, defense of privilege was not available to newspaper; in reporting on content of petition, newspaper was obligated to print substantially correct report. Hoeflicker v. Higginsville Advance, Inc., 818 S.W.2d 650 (Mo.App.1991).

In libel action against credit reporting service alleging that agency issued a false report that plaintiffs had filed for bankruptcy, proper instruction was MAI 23.06(2), not MAI 23.06(1), because agency was entitled to qualified privilege. McDowell v. Credit Bureaus of Southeast Mo., Inc., 747 S.W.2d 630[1] (Mo.1988).

MAI 23.06, Libel, is not to be used in action by public official where malice must be submitted and defined. Rowden v. Amick, 446 S.W.2d 849[1] (Mo.App.1969).

In libel action the existence of a qualified privilege is for the court rather than the jury, and when found to exist plaintiff must include paragraph Fourth to his verdict director. Estes v. Lawton–Byrne–Bruner Ins. Agency Co., 437 S.W.2d 685[3–9] (Mo.App. 1969).

2. Defensive instructions

Error for a defendant to define a phrase not used in plaintiff's verdict director. Lazier v. Pulitzer Pub. Co., 467 S.W.2d 900[3], certiorari denied 404 U.S. 940, 92 S.Ct. 273, 30 L.Ed.2d 253 (1971).

3. Actual malice

In action by public official he must show "actual malice" and that is not covered by paragraph Fourth of MAI 23.06, which should be amended to submit knowledge or serious doubts as to truth. Ramacciotti v. Zinn, 550 S.W.2d 217[14] (Mo.App.1977).

4. Damages

In defamation cases, old rules of per se and per quod do not apply and plaintiff need only plead and prove the unified defamation elements set out in MAI 23.06(1) and 23.06(2), and thus plaintiffs need not concern themselves with whether defamation was per se or per quod nor with whether special damages exist, but must prove actual damages in all cases. Nazeri v. Missouri Valley College, 860 S.W.2d 303 (Mo. banc 1993).

23.06(2)   [1980 New] Verdict Directing—Libel—Plaintiff a Public Official or Public Figure

Your verdict must be for plaintiff if you believe:

First, defendant (*describe act such as "published a newspaper article"*) containing the statement (*here insert the statement claimed to be libelous such as "plaintiff was a convicted felon"*), and [1]

Second, such statement was false, and

Third, defendant (*describe the act of publication such as "published such statement", "wrote such letter", etc.*) either:

with knowledge that it was false, or

with reckless disregard for whether it was true or false at a time when defendant had serious doubt as to whether it was true, and

Fourth, such statement tended to [expose plaintiff to (*select appropriate term or terms such as "hatred", "contempt" or "ridicule"*)] [or] [deprive the plaintiff of the benefit of public confidence and social associations],[2] and

Fifth, such statement was read by (*here insert name of person or persons other than plaintiff or the appropriate generic term such as "the public"*), and

Sixth, plaintiff's reputation was thereby damaged.

* [unless you believe plaintiff is not entitled to recover by reason of Instruction Number _____ (*here insert number of affirmative defense instruction*)].

Notes on Use (1980 New)

1.   If the alleged libelous statement is a lengthy writing such as a newspaper or magazine article or a book, paragraph First may be modified to identify the writing by reference, for example:

First, defendant published the newspaper article identified as plaintiff's exhibit one, and

Also modify the other paragraphs of the instruction by changing the phrase "such statement" to "such article" or other appropriate generic term.

2. Select the appropriate phrase or phrases.

This instruction is intended for use where the plaintiff is a public official or public figure. Use MAI 23.06(1) for a private plaintiff but see the last paragraph of Committee's Comment below as to whether the above instruction (MAI 23.06(2)) is applicable where the statement concerns a private plaintiff involved in a matter of public or general interest.

Use MAI 3.05 for burden of proof and MAI 4.16 as the damage instruction with this verdict director.

* Add if affirmative defense is submitted.

Committee Comment (1990 Revision)

New York Times Company v. Sullivan, 376 U.S. 254, 84 S.Ct. 710, 11 L.Ed.2d 686 (1964), requires actual malice before a recovery may be made in defamation by a public official. The same protection was extended to public figures in *Curtis Publishing Company v. Butts,* 388 U.S. 130, 87 S.Ct. 1975, 18 L.Ed.2d 1094 (1967). The extent to which this protection is available is further defined and to some extent altered by *Rosenbloom v. Metromedia, Inc.,* 403 U.S. 29, 91 S.Ct. 1811, 29 L.Ed.2d 296 (1971), *Gertz v. Robert Welch, Inc.,* 418 U.S. 323, 94 S.Ct. 2997, 41 L.Ed.2d 789 (1974), and *Time, Inc. v. Firestone,* 424 U.S. 448, 96 S.Ct. 958, 47 L.Ed.2d 154 (1976). Paragraphs Second and Third in MAI 23.06(2) reflect the actual malice requirement of *New York Times Company* as the test was further articulated in *St. Amant v. Thompson,* 390 U.S. 727, 88 S.Ct. 1323, 20 L.Ed.2d 262 (1968). The Missouri courts have applied the *New York Times* test on a number of occasions. See *Glover v. Herald Company,* 549 S.W.2d 858 (Mo. banc 1977); *Skain v. Weldon,* 422 S.W.2d 271 (Mo.1967); *Rowden v. Amick,* 446 S.W.2d 849 (Mo.App.1969); and *Whitmore v. Kansas City Star Co.,* 499 S.W.2d 45 (Mo.App.1973).

It is not clear under the present Missouri cases whether the *New York Times* standard of actual malice applies in a Missouri case involving a private plaintiff where the defamatory falsehood concerns matters of public or general interest. In *Rosenbloom v. Metromedia, Inc.,* 403 U.S. 29, 91 S.Ct. 1811, 29 L.Ed.2d 296 (1971), a plurality of the Supreme Court extended the *New York Times* standard to such a situation; this standard was applied by the Missouri court in a similar situation in *Woolbright v. Sun Communications, Inc.,* 480 S.W.2d 864 (Mo.1972). Thereafter, in *Gertz v. Robert Welch, Inc.,* 418 U.S. 323, 94 S.Ct. 2997, 41 L.Ed.2d 789 (1974), the U.S. Supreme Court backed away from the plurality position in *Rosenbloom* and did not require the *New York Times* standard to be applied to a private defamation plaintiff involved in a matter of public or general interest. The Missouri courts could continue to apply this standard in such cases. However, they are probably no longer constitutionally required to do so, and it would appear to be an open question as to what position the Missouri courts will take now that they are free to determine their own position on this issue.

Dicta in *Gertz,* a media defendant case, stated that while there is no constitutional value in false statements of fact there is no such thing as a false idea. *Henry v. Halliburton,* 690 S.W.2d 775 (Mo. banc 1985) adopted that dicta as the law of Missouri and construed the First Amendment protection of ideas to apply to both media and private defendants. The question of fact or idea is a question of law which determines submissibility. It must be decided by the court from the "totality of the circumstances", id., 788, "It is up to the trial judge in the first instance to determine whether the alleged statements are capable of being treated as assertions of fact, although the jury may decide that they were not so understood."

Gertz, was refined in *Milkovich v. Lorain Journal Co.,* 497 U.S. 1, 110 S.Ct. 2695, 111 L.Ed.2d 1 (1990). *Milkovich* held that the above referenced dicta in *Gertz* did not create a wholesale defamation exemption under the First Amendment for anything that might be labeled an "opinion". The test under *Milkovich* for actionability is whether the statement of "opinion" is sufficiently factual to be susceptible of being proved true or false. *Henry v. Halliburton,* supra, should be read in light of *Milkovich.*

In *Philadelphia Newspapers, Inc. v. Hepps,* 475 U.S. 767, 106 S.Ct. 1558, 89 L.Ed.2d 783 (1986), a narrow opinion limited to a private plaintiff suing a media defendant for libel in a matter of public concern, the court shifted the burden of proof on truth-falsity to the plaintiff. Concurring justices would have extended the shift in similar cases against any defendant. Paragraph Second of MAI 23.06(2) already imposes the burden on a public official plaintiff. Prudence would suggest that such a paragraph Second should be included in MAI 23.06(1) when a private plaintiff is suing a media defendant on a publication of public concern. Review of federal decisions later than 1986 should be made when using MAI 23.06(1) against non-media defendants to be sure that the view of the concurring justices in *Philadelphia Newspapers* has not become the majority view.

Library References:

C.J.S. Libel and Slander; Injurious Falsehood § 181.
West's Key No. Digests, Libel and Slander ⚖124(1).

Notes of Decisions

In general　1
Damages　3
Evidentiary support　2

1. In general

Whether privilege exists to report on filing of court petition in circumstances proven is question of law and is not to be submitted to jury; newspaper story stating that defamation plaintiff was defendant in lawsuit was totally inaccurate report of petition filed with court and, thus, defense of privilege was not available to newspaper; in reporting on content of petition, newspaper was obligated to print substantially correct report. Hoeflicker v. Higginsville Advance, Inc., 818 S.W.2d 650 (Mo.App.1991).

In libel action against credit reporting service alleging that agency issued a false report that plaintiffs had filed for bankruptcy, proper instruction was MAI 23.06(2), not MAI 23.06(1), because agency was entitled to qualified privilege. McDowell v. Credit Bureaus of Southeast Mo., Inc., 747 S.W.2d 630[1] (Mo.1988).

2. Evidentiary support

Evidence was insufficient to support jury finding that corporate agent defamed former employee by sending a letter concerning employee's misconduct to party with interest in employee's conduct, where there was no evidence that when agent mailed the letter, he had any reason to doubt or question the information in the letter and, thus, employee failed to prove publication with malice, which is an essential element of employee's claim. Washington v. Thomas, 778 S.W.2d 792 (Mo.App.1989).

3. Damages

In defamation cases, old rules of per se and per quod do not apply and plaintiff need only plead and prove the unified defamation elements set out in MAI 23.06(1) and 23.06(2), and thus plaintiffs need not concern themselves with whether defamation was per se or per quod nor with whether special damages exist, but must prove actual damages in all cases. Nazeri v. Missouri Valley College, 860 S.W.2d 303 (Mo. banc 1993).

23.07 [2000 Revision] Verdict Directing—Malicious Prosecution—For Initiating or Continuing Criminal or Civil Actions

Your verdict must be for plaintiff if you believe:

First, defendant ["instigated", "continued"] [1] a judicial proceeding against plaintiff that terminated in favor of plaintiff, and

Second, in so doing defendant acted maliciously [2] and without reasonable grounds, [3] and

Third, plaintiff was thereby damaged.

*[unless you believe that plaintiff is not entitled to recover by reason of Instruction Number ___ (*here insert number of affirmative defense instruction*)].

Notes on Use (2000 Revision)

1. Select the appropriate term. See *King v. Ryals*, 981 S.W.2d 151 (Mo.App.1998).

2. The term "maliciously" must be defined. See definitions at MAI 16.01(1) and 16.02(2). *Sanders v. Daniel Intern. Corp.*, 682 S.W.2d 803 (Mo. banc 1984); and *Proctor v. Stevens Employment Services, Inc.*, 712 S.W.2d 684 (Mo. banc 1986).

3. The phrase "reasonable grounds" must be defined. See definitions at MAI 16.05 and 16.06.

* Add if affirmative defense is submitted.

Committee Comment (1996 Revision)

See Committee Comment to MAI 23.04.

In cases involving merchants, see § 537.125, RSMo.

Where agency is in issue, see MAI 18.01.

"[T]he constitutive elements of an action for malicious prosecution are: (1) The commencement or prosecution of the proceeding against him or her; (2) its legal causation by the present defendant; (3) its termination in favor of the present plaintiff; (4) the absence of probable cause for such proceeding; (5) the presence of malice therein; and (6) damage to plaintiff by reason thereof." *Bonzo v. Kroger Grocery & Baking Co.*, 344 Mo. 127, 125 S.W.2d 75 (1939); citing *Higgins v. Knickmeyer–Fleer Realty & Investment Co.*, 335 Mo. 1010, 74 S.W.2d 805, 812 (Mo.1934).

In *Sanders v. Daniel International Corp.*, 682 S.W.2d 803 (Mo.banc 1984), the Missouri supreme Court held that the requirement for "malice" to support actual damages in a malicious prosecution case arising out of a criminal prosecution is satisfied by a finding of "legal malice". The *Sanders* case, *supra*, also held that punitive damages in such a malicious prosecution case may only be submitted to a jury if there is evidence of "actual malice" or "malice in fact" as opposed to "legal malice".

In *Sanders*, 682 S.W.2d at 814, the Supreme Court held:

The Restatement of Torts (Second) § 668 (1965) provides: "To subject a person to liability for malicious prosecution, the proceeding must have been initiated primarily for a purpose other than that of bringing an offender to justice." This definition, while not requiring proof of malice in fact, will require proof of legal malice and bring Missouri back into step with the majority of jurisdictions.

In *Proctor v. Stevens Employment Services, Inc.*, 712 S.W.2d 684 (Mo.banc 1986), the Missouri Supreme Court decided that the holding in *Sanders, supra,* does not apply to malicious prosecution actions arising out of a civil case. *Proctor* also held that "malice in law", MAI 16.01(1), is the appropriate definition of "malice" for submission of actual damages under MAI 23.07 in a malicious prosecution case arising out of a civil action.

In *Burnett v. Griffith*, 769 S.W.2d 780, 789 (Mo.banc 1989); the Supreme Court adopted a new MAI 10.01 for submission of punitive damages in intentional tort cases and held that the definition of "malice" in prior MAI 16.01 should no longer be used in connection with the submission of punitive damages. "Malicious prosecution" is an intentional tort. See MAI 10.01 for submission of punitive damages.

Library References:

C.J.S. Malicious Prosecution or Wrongful Litigation § 90.
West's Key No. Digests, Malicious Prosecution ⚖72(1).

Notes of Decisions

————

1. In general

Giving two identical verdict directors which were affirmative converses to mortgagors' malicious prosecution verdict directors was not error in action against mortgagee, where each mortgagor claimed separate damages based on single theory of recovery, and damage claims were virtually independent. Burnett v. GMAC Mortgage Corp., 847 S.W.2d 82 (Mo.App.1992).

In malicious prosecution actions, arising out of criminal proceeding, "the second paragraph of MAI 23.07 should be amended as follows: 'Second, in so doing defendant acted primarily for a purpose other than that of bringing an offender to justice and acted without reasonable grounds, and ...'" Sanders v. Daniel Intern. Corp., 682 S.W.2d 803[8] (Mo. banc 1984).

In action for wrongful sequestration, court correctly refused to give MAI 23.07, *Malicious Prosecution.* Fischer v. MAJ Inv. Corp., 631 S.W.2d 902[2] (Mo.App.1982).

2. Termination

Where defendant had obtained default judgment against plaintiff, allegedly by false return of process, she could not recover for malicious prosecution because the action had not terminated in plaintiff's favor. Proper action was for false return of process. Jackson v. Missouri Rating & Collection Co., 537 S.W.2d 442[1] (Mo.App.1976).

Evidence that defendant dismissed its suit against plaintiff without prejudice warranted a submission that the suit "terminated in favor of plaintiff." McFarland v. Union Finance Co., 471 S.W.2d 497[2, 3] (Mo.App. 1971).

3. Definition

Failure to define the term "malice" was not reversible error in malicious prosecution action where there was no objection and the term "maliciously" was defined. Burnett v. GMAC Mortgage Corp., 847 S.W.2d 82 (Mo. App.1992).

MAI 16.01, a definition of malice in law, is the proper definition of malice in a civil malicious prosecution action. Proctor v. Stevens Employment Services, Inc., 712 S.W.2d 684[5] (Mo. banc 1986).

MAI 16.01 improperly defines the element of malice in a malicious prosecution action arising from criminal proceedings and does not adequately express the degree of culpability required for punitive damages. Sanders v. Daniel Intern. Corp., 682 S.W.2d 803[6–11] (Mo. banc 1984).

Definition of "reasonable grounds" properly refused as argumentative. Boquist v. Montgomery Ward & Co., 516 S.W.2d 769[8–10] (Mo.App.1974).

4. Burden of proof

MAI 3.01 is proper burden of proof instruction in civil malicious prosecution case. Proctor v. Stevens Employment Services, Inc., 712 S.W.2d 684[1] (Mo. banc 1986).

5. Punitive damages

MAI 16.01, a definition of malice in law, does not adequately express degree of culpability required for an award of punitive damages in a malicious prosecution case arising from a civil proceeding. Instead, the jury must be instructed that in order to award punitive damages, "the proceedings must have been initiated or continued primarily for a purpose other than that of securing the proper adjudication of the claim on which they are based." Proctor v. Stevens Employment Services, Inc., 712 S.W.2d 684[6, 7] (Mo. banc 1986).

6. Reasonable grounds

Plaintiff alleging malicious prosecution must prove defendant's want of probable cause to have initiated or to have continued to prosecute original action against malicious prosecution plaintiff. King v. Ryals, 981 S.W.2d 151 (Mo.App.1998).

7. Continuation of malicious proceeding

Trial court should have submitted proposed instruction that malicious prosecution could be based upon either initiation or continuation of malicious proceedings, rather than submit MAI 23.07, which did not require finding of malicious prosecution based upon malicious continuation of proceedings; proposed instruction properly reflected law and facts of case that action in malicious prosecution may be based on malicious continuation of prosecution. King v. Ryals, 981 S.W.2d 151 (Mo.App.1998).

23.08 [1990 Revision] Verdict Directing—Service Letters

Your verdict must be for plaintiff if you believe:

First, plaintiff was employed by defendant [1] for at least 90 days, and

Second, after such employment ended, plaintiff made a written request [2] within a reasonable period of time [3] to (*insert appropriate title or name of person to whom the request must be made under the statute*) for a service letter, and

[Third, defendant did not issue such a letter to plaintiff.] [4]

[Third, defendant did not issue such a letter to plaintiff within 45 days after receipt of such request.] [4]

[Third, defendant's letter did not correctly state [the length of employment] [the true cause for which plaintiff was terminated or quit such employment] [the nature and character of plaintiff's services during such employment.] [5]] [4]

[Third, defendant's letter did not include a statement setting forth [the length of employment] [the true cause for which plaintiff was terminated or quit such employment] [the nature and character of plaintiff's services during such employment.] [5]] [4]

* [unless you believe plaintiff is not entitled to recover by reason of Instruction Number _____ (*here insert number of affirmative defense instruction*)].

Notes on Use (1990 Revision)

1. On rare occasions there may be a factual dispute as to whether defendant was a corporation or had more than seven employees as required by R.S.Mo., § 290.140. If such a factual dispute is appropriate for resolution by the jury, add a paragraph to this verdict directing instruction submitting those issues and renumber the remaining paragraphs.

2. R.S.Mo., § 290.140.1 requires that the plaintiff's written request be by certified mail with specific reference to the statute. If these requisites are in dispute, insert the applicable portion(s) of the following

354

phrase: "by certified mail with specific reference to the service letter statute".

3. R.S.Mo., § 290.140.1 provides that the employee's request must be within a reasonable period of time, but not later than one year. If there is a legitimate factual dispute as to whether the request was made within one year after termination, insert the following phrase: "but not later than one year after such employment ended".

4. Select the appropriate paragraph or paragraphs Third. If more than one is used, they must be submitted in the disjunctive and each must be supported by substantial evidence.

5. Select the appropriate phrase or phrases. If more than one is used, they must be submitted in the disjunctive and each must be supported by the evidence.

* Add if affirmative defense is submitted.

Committee Comment (1990 Revision)

R.S.Mo., § 290.140.2 authorizes nominal damages in some circumstances even in the absence of actual damages. In such a situation, if plaintiff desires an instruction on nominal damages, the following sentence should be added to the actual damage instruction.

> "If you find in favor of plaintiff but do not believe plaintiff sustained compensatory damages, you must award plaintiff nominal damages in the amount of one dollar."

If actual damages are not submissible, nominal damages may still be awarded and serve as the basis for punitive damages where the defendant did not send the requested letter. R.S.Mo., § 290.140(2). In such a case the damage instruction will be:

> "If you find in favor of plaintiff, then you must award plaintiff nominal damages in the amount of one dollar."

In *Hills v. McComas Rentals, Inc.,* 779 S.W.2d 297, 300 (Mo.App. 1989); the Court held that the failure of the service letter to meet all three requirements for the contents of a service letter is equivalent to nonissuance. *Hills* also holds that, if punitive damages are submissible in a service letter case, those punitive damages must be submitted under the standard set forth in MAI 10.01 and *Burnett v. Griffith,* 769 S.W.2d 780 (Mo. banc 1989).

If the corporation does not have a titled officer the statute includes such title or person as may have general supervision or corporate authority to write service letters. *Chrisman v. Terminal R. Ass'n of St. Louis,* 237 Mo.App. 181, 157 S.W.2d 230 (1942); *Turner v. Emerson Electric Mfg. Co.,* 280 S.W.2d 474 (Mo.App.1955).

It is the corporate duty to issue such letter. *Cheek v. Prudential Ins. Co. of America,* 192 S.W. 387 (Mo.1916).

No finding of damage is required since failure to issue a proper letter entitles plaintiff to nominal damages without proof. *Heuer v. John R. Thompson Co., supra; Cook v. Mid–Continent Petroleum Corp.,* 193 S.W.2d 66 (Mo.App.1946).

The statute is to be strictly construed and plaintiff must bring himself within its terms. *Lyons v. St. Joseph Belt Ry. Co.,* 232 Mo.App. 575, 84 S.W.2d 933 (1935), cert. quashed 341 Mo. 733, 108 S.W.2d 351 (1937).

If the request was actually for a report to the Unemployment Compensation Commission then no service letter action exists. *Seiller v. Kiel,* 149 S.W.2d 463 (Mo.App.1941).

Library References:

C.J.S. Labor Relations § 15.
West's Key No. Digests, Labor Relations ☞25.1.

Notes of Decisions

1. In general

Section 290.140, R.S.Mo.1986 provides basis for claim against university for failure to provide service letter to temporary librarian upon failure to renew her employment. Krasney v. Curators of University of Mo., 765 S.W.2d 646, 650–51 (Mo.App.1989).

MAI 23.08 properly requires that a service letter "correctly state the . . . true cause" of plaintiff's discharge; it does not change the substantive law of § 290.140, RSMo., requiring a service letter "truly stating for what cause" defendant discharged plaintiff; there's no substantial difference. Cumby v. Farmland Industries, 524 S.W.2d 132[1] (Mo. App.1975).

Under MAI 23.08 plaintiff need not show the true reason for discharge; that is defendant's burden. Potter v. Milbank Mfg. Co., 489 S.W.2d 197[1] (Mo.1972).

23.09 **[Withdrawn 1980] Verdict Directing—Slander—Not Per Se**

23.10 **[Withdrawn 1980] Verdict Directing—Slander Per Se**

23.10(1) [1980 New] Verdict Directing—Slander— Plaintiff Not a Public Official or Public Figure

Your verdict must be for plaintiff if you believe:

First, defendant stated (*here insert the statement claimed to be slanderous such as "plaintiff was a convicted felon"*), and

Second, defendant was at fault in making such statement, and

Third, such statement tended to [expose plaintiff to (*select appropriate term or terms such as "hatred", "contempt" or "ridicule"*)] [or] [deprive the plaintiff of the benefit of public confidence and social associations],[1] and

Fourth, such statement was heard by (*here insert name of person or persons other than plaintiff who heard the statement*), and

Fifth, plaintiff's reputation was thereby damaged.

* [unless you believe plaintiff is not entitled to recover by reason of Instruction Number _____ (*here insert number of affirmative defense instruction*)].

Notes on Use (1980 New)

1. Select the appropriate phrase or phrases.

This instruction is intended for use in a case involving a private plaintiff, i.e., someone who is neither a public official nor a public figure. See Committee Comment to MAI 23.06(2) as to whether this instruction is applicable where the statement concerns a private plaintiff involved in a matter of public or general interest. Use MAI 23.10(2) in a slander case where plaintiff is a public official or public figure.

It is a question of law for the court to decide whether qualified privilege applies. *Estes v. Lawton–Byrne–Bruner Insurance Agency Co.,* 437 S.W.2d 685 (Mo.App.1969). Use MAI 23.10(2) if the court determines that qualified privilege is applicable.

Use MAI 4.15 as the damage instruction with this verdict director. If punitive damages are submitted, use MAI 3.06 as the burden of proof instruction; if punitive damages are not submitted, use MAI 3.01.

* Add if affirmative defense is submitted.

Committee Comment (1995 Revision)

See Committee Comment to MAI 23.06(1) for a discussion of the federal constitutional standards imposed upon the states in a defamation case involving a plaintiff who is neither a public official nor a public figure. See the Committee Comment to MAI 23.10(2) as to the applicability to slander cases of federal constitutional standards developed in libel cases.

In *Nazeri v. Missouri Valley College,* 860 S.W.2d 303 (Mo. banc 1993), the Court held "in defamation cases the old rules of *per se* and *per quod* do not apply and plaintiff need only to plead and prove the unified defamation elements set out in MAI 23.10(1) and 23.10(2). In short, plaintiffs need not concern themselves with whether the defamation was *per se* or *per quod,* nor with whether special damages exist, but must prove actual damages in all cases."

Nazeri also discusses the types of statements that may qualify as "slanderous" for purposes of paragraph First of MAI 23.10(1) and 23.10(2).

Library References:

C.J.S. Libel and Slander; Injurious Falsehood § 181.
West's Key No. Digests, Libel and Slander ⟨⟩124(1).

Notes of Decisions

1. In general

Plaintiff need only to plead and prove unified defamation elements set out in applicable model jury instructions to establish defamation. Boyd v. Schwan's Sales Enterprises, Inc., 23 S.W.3d 261 (Mo.App.2000).

In defamation cases the old rules of per se and per quod do not apply; plaintiff need only plead and prove the unified defamation elements set out in MAI 23.10(1) and 23.10(2). Thurston v. Ballinger, 884 S.W.2d 22 (Mo.App.1994).

Recovery on a slander claim requires a showing of actual damages. Jenkins v. Revolution Helicopter Corp., Inc., 925 S.W.2d 939 [1996 WL 329926] (Mo.App.1996).

Statement made by director of police academy to police chief, indicating that applicant had cheated on entrance examination, was qualifiedly privileged for purposes of applicant's slander action; trial court therefore erred in failing to instruct on malice; but evidence was insufficient to establish that director acted with actual malice as required to overcome director's qualified privilege. Dvorak v. O'Flynn, 808 S.W.2d 912 (Mo.App.1991).

MAI 23.10(1) is not inadequate due to its failure to require finding by jury that allegedly defamatory statement was false or its failure to require submission to jury of definition of the term "fault." Joseph v. Elam, 709 S.W.2d 517[7] (Mo.App.1986).

Error to submit 23.10(1) where qualified privilege applies, but error not prejudicial where jury in awarding punitive damages found malice sufficient to overcome qualified immunity. Carter v. Willert Home Products, Inc., 714 S.W.2d 506[6, 7] (Mo. banc 1986).

23.10(2) [1980 New] Verdict Directing—Slander— Plaintiff a Public Official or Public Figure

Your verdict must be for plaintiff if you believe:

First, defendant stated (*here insert the statement claimed to be slanderous such as "plaintiff was a convicted felon"*), and

Second, such statement was false, and

Third, defendant (*describe the act of publication such as "published such statement", "wrote the letter", etc.*) either:

with knowledge that it was false, or

with reckless disregard for whether it was true or false at a time when defendant had serious doubt as to whether it was true, and

Fourth, such statement tended to [expose plaintiff to (*select appropriate term or terms such as "hatred", "contempt" or "ridicule"*)] [or] [deprive the plaintiff of the benefit of public confidence and social associations],[1] and

Fifth, such statement was heard by (*here insert name of person or persons other than plaintiff who heard the statement*), and

Sixth, plaintiff's reputation was thereby damaged.

* [unless you believe plaintiff is not entitled to recover by reason of Instruction Number _____ (*here insert number of affirmative defense instruction*)].

Notes on Use (1980 New)

1. Select the appropriate phrase or phrases.

This instruction is intended for use where the plaintiff is a public official or public figure. Use MAI 23.10(1) for a private plaintiff but see the last paragraph of Committee Comment to MAI 23.06(2) as to whether the above instruction (MAI 23.10(2)) is applicable where the statement concerns a private plaintiff involved in a matter of public or general interest.

Use MAI 3.05 for burden of proof and MAI 4.16 as the damage instruction with this verdict director.

* Add if affirmative defense is submitted.

Committee Comment (1995 Revision)

The United States Supreme Court cases extending federal constitutional protection to defamation defendants have not distinguished between libel and slander. *Rosenbloom v. Metromedia, Inc.,* 403 U.S. 29, 91 S.Ct. 1811, 29 L.Ed.2d 296 (1971), involved a television-broadcaster defendant who was afforded the protection of the *New York Times* standard. Neither the Supreme Court nor the Missouri courts have addressed the questions of whether statements broadcast by television are libel or slander or a hybrid. In any event, it cannot be seriously doubted that the federal constitutional protections for defamation defendants extend to slander cases on the same basis as to libel cases. See the Committee Comment to MAI 23.06(2) for a discussion of the federal standard incorporated in MAI 23.06(2) and the above instruction, both of which are substantially similar.

In *Nazeri v. Missouri Valley College,* 860 S.W.2d 303 (Mo. banc 1993), the Court held "in defamation cases the old rules of *per se* and *per quod* do not apply and plaintiff need only to plead and prove the unified defamation elements set out in MAI 23.10(1) and 23.10(2). In short, plaintiffs need not concern themselves with whether the defamation was *per se* or *per quod,* nor with whether special damages exist, but must prove actual damages in all cases."

Nazeri also discusses the types of statements that may qualify as "slanderous" for purposes of paragraph First of MAI 23.10(1) and 23.10(2).

Library References:

C.J.S. Libel and Slander; Injurious Falsehood § 181.
West's Key No. Digests, Libel and Slander ⊕124(1).

Notes of Decisions

1. In general

Verdict directing instruction should have been submitted in action by employee against former employer for allegedly defamatory communication to other employees and customer that employee was terminated for stealing company money; employer's communications to other employees and customer were protected by qualified privilege, but employee made submissible case of actual malice to defeat that privilege. Deckard v. O'Reilly Automotive, Inc., 31 S.W.3d 6 (Mo.App.2000).

Plaintiff need only to plead and prove unified defamation elements set out in applicable model jury instructions to establish defamation. Boyd v. Schwan's Sales Enterprises, Inc., 23 S.W.3d 261 (Mo.App.2000).

In defamation cases the old rules of per se and per quod do not apply; plaintiff need only plead and prove the unified defamation elements set out in MAI 23.10(1) and 23.10(2). Thurston v. Ballinger, 884 S.W.2d 22 (Mo.App.1994).

Evidence was insufficient to establish that officer at police academy in charge of independent applicants acted with malice when he told his superiors that applicant had cheated on his entrance examination, as required to overcome officer's qualified privilege in applicant's slander action; although applicant presented evidence concerning his "connections" within police academy, inference that officer deliberately accused applicant of cheating because of such connections was speculative. Dvorak v. O'Flynn, 808 S.W.2d 912 (Mo.App.1991).

Statements made by employer's employment verifier to finance company that employee had credit complaints as well as judgments and garnishments against her were, as a matter of law, qualifiedly privileged, thus requiring showing of malice. MAI 23.10(2) was thus appropriate instruction, and trial court erred in submitting MAI 23.10(1). Carter v. Willert Home Prods., Inc., 714 S.W.2d 506, 513 (Mo. banc 1986).

23.11 [1981 Revision] Verdict Directing—Tortious Interference With Contract

Your verdict must be for plaintiff if you believe:

First, a contract existed between plaintiff and (*insert name of third party*) which was [breached] [terminated] [1] by (*insert name of third party*), and [2]

Second, defendant caused (*insert name of third party*) to [breach] [terminate] [1] the contract with plaintiff, and

Third, defendant did so intentionally and without justification or excuse, and

Fourth, plaintiff was thereby damaged.

* [unless you believe plaintiff is not entitled to recover by reason of Instruction Number _____ (*here insert number of affirmative defense instruction*)].

Notes on Use (1991 Revision)

1. Select the appropriate term.

2. If defendant's knowledge of the contract is in dispute, insert the following paragraph and renumber the remaining paragraphs.

"Second, defendant knew of such contract, and"

The term "third party" means the one with whom plaintiff had a contract and the one who, at defendant's request, breached or terminated the contract.

* Add if affirmative defense is submitted.

Committee Comment (1991 Revision)

Downey v. United Weatherproofing, 363 Mo. 852, 253 S.W.2d 976, 980–81 (1953), stated:

"It has now come to be the view of a majority of courts in this country that one who maliciously or without justifiable cause induces a person to breach his contract with another may be held responsible to the latter for the damages resulting from such breach. The term 'maliciously' in this connection alludes to malice in its technical legal sense, that is, the intentional doing of a harmful act without justification or excuse, and does not necessarily include actual malice, that is malice in the sense of spite or ill will. . . ."

". . . action will lie for the malicious procurement of the breach of any contract."

See *Community Title Co. v. Roosevelt Federal Savings & Loan Ass'n,* 670 S.W.2d 895 (Mo.App.1984) for discussion of the elements of tortious interference with contract.

Library References:

C.J.S. Torts § 45–54.
West's Key No. Digests, Torts ⚭10(1).

Notes of Decisions

1. In general

Even if real estate salesman who owned one-third share in real estate company was fired by company's shareholders and president so as to remove him from company and force him to sell his common stock at low price under buy-sell agreement, salesman failed to plead sufficient facts establishing absence of justification element of claim for tortious interference with contract, where salesman did not base his claim on breach of buy-sell agreement but rather on his termination, salesman was fired for his unauthorized real estate activities in another state, salesman was not licensed to sell real estate in other state, and salesman was employee-at-will. Murray v. Ray, 862 S.W.2d 931 (Mo. App.1993).

Developer alleging that competitor tortiously interfered with its contract with redevelopment agency was not entitled to jury instruction that competitor could be liable if its actions "contributed to cause" redevelopment agency to terminate contract. White v. Land Clearance for Redevelopment Authority, 841 S.W.2d 691 (Mo.App.1992).

Breach of employment contract. State ex rel. State Dept. of Public Health and Welfare, Div. of Welfare v. Luster, 456 S.W.2d 600[4] (Mo.App.1970).

23.12(1)   [1989 New] Verdict Directing—Conversion— Taking

Your verdict must be for plaintiff if you believe:

First, plaintiff was (*here describe facts which entitled plaintiff to possession—e.g.—"the owner of the watch", "the lessee of the automobile"*), and

Second, defendant took possession of (*here describe the property*) with the intent to exercise some control over (*here describe the property*),[1] and

Third, defendant thereby deprived plaintiff of the right to possession of (*here describe the property*).

* [unless you believe that plaintiff is not entitled to recover by reason of Instruction No. _____ (*here insert number of affirmative defense instruction*)].

Notes on Use (1989 New)

1. In a case which does not involve a wrongful taking, but involves a wrongful appropriation (such as where the owner delivers property to the defendant with instructions that it be used for a certain purpose, but the defendant uses the property contrary to the instructions) modify paragraph Second to submit the facts which are claimed to constitute the wrongful appropriation.

See MAI 32.26 and 32.27 for instructions relating to affirmative defenses of consent and abandonment, respectively. See MAI 23.12(2) relating to conversion by the act of failure to surrender possession.

* Add if affirmative defense is submitted.

Committee Comment (1989 New)

Conversion is the unauthorized assumption of the right of ownership over the personal property of another to the exclusion of the owner's rights; *Maples v. United Savings & Loan Ass'n,* 686 S.W.2d 525 (Mo.App.1985). Conversion is generally concerned with possession, not ownership. The plaintiff must be either the owner or be the person having a right to immediate possession at the time of the conversion; *Hampton v. Stephens,* 691 S.W.2d 287 (Mo.App.1985). To be liable for conversion the defendant must have intended to convert the property to use inconsistent with the owner's right; *Owens v. Automobile Recovery Bureau, Inc.,* 544 S.W.2d 26 (Mo.App.1976).

The unauthorized assumption of the right of ownership may take one of three forms: (1) tortious taking; (2) use or appropriation to use;

or, (3) refusal to surrender possession after demand. Tortious taking involves the defendant's wrongful acquisition of the property. Use or appropriation to use may involve rightful acquisition but unauthorized use, for example a brokerage house properly holding stock for a customer, *but* pledging that stock for its own loan. In neither of these cases is a demand for return a prerequisite to a conversion action; *Brandhorst v. Carondelet Savings & Loan Ass'n*, 625 S.W.2d 696 (Mo.App.1981). The other common form of conversion also involves a rightful possession but the refusal to surrender possession of the property when demanded; *Knight v. M.H. Siegfried Real Estate, Inc.*, 647 S.W.2d 811 (Mo.App. 1982).

Actions for conversion are normally limited to personal property. However, money may be converted if it is placed in the custody of a party for a specific purpose and then misappropriated; *Dillard v. Payne*, 615 S.W.2d 53 (Mo.1981).

Consent and abandonment are complete defenses to an action for conversion. Consent requires words or conduct permitting defendant to take or use the property; *Maples, supra*. Abandonment requires an intent to abandon and an external act by which the intent is carried out; *Chemical Sales Co. v. Diamond Chemical Co.*, 766 F.2d 364 (8th Cir. 1985). Generally, defendant's good faith, motive, lack of knowledge, or mistake of law is no defense to a conversion action; *Coffman v. Faulkner*, 591 S.W.2d 23 (Mo.App.1979); *NIKA Corp. v. City of Kansas City, Mo.*, 582 F.Supp. 343 (W.D.Mo.1983).

Actual damages in a conversion action are the reasonable market value at the time of the conversion, *Weldon v. Town Properties, Inc.*, 633 S.W.2d 196 (Mo.App.1982). As an alternative measure, if property not "stock for sale" nor acquired by the owner in a conventional market, damages may be assessed as "what it will cost the owner to produce or acquire the property at the time of the conversion"; *NIKA Corp., supra*. Punitive damages may be assessed upon a proper showing, though the "good faith" of the defendant may bar punitive recovery; *NIKA Corp., supra*. Where the property is returned before commencement of the lawsuit, the measure of damages is the depreciation in value of the personal property converted between the date of the conversion and the date of return; *Koch Fuels, Inc. v. Cargo of 13,000 Barrels of No. 2 Fuel Oil.*, 530 F.Supp. 1074 (D.C.Mo.1981), aff'd 704 F.2d 1038 (8th Cir.1983).

Library References:

C.J.S. Trover and Conversion § 150–157.
West's Key No. Digests, Trover and Conversion ⚷67.

Notes of Decisions

1. In general

Evidence raised issue for jury on video rental chain's conversion claim against dealer of used video tapes and games; chain presented evidence establishing that it owned video tapes and games recovered from dealer's store, that it never offered seized merchandise for sale, and that all tapes and games seized from dealer's store carried chain's label, and other evidence indicated that dealer attempted to sell chain's property for his own financial gain, and that chain lost revenue during time its property was in dealer's possession. Mertz v. Blockbuster, Inc., 32 S.W.3d 130 (Mo.App.2000).

Verdict director for conversion which charges use of funds "for other purposes" than specified purpose follows model instruction for conversion. Verdict director for conversion that allowed finding of liability even if limited partner's promissory note payment was not diverted to general partner's personal use followed model instruction for conversion, since it instructed that general partner did not use payment for its intended purpose. Stavrides v. Zerjav, 927 S.W.2d 486 (Mo.App.1996).

To establish ownership of allegedly converted property or entitlement to possession of that property, plaintiff must prove that he was either the owner or was entitled to immediate possession of the property at time of alleged conversion. Fehrman v. Pfetzing, 917 S.W.2d 600 (Mo.App.1996).

23.12(2)   [1989 New] Verdict Directing—Conversion— Failure to Surrender Possession

Your verdict must be for plaintiff if you believe:

First, plaintiff was (*here describe facts which entitled plaintiff to possession—e.g.—"the owner of the watch", "the lessee of the automobile"*), and

Second, defendant had possession of (*here describe the property*), and

Third, plaintiff made a demand to defendant for possession of (*here describe the property*), and

Fourth, thereafter defendant intentionally failed to return possession of (*here describe the property*) to plaintiff.

* [unless you believe that plaintiff is not entitled to recover by reason of Instruction No. _____ (*here insert number of affirmative defense instruction*)].

Notes on Use (1989 New)

See MAI 32.27 for submission of the affirmative defense of abandonment.

* Add if affirmative defense is submitted.

Committee Comment (1989 New)

See Committee Comment to MAI 23.12(1).

Library References:

C.J.S. Trover and Conversion § 150–157.
West's Key No. Digests, Trover and Conversion ⚖=67.

Notes of Decisions

1. In general

Towing services' refusal to deliver possession of trailer to owner upon tender of cashier's check for more than amount due for towing and storage was a "conversion" of the trailer. Northland Insurance Co. v. Chet's Tow Service, Inc., 804 S.W.2d 54 (Mo.App.1991).

23.13 [2000 New] Verdict Directing—Retaliatory Discharge or Discrimination—Workers' Compensation

Your verdict must be for plaintiff if you believe:

First, plaintiff was employed by defendant, and

Second, plaintiff filed a workers' compensation claim,[1] and

Third, defendant discharged[2] plaintiff, and

Fourth, the exclusive cause of such discharge[2] was plaintiff's filing of the workers' compensation claim[1] and

Fifth, as a direct result of such discharge[2] plaintiff sustained damage.

Notes on Use (2000 New)

1. Describe the right exercised by the plaintiff under the workers' compensation law if it was other than filing a claim for compensation.

2. If the claim is for discrimination rather than discharge, describe the act of discrimination, such as "reduced plaintiff's rate of pay" or "demoted plaintiff."

Committee Comment (2000 New)

This instruction is for use in a retaliatory discharge case under section 287.780, RSMo. See *Crabtree v. Bugby*, 967 S.W.2d 66 (Mo. banc 1998). Section 287.780 also provides a cause of action to employees who are discriminated against by their employer, but not discharged, for exercising rights under the workers' compensation law. This instruction may be modified to submit acts of discrimination other than discharge where appropriate.

Library References:

C.J.S. Employer-Employee Relationship § 93.
West's Key No. Digests, Master and Servant ⚯44.

24.00

VERDICT DIRECTING—FEDERAL EMPLOYERS' LIABILITY ACT

Analysis of Instructions

Westlaw Electronic Research

See Westlaw Electronic Research Guide preceding the Table of Instructions.

Library References:

C.J.S. Trial § 350–351.
West's Key No. Digests, Trial ☞234(3, 4).

24.01 [1992 Revision] Verdict Directing—F.E.L.A.— Failure to Provide Safe Place to Work

Your verdict must be for plaintiff if you believe:

First, plaintiff was an employee of defendant and a part of his employment in some way closely and substantially affected interstate commerce,[1] and

Second, [with respect to such conditions for work,][2] defendant either failed to provide:[2]

reasonably safe conditions for work, or
reasonably safe appliances, or
reasonably safe methods of work, or
reasonably adequate help, and[3]

Third, defendant in any one or more of the respects submitted in Paragraph Second was negligent,[4] and[5]

Fourth, such negligence[4] resulted in whole or in part in [injury to plaintiff] [the death of (*decedent's name*)].

*[unless you believe plaintiff is not entitled to recover by reason of Instruction Number _____ (*here insert number of affirmative defense instruction*)].

Notes on Use (1992 Revision)

1. Paragraph First will seldom be the issue. Omit this paragraph if this matter is not in issue. If the issue of whether defendant was in interstate commerce is in issue, the instruction must be modified to also submit this issue.

2. The specifications of negligence set forth in this instruction concern conditions of which the defendant had constructive knowledge.

In the event plaintiff submits some act of negligence, constructive knowledge of which is not chargeable to the railroad, there shall be submitted in addition a paragraph providing "Second, conditions for work were not reasonably safe and defendant knew or by using ordinary care could have known of such conditions and that they were not reasonably safe, and". This paragraph should be inserted between existing paragraphs First and Second and the remaining paragraphs should be renumbered accordingly. *Qualls v. St. Louis Southwestern Ry. Co.,* 799 S.W.2d 84 (Mo. banc 1990), cert. denied 499 U.S. 961, 111 S.Ct. 1585, 113 L.Ed.2d 650 (1991). In this situation, existing paragraph Second should also be modified by inserting the bracketed phrase "with respect to such conditions for work", immediately before the phrase "defendant either failed to provide".

3. In the event that negligence charged is based upon the acts of the defendant's employee, the following alternate paragraphs "Second" and "Third" must be used.

"Second, defendant's employee (*characterize the negligent conduct, i.e., failed to keep a careful lookout, etc.*), and"

"Third, defendant's employee was thereby negligent, and".

4. The terms "negligent" and "negligence" must be defined. The term "ordinary care" must be defined if used in accordance with Notes on Use 2. See definitions in Chapter 11.00.

5. In the event that there is only a single submission of negligence under paragraph "Second", then paragraph "Third" must be modified to read as follows:

"Third, defendant was thereby negligent, and"

* Add if affirmative defense is submitted. Do not use this bracketed phrase to submit contributory negligence in an F.E.L.A. case. See MAI 32.07.

Committee Comment (1978 New)

In an F.E.L.A. case, common law negligence rules are controlling *except* that these rules have been modified by F.E.L.A. Because of the "in whole or in part" language of the statute (Title 45, U.S.C.A., Section 51), the traditional doctrine of proximate (direct) cause is not applicable. A railroad is liable if its negligence is only the *slightest* cause of the employee's injury. *Rogers v. Missouri Pac. Ry.*, 352 U.S. 500, 77 S.Ct. 443, 1 L.Ed.2d 493 (1957).

In the traditional negligence case, it is mandatory for the plaintiff to include the word "direct" or "directly" in his instruction because of the proximate (direct) cause requirements. This prevents the jury from awarding damages or finding for plaintiff because of some indirect or contributing causative factors. This is not so with F.E.L.A. The F.E.L.A. "was enacted because the Congress was dissatisfied with the common law duty of the master to his servant. The statute supplants that duty with the far more drastic duty of paying damages for injury or death at work due in whole or in part to the employer's negligence." *Rogers v. Missouri Pac. Ry.*, supra, 352 U.S. 500, 507, 77 S.Ct. 443, 448, 1 L.Ed.2d 493. The test of a jury case under F.E.L.A. is simply "whether the proofs justify within reason the conclusion that employer's negligence played *any part, even the slightest*, in producing injury or death for which damages are sought." (emphasis added). *Rogers v. Mo. Pac. Ry.*, supra, 352 U.S. 500, 506, 77 S.Ct. 443, 448, 1 L.Ed.2d 493. The fact that there may have been a number of causes of the injury is, therefore, irrelevant as long as one cause may be attributable to the railroad's negligence. *Heater v. Chesapeake & O. Ry. Co.*, 497 F.2d 1243, 1246 (7th Cir.1974).

As the United States Supreme Court has stated in *Rogers v. Missouri Pac. Ry.*, supra, in an F.E.L.A. case, the employer railroad is stripped of its common law defenses. The statute is an avowed departure from the rules of common law. Our state Supreme Court has consistently held that the federal interpretation of F.E.L.A. is binding on the Missouri state courts. *Headrick v. Kansas City Southern Ry. Co.*, 305 S.W.2d 478 (Mo.1957); *Adams v. Atchison, T. & S.F. Ry.*, 280 S.W.2d 84 (Mo.1955).

Library References:

C.J.S. Employers' Liability for Injuries to Employees § 341, 343.
West's Key No. Digests, Employers' Liability ⬩261.

Notes of Decisions

In general 1
Conversing 4
Measure of damages 6
Modification 3
Roving commission 5
Scope of employment 2

---

1. In general

MAI 24.01 correctly provides as a basis of negligence the failure to provide reasonably safe appliances to workers under 45 U.S.C.A. § 51 of FELA; rails and switches in railroad yard are "appliances" under section of FELA imposing liability upon railroads for injuries to employees resulting from "any defect or insufficiency due to its negligence in its ... appliances." Gilliam v. Chicago & North Western Transp. Co., 859 S.W.2d 155 (Mo.App.1993).

Approved negligence instruction has been endorsed for use in Federal Employers' Liability Act cases, and there was no error in utilizing it. Robertson v. Burlington Northern R. Co., 785 S.W.2d 626 (Mo.App.1990).

Railroad's contention that MAI 24.01 denied it equal protection of the laws in violation of the 14th Amendment because it singles out and imposes greater liability and burdens upon interstate railroad carriers than it does any other corporate or private individual defendant has been raised before and summarily rejected. Anderson v. Bur-

lington Northern R. Co., 700 S.W.2d 469[18] (Mo.App.1985).

Verdict for recovery for "failure to provide reasonably safe tires" was too general and did not meet requirement that instruction require a finding of a "particular unsafe condition." Searcy v. Neal, 509 S.W.2d 755 [19–20] (Mo.App.1974).

Where defendant had constructive knowledge of condition complained of, it was unnecessary to hypothesize that defendant knew or could have known thereof. Wilmoth v. Chicago, R.I. & P. Ry. Co., 486 S.W.2d 631[11] (Mo.1972).

In action for failure to furnish "reasonably safe conditions for work" plaintiffs' verdict director erroneously submitted that ground without specifying a particular unsafe condition; further, the instruction erroneously allowed recovery if defendant's negligence resulted "in whole or in part" in plaintiff's injury since such "slight negligence" is actionable only in F.E.L.A. cases and MAI 24.01 is suitable only in those cases. Ricketts v. Kansas City Stock Yards Co. of Maine, 484 S.W.2d 216[5, 6] (Mo. banc 1972).

2. Scope of employment

Where as a matter of law evidence showed employee was acting within the scope of his employment it was unnecessary to hypothesize that element in his verdict director. Elliott v. St. Louis Southwestern Ry. Co., 487 S.W.2d 7[11] (Mo.1972).

3. Modification

In instructing jury in Jones Act action on whether towboat owner was negligent for failing to provide reasonably safe methods of work, trial court was not required to include as a material element owner's actual or constructive knowledge of condition which allegedly made work methods unsafe; owner was charged with constructive knowledge of failing to provide reasonably safe methods of work and was not charged with knowledge of existence of condition of defective rubber bumper. Futrell v. Luhr Bros., Inc., 916 S.W.2d 348 (Mo.App.1996).

In action by employee against railroad for injuries sustained in fall while getting off elevator in railroad's office building, evidence concerning railroad's knowledge of continuing defect after visit by elevator repairman was sufficiently disputed to create issue of fact which should have been submitted to the jury, and thus trial court erred in failing to modify verdict director instruction to present that issue. Henry v. Union Pacific Systems, 875 S.W.2d 212 (Mo.App. E.D.1994).

Evidence in FELA action was sufficient to show that railroads had actual or constructive notice of cramped condition within locomotive which led to boilermaker's injury while attempting to install bolt, so that railroads were not entitled to modification of verdict directing instruction to insert separate paragraph requiring finding that railroads knew or by using ordinary care should have known of condition and that it was reasonably likely to cause substantial harm; railroads were chargeable with knowledge of the physical dimensions and location of the bolts on their own locomotives and with procedures used by their employees. Holley v. Missouri Pacific Railroad Co., 867 S.W.2d 610 (Mo.App.1993).

Railroad worker made a submissible case under FELA where the laborer was injured crossing an ice-covered trestle. MAI 24.01 should be modified to include a submission on the actual or constructive knowledge on the part of the railroad with respect to the existence of the dangerous condition where that knowledge is in dispute. Qualls v. St. Louis Southwestern Ry. Co., 799 S.W.2d 84 (Mo. banc 1990).

In employee's negligence action against his tree cutter employers arising when tree felled by one of his employers allegedly struck another tree that in turn struck employee, verdict directing instruction which described series of events leading up to injury but which did not require jury to find particular unsafe act or omission on part of employers that caused injury was erroneous. In dicta, court stated that a modified FELA instruction would not be appropriate for use in a non-FELA, injured employee case. Karnes v. Ray, 809 S.W.2d 738 (Mo.App. 1991).

It was proper for a court to submit constructive knowledge element in third paragraph of jury instruction in railroad employee's Federal Employers' Liability Act case in which employee failed to prove level or duration of noise which could cause injury; where cause of injury could not be said to be commonly known as one that could cause injury shown, employee had burden of proof to show railroad knew or should have known condition was capable of producing injury, even if condition was included in one of specifications for negligence included in jury instruction. Turner v. Norfolk & Western Ry. Co., 785 S.W.2d 569 (Mo. App.1990).

In FELA case not involving violation of a safety rule, verdict-directing instruction must include finding of defendant's constructive knowledge of dangerous condition. White v. St. Louis–San Francisco Ry. Co., 539 S.W.2d 565[12] (Mo.App.1976).

Where plaintiff sought damages for a November 9, 1966 back injury and his evidence showed two earlier back injuries, MAI should have been modified by deleting the words "mentioned in evidence" and substituting therefore the words "of November 9, 1966." Plaintiff's verdict director should have been similarly modified. Russell v. Terminal R.R. Ass'n, 501 S.W.2d 843[2, 6] (Mo. banc 1973).

4. Conversing

Plaintiff's verdict director properly followed MAI 24.01 in submitting that defendant's negligence directly resulted "in whole or in part" in injury to plaintiff. Defendant's converse required that plaintiff sustained damage as a "direct result" of its negligence; held, prejudicially erroneous, since it did not substantially follow the language of the verdict director. Snyder v. Chicago, R.I. & P. Ry. Co., 521 S.W.2d 161[4–8] (Mo.App. 1973).

5. Roving commission

MAI 24.01 as a verdict director does not give the jury a roving commission. Ball v. Burlington Northern R. Co., 672 S.W.2d 358[1] (Mo.App.1984).

6. Measure of damages

Propriety of jury instructions concerning measure of damages in FELA action is issue of substance determined by federal law, and thus fact that instruction on given subject is not to be found in MAI is not dispositive. Holley v. Missouri Pacific Railroad Co., 867 S.W.2d 610 (Mo.App.1993).

Assuming that defendants in FELA action were entitled to submit separate, not-in-MAI instruction on mitigation of damages, instruction tendered was improper where it was abstract in that it did not require any finding by jury or inform jury of how instruction was to impact any finding they were to make, provided no guidance with respect to which party bore burden of proof, was argumentative in purporting to inform jury of what was "required by law," and portion stating that plaintiff was required to try "to eliminate * * * any loss of earnings" was not supported by evidence indicating only that plaintiff might have reduced or ended loss of earnings. Holley v. Missouri Pacific Railroad Co., 867 S.W.2d 610 (Mo.App.1993).

24.02   [1981 Revision] Verdict Directing—F.E.L.A.— Boiler Act Violation

Your verdict must be for plaintiff if you believe:

First, plaintiff was an employee of defendant and a part of his employment in some way closely and substantially affected interstate commerce,[1] and

Second, defendant [used on its line] [permitted use on its line of][2] a [locomotive] [boiler] [tender][3] which was not in proper condition and which could not be safely operated without unnecessary peril of life and limb, and

Third, this use resulted in whole or in part in [injury to plaintiff] [the death of (*decedent's name*)].[2]

* [unless you believe plaintiff is not entitled to recover by reason of Instruction Number _____ (*here insert number of affirmative defense instruction*)].

Notes on Use (1981 Revision)

1. Paragraph First will seldom be the issue. Omit this paragraph if this matter is not in issue. If the issue of whether defendant was in interstate commerce is in issue, the instruction must be modified to also submit this issue.

2. Select the appropriate phrase.

3. Select the appropriate term.

* Add if affirmative defense is submitted.

Library References:

C.J.S. Employers' Liability for Injuries to Employees § 341, 343.
West's Key No. Digests, Employers' Liability ☞261.

24.03 [1981 Revision] Verdict Directing—F.E.L.A. Safety Appliance Act Violation

Your verdict must be for plaintiff if you believe:

First, plaintiff was an employee of defendant and a part of his employment in some way closely and substantially affected interstate commerce,[1] and

Second, defendant [used on its line] [permitted use on its line of][2] a [car] [train] [engine][3] which (*here set out the Safety Appliance Act violation*), and

Third, this use resulted in whole or in part in [injury, to plaintiff] [the death of (*decedent's name*)].[2]

* [unless you believe plaintiff is not entitled to recover by reason of Instruction Number _____ (*here insert number of affirmative defense instruction*)].

Notes on Use (1981 Revision)

1.   Paragraph First will seldom be the issue. Omit this paragraph if this matter is not in issue. If the issue of whether defendant was in interstate commerce is in issue, the instruction must be modified to also submit this issue.

2.   Select the appropriate phrase.

3.   Select the appropriate term.

* Add if affirmative defense is submitted.

Library References:

C.J.S. Employers' Liability for Injuries to Employees § 341, 343.
West's Key No. Digests, Employers' Liability ⟜261.

25.00

VERDICT DIRECTING—BREACH OF WARRANTY AND PRODUCT LIABILITY

Analysis of Instructions

Westlaw Electronic Research

See Westlaw Electronic Research Guide preceding the Table of Instructions.

Library References:

C.J.S. Trial § 350–351.
West's Key No. Digests, Trial ☞234(3, 4).

25.01 [1981 Revision] Verdict Directing—Breach of Warranty of Title to Personalty

Your verdict must be for plaintiff if you believe:

First, defendant sold (*describe the property*) to plaintiff, and

Second, at the time of such sale the (*describe the property*) was in defendant's possession, and

Third, at the time of such sale defendant did not have title to the (*describe the property*), and

Fourth, plaintiff was thereby damaged.

* [unless you believe plaintiff is not entitled to recover by reason of Instruction Number _____ (*here insert number of affirmative defense instruction*)].

Notes on Use (1981 New)

* Add if affirmative defense is submitted.

Committee Comment (1965 New)

In *Schaefer v. Fulton Iron Works Co.,* 158 S.W.2d 452, 455 (Mo.App. 1942), the court said: "... [W]hen personal property is sold at a fair price, there is an implied warranty of title; and, when there is a breach of such warranty, a cause of action arises in favor of the one thereby suffering damage and against the warrantor by reason of such breach."

In *Ivester v. E.B. Jones Motor Company,* 311 S.W.2d 109, 111 (Mo.App.1958), the court said: "There appears to be no dispute about the general rule that there is an implied warranty of title when goods are in possession of a seller at the time of sale." The case also discusses seller's duty to come in and defend purchaser's title and the measure of purchaser's damages.

Library References:

C.J.S. Sales § 315.
West's Key No. Digests, Sales ⊚⇒442(12).

25.02 [1981 Revision] Verdict Directing—Breach of Common Law Implied Warranty of Fitness for Consumption

Your verdict must be for plaintiff if you believe:

First, defendant sold (*describe substance*) for [human] [animal] [1] consumption, and

Second, [plaintiff] [plaintiff's (*describe animals such as "cows"*)][1] [ate] [drank][1] the (*describe the substance*), and

Third, the (*describe substance*) when sold by defendant was not fit for [human] [animal][1] consumption, and

Fourth, as a direct result thereof plaintiff was damaged.

* [unless you believe plaintiff is not entitled to recover by reason of Instruction Number _____ (*here insert number of affirmative defense instruction*)].

Notes on Use (1981 New)

1. Select the appropriate term or phrase.

* Add if affirmative defense is submitted.

Committee Comment (1996 Revision)

MAI 25.03 submits breach of implied warranty of fitness for a particular purpose of products in general under the Uniform Commercial Code. MAI 25.08 submits breach of implied warranty of merchantability (fitness for ordinary purposes) of products in general under the Uniform Commercial Code. The above instruction submits breach of common law implied warranty of fitness of food and drink for human or animal consumption. See §§ 400.1–103 and 400.2–314, RSMo, to determine the extent to which a common law action for implied warranty may be maintained.

In *Midwest Game Co., Inc. v. M.F.A. Milling Co.*, 320 S.W.2d 547, 550 (Mo.1959), the court said: "It is an established rule that in a sale of food for immediate human consumption there is generally an implied warranty that the food is wholesome, is fit for the purpose, and is of merchantable quality. And a buyer of packaged food products may recover from the manufacturer upon an implied warranty of fitness even though there is no express privity of contract between the manufacturer and buyer."

See also *Albers Milling Co. v. Carney*, 341 S.W.2d 117 (Mo.1960).

381

Compare *Green v. Ralston Purina Co.,* 376 S.W.2d 119 (Mo.1964), where plaintiff's evidence did not make a submissible case.

Notes of Decisions

1. In general

Jury instruction in form of MAI 25.02 for farmer's products liability claim against feed producer for damages to cattle due to allegedly contaminated feed—requiring jury to find for farmer if it found that producer sold feed for animal consumption, that cattle ate feed, that feed when sold was not fit for animal consumption, and that, as direct result thereof, farmer was damaged—was not so vague as to give jury roving commission and, thus, was properly given, even though instruction did not specifically refer to aflatoxin, which allegedly caused the damage. Sanders v. Hartville Milling Company, 14 S.W.3d 188 (Mo.App.2000).

Library References:

C.J.S. Products Liability § 93.
West's Key No. Digests, Products Liability ⚬96.1.

25.03 [1980 Revision] Verdict Directing—Breach of Common Law Implied Warranty of Fitness for a Particular Purpose Under Uniform Commercial Code

Your verdict must be for plaintiff if you believe:

First, defendant sold [1] the (*describe the article or product*), and

Second, defendant then knew or should have known of the use for which the (*describe the article or product*) was purchased, and

Third, plaintiff reasonably relied upon defendant's judgment that the (*describe the article or product*) was fit for such use, and

Fourth, when sold [1] by defendant, the (*describe the article or product*) was not fit for such use, and

Fifth, within a reasonable time after plaintiff knew or should have known the product was not fit for such use, plaintiff gave defendant notice thereof,[2] and

Sixth, as a direct result of (*describe the article or product*) being unfit for such use, plaintiff was damaged.

* [unless you believe plaintiff is not entitled to recover by reason of Instruction Number _____ (*here insert number of affirmative defense instruction*)].

Notes on Use (1980 Revision)

1. In the event of a transaction other than a sale which gives rise to a warranty for a particular purpose, substitute the appropriate words.

2. If notice is not required, then omit paragraph Fifth. *See Morrow v. Caloric Appliance Corp.*, 372 S.W.2d 41 (Mo. banc 1963); *Austin v. Western Auto Supply Co.*, 421 S.W.2d 203 (Mo.1967); and discussion in *Crowder v. Vandendeale*, 564 S.W.2d 879 (Mo. banc 1978).

* Add if affirmative defense is submitted.

Committee Comment (1980 Revision)

This instruction is for use in a situation where there is an implied warranty of fitness for a particular purpose under the provisions of the

Uniform Commercial Code enacted by the Missouri General Assembly in 1963. See § 400.2–315, RSMo, and the applicable comments which relate thereto for the requirements necessary to prove an implied warranty of fitness for a particular purpose.

It is well-settled law "that a manufacturer-seller of an article for a particular purpose impliedly warrants that such article will be reasonably fit for that purpose for which it is intended to be used, *if the buyer communicates to the manufacturer-seller the specific purpose for which he wants the article, and if he relies, and has reason to rely, on the producer-seller's skill, judgment and experience to produce an article that will answer the purpose.*" *Southwest Distributors, Inc. v. Allied Paper Bag Corp.*, 384 S.W.2d 838, 841 (Mo.App.1964).

"The statute requires that before there is an implied warranty the buyer must rely on the 'seller's skill or judgment to select or furnish suitable goods.'" *Plasco, Inc. v. Free–Flow Packaging Corp.*, 547 F.2d 86, 90 (8th Cir.1977).

"Missouri law holds: [T]he mere fact of knowledge by the seller of the purpose for which the buyer desired the article is not sufficient to show a reliance by the buyer upon the skill, judgment and experience of the seller to raise an implied warranty of fitness.... Where the buyer understands what he wants and makes an independent examination of the product and tests the product in order to determine its fitness for the intended use, there can be no implied warranty of fitness for a particular purpose. Under the aforesaid circumstances the buyer does not rely on the seller's skill and judgment, but instead relies on his own judgment formed as a result of his examination and tests of the product." *Plasco,* supra, at 91.

"Many cases hold that the manufacturer is liable as a warrantor of fitness for a special purpose though it did not appear that the goods sold were not fit for the purpose for which goods of the sort are naturally adapted." Williston on Contracts, Sale of Land and Personal Property § 989, at 559 (1957).

In an action brought under the provisions of the Uniform Commercial Code, § 400.2–607(3)(a), RSMo, provides "where a tender has been accepted the buyer must within a reasonable time after he discovers or should have discovered any breach notify the seller of breach or be barred from any remedy...." This notice provision may not be required in all causes of action.

A question that may not have been determined is whether there is still a common law cause of action for breach of express warranty. This code provides: "Unless displaced by the particular provisions of this chapter, the principles of law and equity ... shall supplement its provisions." § 400.1–103, RSMo. Therefore, "traditional rights and remedies remain in force unless eliminated by a particular provision of the Uniform Commercial Code." *Roth v. Roth,* 571 S.W.2d 659, 671 (Mo.App.1978).

For a Comment on the requirements of implied warranty of fitness, see 30 Mo.L.Rev. 275 (1965).

Library References:

C.J.S. Sales § 307.
West's Key No. Digests, Sales ⊕446(5).

Notes of Decisions

In general 1
Breach of contract 3
Converse instruction 2

------

1. In general

Where plaintiff submits on strict liability by modified MAI 25.03 it was error to give an instruction absolving defendant if defendant used ordinary care since this introduced the foreign issue of defendant's negligence. Katz v. Slade, 460 S.W.2d 608[1] (Mo.1970).

Verdict director submitting liability for furnishing product not fit for intended use. Plas–Chem Corp. v. Solmica, Inc., 434 S.W.2d 522[4–6] (Mo.1968).

2. Converse instruction

Where plaintiff submitted "fitness" of auto jack for particular purpose, it was error to converse that with instruction exculpating the defendant if injury resulted from the "condition" of the jack. This, because MAI 29.01 [Now 33.01] requires the use of substantially the same language used in the verdict director. Austin v. Western Auto Supply Co., 421 S.W.2d 203[3–5] (Mo.1967).

3. Breach of contract

Where defendant agreed to build home according to plaintiffs' plans and specifications but defectively did so, plaintiffs' proper action was for breach of bilateral contract, not for implied warranty of fitness, and court erred in so submitting plaintiffs' case. Barrett v. Jenkins, 510 S.W.2d 805[1] (Mo.App. 1974).

25.04 [1978 Revision] Verdict Directing—Strict Liability—Product Defect

Your verdict must be for plaintiff if you believe:

First, defendant sold[1] the (*describe product*) in the course of defendant's business, and

Second, the (*describe product*) was then in a defective condition unreasonably dangerous when put to a reasonably anticipated use, and

Third, the (*describe product*) was used in a manner reasonably anticipated, and

Fourth, plaintiff was damaged as a direct result of such defective condition as existed when the (*describe product*) was sold.

* [unless you believe plaintiff is not entitled to recover by reason of Instruction Number _____ (*here insert number of affirmative defense instruction*)].

Notes on Use (1991 Revision)

1. The term "sold" should be modified to cover other situations such as a commercial lease where strict liability is applicable.

* Add if affirmative defense is submitted. If § 537.765, RSMo is applicable, see Chapter 37.00 for submission of comparative fault. Do not use this bracketed phrase to submit comparative fault.

Committee Comment (1978 Revision)

This instruction is intended for use both in cases involving a manufacturing defect and in cases involving a design defect.

Library References:

C.J.S. Products Liability § 93.
West's Key No. Digests, Products Liability ⚖96.1.

Notes of Decisions

In general 1
Comparative fault 8
Contributory fault 6
Conversing 5
Knowledge of defect 4
Modification—Retailer 7
Roving commission   9

Separate verdict directors 3
Strict tort liability 2
"Unreasonably dangerous" 10

_____

1. In general

If instruction was erroneous by failing to find that worker's damage was caused by defect which existed when chemical was sold by defendant, instruction did not prejudice defendant, where it was clear from both instruction and the evidence that if worker was injured due to chemical, it was caused by defect which existed when chemical was sold. Ray v. Upjohn Co., 851 S.W.2d 646 (Mo.App.1993).

MAI No. 25.04 is intended to be used in both manufacturing and in design defect cases. Magnuson v. Kelsey–Hayes Co., 844 S.W.2d 448 (Mo.App.1992).

In product liability cases, jury is not required to be instructed with definition of term "unreasonably dangerous." Speck v. Abell–Howe Co., 839 S.W.2d 623 (Mo.App.1992).

Appellate court approved modification of MAI 25.04 and 25.05 (strict liability) with MAI 19.01 (multiple causes of injury). Menschik v. Mid–America Pipeline Co., 812 S.W.2d 861 (Mo.App.1991).

Second collision case involving enhanced leg injuries to a motorcyclist as a result of a defective fairing following a motor vehicle collision. Indivisible injury rule applied to driver of motor vehicle and manufacturer of fairing in connection with leg injuries. Verdict directing instruction for "enhanced injury" cases approved. McDowell v. Kawasaki Motors Corporation USA, 799 S.W.2d 854 (Mo.App.1990).

Not-in-MAI definition of the term "product" in MAI 25.04, as a "ladder-type track," held to be permissible. Modification of MAI 25.04 with MAI 19.01 held to be proper in stating that the product "directly caused or directly contributed to cause" decedent's death. Eagleburger v. Emerson Electric Co., 794 S.W.2d 210 (Mo.App.1990).

This instruction was intended for use both in cases involving a manufacturing defect and in cases involving a design defect, and there is no Missouri authority requiring definition of the terms "defective" and "unreasonably dangerous." Jarrell v. Fort Worth Steel & Mfg. Co., 666 S.W.2d 828[18, 19] (Mo.App.1984).

In appropriate cases, it is not error to give both MAI 25.04 and 25.05; although the alternative submissions must not be inconsistent with one another and there must be evidence to support each theory. No error where neither of the two theories required proof of a state of fact that would necessarily disprove a state of fact necessary to support the other. Lewis v. Envirotech Corp., 674 S.W.2d 105[5, 6] (Mo.App.1984).

Modified 31.01 (now withdrawn) properly based liability upon submission that car "had a fast idle cam that would break" and was dangerous: unnecessary to further submit detailed evidentiary facts. Rinker v. Ford Motor Co., 567 S.W.2d 655 [4–5] (Mo.App. 1978).

Verdict directors against manufacturer and retailer for defective handgun. Bender v. Colt Industries, 517 S.W.2d 705[2] (Mo.App. 1974).

Modified MAI 25.04 proper in wrongful death action by user's widow against manufacturer only if it submits element that defective electric pump was being used in a reasonably anticipated manner. Court gives proper instruction. Keener v. Dayton Elec. Mfg. Co., 445 S.W.2d 362[7] (Mo.1969).

Modified 25.04 in action against manufacturer concerning the defective armrest against which plaintiff driver was thrown when his car collided with another. Cryts v. Ford Motor Co., 571 S.W.2d 683[11–14] (Mo.App.1978).

2. Strict tort liability

Verdict directors against manufacturer and retailer for defective handgun. Bender v. Colt Industries, 517 S.W.2d 705[2] (Mo.App. 1974).

Where plaintiff submits on strict liability by modified MAI 25.03 it was error to give an instruction absolving defendant if defendant used ordinary care since this introduced the foreign issue of defendant's negligence. Katz v. Slade, 460 S.W.2d 608[1] (Mo.1970).

3. Separate verdict directors

In products liability action against manufacturer and dealer plaintiff properly submitted separate verdict directors against each. Williams v. Ford Motor Co., 494 S.W.2d 678[1–4] (Mo.App.1973).

4. Knowledge of defect

Where plaintiff sued bailor of truck trailer for furnishing a dangerous instrumentality, his verdict director must submit the element of time—that bailor knew of the dangerous condition when he relinquished control. (See Keener v. Dayton Elec. Co., 445 S.W.2d 362[7]). Whitney v. Central Paper Stock Co., 446 S.W.2d 415[1–3] (Mo.App.1969).

5. Conversing

Although plaintiff's verdict director omitted the essential element that he was using the instrument when injured, defendant could properly submit that element in its converse instruction. Mead v. Corbin Equipment, Inc., 586 S.W.2d 388[2] (Mo.App.1979).

In conversing MAI 25.04 defendant entitled to converse "defective condition" of Paragraph Second without also conversing "and therefore dangerous, etc." Lietz v. Snyder Mfg. Co., 475 S.W.2d 105[4–6] (Mo.1972).

6. Contributory fault

Comparative fault does not apply in a strict products liability case, but the giving of MAI 32.23 is not precluded in the appropriate case. Lippard v. Houdaille Industries, Inc., 715 S.W.2d 491[1–3] (Mo. banc 1986).

Although defendant pleaded contributory fault it offered no such instruction, so plaintiff's verdict director properly omitted a "tail" on this affirmative defense. Means v. Sears, Roebuck & Co., 550 S.W.2d 780[2] (Mo. banc 1977).

Action for *negligent* repair of furnace was not a strict liability case. Defendant was entitled to a proper contributory *negligence* instruction. Portman v. Sinclair Oil Co., 518 S.W.2d 625[1] (Mo.1975).

Since negligence is not an element of a manufacturer's strict liability in tort, it is error to give a contributory negligence instruction. Williams v. Ford Motor Co., 454 S.W.2d 611[6, 10–14] (Mo.App.1970).

Unreasonable use of product with knowledge of defect is "contributory fault" and bars recovery. Keener v. Dayton Elec. Mfg. Co., 445 S.W.2d 362[4, 5] (Mo.1969).

7. Modification—Retailer

Plaintiffs' verdict director properly modified MAI 25.04 in action against *retailer,* the only MAI verdict-director being against a *manufacturer.* Means v. Sears, Roebuck & Co., 550 S.W.2d 780[1] (Mo. banc 1977).

8. Comparative fault

Comparative fault does not apply in a strict products liability case, but the giving of MAI 32.23 is not precluded in the appropriate case. Lippard v. Houdaille Industries, Inc., 715 S.W.2d 491[1–3] (Mo. banc 1986).

A combine operator's contributory negligence was not a defense in a strict products liability case against a manufacturer, distributor and retailer. However, contributory fault, MAI 32.23, could be submitted as a complete defense. Love v. Deere & Co., 720 S.W.2d 786[1–2] (Mo.App.1986).

9. Roving commission

Term "dumbwaiter assembly," in instruction provided by repairman injured by falling dumbwaiter, and term "dumbwaiter system," in instruction submitted by seller and installer of dumbwaiter, did not cause jury confusion or give jury roving commission, since terms were defined similarly, and seller/installer neither offered definitional instruction that terms meant the same thing nor offered modified instruction incorporating term preference. Lay v. P & G Health Care, Inc., 37 S.W.3d 310 (Mo.App.2000).

10. "Unreasonably dangerous"

Even assuming Restatement's new risk-utility test was appropriate standard in defective design case, proffered supplemental instruction—defining "unreasonably dangerous" as meaning utility or usefulness outweighed by risks—did not provide any better guidance on test than MAI 25.04 given by trial court and, thus, was appropriately rejected by trial court, since proffered instruction did not address issue of reasonable alternative design raised by risk-utility test. Newman v. Ford Motor Co., 975 S.W.2d 147 (Mo.1998).

25.05 [1978 New] Verdict Directing—Strict Liability—Failure to Warn

Your verdict must be for plaintiff if you believe:

First, defendant sold the (*describe product*) in the course of defendant's business, and

Second, the (*describe product*) was then unreasonably dangerous when put to a reasonably anticipated use without knowledge of its characteristics, and

Third, defendant did not give an adequate warning of the danger, and

Fourth, the product was used in a manner reasonably anticipated, and

Fifth, plaintiff was damaged as a direct result of the (*describe product*) being sold without an adequate warning.

* [unless you believe plaintiff is not entitled to recover by reason of Instruction Number _____ (*here insert number of affirmative defense instruction*)].

Notes on Use (1991 Revision)

* Add if affirmative defense is submitted. If § 537.765, RSMo is applicable, see Chapter 37.00 for submission of comparative fault. Do not use this bracketed phrase to submit comparative fault.

Library References:

C.J.S. Products Liability § 93.
West's Key No. Digests, Products Liability ⬥96.1.

Notes of Decisions

In general 1
Comparative fault 3
Contributory fault 2

_____

1. In general

Term "dumbwaiter assembly," in instruction provided by repairman injured by falling dumbwaiter, and term "dumbwaiter system," in instruction submitted by seller and installer of dumbwaiter, did not cause jury confusion or give jury roving commission, since terms were defined similarly, and seller/installer neither offered definitional instruction that terms meant the same thing nor offered modified instruction incorporating term preference. Lay v. P & G Health Care, Inc., 37 S.W.3d 310 (Mo.App.2000).

Product user failed to prove element of causation in failure to warn product liability case and instruction on failure to warn should not have been submitted to jury; product user failed to show that a warning on air compressor instructing users that compressor created spark that could ignite flammable fumes would have altered product user's behavior as related to the accident where product user knew that there was danger of explosion if gas fumes accumulated in shop where accident occurred. Arnold v. Ingersoll–Rand Co., 834 S.W.2d 192 (Mo. 1992).

Appellate court approved modification of MAI 25.04 and 25.05 (strict liability) with MAI 19.01 (multiple causes of injury). Menschik v. Mid–America Pipeline Co., 812 S.W.2d 861 (Mo.App.1991).

In appropriate cases, it is not error to give both MAI 25.04 and 25.05; although the alternative submissions must not be inconsistent with one another and there must be evidence to support each theory. No error where neither of the two theories required proof of a state of fact that would necessarily disprove a state of fact necessary to support the other. Lewis v. Envirotech Corp., 674 S.W.2d 105[5, 6] (Mo.App.1984).

2. Contributory fault

Comparative fault does not apply in a strict products liability case, but the giving of MAI 32.23 is not precluded in the appropriate case. Lippard v. Houdaille Industries, Inc., 715 S.W.2d 491[1–3] (Mo. banc 1986).

3. Comparative Fault

Comparative fault does not apply in a strict products liability case, but the giving of MAI 32.23 is not precluded in the appropriate case. Lippard v. Houdaille Industries, Inc., 715 S.W.2d 491[1–3] (Mo. banc 1986).

25.06 [1990 Withdrawn] Verdict Directing—Products Liability—Negligently Furnishing Dangerous Instrumentality or Product

(This instruction and the Notes on Use thereto are withdrawn. See MAI 25.09, 25.10(A) and 25.10(B).)

25.07 [1991 Revision] Verdict Directing—Breach of Express Warranty Under Uniform Commercial Code

Your verdict must be for plaintiff if you believe:

First, defendant sold[1] and plaintiff[2] purchased[1] (*here describe the article or product*), and

Second, defendant represented [by (*here insert conduct claimed to have constituted a representation*)][3] that (*here insert the representation claimed to be an express warranty under* § 400.2–313, RSMo), and

Third, such representation [was made to induce plaintiff to purchase][1] [or] [was a material factor in plaintiff's decision to purchase][1] the (*describe the article or product*),[4] and

Fourth, the (*describe the article or product*) did not conform to such representation made by defendant, and

Fifth, within a reasonable time after plaintiff knew or should have known of such failure to conform, plaintiff gave defendant notice thereof, and

Sixth, as a direct result of such failure to conform, plaintiff was damaged.

* [unless you believe plaintiff is not entitled to recover by reason of Instruction Number _____ (*here insert number of affirmative defense instruction*)].

Notes on Use (1991 Revision)

1. In the event of a transaction other than a sale as to which there is an express warranty, substitute the appropriate words.

2. If the injured party was not the purchaser of the goods but is a natural person who is a member of the family or household of the buyer or was a guest in the buyer's home and it was reasonable to expect that such person would use, consume, or be affected by the goods, the instruction should be modified as follows:

(a) In paragraph First change "plaintiff" to the name of the buyer.

(b) Insert the following paragraphs as paragraph Second and Third and renumber the remaining paragraphs:

Second, plaintiff [was a member of (*name of purchaser*)'s family] [was a member of (*name of purchaser*)'s household] [was a guest in (*name of purchaser*)'s home], and

Third, defendant should have reasonably expected that such a person would [use] [consume] [be affected by] (*describe the article or product*), and

See § 400.2–318, RSMo.

3. Insert bracketed phrase when the representation is based on conduct other than an express statement of the alleged representation.

4. Plaintiff may select either or both phrases. If both are used, submit in the disjunctive and the evidence must support each.

* Add if affirmative defense is submitted.

Committee Comment (1991 Revision)

This instruction is for use in an express warranty case in which the Uniform Commercial Code enacted by the Missouri General Assembly in 1963 is applicable. See § 400.2–313, RSMo, and the applicable comments which relate thereto for the requirements necessary to prove an express warranty. For a discussion of the requirements of express warranty in Missouri, also see *Interco Inc. v. Randustrial Corp.,* 533 S.W.2d 257 (Mo.App.1976). Although no particular reliance on an express warranty is necessary, the UCC requires that it be part of the "basis of the bargain." *Interco,* supra, at 262. Express warranties are more than expressions of opinion and are properly regarded as expressions of fact. "Ordinarily . . . the question of whether there has been a breach of warranty is a factual matter to be determined by the trier of fact." *Interco,* supra, at 263.

Regarding the requirement of notice, see § 400.2–607(3)(a), RSMo.

Section 400.2–725(1), RSMo, requires that actions for breach of a sale contract be brought within four years after the cause of action has accrued.

By express disclaimer, warranties may be limited or eliminated and the parties may reduce the period of limitations but not extend it. However, the court may refuse to enforce any contract term which is unconscionable. See §§ 400.2–316 and 400.2–302, RSMo.

Library References:

C.J.S. Sales § 307.
West's Key No. Digests, Sales ⟲446.

Notes of Decisions

In general   1
Evidentiary support   2

─────────

1. In general

Verdict director that tracked the language of MAI 25.07 without modification was not prejudicially vague, ambiguous, or erroneous; there is no requirement to instruct the jury that it find that the alleged representations or warranties were false when made. Carpenter v. Chrysler Corporation, 853 S.W.2d 346 (Mo.App.1993).

2. Evidentiary support

Automobile purchasers made submissible case on their claim for breach of express warranty and common law fraud where purchasers sufficiently established that statements of car dealer's salesman falsely described a car's condition, that car dealer did not disclose to purchasers certain repairs made to the car prior to its sale, that the statements were representations of fact and not mere puffing, that the misrepresentations were material, and that the purchasers reasonably relied upon them. Carpenter v. Chrysler Corporation, 853 S.W.2d 346 (Mo. App.1993).

25.08 [1980 New] Verdict Directing—Breach of Implied Warranty of Merchantability Under Uniform Commercial Code

Your verdict must be for plaintiff if you believe:

First, defendant sold [1] and plaintiff [2] purchased [1] (*describe the article or product*), and

Second, when sold by defendant (*describe the article or product*) was not fit for one of its ordinary purposes,[3] and

Third, plaintiff used such (*describe the article or product*) for such a purpose, and [4]

Fourth, within a reasonable time after plaintiff knew or should have known the product was not fit for such purpose, plaintiff gave defendant notice thereof, and

Fifth, as a direct result of such (*describe the article or product*) being unfit for such purpose, plaintiff was damaged.

* [unless you believe plaintiff is not entitled to recover by reason of Instruction Number _____ (*here insert number of affirmative defense instruction*)].

Notes on Use (1991 Revision)

1. In the event of a transaction other than a sale which gives rise to an implied warranty of merchantability, substitute the appropriate words.

2. If the injured party was not the purchaser of the goods but is a natural person who is a member of the family or household of the buyer or was a guest in the buyer's home and it was reasonable to expect that such person would use, consume, or be affected by the goods, the instruction should be modified as follows:

(a) In paragraph First change "plaintiff" to the name of the buyer.

(b) Insert the following paragraphs as paragraph Second and Third and renumber the remaining paragraphs:

Second, plaintiff [was a member of (*name of purchaser*)'s family] [was a member of (*name of purchaser*)'s household] [was a guest in (*name of purchaser*)'s home], and

Third, defendant should have reasonably expected that such a person would [use] [consume] [be affected by] (*describe the article or product*), and

See § 400.2–318, RSMo.

3. Although the most common claim for breach of the implied warranty of merchantability is that the article was not fit for the ordinary purposes for which such goods are used, the Uniform Commercial Code, § 400.2–314, RSMo, provides five other requirements for goods to be merchantable. In the event the breach proved is one other than fitness for the ordinary purposes, paragraphs Third and Fourth must be modified to state the statutory basis of the breach proved, which are stated in § 400.2–314(2)(a), (b), (d), (e), or (f), RSMo.

4. Omit this paragraph and renumber the remaining paragraphs if plaintiff learns that the goods are unfit by means other than use, such as by an initial inspection.

Submit the following as paragraph Second and renumber the remaining paragraphs if the issue of whether the defendant is a merchant is an appropriate issue in the case:

Second, defendant was a merchant with respect to such (*describe the article or product*), and

* Add if affirmative defense is submitted.

Committee Comment (1991 Revision)

This instruction is for use in an implied warranty case in which the Uniform Commercial Code enacted by the Missouri General Assembly in 1963 is applicable. See § 400.2–314, RSMo, and the applicable comments which relate thereto for the requirements necessary to prove an implied warranty.

Since the decision of *Morrow v. Caloric Appliance Corp.*, 372 S.W.2d 41 (Mo. banc 1963), a consumer may recover for breach of implied warranty against the manufacturer despite lack of privity.

"The *Uniform Commercial Code* does not attempt any definitive resolution of the privity of contract problem, but leaves the matter to the decidedly non-uniform development of the common law in the various states. The UCC restricts its treatment of the subject to a relatively small area. Section 400.2–318 provides that warranties by a seller extend not only to the buyer, but also to members of the buyer's household and guests therein 'if it is reasonable to expect that such person may use, consume or be affected by the goods.' This extension includes only those 'injured in person' by the breach." 30 Mo.L.Rev. 259, 279–80 (1965).

Library References:

C.J.S. Sales § 307.
West's Key No. Digests, Sales ⟜446.

Notes of Decisions

In general 1
Affirmative defense 3
Modification 2

_____

1. In general

Verdict-directing instruction for breach of implied warranty did not have to contain definitional instructions on terms "used" and "fit for one of its ordinary purposes." Christensen v. R.D. Sell Const. Co., 774 S.W.2d 535 (Mo.App.1989).

2. Modification

In homeowner's suit against builder, breach of implied warranty that house was suitable for ordinary purposes was properly submitted under MAI 25.08. Lieber v. Bridges, 650 S.W.2d 688[3] (Mo.App.1983).

3. Affirmative defense

Where an affirmative defense has evidentiary support and is therefore properly included, the failure to include in the verdict-director the phrase "unless you believe plaintiff is not entitled to recover by reason of Instruction No. _____," more commonly referred to as a "tail," is reversible error. Lieber v. Bridges, 650 S.W.2d 688[4] (Mo. App.1983).

25.09   [1990 New] Verdict Directing—Products Liability—Negligent Manufacture, Design, or Failure to Warn

Your verdict must be for plaintiff if you believe [1]:

First, defendant [manufactured] [designed] [2] the (*describe product*), and

Second, the (*describe product*) (*here describe alleged defect or hazard*), and

Third, defendant failed to use ordinary care [3] to [either] [[manufacture] [design] [2] the (*describe product*) to be reasonably safe] [[or] adequately warn of the risk of harm from (*here describe alleged defect or hazard*)],[4] and

Fourth, as a direct result of such failure[, in one or more of the respects submitted in paragraph Third],[4] plaintiff sustained damage.

* [unless you believe plaintiff is not entitled to recover by reason of Instruction Number _____ (*here insert number of affirmative defense instruction*)].

Notes on Use (1990 New)

1. Where comparative fault is submissible, modify this instruction in accordance with MAI 37.01.

2. Select appropriate term.

3. The phrase "ordinary care" must be defined. See definition at MAI 11.05. MAI 11.10 II may be appropriate in some situations.

4. Select one or both phrases. If both phrases are used, they must be submitted in the disjunctive and each must be supported by the evidence.

* Add if affirmative defense is submitted. This bracketed material should not be used to submit comparative fault.

Committee Comment (1990 New)

This instruction is for submission of a negligence theory of product liability. See § 395, Restatement of Torts (Second) (1965) which was referenced in *Stevens v. Durbin–Durco, Inc.,* 377 S.W.2d 343, 346 (Mo. 1964); §§ 388 and 392, Restatement of Torts (Second) (1965) were approved in *Morris v. Shell Oil Company,* 467 S.W.2d 39, 42 (Mo.1971);

and *Ridenhour v. Colson Caster Corp.*, 687 S.W.2d 938, 945 (Mo.App. 1985), respectively. See MAI 25.10(A) and 25.10(B). Each Restatement section has different substantive elements.

Library References:

C.J.S. Products Liability § 93.
West's Key No. Digests, Products Liability ⚶96.1.

25.10(A) [1990 New] Verdict Directing—Negligently Supplying Dangerous Instrumentality

Your verdict must be for plaintiff if you believe [1]:

First, defendant supplied (*here describe instrumentality supplied, such as automobile, hair dye, etc.*) for use, and

Second, the (*describe instrumentality*) (*here describe defect or hazard such as "had a wheel constructed with improperly tempered steel which had a propensity to break"; "included an ingredient which would cause systemic damage in certain persons", etc.*) and was therefore dangerous when put to a reasonably expected use, and

Third, the (*describe instrumentality*) was put to a reasonably expected use, and

Fourth, defendant had no reason to believe that those for whose use the (*describe instrumentality*) was supplied would realize its dangerous condition, and

Fifth, defendant knew or had information from which defendant, in the exercise of ordinary care,[2] should have known of such dangerous condition, and

Sixth, defendant failed to adequately warn of such dangerous condition, and

Seventh, defendant was thereby negligent,[3] and

Eighth, as a direct result of such negligence,[3] plaintiff sustained damage.

* [unless you believe plaintiff is not entitled to recover by reason of Instruction Number _____ (*here insert number of affirmative defense instruction*)].

Notes on Use (1990 New)

    1. Where comparative fault is submissible, modify this instruction in accordance with MAI 37.01.

    2. The phrase "ordinary care" must be defined. See definition at MAI 11.05.

    3. The terms "negligent" and "negligence" must be defined. See definitions in Chapter 11.00.

* Add if affirmative defense is submitted. This bracketed material should not be used to submit comparative fault.

Committee Comment (1995 New)

Sections 388 and 392, Restatement (Second) of Torts (1965) were approved in *Morris v. Shell Oil Company,* 467 S.W.2d 39, 42 (Mo.1971), and *Ridenhour v. Colson Caster Corp.,* 687 S.W.2d 938, 945 (Mo.App. 1985), respectively. Each Restatement section has different substantive elements. This instruction is for submission under § 388. See MAI 25.10(B) for submission under § 392.

Section 388 of the Restatement uses the terms "dangerous for the use for which it is supplied." Comment "e" of the Restatement explains the term "use" by the language "... but the chattel must be put to a use to which the supplier has reason to expect it to be put."

Paragraph Fifth uses the phrase "had information from which defendant, in the exercise of ordinary care, should have known" as the equivalent of the phrase "had reason to know" as defined in Restatement (First) and (Second) of Torts § 12. The Committee has opted to use this equivalent phrase rather than "had reason to know" because it is thought that the phrase "had reason to know" may be confusing or misleading to the jury.

Notes of Decisions

1. In general

MAI 25.10A, on supplying of dangerous instrumentality, does not apply to gratuitous bailments. Bailey v. Innovative Management & Inv., Inc., 916 S.W.2d 805 (Mo.App.1995).

In action by electricity customer against supplier to recover for injuries received while attempting to install transformer fuse, instruction was improper where it failed to require the jury to find that furnishing the fuse to customer presented a foreseeable risk of injury and that supplier knew or in the exercise of the highest degree of care should have known of the risk and failed to warn of it; modifications of MAI 25.10(A) would appear to be appropriate to this case. Mobley v. Webster Elec. Co-op., 859 S.W.2d 923 (Mo.App.1993).

Transformer fuse was not dangerous, and thus customer who was injured while attempting to install it could not recover on theory of negligently furnishing dangerous instrumentality. Mobley v. Webster Elec. Co-op., 859 S.W.2d 923 (Mo.App.1993).

Restatement (Second) of Torts § 392 provides a cognizant legal theory of recovery for negligent failure to warn. The elements under § 392 are: (1) a supplier who supplies; (2) a chattel for supplier's business purposes; (3) the chattel is used in the manner for which and by persons for whose use it was supplied; (4) the chattel was defective, the defect was discoverable on inspection, and the defect caused the accident; and (5) the supplier failed to inspect and failed to inform of the defect. Plaintiff's proposed instruction did not set forth all of these necessary elements and was properly refused. Steenrod v. Klipsch Hauling Co., 789 S.W.2d 158, 168 (Mo.App.1990).

Library References:

C.J.S. Products Liability § 93.
West's Key No. Digests, Products Liability ⚏96.1.

25.10(B)   **[1995 Revision] Verdict Directing—Negligently Supplying Dangerous Instrumentality for Supplier's Business Purposes**

Your verdict must be for plaintiff if you believe [1]:

First, defendant supplied (*here describe instrumentality supplied, such as automobile, hair dye, etc.*) for use, and

Second, the (*describe instrumentality*) (*here describe defect or hazard such as "had a wheel constructed, with improperly tempered steel that had a propensity to break"; "included an ingredient that would cause systemic damage in certain persons", etc.*) and was therefore dangerous when put to a reasonably expected use, and

Third, the (*describe instrumentality*) was put to a reasonably expected use, and

Fourth, defendant knew or in the exercise of ordinary care [2] could have known of such dangerous condition, and

Fifth, defendant failed to exercise ordinary care [2] to [either] [make the condition reasonably safe] [or adequately warn of it] [3], and

Sixth, as a direct result of such failure, plaintiff sustained damage.

* [unless you believe plaintiff is not entitled to recover by reason of Instruction Number _____ (*here insert number affirmative defense instruction*)].

Notes on Use (1990 New)

1. Where comparative fault is submissible, modify this instruction in accordance with MAI 37.01.

2. The phrase "ordinary care" must be defined. See definition at MAI 11.05.

3. Select one or both phrases. If both phrases are used, they must be submitted in the disjunctive and each must be supported by the evidence.

* Add if affirmative defense is submitted. This bracketed material should not be used to submit comparative fault.

Committee Comment (1995 Revision)

Sections 388 and 392, Restatement (Second) of Torts (1965) were approved in *Morris v. Shell Oil Company,* 467 S.W.2d 39, 42 (Mo.1971), and *Ridenhour v. Colson Caster Corp.,* 687 S.W.2d 938, 945 (Mo.App. 1985), respectively. Each Restatement section has different substantive elements. This instruction is for submission under § 392. See MAI 25.10(A) for submission under § 388.

Section 388 of the Restatement uses the terms "dangerous for the use for which it is supplied." Comment "e" of the Restatement explains the term "use" by the language ". . . but the chattel must be put to a use to which the supplier has reason to expect it to be put". Comment "a" to § 392 of the Restatement incorporates by reference the rationale expressed in the comments to § 388.

The 1995 Revision to this instruction changed the phrase "should have known" to "could have known" on the issue of constructive notice. Some MAI instructions had used one of the phrases and other instructions had used the other phrase. Questions had arisen as to whether "should have known" imposed a higher burden than "could have known". See *Benton v. City of Rolla,* 872 S.W.2d 882 (Mo.App.1994), and *Burrell v. Mayfair–Lennox Hotels, Inc.,* 442 S.W.2d 47 (Mo.1969). For consistency, the Committee has opted to use the phrase "could have known" to the extent possible in the context of constructive notice. Other instructions, such as MAI 10.07, paragraph Second of MAI 22.01, MAI 22.07, and MAI 25.10(A), continue to use the phrase "should have known" because that phrase is part of a "knew or had reason to know" standard as explained in the Committee Comments to those instructions.

Library References:

C.J.S. Products Liability § 93.
West's Key No. Digests, Products Liability ⚷96.1.

Notes of Decisions

1. In general

Ankle bracelet for monitoring parolee, which device had previously sent false alarms, was not dangerous instrumentality, for purposes of negligence suit brought against monitoring corporation by widow and son of man killed in automobile accident involving intoxicated parolee, where device was not defective, and false alarms were corrected by placing the receiver in another location within the house. Trout v. General Sec. Services Corp., 8 S.W.3d 126 (Mo.App. 1999).

Error in dismissing claims against city was harmless, where verdict directions instruction under MAI 31.16 given on remaining claim was practically identical to instructions under MAI 22.05 and 25.10(B) from which plaintiff would have been required to choose if other claims had not been dismissed and jury returned verdict in city's favor; under circumstances, dismissal of those claims did not affect outcome of case. Benton v. City of Rolla, 872 S.W.2d 882 (Mo.App.1994).

Transformer fuse was not dangerous, and thus customer who was injured while attempting to install it could not recover on theory of negligently furnishing dangerous instrumentality. Mobley v. Webster Elec. Co-op., 859 S.W.2d 923 (Mo.App.1993).

26.00

VERDICT DIRECTING—CONTRACT

Analysis of Instructions

Westlaw Electronic Research

See Westlaw Electronic Research Guide preceding the Table of Instructions.

Library References:

C.J.S. Trial § 350–351.
West's Key No. Digests, Trial ☞234(3, 4).

26.01 [1980 Revision] Verdict Directing—Breach of Unilateral Contract

Your verdict must be for plaintiff if you believe:

First, defendant offered to (*set out essential terms of offer*) if plaintiff would (*set out terms of plaintiff's performance*), and

Second, plaintiff performed the act[s] called for in such offer with intent to accept such offer, and

Third, defendant knew of such performance, and

Fourth, defendant thereafter did not perform what he had so offered, and

Fifth, plaintiff was thereby damaged.

* [unless you believe plaintiff is not entitled to recover by reason of Instruction Number _____ (*here insert number of affirmative defense instruction*)].

Notes on Use (1980 Revision)

* Add if affirmative defense is submitted.

Library References:

C.J.S. Contracts § 795.
West's Key No. Digests, Contracts ⚭353(1).

Notes of Decisions

In general 1
Consideration   4
Definition 3
Evidentiary support 2

―――――

1.   In general

Where terms of agreement are in dispute, verdict-directing instruction must hypothesize proponent's version of agreement actually made, and failure to do so is prejudicial error. Cranor v. Jones Co., 921 S.W.2d 76 (Mo.App.1996).

Jury instruction regarding diminished fair market property value, due to the builder's failure to grade the property pursuant to a contract, was not misleading or confusing to the jury, nor was the ability of the jury to grant damages for "loss of use" without defining that term. Kaiser v. Kadean Const. Co., 719 S.W.2d 892[1, 5] (Mo.App.1986).

Breach of contract verdict director submitting only "defendant's contract obligations were not met" erroneous for failure to state the nature of the breach. Tainter v. Graham, 579 S.W.2d 143[1, 2] (Mo.App.1979).

Plaintiffs' not-in-MAI verdict director for breach of house building contract, patterned after MAI 26.01, arguably erroneous when terms of contract were in dispute. Defendants' contention that some form of MAI 26.06 should have been used failed for not informing court how that could have been done without transgressing Rule 70.02(a). Forsythe v. Starnes, 554 S.W.2d 100[1, 2] (Mo.App.1977).

Verdict director on bilateral contract of employment. Vondras v. Titanium Research & Development Co., 511 S.W.2d 883, 885 (Mo. App.1974).

Verdict director for damage by surface water. Genova v. Kansas City, 497 S.W.2d 555[2] (Mo.App.1973).

Where plaintiff's case for breach of contract was based on three elements it was error to omit the connective "and" between paragraphs of plaintiff's Not–in–MAI verdict director. R–Way Furniture Co. v. Powers Interiors, Inc., 456 S.W.2d 632[9–12] (Mo. App.1970).

2. Evidentiary support

Paragraph First of MAI 26.01, Breach of Unilateral Contract, had evidentiary support if defendant's proposal could be reasonably inferred from the testimony. James v. Turilli, 473 S.W.2d 757[10, 11] (Mo.App.1971).

3. Definition

Accurate definition of "substantially performed," which is a legal and technical term. Forsythe v. Starnes, 554 S.W.2d 100[5–7] (Mo.App.1977).

4. Consideration

MAI 26.01 properly instructed jury that it had to find performance with intent to accept offer; separate finding of consideration was not necessary. Cook v. Coldwell Banker/Frank Laiben Realty Co., 967 S.W.2d 654 (Mo.App.1998).

26.02 [1980 Revision] Verdict Directing—Breach of Bilateral Contract—Breach Sole Issue

Your verdict must be for plaintiff if you believe:

First, defendant did not (*here insert the nature of the breach*), and

Second, because of such failure, defendant's contract obligations were not performed, and

Third, plaintiff was thereby damaged.

* [unless you believe that plaintiff is not entitled to recover by reason of Instruction Number _____ (*here insert number of affirmative defense instruction*)].

Notes on Use (1980 Revision)

This instruction is applicable only when there is no dispute concerning the terms of the agreement and the defendant's obligation to perform his agreement.

* Add if affirmative defense is submitted.

Library References:

C.J.S. Contracts § 795.
West's Key No. Digests, Contracts ☞353(1).

Notes of Decisions

In general 1
Affirmative defense 3
Contract terms disputed 2
Contract to loan money 6
Damages 4
Definition 7
Modified; sales contract 5
Modification 8

———

1. In general

Building owner's submission of instruction patterned after approved instruction concerning breach of undisputed contract terms, rather than based on approved instruction concerning dispute over contract terms and breach of contract, resulted in prejudicial error. Porta–Fab Corp. v. Young Sales Corp., 943 S.W.2d 686 (Mo.App.1997).

In customer's breach of contract action against bank, trial court properly used as verdict-directing instruction approved in-

struction to be used for breach of bilateral contract action where breach is sole issue, rather than approved instruction to be used in breach of contract action when terms of agreement and its breach are at issue; although terms of agreement between bank and customer were disputed, that dispute was not determinative of the issues as submitted by the parties. McMillan v. First State Bank of Joplin, 935 S.W.2d 329 (Mo.App. 1996).

MAI 26.06 was not proper instruction where plaintiff was prevented from performing contract by defendants; MAI 26.06 only addresses a situation where plaintiff fully performed; giving of instruction modified after MAI 26.02 was not reversible error. Smith Moore & Co. v. J.L. Mason Realty & Inv., Inc., 817 S.W.2d 530 (Mo.App.1991).

A verdict director instruction patterned after MAI 26.02 for breach of contract will be proper if it accurately describes the nature of the breach. George K. Baum Properties, Inc. v. Columbian Nat. Title Ins. Co., 763 S.W.2d 194, 200, 202 (Mo.App.1988).

Any error in verdict director omitting element that policy was in force was cured by reference to instruction on affirmative defense of misrepresentation. Crewse v. Shelter Mut. Ins. Co., 706 S.W.2d 35[5] (Mo.App. 1985).

In breach-of-contract action, absence from defendant's verdict director on counterclaim of essential element of excused delay in performance was cured by fact that the contested element of excusable delay was necessarily addressed by the jury in finding against plaintiff on its claim under plaintiff's verdict director as conversed by defendant's instruction defining that term. Seuf, Inc. v. Bartlett, 665 S.W.2d 31[2] (Mo.App.1984).

MAI 26.02 is intended to be used in situations where the existence and terms of the contract are undisputed and the jury is to decide only the issues of breach and resulting damages. Buder v. Martin, 657 S.W.2d 667[1] (Mo.App.1983).

Failure to submit disputed and essential element of substantial performance constituted an impermissible deviation from MAI 26.02. Reed Stenhouse, Inc. of Missouri v. Portnoy, 642 S.W.2d 947 (Mo.App.1982).

Where interpretation of contract terms were in dispute, submission of instruction patterned after MAI 26.02 was prejudicial error. Reed Stenhouse, Inc. of Missouri v. Portnoy, 642 S.W.2d 947[8] (Mo.App.1982).

MAI 26.02 covers cases where the only issues are breach and resultant damage; where the issues are what agreement was made and if breached, MAI 26.06 is the proper instruction. Braun v. Lorenz, 585 S.W.2d 102[1–3] (Mo.App.1979).

MAI 26.02 is to be used where the existence and terms of a contract are undisputed and the sole issue is whether defendant breached the contract. Laclede Investment Corp. v. Kaiser, 541 S.W.2d 330[11] (Mo. App.1976).

MAI 26.02 is designed for cases where terms of contract are undisputed. North County School Dist. R–1 v. Fidelity & Deposit Co., 539 S.W.2d 469[11] (Mo.App.1976).

Where defendant agreed to build home according to plaintiffs' plans and specifications but defectively did so, plaintiffs' proper action was for breach of bilateral contract, not for implied warranty of fitness, and court erred in so submitting plaintiffs' case. Barrett v. Jenkins, 510 S.W.2d 805[1] (Mo.App. 1974).

In suit on express contract for agreed price for building a garage the court properly submitted plaintiff "substantially performed" the contract. Defendant was entitled to converse that specific element but was not entitled to base a converse on three separately described construction defects. Bullock Co. v. Allen, 493 S.W.2d 5[5–7] (Mo.App.1973).

Approved not-in-MAI verdict director based on bilateral contract hypothesizing offer, acceptance and breach. Hinkeldey v. Cities Service Oil Co., 470 S.W.2d 494, 496 (Mo.1971).

Where plaintiff's case for breach of contract was based on three elements it was error to omit the connective "and" between paragraphs of plaintiff's Not–in–MAI verdict director. R–Way Furniture Co. v. Powers Interiors, Inc., 456 S.W.2d 632[9–12] (Mo. App.1970).

Where plaintiffs granted powerline easement for defendant's promise to pay stated amount for each pole installed it was error to give plaintiffs' not-in-MAI instructions authorizing recovery for difference between before and after values, since plaintiffs' recovery was limited to breach of defendant's promise to pay agreed amount. Shelton v. M & A Elec. Power Co-op., 451 S.W.2d 375[1, 6] (Mo.App.1970).

In suit on an oral promise asserted by plaintiff and denied by defendant it was sufficient to submit a not-in-MAI verdict director hypothesizing the ultimate issue "the defendant agreed to pay cash ... for said property" and failed to do so to plaintiff's damage. Verdict director approved. Gottlieb v. Hyken, 448 S.W.2d 617[1–3] (Mo.1970).

In suit against repairman where elements of reasonable time and damages were the only issues, a not-in-MAI verdict director which included undisputed evidentiary facts violated Rule 70.01(e) concerning submission of only the disputed, ultimate facts. Pavyer Printing Mach. Works v. South Side Roofing Co., 446 S.W.2d 445[7–9] (Mo.App. 1969).

In suit on implied contract, verdict director should not have required the jury to find the existence of an "implied contract", that being a legal question, but should have merely hypothesized the ultimate fact of the parties' agreement. Kosher Zion Sausage Co. of Chicago v. Roodman's, Inc., 442 S.W.2d 543[7, 8] (Mo.App.1969).

2. Contract terms disputed

MAI 26.02 did not have to hypothesize terms of agreement with regard to self-insured employer's breach-of-contract claim against insurance brokers to obtain stop-loss medical policy with active-at-work provision; brokers admitted material terms of contract. A.G. Edwards & Sons, Inc. v. Drew, 978 S.W.2d 386 (Mo.App.1998).

It was prejudicial error to give verdict directing instruction based on MAI 26.02 in contract dispute over corporation's payment of additional funds into travel agent's escrow account where parties disputed whether contract required corporation to pay second deposit into account if there were enough funds to recover cost of actual number of trips in corporation's incentive travel program; MAI 26.02 is intended for use in situations where existence and terms of contract are undisputed and the sole question for jury to decide is whether defendant has breached that contract and, if so, the damage resulting; MAI 26.06 is to be used where the terms of the agreement and its breach are at issue. James O'Brien & Associates, Inc. v. American Sportsman Travel, Inc., 819 S.W.2d 62 (Mo.App.1991).

Where terms of contract were disputed it was error to give MAI 26.02 submitting only defendant's breach. Varn Co. v. Hamiltonian Fed. Sav. & Loan Ass'n, 488 S.W.2d 649[3] (Mo.1973).

Breach of contract verdict director submitting only "defendant's contract obligations were not met" erroneous for failure to state

the nature of the breach. Tainter v. Graham, 579 S.W.2d 143[1, 2] (Mo.App.1979).

3. Affirmative defense

Where defendant got an affirmative defense instruction submitting facts justifying his termination of a contract the instruction should also have submitted that defendant did in fact terminate the contract. Beuc v. Morrissey, 463 S.W.2d 851[2–6] (Mo. banc 1971).

Defendant's theory that unreasonable working conditions justified her in breaching employment contract was properly submitted by a Third–Method Converse. State ex rel. State Department of Public Health and Welfare, Division of Welfare v. Luster, 456 S.W.2d 600[3] (Mo.App.1970).

4. Damages

Plaintiff's verdict director on breach of contract must submit the fact that plaintiff was damaged by the breach. Beuc v. Morrissey, 463 S.W.2d 851[7] (Mo. banc 1971).

5. Modified; sales contract

Where action on a construction contract was based on failure to construct roof in a workmanlike manner, MAI 26.02 improperly omitted that element and erroneously conditioned plaintiff's recovery on whether the roof leaked. North County School Dist. R–1 v. Fidelity & Deposit Co., 539 S.W.2d 469[10] (Mo.App.1976).

Seller's verdict director against defaulting buyer. R.R. Waites Co. v. E.H. Thrift Air Conditioning, Inc., 510 S.W.2d 759[1–3] (Mo. App.1974).

6. Contract to loan money

Verdict director on breach of contract to loan money. Levey v. Roosevelt Fed. Sav. & Loan Ass'n, 504 S.W.2d 241[11] (Mo.App. 1973).

7. Definition

Accurate definition of "substantially performed," which is a legal and technical term. Forsythe v. Starnes, 554 S.W.2d 100[5–7] (Mo.App.1977).

8. Modification

Because of unique factual issues created by lease addendum releasing tenant of duty to restore premises to their original condition, but preserving tenant's liability for "remediation of any environmental issues," trial court properly modified MAI 26.02, relating to landlord's breach of contract claim, to include additional requirement that landlord could prevail only if jury found that alleged oil deposits left by tenant constituted "environmental issue." Shutt v. Chris Kaye Plastics Corp., 962 S.W.2d 887 (Mo.1998).

Modified MAI 26.02 could be submitted with applicable Illinois substantive law so long as instruction did not contain abstract statements of law. Shop 'N Save Warehouse Foods, Inc. v. Soffer, 918 S.W.2d 851 (Mo.App.1996).

No approved instruction covers an action for breach of warranty for workmanlike performance and, therefore, a non-MAI or modified instruction is required under Rule 70.02(e). The court approved the use of a modification of MAI 26.02. Crank v. Firestone Tire & Rubber Co., 692 S.W.2d 397[7] (Mo.App.1985).

Words in instructions which are in common usage and are generally understood need not be defined. Court noted frequent instructional use of "workmanlike manner" without definition. Steffens v. Paramount Properties, Inc., 667 S.W.2d 725[3] (Mo.App. 1984).

26.03 [1969 New] Verdict Directing—Action on Account

Your verdict must be for plaintiff if you believe:

First, at defendant's request plaintiff furnished [to defendant] [to (*name of third party*)]¹ certain (*describe goods furnished*) between _____, 19__ and _____, 19__, and

Second, plaintiff charged a total of $_____ for such goods, and

Third, plaintiff's charges were reasonable.

* [unless you believe plaintiff is not entitled to recover by reason of Instruction Number _____ (*here insert number of affirmative defense instruction including defense of payment*)].

Notes on Use (1969 New)

1. Select appropriate term.

* Add if affirmative defense is submitted.

Library References:

C.J.S. Account, Action on § 44–49.
West's Key No. Digests, Account, Action on ⊆8.

Notes of Decisions

In general 1
Evidentiary support 3
Measure of damages 2

1. In general

Verdict-directing pattern instruction for action on account was properly given in excavator's action to recover payment against property owners who allegedly hired excavator to conduct lake excavation project, rather than instruction relating to breach of contract, although it was not clear whether parties had ever reached agreement as to project, as action on account was pled, and facts existed to support that claim. Raysik v. Standiford, 944 S.W.2d 288 (Mo.App.1997).

Trial court should have given instruction for quantum meruit, not for action on account, in attorney's action to recover attorney fees, where no express contract existed between attorney and client. Kalish v. Smith, 824 S.W.2d 35 (Mo.App.1991).

An action on a "time plus materials" contract possess all of the classic indices of an action on an account for which MAI 26.03 was specifically drafted. Wehrend v. Roknick, 664 S.W.2d 247[2] (Mo.App.1983).

2. Measure of damages

In home builder's action for balance of price of house, MAI 4.04 was proper damage instruction with MAI 26.03. Wehrend v. Roknick, 664 S.W.2d 247[4] (Mo.App.1983).

Where plaintiff submitted on MAI 26.03—Action on Account, its proper damage instruction was MAI 4.04. Hereford Concrete Products v. Aerobic Services, 565 S.W.2d 176[4–5] (Mo.App.1978).

3. Evidentiary support

Evidence including testimony of plaintiff's comptroller and computer-generated account statement listing invoices for goods sold and delivered to defendant that were unpaid as of August 10, 1990 were sufficient to make submissible case in action on account, even though plaintiff's comptroller admitted that final statement did not contain bottom line showing what was due and owing at time of trial. Helmtec Industries, Inc. v. Motorcycle Stuff, Inc., 857 S.W.2d 334 (Mo.App.1993).

26.04 [1981 Revision] Verdict Directing—Account Stated—Matured Debts

Your verdict must be for plaintiff if you believe:

First, after the transaction mentioned in evidence plaintiff and defendant agreed that the stated sum of $_____ was the amount defendant owed plaintiff, and

Second, thereafter defendant [failed] [refused] [1] to pay this stated sum.

* [unless you believe that plaintiff is not entitled to recover by reason of Instruction Number _____ (*here insert number of affirmative defense instruction including affirmative defense of payment*)].

Notes on Use (1981 Revision)

1. Select appropriate term.

* Add if affirmative defense is submitted.

Library References:

C.J.S. Account Stated § 41, 51.
West's Key No. Digests, Account Stated ⊙20(2).

Notes of Decisions

1. In general

Verdict director on account stated, negating affirmative defenses of payment and statute of limitations. Schwartz v. Fein, 471 S.W.2d 679[3] (Mo.App.1971).

26.05 [1980 Revision] Verdict Directing—Quantum Meruit—Goods or Services Furnished

Your verdict must be for plaintiff if you believe:

First, plaintiff furnished (*here describe generally the goods or the services*) to defendant, and

Second, defendant accepted such [goods] [services].[1]

* [unless you believe that plaintiff is not entitled to recover by reason of Instruction Number _____ (*here insert number of affirmative defense instruction*)].

Notes on Use (1980 Revision)

1. Select appropriate term.

* Add if affirmative defense is submitted.

Committee Comment (1991 New)

This remedy goes under a variety of names including quantum valebant which was one of the common counts in an action of assumpsit. It is sometimes called quasi contract. The court in discussing this remedy in *Bennett v. Adams,* 362 S.W.2d 277, 281 (Mo.App.1962) said:

> Contracts really implied in law are those which are imposed, or created, without regard to promise or intention of the party to be bound. The assent rests solely in legal fiction, and the liability created thereunder rests simply in reason and justice. The fictitious implication of agreement to pay the reasonable value arises (as one example) when services or things necessary to the recipient are furnished to an incompetent person. The fictitious contract is based primarily upon a benefit conferred upon the recipient of the goods or services. Running through all the cases which involve quantum meruit by reason of contract implied in law are the words "valuable" and "beneficial" services.

For a real estate commission case without a contract, see *Williams v. Enochs,* 742 S.W.2d 165 (Mo.banc 1987), where the Court recommended a modification which combined MAI 29.02 (Sale Consummated—Agreed Commission) with MAI 26.05.

Library References:

C.J.S. Account, Action on § 44–49.
West's Key No. Digests, Account, Action on ⟜8.

Notes of Decisions

In general   1
Evidentiary support   2

---

1. In general

Instruction on theory of quantum meruit was improper in excavator's action on account against property owners, because owners did not accept services provided by excavator. Raysik v. Standiford, 944 S.W.2d 288 (Mo.App.1997).

Trial court should have given instruction for quantum meruit, not for action on account, in attorney's action to recover attorney fees, where no express contract existed between attorney and client. Kalish v. Smith, 824 S.W.2d 35 (Mo.App.1991).

Pattern jury instruction for "action for quantum meruit" is appropriate for use when legal relationship between party is contract implied in law or quasi-contract, but not where remedy of quantum meruit may be pursued for breach of express contract. Westerhold v. Mullenix Corp., 777 S.W.2d 257 (Mo.App.,1989).

Not-in-MAI verdict director properly given in quantum meruit action submitted before adoption of MAI 26.05, the quantum meruit verdict director. Kaiser v. Lyon Metal Products, Inc., 461 S.W.2d 893[5] (Mo.App.1970).

Including the words "emergency repairs" in paragraph First was harmless error under the facts. Kranz v. Kansas City, 573 S.W.2d 88[4] (Mo.App.1978).

Modified MAI 26.05 to submit plaintiff's claim for services rendered beyond agreed salary, and modified damages instruction for same. Austin v. Kansas City General Hospital, 570 S.W.2d 752[3, 4] (Mo.App.1978).

2. Evidentiary support

Plaintiff contracted and was paid for specific work at stated price, but sued for "extras" done on estimated basis. Plaintiff's properly submitted on quantum meruit; not error to submit without reference to contract price. Bodde v. Burnham, 588 S.W.2d 516[2–5] (Mo.App.1979).

26.06 [1981 Revision] Verdict Directing—Breach of Bilateral Contract—Terms and Breach in Issue

Your verdict must be for plaintiff if you believe:

First, plaintiff and defendant entered into an agreement whereby plaintiff agreed (*set out plaintiff's agreement*) and defendant agreed (*set out defendant's agreement*), and

Second, plaintiff performed his agreement, and

Third, defendant failed to perform his agreement, and

Fourth, plaintiff was thereby damaged.

* [unless you believe plaintiff is not entitled to recover by reason of Instruction Number _____ (*here insert number of affirmative defense instruction*)].

Notes on Use (1980 Revision)

* Add if affirmative defense is submitted.

Committee Comment (1973 New)

See: *Gottlieb v. Hyken*, 448 S.W.2d 617 (Mo.1970).

Library References:

C.J.S. Contracts § 795.
West's Key No. Digests, Contracts ⊙353(1).

Notes of Decisions

In general 1
Conversing 2

_____

1. In general

Jury instruction given at trial on conditions for verdict for building owner against roofing contractor for breach of settlement agreement failed to substantially track Missouri Approved Instruction (MAI) elements requiring identification of building owner's obligations under agreement and requiring jury to find that owner performed those obligations. Porta–Fab Corp. v. Young Sales Corp., 943 S.W.2d 686 (Mo.App.1997).

Verdict-directing pattern instruction for action on account was properly given in excavator's action to recover payment against property owners who allegedly hired excavator to conduct lake excavation project, rather than instruction relating to breach of contract, although it was not clear whether parties had ever reached agreement as to project, as action on account was pled, and facts existed to support that claim. Raysik v. Standiford, 944 S.W.2d 288 (Mo.App.1997).

In customer's breach of contract action against bank, trial court properly used as

417

verdict-directing instruction approved instruction to be used for breach of bilateral contract action where breach is sole issue, rather than approved instruction to be used in breach of contract action when terms of agreement and its breach are at issue; although terms of agreement between bank and customer were disputed, that dispute was not determinative of the issues as submitted by the parties. McMillan v. First State Bank of Joplin, 935 S.W.2d 329 (Mo.App. 1996).

Instruction, which directed jury to reach verdict for agent in agent's anticipatory breach of contract action against professional football player following player's retention of another agent, if jury believed that parties "agreed" that agent would serve as player's contract advisor, and that player failed to perform his "agreement," was neither prejudicial nor plain error; though player claimed that the instruction improperly assumed facts in issue by using words "agreed" and "agreement," pattern instruction required jury to determine existence of binding agreement by finding that both parties had agreed, and trial court had submitted at player's request a true converse instruction with respect to the challenged issue. Total Economic Athletic Management of America v. Pickens, 898 S.W.2d 98 (Mo.App. W.D.,1995).

If plaintiff has not fully performed to exact and original contract specifications, instruction on full performance may not be used. Lindsey Masonry Co., Inc. v. Jenkins & Associates, Inc., 897 S.W.2d 6 (Mo.App. W.D. 1995).

Failure to identify agreement for sale of chiropractic practice by date in jury instruction on breach of contract did not deviate from MAI 26.06; although more than one agreement was in evidence, there was no dispute at trial as to which agreement was at issue; instruction did not prejudice buyers, as buyers failed to object to instruction at trial, converse instruction required jury to focus on agreement in question, and sellers' counsel advised jury several times in closing argument as to which agreement was at issue. Dierker Associates, D.C., P.C. v. Gillis, 859 S.W.2d 737 (Mo.App.1993).

Alternate constructions of ambiguous indemnification provision in shareholder agreement were not required to be submitted to jury; although jury instruction deviated slightly from MAI 26.02 and failed to require finding that defendant agreed to formula advanced by plaintiff, instructions stated that plaintiff and defendant entered into agreement and defendant failed to perform, enabling reasonable juror to understand that both plaintiff and defendant agreed to formula submitted in instruction. Graham v. Goodman, 850 S.W.2d 351 (Mo.1993).

It was prejudicial error to give verdict directing instruction based on MAI 26.02 in contract dispute over corporation's payment of additional funds into travel agent's escrow account where parties disputed whether contract required corporation to pay second deposit into account if there were enough funds to recover cost of actual number of trips in corporation's incentive travel program; MAI 26.02 is intended for use in situations where existence and terms of contract are undisputed and the sole question for jury to decide is whether defendant has breached that contract and, if so, the damage resulting; MAI 26.06 is to be used where the terms of the agreement and its breach are at issue. James O'Brien & Associates, Inc. v. American Sportsman Travel, Inc., 819 S.W.2d 62 (Mo.App.1991).

MAI 26.06 was not proper instruction where plaintiff was prevented from performing contract by defendants; MAI 26.06 only addresses a situation where plaintiff fully performed; giving of instruction modified after MAI 26.02 was not reversible error. Smith Moore & Co. v. J.L. Mason Realty & Inv., Inc., 817 S.W.2d 530 (Mo.App.1991).

Verdict director should have submitted dispute over what entitled sales representative to commissions on an account; verdict director only submitted undisputed terms of representative's agreement to be sales representative for carrier and carrier's agreement to pay five percent sales commission on gross revenue produced by representative's accounts, but all facts submitted in director could be resolved in favor of representative without any finding that he procured any account. Penberthy v. Nancy Transp., Inc., 804 S.W.2d 404 (Mo.App. 1991).

In a breach of contract action where plaintiff was seeking damages for breach of both a written agreement and a subsequent oral agreement, it may have been improper to submit both contracts in one verdict-director, rather than in two separate instructions, but the plaintiff suffered no prejudice as a result. Aluminum Prods. Enters., Inc. v. Fuhrmann Tooling & Mfg. Co., 758 S.W.2d 119, 125 (Mo.App.1988).

In action for damages for breach of contract, where the terms of agreement were in dispute, trial court erred in submitting verdict-directing instruction based on MAI 26.06 that did not hypothesize plaintiff's version of the agreement and require jury to make a finding in that regard. Schlemer v. Connell Agencies of Kimberling City, Inc., 741 S.W.2d 307[1] (Mo.App.1987).

Submission of a quantum meruit theory by a verdict director submitting breach of a bilateral contract was error, and such error was compounded by the use of a bilateral contract verdict director with a quantum meruit damages instruction. Instructions which intermingle inconsistent guides for recovery are prejudicially erroneous. Hall v. Cooper, 691 S.W.2d 507[1, 7] (Mo.App.1985).

MAI 26.06 is appropriate where the jury issues are what agreement was made and whether the agreement was reached. Boswell v. Steel Haulers, Inc., 670 S.W.2d 906[7] (Mo.App.1984).

Where terms of an agreement are in dispute, the verdict directing instruction must hypothesize the proponent's version of the agreement actually made. Failure to submit to jury defendant's proposed construction of language previously held ambiguous by court was prejudicial error. Reed Stenhouse, Inc. of Missouri v. Portnoy, 642 S.W.2d 947[6, 7] (Mo.App.1982).

MAI 26.02 covers cases where the only issues are breach and resultant damage; where the issues are what agreement was made and if breached, MAI 26.06 is the proper instruction. Braun v. Lorenz, 585 S.W.2d 102[1–3] (Mo.App.1979).

Plaintiffs' not-in-MAI verdict director for breach of house building contract, patterned after MAI 26.01, erroneous when terms of contract were in dispute. A modified MAI 22.06 would have been proper. Forsythe v. Starnes, 554 S.W.2d 100[1, 2] (Mo.App. 1977).

Breach of agreement to pay fee for obtaining employment. S.P. Personnel Associates, etc., v. Hospital Building & Equipment Co., Inc., 525 S.W.2d 345[4–7] (Mo.App. 1975).

Verdict director in action on contract to support illegitimate child. S-- v. W--, 514 S.W.2d 848[852] (Mo.App.1974).

Affirmative defense of duress in executing contract. S-- v. W--, 514 S.W.2d 848, 852 (Mo.App.1974).

Where terms of contract were disputed it was error to give MAI 26.02 submitting only defendant's breach. Varn Co. v. Hamiltonian Fed. Sav. & Loan Ass'n, 488 S.W.2d 649[3] (Mo.1973).

2. Conversing

Plaintiff's modified MAI 26.06 hypothesized defendant's agreement to pay him commissions; defendant's converse directed a verdict if plaintiff was "not entitled to commissions." Condemned as a roving commission which did not negate an essential element of plaintiff's case. Lawrie v. Continental Cas. Co., 555 S.W.2d 347 (Mo. App.1977).

26.07 [1981 Revision] Verdict Directing—Breach of Bilateral Contract—When Substantial Performance Sufficient

Your verdict must be for plaintiff if you believe:

First, plaintiff and defendant entered into an agreement whereby plaintiff agreed (*set out plaintiff's agreement*) and defendant agreed (*set out defendant's agreement*), and

Second, plaintiff substantially performed [1] his agreement [in a workmanlike manner],[2] and

Third, defendant failed to perform his agreement, and

Fourth, plaintiff was thereby damaged.

* [unless you believe plaintiff is not entitled to recover by reason of Instruction Number _____ (*here insert number of affirmative defense instruction*)].

Notes on Use (1980 New)

1. The phrase "substantially performed" must be defined. See definition in MAI 16.04.

2. Submit bracketed clause only when quality of workmanship is in issue.

Caution: This instruction is not proper in all contract cases. This instruction may be used only in cases where substantial performance is legally sufficient. Use MAI 26.06 where substantial performance may not be submitted. Use MAI 4.08 as the damage instruction where substantial performance is submitted.

* Add if affirmative defense is submitted.

Committee Comment (1980 New)

This instruction would be appropriate where recovery is sought on a building contract. *Cross v. Robinson,* 281 S.W.2d 22 (Mo.App.1955); *McAlpine Co. v. Graham,* 320 S.W.2d 951 (Mo.App.1959); *Julian v. Kiefer,* 382 S.W.2d 723 (Mo.App.1964); *State ex rel. Stites v. Goodman,* 351 S.W.2d 763 (Mo.banc 1961); *Southwest Engineering Co. v. Reorganized School District R–9,* 434 S.W.2d 743 (Mo.App.1968); *Vic Koepke Excav. & Grading Co. v. Kodner Dev. Co.,* 571 S.W.2d 253 (Mo. banc 1978).

Library References:

C.J.S. Contracts § 795.
West's Key No. Digests, Contracts ⚯353(1).

Notes of Decisions

1. In general

"Substantial performance" jury instruction was properly submitted in subcontractor's breach of contract action against general contractor, despite subcontractor's claim that each of three allegedly breaches of contract was sufficient to give rise to claim of total breach of agreement; project was uncompleted, no term of parties' contract was in dispute, and, in any event, subcontractor was not prejudiced thereby, as finding that it "substantially performed" was lesser burden of proof. Lindsey Masonry Co., Inc. v. Jenkins & Associates, Inc., 897 S.W.2d 6 (Mo. App. W.D.1995).

A court may properly submit MAI 26.07 when substantial performance upon the part of the plaintiff is legally sufficient to support a verdict in plaintiff's favor where defendant has breached its contractual obligations. It is impermissible to modify MAI 26.07 to require the jury to evaluate whether defendant substantially performed their agreement. Kim v. Conway & Forty, Inc., 772 S.W.2d 723, 727 (Mo.App.1989).

27.00

VERDICT DIRECTING—EJECTMENT

Analysis of Instructions

Westlaw Electronic Research

See Westlaw Electronic Research Guide preceding the Table of Instructions.

Library References:

27.01 [1981 Revision] Verdict Directing—Ejectment Against a Stranger

Your verdict must be for plaintiff if you believe:

First, defendant was in possession of the premises claimed by plaintiff on (*state the date action for ejectment was commenced*), and

Second, plaintiff had the right to possession of the premises on that date by reason of (*set out basis of right to possession*).

* [unless you believe plaintiff is not entitled to recover by reason of Instruction Number _____ (*here insert number of affirmative defense instruction*)].

Notes on Use (1981 Revision)

This instruction is to be used in cases in which the plaintiff claims either nominal damages or substantial damages. The finding of a right to possession carries with it the right to at least nominal damages. *Curd v. Reaban,* 232 S.W.2d 389 (Mo.1950).

* Add if affirmative defense is submitted.

Library References:

C.J.S. Ejectment § 118.
West's Key No. Digests, Ejectment ☞110.

Notes of Decisions

1. In general

Landowners could not recover from adjoining landowners in ejectment action brought to determine boundary between their properties, absent evidence that adjoining landowners were in possession of disputed area. Allen v. Welch, 770 S.W.2d 521, 523 (Mo.App.1989).

Verdict directing instruction on ejectment erroneous for failure to negate defensive instruction on title by limitation. Kammerer v. Cella, 585 S.W.2d 552[5] (Mo.App.1979).

27.02 [1981 Revision] Verdict Directing—Ejectment Against Co-tenant

Your verdict must be for plaintiff if you believe:

First, defendant was in possession of the premises claimed by plaintiff on (*state the date action for ejectment was commenced*), and

Second, plaintiff had the right to [joint] [1] possession on that day by reason of (*set out basis of right to possession or joint possession*), and

Third, defendant (*set out the conduct of the defendant amounting to a total denial of plaintiff's right to entry and possession as a co-tenant, such as "barred plaintiff from the premises" or "ousted plaintiff from the premises"*).

* [unless you believe plaintiff is not entitled to recover by reason of Instruction Number _____ (*here insert number of affirmative defense instruction*)].

Notes on Use (1981 Revision)

1. Insert if appropriate to avert requirement that plaintiff co-tenant or joint tenant must be found entitled to exclusive possession.

This instruction is to be used by a plaintiff claiming either nominal damages or substantial damages.

* Add if affirmative defense is submitted.

Library References:

C.J.S. Ejectment § 118.
West's Key No. Digests, Ejectment ☞110.

27.03 [1978 New] Verdict Directing—Ejectment— Damages Only

Your verdict must be for plaintiff if you believe:

First, defendant was in possession of the premises claimed by plaintiff on (*state the date action for ejectment was commenced*), and

Second, plaintiff had the right to [joint] [1] possession of the premises on that day by reason of (*state basis of right to possession or joint possession, such as "being a tenant" or "being a joint tenant"*), and

Third, defendant had knowledge of plaintiff's claim to possession of the premises on (*insert date*), and

Fourth, defendant remained in possession thereafter. [2]

* [unless you believe plaintiff is not entitled to recover by reason of Instruction Number _____ (*here insert number of affirmative defense instruction*)].

Notes on Use (1978 New)

1. Insert if appropriate to avert requirement that plaintiff co-tenant or joint tenant must be found entitled to exclusive possession.

2. If action is against a co-tenant, use this Paragraph Third in lieu of Paragraphs Third and Fourth above:

"Third, the defendant (*set out the conduct of defendant amounting to a total denial of plaintiff's right to entry and possession as co-tenant, such as 'ousted plaintiff from the premises'*)".

* Add if affirmative defense is submitted.

Committee Comment (1978 New)

The right to possession on the day the action for ejectment is commenced must exist or ejectment will not lie; however, if the right to possession is based on a lease or other terminable right, the right to possession may no longer exist at the time of trial. If plaintiff's right to possession has terminated, he cannot be granted a writ of possession. His only claim remaining will be for damages. This is the instruction approved for use in that circumstance.

Library References:

C.J.S. Ejectment § 118.
West's Key No. Digests, Ejectment ☞110.

Notes of Decisions

1. In general

In action seeking damages for interference with easement, jury should not have been instructed based on ejectment damage instruction MAI 27.03. Liability for damages caused by interference or obstruction of easement is based upon nuisance instruction MAI 22.06. Gilbert v. K.T.I., Inc., 765 S.W.2d 289, 294, 297 (Mo.App.1988).

27.04 [1981 Revision] Verdict Directing—Ejectment—Counterclaim for Value of Improvements

If your verdict is for plaintiff on his claim for possession of the premises, your verdict must be for defendant on his counterclaim if you believe:

First, defendant entered into possession of the premises under a good faith [1] claim of title to the premises and without knowledge of plaintiff's claim to possession, and

Second, the improvements were made in good faith [1] on the premises prior to defendant's having notice of plaintiff's claim to possession of the premises.

* [unless you believe defendant is not entitled to recover by reason of Instruction Number _____ (*here insert number of affirmative defense instruction*)].

Notes on Use (1981 Revision)

1. The phrase "good faith" must be defined. See definition in MAI 16.03.

* Add if affirmative defense is submitted.

Committee Comment (1978 New)

The right of the defendant to recover for improvements is provided for in § 524.160, RSMo. Section 524.170, RSMo requires that the defendant show that the improvements were made in good faith. Sections 524.190 through 524.230, RSMo provide for alternate remedies such as relinquishing the improved land to the defendant but requiring him to pay the plaintiff the value of the land or for partition between plaintiff and defendant. If these remedies are at issue, some modifications of the instructions may be required.

Library References:

C.J.S. Ejectment § 118.
West's Key No. Digests, Ejectment ☜110.

28.00

VERDICT DIRECTING—SERVICES
FURNISHED DECEDENT

Analysis of Instructions

Westlaw Electronic Research

See Westlaw Electronic Research Guide preceding the Table of Instructions.

Library References:

   C.J.S. Trial § 350–351.
   West's Key No. Digests, Trial ☞234(3, 4).

28.00 [1980 Revision] Verdict Directing—Services Furnished Decedent—General Comment

Actions to recover for services to decedents can be divided into two kinds. In one, the plaintiff is *not* in a family relationship with the decedent and is hereinafter called a stranger. (MAI 28.03 and 28.04). In the other, the plaintiff *is* in a family relationship with the decedent. (MAI 28.01 and 28.02).

Actions by Stranger

"Absent a family relationship, where one performs valuable services for another, the benefit of which has been received and enjoyed by him, the law presumes an intention on the part of the former to charge and the latter to pay the reasonable value thereof...." *Smith v. Estate of Sypret,* 421 S.W.2d 9, 14 (Mo.1967).

When a stranger furnishes services to a decedent which decedent accepts, the rule of quantum meruit allows recovery and is barred if the defendant establishes an intent by the stranger to make a gift. This is an affirmative defense. *Lauf v. Wiegersen,* 17 S.W.2d 369, 371 (Mo.App.1929).

Defense Instructions Where Plaintiff Is a Stranger

When claim is made by a stranger, the defendant may offer the affirmative defense of payment using MAI 32.14 or the affirmative defense that services were furnished gratuitously, using MAI 32.15.

Actions by Persons in a Family Relationship

When services are performed by one who is in a family relationship with decedent, "recovery must be upon an express contract, or from evidence from which it can be reasonably concluded that there was a distinct understanding and agreement, understood and acted upon between the parties, a contract established on inference rather than implication." *Smith v. Davis' Estate,* 206 Mo.App. 446, 459, 230 S.W. 670, 673 (1921). *See also Kopp v. Traders Gate City Nat. Bank,* 357 Mo. 659, 665, 210 S.W.2d 49, 51 (banc

1948); *Lipperd v. Lipperd's Estate,* 181 Mo.App. 106, 163 S.W. 934 (1914).

In *Steva v. Steva,* 332 S.W.2d 924, 926 (Mo.1960), the term "family," within the rule under discussion, was defined as "a collective body of persons under one head and one domestic government, who have reciprocal, natural, or moral duties to support and care for each other." For further definition see *Smith v. Estate of Sypret,* 421 S.W.2d 9, 14 (Mo.1967).

If plaintiff admits he was in a "family relationship" with decedent, or if this relationship is in issue, plaintiff may submit on the basis of express contract, using MAI 28.01, or on a contract implied by the conduct of the parties, using MAI 28.02.

Defense Instructions Where Plaintiff Is In a Family Relationship

As recovery by one admittedly in a family relationship can only be had on the basis of an express or implied contract, defendants would normally converse one or more elements of the plaintiff's case in the same manner as other contract actions are conversed. Or, defendant may submit the affirmative defense of payment, MAI 32.14.

Defense Instructions

See affirmative defense instructions, MAI 32.14 to 32.16.

Damages

MAI 4.07 should be used. See *Ridinger v. Harbert,* 409 S.W.2d 764, 768 (Mo.App.1966).

Library References:

C.J.S. Executors and Administrators § 398–399.
West's Key No. Digests, Executors and Administrators ☞205, 206(1), 451(3).

28.01 [1969 New] Verdict Directing—Recovery for Services Furnished Decedent Under Express Contract Where Family Relationship Is Admitted or an Issue

Your verdict must be for plaintiff if you believe:

First, plaintiff and (*name of decedent*) agreed that plaintiff would (*here describe services performed*) and (*name of decedent*) would pay for such services, and

Second, these services were thereafter furnished to (*name of decedent*) by plaintiff.

* [unless you believe plaintiff is not entitled to recover by reason of Instruction Number _____ (*here insert number of affirmative defense instruction*)].

Notes on Use (1991 Revision)

* Add if affirmative defense is submitted.

Caution. Lawyers must be sure that they have evidence of an express contract before using this instruction. If the evidence shows only an agreement by implication, MAI 28.02 should be used.

Committee Comment (1969 New)

See General Comment at MAI 28.00.

Library References:

C.J.S. Executors and Administrators § 399.
West's Key No. Digests, Executors and Administrators ☞206(1), 451(3).

28.02 [1969 New] Verdict Directing—Recovery for Services Furnished Decedent Under Implied Contract Where Family Relationship Is Admitted or an Issue

Your verdict must be for plaintiff if you believe:

First, plaintiff furnished valuable services to (*name of decedent*), and

Second, (*name of decedent*) accepted the benefits of such services, and

Third, the conduct and relationship of plaintiff and (*name of decedent*) was such as to imply an agreement that payment would be made for such services.

* [unless you believe plaintiff is not entitled to recover by reason of Instruction Number _____ (*here insert number of affirmative defense instruction*)].

Notes on Use (1969 New)

* Add if affirmative defense is submitted.

Caution. This is not a quantum meruit recovery. The record must contain evidence "from which it may reasonably be inferred that there was an agreement or mutual understanding the claimant was to be remunerated for the services rendered." *Kopp v. Traders Gate City National Bank*, 357 Mo. 659, 210 S.W.2d 49, 51 (banc 1948).

Committee Comment (1969 New)

See General Comment at MAI 28.00.

Library References:

C.J.S. Executors and Administrators § 399.
West's Key No. Digests, Executors and Administrators ☞206(2), 451(3).

Notes of Decisions

1. In general

Where plaintiff went to jury on MAI 28.02, *Implied Contract,* it was error to give defendant's MAI 32.16, appropriate only where plaintiff submits on *Quantum Meruit.* Sturgeon v. Estate of Wideman, 631 S.W.2d 55 (Mo.App.1981).

28.03 [1969 New] Verdict Directing—Action Against Estate by One Admittedly Not in a Family Relationship

Your verdict must be for plaintiff if you believe:

First, plaintiff furnished to (*name of decedent*) valuable services, and

Second, (*name of decedent*) accepted the benefits of such services.

* [unless you believe plaintiff is not entitled to recover by reason of Instruction Number _____ (*here insert number of affirmative defense instruction*)].

Notes on Use (1969 New)

* Add if affirmative defense is submitted.

Committee Comment (1969 New)

See General Comment at MAI 28.00.

Library References:

C.J.S. Executors and Administrators § 398.
West's Key No. Digests, Executors and Administrators ☞205, 451(3).

Notes of Decisions

1. In general

Instruction given by trial court in farmer's action to recover the fair value of services he performed on behalf of his neighbor was not improper for failing to inform jurors that services had to be rendered at neighbor's request. Jones v. Estate of McReynolds, 762 S.W.2d 854, 856 (Mo.App.1989).

28.04 [1969 New] Verdict Directing—Quantum Meruit Recovery Sought Where Family Relationship Is an Issue

Your verdict must be for plaintiff if you believe:

First, plaintiff furnished to (*name of decedent*) valuable services, and

Second, (*name of decedent*) accepted the benefits of such services.

* [unless you believe that plaintiff is not entitled to recover by reason of Instruction Number _____ (*here insert number of affirmative defense instruction*)].

Notes on Use (1969 New)

* Add if affirmative defense is submitted.

Committee Comment (1969 New)

Where plaintiff has no evidence of an express contract or a contract implied from the conduct of the parties he must rely on quantum meruit to recover.

Plaintiff is entitled to recover on the above facts unless some affirmative defense is shown. The existence of a family relationship is an affirmative defense. In *Muench v. South Side National Bank,* 251 S.W.2d 1, 4 (Mo.1952) the court said:

Defendant does not plead the existence of a family relationship, giving rise to the presumption that the services were gratuitous, but denies everything. Such a defense is special and affirmative, is in the nature of confession and avoidance and should have been pleaded, if it were to be relied upon.

Defendants should submit the issue by using MAI 32.16.

It is not clear whether a child may recover in quantum meruit for services furnished a parent even though the child and parent were not living in the same household when the services were rendered. See General Comment at 28.00. For this reason it may be safer for a child to sue on a contract implied in fact using the form shown at MAI 28.02.

Library References:

C.J.S. Executors and Administrators § 399.
West's Key No. Digests, Executors and Administrators ⚷206(1), 451(3).

29.00

VERDICT DIRECTING—REAL
ESTATE COMMISSION

Analysis of Instructions

Westlaw Electronic Research

See Westlaw Electronic Research Guide preceding the Table of Instructions.

Library References:

C.J.S. Trial § 350–351.
West's Key No. Digests, Trial ☞234(3, 4).

29.01   [1978 Revision] Verdict Directing—Real Estate Commission—Sale Not Consummated

Your verdict must be for plaintiff if you believe:

First, plaintiff was a licensed real estate broker, and

Second, plaintiff and defendant agreed that plaintiff should receive _____% of the sale price as commission if plaintiff produced a purchaser [1] [who was ready, willing and able] [2] to purchase [1] the property for $_____ (*plus any other terms of purchase which are in issue*), and

Third, plaintiff did produce a purchaser [1] [who was ready, willing and able] [2] to purchase [1] for such price (*and on such terms*) [3] and so informed defendant.

*[unless you believe plaintiff is not entitled to recover by reason of Instruction Number _____ (*here insert number of affirmative defense instruction*)].

Notes on Use (1978 Revision)

1. If a lessee was produced substitute the words "tenant" "rent" and "rental".

2. Submit only where sale was not completed.

3. Add this phrase if additional terms of agreement submitted in Paragraph Second.

* Add if affirmative defense is submitted.

Committee Comment (1996 Revision)

In regard to the question of whether or not the plaintiff is a licensed real estate broker, § 339.160, RSMo provides:

No person, partnership, corporation or association engaged within this state in the business or acting in the capacity of a real estate broker or real estate salesperson shall bring or maintain an action in any court in this state for the recovery of compensation for services rendered in the buying, selling, exchanging, leasing, renting or negotiating a loan upon any real estate without alleging and proving that such person, partnership, corporation, or association was a licensed real estate broker or salesperson at the time when the alleged cause of action arose.

For action by one who does not hold himself out as a real estate broker, *see Dolan v. Ramacciotti,* 462 S.W.2d 812 (Mo.1970).

See Reed Schmidt and Assoc. v. Carafiol Furniture Co., 469 S.W.2d 876 (Mo.App.1971) where a new trial was granted based upon plaintiff's failure to allege and prove that it was a licensed real estate broker, even though the question was first raised when the instructions were being considered and the issue does not appear to have been in dispute. But see *Dickey Co. v. Kanan,* 537 S.W.2d 430 (Mo.App.1976).

Paragraph Second contains the phrase "... a purchaser who was ready, willing and able to purchase ...," proof of which may properly be omitted if the seller has entered into a contract with the buyer for the sale; *Kelly v. Craigmiles,* 460 S.W.2d 577 (Mo.1970).

In *Blackburn–Ens, Inc. v. Roberts,* 379 S.W.2d 630, 633 (Mo.App. 1964) the court quoted an earlier opinion saying, "the general rule is that if a broker procures a purchaser who is ready, willing and able to buy on the seller's terms, the broker is entitled to his commission whether or not the sale is consummated." See also *Lund v. Dalton,* 384 S.W.2d 825 (Mo.App.1964).

Rule 55.08 states that payment is an affirmative defense.

Real estate contracts vary in content and lawyers must be sure to submit to the jury any additional issues which their special cases may contain. "Usually, a broker earns his commission when he produces a purchaser ready, willing and able to purchase upon the terms specified by the owner, whether the transaction be closed or not, or upon terms satisfactory to the owner. However, owners and their brokers, like others, may by their expressed contract condition liability upon prescribed events, contingencies or conditions precedent." *Tant v. Gee,* 348 Mo. 633, 154 S.W.2d 745, 747 (1941).

See also: *Sargent v. Wekenman,* 374 S.W.2d 635, 639 (Mo.App.1964) where an instruction was held erroneous because it failed to hypothesize that plaintiff produced a lessee who would take on the conditions imposed by the lessor. The court said: "... In order to recover his commission a real estate broker must show that he produced a buyer ready, willing and able to buy on the terms set by the owner or those satisfactory to him.... And the same rule applies to a broker employed to find a lessee."

Library References:

C.J.S. Brokers § 228.
West's Key No. Digests, Brokers ☜88(7).

Notes of Decisions

Modification 1
Terms of agreement 2

1. Modification

Where defendant-owner accepted customer produced by broker, MAI 29.01 was properly modified by deleting the ready-willing-and-able clause and hypothesizing that the customer had executed a contract to buy owner's land. Kelly v. Craigmiles, 460 S.W.2d 577[1] (Mo.1970).

Broker's verdict director necessarily modified in action seeking commission from a purchaser. This was not an improper deviation from an applicable MAI. Reed Schmidt & Associates, Inc., v. Carafiol Furniture Co., 469 S.W.2d 876[6] (Mo.App.1971).

Where defendant-owner improperly introduced evidence that sales contract was breached after defendant had accepted the buyer broker had produced, court properly gave a cautionary instruction that breach did not affect broker's right to commission. Kelly v. Craigmiles, 460 S.W.2d 577[2] (Mo. 1970).

2. Terms of agreement

Undisputed terms of purchase of apartment building need not have been included in instruction based on MAI 29.01 in broker's action to recover commission. Meridian Interests, Inc. v. J.A. Peterson Enterprises, Inc., 693 S.W.2d 179 (Mo.App.1985).

Where terms of agency contract were disputed, the ultimate facts of the terms should have been hypothesized. Zellmer Real Estate, Inc. v. Brooks, 559 S.W.2d 594 (Mo. App.1977).

29.02 [1978 Revision] Verdict Directing—Real Estate Commission—Sale Consummated—Agreed Commission

Your verdict must be for plaintiff if you believe:

First, plaintiff was a licensed real estate broker, and

Second, plaintiff and defendant agreed that plaintiff should receive _____ % of the sale price of defendant's property as commission if defendant's property was sold as a result of plaintiff's efforts, and

Third, defendant sold the property as a direct result of plaintiff's efforts.

* [unless you believe plaintiff is not entitled to recover by reason of Instruction Number _____ (*here insert number of affirmative defense instruction*)].

Notes on Use (1978 Revision)

* Add if affirmative defense is submitted.

This instruction is appropriate where the only issues are whether defendant hired plaintiff to sell his property and whether plaintiff was the procuring cause of the sale.

Committee Comment (1991 Revision)

In *Ingram v. Clemens*, 350 S.W.2d 823 (Mo.App.1961), defendants contended that plaintiff's verdict-directing instruction was erroneous because it failed to hypothesize that the acts of plaintiff were the procuring and inducing cause of the sale. The court said:

> The Instruction told the jury that if they found from the evidence that defendants listed their ... farm ... for sale with the plaintiff ... as their agent, and agreed with the plaintiff that if he would find a purchaser therefor, and a sale was made to said purchaser, the defendants ... would pay to the plaintiff the sum of 5% commission ...; and if the jury further found ... that plaintiff did find and did procure ... purchasers ... and that the said (purchasers) did buy ... the verdict would be for plaintiff. Id. at 824.

The instruction was held to have submitted every essential fact.

See *Reed Schmidt & Assoc. v. Carafiol Furniture Co.*, 469 S.W.2d 876 (Mo.App.1971) where a new trial was granted based upon plaintiff's failure to allege and prove that it was a licensed real estate broker, even though the question was first raised when the instructions were being considered and the issue does not appear to have been in dispute. But see *Dickey Co. v. Kanan,* 537 S.W.2d 430 (Mo.App.1976).

For a real estate commission case without a contract, see *Williams v. Enochs,* 742 S.W.2d 165 (Mo. banc 1987), where the Court recommended a modification which combined MAI 29.02 with MAI 26.05 (Quantum Meruit).

Library References:

C.J.S. Brokers § 228.
West's Key No. Digests, Brokers ☞88(7).

Notes of Decisions

Evidentiary support   1
Implied contracts   2

1. Evidentiary support

Error to give verdict director submitting alternate hypothesis for means of payment when only one had evidentiary support. Dickey Co. v. Kanan, 486 S.W.2d 33[5] (Mo. App.1972).

2. Implied contracts

MAI 29.02, addressing whether real estate broker is entitled to commission under express contract, does not apply to issue of commission under implied contract. Incentive Realty, Inc. v. Hawatmeh, 983 S.W.2d 156 (Mo.App.1998).

29.03 [1978 Revision] Verdict Directing—Real Estate Commission—Sale Consummated—No Agreed Commission

Your verdict must be for plaintiff if you believe:

First, plaintiff was a licensed real estate broker, and

Second, defendant employed plaintiff to sell defendant's property, and

Third, defendant's property was sold as a direct result of plaintiff's efforts.

* [unless you believe plaintiff is not entitled to recover by reason of Instruction Number ______ (*here insert number of affirmative defense instruction*)].

Notes on Use (1978 Revision)

* Add if affirmative defense is submitted.

Committee Comment (1978 Revision)

In *Groves Bros. & Co. v. Schell,* 379 S.W.2d 857 (Mo.App.1964) plaintiff obtained a lessee for defendant's property. No commission was agreed upon. Plaintiff's verdict-directing instruction was challenged but affirmed on appeal. The court said at page 860:

> A verdict directing instruction must hypothesize all of the elements of plaintiff's case essential for him to recover.... The instruction requires that the jury find the employment of plaintiff by defendant to lease the property, that plaintiff first solicited Mr. Lillis as a lessee and brought his name to defendant as a prospective lessee and that Mr. Lillis did lease the property from defendant. Those are the essential facts required to be found in this case.

See also *O'Neal v. Mavrakos Candy Co.,* 364 Mo. 467, 263 S.W.2d 430 (banc 1953) where the elements of recovery on quantum meruit are discussed.

See *Reed Schmidt & Assoc. v. Carafiol Furniture Co.,* 469 S.W.2d 876 (Mo.App.1971) where a new trial was granted based upon plaintiff's failure to allege and prove that it was a licensed real estate broker, even though the question was first raised when the instructions were being considered and the issue does not appear to have been in dispute. But see *Dickey Co. v. Kanan,* 537 S.W.2d 430 (Mo.App.1976).

Library References:

C.J.S. Brokers § 228.
West's Key No. Digests, Brokers ⚷88(7).

29.04 [1978 Revision] Verdict Directing—Real Estate Commission—Sale Consummated—Exclusive Right to Sell

Your verdict must be for plaintiff if you believe:

First, plaintiff was a licensed real estate broker, and

Second, plaintiff and defendant agreed that for _____ days plaintiff should have the exclusive right to sell defendant's property and that plaintiff would use reasonable efforts to sell it, and

Third, defendant agreed that if the property was sold within the exclusive sale period he would pay plaintiff _____ % of the sale price, and

Fourth, defendant's property was sold within the exclusive sale period.

* [unless you believe plaintiff is not entitled to recover by reason of Instruction Number _____ (*here insert number of affirmative defense instruction*)].

Notes on Use (1978 Revision)

* Add if affirmative defense is submitted.

Committee Comment (1978 Revision)

"In the absence of any contractual provision to the contrary, the general rule is that when the owner of real estate places it in the hands of a broker for sale he does not thereby relinquish his right to sell the property himself or through a second broker, without the first broker's aid, and without being liable to the first broker for any commission.

"A different situation exists if the right to sell granted to the broker is exclusive, or if the contract provides for the broker to be compensated regardless of who may make the sale during the term of the contract. In such event the owner would be liable to the broker for the commission specified in the contract if the sale was made either by the owner alone or through another broker." *Byers Bros. Real Estate & Ins. Agency Inc. v. Campbell,* 329 S.W.2d 393, 396 (Mo.App.1959). See also *Lund v. Dalton,* 384 S.W.2d 825 (Mo.App.1964).

See *Reed Schmidt & Assoc. v. Carafiol Furniture Co.,* 469 S.W.2d 876 (Mo.App.1971) where a new trial was granted based upon plaintiff's failure to allege and prove that it was a licensed real estate broker, even though the question was first raised when the instructions were being considered and the issue does not appear to have been in dispute. But see: *Dickey Co. v. Kanan,* 537 S.W.2d 430 (Mo.App.1976).

Library References:

C.J.S. Brokers § 228.
West's Key No. Digests, Brokers ⊙88(7).

29.05   [Withdrawn 1980] Verdict Directing—Real Estate Commission—Sale Prevented by Owner

30.00

VERDICT DIRECTING—THIRD PARTY PLAINTIFF

Analysis of Instructions

Westlaw Electronic Research

See Westlaw Electronic Research Guide preceding the Table of Instructions.

Library References:

C.J.S. Trial § 350–351.
West's Key No. Digests, Trial ⚎234(3, 4).

30.01 [1969 New] Verdict Directing—Third Party Plaintiff—Surety Against Principal

If your verdict is in favor of (*plaintiff's name*) and against (*surety*) then your verdict must also be for (*surety*) against (*principal*) for the same amount.

* [unless you believe (*surety*) is not entitled to recover by reason of Instruction Number _____ (*here insert number of affirmative defense instruction*)].

Notes on Use (1980 Revision)

* Add if affirmative defense is submitted.

In most cases the basic duty to indemnify will not be in dispute. If such a dispute exists the instruction must be modified to submit the ultimate issues in dispute.

Committee Comment (1969 New)

A number of Missouri cases have held that the surety cannot recover from the principal until the surety has paid.

Rule 52.11 authorizing impleading one who is or *may* be liable to defendant for all or part of plaintiff's claim against defendant appears to supersede the earlier view.

The federal equivalent, Federal Rule 14, has been construed to authorize such impleader actions.

In *American Surety Co. v. Morton*, 22 F.R.D. 261 (E.D.Ill.1958), the court said:

It is axiomatic that a surety is subrogated and succeeds to the right owned by the party whose obligation the surety becomes liable to pay. Therefore, it would seem that where, as here, the surety is made defendant in an action as a result of the defalcation of the party whose obligation the surety has guaranteed, that surety may properly make such party a third-party defendant to an action in which the surety is charged or is attempted to be charged for the obligation.

In *Glens Falls Indemnity Co. v. Atlantic Building Corp.*, 199 F.2d 60 (4th Cir.1952), the court said:

It is true in South Carolina and elsewhere that the right of subrogation may not be recognized unless the party asserting it has paid the debt on which the right of subrogation is based. American Surety Co. v. Hamrick Mills, 191 S.C. 362, 4 S.E.2d 308, 124 A.L.R. 1147. But this rule applies when the indemnitor brings a separate suit against the person whose action has caused the loss. Rule 14 was designed to prevent this circuity of action and to enable the rights of an indemnitee against an indemnitor and the rights of the latter against a wrongdoer to be finally settled in one and the same suit. It is generally held that it is no obstacle to a third party action that the liability, if any, of the third party defendant can be established only after that of the original defendant and after the satisfaction of the plaintiff's claim, where subrogation is the basis of the claim.

See also: Barron and Holtzoff, Federal Practice and Procedure, § 421 et seq., and Moore, Federal Practice ¶ 14.08 and ¶ 14.10.

Notes of Decisions

1. In general

MAI 27.01 [Now 30.01] properly modified as a verdict director against third-party defendant where jury found for plaintiff against defendant (third-party plaintiff). Kahn v. Prahl, 414 S.W.2d 269[1, 5] (Mo.1967).

30.02 [1969 New] Verdict Directing—Third Party Plaintiff—Master Against Servant

If your verdict is in favor of (*plaintiff's name*) and against (*master's name*) then your verdict must also be in favor of (*master's name*) against (*servant's name*) for the same amount.

* [unless you believe (*master's name*) is not entitled to recover by reason of Instruction Number _____ (*here insert number of affirmative defense instruction*)].

Notes on Use (1969 New)

* Add if affirmative defense is submitted.

This instruction may be used where master brings in servant as a third party defendant or where master and servant are sued jointly and master cross-claims against servant.

Committee Comment (1969 New)

In *State ex rel. Algiere v. Russell,* 359 Mo. 800, 223 S.W.2d 481 (banc 1949), the Court quoted with approval the following statement from the Restatement of Agency:

"Unless he has been authorized to act in the manner in which he acts, the agent who subjects his principal to liability because of a negligent or other wrongful act is himself subject to liability to the principal for the loss which results therefrom. This includes the payment of damages by the principal to the third person, . . . Thus, a servant who, while acting within the scope of his employment, negligently injures a third person, although personally liable to such person, is also subject to liability to the principal if the principal is thereby required to pay damages."

30.03 [1969 New] Verdict Directing—Third Party Plaintiff—Retailer Against Wholesaler

If your verdict is in favor of (*plaintiff's name*) and against (*defendant's name*) then your verdict must also be for (*defendant's name*) against (*third party defendant's name*) for the same amount if you believe:

First, (*third party defendant's name*) sold the (*describe the substance*) to (*defendant's name*) to be retailed by him to others who would [drink] [eat][1] it, and

Second, that (*describe the substance*) when sold by (*third party defendant's name*) to (*third party plaintiff's name*) was not fit for [human] [animal][1] consumption.

* [unless you believe (*third party plaintiff's name*) is not entitled to recover by reason of Instruction Number _____ (*here insert number of affirmative defense instruction*)].

Notes on Use (1991 Revision)

1. Select the appropriate term.

* Add if affirmative defense is submitted.

This instruction may be used where manufacturer is brought in as a third-party defendant or where retailer and manufacturer are sued as joint defendants and retailer cross-claims against manufacturer in a case brought under MAI 25.02 breach of common law implied warranty of fitness for consumption. In cases involving comparative fault, see Chapter 37.00 and MAI 4.12, 4.13 and 4.14.

31.00

VERDICT DIRECTING—MISCELLANEOUS

Analysis of Instructions

Westlaw Electronic Research

See Westlaw Electronic Research Guide preceding the Table of Instructions.

Library References:

C.J.S. Trial § 350–351.
West's Key No. Digests, Trial ☞234(3, 4).

453

31.01 [Withdrawn 1978] Verdict Directing—Negligently Furnishing Dangerous Instrumentality or Product

(MAI 31.01 was withdrawn, revised, and renumbered MAI 25.06. MAI 25.06 was withdrawn in 1990. See MAI 25.09, 25.10(A) and 25.10(B).)

31.02(1) [1997 Revision] Verdict Directing—Res Ipsa Loquitur—Pedestrian

Your verdict must be for plaintiff if you believe:

First, defendant was the driver of the automobile, and

Second, the automobile left the street and ran across the sidewalk, and

Third, from the fact of such occurrence and the reasonable inferences therefrom, such occurrence was directly caused by defendant's negligence[1], and

Fourth, as a direct result of such negligence[1], plaintiff sustained damage.

Notes On Use (1997 Revision)

1. The terms "negligent" and "negligence" must be defined. See Definitions in Chapter 11.00.

For cases where joint control is in issue, see Notes on Use under MAI 31.02(3).

Committee Comment (1997 Revision)

See Committee Comment to MAI 31.02(3) for further discussion of the doctrine of "res ipsa loquitur."

In those rare cases where a complete affirmative defense may be submissible in a res ipsa loquitur case, an affirmative defense tail such as that shown in brackets at the end of MAI 17. 01 must be added to this instruction. See *Cannamore v. Bi–State Development Agency,* 469 S.W.2d 664 (Mo.App.1971), reversed on other ground 484 S.W.2d 308 (Mo.banc 1972) and *Lawley v. Kansas City,* 516 S.W.2d 829, 835 (Mo. App.1974).

Where agency is in issue see MAI 18.01.

Where suit involves multiple causes of damage, see MAI 19.01.

Where suit is for loss of services or medical expenses of dependent see MAI 31.04.

Only in unusual circumstances is the res ipsa loquitur doctrine available in malpractice cases; Zumwalt v. Koreckij, 24 S.W.3d 166 (Mo.App.2000); and *Hasemeier v. Smith,* 361 S.W.2d 697 (Mo.banc 1962).

Library References:

C.J.S. Motor Vehicles § 530.
West's Key No. Digests, Automobiles ☞246(1).

Notes of Decisions

In general   1
Defining negligence   3
Modification   2

1. In general

Where defendant drove off the roadway, struck a culvert and then veered back onto the roadway, and struck plaintiff on wrong side of the road, plaintiff's case should have been submitted by MAI 17.13, wrong side of the road, rather than by MAI 31.02(1), res ipsa loquitur.   Dwyer v. Moss, 462 S.W.2d 645 (Mo. banc 1971).

MAI 26.02 [Now 31.02] not an unconstitutional change in rules of evidence.   Stemme v. Siedhoff, 427 S.W.2d 461[7–9] (Mo.1968).

Where passenger's case was tried on theory that bus driver negligently failed to keep a lookout for a depression, MAI 17.05 was appropriate, and it was error to submit plaintiff's case on a modified MAI 17.01–26.02(1) [Now 31.02(1)] hypothesizing driver negligently drove into the depression.   The instruction given would unduly extend the res ipsa doctrine.   Routt v. Bi–State Transit Development Agency, 423 S.W.2d 202[1, 2] (Mo.App.1967).

Error to combine general negligence (driving off road) with specific negligence (failure to keep a lookout).   Skiles v. Schlake, 421 S.W.2d 244[4] (Mo.1967).

2. Modification

Res ipsa submission proper where plaintiff ran into defendant's car after defendant left the highway, returned, and stopped in plaintiff's path.   Scott v. Club Exchange Corp., 560 S.W.2d 289[1, 6–7] (Mo.App.1977).

Proper res ipsa instruction in workman's action against city where heavy object slipped from sling affixed by other employees.   Lawley v. Kansas City, 516 S.W.2d 829[6–7] (Mo.App.1974).

Where defendant's car *skidded* off the wrong side of the highway plaintiff was entitled to a res ipsa verdict director.   Silver v. Curtis, 490 S.W.2d 412[1–2] (Mo.App.1972).

In res ipsa action by tenant against landlord for injuries from leaking hot water pipe, it was unnecessary, although harmless, to further hypothesize the elements of defendant's superior knowledge and the unlikelihood of the occurrence if defendant had used due care;   under the evidence in this case those two elements were for the court to determine, not the jury.   Niman v. Plaza House, Inc., 471 S.W.2d 207[3] (Mo. banc 1971).

Proper modification of res ipsa verdict director suggested in customer's action against beautician.   Epps v. Ragsdale, 429 S.W.2d 798[10] (Mo.App.1968).

Plaintiff passenger's verdict director submitting modified MAI 26.02(1) [Now 31.02(1)] (driving off highway).   Stemme v. Siedhoff, 427 S.W.2d 461, 463–4 (Mo.1968).

3. Defining negligence

Defining the term "negligence" used in a res ipsa verdict director was mandatory.   Cunningham v. Hayes, 463 S.W.2d 555[13–15] (Mo.App.1971).

31.02(2) [1997 Revision] Verdict Directing—Res Ipsa Loquitur—Bus Passenger

Your verdict must be for plaintiff if you believe:

First, defendant was the [driver] [operator][1] of the bus, and

Second, the bus made a sudden and unusual [stop] [swerve] [jerk] [lurch][1], and

Third, from the fact of such occurrence and the reasonable inferences therefrom, such occurrence was directly caused by defendant's negligence[2], and

Fourth, as a direct result of such negligence[2], plaintiff sustained damage.

Notes on Use (1997 Revision)

1. Select the appropriate term.

2. The terms negligent and "negligence" must be defined. See Definitions in Chapter 11.00. For cases where joint control is in issue see Notes on Use under MAI 31.02(3).

Committee Comment (1997 Revision)

See Committee Comment to MAI 31.02(3) for further discussion of the doctrine of "res ipsa loquitur."

In those rare cases where a complete affirmative defense may be submissible in a res ipsa loquitur case, an affirmative defense tail such as that shown in brackets at the end of MAI 17. 01 must be added to this-instruction. See *Cannamore v. Bi–State Development Agency,* 469 S.W.2d 664 (Mo.App.1971), reversed on other ground 484 S.W.2d 308 (Mo.banc 1972) and *Lawley v. Kansas City,* 516 S.W.2d 829, 835 (Mo. App.1974).

Where agency is in issue, see MAI 18.01.

Where suit involves multiple causes of damage, see MAI 19.01.

Where suit is for loss of services or medical expenses of dependent, see MAI 31.04.

Only in unusual circumstances is the res ipsa loquitur doctrine available in malpractice cases; Zumwalt v. Koreckij, 24 S.W.3d 166 (Mo.App.2000); and *Hasemeier v. Smith,* 361 S.W.2d 697 (Mo.banc 1962).

Library References:

C.J.S. Carriers § 586.
West's Key No. Digests, Carriers ☞321(1).

Notes of Decisions

In general 1
Conversing 5
Defining negligence 3
Evidentiary support 2
Modification 4

---

1. In general

Instruction in suit against bus company that driver "operated the bus before plaintiff was seated" was a roving commission and did not adequately describe the act of neglect on the part of the driver. Spring v. Kansas City Area Transportation Authority, 813 S.W.2d 386 (Mo.App.1991).

Plaintiff guest-passenger properly submitted res ipsa loquitur against host driver and primary negligence against road contractor. Morris v. Israel Bros., 510 S.W.2d 437[11, 12] (Mo.1974).

Error to submit on res ipsa (MAI 26.02(2) [Now 31.02(2)]) against two defendants when each is in control of a separate instrumentality. Willis v. Terminal Railroad Ass'n of St. Louis, 421 S.W.2d 220[5] (Mo.1967).

Use of MAI 26.02(2) [Now 31.02(2)], Res Ipsa Verdict Director, held mandatory; follows substantive law of McCloskey v. Koplar, 329 Mo. 527, 46 S.W.2d 557[2] (1932). (Instruction properly omits statement by court that facts warrant an inference of negligence.) Brown v. Bryan, 419 S.W.2d 62[3–5] (Mo.1967).

2. Evidentiary support

Evidence supported submission of "sudden and unusual jerk" although witnesses did not use those precise words in describing the occurrence. Dennis v. Sears, Roebuck & Co., 461 S.W.2d 325[3] (Mo.App. 1970).

3. Defining negligence

Defining the term "negligence" used in a res ipsa verdict director was mandatory. Cunningham v. Hayes, 463 S.W.2d 555[13–15] (Mo.App.1971).

4. Modification

Res ipsa loquitur properly applied in fire case where defendant had control and superior knowledge of combustible materials.

Cohen v. Archibald Plumbing & Heating Co., 555 S.W.2d 676 (Mo.App.1977).

Personal injury action for damage to ear by explosive sound from telephone properly submitted by modified MAI 31.02(2). Instrumental control properly described by phrase that defendant was "operator of the telephone system." McDowell v. Southwestern Bell Tel. Co., 546 S.W.2d 160[6] (Mo.App. 1976).

Proper res ipsa instruction in workman's action against city where heavy object slipped from sling affixed by other employees. Lawley v. Kansas City, 516 S.W.2d 829[6–7] (Mo.App.1974).

In res ipsa action by tenant against landlord for injuries from leaking hot water pipe, it was unnecessary, although harmless, to further hypothesize the elements of defendant's superior knowledge and the unlikelihood of the occurrence if defendant had used due care; under the evidence in this case those two elements were for the court to determine, not the jury. Niman v. Plaza House, Inc., 471 S.W.2d 207[3] (Mo. banc 1971).

5. Conversing

Defendant may *disjunctively* converse two elements of plaintiff's res ipsa verdict director i.e., the sudden jerk and negligent causation. Sabbath v. Marcella Cab Co., 536 S.W.2d 939[12] (Mo.App.1976).

Plaintiff's res ipsa submission required jury first to believe bus made a sudden stop *and* second, to believe such movement was the result of defendant's negligence. Defendant's converse directed a verdict if the jury did not believe both those two hypotheses. The jury could not disbelieve the first and also disbelieve the second, but the trial court improperly granted plaintiff a new trial on the ground the converse was confusing since it was not prejudicial to plaintiff. Wims v. Bi-State Development Agency, 484 S.W.2d 323[1, 2] (Mo. banc 1972).

31.02(3) [1997 Revision] Verdict Directing—Res Ipsa Loquitur—General

Your verdict must be for plaintiff if you believe:

First, defendant (*here describe defendant's control, right to control, or management of the instrumentality involved*), and

Second, (*here describe the occurrence, event or incident, which is alleged to be the type that does not ordinarily happen when those in charge use due care*), and

Third, from the fact of such occurrence and the reasonable inferences therefrom, such occurrence was directly caused by defendant's negligence [1], and

Fourth, as a direct result of such negligence[1], plaintiff sustained damage.

Notes On Use (1997 Revision)

1. The terms "negligent" and "negligence" must be defined. See Definitions in Chapter 11.00.

The res ipsa loquitur doctrine can be applicable to those in joint control, or with joint right of control (e.g. landlords and tenants or contractors doing work on landowner's property). However, these submissions will be on different factual theories. See *McGowen v. Tri-County Gas Co.*, 483 S.W.2d 1 (Mo.1972); *Barb v. F.I.E.*, 281 S.W.2d 297, 303 (Mo.1955); *Bone v. G.M.C.*, 322 S.W.2d 916, 921 (Mo.1959); *Kelly v. Laclede Real Estate & Inv. Co.*, 348 Mo. 407, 155 S.W.2d 90, 96 (1941). In such cases, the res ipsa loquitur general instruction may be used to submit the appropriate factual theory against each of the defendants in separate verdict directing instructions with Paragraph Fourth modified in accordance with MAI 19.01.

Committee Comment (1997 Revision)

In *Martin v. City of Washington*, 848 S.W.2d 487, 495 (Mo.banc 1993); the Supreme Court states:

Res ipsa loquitur is a rule of evidence that permits the jury to infer negligence without direct proof. *Frazier v. Ford Motor Co.*, 365 Mo. 62, 276 S.W.2d 95, 98 (banc 1955). The doctrine supplies circumstantial evidence of a breach when the plaintiff lacks the facts to plead the specific negligent conduct that constituted the breach. In effect, res ipsa loquitur carries the plaintiff over the breach hurdle. It can not, however, leap over the causation hurdle.

In *Cremeens v. Kree Institute of Electrolysis*, 689 S.W.2d 839, 842 (Mo.App. E.D.1985); the court of appeals held that the doctrine of res ipsa loquitur applies when (a) the instrumentality involved was under the management and control of the defendant; (b) the defendant possesses a superior knowledge or means of information as to the cause of the occurrence; and (c) the occurrence resulting in injury was such as does not ordinarily happen if those in charge use due care. In *Cremeens*, Id. at 842, the court also stated that the third element is a question of law since it is a judicial function to determine whether a certain set of circumstances does, as a matter of law, permit the inference of negligence. See also, *Epps v. Ragsdale*, 429 S.W.2d 798, 800 (Mo.App. E.D.1968).

In *Niman v. Plaza House, Inc.*, 471 S.W.2d 207, 213 (Mo.1971); the supreme court stated that the issues of defendant's superior knowledge, and that the occurrence does not usually happen in the absence of negligence, need not be submitted to the jury. The presence of two defendants does not preclude the use of res ipsa loquitur, so long as on the facts of the case the jury could reasonably find that either or both of the defendants were in control of the instrumentality, so as to make the application of res ipsa loquitur proper. *Bass v. Nooney Co.*, 646 S.W.2d 765, 768 (Mo.banc 1983).

In those rare cases where a complete affirmative defense may be submissible in a res ipsa loquitur case, an affirmative defense tail such as that shown in brackets at the end of MAI 17. 01 must be added to this instruction. See *Cannamore v. Bi–State Development Agency*, 469 S.W.2d 664 (Mo.App.1971), rev'd on other ground, 484 S.W.2d 308 (Mo.banc 1972) and *Lawley v. Kansas City*, 516 S.W.2d 829, 835 (Mo. App.1974).

Where agency is in issue, see MAI 18.01.

Where suit involves multiple causes of damage, see MAI 19.01.

Where suit is for loss of services or medical expenses of dependent, see MAI 31.04.

Only in unusual circumstances is the res ipsa loquitur doctrine available in malpractice cases; Zumwalt v. Koreckij, 24 S.W.3d 166 (Mo.App.2000); and *Hasemeier v. Smith*, 361 S.W.2d 697 (Mo.banc 1962).

Library References:

C.J.S. Negligence § 871–875.
West's Key No. Digests, Negligence ⊜1720.

Notes of Decisions

1. In general

Standard res ipsa loquitur instruction, although appropriately used for bailment actions, is not necessarily a "bailment" instruction and is properly used in negligence cases. Jungerman v. City of Raytown, 925 S.W.2d 202 (Mo.1996).

Verdict directing instruction combining MAI 31.11 (UM) with MAI 31.02(3) (Res Ipsa Loquitor) approved. Hale v. American Family Mut. Ins. Co., 927 S.W.2d 522 (Mo.App. 1996).

MAI 31.02(3), although appropriately used for bailment actions, is not necessarily a "bailment" instruction; rather, it is a general res ipsa loquitur instruction that is properly used in negligence cases with facts fitting the MAI 31.02(3) pattern. Jungerman v. City of Raytown, 925 S.W.2d 202 (Mo.1996).

Jury instruction term "occurrence" was sufficiently described where there was only one relevant, compensable event involved and occurrence referenced an automobile accident which was sufficiently described elsewhere in same instruction. Hansen v. James, 847 S.W.2d 476 (Mo.App.1992).

Instruction in negligence action arising out of incident in which parked car rolled down hill into building was not defective for failing to correctly hypothesize element of control and element of superior knowledge required for submission on res ipsa loquitur; facts hypothesized in instruction supported inference that defendant had the right to control and, in fact, did control the automobile, and other facts hypothesized in instruction described an occurrence of the type which does not ordinarily happen when those in charge use due care. Housing Auth. of City of Rolla v. Kimmel, 771 S.W.2d 932, 939 (Mo.App.1989).

MAI 31.02(3) approved and not subject to attack on the basis that it does not correctly hypothesize the elements of control or superior knowledge. Housing Authority of City of Rolla v. Kimmel, 771 S.W.2d 932 (Mo.App. 1989).

Res ipsa loquitur instruction was proper in personal injury action, even though it did not require defendant to have exclusive control of instrumentality. Johnson v. National Super Markets, Inc., 752 S.W.2d 809, 814 (Mo. App.1988).

Error to submit instruction on punitive damages, where plaintiff's general negligence claim was based upon res ipsa loquitur, which did not require jury to find any specific negligent conduct. Johnson v. National Super Markets, Inc., 710 S.W.2d 455[2] (Mo.App.1986).

Error to refuse proper res ipsa instruction and give instead a not-in-MAI lack of control instruction. Sams v. Green, 591 S.W.2d 15[4] (Mo.App.1979).

31.03   [1981 Revision] Verdict Directing—Explosives

Your verdict must be for plaintiff if you believe:

First, defendant intentionally [1] exploded (*describe explosive such as dynamite*), and

Second, as a direct result of such explosion plaintiff was damaged.

* [unless you believe plaintiff is not entitled to recover by reason of Instruction Number _____ (*here insert number of affirmative defense instruction*)].

Notes on Use (1981 Revision)

1.   Omit the word "intentionally" if this matter is not in issue.

* Add if affirmative defense is submitted.

Committee Comment (1996 Revision)

In *Summers v. Tavern Rock Sand Co.,* 315 S.W.2d 201, 203 (Mo. 1958), the court said:

> In this state "blasting is regarded as a work which one may lawfully do, providing he avoids injuring persons or property, and subject to his obligation to pay damages for any injury inflicted by his blasting." *Schaefer v. Frazier–Davis Const. Co.,* Mo.App., 125 S.W.2d 897. And in this state when damage to property is by vibration or concussion from blasting there is an invasion of the premises and liability irrespective of negligence quite as if the blasting had cast rocks or debris thereon.

See Restatement (Second) of Torts §§ 519 and 520 (1965).

Library References:

C.J.S. Explosives § 4.
West's Key No. Digests, Explosives ☞7.

Notes of Decisions

1. Intention

Where defendant's *intention* to explode dynamite was not in dispute but plaintiffs included that element in their verdict director they assumed an unnecessary, harmless burden. Donnell v. Vigus Quarries, 526 S.W.2d 314[8, 9] (Mo.App.1975).

31.04 [1991 Revision] Verdict Directing—Loss of Consortium, Loss of Services or Medical Expenses—Spouse or Child Injured—For EITHER Comparative Fault or Non–Comparative Fault Submissions

If you [find in favor of plaintiff (*name of plaintiff with primary claim*) on [his] [her] [1] claim for personal injuries] [2] [assess a percentage of fault to [any] [3] defendant] [4] and if you believe that plaintiff (*name of plaintiff with derivative claim*) sustained damage as a direct result of injury to [his] [her] [husband] [wife] [child] [1] then in your verdict you must find that plaintiff (*name of plaintiff with derivative claim*) did sustain such damage.

Notes on Use (1991 New)

1. Select appropriate word(s).
2. Use this bracketed phrase in a non-comparative fault case.
3. Insert if more than one defendant.
4. Use this bracketed phrase in a comparative fault case.

Committee Comment (1991 New)

This verdict directing instruction is for use in submitting a derivative claim for loss of consortium, loss of services or medical expenses on behalf of a spouse or a child where the derivative claim is joined in the same lawsuit with the primary claim. In such a situation, the jury determines negligence issues under the verdict directing instruction submitting the primary claim and the only additional element which needs to be decided on the derivative claim is whether the spouse (or parent) sustained damage due to injury to the injured spouse (or child).

See MAI 4.18 for the damage instruction to be used in conjunction with this instruction in a non-comparative fault case and MAI 37.08 for the damage instruction to be used with this instruction in a comparative fault case. See MAI 36.23 and MAI 37.09 for the appropriate verdict for non-comparative fault and comparative fault cases respectively.

In the rare case in which the derivative claim is tried separately (primary claim not joined), the verdict directing instruction will need all elements of negligence and damage. Thus, if MAI 17.01 is used in such a non-comparative fault case, the verdict directing instruction would read as follows:

Your verdict must be for plaintiff (*name of plaintiff with derivative claim*) if you believe:

First, defendant violated the traffic signal, and

Second, defendant was thereby negligent,[1] and

Third, as a direct result of such negligence,[1] plaintiff's [husband] [wife] [child] [2] was injured and plaintiff thereby sustained damage.

1. Where the term "negligent" or "negligence" is used, it must be defined. See Chapter 11.00.

2. Select the appropriate term.

A similar instruction, modified for a comparative fault case, should be given in a comparative fault case in which the derivative claim is tried without joinder of the primary claim. See Chapter 37.00 for the modifications necessary to submit comparative fault.

Library References:

C.J.S. Parent and Child § 137–140, 142, 151–152.
West's Key No. Digests, Husband and Wife ⊗235(3); Parent and Child ⊗7(1, 14).

Notes of Decisions

In general 1
Form of verdict 2

———

1. In general

Spouse is not entitled to judgment on claim for loss of consortium merely because injured spouse was found entitled to recover. Consortium claimant is not entitled to nominal damages. Lear v. Norfolk & Western Ry. Co., 815 S.W.2d 12 (Mo.App.1991).

The Missouri Supreme Court refused to recognize a cause of action for loss of parental consortium (consortium action by child due to injury to parent) or filial consortium (consortium action by sibling due to injury to another sibling). Powell v. American Motors Corp., 834 S.W.2d 184 (Mo. banc 1992).

In consortium damage instruction use of "thereby" as in MAI 31.04 instead of "as the direct result of such injury" as in MAI's 35.05 and 35.06 not error. Penn v. Columbia As-

phalt Co., 513 S.W.2d 679[19] (Mo.App. 1974).

In consortium case it was prejudicially erroneous to omit "thereby" from damage clause. Joly v. Wippler, 449 S.W.2d 565[2] (Mo.1970).

Where husband and wife joined in action for his injuries and her loss of consortium, it was error to submit verdict director without adding the damage-to-wife clause of MAI 26.04 [Now 31.04] (consortium damage); prejudice presumed. Robben v. Peters, 427 S.W.2d 753[1] (Mo.App.1968).

2. Form of verdict

Where there was undisputed evidence of a wife's loss of consortium and jury found for injured husband but against wife, the verdict against her was void for inconsistency. Foster v. Rosetta, 443 S.W.2d 183[4] (Mo.1969).

31.05 [1981 Revision] Verdict Directing—Eminent Domain

Your verdict must be for defendant if you believe that defendant has been damaged by either or both of the following:

1. The taking of the property [rights].[1]

2. The use[s] which plaintiff has the right to make of the property [rights] [1] taken.

* [unless you believe defendant is not entitled to recover by reason of Instruction Number _____ (*here insert number of affirmative defense instruction*)].

Notes on Use (1981 Revision)

1. Use bracketed term where easements etc., are taken rather than the fee.

This verdict directing instruction is to be used in condemnation cases where the condemning authority offers evidence that the property owner sustained no damage from the taking.

* Add if affirmative defense is submitted.

Library References:

C.J.S. Eminent Domain § 308–309.
West's Key No. Digests, Eminent Domain ☞222(1).

Notes of Decisions

1. In general

In condemnation proceeding where condemning authority acknowledged that property owners sustained some damages, instruction patterned from MAI 31.05 would be improper and was properly refused. City of Lake Ozark v. Campbell, 745 S.W.2d 799 [5] (Mo.App.1988).

MAI 26.05 [Now 31.05] improper where condemnor concedes defendant suffered some damage by the taking. State ex rel. Kansas City Power & Light Co. v. Campbell, 433 S.W.2d 606[1] (Mo.App.1968).

31.06 [1978 Revision] Verdict Directing—Will Contest

Your verdict must be that the document in issue is [the codicil to] the last will and testament of (*name of testator*) if you believe:

> First, the document was signed by (*name of testator*)[1] and declared by him to be [the codicil to] his last will and testament, and

> Second, that at the time of signing, (*name of testator*) was of sound and disposing mind and memory,[2] and

> Third, that the document was attested by at least two [competent][3] witnesses, signing their names to the document in his presence and at his request.

* [unless you believe the document in issue is not [the codicil to] the last will and testament of (*name of testator*) by reason of Instruction Number _____ (*here insert number of affirmative defense instruction*)].

Notes on Use (1978 Revision)

1. In those rare cases where testator did not sign, but directed the signing by another in his presence, substitute the words: "The document was signed by (*insert name of person who signed*) at (*name of testator*)'s direction and in his presence."

2. The phrase "sound and disposing mind and memory" must be defined. See definition in MAI 15.01.

3. The term "competent" may be omitted if the competency of the witness is not in issue.

* Add if affirmative defense is submitted.

Committee Comment (1995 Revision)

The burden is on the proponent of a will to establish "... that said instrument was executed and signed by (decedent) as and for her last will; that the signatures of the attesting witnesses were placed on such paper in her presence, and at her request or with her consent; and that at the time she executed the same she was of sound and disposing mind and memory." *Gordon v. Burris,* 153 Mo. 223, 54 S.W. 546, 548 (1899).

These issues need not be submitted to the jury unless contestants offer proof to the contrary. In *Fletcher v. Henderson,* 333 Mo. 349, 62 S.W.2d 849 (1933), the Court said:

It was therefore incumbent upon the proponents of the will in the first instance to make proof of the due execution of the will, i.e., compliance with all the requirements and formalities prescribed by statute, and that the testator was at the time of sound mind. When this was done "the weight of the evidence was against the contestant" and then it "became necessary," in order for contestants "to obtain a submission" to the jury of either, that the instrument was not duly executed or testamentary incapacity, as an issue, "to adduce some substantial evidence tending to support" such affirmation "in total default of which" the trial judge could properly direct a finding on such issue in favor of proponents.

To the same effect is *Switzer v. Switzer,* 373 S.W.2d 930 (Mo.1964), where the Court said:

Wills are solemn acts, designed to accomplish a testator's last wishes, and should be overturned only on proper and substantial evidence.

In *Pasternak v. Mashak,* 392 S.W.2d 631 (Mo.App.1965), the court said:

There is no substantial evidence in this record that the testatrix lacked testamentary capacity at the time the will was executed, and that issue should not have been submitted to the jury.

Where only a partial invalidity of a will is claimed under § 473.081, RSMo, this instruction should not be given since only the validity of part of the will is contested. In such a case, see MAI 31.21, 31.22 and 36.17(B).

Library References:

C.J.S. Wills § 468.
West's Key No. Digests, Wills ⌖329.

Notes of Decisions

In general 1
Conversing 3
Modification 4
Not in MAI 2

———

1. In general

In a will contest it was error to put burden of proof on contestant to show decedent was of unsound mind; that burden rests on proponents throughout the trial. Brug v. Manufacturers Bank & Trust Co., 461 S.W.2d 269[8] (Mo. banc 1970).

2. Not in MAI

Use of a pre-MAI definition of "sound and disposing memory" which used in the name of the testatrix instead of "a person" in the first paragraph was not prejudicial error. Arterburn v. Meadows, 451 S.W.2d 85 [1] (Mo. 1970).

3. Conversing

Since the purpose of MAI is to submit fact issues accurately and concisely, a rambling, argumentative pre-MAI-type defense instruction in a will contest was properly refused. Barnes v. Marshall, 467 S.W.2d 70 [10–11] (Mo.1971).

Contestants' wordy instruction on testamentary capacity which failed to submit ultimate issue was properly refused. Earney v. Clay, 462 S.W.2d 672[2] (Mo.1971).

Third–Method converse submitting issue of insane delusion in will contest was error when unsupported by substantial evidence. Byars v. Buckley, 461 S.W.2d 817[4] (Mo. 1970).

4. Modification

In a will contest, including the bracketed word "competent" in proponent's verdict director, unnecessary because not in issue; was harmless error. Martin v. Martin, 513 S.W.2d 756[1] (Mo.App.1974).

31.07 [1978 Revision] Verdict Directing—Amount of Damages Only Issue

Under the law, defendant is liable to plaintiff for damages in this case. Therefore, you must find the issues in favor of plaintiff and award plaintiff such sum as you believe will fairly and justly compensate plaintiff for any damages you believe he sustained [and is reasonably certain to sustain in the future][1] as a direct result of the occurrence[2] mentioned in the evidence.

Notes on Use (1996 Revision)

1. This may be added if supported by the evidence.

2. When the evidence discloses a compensable event and a non-compensable event, both of which are claimed to have caused damage, the term "occurrence" may need to be modified. See *Vest v. City National Bank & Trust Co.*, 470 S.W.2d 518 (Mo.1971). When the term "occurrence" is modified, substitute some descriptive phrase which specifically describes the compensable event or conduct. As an example, if plaintiff sustained damages in an automobile collision but also had a non-compensable illness, the instruction may be modified to read "... as a direct result of the automobile collision." Other modifications may also be appropriate.

This instruction should be used only in those rare cases where defendant is liable as a matter of law and the only issue is the amount of damages. It is not applicable where defendant claims there was no damage.

See the case of *Copeland v. Compton*, 914 S.W.2d 378 (Mo.App. S.D.1996) for a discussion of the difference between an admission of negligence and an admission of liability. This instruction is not to be used in a case where defendant concedes negligence, as opposed to admitting liability. In a case where defendant admits negligence, but disputes causation, the usual verdict director for that type of negligence action should be used, but the elements which are not disputed (negligence) should be omitted. For example, in a rear end automobile accident case wherein negligence is admitted, the verdict director would be a modified 17.16, and would read as follows:

Your verdict must be for plaintiff if you believe as a direct result of the collision mentioned in the evidence, plaintiff sustained damage.

See, *Lauber v.Buck*, 615 S.W.2d 89 (Mo.App. E.D.1981).

Notes of Decisions

In general 1
Retrial on damage only 2

————

1. In general

Where it was stipulated defendant was negligent and the only issue to be tried was the extent of plaintiff's damages, the court properly gave MAI 31.07. Booth v. Rauch, 525 S.W.2d 376 (Mo.App.1975).

2. Retrial on damage only

Where new trial was had on issue of damages only and liability and causation were no longer in issue, MAI 4.01 was inapplicable and was properly modified by deleting the opening words "If you find the issues in favor of the plaintiff, then ..." Reynolds v. Arnold, 443 S.W.2d 793[3, 4] (Mo.1969).

31.08 [1978 Revision] Verdict Directing—Life Insurance Policy

Your verdict must be for plaintiff if you believe:

First, defendant issued its policy of life insurance to (*insert name of decedent*), and

Second, the policy was in force on (*the date of death*) when (*insert name of decedent*) died, and

Third, plaintiff then was the beneficiary of the policy. [and] [1]

* [unless you believe plaintiff is not entitled to recover by reason of Instruction Number _____ (*here insert number of affirmative defense instruction*)].

Notes on Use (1978 Revision)

1. In those cases where there is an issue involving proof of a material fact which is an essential element of the plaintiff's case (for example, an issue as to whether a death resulted from accidental means when the policy covers only accidental death) a paragraph requiring a finding on such material fact must be added, e.g.,

"Fourth, the death of (*insert name of decedent*) was (*here insert policy condition, such as 'a result of accidental means'*)."

* Add if affirmative defense is submitted. For example MAI 32.24.

Library References:

West's Key No. Digests, Insurance ⇒3579.

Notes of Decisions

In general 1
Definitions 2

_____

1. In general

In action on accident insurance policy plaintiff's verdict director erroneously hypothesized.... [T]he activity engaged in by plaintiff was within the terms of the policy since that submitted a question of law. Crawford v. Mid–America Ins. Co., 488 S.W.2d 255[4] (Mo.App.1972).

In case on insurance policy the cause of damage was a factual issue and it was error to submit an hypothesis that "plaintiff sustained a loss within the terms of the policy." That was a legal question and the instruction was a roving commission. Esmar v. Zurich, Ins. Co., 485 S.W.2d 417[5] (Mo.1972).

2. Definitions

Because accidental death policy term, "to the exclusion of all other causes," has meaning in law different than it has in common parlance, its legal meaning should be defined to jury. Brock v. Firemens Fund of America Ins. Co., 637 S.W.2d 824[2, 3] (Mo. App.1982).

471

In suit on accidental death policy, the term "course of employment" as used in instruction defining "non-occupational injury" was plain and unambiguous and the jury needed no instruction to define it. Brock v. Firemens Fund of America Ins. Co., 637 S.W.2d 824[5] (Mo.App.1982).

31.09 [1978 New] Verdict Directing—Insurance Policy on Property

Your verdict must be for plaintiff if you believe:

First, defendant issued its policy to plaintiff on (*here describe property*) covering loss due to (*here describe applicable coverage, e.g., fire, collision, or windstorm*), and

Second, such property was damaged by (*here insert applicable coverage*), and

Third, the policy was in force on the date of such loss.

* [unless you believe plaintiff is not entitled to recover by reason of Instruction Number _____ (*here insert number of affirmative defense instruction*)].

Notes on Use (1978 New)

* Add if affirmative defense is submitted. For example MAI 32.24.

Library References:

West's Key No. Digests, Insurance ⊂⊃3579.

Notes of Decisions

1. In general

Insurer bears burden of proof on issue of prejudice from insured's failure to comply with policy condition such as duty to cooperate and submit to examination under oath. Nichols v. Preferred Risk Group, 44 S.W.3d 886 (Mo.App.2001).

To recover under fire insurance policy, claimant must establish (1) that insurance company issued its policy to claimant on property covering loss from fire; (2) that such property was damaged by fire; and (3) that policy was in force on date of fire. Travers v. Universal Fire & Cas. Ins. Co., 34 S.W.3d 156 (Mo.App.2000).

In referring to language used in an instruction patterned after MAI 31.09, the court held that the words "all" and "risks" need not be defined. Missouri Commercial Inv. v. Employers Mut. Cas., 680 S.W.2d 397[13] (Mo. App.1984).

Where an insured's recovery depends upon proof that he had an insurable interest, these facts must be submitted in the verdict directing instruction even though they are not specifically set out in the model MAI instruction. Glover v. Missouri Property Ins. Placement, 676 S.W.2d 66[5] (Mo.App. 1984).

In referring to language used in an instruction patterned after MAI 31.09, the court held that the words "all" and "risks" need not be defined. Missouri Commercial Inv. v. Employers Mut. Cas., 680 S.W.2d 397[13] (Mo. App.1984).

Plaintiffs' verdict director, by failing to submit to the jury the issue of ownership, patently assumed a highly controverted issue of fact permeating the entire case and for this reason was inherently prejudicial. Duncan v. Andrew County Mut. Ins. Co., 665 S.W.2d 13[2] (Mo.App.1983).

31.10 [1978 Revision] Verdict Directing—Uninsured Motor Vehicle—General Comment

Uninsured motorist insurance cases combine tort liability and contract liability into one action. The obligation of the uninsured motorist to respond in money damages is governed by tort rules and that of the insurer is governed by contract (treaty and law). Under Section 379.203, RSMo and current policy provisions, recovery can be made in uninsured motor vehicle cases only when the damages result from "bodily injury, sickness or disease, including death."

It is the function of the jury to assess the plaintiff's damages and the tort-feasor is liable for the total amount. Use MAI 4.01 or other applicable damage instruction. When the insurance company is found liable, the amount of the judgment against it is a matter of law to be determined by the court. In most instances, it will be set by the policy limits unless the verdict and judgment against the tort-feasor is less than the policy limits.

Where the suit is against the insurance company only in an uninsured motor vehicle situation, the measure of damages instruction MAI 4.11 should be used. This instruction does not assess damages against the defendant, but sets the amount of damages sustained by the plaintiff as a result of the collision. If the amount of damages is over the applicable policy limits, the court will enter judgment in the amount of the applicable policy limit. If the damages sustained by plaintiff are less than the policy limit, the court will then enter judgment in that amount.

Verdict form MAI 36.14 should be used where the insurance company is sued as the only defendant in uninsured motor vehicle situations.

The jury will assess by its general verdict the amount of damages. The court, as a matter of law, will enter judgment against the tort-feasor for the full amount.

The court will enter judgment upon the jury's verdict against the uninsured motor vehicle insurance carrier only in such amount as its liability appears as a matter of law, including questions of stacking.

Library References:

West's Key No. Digests, Insurance ⊂⇒3579.

31.11   [1996 Revision] Verdict Directing—Uninsured Motor Vehicle—Insurer Only Defendant

Your verdict must be for plaintiff if you believe:

First, (*name of operator of uninsured motor vehicle*) was the operator of an uninsured motor vehicle,[1] and

Second, (*name of operator*) violated the traffic signal,[2] and

Third, (*name of operator*) was thereby negligent,[3] and

Fourth, as a direct result of such negligence [3] plaintiff sustained damage. [and] [4]

* [unless you believe plaintiff is not entitled to recover by reason of Instruction Number _____ (*here insert number of affirmative defense instruction*)].

Notes on Use (1988 Revision)

1. The phrase "uninsured motor vehicle" must be defined. See definitions of this phrase in MAI 12.01.

2. Select appropriate specification[s] of negligence from Chapter 17.00. For submitting multiple negligent acts, use the form used in MAI 17.02.

3. The terms "negligent" and "negligence" must be defined. See definitions in Chapter 11.00.

4. In those cases where the existence of the policy is in issue, the following paragraph must be added:

"Fifth, a policy providing uninsured motorist coverage for plaintiff existed at the time of the occurrence."

Section 379.203, RSMo, requires uninsured motor vehicle coverage whether or not there was physical contact between the uninsured motor vehicle and the insured or the insured's vehicle. That statute also requires coverage although the identity of the owner or operator of such vehicle cannot be identified because the vehicle left the scene of the occurrence. In such situations, the definition of "uninsured motor vehicle" in MAI 12.01 IV must be used along with MAI 31.11, modified to read as follows:

Your verdict must be for plaintiff if you believe:

First, the operator of an uninsured motor vehicle [1] violated the traffic signal,[2] and

Second, the operator of said vehicle was thereby negligent,[3] and

Third, as a direct result of such negligence[3] plaintiff sustained damage.

* Add if affirmative defense is submitted. Do not use to submit comparative fault of the plaintiff.

Library References:

West's Key No. Digests, Insurance ⊗−3579.

Notes of Decisions

1. In general

MAI 31.11 does not make the presence or absence of "accident" an issue in uninsured motorist cases; jury is not required to find that injuries are the result of an "accident." Thornburg v. Farmers Ins. Co., 859 S.W.2d 847 (Mo.App.1993).

31.12   [1978 New] Verdict Directing—Uninsured Motor Vehicle—Insurer and Uninsured Driver Joined

If you find the issues for plaintiff under Instruction Number _____ (*here insert number of verdict directing instruction against the uninsured driver*), your verdict must be for plaintiff and against defendant (*insert name of insurance company*) if you believe (*insert name*) was the operator of an uninsured motor vehicle.[1]

* [unless you believe plaintiff is not entitled to recover by reason of Instruction Number _____ (*here insert number of affirmative defense instruction*)[2]].

Notes on Use (1978 New)

1. The phrase "uninsured motor vehicle" must be defined. See definitions of this phrase in MAI 12.01.

2. The legal right to recovery against the uninsured motor vehicle operator will have been decided. Only affirmative policy defenses should be inserted, for example, MAI 32.24.

This instruction submits against insurer when the uninsured operator is joined; the submission against the uninsured operator must be made by a 17.00 series or other applicable instruction.

* Add if affirmative defense is submitted. Do not use this bracketed phrase to submit comparative fault of the plaintiff.

Library References:

West's Key No. Digests, Insurance ☞3579.

31.13 [1996 Revision] Verdict Directing—Uninsured Motor Vehicle—Hit-and-Run Vehicle

Your verdict must be for plaintiff if you believe:

First, (select appropriate term, i.e., plaintiff or the vehicle occupied by plaintiff) was struck by a hit-and-run vehicle,[1] and

Second, the operator of the hit-and-run vehicle violated the traffic signal,[2] and

Third, the operator of the hit-and-run vehicle was thereby negligent,[3] and

Fourth, as a direct result of such negligence,[3] plaintiff sustained damage. [and][4]

* [unless you believe plaintiff is not entitled to recover by reason of Instruction Number _____ (here insert number of affirmative defense instruction).]

Notes on Use (1988 Revision)

This instruction may be given in lieu of MAI 31.11 if the policy has specific language relating to "hit-and-run" vehicle.

1. The phrase "hit-and-run vehicle" must be defined. See definition of this phrase in MAI 12.02.

2. Select the appropriate specification[s] of negligence from Chapter 17.00. For submitting multiple negligent acts, use the form shown in MAI 17.02.

3. The terms "negligent" and "negligence" must be defined. See definitions in Chapter 11.00.

4. In those cases where the existence of the policy is in issue, the following phrase must be added:

"Fifth, a policy providing uninsured motorist coverage for plaintiff existed at the time of the occurrence."

* Add if affirmative defense is submitted. Do not use to submit comparative fault of the plaintiff.

Library References:

West's Key No. Digests, Insurance ⟶3579.

31.14 [2000 Revision] Verdict Directing—Commitment for Mental Illness

Your verdict must be that respondent should be detained for treatment if you believe:

First, respondent is mentally ill,[1] and

Second, as a result of such mental illness,[1] respondent presents a substantial risk of serious physical harm to [himself] [others].[2]

Notes on Use (2000 Revision)

1. The phrases "mentally ill" and "mental illness" must be defined. See definition in MAI 16.07.

2. Select the term supported by the evidence. If both are supported by the evidence, they may be submitted in the alternative.

Committee Comment (2000 Revision)

On hearings for commitment for treatment and extensions of commitments there are three questions of fact that must be decided upon clear and convincing evidence:

1. Is the respondent mentally ill?

2. If so, as a result is he likely to harm himself or others?

3. Is there an agreeing, appropriate facility for his treatment?

When a jury is called, the jury decides only the first two questions and, if both are found in the affirmative, the court must determine in the affirmative the third question of the availability of an appropriate consenting treatment facility before it can make its order of detention. Section 632.350, RSMo.

See Section 632.005.(9), RSMo.

Library References:

C.J.S. Insane Persons § 49, 54, 59–64, 66–70.
West's Key No. Digests, Mental Health ⊙=41.

31.15 [1992 New] Verdict Directing—Inherently Dangerous Activity—Liability of Employer of Independent Contractor

Your verdict must be for plaintiff and against (*state the name of the employer of the independent contractor*) if you believe:

First [1], (*here describe the allegedly inherently dangerous activity*) was an inherently dangerous activity [2], and

Second, during such activity, (*state the name of independent contractor*) either:

failed to (*here state the special precaution the independent contractor failed to take*), or

failed to (*here insert alternative failure*), and

Third, (*state the name of independent contractor*), in one or more of the respects submitted in Paragraph Second, was thereby negligent [3], and

Fourth, such negligence [3] and the danger inherent in such activity combined to directly cause [4] damage to plaintiff.

* [unless you believe plaintiff is not entitled to recover by reason of Instruction Number _____ (*here insert number of affirmative defense instruction*)].

Notes on Use (1992 New)

1. Where there is a dispute as to whether the allegedly inherently dangerous activity is in fact called for by the nature of the work to be performed under the contract, an additional paragraph must be inserted as paragraph First and the remaining paragraphs should be renumbered. It is not clear under Missouri cases whether the "inherently dangerous activity" doctrine is formulated under Restatement of Torts or Restatement (Second) of Torts.

If Restatement of Torts applies, the additional paragraph that must be inserted as paragraph First is as follows:

"the (*here describe the allegedly inherently dangerous activity*) was reasonably necessary to the performance of the work (*state the name of independent contractor*) was hired to do, and"

If Restatement (Second) of Torts applies, the additional paragraph that must be inserted as paragraph First is as follows:

481

"the (*here describe the allegedly inherently dangerous activity*) was reasonably likely during the performance of the work by (*state the name of independent contractor*), and"

2. The term "inherently dangerous activity" must be defined. See MAI 16.08.

3. The terms "negligence" and "negligent" must be defined. See definition in Chapter 11.00.

4. Where applicable, this paragraph may be modified in accordance with MAI 19.01.

* Add if affirmative defense is submitted. This bracketed phrase should not be used to submit comparative fault. See MAI 37.01.

Committee Comment (1996 Revision)

In *Ballinger v. Gascosage Elec. Co-op.*, 788 S.W.2d 506 (Mo. banc 1990), the Court reviewed prior Missouri cases involving the "inherently dangerous activity" doctrine and set forth the elements necessary to support a claim against an employer of an independent contractor arising out of the performance of the activity by the independent contractor.

The "inherently dangerous activity" doctrine is limited in scope and the initial determination of whether the doctrine may apply to the activity in a particular case is for the court. *Nance v. Leritz*, 785 S.W.2d 790 (Mo.App.1990); *Sullivan v. St. Louis Station Associates*, 770 S.W.2d 352 (Mo.App.1989); and *Floyd v. Benson*, 753 S.W.2d 945 (Mo.App. 1988).

In *Zueck v. Oppenheimer Gateway Properties*, 809 S.W.2d 384 (Mo. banc 1991), the Court held:

"We hold that the inherently dangerous exception no longer applies to employees of independent contractors covered by workers' compensation and overrule *Mallory* v. *Louisiana Pure Ice & Supply Co.*, 320 Mo. 95, 6 S.W.2d 617 (Mo. banc 1928) and cases following *Mallory*, including *Ballinger v. Gascosage Electric Cooperative*, 788 S.W.2d 506 (Mo. banc 1990), to the extent that those cases are inconsistent with this opinion."

In *Matteuzzi v. Columbus Partnership, L.P.*, 866 S.W.2d 128 (Mo. banc 1993), the Supreme Court held that *Zueck*, supra, applies not only to the vicarious liability of the landowner, but also to a direct negligence action against the landowner by the employee of an independent contractor engaged in an inherently dangerous activity. In *State ex rel. Anheuser-Busch v. Mummert*, 887 S.W.2d 736, 738 (Mo.App. E.D.1994), the court stated:

"To summarize, an employee of an independent contractor hired by a landowner to perform an inherently dangerous activity on landowner's property has no cause of action against the landowner for injuries sustained while performing such activity under either the vicarious liability theory or the direct negligence theory where the employee was covered by workers' compensation."

See also Restatement (Second) of Torts § 416–429.

Library References:

C.J.S. Employers' Liability for Injuries to Employees § 341, 343.
West's Key No. Digests, Employers' Liability ⊷261.

31.16   [1995 Revision] Verdict Directing—Waiver of Sovereign Immunity—Dangerous Condition of Public Entity's Property—Actual or Constructive Notice

Your verdict must be for plaintiff if you believe [1]:

First, (*here describe condition that made the public entity's property dangerous, such as "there was oil on the gymnasium floor" or "the table saw was unguarded"*), and as a result the defendant's (*describe property, such as "gymnasium floor" or "table saw"*) was not reasonably safe, and

Second, defendant knew or by using ordinary care [2] could have known of this condition in time to [remedy] [warn of] [3] such condition, and

Third, defendant failed to use ordinary care [2] to [remedy] [warn of] [3] such condition, and

Fourth, as a direct result of such failure, plaintiff sustained damage.

* [unless you believe plaintiff is not entitled to recover by reason of Instruction Number _____ (here insert number of affirmative defense instruction)].

Notes on Use (1992 New)

1. Where comparative fault is submissible, modify this instruction in accordance with MAI 37.01. For submission of plaintiff's comparative fault for failure to keep a careful lookout, see MAI 32.28.

2. The phrase "ordinary care" must be defined. See definition at MAI 11.05.

3. Select one or more of these phrases. If both phrases are used, they must be submitted in the disjunctive and each must be supported by the evidence. Other submissions of negligence, such as "barricade it", "remove it", or other appropriate submission, may also be proper if supported by the facts of the case.

* Add if affirmative defense is submitted. This bracketed material should not be used to submit comparative fault. See MAI 37.01.

Committee Comment (1995 Revision)

This verdict directing instruction is for use in cases under § 537.600.1(2), RSMo, relating to a dangerous condition of property of which a public entity has actual or constructive notice. In cases in which the dangerous condition of the property is created by an employee of the public entity as described in § 537.600.1(2), see MAI 31.17.

Where suit involves multiple causes of damages, see MAI 19.01.

Where suit is for wrongful death, see MAI 20.01 and 20.02.

Where suit involves a dangerous condition on private land, see MAI 22.03.

Where suit is for loss of services or medical expenses of dependent, see MAI 31.04.

Where suit involves liability of an adjoining landowner for a dangerous condition created or enhanced by the adjoining landowner on a public sidewalk, see MAI 22.09.

The 1995 Revision to this instruction changed the phrase "should have known" to "could have known" on the issue of constructive notice. Some MAI instructions had used one of the phrases and other instructions had used the other phrase. Questions had arisen as to whether "should have known" imposed a higher burden than "could have known". See *Benton v. City of Rolla,* 872 S.W.2d 882 (Mo.App.1994), and *Burrell v. Mayfair–Lennox Hotels, Inc.,* 442 S.W.2d 47 (Mo.1969). For consistency, the Committee has opted to use the phrase "could have known" to the extent possible in the context of constructive notice. Other instructions, such as MAI 10.07, paragraph Second of MAI 22.01, MAI 22.07, and MAI 25.10(A), continue to use the phrase "should have known" because the phrase is part of a "knew or had reason to know" standard as explained in the Committee Comments to those instructions.

Library References:

C.J.S. Municipal Corporations § 868.
West's Key No. Digests, Municipal Corporations ☞822.

Notes of Decisions

In general   1
Proximate cause   2

_____

1. In general

Error in dismissing claims against city was harmless, where verdict directing instruction under MAI 31.16 given on remaining claim was practically identical to instructions under MAI 22.05 and 25.10(B) from which plaintiff would have been required to choose if other claims had not been dismissed and jury returned verdict in city's favor; under circumstances, dismissal of those claims did not affect outcome of case. Benton v. City of Rolla, 872 S.W.2d 882 (Mo.App.1994).

2. Proximate cause

Modification of MAI 31.16 from "as a direct result of such failure, plaintiff sustained damages," to "such failure directly caused or directly contributed to cause the fatal injury," was not misleading or prejudicial; change was due to comparative fault nature of wrongful death action by survivors of fatal automobile accident against Highway and

Transportation Commission (MHTC). Linton
v. Missouri Highway and Transp. Com'n, 980
S.W.2d 4 (Mo.App.1998).

31.17 [1992 New] Verdict Directing—Waiver of Sovereign Immunity—Dangerous Condition of Public Entity's Property Created by Employee

Your verdict must be for plaintiff if you believe [1]:

First, (*here describe condition that made the public entity's property dangerous, such as "there was oil on the gymnasium floor" or "the table saw was unguarded"*), and as a result the defendant's (*describe property, such as "gymnasium floor" or "table saw"*) was not reasonably safe, and

Second, such condition was created by an employee of (*name of public entity*) within the scope and course of employment [2], and

Third, the employee was thereby negligent [3], and

Fourth, as a direct result of such negligence [3], plaintiff sustained damage.

* [unless you believe plaintiff is not entitled to recovery by reason of Instruction Number _____ (*here insert number of affirmative defense instruction*)].

Notes on Use (1992 New)

1. Where comparative fault is submissible, modify this instruction in accordance with MAI 37.01. For submission of plaintiff's comparative fault for failure to keep a careful lookout, see MAI 32.28.

2. Delete the phrase "within the scope and course of employment" if not in issue. If in issue, the phrase must be defined. See Chapter 13.00 and particularly MAI 13.05, which will fit the facts of most cases.

3. The terms "negligent" and "negligence" must be defined. See definitions in Chapter 11.00.

* Add if affirmative defense is submitted. This bracketed material should not be used to submit comparative fault. See MAI 37.01.

Committee Comment (1993 Revision)

This verdict directing instruction is for use in cases under § 537.600.1(2), RSMo, relating to a dangerous condition of property created by an employee of a public entity. For cases in which the dangerous condition of property is one premised upon actual or constructive notice to the public entity as described in § 537.600.1(2), see MAI 31.16.

Where suit involves multiple causes of damages, see MAI 19.01.

Where suit is for wrongful death, see MAI 20.01 and 20.02.

Where suit involves a dangerous condition on private land, see MAI 22.03.

Where suit is for loss of services or medical expenses of a dependent, see MAI 31.04.

Where suit involves liability of an adjoining landowner for a dangerous condition created or enhanced by the adjoining landowner on a public sidewalk, see MAI 22.09.

Library References:

C.J.S. Municipal Corporations § 868.
West's Key No. Digests, Municipal Corporations ☞822.

31.18 [1994 New] Verdict Directing—Paternity Actions—No Statutory Presumption

Your verdict must be that (*state the name of the putative father*) is the natural father of (*state the name of the child*) if you believe:

First, (*state the name of the putative father*) and (*state the name of the child's natural mother*) had sexual intercourse, and

Second, that (*state the name of the child*) was conceived as a result of such sexual intercourse between (*state the name of the putative father*) and (*state the name of the mother*).

Committee Comment (1998 Revision)

This paternity verdict directing instruction is not be used to submit the statutory presumptions in section 210.822, RSMo.

The burden of proof is on the party seeking to establish paternity. See MAI 3.08. Use verdict form MAI 36.28.

For paternity actions in which a statutory presumption applies, see MAI 31.19 for the verdict directing instruction. If clear and convincing evidence rebutting the statutory presumption is presented, see MAI 31.20.

This instruction and MAI 31.19 (submitting a statutory presumption) may be submitted in the alternative in an appropriate case.

MAI 3.08, MAI 31.18, MAI 31.19, MAI 31.20, and MAI 36.28 were drafted for civil paternity actions under sections 210.817 et seq., RSMo. Effective July 1, 1997, section 210.839.4 was amended to provide that no party in such a paternity action has a right to trial by jury. The Committee has chosen not to withdraw these instructions and the related verdict form in the event that they are instructive or perhaps useful in the future since the Supreme Court has held that the Parentage Act (sections 210.817 et seq.) is not the exclusive means to determine paternity. *Matter of Nocita*, 914 S.W.2d 358 (Mo. banc 1996).

Library References:

C.J.S. Children Out-of-Wedlock § 116.
West's Key No. Digests, Children Out-of-Wedlock ⊙60.

31.19 [1994 New] Verdict Directing—Paternity Actions—Statutory Presumption

In your verdict you must find that (*state the name of putative father*) is the natural father of (*state the name of child*) if you believe (*here set out facts which give rise to the statutory presumption, such as "(name of child) was born during the marriage of (name of mother) and (name of putative father)"*) [1].

* [unless you believe that (*state the name of putative father*) is not the natural father of (*state the name of child*) by reason of Instruction Number _____ (*here insert number of rebuttal instruction*).]

Notes on Use (1994 New)

1. Insert those ultimate facts necessary to establish any of the statutory presumptions set out in § 210.822, RSMo.

* Add this bracketed phrase only if plaintiff submits a statutory presumption of paternity and defendant submits a rebuttal of that statutory presumption under MAI 31.20.

Committee Comment (1998 Revision)

This paternity verdict directing instruction is to be used to submit any of the statutory presumptions in section 210.822, RSMo. See burden of proof instruction MAI 3.08 and MAI 36.28.

If clear and convincing evidence rebutting the statutory presumption is presented, see MAI 31.20. For paternity actions not relying on a statutory presumption, see MAI 31.18.

This instruction and a verdict directing instruction based on MAI 31.18 may be submitted in the alternative in an appropriate case.

MAI 3.08, MAI 31.18, MAI 31.19, MAI 31.20, and MAI 36.28 were drafted for civil paternity actions under sections 210.817 et seq., RSMo. Effective July 1, 1997, section 210.839.4 was amended to provide that no party in such a paternity action has a right to trial by jury. The Committee has chosen not to withdraw these instructions and the related verdict form in the event that they are instructive or perhaps useful in the future since the Supreme Court has held that the Parentage Act (sections 210.817 et seq.) is not the exclusive means to determine paternity. *Matter of Nocita*, 914 S.W.2d 358 (Mo. banc 1996).

Library References:

C.J.S. Children Out-of-Wedlock § 116.
West's Key No. Digests, Children Out-of-Wedlock ⬥60.

31.20 [1994 New] Verdict Directing—Paternity Actions—Rebuttal of Statutory Presumption

In your verdict you must not find that (*state the name of putative father*) is the natural father of (*state the name of child*) if you believe (*here set out facts which rebut the presumption that defendant is the natural father, such as, "(state name of putative father) was sterile"*) [1].

Notes on Use (1994 New)

1. Here insert those facts, which must be shown by clear and convincing evidence under § 210.822.2, RSMo, that rebut the statutory presumption submitted under MAI 31.19.

Committee Comment (1998 New)

MAI 3.08, MAI 31.18, MAI 31.19, MAI 31.20, and MAI 36.28 were drafted for civil paternity actions under sections 210.817 et seq., RSMo. Effective July 1, 1997, section 210.839.4 was amended to provide that no party in such a paternity action has a right to trial by jury. The Committee has chosen not to withdraw these instructions and the related verdict form in the event that they are instructive or perhaps useful in the future since the Supreme Court has held that the Parentage Act (sections 210.817 et seq.) is not the exclusive means to determine paternity. *Matter of Nocita*, 914 S.W.2d 358 (Mo. banc 1996).

Library References:

C.J.S. Children Out-of-Wedlock § 116.
West's Key No. Digests, Children Out-of-Wedlock ⊙—60.

31.21 [1995 New] Verdict Directing—Partial Invalidity of Will Due to Fraud

In your verdict, you must find that the contested part of the last will and testament of (*name of testator*) providing for (*here insert description of the challenged provision of the will*) is not valid if you believe:

First, (*insert name of person committing fraud*) represented to (*name of testator*) that (*here state the allegedly false representation*), and

Second, such representation was false, and

Third, (*insert name of person committing fraud*) knew such representation was false, and

Fourth, such representation was intended to and did deceive (*name of testator*), and

Fifth, (*name of testator*) relied upon such representation, and

Sixth, (*name of testator*) was induced to include the contested part of the will by reason of such representation.

Notes on Use (1995 New)

This instruction will be used where the validity of part of a will is contested for fraud in accordance with § 473.081, RSMo. Where the entire will is challenged under § 473.083, RSMo, see MAI 32.17 and 32.18.

Section 473.081 provides for multiple grounds for partial invalidity of a will. See MAI 31.22 regarding partial invalidity of a will due to undue influence. Other grounds of partial invalidity set forth in § 473.081, RSMo, will require submission in accordance with developing substantive law and the method for submission demonstrated in MAI 31.21, 31.22 and 36.17(B).

Library References:

C.J.S. Wills § 468.
West's Key No. Digests, Wills ⊙―329.

31.22 [1995 New] Verdict Directing—Partial Invalidity of Will Due to Undue Influence

In your verdict, you must find that the contested part of the last will and testament of (*name of testator*) providing for (*here insert description of the challenged portion of the will*) is not valid if you believe that (*name of testator*) included the contested part of the will as a result of the undue influence[1] of (*here insert the name of the person who allegedly exerted the undue influence.*)

Notes on Use (1995 New)

1. The phrase "undue influence" must be defined. See MAI 15.03.

This instruction will be used where the validity of part of a will is contested for undue influence in accordance with § 473.081, RSMo. Where the entire will is challenged under § 473.083, RSMo, see MAI 32.17 and 32.18.

Section 473.081 provides for multiple grounds for partial invalidity of a will. See MAI 31.21 for partial invalidity of a will due to fraud. Other grounds of partial invalidity set forth in § 473.081, RSMo, will require submission in accordance with developing substantive law and the method of submission demonstrated in MAI 31.21, 31.22 and 36.17(B).

Library References:

C.J.S. Wills § 468.
West's Key No. Digests, Wills ⚖329.

493

31.23 [2000 New] Verdict Directing—Negligent Infliction of Emotional Distress

In a verdict directing instruction submitting negligent infliction of emotional distress, the essential elements are:

, such [negligence] [failure][1] involved an unreasonable risk of causing emotional distress, and

, defendant knew or by using ordinary care[2] could have known of such risk, and

, as a direct result[3] of such [negligence] [failure][1], plaintiff sustained medically diagnosable and significant emotional distress.

The above paragraphs would be substituted for the "damage" paragraph of an applicable verdict directing instruction. Thus, if verdict directing instruction 31.02(3) (*res ipsa loquitur*) were to be modified for a negligent infliction of emotional distress case to submit the case against the owner of the elevator in *Bass v. Nooney Co.*, 646 S.W.2d 765 (Mo. banc 1983), it would read as follows:

Your verdict must be for plaintiff if you believe:[4]

First, defendant owned the elevator, and

Second, the elevator stalled between floors, and

Third, from the fact of such occurrence and the reasonable inferences therefrom, such occurrence was directly caused by defendant's negligence[1],

Fourth, such negligence[1] involved an unreasonable risk of causing emotional distress, and

Fifth, defendant knew or by using ordinary care[2] could have known of this risk, and

Sixth, as a direct result[3] of such negligence, plaintiff sustained medically diagnosable and significant emotional distress.

* [unless you believe that plaintiff is not entitled to recover by reason of Instruction Number ____ (*here insert number of affirmative defense instruction*)].

Notes on Use (2000 New)

1. Select the appropriate term. The terms "negligent" and "negligence" must be defined. See definitions in Chapter 11.00.

2. The term "ordinary care" must be defined. See definitions in Chapter 11.00.

3. Where suit involves multiple causes of damage, see MAI 19.01.

4. For modification of verdict directing instructions to submit comparative fault, see MAI 37.01.

* Add if affirmative defense is submitted. This bracketed material should not be used to submit comparative fault. See MAI 37.01.

Committee Comment (2000 New)

In *Bass v. Nooney Co*, 646 S.W.2d 765, 772–73 (Mo. banc 1983), the Supreme Court of Missouri held: "Instead of the old impact rule, a plaintiff will be permitted to recover for emotional distress provided: (1) the defendant should have realized that his conduct involved an unreasonable risk of causing the distress; and (2) the emotional distress or mental injury must be medically diagnosable and must be of sufficient severity to be medically significant."

In *K.G. v. R.T.R.*, 918 S.W.2d 795 (Mo. banc 1996), the Court observed: "To plead an action for negligent infliction of emotional harm, a plaintiff must allege the duty exists, that the defendant should have realized that his conduct involved an unreasonable risk of causing emotional distress, and the distress or mental injury must be medically diagnosable and must be of sufficient severity so as to be medically significant." 918 S.W.2d at 800.

Asaro v. Cardinal Glennon Memorial Hosp., 799 S.W.2d 595, 597–98 (Mo. banc 1990), imposes a "zone of danger" requirement when the claim arises from observing an injury to a third person. The Committee takes no position as to whether, in a third-party injury case such as *Asaro,* the emotional distress must be medically diagnosable and medically significant. Compare *Jackson v. Christian Hosp.*, 823 S.W.2d 137 (Mo.App.1992), and *Sale v. Slitz*, 998 S.W.2d 159 (Mo.App.1999), relating to damages in a case involving "right of sepulchre."

See also Restatement (Second) Torts, Section 313.

Library References:

C.J.S. Negligence § 871–875.
West's Key No. Digests, Negligence ⟐1720.

32.00

AFFIRMATIVE DEFENSES

Analysis of Instructions

Westlaw Electronic Research

See Westlaw Electronic Research Guide preceding the Table of Instructions.

AFFIRMATIVE DEFENSES

Library References:

C.J.S. Assault and Battery § 51; False Imprisonment § 60; Libel and Slander, Injurious Falsehood § 181; Motor Vehicles §§ 533–550; Negligence §§ 293–300.

West's Key No. Digests, Assault and Battery ⚭43(2); Automobiles ⚭246(23–37); False Imprisonment ⚭40; Libel and Slander ⚭124(7); Negligence ⚭141(1–12).

32.01 [1991 New] Affirmative Defenses—Generally

Some of the instructions in Chapter 32 are comparative fault instructions. Contributory negligence instructions as they existed in previous editions of MAI prior to the adoption of comparative fault have been revised to conform to the method of submission in MAI 37.02. Numbering of those instructions has remained the same for purposes of historical consistency.

Other instructions in this Chapter are complete affirmative defenses.

MAI 32.07 (Contributory Negligence—FELA) has not been revised in the manner provided in MAI 37.02 because FELA is a matter of federal law. See the Committee explanation in the Committee Comments to MAI 8.01 and 8.02.

Annotations to instructions prior to the adoption of comparative fault remain in this edition.

Library References:

C.J.S. Negligence § 292.
West's Key No. Digests, Negligence ⊕141.

32.01(1)　[1991 Revision] Comparative Fault—Single Negligent Act Submitted

In your verdict you must assess a percentage of fault to plaintiff [, whether or not defendant was partly at fault,] [1] if you believe:

First, plaintiff drove at an excessive speed, and

Second, plaintiff was thereby negligent,[2] and

Third, such negligence [2] of plaintiff directly caused or directly contributed to cause any damage plaintiff may have sustained.

Notes on Use (1991 Revision)

1. This bracketed phrase may be added at defendant's option.

2. The terms "negligent" and "negligence" must be defined. See definitions in Chapter 11.00.

This sample instruction submits a single act of comparative fault. If more than one act is submitted in the disjunctive, use MAI 32.01(2). For other specifications of negligence which may be hypothesized in a comparative fault instruction, see Chapter 17.00.

See Chapter 37.00 and Illustration 35.14 with regard to comparative fault generally.

Library References:

C.J.S. Negligence § 871, 891, 900–901.
West's Key No. Digests, Negligence ⊙1746.

Notes of Decisions

In general 1
Agency 13
Amendment for dual submissions 4
Apparent danger 12
Contributory fault 8
Degree of care 7
Deviation 2
Evidentiary support 9
Knowledge 11
Modification 3
Parking 17
Proximate cause 10
Railway crossing 18
Right of way 14
Roving commission 6
Separate instructions 5
Unlighted vehicle 16
Wrong side of road 15

1. In general

It is permissible for defendant to rely on multiple defenses even though inconsistent; while plaintiff may not predicate recovery upon theory that is contrary to his own positive evidence, defendant pleading both general denial and comparative fault has right to submit comparative fault to jury even though issue contradicts some of defendant's own positive evidence. Michael v. Kowalski, 813 S.W.2d 6 (Mo.App.1991).

Error in giving a comparative fault instruction harmless where jury found no negligence on the part of defendant. Hyman v. Robinson, 713 S.W.2d 300[1, 2] (Mo.App. 1986).

Evidence must show allegedly negligent act was proximate cause of injury. Cella v. Evangelical Deaconess Society of St. Louis, 581 S.W.2d 881[2, 3] (Mo.App.1979).

Evidence supported defendant's contributory negligence instruction on (a) rearend collision, (b) failure to keep a lookout, and (c) following too closely. Pitezel v. Danielson, 571 S.W.2d 694[1–4] (Mo.App.1978).

Defendant may submit both a converse and contributory negligence. Van Dyke v. Major Tractor & Equipment Co., 557 S.W.2d 11[7, 8] (Mo.App.1977).

Contributory negligence instruction must hypothesize facts which negate an essential element of plaintiff's case. Portman v. Sinclair Oil Co., 518 S.W.2d 625 (Mo.1975).

Plaintiff need not negate contributory negligence where defendant did not submit an instruction on that defense. Lawley v. Kansas City, 516 S.W.2d 829[10] (Mo.App. 1974).

Avoidance of statute of limitation. Smile v. Lawson, 506 S.W.2d 400[4, 5] (Mo.1974).

Failure to define "ordinary care" used in contributory negligence instruction was not necessarily prejudicial. Robinett v. Kansas City Power & Light Co., 484 S.W.2d 506[2,3] (Mo.App.1972).

Defendant properly allowed to submit both a converse and affirmative defense instruction. Fehlbaum v. Newhouse Broadcasting Corp., 483 S.W.2d 664[6] (Mo.App.1972).

Failure of plaintiff's verdict director to negate defendant's given contributory negligence instruction was not error where defendant's pleading and the evidence did not warrant the giving of the contributory negligence instruction. Mulliken v. Presley, 442 S.W.2d 153[6] (Mo.App.1969).

Defendant may properly submit contributory negligence, but not *concurrent* negligence. Moore v. Quality Dairy Co., 425 S.W.2d 261[10] (Mo.App.1968).

Defendant not entitled to instruction on *concurrent* negligence of plaintiff and defendant. Harris v. Quality Dairy, 423 S.W.2d 8[1–3] (Mo.App.1967).

Defendant may submit affirmative defense or converse, or both. Jefferson v. Biggar, 416 S.W.2d 933[4] (Mo.1967).

2. Deviation

Omission of the connecting word "and" between paragraphs of a verdict director held not to be prejudicial error. Goff v. St. Luke's Hosp. of Kansas City, 753 S.W.2d 557 (Mo.banc 1988).

Omission of "for damages" from bracketed phrase not presumptively prejudicial where it was not possible that jury would confuse plaintiff's claim for damages with his claims on how the collision occurred. Griffon v. Northcott, 655 S.W.2d 883[3, 4] (Mo. App.1983).

Evidence supported defendant's contributory negligence instruction on (a) rearend collision, (b) failure to keep a lookout, and (c) following too closely. Pitezel v. Danielson, 571 S.W.2d 694[1–4] (Mo.App.1978).

Omission of "and" between numbered paragraphs was presumptively error. Kirkendall v. Townsend, 559 S.W.2d 561 (Mo. App.1977).

Deviation from paragraph Third of contributory negligence instruction by omitting the word "directly" qualifying the word "caused" was prejudicially erroneous. Meredith v. Missouri Pacific Ry. Co., 467 S.W.2d 79[4] (Mo.1971).

MAI 28.01 [Now 32.01] submitted First, failure to keep a lookout, and "Second, . . . was negligence." Error for failure to use the connecting words "in the respect submitted in paragraph First." Gousetis v. Bange, 425 S.W.2d 91[4] (Mo.1968).

3. Modification

Rear-end instruction may be used by defendant driver to submit *contributory negligence* of plaintiff-driver of following car. Mueller v. Storbakken, 583 S.W.2d 179[1–4, 7] (Mo. banc 1979).

In slip-and-fall case defendant was entitled to its own modified contributory negligence instruction on plaintiff's contributory negligence in failing to keep a careful lookout. Refusal was error, not waived by the requirement in plaintiff's verdict director that he had neither actual nor constructive knowledge of the dangerous condition. Wyatt v. Southwestern Bell Telephone Co., 573 S.W.2d 386[8, 9] (Mo.App.1978).

In slip and fall case, defendants' modified contributory negligence instruction erroneously enlarged upon the "failed to keep a careful lookout" language, was prolix and erroneous. Shackman v. Lincoln Property Co., 556 S.W.2d 50[2] (Mo.App.1977).

Pedestrian v. Motorist. Defendant's contributory negligence submitting that plaintiff negligently moved into motorist's path when she could have seen him and avoided contact approved in substance as submitting that plaintiff left a place of safety and entered a dangerous position. Anderson v. Sellers, 521 S.W.2d 33[1] (Mo.App.1975).

A modified MAI or a Not–in–MAI instruction on contributory negligence must conform to the philosophy of MAI. Holt v. Myers, 494 S.W.2d 430[10–12] (Mo.App.1973).

Where plaintiff was injured by beam falling from hoist, defendant properly modified MAI 32.01 by hypothesizing plaintiff's constructive knowledge of danger and negligence in moving from a position of safety to one of danger. Kraus v. Auxvasse Stone & Gravel Co., 444 S.W.2d 434[4] (Mo.1969).

Defendant's contributory negligence verdict director properly submitted "suddenly turned to the left [changing lanes] at a time when such movement could not be made with reasonable safety." McDaniels v. Hall, 426 S.W.2d 751[8] (Mo.App.1968).

4. Amendment for dual submissions

Plaintiff submitted both primary and humanitarian negligence; defendant's contributory negligence instruction referred to plaintiff's primary negligence instruction but erroneously failed to change "verdict" to "finding" as required by Notes on Use, which must be "religiously followed." Ronan v. Reidel, 510 S.W.2d 762[1–2] (Mo. App.1974).

5. Separate instructions

Even where plaintiff submits more than one theory of recovery against multiple defendants (e.g. strict liability and negligence), defendants are only entitled to a single comparative fault instruction against plaintiff. Under Missouri principles of comparative fault, plaintiff's negligence is not compared with that of defendant A and then again with that of defendant B, but rather it is compared with the cumulative fault of all defendants. Egelhoff v. Holt, 875 S.W.2d 543 (Mo.banc 1994).

Submission of separate contributory negligence instructions (comparative fault) by each defendant held to be erroneous, but not prejudicial under the facts of this case. Cornell v. Texaco, Inc., 712 S.W.2d 680 (Mo. banc 1986).

6. Roving commission

In bricklayer's action against employer for failure to furnish a safe place to work, a contributory negligence instruction authorized a defendant's verdict if plaintiff "knew of the conditions for work." This was a roving commission since it failed to submit what plaintiff did or failed to do that was negligent. Todd v. Watson, 501 S.W.2d 48[1–4] (Mo.1973).

Instruction hypothesizing plaintiff's contributory negligence in riding on an open truck bed without hypothesizing the surrounding circumstances was error. Ballew v. Schlotzhauer, 492 S.W.2d 774[1] (Mo.1973).

Contributory negligence instruction in quick-draw case was erroneous as a roving commission for submitting that decedent's mere act of engaging in the contest could be negligent. Turpin v. Shoemaker, 427 S.W.2d 485, 488, 491 (Mo.1968).

Contributory negligence submission that "plaintiff's conduct was negligent" did not submit the ultimate fact in issue and was condemned as a roving commission. Pollard v. General Elevator Engineering Co., 416 S.W.2d 90[5] (Mo.1967).

7. Degree of care

The Notes on Use to MAI 17.04 indicate that one or more of the specifications provided therein may be submitted as an act of contributory negligence as well, but they also provide that the phrase "highest degree of care" must be defined. The language is mandatory, not permissive, and failure to follow is presumed to be error. Kindle v. Keene, 676 S.W.2d 82[2] (Mo.App.1984).

In suit by tenant's invitee against landlord the court properly gave MAI 32.01 to present the issue of plaintiff's contributory negligence in failing to keep a careful lookout; that phrase properly imposed a duty of ordinary care. Helfrick v. Taylor, 440 S.W.2d 940[4] (Mo.1969).

8. Contributory fault

Whether contributory negligence instruction confused jury by improperly assuming controverted fact is tested by principle of "reasonable men" construction. Kewanee Oil Co. v. Remmert–Werner, Inc., 508 S.W.2d 23[2–4] (Mo.App.1974).

Unreasonable use of product with knowledge of defect is "contributory fault" and bars recovery. Keener v. Dayton Elec. Mfg. Co., 445 S.W.2d 362[4, 5] (Mo.1969).

9. Evidentiary support

It is prejudicial error to submit an instruction on contributory negligence where there is no substantial evidence to support it. The same rule applies with respect to the negligence of a plaintiff in a comparative negligence context. Finninger v. Johnson, 692 S.W.2d 390[2, 3] (Mo.App.1985).

Where defendant failed to supply the element of causation in regard to plaintiff's alleged excessive speed, submission of excessive speed as an assignment of contributory negligence was error. Roper v. Archibald, 680 S.W.2d 743[8] (Mo.App.1984).

Error to submit failure to sound a horn where only evidence was answer of witness that she did not recall hearing a horn. Baker v. Brinker, 585 S.W.2d 256[1–4] (Mo.App. 1979).

Pedestrian hit by defendant's car at highway's edge, as she fell or was pushed into highway. Contributory negligence instruction erroneously submitted plaintiff "moved" into defendant's path since there was no evidence plaintiff moved *voluntarily.* Kuhlmann v. Rowald, 549 S.W.2d 583 (Mo.App. 1977).

Contributory negligence instruction submitting defendant's multiple disjunctive acts must have evidentiary support for each. Saupe v. Kertz, 523 S.W.2d 826[4–5] (Mo. banc 1975).

Instruction hypothesizing plaintiff's contributory negligence in riding on an open truck bed without hypothesizing the surrounding circumstances was error. Ballew v. Schlotzhauer, 492 S.W.2d 774[1] (Mo.1973).

Submission of failure to swerve properly refused absent showing of available time and space. Middleman v. Complete Auto Transit, Inc., 486 S.W.2d 456[3] (Mo. banc 1972).

Where rear-ended plaintiff had adequate warning that preceding car was going to slow down and turn but suddenly braked and stopped without signalling, her contributory negligence was properly submitted by MAI 32.01–17.12. Schoessel v. Robertson, 480 S.W.2d 95[1, 2] (Mo.App.1972).

Each element of a disjunctive contributory negligence instruction must be supported by evidence. Shaffer v. Kansas City Transit, Inc., 463 S.W.2d 606[1] (Mo.App.1971).

Fact that plaintiff walked into the path of a clearly visible automobile is sufficient to support an instruction on failing to keep a careful lookout. Young v. Grotsky, 459 S.W.2d 306[5] (Mo.1970).

Evidence must show a causal connection between negligent act and injury; where plaintiff-driver knew approaching school bus was going to stop, driver improperly submitted negligence of approaching bus driver in thereafter giving another belated signal to stop. Pruneau v. Cain, 458 S.W.2d 265[1] (Mo.1970).

Sufficiency of evidentiary support for contributory negligence submission is measured by defendant's evidence and is not limited to plaintiff's evidence. Creager v. Chilson, 453 S.W.2d 941[12] (Mo.1970).

Contributory negligence instruction must have evidentiary support. Ryan v. Manheimer, 435 S.W.2d 366 (Mo.1968).

Defendant's MAI 28.01 [Now 32.01]– 17.05–17.12 (contributory negligence involving lookout and sudden stop) proper in form, but erroneous where there was no evidence that plaintiff's stop was sudden. Markle v. Fallek, 424 S.W.2d 756[1] (Mo.App.1968).

10. Proximate cause

Error to give MAI 28.01 [Now 32.01]–1711 as contributory negligence (slowing suddenly without warning) where (1) defendant was vague as to whether plaintiff's brake lights did go on, and (2) defendant was not looking and would not have seen the lights if they were on. Brassfield v. Sears, 421 S.W.2d 321[2, 4] (Mo.1967).

11. Knowledge

Contributory negligence instruction erroneously omitted element of plaintiff's knowledge and appreciation of danger. Howard v. Research Hospital & Medical Center, Inc., 563 S.W.2d 111[3] (Mo.App.1978).

Hotel guest injured in common area need not show lack of knowledge of defect (MAI 22.05, Tenant Injured, etc.), and court erred in requiring plaintiff to so show (MAI 22.03, Invitee Injured, etc.). Defendant could have submitted guest's contributory negligence under guest submission. Wilder v. Chase Resorts, Inc., 543 S.W.2d 527[1] (Mo.App. 1976).

Where plaintiff acknowledged she knew dangerous condition of step, a modified contributory negligence instruction properly omitted a requirement plaintiff knew of dangerous condition. Weisman v. Herschend Enterprises, 509 S.W.2d 32[2, 3] (Mo.1974).

In bricklayer's action against employer for failure to furnish a safe place to work, a contributory negligence instruction authorized a defendant's verdict if plaintiff "knew of the conditions for work." This was a roving commission since it failed to submit what plaintiff did or failed to do that was negligent. Todd v. Watson, 501 S.W.2d 48[1–4] (Mo.1973.)

Where plaintiff was injured by cave-in of ditch where he was working defendants' contributory negligence instruction properly hypothesized that ditch was dangerous and plaintiff had actual or constructive knowledge of danger, and plaintiff was negligent. Koirtyohann v. Washington Plumbing & Heating Co., 494 S.W.2d 665[1–3] (Mo.App. 1973).

In slip and fall case defendant properly modified MAI 32.01 to exonerate defendant if

plaintiff failed to keep a careful lookout; unnecessary to also submit plaintiff's knowledge of readily apparent danger. Fehlbaum v. Newhouse Broadcasting Corp., 483 S.W.2d 664[4] (Mo.App.1972).

When plaintiff's contributory negligence vel non depends not only on his knowledge of surrounding condition but also on his appreciation of the dangerous nature of those conditions, MAI 32.01 must be modified to submit the latter element. Koirtyohann v. Washington Plumbing & Heating Co., 471 S.W.2d 217[5, 6] (Mo.1971).

Plaintiff-invitee's actual or constructive knowledge of danger properly submitted by a not–in–MAI contributory negligence instruction. Cover v. Phillips Pipe Line Co., 454 S.W.2d 507[1–3] (Mo.1970).

Verdict-director basing liability on defendant's negligent failure to warn plaintiff was erroneous in omitting element of plaintiff's lack of knowledge of danger. Cover v. Phillips Pipe Line Co., 454 S.W.2d 507[11] (Mo. 1970).

It is contributory negligence to fly an overweight airplane only if flyer has actual or constructive knowledge of the overweight, and it is error to omit that element from a verdict director. Bledsoe v. Northside Supply & Development Co., 429 S.W.2d 727[5] (Mo.1968).

Contributory negligence instruction in slip-and-fall case erroneous for omission of a requirement that plaintiff had actual or constructive knowledge of dangerous condition. Davidson v. International Shoe Co., 427 S.W.2d 421[4, 5] (Mo.1968).

12. Apparent danger

Contributory negligence instruction erroneously omitted element of plaintiff's knowledge and appreciation of danger. Howard v. Research Hospital & Medical Center, Inc., 563 S.W.2d 111[3] (Mo.App.1978).

Where plaintiff acknowledged she knew dangerous condition of step, a modified contributory negligence instruction properly omitted a requirement plaintiff knew of dangerous condition. Weisman v. Herschend Enterprises, 509 S.W.2d 32[2, 3] (Mo.1974).

In slip and fall case defendant properly modified MAI 32.01 to exonerate defendant if plaintiff failed to keep a careful lookout; unnecessary to also submit plaintiff's knowledge of readily apparent danger. Fehlbaum v. Newhouse Broadcasting Corp., 483 S.W.2d 664[4] (Mo.App.1972).

When plaintiff's contributory negligence vel non depends not only on his knowledge of surrounding condition but also on his appreciation of the dangerous nature of those conditions, MAI 32.01 must be modified to submit the latter element. Koirtyohann v. Washington Plumbing & Heating Co., 471 S.W.2d 217[5, 6] (Mo.1971).

Plaintiff's contributory negligence properly submitted by incorporating MAI 17.04—Failure to Act After Danger Apparent—in MAI 32.01. Creager v. Chilson, 453 S.W.2d 941[12] (Mo.1970).

13. Agency

Where evidence did not show plaintiff's driver was her agent it was error to give a contributory negligence instruction. McAuliffe v. Vondera, 494 S.W.2d 692[1, 2] (Mo. App.1973).

Where wife-passenger and co-owner of car being driven by her husband was injured in a collision with defendant it was error to instruct on contributory negligence of husband since his negligence is no longer attributable to her. (Stover v. Patrick, 459 S.W.2d 393). Dickey v. Nations, 479 S.W.2d 208[3–5] (Mo.App.1972).

Where defense of contributory negligence depends on driver's being plaintiff's agent, it is error to submit a contributory negligence instruction without hypothesizing and defining agency. Sanfilippo v. Bolle, 432 S.W.2d 232[2] (Mo.1968).

14. Right of way

Pedestrian v. motorist, contributory negligence instruction need not define "place of safety" or "immediate path." Frantz v. State Farm Mutual Auto. Ins. Co., 526 S.W.2d 345[3, 5] (Mo.App.1975).

Modified MAI 28.01 [Now 32.01]–14.02 proper as a defensive failure to yield right-of-way instruction against MAI 17.01 (violation of traffic signal) where there was evidence traffic signals were not working. Jefferson v. Biggar, 416 S.W.2d 933[4–6] (Mo.1967).

In pedestrian's action against motorist, the motorist was entitled to a modified MAI 28.01 [Now 32.01(2)] on plaintiff's contributory negligence for failure to yield right-of-way contrary to city ordinance. Morris v. Duker, 414 S.W.2d 77[7–10] (Mo.1967).

Contributory negligence instruction defining right-of-way by MAI 14.05 was proper where plaintiff drove into through highway, creating an immediate hazard. Todd v. Presley, 413 S.W.2d 173[5] (Mo.1967).

15. Wrong side of road

Defendant not in error in submitting her counterclaim on MAI 32.01 (*drove* on the wrong side of the road) since it had not been amended to conform to MAI 17.13, amended (*was* on the wrong side of the road). Pittock v. Gardner, 530 S.W.2d 217[3] (Mo. banc 1975).

16. Unlighted vehicle

Defendant properly submitted that plaintiff operated an unlighted vehicle at night on the highway and was thereby contributorily negligent. (Common law negligence.) Burt v. Becker, 497 S.W.2d 411[1–2] (Mo.1973).

17. Parking

Not-in-MAI contributory negligence instruction properly submitted parking or standing on highway without lights. Stigers v. Harlow, 419 S.W.2d 41[6, 7] (Mo.1967).

18. Railway crossing

PSC Rule 43C requiring motorist to reduce speed when approaching crossing properly used in contributory negligence instruction. Silvey v. Missouri Pac. Ry. Co., 445 S.W.2d 354[8] (Mo.1969).

32.01(2) [1991 Revision] Comparative Fault—Multiple Negligent Acts Submitted

In your verdict you must assess a percentage of fault to plaintiff [, whether or not defendant was partly at fault,][1] if you believe:

First, either:

plaintiff failed to keep a careful lookout, or

plaintiff drove at an excessive speed, or

plaintiff was following the defendant's car too closely, and

Second, plaintiff, in any one or more of the respects submitted in Paragraph First, was thereby negligent,[2] and

Third, such negligence[2] of plaintiff directly caused or directly contributed to cause any damage plaintiff may have sustained.

Notes on Use (1991 Revision)

1. This bracketed phrase may be added at defendant's option.

2. The terms "negligent" and "negligence" must be defined. See definitions in Chapter 11.00.

This sample instruction submits three separate specifications of negligence in the disjunctive. If defendant submits a single specification of negligence, use MAI 32.01(1). For other specifications of negligence which may be hypothesized in a comparative fault instruction, see Chapter 17.00.

See Chapter 37.00 and illustration 35.14 with regard to comparative fault generally.

Library References:

C.J.S. Negligence § 871, 891, 900–901.
West's Key No. Digests, Negligence ⚷1746.

Notes of Decisions

In general 1
Disjunctive submission 3
Evidentiary support 4
Modification 2
Multiple defendants 5

1. In general

Plaintiff's multi-faceted contributory negligence instruction analyzed and denied. Dorrin v. Union Elec. Co., 581 S.W.2d 852[5–13] (Mo.App.1979).

Instruction submitting two grounds of contributory negligence, one of which was unpleaded, was properly refused. Zipp v. Gasen's Drug Stores, Inc., 449 S.W.2d 612[12] (Mo.1970).

Where plaintiff submitted both primary and humanitarian negligence, it was error to (1) converse plaintiff's primary verdict director and (2) give defendant's contributory negligence instruction without limiting each to plaintiff's primary negligence submission. Payton v. Bi–State Development Agency, 417 S.W.2d 522[3–6] (Mo.App.1967).

2. Modification

Verdict director should have allowed jury to find specific manner, based upon evidence, in which contributorily negligent plaintiff failed to heed warning, i.e., "failed to stop," etc.; abstract instruction gave jury roving commission. Mott v. Missouri Pacific Railroad Co., 926 S.W.2d 81 (Mo.App.1996).

When there was no evidence plaintiffs failed to give a warning signal, defendant's contributory negligence instruction, combining MAI 32.01 with modifications of MAI 17.11 (slowing without adequate warning) and MAI 17.12 (stopping without adequate warning), was erroneous for substituting the words "at a time when it was not reasonably safe to do so." Burton v. Bi–State Development Agency, 468 S.W.2d 4 (Mo.1971).

Where plaintiff was injured while disconnecting a trailer from defendant's tractor, MAI 32.01 was properly modified to submit plaintiff's contributory negligence in failing to unfasten a safety chain or telling defendant it was safe to move the tractor. Newsom v. Crockett, 453 S.W.2d 674[4] (Mo.App.1970).

3. Disjunctive submission

Erroneous inclusion of one assignment of contributory negligence in multiple disjunctive submission was prejudicial. Roper v. Archibald, 680 S.W.2d 743[9] (Mo.App. 1984).

A not-in-MAI contributory negligence instruction properly submitted, in the conjunctive, plaintiff's failure to keep a careful lookout and permitting his truck to contact an electric wire that was in plain view. Robinett v. Kansas City Power & Light Co., 484 S.W.2d 506[4, 5] (Mo.App.1972).

Affirmative defenses were not inconsistent in disjunctively submitting (1) that corporate plaintiff knew of danger and failed to warn its driver or (2) that driver knew of danger and negligently failed to avoid it. Cover v. Phillips Pipe Line Co., 454 S.W.2d 507[5] (Mo. 1970).

Defendant's contributory negligence instruction (MAI 28.01 [Now 32.01]–17.06) submitting plaintiff's failure to keep a lookout or failure to signal. Lands v. Boyster, 417 S.W.2d 942 [l.c. 944] (Mo.1967).

Contributory negligence verdict director submitting failure to keep a lookout or failure to yield right-of-way at intersection. Bauser v. Denoble, 412 S.W.2d 409[3] (Mo.1967).

4. Evidentiary support

Where defendant failed to supply the element of causation in regard to plaintiff's alleged excessive speed, submission of excessive speed as an assignment of contributory negligence was error. Roper v. Archibald, 680 S.W.2d 743[8] (Mo.App.1984).

Contributory negligence instruction submitting defendant's multiple disjunctive acts must have evidentiary support for each. Saupe v. Kertz, 523 S.W.2d 826[4–5] (Mo. banc 1975).

5. Multiple defendants

Only single comparative fault instruction should be given where there are two defendants, even if their liability is premised on different theories; plaintiff's negligence is compared to cumulative negligence of all defendants. Egelhoff v. Holt, 875 S.W.2d 543 (Mo. banc 1994).

32.01(3) [1991 Revision] Comparative Fault—Wrongful Death

In your verdict you must assess a percentage of fault to decedent [, whether or not defendant was partly at fault,][1] if you believe:

First, either:

decedent failed to keep a careful lookout, or

decedent drove at an excessive speed, or

decedent was following the defendant's car too closely, and

Second, decedent, in any one or more of the respects submitted in Paragraph First, was thereby negligent,[2] and

Third, such negligence[2] of decedent directly caused or directly contributed to cause the death of decedent.

Notes on Use (1991 Revision)

1. This bracketed phrase may be added at defendant's option.

2. The terms "negligent" and "negligence" must be defined. See definitions in Chapter 11.00.

This instruction is for use in a wrongful death case. It submits the conduct of the decedent as the basis for comparative negligence and requires that the negligence directly cause or directly contribute to cause the death.

This sample instruction submits three separate specifications of negligence in the disjunctive. If defendant submits a single specification of negligence, modify Paragraph Second to use the format of Paragraph Second of MAI 32.01(1). For other specifications of negligence which may be hypothesized in a comparative fault instruction, see Chapter 17.00.

See Chapter 37.00 and illustration 35.14 with regard to comparative fault generally.

Library References:

C.J.S. Motor Vehicles § 530.
West's Key No. Digests, Automobiles ☞246.

32.02 [1991 Revision] Comparative Fault—Guest Passenger—Failure to Warn Driver of Known Dangers

In your verdict you must assess a percentage of fault to plaintiff [, whether or not defendant was partly at fault,][1] if you believe:

First, plaintiff knew that he was in immediate danger, and

Second, plaintiff thereafter had time to warn (*name of driver*) and failed to do so, and

Third, plaintiff was thereby negligent,[2] and

Fourth, such negligence[2] directly caused or directly contributed to cause any damage plaintiff may have sustained.

Notes on Use (1991 Revision)

1. This bracketed phrase may be added at defendant's option.

2. The terms "negligent" and "negligence" must be defined. See definitions in Chapter 11.00.

Caution: The standard of care applied to a passenger is only ordinary care, *Happy v. Blanton,* 303 S.W.2d 633, 639 (Mo.1957), while drivers are required to use the highest degree of care. Lawyers must be careful to avoid an accidental misdirection when two completely different definitions of negligence apply in a single case. See MAI 11.08 submitting separate standards of care in a single instruction.

See Chapter 37.00 and Illustration 35.14 with regard to comparative fault generally.

Committee Comment (1969 New)

Caution: This instruction applies in a very limited area. It will be error to give it unless the evidence clearly supports its submission. In *Heifner v. Sparks,* 392 S.W.2d 1, 4 (Mo.App.1965) the court said:

It is common knowledge that passengers do largely rely upon the driver who has the exclusive control of a motor vehicle and under ordinary circumstances have the right so to do. As was said in Ketcham v. Thomas, 283 S.W.2d 642, 645: "In the absence of visible lack of caution of the driver or known imminence of danger, a guest may ordinarily rely upon a driver who has exclusive control of the vehicle, Toburen v. Carter, supra, 273 S.W.2d 161 at page 164, and it is a matter of common knowledge that under ordinary circumstances such occupants do largely rely upon the driver, who has the exclusive control and management of the vehicle, and who is exercising the required degree of care. . . . "

In *Happy v. Blanton,* 303 S.W.2d 633, 638 (Mo.1957) the Missouri Supreme Court held that it was error to instruct the jury that the passenger could not entrust herself to the driver and authorized the jury to find that failure of the passenger to keep a lookout and warn was negligent. The court said:

> The giving of this instruction was error. It requires that in the exercise of ordinary care, plaintiff, as a guest passenger, had to maintain a lookout and warn the driver of the automobile in which she was riding of dangerous situations she could have seen if she had maintained a lookout even though the driver of the automobile had been exercising the highest degree of care and plaintiff had no reason to believe he would not continue to do so. This is not a correct statement of the legal duty of a guest passenger in an automobile. Only mischief and confusion could result from a requirement that in the exercise of ordinary care every guest passenger must at all times be a "back seat driver."

This language has been quoted with approval in *Cunningham v. Pulver,* 327 S.W.2d 227 (Mo.1959); *Brooks v. Mock,* 330 S.W.2d 759 (Mo.1959); *Lamfers v. Licklider,* 332 S.W.2d 882 (Mo.1960); *Stone v. Engler,* 349 S.W.2d 38 (Mo.1961).

Library References:

C.J.S. Motor Vehicles § 530.
West's Key No. Digests, Automobiles ⚖246.

Notes of Decisions

In general 1
Modification 2

———

1. In general

Driver's not-in-MAI submission of passenger's contributory negligence in failing to request driver to reduce speed properly defined passenger's negligence as failure to use ordinary care. Underwood v. Crosby, 447 S.W.2d 566[5] (Mo. banc 1969).

2. Modification

MAI 32.03 modified to fit non-automotive case. George v. Gross and Janes Co., 634 S.W.2d 579[1] (Mo.App.1982).

32.03 [1991 Revision] Comparative Fault—Guest Passenger—Failure to Warn Driver of Dangers Which Were "Reasonably Apparent"

In your verdict you must assess a percentage of fault to plaintiff [, whether or not defendant was partly at fault,] [1] if you believe:

First, plaintiff knew facts from which it was reasonably apparent that he was in immediate danger, and

Second, plaintiff had time to warn (*name of driver*) and failed to do so, and

Third, plaintiff was thereby negligent,[2] and

Fourth, such negligence [2] directly caused or directly contributed to cause any damage plaintiff may have sustained.

Notes on Use (1991 Revision)

1. This bracketed phrase may be added at defendant's option.

2. The terms "negligent" and "negligence" must be defined. See definitions in Chapter 11.00.

See Notes on Use for MAI 32.02 regarding the appropriate standard of care.

See Chapter 37 and Illustration 35.14 with regard to comparative fault generally.

Committee Comment (1969 New)

In *Toburen v. Carter,* 273 S.W.2d 161, 164 (Mo.1954) and in other cases, the Missouri Supreme Court has talked about the passenger's duty to warn of dangers which are "known" and also those dangers which are "reasonably manifest."

In *Happy v. Blanton,* 303 S.W.2d 633, 638 (Mo.1957) the Supreme Court held that a passenger has no duty to keep a lookout. "Reasonably manifest" is therefore something other than that which could have been discovered had the passenger been looking. The Committee concluded that the term "reasonably manifest" was intended to apply to a passenger who was looking but who negligently failed to appreciate and warn of the danger of the condition seen. The Committee substituted the term "reasonably apparent" because it is more apt to be understood by lay jurors.

511

See also Committee Comment following MAI 32.02.

Library References:

C.J.S. Motor Vehicles § 530.
West's Key No. Digests, Automobiles ☞246.

Notes of Decisions

1. In general

Instruction submitting plaintiff-passenger's contributory negligence in failing to warn defendant-driver of impending danger. Worley v. Tucker Nevils, Inc., 503 S.W.2d 417[3] (Mo. banc 1973).

In an instruction submitting plaintiff guest-passenger's contributory negligence by failing to warn driver, it was error to submit

constructive knowledge of danger. Denny v. Mathieu, 452 S.W.2d 114[5] (Mo. banc 1970).

Driver's not-in-MAI submission of passenger's contributory negligence in failing to request driver to reduce speed properly defined passenger's negligence as failure to use ordinary care. Underwood v. Crosby, 447 S.W.2d 566[5] (Mo. banc 1969).

32.04 [1991 Revision] Comparative Fault—Guest Passenger—Interfering With Driver

In your verdict you must assess a percentage of fault to plaintiff [, whether or not defendant was partly at fault,] [1] if you believe:

First, plaintiff (*here insert act which was interference, such as, "diverted the attention of the driver"*), and

Second, plaintiff was thereby negligent,[2] and

Third, such negligence [2] directly caused or directly contributed to cause any damage plaintiff may have sustained.

Notes on Use (1991 Revision)

1. This bracketed phrase may be added at defendant's option.

2. The terms "negligent" and "negligence" must be defined. See definitions in Chapter 11.00.

See Notes on Use for MAI 32.02 regarding the appropriate standard of care.

See Chapter 37.00 and Illustration 35.14 with regard to comparative fault generally.

Committee Comment (1969 New)

See Committee Comment following MAI 32.02 and particularly the *Caution* therein.

See also *Swinger v. Bell,* 373 S.W.2d 30 (Mo.1963) where passenger allegedly diverted driver's attention and *La Fata v. Busalaki,* 291 S.W.2d 151 (Mo.1956) where plaintiff sat so close to the driver as to impair driver's ability to steer the car.

Library References:

C.J.S. Motor Vehicles § 533, 543.
West's Key No. Digests, Automobiles ☞246(36).

32.05 [1991 Revision] Comparative Fault—Guest Passenger—Riding With Intoxicated Driver

In your verdict, you must assess a percentage of fault to plaintiff [, whether or not defendant was partly at fault,] [1] if you believe:

First, at the time plaintiff [entered] [remained in] [2] defendant's automobile, the defendant was intoxicated to the extent that defendant's driving ability was impaired, and

Second, plaintiff [entered] [remained in] [2] defendant's automobile knowing that defendant was in such an intoxicated condition, and

Third, plaintiff was thereby negligent,[3] and

Fourth, such negligence [3] and the impaired driving ability of defendant directly caused or directly contributed to cause any damage plaintiff may have sustained.

Notes on Use (1991 Revision)

1. This bracketed phrase may be added at defendant's option.

2. Select appropriate term or phrase.

3. The terms "negligent" and "negligence" must be defined. See definitions in Chapter 11.00.

See Notes on Use for MAI 32.02 regarding the appropriate standard of care.

See Chapter 37.00 and Illustration 35.14 with regard to comparative fault generally.

Library References:

C.J.S. Motor Vehicles § 533, 543.
West's Key No. Digests, Automobiles ⟐246(36).

Notes of Decisions

1. Modification

MAI 32.05, modified for submission of plaintiff's contributory negligence in riding in a car when he knew the driver intended to drive at an excessive speed, was erroneous in failing to submit defendant did in fact drive at excessive speed. Waters v. Storms, 501 S.W.2d 42[2] (Mo.1973).

32.06 [1991 Revision] Comparative Fault—Malpractice

In your verdict you must assess a percentage of fault to plaintiff [, whether or not defendant was partly at fault,] [1] if you believe:

First, plaintiff (*here set out act of contributory negligence complained of, such as, "failed to inform defendant of her allergy to penicillin"*), and

Second, plaintiff was thereby negligent,[2] and

Third, such negligence [2] of plaintiff directly caused or directly contributed to cause any damage plaintiff may have sustained.

Notes on Use (1991 Revision)

1. This bracketed phrase may be added at defendant's option.

2. The terms "negligent" and "negligence" must be defined. See definitions in Chapter 11.00.

See Chapter 21.00 for instructions in actions against health care providers.

Committee Comment (1996 Revision)

Caution: This instruction should not be used where the patient's negligent acts merely aggravate the damages. In *Sanderson v. Holland,* 39 Mo.App. 233 (1889), the court said: "While then it is a good defense, in an action for negligence, that the negligence of the plaintiff, *at the time of the injury,* contributed to produce the injury, yet 'it is no answer to an action, that the injured party, subsequent to the injury, was guilty of negligence which aggravated it. The negligence that will constitute a defense must have concurred in *producing* the injury.' "

See also: *Steele v. Woods,* 327 S.W.2d 187 (Mo.1959), and Van Vacter v. Hierholzer, 865 S.W.2d 355 (Mo.App. W.D.1993).

Library References:

C.J.S. Physicians, Surgeons, and other Health-Care Providers § 97–100, 124.
West's Key No. Digests, Physicians and Surgeons ⚖18.100.

Notes of Decisions

In general 1
Modification 2

———

1. In general

Principle of comparative fault in failure of patient to follow physician instructions should also apply to failure to follow hospital nurse's instructions; however, hospital's requested instruction concerning patient's failure to turn over to allow nurse to check his condition and to check a heating pad was properly refused in action involving burns from the heating pad where hospital offered no evidence that patient could turn and it was not shown whether patient had already been burned by the heating pad by the time of the nurse's request. Hackathorn v. Lester E. Cox Medical Center, 824 S.W.2d 472 (Mo. App.1992).

Evidence in medical malpractice action did not justify physician's affirmative converse instruction, which effectively required the jury to find for the physician if it believed the patient had failed to tell physician about left-sided symptoms prior to her stroke; affirmative converse instruction must be supported by independent evidence and the facts submitted must be sufficient in law to defeat plaintiff's claim; facts that merely relate to negligence or possible comparative fault on the part of the plaintiff do not amount to matters to be submitted as an affirmative converse instruction. Hiller v. Diestelhorst, 820 S.W.2d 522 (Mo.App.1991).

2. Modification

In malpractice action for damages to real estate, rather than personal injuries, defendant properly modified MAI 32.06 by deleting the words "injuries and" from the Paragraph Third clause reading "... the injuries and damages plaintiff may have sustained." Siteman v. Woodward–Clyde & Associates, Inc., et al., 503 S.W.2d 141[1–3] (Mo.App. 1973).

32.07 [Withdrawn 1996] Affirmative Defenses—Contributory Negligence—F.E.L.A.

(This instruction and its Notes on Use are withdrawn. See MAI 32.07(A) for submission of the affirmative defense of mitigation of damages in an F.E.L.A. case and MAI 32.07(B) for submission of the affirmative defense of contributory negligence in an F.E.L.A. case.)

Library References:

C.J.S. Employers' Liability for Injuries to Employees § 341, 343.
West's Key No. Digests, Employers' Liability ⊕261.

32.07(A) [1996 New]—Affirmative Defenses—Failure to Mitigate Damages—F.E.L.A.

If you find in favor of plaintiff, you must find that plaintiff failed to mitigate damages if you believe:

First, plaintiff (insert act sufficient to constitute failure to mitigate, such as "failed to return to work"), and

Second, plaintiff thereby failed to use ordinary care[1], and[2]

Third, plaintiff thereby sustained damage which would not have occurred otherwise.

Notes on Use (1996 New)

1. The term "ordinary care" must be defined. See definitions in Chapter 11.00.

2. If more than one specification of failure to mitigate damages is appropriately submitted, modify Paragraph First to submit such specifications in the disjunctive and modify Paragraph Second to read:

"Second, plaintiff, in one or more of the respects submitted in Paragraph First, thereby failed to use ordinary care, and"

Committee Comment (1996 New)

Federal substantive law governs F.E.L.A. cases adjudicated in State Court. *St. Louis Southwestern Ry. Co. v. Dickerson*, 470 U.S. 409, 411, 105 S.Ct. 1347, 1348, 84 L.Ed.2d 303, 306 (1985). Under federal law, plaintiff's failure to mitigate damages is an affirmative defense which must be pleaded and proved by defendant, and defendant is entitled to a separate instruction on mitigation of damages if supported by substantial evidence. *Kauzlarich v. Atchison, Topeka, and Santa Fe Ry. Co.*, 910 S.W.2d 254 (Mo. banc 1995).

See MAI 8.02 for appropriate modification of the damage instruction in an F.E.L.A. case in which failure to mitigate damages is submissible.

Library References:

C.J.S. Employers' Liability for Injuries to Employees § 341, 343.
West's Key No. Digests, Employers' Liability ⚖261.

32.07(B) [1996 Revision]—Affirmative Defenses— Contributory Negligence—F.E.L.A.

You must find plaintiff contributorily negligent if you believe:

First, plaintiff (characterize the act of negligence, such as "failed to keep a lookout for oncoming trains"), and

Second, plaintiff was thereby negligent,[1] and[2]

Third, such negligence[1] of plaintiff directly contributed to cause his injury.

Notes on Use (1996 New)

1. The terms "negligent" and "negligence" must be defined. See definitions in Chapter 11.00.

2. If more that one specification of negligence is submitted, modify Paragraph First to submit such specifications in the disjunctive and modify Paragraph Second to read:

"Second, plaintiff, in any one or more of the respects submitted in Paragraph First, was thereby negligent, and"

If contributory negligence is submitted, see MAI 8.01 and 8.02 for appropriate modification of the damage instruction in an F.E.L.A. case.

Committee Comment (1996 New)

This instruction is the same as prior MAI 32.07.

Library References:

C.J.S. Employers' Liability for Injuries to Employees § 341, 343.
West's Key No. Digests, Employers' Liability ☞261.

32.08 [1969 New] Affirmative Defenses—Battery Actions—Consent

Your verdict must be for defendant if you believe that plaintiff, by words or conduct, consented to the acts of defendant and the reasonable consequences thereof.

Committee Comment (1969 New)

See Restatement (Second) of Torts § 13 Comments g and h; § 18 Comment g; § 49 to § 60; § 69 (1965).

"It is well settled law that if a man voluntarily enters a fight, not in self defense, and gets the worst of it, he cannot recover damages, unless the beating given him by defendant was excessive or unreasonable." *Mitchell v. United Railways Co.,* 125 Mo.App. 1, 102 S.W. 661, 664 (1907). Compare: *Jones v. Gale,* 22 Mo.App. 637 (Mo.App.1886).

The courts of the United States are divided on the question of whether one who consents to a fight may recover. The Missouri Supreme Court has not yet spoken. See Note, 3 Mo.L.Rev. 44 (1938).

Library References:

C.J.S. Assault and Battery § 51.
West's Key No. Digests, Assault and Battery ☞43(2).

32.09 [1969 New] Affirmative Defenses—Battery Actions—Ejecting Trespasser

Your verdict must be for defendant if you believe:

First, plaintiff [was] [1] [remained] [2] on defendant's premises without permission, and

Second, defendant by (*here insert defensive measures such as "striking" "shoving"*) plaintiff, used only such force as was reasonable and necessary to remove plaintiff from the premises.

Notes on Use (1969 New)

1. This term should be used where plaintiff improperly entered defendant's premises.

2. This term should be used where plaintiff lawfully entered defendant's premises but declined to leave when requested to do so.

Committee Comment (1969 New)

Whether the trespasser was requested to leave before being forcibly ejected goes to the issue of what was reasonable and necessary and therefore is not set out as a separate element.

See Restatement (Second) of Torts §§ 77–83 (1965).

See *Hartman v. Hoernle,* 201 S.W. 911 (Mo.App.1918); *Robbs v. Missouri Pac. Ry. Co.,* 210 Mo.App. 429, 242 S.W. 155 (1922); *Cunningham v. Reagan,* 273 S.W.2d 174 (Mo.1954).

Library References:

C.J.S. Assault and Battery § 51.
West's Key No. Digests, Assault and Battery ☞43(2).

Notes of Decisions

In general 1
Definition 2

———

1. In general

Commercial vehicle inspector at state truck weighing station had authority to request truck driver to leave the scale house and had right to use reasonable force to cause driver to leave when driver refused to do so, and thus, jury instruction to that effect was permissible in driver's action alleging intentional striking and shoving. Billings v. Stanley, 759 S.W.2d 277, 279 (Mo.App. 1988).

2. Definition

The "necessary means" to effect an arrest need not be defined. Davis v. Moore, 553 S.W.2d 559[1, 2] (Mo.App.1977).

32.10   [1969 New] Affirmative Defenses—Battery Actions—Resisting Invasion of Property

Your verdict must be for defendant if you believe:

First, plaintiff attempted to (*here describe unlawful act such as "enter defendant's home" or "take defendant's property"*) when he had no right to do so, and

Second, defendant (*here describe defensive measures such as "struck plaintiff"*) for the purpose of resisting plaintiff's attempt, and

Third, defendant used only such force as was reasonable and necessary to prevent plaintiff from (*here repeat act described in Paragraph First*).

Committee Comment (1969 New)

Restatement (Second) of Torts § 77 (1965) says that the right to commit a battery in defense of property is conditioned upon defender's:

1.   Reasonable belief that the intrusion can be prevented only by force.

2.   Use of only reasonable force to protect the intrusion.

3.   First making a request to the intruder to leave unless such a request is impractical.

It is the Committee's view that all three elements bear on the issue of the reasonableness of defender's action and therefore should be combined under the phrase "... used only such force as was reasonable and necessary ...."

In *Hartman v. Hoernle,* 201 S.W. 911, 912 (Mo.App.1918), the court said: "... there can be no doubt that while defendant was entitled to resist the trespass upon his land, and the taking of his melons, he was not warranted in using more force than was necessary to eject the trespassers or to protect his property, and particularly not justified in unnecessarily assaulting plaintiff with a deadly weapon."

See also *Morgan v. Durfee,* 69 Mo. 469 (1879); Restatement (Second) of Torts §§ 77–82 (1965); 25 A.L.R. 537.

Library References:

C.J.S. Assault and Battery § 51.
West's Key No. Digests, Assault and Battery ☞43(2).

32.11 [1998 Revision] Affirmative Defenses—Battery Actions—Self-Defense

Your verdict must be for defendant if you believe:

First, defendant had reasonable cause to apprehend and did apprehend [great bodily harm from plaintiff] [bodily harm from plaintiff] [offensive contact from plaintiff][1] (*if to some other person such as defendant's wife, insert "to defendant's wife"*), and

Second, defendant did not create the situation that caused [his] [her] apprehension, and

Third, the (*describe act of defendant, such as "striking of plaintiff"*), was in defense against this apprehended [great bodily harm] [bodily harm] [offensive contact][1] and

Fourth, defendant used only such force as was reasonable and necessary.

Notes on Use (1981 Revision)

1. Select the phrase appropriate to the force used.

Committee Comment (1981 Revision)

Self-defense must be affirmatively pleaded or it is waived. *Atchison v. Procise,* 24 S.W.2d 187 (Mo.App.1930).

"The law does not permit a person voluntarily to seek or invite a combat, or to put himself in the way of being assaulted, so that when hard pressed he may have a pretext for injuring his assailant ... if the necessity for defending himself was of defendant's own creation, it did not operate to excuse him. The self-defense instructions given on his behalf should have been qualified accordingly." *Lehman v. Lambert,* 329 Mo. 1147, 49 S.W.2d 65, 68 (1932).

See also *Lawrence v. Womack,* 23 S.W.2d 190 (Mo.App.1930); *O'Shea v. Opp,* 341 Mo. 1042, 111 S.W.2d 40 (1937); *Duncan v. Moore,* 219 Mo.App. 374, 271 S.W. 847 (1925).

The defendant party must have "reasonable cause" for believing he is in danger. *Daggs v. St. Louis–S.F. Ry. Co.,* 326 Mo. 555, 31 S.W.2d 769 (1930), appeal following rehearing, 51 S.W.2d 164 (Mo.App.1932).

The act of self-defense must be commensurate with the apprehension of harm. See *Martin v. Yeoham,* 419 S.W.2d 937 (Mo.App.1967).

See generally Restatement (Second) of Torts §§ 63–71 (1965). As to protection of third parties see § 76.

Library References:

C.J.S. Assault and Battery § 51.
West's Key No. Digests, Assault and Battery ⚓43(2).

Notes of Decisions

1. Modification

Where defendant *shot* plaintiff, Paragraph First of his self-defense instruction should be modified to require a finding defendant believed he was in imminent danger of death or great bodily harm. Martin v. Yeoham, 419 S.W.2d 937[12] (Mo.App.1967).

32.12 [1969 New] Affirmative Defenses—Libel and Slander—Truth

Your verdict must be for defendant if you believe that the statement (*here repeat statement contained in plaintiff's verdict directing instruction*) was substantially true.

Committee Comment (1988 Revision)

Mo.Const. Art. I, section 8, states: "... in all suits and prosecutions for libel or slander the truth thereof may be given in evidence; and in suits and prosecutions for libel the jury, under the direction of the court, shall determine the law and the facts."

In *Kleinschmidt v. Johnson*, 183 S.W.2d 82, 86 (Mo.1944), the court said: "The [trial] court instructed the jury to find for the defendants if, inter alia, 'you find from the evidence that the article, in substance, was true, ...' It was not necessary that the precise facts stated in the alleged defamatory article should be found to be literally true. Slight inaccuracies of expression are immaterial if the defamatory charge is true in substance.... The term 'in substance' is not such as would require a definition."

See verdict directing instructions at MAI 23.06(1) and MAI 23.10(1).

Library References:

C.J.S. Libel and Slander; Injurious Falsehood § 181.
West's Key No. Digests, Libel and Slander ⊜124(7).

Notes of Decisions

1. In general

Disparate testimony re truth of statement warranted giving of MAI 32.12. Ramacciotti v. Zinn, 550 S.W.2d 217[6] (Mo.App.1977).

Defensive instructions in libel case must conform to MAI or the philosophy of MAI. Skain v. Weldon, 422 S.W.2d 271[1] (Mo. 1967).

Defendant's instructions in libel case on "fair comment" about a public official condemned as (1) abstract statements, (2) argumentative, and (3) "lecturing type" instructions. Instructions not justified by the fact they were quoted from Supreme Court opinions. Skain v. Weldon, 422 S.W.2d 271[1] (Mo.1967).

32.13 [1978 Revision] Affirmative Defenses—False Imprisonment—Shoplifting

Your verdict must be for defendant if you believe:

First, defendant was engaged in mercantile trade, and

Second, defendant had reasonable cause to believe that plaintiff wrongfully had taken or was taking merchandise or money, and [1]

Third, plaintiff's restraint was made in a reasonable manner and for a reasonable length of time for the purpose of investigation.

Notes on Use (1978 New)

1. If the defendant wishes to submit upon the evidentiary presumption of reasonable cause for detention arising from evidence of willful concealment of merchandise provided for in § 537.125.3, RSMo, the following alternative Paragraph Second may be substituted:

"Second, plaintiff willfully concealed (describe concealed merchandise, such as 'the watch' and state place of concealment such as 'in his pocket'), and"

Committee Comment (1978 Revision)

This instruction submits the defense provided for in § 537.125, RSMo. See Annot., 86 A.L.R.2d 435 (1962) for cases construing similar statutes. See *Schwane v. The Kroger Company*, 480 S.W.2d 113 (Mo. App.1972) construing the statutory presumption for willful concealment.

For the common law defense see *Teel v. May Dept. Stores Co.*, 348 Mo. 696, 155 S.W.2d 74 (1941) citing Restatement (First) of Torts §§ 77–80 (1934), appeal following rehearing, 352 Mo. 127, 176 S.W.2d 440 (1943). The case is discussed in 8 Mo.L.Rev. 336 (1943) and 14 Mo.Bar J. 310 (1943).

Library References:

C.J.S. False Imprisonment § 60.
West's Key No. Digests, False Imprisonment ⟨≈⟩40.

Notes of Decisions

In general   1
Modification   2

1. In general

In an action for false arrest trial court properly refused defendants' affirmative defense instruction, MAI 32.13, where defendants were attempting to use plaintiff's evidence to support a theory inconsistent with their own theory of defense. Stewart v. K–Mart Corp., 747 S.W.2d 205[4] (Mo.App.1988).

MAI 23.04 (verdict director) and 28.10 [Now 32.13] (affirmative defense) properly submitted case of customer's arrest by off-duty policeman working as defendant's security officer. Nelson v. R.H. Macy & Co., 434 S.W.2d 767[5, 12] (Mo.App.1968).

2. Modification

Modification of Paragraph Second improperly added the clause "... may have committed...." Bergel v. Kassebaum, 577 S.W.2d 863[5, 6] (Mo.App.1978).

32.14   [1969 New] Affirmative Defenses—Payment for Services Furnished Decedent

Your verdict must be for defendant if you believe that plaintiff has already been paid for all services furnished to (*name of decedent*).

Committee Comment (1969 New)

Payment is an affirmative defense, Rule 55.08, Mo.R.Civ.Proc.

Library References:

C.J.S. Executors and Administrators § 489.
West's Key No. Digests, Executors and Administrators ☞253.

Notes of Decisions

1. In general

Patient and patient's husband were not entitled to affirmative defense instruction of payment in hospital's action to collect for unpaid medical bills, where there was no evidence that full payment had been made. St. Francis Medical Center v. Sheffer, 892 S.W.2d 394 (Mo.App. E.D.1995).

32.15 [1969 New] Affirmative Defenses—Gratuitous Furnishing of Services

Your verdict must be for defendant if you believe that at the time the services were furnished to (*name of decedent*) plaintiff did not intend to make a charge for his services.

Committee Comment (1969 New)

See General Comment at MAI 28.00.

Gratuitous furnishing of services is an affirmative defense. In *Lauf v. Wiegersen,* 17 S.W.2d 369, 371 (Mo.App.1929) the court said:

> The rule is that, where the family relationship does not exist, the burden is upon the party who accepts services of the character shown in this case to prove that they were rendered gratuitously . . .

This instruction is intended for use in conversing actions by strangers. Where suit is brought by one in a family relationship, claimant will have to prove a contract and such would be the issue normally conversed.

Library References:

C.J.S. Executors and Administrators § 489.
West's Key No. Digests, Executors and Administrators ☜253.

Notes of Decisions

1. In general

In quantum meruit claim for services rendered to unmarried cohabitant where status as "stranger" was in dispute, court erred by refusing to give defendant's requested instruction based on MAI 32.15 in addition to MAI 32.16. Kirk v. Estate of Garr, 732 S.W.2d 255 (Mo.App.1987).

32.16 [1969 New] Affirmative Defenses—Family Relationship

Your verdict must be for defendant if you believe that at the time the services were furnished to (*name of decedent*) there existed between the plaintiff and (*name of decedent*) such a relationship that there was a natural or moral obligation to support and care for each other.

Notes on Use (1969 New)

To be used as a defense to MAI 28.04 *only*.

Committee Comment (1969 New)

In *Smith v. Estate of Sypret*, 421 S.W.2d 9, 14 (Mo.1967) it is stated, "... to constitute a 'family' there must be (1) a social status, (2) there must be a head who has a right, at least in a limited way, to direct and control those gathered into the household, and (3) this head must be obligated either legally or morally to support the other members, and (4) there must be a corresponding state of at least partial dependence of the other members for this support."

Library References:

C.J.S. Executors and Administrators § 489.
West's Key No. Digests, Executors and Administrators ⚷253.

Notes of Decisions

1. In general

In quantum meruit claim for services rendered to unmarried cohabitant where status as "stranger" was in dispute, court erred by refusing to give defendant's requested instruction based on MAI 32.15 in addition to MAI 32.16. Kirk v. Estate of Garr, 732 S.W.2d 255 (Mo.App.1987).

Where plaintiff went to jury on MAI 28.02, *Implied Contract,* it was error to give defendant's MAI 32.16, appropriate only where plaintiff submits on *Quantum Meruit.* Sturgeon v. Estate of Wideman, 631 S.W.2d 55 (Mo.App.1981).

32.17 [1995 Revision] Affirmative Defenses—Will Contest—Fraud Invalidating Will

Your verdict must be that the document in issue is not the last will and testament of (*name of testator*) if you believe:

First, (*insert name of person committing fraud*) represented to (*name of testator*) that (*here state the allegedly false representation*), and

Second, such representation was false, and

Third, (*insert name of person committing fraud*) knew such representation was false, and

Fourth, such representation was intended to and did deceive (*name of testator*), and

Fifth, (*name of testator*) relied upon such representation, and

Sixth, (*name of testator*) was induced to sign the document in issue by reason of such representation.

Notes on Use (1995 New)

This instruction will be used where the validity of the entire will or codicil is contested under § 473.083, RSMo. Where only part of the will is contested under § 473.081, RSMo, see MAI 31.21.

Library References:

C.J.S. Wills § 473.
West's Key No. Digests, Wills ☜332.

Notes of Decisions

1. Modification

Proper verdict-directing instruction submitting testator's intent to cancel will by making alterations. Watson v. Landvatter, 517 S.W.2d 117[10] (Mo. banc 1974).

32.18 [1969 New] Affirmative Defenses—Will Contest—Undue Influence

Your verdict must be that the document in issue is not the last will and testament of (*name of testator*) if you believe that (*name of testator*) signed the document as a result of the undue influence [1] of (*here insert the name of the person who allegedly exerted the undue influence*).

Notes on Use (1995 Revision)

1. The phrase "undue influence" must be defined. See definition at MAI 15.03.

2. This instruction will be used where the validity of the entire will or codicil is contested under § 473.083, RSMo. Where only part of the will is contested under § 473.081, RSMo, see MAI 31.21, 31.22 and 36.17(B).

Library References:

C.J.S. Wills § 473.
West's Key No. Digests, Wills ⇒332.

Notes of Decisions

1. In general

Settlor's petition for declaratory judgment that family trust had been properly revoked could not be denied on grounds of undue influence, when settlor's son, as trustee, failed to plead affirmative defense of undue influence at any stage in proceedings, and settlor did not impliedly consent to trying such defense. Holdener v. Fieser, 971 S.W.2d 946 (Mo.App.1998).

Affirmative defense of undue influence. Martin v. Martin, 513 S.W.2d 756 (Mo.App. 1974).

32.19   [1981 Revision] Affirmative Defenses—Life Insurance—Misrepresentation of Material Fact—Not Warranted

Your verdict must be for defendant if you believe:

First, decedent represented in the application for the policy that (*here insert the statement, such as "he had not previously had heart trouble"*), and

Second, decedent intended that defendant rely upon the representation in issuing the policy, and

Third, the representation was false, and

Fourth, decedent [knew that the representation was false] [did not know whether the representation was true or false],[1] and

Fifth, defendant relied on the representation in issuing the policy, and

Sixth, such (*here insert a description of the matter referred to in the representation*) contributed to the death of decedent.

Notes on Use (1981 New)

1.   Select the appropriate phrase.

Caution: This instruction contains the elements of fraud which must be submitted if the policy application does not warrant that the matters referred to in the application are true. If it does, use MAI 32.20.

Committee Comment (1981 Revision)

See the Committee Comment following MAI 32.20 pertaining to the basis for the two defenses involving misrepresentation.

Section 376.580, RSMo is applicable to both defenses. It provides:

Misrepresentation. No misrepresentation made in obtaining or securing a policy of insurance on the life or lives of any person or persons, citizens of this state, shall be deemed material, or render the policy void, unless the matter misrepresented shall have actually contributed to the contingency or event on which the policy is to become due and payable, and whether it so contributed in any case shall be a question for the jury.

Library References:

West's Key No. Digests, Insurance ⟜3579.

Notes of Decisions

1. In general

Any error in verdict director omitting element that policy was in force was cured by reference to instruction on affirmative defense of misrepresentation. Crewse v. Shelter Mut. Ins. Co., 706 S.W.2d 35[5] (Mo.App. 1985).

32.20 [1981 Revision] Affirmative Defenses—Life Insurance—Breach of Warranty

Your verdict must be for defendant if you believe:

First, decedent represented in the application for the policy that (*here insert the statement, such as "he had not previously had heart trouble"*), and

Second, the representation was false, and

Third, such (*here insert a description of the matter referred to in the application*) contributed to the death of decedent.

Notes on Use (1969 New)

Caution: This instruction is appropriate only "where material representations made in an application for a policy of life insurance are warranted to be true, or the policy is conditioned upon the truth of the representations, or provides that the falsity of the representations shall avoid the policy." See Committee Comment which follows.

Committee Comment (1969 New)

Where an action is brought to recover benefits under a life insurance policy, two distinct defenses may be available to the insurer. Insurer may defend on breach of a condition warranted to be true, and it may defend on the basis of misrepresentation of a material fact. When the defense is breach of a condition warranted to be true, the insurer may avoid liability without showing that the insured was guilty of fraud because the policy is *conditioned* upon the truth of the warranty or representation. To the contrary, the element of fraud must be established and submitted when the defense is one of false representation where no such warranty or policy condition exists.

The rule has been explained in *Dixon v. Business Men's Assurance Co.,* 365 Mo. 580, 285 S.W.2d 619, 625 (1955) as follows:

The rule in this state, as we understand it, is that where material representations made in an application for a policy of life insurance are warranted to be true, or the policy is conditioned upon the truth of the representations, or provides that the falsity of the representations shall avoid the policy, then the representations, if in fact untrue, will avoid the policy, though the representations were innocently made. This is so because such is the contract. The insurer is entitled to stand on the contract as written, and the innocence of the insured in making the representations is a matter of no concern. But where there is no such warranty or provision in the policy a misrepresentation, in order to avoid the policy must have been fraudulently made. This is the rule applicable to contracts generally, and we see no reason why an exception should be made with respect to insurance contracts. . . .

Defendant invokes the rule, announced in the decisions, that the statute, section 5732, R.S.1929, Mo.St.Ann. § 5732, p. 4373 [RSMo § 376.580], providing that no misrepresentations made in obtaining or securing a policy of life insurance shall be deemed material, or render the policy void, unless the matter misrepresented shall have actually contributed to the contingency or event on which the policy is to become due and payable, applies alike to warranties and representations, and draws no distinction between innocent and fraudulent misrepresentations. We are unable to see how this rule helps defendant. Obviously, the statute does not disturb the law of insurance contracts except in that it avoids defenses founded on misrepresentations when the matter misrepresented does not contribute to the contingency or event on which the policy is to become due and payable. The purpose of the statute is to aid, not to hinder, the insured—to limit, not to extend, the rights of the insurer. Houston v. Metropolitan Life Ins. Co., 232 Mo.App. 195, 205, 97 S.W.2d 856, 860 (1936).

A similar requirement applicable to accident and health policies is in Section 376.783.3, RSMo which requires that false statements in policy applications cannot bar recovery unless such statements are material to the hazard assumed, or the acceptance of the risk.

Library References:

West's Key No. Digests, Insurance ⚷3579.

Notes of Decisions

1. In general

Instruction is only applicable when coverage application answers are warranted to be true, or policy is conditioned on truthful answers. Barrera v. Individual Assurance Co., 829 S.W.2d 14 (Mo.App.1992).

32.21 [1978 Revision] Affirmative Defenses—Release

Your verdict must be for defendant if you believe:

First, plaintiff signed and delivered the release to defendant, and

Second, plaintiff was paid $_____ [1] for such release.

* [unless you find for plaintiff under Instruction Number _____ (*here insert number of plaintiff's instruction which hypothesizes that the release is not effective, such as MAI 32.22*)].

Notes on Use (1978 New)

1. If plaintiff's consideration was something other than money, modify Paragraph Second to describe the consideration received.

This instruction is to be given only when there is a disputed issue as to whether plaintiff gave a release. If the plaintiff disputes executing the release and claims in the alternative that if a release was given, it was obtained by fraud, then this instruction should be given along with the bracketed phrase shown. If the plaintiff admits he gave the release for consideration but claims that it was obtained by fraud, then neither this instruction nor MAI 32.22 should be given. The issues which would otherwise be given in MAI 32.22 should be added to plaintiff's verdict director. See Notes on Use, MAI 32.22.

* Add in the event plaintiff submits an avoidance of release.

Library References:

C.J.S. Release § 86.
West's Key No. Digests, Release ☞59.

Notes of Decisions

1. In general

Release instruction properly refused where plaintiff's evidence was that release given was for a different, prior injury. Woodford v. Illinois Central Gulf R. Co., 518 S.W.2d 712 [6–9] (Mo.App.1974).

32.22 [1978 Revision] Affirmative Defenses—Avoidance of Affirmative Defense—Release Obtained by Fraud

Your finding must be for plaintiff on the defense of release submitted in Instruction Number _____ (*here insert number of the affirmative defense instruction which submits release*) if you believe:

First, defendant represented (*here insert the factual representation allegedly made in connection with the release*), and

Second, the representation was false, and

Third, [defendant knew it was false] [or] [defendant did not know whether it was true or false],[1] and

Fourth, the representation was material to the execution of the release by plaintiff, and

Fifth, plaintiff relied on the representation in executing the release.

Notes on Use (1978 Revision)

1. Plaintiff may use either or both bracketed phrases at his option. If both phrases are used they should be submitted in the disjunctive.

This instruction is to be given only when the plaintiff disputes executing the release and claims in the alternative that if a release was given, it was obtained by fraud. If the plaintiff admits he gave the release for consideration but claims that it was obtained by fraud, then neither this instruction nor MAI 32.21 should be given. The issues which would otherwise be submitted by this instruction should be added to plaintiff's verdict director.

Committee Comment (1969 New)

See *Southwest Pump & Machinery Co. v. Jones,* 87 F.2d 879 (8th Cir.1937) and *Pevesdorf v. Union Electric Light & Power Co.,* 333 Mo. 1155, 64 S.W.2d 939 (1933).

Library References:

C.J.S. Release § 86.
West's Key No. Digests, Release ☞59.

Notes of Decisions

1. In general

Where contested issues of right to rely and element of intent were omitted from plaintiff's verdict director, patterned after MAI 32.22, new trial was required. Bockover v. Stemmerman, 708 S.W.2d 179[2, 3] (Mo.App. 1986).

32.23   [1978 Revision] Affirmative Defenses—Product Liability—Strict   Liability—Contributory Fault

Your verdict must be for defendant if you believe:

First, when the (*describe product*) was used, plaintiff knew of the danger as submitted in Instruction[s] Number _____ [and _____] [1] and appreciated the danger of its use, and

Second, plaintiff voluntarily and unreasonably exposed himself to such danger, and

Third, such conduct directly caused or directly contributed to cause any damage plaintiff may have sustained.

Notes on Use (1978 Revision)

1. If plaintiff submits under both MAI 25.04 (Strict Liability–Product Defect) and MAI 25.05 (Strict Liability–Failure to Warn) use the bracket so that this instruction will refer to both verdict directors; the defense submitted under this instruction is a defense to both theories of recovery.

Caution: This instruction must be modified if plaintiff submits more than one danger.

Committee Comment (1991 Revision)

See *Keener v. Dayton Electric Mfg. Co.*, 445 S.W.2d 362 (Mo.1969) and *Williams v. Ford Motor Co.*, 454 S.W.2d 611, 617–620 (Mo.App. 1970).

In *Lippard v. Houdaille Industries, Inc.*, 715 S.W.2d 491 (Mo. banc 1986), the Supreme Court of Missouri held that comparative fault does not apply to the plaintiff's claim based on strict liability in tort but that MAI 32.23 may be given as a complete defense to a strict liability claim where supported by adequate evidence.

Changes in tort law effected by the provisions of § 537.765, RSMo, applicable to the doctrines of comparative fault and strict liability, and the abolition of contributory fault as a complete defense, apply only to causes of action accruing after July 1, 1987. If § 537.765, is applicable, see Chapter 37.00 for submission of comparative fault.

Library References:
C.J.S. Products Liability § 93.
West's Key No. Digests, Products Liability ⊚⇒96.1.

Notes of Decisions

1. In general

There was sufficient evidence to warrant giving of instruction on product user's contributory fault in product liability case arising out of explosion caused by spark created by air compressor which ignited gas fumes; there was evidence that product user engaged in behavior that he knew could cause explosion, including evidence that product user was aware of danger of an accumulation of gas fumes, that any spark could cause fumes to explode, and that electrical products give off sparks. Arnold v. Ingersoll–Rand Co., 834 S.W.2d 192 (Mo.1992).

Jury question existed as to whether asbestos insulator, who brought products liability action against successor to asbestos manufacturer, was guilty of contributory fault with respect to his asbestosis, even though insulator continued to work with asbestos after learning that asbestosis was possibility from exposure to asbestos, and failed to wear mask or respirator, where insulator had already worked in asbestos industry for 20 years, and there was no evidence of insulator's understanding of level of danger, nature of danger, or who was at risk. Angotti v. Celotex Corp., 812 S.W.2d 742 (Mo.App. 1991).

Defense of contributory fault as a complete bar to recovery could be submitted to jury in products liability action against manufacturer of silage wagon by farm worker who lost his arm after his clothing became caught in wagon, given farm worker's extensive familiarity with operations of the wagon and his awareness of danger poised by rotating blades when he tried to repair broken chain while power was engaged. Harper v. NAMCO, Inc., 765 S.W.2d 634, 637–38 (Mo.App. 1989).

A combine operator's contributory negligence was not a defense in a strict products liability case against a manufacturer, distributor and retailer. However, contributory fault, MAI 32.23, could be submitted as a complete defense. Love v. Deere & Co., 720 S.W.2d 786 [1–2] (Mo.App.1986).

Comparative fault does not apply in a strict products liability case, but the giving of MAI 32.23 is not precluded in the appropriate case. Lippard v. Houdaille Industries, Inc., 715 S.W.2d 491[1–3] (Mo. banc 1986).

Jury instruction was not proper submission of "contributory fault" in products liability case, where it introduced negligence concepts. Barnes v. Tools & Machinery Builders, Inc., 715 S.W.2d 518[2] (Mo. banc 1986).

Action for *negligent* repair of furnace was not a strict liability case, so defendant was not entitled to a contributory fault instruction. Portman v. Sinclair Oil Co., 518 S.W.2d 625[1] (Mo.1975).

32.24 [1978 New] Affirmative Defenses—Insurance Policy Defense

Your verdict must be for defendant if you believe:

First, plaintiff (*describe violated policy condition, e.g., "failed to submit a proof of loss to defendant within the time prescribed by the policy"*), and

Second, defendant was thereby prejudiced.

Committee Comment (1978 New)

This instruction should not be given unless there is evidence of a material breach of a policy condition. *Greer v. Zurich Insurance Co.*, 441 S.W.2d 15 (Mo.1969).

Library References:

West's Key No. Digests, Insurance ⊕3579.

Notes of Decisions

1. In general

Insurer bears burden of proof on affirmative defense that insured failed to comply with policy condition. Nichols v. Preferred Risk Group, 44 S.W.3d 886 (Mo.App.2001).

Instruction requiring verdict for insurer if insured's violation of policy condition preju- dices insurer is inapplicable when condition is notice provision and delay in notice was due to insured's incapacity; when delay is due to incapacity, prejudice is only one factor in determination of reasonableness of delay. Tresner v. State Farm Ins. Co., 913 S.W.2d 7 (Mo.1995).

32.25 [1981 New] Affirmative Defenses—Warranty— Exclusion of Implied Warranty Under UCC

Your verdict must be for defendant if you believe [either]: (*insert one or more* [1] *of the following*)

defendant [here set out or describe the statement or writing relied on by defendant to exclude the warranty],[2] or

defendant sold (*describe the article or product*) "as is",[3] or

the warranty was excluded by the course of dealings [4] between plaintiff and defendant, or

[plaintiff examined and accepted the goods] [plaintiff refused to examine the goods] [5] and the failure of the goods to conform was the type of defect which an examination by plaintiff ought to have revealed.

Notes on Use (1981 New)

1. If more than one basis for the exclusion is submitted, they must be submitted in the disjunctive.

2. The statement disclaiming the implied warranty of merchantability must contain the word merchantability. § 400.2–316(2), RSMo. In the case of a writing, whether a disclaimer is "conspicuous" is a matter for the court to decide. § 400.1–201(10), RSMo.

3. See § 400.2–316(3)(a), RSMo, for other phrases which can operate to exclude all implied warranties.

4. See § 400.2–316(3)(c), RSMo, for alternate methods of excluding all implied warranties.

5. Select the appropriate phrase.

Committee Comment (1981 New)

See Uniform Commercial Code Comment to § 400.2–316, RSMo.

Library References:

C.J.S. Sales § 307.
West's Key No. Digests, Sales ☞446(1).

32.26 [1990 New] Affirmative Defense—Conversion— Consent

Your verdict must be for defendant if you believe that plaintiff by words or conduct permitted defendant to take possession of (*here describe property*).

Notes on Use (1990 New)

This instruction may only be used as an affirmative defense to a conversion by a wrongful taking as submitted in MAI 23.12(1).

Library References:

C.J.S. Trover and Conversion § 150–157.
West's Key No. Digests, Trover and Conversion ☞67.

32.27 [1990 New] Affirmative Defense—Conversion—Abandonment

Your verdict must be for defendant if you believe:

First, plaintiff (*here describe act(s) claimed to constitute abandonment such as "left the property in the apartment after the lease expired"*), and

Second, plaintiff intended to abandon (*here describe the property*).

Notes on Use (1990 New)

Caution: Where a motor vehicle or trailer is involved, *see,* § 301.210 RSMo and *Jones v. Ford Motor Credit Company,* 607 S.W.2d 179 (Mo.App.1980), in connection with submitting affirmative defense of abandonment. This may apply to other property with statutory title requirements.

This instruction may be used as an affirmative defense to any type of conversion case, see MAI 23.12(1) and 23.12(2).

Library References:

C.J.S. Trover and Conversion § 150–157.
West's Key No. Digests, Trover and Conversion ☞67.

32.28 [1995 Revision] Comparative Fault—Invitee Injured—Failure to Keep a Lookout

In your verdict you must assess a percentage of fault to plaintiff [whether or not defendant was partly at fault] [1] if you believe:

First, plaintiff knew or by using ordinary care [2] could have known that there was (*here describe substance on floor that caused the fall*) on the floor of defendant's store and as a result the floor was not reasonably safe, and

Second, plaintiff failed to use ordinary care [2] to keep a careful lookout [3], and

Third, such failure directly caused or directly contributed to cause any damage plaintiff may have sustained.

Notes on Use (1989 New)

1. The bracketed phrase may be used at defendant's option.

2. The phrase "ordinary care" must be defined. See definition at MAI 11.05.

3. A "lookout" submission may not be appropriate in all cases. If supported by the evidence and the applicable law, another appropriate act or omission may be submitted.

Committee Comment (1995 Revision)

For discussion of a possessor's duty, obviousness of a dangerous condition, and comparative fault, see *Harris v. Niehaus*, 857 S.W.2d 222 (Mo. banc 1993); *Patton v. May Dept. Stores Co.*, 762 S.W.2d 38 (Mo. banc 1988); *Cox v. J.C. Penney Co., Inc.*, 741 S.W.2d 28 (Mo. banc 1987); *Hefele v. National Super Markets, Inc.*, 748 S.W.2d 800 (Mo.App.1988); and §§ 343 and 343A(1), Restatement (Second) of Torts (1965).

This instruction has not been formulated to submit plaintiff's fault based on conduct other than that associated with the failure to discover a dangerous condition.

The 1995 Revision to this instruction changed the phrase "should have known" to "could have known" on the issue of constructive notice. Some MAI instructions had used one of the phrases and other instructions had used the other phrase. Questions had arisen as to whether "should have known" imposed a higher burden than "could have known". See *Benton v. City of Rolla,* 872 S.W.2d 882 (Mo.App.1994), and *Burrell v. Mayfair–Lennox Hotels, Inc.,* 442 S.W.2d 47 (Mo.1969). For consistency, the Committee has opted to use the phrase "could have known" to the extent possible in the context of constructive notice. Other instructions, such as MAI 10.07, paragraph Second of MAI 22.01, MAI 22.07, and MAI 25.10(A), continue to use the phrase "should have known" because that phrase is part of a "knew or had reason to know" standard as explained in the Committee Comments to those instructions.

Library References:

C.J.S. Negligence § 871–875.
West's Key No. Digests, Negligence ☞1720.

32.29 [2002 New] Affirmative Defenses—Failure to Mitigate Damages

If you find in favor of plaintiff, you must find that plaintiff failed to mitigate damages if you believe:

First, plaintiff (*insert act sufficient to constitute failure to mitigate, such as "failed to return to work"*), and

Second, plaintiff thereby failed to use ordinary care,[1] and[2]

Third, plaintiff thereby sustained damage that would not have occurred otherwise.

Notes on Use (2002 New)

1. The term "ordinary care" must be defined. See definitions in Chapter 11.00.

2. If more than one specification of failure to mitigate damages is appropriately submitted, modify Paragraph First to submit such specifications in the disjunctive and modify Paragraph Second to read:

"Second, plaintiff, in one or more of the respects submitted in Paragraph First, thereby failed to use ordinary care, and ".

Committee Comment (2002 New)

In the past, varied approaches have been suggested for the manner of instructing on the issue of mitigation of damages. For example, the plurality opinion in *Love v. Park Lane Medical Center*, 737 S.W.2d 720 (Mo. banc 1987), suggested using a comparative fault approach. The product liability statute, section 537.765, RSMo, also could be read to suggest a comparative fault approach. *Tillman v. Supreme Exp. & Transfer, Inc.*, 920 S.W.2d 552 (Mo.App.1996), seemed to indicate that MAI 6.01 is the correct approach, although it also observed that MAI 6.01 is limited to wrongful death cases.

In fact, rather than the doctrine of avoidable consequences, MAI 6.01 submits a completely different type of mitigation (mitigating circumstances attendant upon the fatal injury in a wrongful death case pursuant to section 537.090, RSMo.). *Tillman* also rejected the comparative fault approach to mitigation of damages. In order to avoid potential inconsistencies in alternative methods of submission (comparative fault approach in some cases, the FELA approach in other cases, and yet other possible approaches in other cases), the Committee has concluded that it is best to adopt a uniform approach to the submission of the doctrine of mitigation of damages in all cases as reflected in MAI 32.29 and the revision of MAI 4.01. This approach is both legally and logically correct and consistent with the approach already taken in FELA cases (See MAI 32.07(A) and MAI 8.02). It is also in compliance with the mandate of section 537.765 that failure to mitigate damages "shall diminish proportionately the amount awarded as compensatory damages ...''; thus, the method of submission of mitigation of damages in a product liability case should also utilize the approach taken in MAI 32.29 and MAI 4.01.

Library References:

C.J.S. Negligence § 871–875.
West's Key No. Digests, Negligence ⬡1720.

33.00

CONVERSE INSTRUCTIONS

Analysis of Instructions

Westlaw Electronic Research

See Westlaw Electronic Research Guide preceding the Table of Instructions.

Library References:

C.J.S. Trial § 303.
West's Key No. Digests, Trial ☞203(3).

551

33.01 [1996 Revision] Converse Instructions—General Comment

Cases prior to MAI recognized that a defendant is entitled to a converse of plaintiff's verdict directing instruction. *Frazier v. Ford Motor Company,* 365 Mo. 62, 276 S.W.2d 95 (1955).

A true converse instruction does not need testimony to support it "because, absent a judicial admission, ... the credibility of the witnesses giving oral testimony establishing the affirmative remains for the jury." *Kimbrough v. Chervitz,* 353 Mo. 1154, 186 S.W.2d 461, 464 (1945).

In *Dell'Aria v. Bonfa,* 307 S.W.2d 479, 480 (Mo.1957), the Missouri Supreme Court said: "[a defendant] may submit the exact converse of plaintiff's submission, *Janssens v. Thompson,* 360 Mo. 351, 228 S.W.2d 743 (Mo.banc 1950) or the converse of any one of the elements essential to plaintiff's recovery, *McCarty v. Milgram Food Stores, Inc.,* 252 S.W.2d 343 (Mo.1952), or he can submit facts (*supported by the evidence*) which would disprove one or more of the factual elements essential to a recovery by plaintiff. *Liebow v. Jones Store Co.,* 303 S.W.2d 660 (Mo.1957)." For an extensive discussion of Converse Instructions under MAI, see Note, 42 Mo.L.Rev. 175 (1977).

Verdict directing instructions of plaintiffs (*and cross claimants and counterclaimants*) may be conversed in one of the following two ways:

True Converse

An instruction beginning "Your verdict must be for defendant unless you believe" followed by one or more propositions submitted by the verdict directing instruction and in substantially the same language used in the verdict directing instruction. It is important to understand that the converse instructions shown in Illustrations 33.03, 33.04, 33.06 and 33.15 are merely illustrations of the method by which the "unless you believe" introductory language is to be combined with language from the verdict director being conversed. Unlike other forms of instructions shown in this book, it is not safe to select a complete converse instruction from Chapter 33 for use in particular litigation because the language of the verdict director in the litigation involved is likely to differ from the examples shown in the book. The form book for the language of the converse instruction, other than the introductory phrase, is the verdict director itself.

If a defendant converses more than one element of a verdict director, the converse instruction should use the same connecting term (*and* vs. *or*) as used in the verdict director. In other words, in conversing conjunctive submissions, the converse uses "and" between elements; in conversing disjunctive submissions, it uses "or". Thus, the principle that all of the language of the converse instruction except the preliminary phrase is to be taken from the verdict director covers the selection of the appropriate connecting term as well as the other language of the elements being conversed. This simple rule will avoid any error or ambiguity in selecting the proper connecting term, whether conversing conjunctive or disjunctive submissions. See the discussion in 42 Mo.L.Rev. 175 at 181–83 (1977).

A true converse instruction requires no independent evidence to support it. The defendant's converse instruction rests upon his contention that the plaintiff has failed to prove some portion of his case; it is the device with which the defendant seeks to emphasize one or more of the elements of the case upon which the plaintiff has the burden of proof. Unlike an affirmative converse instruction, there is *no* requirement that the verdict director contain a phrase, commonly referred to as an "affirmative defense" tail, which refers the jury directly from the verdict director to the true converse instruction.

The defendant has the option to converse one or more elements of the verdict director. The only limitation on defendant's right to converse as much or as little of the verdict director as desired is with respect to disjunctive submissions. If defendant elects to converse any element which is submitted by the verdict director in the disjunctive, he must converse all such disjunctive elements. For example, if plaintiff submits that defendant either "failed to keep a careful lookout or drove at an excessive speed," a converse stating that "Your verdict must be for defendant unless you believe defendant drove at an excessive speed" would be improper because it deprives the plaintiff of the opportunity for a verdict if the jury does not believe excessive speed but finds defendant failed to keep a proper lookout. A proper converse of excessive speed must also converse lookout. Defendant may converse all of the disjunctive submissions only or may combine his converse of the disjunctive submissions with one or more additional conjunctive submissions from the verdict director. If defendant elects not to converse any of the disjunctive submissions, he may converse one or more of the remaining conjunctive submissions as he sees fit.

Affirmative Converse

The other type of converse instruction provided is an instruction beginning "Your verdict must be for defendant if you believe" followed by a hypothesized ultimate issue which, if true, would defeat plaintiff's claim. See *Hiers v. Lemley*, 834 S.W.2d 729 (Mo.banc 1992); and Notes on Use and Committee Comment to MAI 33.05(1). Use of this form requires independent evidence to support it. However, unlike a true converse instruction, there *is* a requirement that the verdict director contain a phrase, commonly referred to as an "affirmative defense" tail, which refers the jury directly from the verdict director to the affirmative converse instruction. The facts hypothesized in an affirmative converse instruction must be sufficient in law to defeat the plaintiff's claim. *Shepard v. Ford Motor Company*, 457 S.W.2d 255 (Mo.App.1970). The affirmative converse instruction should not be used to submit in the affirmative the same issue in substantially the same language as has already been submitted in the verdict directing instruction. Use a true converse instruction to converse an element submitted by the verdict director. See *Stover v. Patrick*, 459 S.W.2d 393 (Mo.banc 1970) and *Oliver v. Bi–State Development Agency*, 494 S.W.2d 49 (Mo.1973).

Types of Converse Instructions Withdrawn

The "If you do not believe" format for a true converse instruction and the general converse instruction (MAI 33.13) are withdrawn because limitations placed on their use under the prior rules resulted in only a limited number of cases in which they could be safely used and added substantially to the complexity of the rules governing the use of converse instructions. Since other instructions are available to accomplish the same purposes with less difficulty, these converse instruction methods will no longer be used.

Conversing Alternative Verdict Directors

If plaintiff submits against defendant under alternative verdict directing instructions, defendant should modify the accepted converse instruction format to read as follows:

> Your finding must be for defendant under Instruction Number _____ (*insert the number of the verdict director being conversed*) "unless you believe" followed by one or more of the propositions submitted by the verdict directing instruction being conversed.

Use of the word "finding" in lieu of the word "verdict" avoids directing a verdict for the defendant if plaintiff prevails upon one alternative theory but not on the other.

How Many Converse Instructions Will Be Allowed?

Each defendant will be allowed one converse instruction to respond to each verdict directing instruction directed to such defendant. No defendant will be required to join with any other defendant in a converse instruction. However, if two or more defendants wish to join in the same converse instruction, they may do so in appropriate situations by modifying the opening phrase to read, "Your verdict must be for [both] [all] defendants if you believe...." If a defendant joins with other defendants in a converse instruction, such instruction counts fully against each such defendant in determining the allowable number of instructions for each such defendant.

If one plaintiff submits against two defendants, each such defendant will be allowed one converse instruction in which to respond to the plaintiff's claim. This will occur whether plaintiff submits against both defendants in a single verdict directing instruction or against each defendant in a separate verdict directing instruction. By the same token, if a plaintiff submits alternative theories in two verdict directing instructions against a defendant, such defendant will be allowed two converse instructions, one in which to respond to each such verdict directing instruction. The fact that two verdict directing instructions against one or more defendants may contain similar language or common theories of recovery shall not deprive each defendant of the opportunity to use one converse instruction for each verdict director directed to such defendant. This rule is intended to operate on a strictly mechanical basis. In a few instances, this rule will allow a greater number of converse instructions than was the case under prior rules but whatever detriment may result therefrom is more than outweighed by the simplicity of a simple mechanical rule as to the allowable number of converse instructions in a particular case.

CONVERSE INSTRUCTIONS IN COMPARATIVE FAULT CASES

Converse instructions are available to both the plaintiff and the defendant in a comparative fault case. *See* MAI 37.04 for the appropriate format. A plaintiff is entitled to converse the comparative fault instruction submitting plaintiff's fault in the same manner in which a defendant may converse the verdict director submitting the defendant's fault. Since in a comparative fault case, the jury does not return a verdict in favor of either party, the converse instruction does not direct the jury in terms of returning a verdict in favor of either party. Rather, the converse instruction directs the jury that "In your verdict you must not assess a percentage of fault to. . . ." The other rules concerning such matters as the number of converse instructions allowed, the submissions which may or must be conversed, and the use of the various types of converse instructions apply in a comparative fault case in the same manner as in a non-comparative fault case.

Notes of Decisions

In general 1
Conjunctive submission 13

-----

1. In general

No error arose from train conductor's decision to converse negligence element of railroad's verdict director on FELA claim, as opposed to element setting forth specific acts of conductor's negligence as hypothesized in verdict director. Burrus v. Norfolk and Western Ry. Co., 977 S.W.2d 39 (Mo. App.1998).

Defendant is entitled to converse of plaintiff's verdict directing instruction. Gilleylen v. Surety Foods, Inc., 963 S.W.2d 15 (Mo.App. 1998).

To benefit from true converse instruction, truck owner sued in rear-end collision case was not required to present evidence or instruct jury in conformance with oral arguments defendant made at trial, since credibility of witness giving oral testimony establishing the affirmative remained for jury, absent judicial admission. Gilleylen v. Surety Foods, Inc., 963 S.W.2d 15 (Mo.App.1998).

In action by minor patient's parent against abortion provider to recover for patient's suicide after abortion, instruction that was phrased in the language of an affirmative converse failed to comply with MAI 33.01 and was accordingly erroneous, since instruction did not hypothesize independent evidence to defeat plaintiff's claim and since instruction conversed the propositions submitted in verdict directing instruction; but instructional error was harmless since plaintiff failed to make submissible case. Eidson v. Reproductive Health Services, 863 S.W.2d 621 (Mo.App.1993).

Giving of converse instruction in medical malpractice action was prejudicial error where converse instruction failed to follow the language of the verdict director; the verdict director stated that the negligence "directly caused or directly contributed to cause" the damage, whereas the converse instruction stated that the damage was a "direct result of such negligence." Hiers v. Lemley, 834 S.W.2d 729 (Mo.1992).

Affirmative converse instruction to a verdict directing instruction on vexatious refusal to pay pursuant to a contract of suretyship was properly refused where the affirmative converse merely submitted in the affirmative the same issue as submitted in the verdict directing instruction. Howard Const. Co. v. Teddy Woods Const. Co., 817 S.W.2d 556 (Mo.App.1991).

In making comparison between verdict directing instruction and converse instruction, to determine validity of converse instruction, the court should not be hypertechnical about language utilized but should be concerned about meaning of instruction to average juror; significance of any language variation between verdict director and converse is in whether same legal theory is contained in both instructions. Sandza v. City of Des Peres, 768 S.W.2d 582, 583–85 (Mo.App. 1989).

General or true converse instruction is characterized by use of words "unless you believe" followed by some or all of propositions submitted in plaintiff's verdict directive instruction. True converse instruction relates back to plaintiff's verdict director and should emphasize necessity for jury to believe certain propositions upon which plaintiff must sustain burden of proof before recovery may be awarded; true conversion instruction may or may not include "tail" referring, for proposition in question, to plaintiff's verdict director. Powers v. Ellfeldt, 768 S.W.2d 142, 145 (Mo.App.1989).

"True converse" jury instruction is one that requires no independent evidence for support, but rests rather upon contention that plaintiff failed burden to prove some element of case. Palcher v. J.C. Nichols Co., 783 S.W.2d 166 (Mo.App.1990).

Where plaintiff submitted failure to use the "highest degree of care", error to give defendant's converse based only on defendant's "negligence". Doyle v. Bi–State Dev. Agency, 628 S.W.2d 695[2] (Mo.App.1982).

When defendants are jointly liable for the negligence of either, it was error to give their converse instruction requiring a finding *both* were negligent. Swindell v. J.A. Tobin Construction Co., 629 S.W.2d 536[10] (Mo.App. 1981).

In suit by husband and wife it was error to give defendant's converse instruction to find for defendant unless both plaintiffs sustained damages. Conger v. Queen City Food & Vending, Inc., 591 S.W.2d 161[4] (Mo.App. 1979).

Although plaintiff's verdict director omitted the essential element that he was *using* the instrument when injured, defendant could properly submit that element in its converse instruction. Mead v. Corbin Equipment, Inc., 586 S.W.2d 388 (Mo.App.1979).

Where plaintiff submitted on both lookout and on exceeding speed limit, the latter being negligence per se, it was error to give defendant's single converse instruction, since that was not a defense to plaintiff's per se submission. Croak v. Wines, 574 S.W.2d 525 (Mo.App.1978).

Defendant may submit both a converse and contributory negligence. Van Dyke v. Major Tractor & Equipment Co., 557 S.W.2d 11[7, 8] (Mo.App.1977).

Slip-and-fall case. Where plaintiff's verdict director unnecessarily included concealed element of causation, it was not error to give defendant's instruction conversing that element. Young v. Jefferson Hotel Corp., 541 S.W.2d 32[11] (Mo.App.1976).

Bailee's third-method converse submitting its use of ordinary care. Broadview Leasing Co. v. Cape Central Airways, Inc., 539 S.W.2d 553, 558 (Mo.App.1976).

Defendant's confusing converse instruction not prejudicial to plaintiff. Sabbath v. Marcella Cab Co., 536 S.W.2d 939[14] (Mo. App.1976).

Where plaintiff's verdict director submitted facts constituting negligence per se and did not require a finding defendant was negligent, it was error to give defendant's converse to find for defendant if he was not negligent as submitted in plaintiff's verdict director. Oventrop v. Bi–State Development Agency, 521 S.W.2d 488[10] (Mo.App.1975).

Where plaintiff's verdict director *unnecessarily* submitted the element of defendant's negligence defendant properly conversed that element. Invited error. Arbuthnot v. Charlton, 512 S.W.2d 464[3] (Mo.App.1974).

A true converse instruction requires no evidentiary support. Arbuthnot v. Charlton, 512 S.W.2d 464[1, 2] (Mo.App.1974).

True converse instruction conversing the element of defendant's negligence as in 33.03(2) does not require evidentiary support. Strickner v. Brown, 491 S.W.2d 253[2] (Mo.1973).

True converse instruction does not require evidentiary support. Price v. Bangert Bros., 490 S.W.2d 53[9] (Mo.1973).

Defendant properly allowed to submit both a converse and affirmative defense instruction. Fehlbaum v. Newhouse Broadcasting Corp., 483 S.W.2d 664[6] (Mo.App.1972).

Defendant may converse part of plaintiff's submission and also submit plaintiff's contributory negligence as an affirmative defense. Moore v. Parks, 458 S.W.2d 344[9] (Mo.1970).

Where status of plaintiff while visiting defendant church presented a critical factual issue of her status as an invitee or a licensee the trial court defined "invitee" and also gave an affirmative converse instruction for defendant submitting the elements of plaintiff's status as a "licensee". Claridge v. Watson Terrace Christian Church of St. Louis, 457 S.W.2d 785[1] (Mo. banc 1970).

Where plaintiff's verdict director submits defendant's failure to use "ordinary care," such as MAI 22.03"," Invitee Injured, defendant's converse must be in substantially the same language, and it is error to converse "negligence" since that word was not used in plaintiff's verdict director. Brewer v. Swift & Co., 451 S.W.2d 131[1] (Mo. banc 1970).

In action against truck owner for his driver's negligence it was error to give a converse instruction exonerating the owner unless the jury believed the owner was negligent; it should have submitted the driver's lack of negligence. Denny v. Mathieu, 452 S.W.2d 114[6] (Mo. banc 1970).

Defendant may submit affirmative defense or converse, or both. Jefferson v. Biggar, 416 S.W.2d 933[4] (Mo.1967).

By a true converse instruction a defendant may submit only an exact converse of all or essential elements of plaintiff's verdict director. Ridinger v. Harbert, 409 S.W.2d 764[7–8] (Mo.App.1966).

2. Partial converse

Although plaintiff submits two acts as being negligent defendant may converse negligence generally. O'Riley v. Coffelt, 588 S.W.2d 203[2] (Mo.App.1979).

A converse instruction may converse any one or all of the essential elements of the plaintiff's verdict director. Anderson v. Cahill, 528 S.W.2d 742[3] (Mo. banc 1975).

Where plaintiff's verdict director *unnecessarily* submitted the element of defendant's negligence defendant properly conversed that element. Invited error. Arbuthnot v. Charlton, 512 S.W.2d 464[3] (Mo.App.1974).

In conversing MAI 25.04 defendant entitled to converse "defective condition" of Paragraph Second without also conversing "and therefore dangerous, etc." Lietz v. Snyder Mfg. Co., 475 S.W.2d 105[4–6] (Mo.1972).

In products liability case defendant may converse the separate element that defective article was being used in a manner reasonably anticipated. Keener v. Dayton Elec. Mfg. Co., 445 S.W.2d 362[7] (Mo.1969).

Defendant has a right to converse the single element of negligence in plaintiff's right-of-way submission. Morris v. Duker, 414 S.W.2d 77[11] (Mo.1967).

Defendant may converse the single element of negligence in plaintiff's verdict director. Birmingham v. Smith, 420 S.W.2d 514[5] (Mo.1967).

3. Modification

Where plaintiff properly departed from MAI in his verdict director, defendant was not restricted to one of the MAI converse instructions but could properly modify his converse instruction to match plaintiff's submission. Proper, because there was no *applicable* MAI converse instruction. Morris v. Klein, 400 S.W.2d 461[1–3, 5] (Mo.App.1966).

4. Negating

"Unless you believe" tail of verdict directing instruction is not necessary to negate defendant's true converse instruction, but doing so is harmless error. Walkley v. Sears, Roebuck & Co., 536 S.W.2d 169[2, 3] (Mo.App.1976).

Plaintiff's modified MAI 26.06 hypothesized defendant's agreement to pay him commissions; defendant's converse directed a verdict if plaintiff was "not entitled to commissions." Condemned as a roving commission which did not negate an essential element of plaintiff's case. Lawrie v. Continental Cas. Co., 555 S.W.2d 347 (Mo. App.1977).

5. Sole cause

Converse instruction adequately covers defense of sole cause. Birmingham v. Smith, 420 S.W.2d 514[2] (Mo.1967).

6. Language

A true converse prefaced by "your verdict must be for defendant, unless you believe," must submit the proposition of the verdict director in substantially the same language used in the verdict director to avoid distortion of the legitimate burden of proof. Sall v. Ellfeldt, 662 S.W.2d 517[2] (Mo.App.1983).

Where plaintiff submitted failure to use the "highest degree of care", error to give defendant's converse based only on defendant's "negligence". Doyle v. Bi–State Dev. Agency, 628 S.W.2d 695[2] (Mo.App.1982).

Defendant may *disjunctively* converse two elements of plaintiff's res ipsa verdict director—the sudden jerk and negligent causation. Sabbath v. Marcella Cab Co., 536 S.W.2d 939[12] (Mo.App.1976).

Error to give a converse instruction that does not converse the verdict director in "substantially the same language." Anderson v. Cahill, 528 S.W.2d 742[4] (Mo. banc 1975).

Where plaintiff's verdict director submitted facts constituting negligence per se and did not require a finding defendant was negligent, it was error to give defendant's converse to find for defendant if he was not negligent as submitted in plaintiff's verdict director. Oventrop v. Bi–State Development Agency, 521 S.W.2d 488[10] (Mo.App.1975).

Plaintiff's verdict director properly followed MAI 24.01 in submitting that defendant's negligence directly resulted "in whole or in part" in injury to plaintiff. Defendant's converse required that plaintiff sustained damage as a "direct result" of its negligence; held, prejudicially erroneous since it did not substantially follow the language of the verdict director. Snyder v. Chicago, R.I. & P. Ry. Co., 521 S.W.2d 161[4–8] (Mo.App. 1973).

In suit on express contract for agreed price for building a garage the court properly submitted plaintiff "substantially performed" the contract. Defendant was entitled to converse that specific element but was not entitled to base a converse on three separately described construction defects. Bullock Co. v. Allen, 493 S.W.2d 5[5–7] (Mo.App.1973).

Converse to Not-in-MAI verdict director approved where it used substantially, although not identically, the same language as the verdict director. Durbin–Durco, Inc. v. Blades Mfg. Corp., 455 S.W.2d 449[6] (Mo. 1970).

Where plaintiffs' verdict-director MAI 22.03 submitted defendant's failure to use ordinary care it was error to give defendant's MAI 33.02(2) conversing *negligence* since the converse was not in substantially the same language as plaintiff's verdict director. Frogge v. Nyquist Plumbing & Ditching Co., 453 S.W.2d 913[6] (Mo. banc 1970).

Rule that converse instruction must be in substantially the same words as verdict director is not violated by use of different words having the same meaning. Bartleman v. Humphrey, 441 S.W.2d 335[25] (Mo. 1969).

While true converse must use substantially the same language as verdict director, only differences affecting the meaning are erroneous. Plas–Chem Corp. v. Solmica Inc., 434 S.W.2d 522[7] (Mo.1968).

True converse in words differing from verdict director held confusing and erroneous.

Reichman v. Camden Fire Ins. Ass'n, 427 S.W.2d 729[3] (Mo.App.1968).

Where plaintiff in a products liability case submitted "fitness" of auto jack for particular purpose (MAI 25.03), it was error to converse that with instruction exculpating the defendant if injury resulted from the "condition" of the jack. This, because MAI 29.01 [Now 33.01] requires substantially the same language used in the verdict director. Austin v. Western Auto, 421 S.W.2d 203[3–5] (Mo.1967).

MAI 29.01 [Now 33.01] requires a true converse be "in substantially the same language" used in the verdict director. Bollman v. Kark Rendering Plant, 418 S.W.2d 39[17, 18] (Mo.1967).

7. Definitions

Where court gave MAI 16.01 defining malice, defendant was not entitled to a converse definition. Duensing v. Huscher, 431 S.W.2d 169[5] (Mo.1968).

8. Damages

In suit by husband and wife it was error to give defendant's converse instruction to find for defendant unless both plaintiffs sustained damages. Conger v. Queen City Food & Vending, Inc., 591 S.W.2d 161[4] (Mo.App. 1979).

In wrongful death case it is error to give separate converse instructions, one conversing negligence and the other conversing damages. Higgins v. Gosney, 435 S.W.2d 653[8–9] (Mo.1968).

Where plaintiff mother gave MAI 20.01 in action for wrongful death of son omitting finding that plaintiff suffered damages (because nominal damages are presumed), and MAI 5.01 on her measure of damages, it was error for defendant to separately converse the element of damages. Aubuchon v. La-Plant, 435 S.W.2d 648[5–8] (Mo.1968).

Defendant not entitled to a separate instruction conversing plaintiff's damage instruction. Pauling v. Rountree, 412 S.W.2d 545[9] (Mo.App.1967).

9. Only one converse—in general

Giving of converse instructions in medical malpractice action was prejudicial error where instructions combined true converse instruction, using the disjunctive "or," with an affirmative converse instruction; each defendant is allowed only one converse instruction to respond to each verdict directing instruction directed to such defendant. Hiers v. Lemley, 834 S.W.2d 729 (Mo.1992).

Where plaintiff submitted separate verdict directors against four defendants, each defendant was entitled to a separate converse instruction. Demko v. H & H Inv. Co., 527 S.W.2d 382[5–8] (Mo.App.1975).

Defendant entitled to only one converse of plaintiff's verdict director. Potter v. Milbank Mfg. Co., 489 S.W.2d 197[8, 9] (Mo.1972).

Where defendant got a true converse it was proper to refuse an affirmative Third–Method Converse presenting the same defense, since MAI 33.01 says a verdict director may be conversed in one of three ways. Bishop v. Goldschmidt, 436 S.W.2d 47[8] (Mo.App.1968).

Where court gave defendant's overall converse by MAI 29.06(6) [Now 33.06(6)], it was error to specifically converse negligence with MAI 29.04(1) [Now 33.04(1)]. Murphy v. Land, 420 S.W.2d 505[1] (Mo.1967).

Error to give three converse instructions directed against plaintiff's MAI 17.14 (slackening and swerving). Nugent v. Hamilton & Son, 417 S.W.2d 939[2, 3] (Mo.1967).

Defendant entitled to only one converse to meet plaintiff's verdict director. Temple v. Atchison, T. & S.F. Ry., 417 S.W.2d 97, 99 (Mo.1967).

10. Only one converse—Joint plaintiffs

Separate negative converse instructions to husband's personal injury claim and wife's loss of consortium claim, both founded on a strict liability theory, were proper, because MAI 2.05 now mandates separate packaging of instructions and defendants could converse each claim without prejudicial error. Johnston v. Allis–Chalmers Corp., 736 S.W.2d 544[1] (Mo.App.1987).

Plaintiff-husband and wife properly gave separate verdict directors since their damage submissions differed. Defendant erroneously gave one converse instruction to find for defendant unless plaintiffs were injured; separate converse instructions required since damages differed. Burrow v. Moyer, 519 S.W.2d 568[4–8] (Mo.App.1975).

Where plaintiffs husband and wife submitted separate verdict directors defendant was entitled to only one converse on plaintiffs'

theory of recovery, and it was error to give defendant's two general converses (MAI 33.03) since that doubly conversed plaintiff's theory of recovery. (Defendant could have given one converse on plaintiffs' theory of recovery and one converse on wife's separate damage element.) Wyatt v. Southwestern Bell Tel. Co., 514 S.W.2d 366 (Mo.App. 1974).

11. Only one converse—Joint defendants

Where defendants are liable jointly, if at all, they must join in one converse instruction. Scheele v. American Bakeries, 427 S.W.2d 361[1] (Mo.1968).

12. Disjunctive submission

Defendant may *disjunctively* converse two elements of plaintiff's res ipsa verdict director—the sudden jerk and negligent causation. Sabbath v. Marcella Cab Co., 536 S.W.2d 939[12] (Mo.App.1976).

Plaintiff's res ipsa submission required jury first to believe bus made a sudden stop *and* second, to believe such movement was the result of defendant's negligence. Defendant's converse directed a verdict if the jury did not believe both those two hypotheses. The jury could not disbelieve the first and also disbelieve the second, but the trial court improperly granted plaintiff a new trial on the ground the converse was confusing since it was not prejudicial to plaintiff. Wims v. Bi–State Development Agency, 484 S.W.2d 323[1, 2] (Mo. banc 1972).

13. Conjunctive submission

Defendant has the option to converse one or more of the elements of a verdict-director when the elements are submitted in the conjunctive. Kennedy v. Bi–State Development Agency, 668 S.W.2d 260[5, 6] (Mo.App. 1984).

Error to give three converse instructions directed against plaintiff's MAI 17.14 (slackening and swerving). Nugent v. Hamilton & Son, 417 S.W.2d 939[2, 3] (Mo.1967).

14. Disjunctive converse

Submission of insurers' disjunctive converse instruction was improper as instruction was an affirmative converse and there was *no* evidence to support its submission. Petterson v. State Farm General Ins. Co., 701 S.W.2d 764[1, 2] (Mo.App.1985).

Plaintiff's res ipsa submission required jury first to believe bus made a sudden stop *and* second, to believe such movement was the result of defendant's negligence. Defendant's converse directed a verdict if the jury did not believe both those two hypotheses. The jury could not disbelieve the first and also disbelieve the second, but the trial court improperly granted plaintiff a new trial on the ground the converse was confusing since it was not prejudicial to plaintiff. Wims v. Bi–State Development Agency, 484 S.W.2d 323[1, 2] (Mo. banc 1972).

Where plaintiff submitted disjunctively employer's negligence and negligence of defendant's employee, defendant erred in conversing only defendant's negligence since this absolved defendant from liability for its employee's negligence. Davis v. St. Louis Southwestern Ry. Co., 444 S.W.2d 485[4] (Mo.1969).

Where plaintiff submitted two disjunctive acts of negligence they should have been conversed with "unless you believe" and it was confusing to converse with "if you do not believe." Davis v. St. Louis Southwestern Ry. Co., 444 S.W.2d 485[3] (Mo.1969).

Where plaintiff's verdict director is a disjunctive submission, it is error for defendant's "Third Method" converse to direct a verdict on failure to find one of the two submissions. Travagliante v. J.W. Wood Realty Co., 425 S.W.2d 208[2–7] (Mo.1968).

15. Primary humanitarian submission

When plaintiff submitted both primary and humanitarian negligence, it was error to (1) converse plaintiff's primary verdict director and (2) give defendant's contributory negligence instruction without limiting each to plaintiff's primary negligence submission. Payton v. Bi–State Development Agency, 417 S.W.2d 522[3–6] (Mo.App.1967).

Where plaintiff submits on two theories, defendant's converse instruction may not ignore either and must specify the instruction being conversed. Griffith v. Saavedra, 409 S.W.2d 665[3] (Mo.1966).

16. Products liability

Although plaintiff's verdict director omitted the essential element that he was *using* the instrument when injured, defendant could properly submit that element in its converse instruction. Mead v. Corbin Equipment Inc., 586 S.W.2d 388 (Mo.App.1979).

In conversing MAI 25.04 defendant entitled to converse "defective condition" of Paragraph Second without also conversing "and therefore dangerous, etc." Lietz v. Snyder Mfg. Co., 475 S.W.2d 105[4–6] (Mo.1972).

AFFIRMATIVE CONVERSE
Notes of Decisions

In general 1
Burden of proof 3
Invalid defense 4
Will contest 2

---

1. In general

Affirmative converse instruction is suspect unless the converse submits a contested ultimate issue that was omitted from or assumed as true in the verdict director; affirmative converse instruction is not favored and should only be given if supported by the evidence. Hiers v. Lemley, 834 S.W.2d 729 (Mo.1992).

Giving of affirmative converse instruction in medical malpractice action was prejudicial error where converse instructions were used as means of conversing, in different language, the very same issues submitted in verdict director instruction; affirmative converse instructions were misleading and therefore prejudicial where instructions failed to make clear that defendant-doctor was held to standards of his profession. Hiers v. Lemley, 834 S.W.2d 729 (Mo.1992).

Not-in-MAI affirmative converse instruction given by trial court in customer's action against bank for breaching alleged loan commitment agreement, in which trial court instructed jurors that their verdict must be for bank if they believed there were conditions to bank's approval of loan, was in nature of roving commission that required reversal of judgment in bank's favor, where trial court failed to specify what those conditions might be or otherwise to circumscribe jurors' discretion. Duncan v. First State Bank of Joplin, 848 S.W.2d 566 (Mo.App.1993).

Where plaintiff's verdict director does not require finding defendant negligent, it is error to give a converse which directs a finding for defendant if he was not negligent since a converse instruction must be in substantially the same language as the verdict director. The court, however, noted that defendant was entitled to an instruction on justification or excuse, and indicated that the error in defendant's converse instruction would have been avoided if it had been reworded, making it an affirmative converse. Cowell v. Thompson, 713 S.W.2d 52[1, 5, 6] (Mo.App. 1986).

The facts hypothesized in an affirmative converse instruction must be sufficient in law to defeat plaintiff's claim. Because defendants' hypothetical facts merely eliminate two of many ways to show unreasonable land use, the converses were properly rejected. Frank v. Environmental Sanitation Management, 687 S.W.2d 876[9] (Mo. banc 1985).

Although there is no requirement that a "tail" be used for affirmative converse instructions, use of such does not lead to a per se reversal. Shearin v. Fletcher/Mayo/Associates, 687 S.W.2d 198[5, 6] (Mo.App.1984).

The facts hypothesized in an affirmative converse instruction must be sufficient in law to defeat plaintiff's claim. Linkogel v. Baker Protective Services, Inc., 659 S.W.2d 300[1] (Mo.App.1983).

Affirmative Converse submitted facts, supported by independent evidence, which would defeat plaintiff's claim. Associated Underwriters, Inc. v. Mercantile Trust Co., 576 S.W.2d 343[1] (Mo.App.1978).

Action for invasion of privacy by opening another's mail. Publication of information not essential and Affirmative Converse instruction so requiring was error. Corcoran v. Southwestern Bell Telephone Co., 572 S.W.2d 212[7–9] (Mo.App.1978).

Defendant's converse instruction submitting ice and snow was a general condition.

Carden v. Lester E. Cox Med. Center, 519 S.W.2d 338[8] (Mo.App.1975).

Affirmative converse must hypothesize facts which if true disprove an essential element of plaintiff's verdict director. Restaurant Industries, Inc. v. Lum's, Inc., 495 S.W.2d 668[2, 3] (Mo.App.1973).

Where plaintiff properly submitted MAI 17.13, driving on wrong side of the road, and defendant testified she skidded across the center line, it was error to give defendant's affirmative defense instruction exonerating her if she skidded. (This would have been error even had defendant further submitted that her skidding was not negligent.) Such an instruction is akin to an accident instruction condemned by MAI 1.01 and a sole-cause instruction condemned by MAI 1.03. Defendant should be limited to conversing negligence by MAI 33.02(2), and then arguing non-negligent skidding. Stover v. Patrick, 459 S.W.2d 393[1, 2] (Mo. banc 1970).

In an affirmative converse instruction a defendant may submit "its own theory of the case" and need not *directly* negate the plaintiff's theory, but the fact hypothesized in defendant's instruction must be a fact which, if true, would defeat plaintiff's claim. Shepard v. Ford Motor Co., 457 S.W.2d 255[1] (Mo.App.1970).

Defendant's theory that unreasonable working conditions justified her in breaching employment contract was properly submitted by an Affirmative Converse. State ex rel. State Department of Public Health and Welfare, Division of Welfare v. Luster, 456 S.W.2d 600[3] (Mo.App.1970).

Where defendant got a true converse it was proper to refuse an affirmative converse presenting the same defense, since MAI 33.01 says a verdict director may be conversed in one of three ways. Bishop v. Goldschmidt, 436 S.W.2d 47[8] (Mo.App. 1968).

Defendant's theory that passenger had already walked away from cab when she slipped was properly submitted by an affirmative if-you-believe converse. Wilson v. Checker Cab, 431 S.W.2d 122[1] (Mo.1968).

Evidence warranting, insurer may submit by affirmative converse that loss was caused by an element not covered by its policy. (Its own theory of the case.) Reichman v. Camden Fire Ins. Ass'n, 427 S.W.2d 729[1–2] (Mo.App.1968).

MAI 29.01 [Now 33.01] requires a true converse be "in substantially the same language" used in the verdict director. But in an affirmative converse, a defendant may submit his own theory and need not directly negate the plaintiff's theory. Bollman v. Kark Rendering Plant, 418 S.W.2d 39[17, 18] (Mo. 1967).

In verdict directors plaintiff must negate affirmative defenses, but need not negate defendant's converse instruction even if it uses the affirmative if-you-believe converse. Bollman v. Kark Rendering Plant, 418 S.W.2d 39[18] (Mo.1967).

Rear-ended plaintiff submitted under MAI 17.16. Defendant's excuse was unexpected slide and brake failure. The court gave defendant's MAI 29.02(3) [Now 33.02(3)] conversing negligence. Defendant also offered, but the court refused, an if-you-believe converse instruction hypothesizing the unexpected slide and brake failure. Refusal upheld because defendant was entitled to only one instruction conversing negligence. Suchara v. St. Louis Public Service Co., 410 S.W.2d 93[1] (Mo.App.1966).

2. Will contest

Affirmative converse submitting issue of insane delusion in will contest was error when unsupported by substantial evidence. Byars v. Buckley, 461 S.W.2d 817 (Mo. 1970).

3. Burden of proof

MAI 3.01 need not be modified to meet defendant's burden of proof or affirmative converse instruction. Restaurant Industries, Inc. v. Lum's Inc., 495 S.W.2d 668[5] (Mo. App.1973).

4. Invalid defense

Third-method converse erroneous in hypothesizing fact which as a matter of law is not a defense to plaintiff. Moranz v. Schiller, 525 S.W.2d 785[1–4] (Mo.App.1975).

33.02 [Withdrawn 1980] Converse Instructions—Instructions Conversing Verdict Directing 17.01 Using "If You Do Not Believe" Introduction

(See MAI 33.01—General Comment.)

33.03 [1995 Revision] Converse Instructions—Instructions Conversing Verdict Directing 17.01 Using "Unless You Believe" Introduction

33.03(1)
(Conversing Fact on Which Negligence is Predicated)

Your verdict must be for defendant unless you believe defendant violated the traffic signal.

33.03(2)
(Conversing Negligence)

Your verdict must be for defendant unless you believe defendant was negligent [1] [as submitted in Instruction Number _____].[2]

33.03(3)
(Conversing Damages)

Your verdict must be for defendant unless you believe plaintiff sustained damage.

33.03(4)
(Conversing Negligence and Causation)

Your verdict must be for defendant unless you believe defendant was negligent [1] [as submitted in Instruction Number _____],[2] and as a direct result of such negligence,[1] plaintiff sustained damage.

33.03(5)
(Conversing Damages and Causation)

Your verdict must be for defendant unless you believe defendant was negligent [1] [as submitted in Instruction Number _____],[2] and as a direct result of such negligence,[1] plaintiff sustained damage.

33.03(6) [3]
(Conversing Causation Submitted With MAI 19.01 (First Alternate))

Your verdict must be for defendant unless you believe that defendant's negligence [1] [as submitted in Instruction

Number _____][2] directly caused or directly contributed to cause damage to plaintiff.

33.03(7)[3]
(Conversing Negligence and Causation Submitted With MAI 19.01 (First Alternate))

Your verdict must be for defendant unless you believe that defendant was negligent[1] [as submitted in Instruction Number _____][2] and such negligence[1] directly caused or directly contributed to cause damage to plaintiff.

Notes on Use (1995 Revision)

1. The terms "negligent" and "negligence" must be defined. See definitions in Chapter 11.00.

2. This bracketed material may be included at the option of the defendant.

Caution: The above instructions are examples of the proper method for combining the "unless you believe" introductory phrase with the language from the portion of the verdict director selected to be conversed. These examples are not approved instructions for any particular litigation since the proper language for a converse instruction in any particular litigation depends upon the verdict director being conversed. See MAI 33.01 Converse Instructions—General Comment for rules concerning the use of converse instructions including the use of language from the verdict director in the converse instruction, modifications for conversing alternative verdict directors and limitations upon the number of allowable converse instructions.

3. In *Hiers v. Lemley,* 834 S.W.2d 729 (Mo. banc 1992), the Supreme Court held that a converse that required a verdict for defendant unless the jury found causation "as a direct result of" defendant's negligence was prejudicially erroneous where the verdict directing instruction submitted causation with an MAI 19.01 modification as "directly caused or directly contributed to cause". If the verdict directing instruction is modified with the second alternate in MAI 19.01, the converse instruction should utilize substantially the same language to converse causation. Where one of the alternates in MAI 19.01 is modified in a verdict director to fit a submission such as in death cases, premises cases, products cases, or malpractice cases, the converse instruction should utilize substantially the same modified language as used in the verdict directing instruction.

Notes of Decisions

---

1. In general

Although the words of MAI 33.03(2) differ from the words of MAI 33.04(1), the instructions do not differ in substance. Ernst v. Emerick, 525 S.W.2d 573[1] (Mo.App.1975).

2. Conversing damages

Two plaintiffs gave four verdict directors against two defendants, each on the same theory of recovery. *Each* defendant gave two converse instructions, one against each plaintiff. No error. Saveway Oil Co. v. Sears, Roebuck & Co., 560 S.W.2d 325[1, 3] (Mo.App.1977).

True converse instruction conversing the element of defendant's negligence as in 33.03(2) does not require evidentiary support. Strickner v. Brown, 491 S.W.2d 253[2] (Mo.1973).

In condemnation suit where there was no evidence of special benefits, some damage is presumed, and it was error to give plaintiff's MAI 33.03(3) conversing damages since that converse is designed to converse the damage element of a plaintiff's verdict director in a suit for damages, not the plaintiff's measure of damage instruction which cannot be conversed. City of Gladstone v. Hamilton, 463 S.W.2d 622 (Mo.App.1971).

Where plaintiff properly submitted MAI 17.13, driving on wrong side of the road, and defendant testified she skidded across the center line, it was error to give defendant's affirmative defense instruction exonerating her if she skidded. (This would have been error even had defendant further submitted that her skidding was not negligent.) Such an instruction is akin to an accident instruction condemned by MAI 1.01 and a sole-cause instruction condemned by MAI 1.03. Defendant should be limited to conversing negligence by MAI 33.02, and then arguing non-negligent skidding. Stover v. Patrick, 459 S.W.2d 393[1, 2] (Mo. banc 1970).

3. Separate verdict directors

Error for defendant to give only one converse instruction where plaintiffs husband and wife submitted separate verdict directors on their individual damages. Long v. REA Express Co., 573 S.W.2d 62[6–8] (Mo.App. 1978).

Where plaintiffs husband and wife submitted separate verdict directors defendant was entitled to only one converse on plaintiffs' theory of recovery, and it was error to give defendant's two general converses (MAI 33.03) since that doubly conversed plaintiff's theory of recovery. (Defendant could have given one converse on plaintiffs' theory of recovery and one converse on wife's separate damage element.) Wyatt v. Southwestern Bell Tel. Co., 514 S.W.2d 366 (Mo.App. 1974).

Where plaintiff had separate verdict directors for false arrest and malicious prosecution it was proper to give two converse instructions, one for each verdict director. Brown v. Jones Store, 493 S.W.2d 39[6, 7] (Mo.App.1973).

4. Causation

Truck owner's true converse instruction in rear-end collision case, providing "Your verdict must be for the defendant unless you believe ...," was proper, where it conformed exactly to format of MAI 33.03(4), and directly conversed language of injured motorist's verdict director. Gilleylen v. Surety Foods, Inc., 963 S.W.2d 15 (Mo.App.1998).

33.04 [1995 Revision] Converse Instructions—Instructions Conversing Verdict Directing 17.02 Using "Unless You Believe" Introduction

33.04(1)
(Conversing Negligence)

Your verdict must be for defendant unless you believe defendant was negligent [1] [as submitted in Instruction Number _____].[2]

33.04(2)
(Conversing Damages)

Your verdict must be for defendant unless you believe plaintiff sustained damage.

33.04(3)
(Conversing Causation)

Your verdict must be for defendant unless you believe that as a direct result of defendant's negligence [1] [as submitted in Instruction Number _____],[2] plaintiff sustained damage.

33.04(4)
(Conversing Damages and Causation)

Your verdict must be for defendant unless you believe defendant was negligent [1] [as submitted in Instruction Number _____],[2] and as a direct result of such negligence,[1] plaintiff sustained damage.

33.04(5)
(Conversing All Disjunctive Specifications of Negligence)

Your verdict must be for defendant unless you believe either defendant failed to keep a careful lookout, or defendant drove at an excessive speed, or defendant's automobile was on the wrong side of the road.

33.04(6)[3]
(Conversing Causation Submitted With MAI 19.01 (First Alternate))

Your verdict must be for defendant unless you believe that defendant's negligence[1] [as submitted in Instruction Number _____][2] directly caused or directly contributed to cause damage to plaintiff.

33.04(7)[3]
(Conversing Negligence and Causation Submitted With MAI 19.01 (First Alternate))

Your verdict must be for defendant unless you believe that defendant was negligent[1] [as submitted in Instruction Number _____][2] and such negligence[1] directly caused or directly contributed to cause damage to plaintiff.

Notes on Use (1995 Revision)

1. The terms "negligent" and "negligence" must be defined. See definitions in Chapter 11.00.

2. This bracketed material may be included at the option of the defendant.

Caution: The above instructions are examples of the proper method for combining the "unless you believe" introductory phrase with the language from the portion of the verdict director selected to be conversed. These examples are not approved instructions for any particular litigation since the proper language for a converse instruction in any particular litigation depends upon the verdict director being conversed. See MAI 33.01 Converse Instructions—General Comment for rules concerning the use of converse instructions including the use of language from the verdict director in the converse instruction, modifications for conversing alternative verdict directors and limitations upon the number of allowable converse instructions.

3. In *Hiers v. Lemley,* 834 S.W.2d 729 (Mo. banc 1992), the Supreme Court held that a converse that required a verdict for defendant unless the jury found causation "as a direct result of" defendant's negligence was prejudicially erroneous where the verdict directing instruction submitted causation with an MAI 19.01 modification as "directly caused or directly contributed to cause". If the verdict directing instruction is modified with the second alternate in MAI 19.01, the converse instruction should utilize substantially the same language to converse causation. Where one of the alternates in MAI 19.01 is modified in a verdict director to fit a submission such as in death cases, premises cases, products cases, or malpractice cases, the converse instruction should utilize substantially the same modified language as used in the verdict directing instruction.

Notes of Decisions

In general 1
Language 3
Separate verdict directors 2

———

1. In general

Although plaintiff submits two acts as being negligent defendant may converse negligence generally. O'Riley v. Coffelt, 588 S.W.2d 203[2] (Mo.App.1979).

Where plaintiff's verdict director submits in Paragraph First disjunctive acts, defendant may separately converse Paragraph Second submitting that defendant was negligent. Graeff v. Baptist Temple of Springfield, 576 S.W.2d 291[4] (Mo. banc 1978).

Where plaintiff had separate verdict directors for false arrest and malicious prosecution it was proper to give two converse instructions, one for each verdict director. Brown v. Jones Store, 493 S.W.2d 39[6, 7, 8] (Mo.App.1973).

Where plaintiff submitted two disjunctive acts of negligence they should have been conversed with "unless you believe" and it was confusing to converse with "if you do not believe." Davis v. St. Louis Southwestern Ry. Co., 444 S.W.2d 485[3] (Mo.1969).

Where plaintiff submitted disjunctively employer's negligence and negligence of defendant's employee, defendant erred in conversing only defendant's negligence since this absolved defendant from liability for its employee's negligence. Davis v. St. Louis Southwestern Ry. Co., 444 S.W.2d 485[4] (Mo.1969).

When defendant got an overall converse by MAI 29.06(6) [Now 33.06(6)], it was error to specifically converse negligence with MAI 29.04(1) [Now 33.04(1)]. Murphy v. Land, 420 S.W.2d 505[1] (Mo.1967).

2. Separate verdict directors

Where plaintiffs husband and wife submitted separate verdict directors defendant was entitled to only one converse on plaintiffs' theory of recovery, and it was error to give defendant's two general converses (MAI 33.03) since that doubly conversed plaintiff's theory of recovery. (Defendant could have given one converse on plaintiffs' theory of recovery and one converse on wife's separate damage element.) Wyatt v. Southwestern Bell Tel. Co., 514 S.W.2d 366 (Mo.App. 1974).

In suit by husband and wife it was error to give defendant's converse instruction to find for defendant unless both plaintiffs sustained damages. Conger v. Queen City Food & Vending, Inc., 591 S.W.2d 161[6] (Mo.App. 1979).

3. Language

Trial court erred in submitting defendant's requested converse instruction, since converse instruction did not employ substantially the same language used in verdict director. The error was harmless since instruction merely substituted definition for the term "negligence." McCarthy v. Cullom, 634 S.W.2d 494[1] (Mo.App.1982).

33.05 [Withdrawn 1988] Converse Instructions—Conversing Verdict Directing Using Affirmative Converse—"If You Believe" Introduction

(MAI 33.05 and the Notes on Use thereto are withdrawn and replaced by MAI 33.05(1) and the Notes on Use thereto.)

33.05(1) [1993 Revision] Converse Instructions— Conversing Verdict Directing Instruction Using Affirmative Converse—"If You Believe" Introduction

Your verdict must be for defendant if you believe (*here insert the ultimate issue assumed as true or erroneously omitted from plaintiff's verdict director*).

Notes On Use (1996 Revision)

Caution: *Hiers v. Lemley,* 834 S.W.2d 729 (Mo. banc 1992), held that "[A]n affirmative converse instruction is appropriate where the verdict director assumes as true or omits a disputed ultimate issue[.]", and "[A]n affirmative converse instruction may be appropriate where it is used by a defendant to submit an ultimate issue that was erroneously excluded from plaintiff's verdict director."

Use of this form carries with it the risk of nonpersuasion because the jurors are told in the burden of proof instruction that if they do not form a belief on a proposition, that proposition fails. Use of this type of converse instruction requires independent evidence to support the facts submitted. These facts must be sufficient in law to defeat the plaintiff's claim. See *Shepard v. Ford Motor Company,* 457 S.W.2d 255 (Mo.App. 1970). *Hiers* does not suggest that defendant is obligated to tender an affirmative converse instruction to cure a plaintiff's verdict director that omits an essential ultimate issue; the defendant is entitled to make an appropriate objection to such a verdict director and stand on that objection. 834 S.W.2d at 735, n. 3.

The affirmative converse instruction should not be used to submit in the affirmative the same issue as has already been submitted in the verdict directing instruction. See *Stover v. Patrick,* 459 S.W.2d 393 (Mo. banc 1970), and *Oliver v. Bi-State Development Agency,* 494 S.W.2d 49 (Mo.1973). Use a true converse instruction to converse an element that is submitted by the verdict director.

Caution: Where an affirmative converse instruction is properly submitted, the verdict director must be modified by adding a phrase, commonly referred to as an "affirmative defense" tail, which refers the jury directly from the verdict director to the affirmative converse instruction. No such "tail" is required when a true converse instruction is submitted. See the discussion in MAI 33.01.

Committee Comment (1993 New)

In *Wilson v. Checker Cab Company,* 431 S.W.2d 122 (Mo.1968), where the plaintiff claimed that the defendant was negligent because its driver either stopped so that plaintiff stepped out onto a patch of ice or started the cab before she had fully alighted, the court approved the following affirmative converse instruction:

"Your verdict must be for defendant if you believe plaintiff fell after she had alighted from the defendant's taxicab and traveled approximately twenty feet from said taxicab."

However, the Supreme Court in *Hiers* described the affirmative converse instruction in *Wilson* as violating "a fundamental rule of our scheme of approved instructions," and criticized the holding in *Wilson* as "highly questionable."

The affirmative converse instruction may be used to submit an ultimate fact that, if true, would defeat plaintiff's submission. The affirmative converse instruction may also be used to submit legal excuse or justification when plaintiff submits on negligence per se. See MAI 33.05(2) and *Cowell v. Thompson*, 713 S.W.2d 52 (Mo.App.1986).

Notes of Decisions

1. In general

Instruction, as modified by court, directing jury to find for defendant if it believed that defendant's wife was sole owner and operator of roofing company and contracted for goods supplied by plaintiff, was better statement of law than converse submitted by defendant, instructing jury to find for defendant if it believed that defendant's wife owned and operated roofing business and contracted for goods supplied by plaintiff. Petry Roofing Supply, Inc. v. Sutton, 839 S.W.2d 337 (Mo.App.1992).

Evidence in medical malpractice action did not justify physician's affirmative converse instruction, which effectively required the jury to find for the physician if it believed the patient had failed to tell physician about left-sided symptoms prior to her stroke; affirmative converse instruction must be supported by independent evidence and the facts submitted must be sufficient in law to defeat plaintiff's claim; facts that merely relate to negligence or possible comparative fault on the part of the plaintiff do not amount to matters to be submitted as an affirmative converse instruction. Hiller v. Diestelhorst, 820 S.W.2d 522 (Mo.App.1991).

Affirmative converse instruction to a verdict directing instruction on vexatious refusal to pay pursuant to a contract of suretyship was properly refused where the affirmative converse merely submitted in the affirmative the same issue as submitted in the verdict directing instruction. Howard Const. Co. v. Teddy Woods Const. Co., 817 S.W.2d 556 (Mo.App.1991).

Characteristics of affirmative converse instruction are use of words "if you believe" and submission of proposition which does not appear in plaintiff's verdict directing instruction. Function of affirmative converse instruction is to permit defendant to present his theory of case without being required to directly negate plaintiff's theories; because affirmative converse instruction introduces different ultimate fact into instructions, it does not conclude with "tail" referring to plaintiff's verdict directing instruction as does true converse instruction. Affirmative converse instruction requires that defendant submit hypothesized ultimate issue which, if true, would defeat plaintiff's claim. Because defendant bears burden of proof on proposition submitted in affirmative converse instruction, that instruction is appropriate for use only when defendant has carried his burden to produce and relies on independent evidence supporting facts submitted in converse instruction. It is error to submit by affirmative converse instruction the same issues submitted in plaintiff's verdict director. Powers v. Ellfeldt, 768 S.W.2d 142, 145 (Mo. App.1989).

An affirmative converse instruction should not be used to submit the same issue submitted in the verdict directing instruction. Fidelity & Deposit Co. v. Fleischer, 772 S.W.2d 809, 817 (Mo.App.1989).

In view of omission from plaintiff's verdict director of express requirement that jury make a finding on the contested issue of whether her slip and fall occurred on landowners' property, landowners properly submitted the issue by means of an affirmative converse instruction rather than a converse instruction which directly followed the language of plaintiff's verdict director. McMullin v. Politte, 780 S.W.2d 94 (Mo.App.1989).

An affirmative converse instruction must submit and hypothesize ultimate fact issue which if true defeats plaintiff's claim. A defendant has the option of submitting his theory of the case through the use of an affirmative converse instruction, but when he does, he must carry his burden of persuasion by producing independent evidence supporting those facts submitted in the instruction. Tierney v. Berg, 679 S.W.2d 919[3, 4] (Mo.App.1984).

The facts hypothesized in an affirmative converse instruction must be sufficient in law to defeat plaintiff's claim. Linkogel v. Baker Protective Services, Inc., 659 S.W.2d 300[1] (Mo.App.1983).

Affirmative converse may be used to submit an ultimate fact which, if true, would defeat plaintiff's submission; it is improperly used to hypothesize factual issues not submitted by and essential to plaintiff's submission. Oliver v. Bi–State Dev. Agency, 494 S.W.2d 49[1–3] (Mo.1973).

Affirmative converse must have independent evidence to support it. Koirtyohann v. Washington Plumbing & Heating Co., 471 S.W.2d 217[7] (Mo.1971).

33.05(2) [2002 Revision] Converse Instructions—Affirmative Converse—Legal Justification for Negligence Per Se

Your verdict must be for defendant if you believe:

First, [defendant's automobile was on the wrong side of the road][1] because (*here set forth circumstances constituting legal justification or excuse*), and[1]

Second, defendant was not thereby negligent[2].

Notes On Use (2002 Revision)

1. This bracketed phrase is to be used to submit that element of plaintiff's verdict directing instruction which constitutes "negligence per se".

2. The terms "negligent" and "negligence" must be defined. See definitions in Chapter 11.00.

This instruction may only be used where plaintiff submits on negligence per se and only if it is supported by the evidence and the facts show that legal justification or excuse is applicable.

Caution: Where an affirmative converse instruction is properly submitted, the verdict director must be modified by adding a phrase, commonly referred to as an "affirmative defense" tail, which refers the jury directly from the verdict director to the affirmative converse instruction. No such "tail" is required when a true converse instruction is submitted. See the discussion in MAI 33.01.

Committee Comment (2002 Revision)

Caution: In order to submit this instruction, the trial court must determine that the circumstances relied upon by the defendant constitute a legal justification or excuse under Missouri law. "In general, legal justification or excuse requires proof of circumstances beyond the defendant's control and not the result of the defendant's negligence which justify or excuse strict compliance with the statute." *Egenreither v. Carter,* 23 S.W.3d 641, 645 (Mo.App. E.D.2000).

A problem in submitting a converse instruction may arise when the plaintiff submits a negligence per se theory such as MAI 17.17, or 17.18, where the term "negligence" is not mentioned, because the duty is imposed by regulation, statute, or ordinance. *Breeding v. Dodson Trailer Repair,* 679 S.W.2d 281, 287 (Mo. banc 1984); *Cowell v. Thompson,* 713 S.W.2d 52 (Mo.App.1986). Where plaintiff's verdict director does not require a finding of negligence, it is error to give a converse concerning negligence of the defendant. *Oventrop v. Bi–State Development Agency,* 521 S.W.2d 488 (Mo.App.1975). However, the defendant is entitled to instruct on legal justification or excuse, *Ruediger v. American Bus Lines, Inc.,* 426 S.W.2d 4 (Mo.1967), and may desire to use a converse instruction including the term "negligence," and thus be unable to properly submit a converse in substantially the same language as the plaintiff's verdict director. *Anderson v. Cahill,* 528 S.W.2d 742, 746 (Mo. banc 1975). In these circumstances an affirmative converse, not a true converse, is needed. An affirmative converse, unlike a true converse, should not and does not use the same language submitted by the plaintiff's verdict director. *Cowell v. Thompson,* 713 S.W.2d 52 (Mo. App.1986). Such an affirmative converse under these circumstances does not run contrary to MAI 1.01.

Library References:

C.J.S. Motor Vehicles § 530.
West's Key No. Digests, Automobiles ⟜246.

Notes of Decisions

1. In general

Model jury instruction likely misstates law for availability of converse instruction in negligence per se cases, where instruction does not require that jury find that facts constituting legal justification or excuse actually exist, but, rather, as drafted, it merely requires jury to find defendant exercised ordinary care or highest degree of care, and where statute or ordinance imposes affirmative duty beyond ordinary care, submission of that instruction would appear to impermissibly substitute ordinary care for standard of care established by legislature, and model jury instruction also fails to require that defendant must establish both circumstances beyond her control and freedom from negligence as required to establish legal justification or excuse. Egenreither v. Carter, 23 S.W.3d 641 (Mo.App.2000).

Defendant is not entitled to submit converse instruction patterned on MAI 33.05(2), regardless of nature of her explanation for failing to conform to statute, but she may submit converse instruction only if explanation constitutes legal justification or excuse; in general, legal justification or excuse requires proof of circumstances beyond defendant's control and not the result of defendant's negligence, which circumstances justify or excuse strict compliance with the statute. Egenreither v. Carter, 23 S.W.3d 641 (Mo.App.2000).

Compliance with leash law was not rendered impossible by any circumstance beyond defendant's control, so that defendant's explanation for failure to conform to leash law did not constitute legal justification or excuse for which she would be entitled to converse instruction on negligence per se claim submitted by victim of dog bite; fact that defendant was not at home when incident occurred did not relieve her of affirmative obligation imposed by leash law to insure that dog either remained in yard or was restrained on leash by responsible person, so as to prevent it from biting anyone, and in fact, evidence showed that defendant failed to use available dog pen to restrain dog. Egenreither v. Carter, 23 S.W.3d 641 (Mo. App.2000).

In personal injury action involving wrong side of the road case, it was reversible error to submit verdict directing instruction that withheld element of negligence from consideration where negligence per se theory of liability was not tried by consent; even though driver's guilty plea to traffic violation was admissible, submission of instruction based on negligence per se was improper where driver did not plead a statutory violation or negligence per se theory of liability. Myers v. Morrison, 822 S.W.2d 906 (Mo.App. 1991).

33.06 [Withdrawn 1990] Converse Instructions—Humanitarian Converse Instructions

33.07 [Withdrawn 1980] Converse Instructions—Issue of Sound and Disposing Mind and Memory

33.08 [Withdrawn 1980] Converse Instructions—Issue of Furnishing Services and Agreement to Pay

33.09 [Withdrawn 1980] Converse Instructions—Issue of Implied Agreement to Pay

33.10 [Withdrawn 1980] Converse Instructions—Issue of Plaintiff Furnishing Services

33.11 [Withdrawn 1980] Converse Instructions—Issue of Express Contract

33.12 [Withdrawn 1980] Converse Instructions—Conversing Issue of Accepting Benefits of Services

33.13 [Withdrawn 1980] Converse Instructions—General Converse

33.14 [Withdrawn 1980] Converse Instructions—Conversing Verdict Directing 22.02, 22.03, 22.04 and 22.05. Using "If You Do Not Believe" Introduction

(With respect to 33.06–33.14, all withdrawn, see MAI 33.01, General Comment).

33.15 [1995 Revision] Converse Instructions—Instructions Conversing Verdict Directing 22.02, 22.03, 22.04 and 22.05 Using "Unless You Believe" Introduction

33.15(1)
(Conversing Failure to Use Ordinary Care)

Your verdict must be for defendant unless you believe defendant failed to use ordinary care[1] [as submitted in Instruction Number _____].[2]

33.15(2)
(Conversing Causation)

Your verdict must be for defendant unless you believe plaintiff sustained damage as a direct result of defendant's failure to use ordinary care[1] [as submitted in Instruction Number _____].[2]

33.15(3)
(Conversing Negligence and Causation)

Your verdict must be for defendant unless you believe defendant failed to use ordinary care[1] [as submitted in Instruction Number _____],[2] and that as a direct result of such failure plaintiff sustained damage.

33.15(4)
(Conversing Damages)

Your verdict must be for defendant unless you believe plaintiff sustained damage.

33.15(5) [3]
(Conversing Causation Submitted With MAI 19.01 (First Alternate))

Your verdict must be for defendant unless you believe that defendant's failure to use ordinary care[1] [as submitted in Instruction Number _____][2] directly caused or directly contributed to cause damage to plaintiff.

33.15(6) [3]

(Conversing Negligence and Causation Submitted With MAI 19.01 (First Alternate))

Your verdict must be for defendant unless you believe that defendant failed to use ordinary care [1] [as submitted in Instruction Number _____] [2] and such failure directly caused or directly contributed to cause damage to plaintiff.

Notes on Use (1996 Revision)

1. The term "ordinary care" must be defined. See definitions in MAI 11.05 and 11.07.

2. This bracketed material may be included at the option of the defendant.

Caution: The above instructions are examples of the proper method for combining the "unless you believe" introductory phrase with the language from the portion of the verdict director selected to be conversed. These examples are not approved instructions for any particular litigation since the proper language for a converse instruction in any particular litigation depends upon the verdict director being conversed. See MAI 33.01 Converse Instructions—General Comment for rules concerning the use of converse instructions including the use of language from the verdict director in the converse instruction, modifications for conversing alternative verdict directors and limitations upon the number of allowable converse instructions.

3. In *Hiers v. Lemley,* 834 S.W.2d 729 (Mo. banc 1992), the Supreme Court held that a converse that required a verdict for defendant unless the jury found causation "as a direct result of" defendant's negligence was prejudicially erroneous where the verdict directing instruction submitted causation with an MAI 19.01 modification as "directly caused or directly contributed to cause". If the verdict directing instruction is modified with the second alternate in MAI 19.01, the converse instruction should utilize substantially the same language to converse causation. Where one of the alternates in MAI 19.01 is modified in a verdict director to fit a submission such as in death cases, premises cases, products cases, or malpractice cases, the converse instruction should utilize substantially the same modified language as used in the verdict directing instruction.

33.16 [1991 New] Converse Instructions—Damages— Exemplary

33.16(1)
(Conversing 10.01—Intentional Tort Constituting Outrageous Conduct)

You must not award plaintiff an additional amount as punitive damages under Instruction Number _____ (*here insert number of punitive damage instruction*) unless you believe the conduct of defendant as submitted in Instruction Number _____ (*here insert plaintiff's verdict directing instruction based on intentional tort*) was outrageous because of defendant's evil motive or reckless indifference to the rights of others.

33.16(2)
(Conversing 10.02—Negligence Constituting Conscious Disregard for Others)

You must not award plaintiff an additional amount as punitive damages under Instruction Number _____ (*here insert number of punitive damage instruction*) unless you believe the conduct of defendant as submitted in Instruction Number _____ (*here insert plaintiff's verdict directing instruction based on negligence*) showed complete indifference to or conscious disregard for the safety of others.

33.16(3)
(Conversing 10.04—Strict Liability Failure to Warn— Knowledge Constituting Conscious Disregard for Others)

You must not award plaintiff an additional amount as punitive damages under Instruction Number _____ (*here insert number of punitive damage instruction*) unless you believe:

> First, at the time defendant sold the (*describe product*) defendant knew of the danger submitted in Instruction Number _____ (*here insert number of plaintiff's strict liability verdict directing instruction*), and

Second, defendant thereby showed complete indifference to or conscious disregard for the safety of others.

33.16(4)
(Conversing 10.07—Negligence—Specific Acts and Knowledge Constituting Conscious Disregard for Others)

You must not award plaintiff an additional amount as punitive damages under Instruction Number _____ (*here insert number of punitive damage instruction*) unless you believe:

First, (*here insert the specific act or omission that supports submission of punitive damages*), and

Second, defendant knew or had information from which defendant, in the exercise of ordinary care,[1] should have known that such conduct created a high degree of probability of injury, and

Third, defendant thereby showed complete indifference to or conscious disregard for the safety of others.

Notes on Use (1991 New)

1. The phrase "ordinary care" must be defined. See Chapter 11.

Under *Menaugh v. Resler Optometry, Inc.,* 799 S.W.2d 71 (Mo. banc 1990), the defendant is entitled to a converse of the punitive damage instruction.

The above instructions are examples of the proper method of combining the "unless you believe" introductory phrase with the language from the punitive damages instructions that may be submitted in intentional tort, negligence and strict liability cases. See MAI 33.01 Converse Instructions—General Comment, for rules concerning the use of converse instructions. Where punitive damages are submitted, the defendant would be entitled to a converse instruction to the punitive damage instruction as well as a converse instruction to the verdict director.

Library References:

C.J.S. Damages § 177.
West's Key No. Digests, Damages ☞210.

34.00

WITHDRAWAL INSTRUCTIONS

Analysis of Instructions

Westlaw Electronic Research

See Westlaw Electronic Research Guide preceding the Table of Instructions.

Library References:

C.J.S. Trial § 305.
West's Key No. Digests, Trial ☞203(4).

34.01 [1978 Revision] Withdrawal Instructions—General Comment

A withdrawal instruction is only to be given when during the course of the trial a false issue, improper evidence, or evidence of an abandoned issue has been injected. The purpose of a withdrawal instruction may be served by the court sustaining a motion to strike and admonishing the jury to disregard the evidence. However, in certain instances, the trial court may determine that such action is inadequate, inappropriate or untimely and that a written instruction is necessary.

The court may properly give a withdrawal instruction when it has received evidence upon an issue which is later abandoned either by choice or by reason of inadequate proof for final submission to the jury. The instruction to be given is that the issue is no longer open for the jury's consideration.

Evidence, rather than an entire issue, may also properly be withdrawn by instruction. In the event evidence, rather than an issue, is sought to be withdrawn from the jury's consideration, care must be taken that such evidence does not also concern an issue still before the jury.

Notes of Decisions

1. In general

Withdrawal instructions may be given when evidence on issue has been received but there is inadequate proof for submission of issue to jury; when there is evidence presented which might mislead jury in its consideration of case as pleaded and submitted; when there is evidence presented directed to issue that is abandoned; when there is evidence of such character that might easily raise false issue; or when appropriate to clarify damages for jury. Stevens v. Craft, 956 S.W.2d 351 (Mo.App. S.D. 1997).

Determining whether to give withdrawal instruction is matter within trial court's discretion. Stevens v. Craft, 956 S.W.2d 351 (Mo. App. S.D.1997).

Use of withdrawal instruction is to avoid misleading jury on specious issue. Bailey v. Norfolk and Western Ry. Co., 942 S.W.2d 404 (Mo.App.1997).

MAI 34.01 may be given when evidence on issue has been received, but there is inadequate proof given for final submission of issue to jury; withdrawal instructions should be given when there is evidence which might mislead jury in its consideration of case as pleaded and submitted. Arnold v. Ingersoll–Rand Co., 908 S.W.2d 757 (Mo. App.1995).

Giving or refusing to give withdrawal instruction is discretionary and reviewable for abuse, which occurs when trial court's ruling is clearly against logic and circumstances and is so arbitrary and unreasonable as to shock sense of justice and indicate lack of careful consideration. Shady Valley Park & Pool, Inc. v. Fred Weber, Inc., 913 S.W.2d 28 (Mo.App.1995).

Abandonment of issue whether excessive train speed caused collision with car did not entitle railroad company to withdrawal of speed evidence from jury; evidence of train speed was used to calculate braking distance, how long bell, horn, and whistle could have sounded before train struck car, and train speed and automobile speed were also relevant to driver's ability to keep lookout and to react if he heard whistle; trial court did not abuse its discretion in refusing withdrawal instructions that were too broad. Elfrink v. Burlington Northern Railroad Co., 845 S.W.2d 607 (Mo.App.1992).

Trial court was not required to give withdrawal instructions involving loss of visibility evidence, effective median barrier, loss of traffic, circuitous travel, loss of business by tenants, loss of rental income and inconvenience of travel in condemnation case involving property used for shopping center; the elements were relevant to theory that the taking involved loss of access destroying future use. State ex rel. Missouri Highway and Transp. Com'n v. Jim Lynch Toyota, Inc., 830 S.W.2d 481 (Mo.App.1992).

Use of withdrawal instructions is to avoid misleading jury on specious issue; the giving or refusal of withdrawal instructions is up to discretion of trial judge. Bradley v. Browning–Ferris Ind., 779 S.W.2d 760 (Mo. App.1989).

Trial court did not err in refusing to submit instruction withdrawing from consideration all evidence of misuse or evidence of plaintiff's fault since evidence was properly admitted for the consideration of the jury in determining the existence of a defect and the causation of the accident. Earll v. Consolidated Aluminum Corp., 714 S.W.2d 932[5] (Mo.App.1986).

Where there is evidence in the case which might raise a false issue, it is reversible error for the court to fail to give an instruction withdrawing such evidence from the jury's consideration. Harris v. Washington, 654 S.W.2d 303[13] (Mo.App.1983).

Purpose of withdrawal instruction is to avoid misleading and confusing the jury because of some spurious issue raised by testimony. The instruction is given at the discretion of the trial court, and where there was no reasonable likelihood that the jury would be in any way confused or misled, refusal of the withdrawal instruction was not an abuse of discretion and was not reversible error. Weisbach v. Vargas, 656 S.W.2d 797[1–3] (Mo.App.1983).

Permissible but not mandatory. Where condemnee objected to court's erroneous admission of evidence of general benefits, condemnee did not waive the error by failing to offer a withdrawal instruction. State ex rel. State Hwy. Com'n v. Johnson, 544 S.W.2d 276[2] (Mo.App.1976).

Where evidence on a false issue was developed in evidence, giving a withdrawal instruction was discretionary. Schmid v. Langenberg, 526 S.W.2d 940[2–5] (Mo.App. 1975).

34.02 [1978 Revision] Withdrawal Instructions—Issues and Evidence

The [evidence] [matter] [issue] [fact] [1] of (*here insert withdrawn issue such as "the plaintiff's hospital and medical bills"*) is withdrawn from the case and you are not to consider such [evidence] [matter] [issue] [fact] [1] in arriving at your verdict.

Notes on Use (1969 New)

1. Select appropriate term.

Committee Comment (1969 New)

In *Roberts v. Emerson Electric Manufacturing Co.*, 362 S.W.2d 579, 582 (Mo.1962), plaintiff sued for failure of defendant, his employer, to give him a proper service letter of dismissal. The court said:

Paragraph 14 assigns error in the giving of Instruction 3, which follows: "The Court instructs the jury that this action is not one for damages for wrongful discharge of plaintiff by defendant, and the question as to whether plaintiff was rightfully or wrongfully discharged by defendant is not material to any of the issues in this action and should not be considered in your deliberations." Instruction 3 was a cautionary instruction intended to guard against the consideration of a false issue. "It is not only the office of instructions to inform the jury as to the law of the issues raised, but, where the evidence is of a character as might easily lead to the raising of a false issue, the court ought to guard against such an issue by appropriate instructions." *Estes v. Desnoyers Shoe Co.*, 155 Mo. 577, 56 S.W. 316.

If specific evidence of general benefits is improperly admitted, such evidence may be withdrawn by an instruction patterned after MAI 34.02. MAI 34.03 may be used in addition thereto.

While MAI 34.02 is called a "withdrawal" instruction, its use is not limited to withdrawing evidence which is accidently or improperly admitted. It is intended rather to clarify what the jury is to consider in assessing damages. Instructions patterned after MAI 34.01 are intended to withdraw a specific matter which might otherwise mislead the jury. MAI 34.03 may be given at the defendant's option while MAI 34.02 may be given only at the discretion of the trial judge.

Library References:

C.J.S. Trial § 305.
West's Key No. Digests, Trial ⊸203(4).

Notes of Decisions

_____

1. In general

Medical malpractice defendant was not entitled to instruction withdrawing from jury's consideration fact that defendant did not order CAT scan prior to surgery, even though plaintiff's expert could not state whether failure caused or contributed to injury; issue was not abandoned, and remained relevant to issue of whether standard of care was followed. Klaus v. Deen, 883 S.W.2d 904 (Mo.App. E.D., 1994).

Even though propane gas explosion plaintiff had abandoned negligence theory based on defendant's failure to train distributors, failure to train evidence remained relevant to plaintiff's failure to warn-strict liability issue, and thus denial of withdrawal instruction was proper. Heifner v. Synergy Gas Corp., 883 S.W.2d 29 (Mo.App. S.D., 1994).

Use of MAI 34.02 is not limited to withdrawing evidence which is accidently or improperly admitted; it is intended rather to clarify what jury is to consider in assessing damages and is intended to withdraw specific matter which might otherwise mislead jury. Dillard v. Atchison, Topeka and Santa Fe Railway Co., 882 S.W.2d 211 (Mo.App.1994).

In condemnation proceeding, it was not error for trial court to refuse to give MAI 34.02, which would have withdrawn the issue of traffic from the jury's consideration, where the evidence that there would be increased traffic passing the condemnee's property was admissible for the purpose of showing impact on property's highest and best use. State ex rel. Missouri Highway and Transp. Com'n v. Jim Lynch Toyota, Inc., 854 S.W.2d 490 (Mo.App.1993).

In action arising from automobile accident, trial court did not abuse discretion in failing to give requested withdrawal instruction on issue of whether plaintiff motorist could sustain degenerative changes in knee as result of limited ankle movement where evidence of that issue was before jury. Seabaugh v.

Milde Farms, Inc., 816 S.W.2d 202 (Mo. 1991).

Trial court in condemnation suit did not abuse its discretion in giving withdrawal instruction barring jury from considering testimony of condemnor's expert except as it rebutted condemnee's evidence where the sales relied on by the expert for purposes of valuing property were not comparable to the property in question and where the expert's opinion of value after taking was unsupported. State ex rel. Missouri Highway and Transp. Com'n v. Union Realty and Securities Co., 827 S.W.2d 768 (Mo.App.1992).

In homeowner's suit against builder based on breach of implied warranty of suitability, trial court erred in not submitting withdrawal instruction since testimony regarding what builder should have done was irrelevant. Lieber v. Bridges, 650 S.W.2d 688[1] (Mo. App.1983).

Where plaintiff in medical malpractice had on cross-examination questioned defendant's medical witnesses about their agreement or disagreement with statements in medical texts, the court properly instructed the jury that readings to which _no witness agreed_ "are not evidence". Berring v. Jacob, 595 S.W.2d 412[4] (Mo.App.1980).

Not-in-MAI withdrawal instruction in wrongful death action regarding widow's re-marriage. Salsberry v. Archibald Plumbing & Heating Co., Inc., 587 S.W.2d 907[18] (Mo. App.1979).

Withdrawal instruction to disregard elements of damage is presumptively effective. Green v. Crunden Martin Mfg. Co., 575 S.W.2d 930[8, 9] (Mo.App.1978).

Permissible but not mandatory. Where condemnee objected to court's erroneous admission of evidence of general benefits, condemnee did not waive the error by failing to offer a withdrawal instruction. State ex rel. State Hwy. Comm'n v. Johnson, 544 S.W.2d 276[2] (Mo.App.1976).

Where court erroneously admitted evidence of workmen's compensation received by injured plaintiff, refusal to give her withdrawal instruction was reversible error. Womack v. Crescent Metal Products, 539 S.W.2d 481[2–4] (Mo.App.1976).

Giving or refusing withdrawal instruction is discretionary and error only when abused. Helming v. Adams, 509 S.W.2d 159[13, 15] (Mo.App.1974).

In condemnation case court properly refused to withdraw evidence of construction damage which could have been anticipated at time of taking. Northeast Missouri Electric Power Co-op v. Cary, 485 S.W.2d 862[4] (Mo.App.1972).

When evidence is admissible against one defendant but not the other the latter is entitled to an instruction limiting the extent of that evidence. Wors v. Glasgow Village Supermarket, 460 S.W.2d 583[3] (Mo.1970).

Where defendant's instruction withdrew three items of plaintiff's damages but one of those three items was compensable, the withdrawal instruction was properly refused, and the court had no duty to correctly modify the instruction. Wors v. Glasgow Village Supermarket, 460 S.W.2d 583[5, 6] (Mo.1970).

Where court admitted evidence of rental income but that element was not considered by subsequent value witnesses, trial court properly gave withdrawal instruction not to consider evidence of rental income. State ex rel. State Highway Commission v. Franklin, 456 S.W.2d 26[1–3] (Mo.1970).

Where plaintiff's evidence of medical expense was improperly admitted over defendant's objection of no causation, the court erred in refusing defendant's withdrawal instruction. DeMoulin v. Kissir, 446 S.W.2d 162 [5–7] (Mo.App.1969).

Where condemnor feared evidence of amount of gravel sold from condemned land would be misunderstood by the jury, condemnor should have offered a "withdrawal or delimiting instruction." State ex rel. State Highway Commission v. Yackel, 445 S.W.2d 389[7] (Mo.App.1969).

Withdrawal instruction MAI 34.02 given to withdraw part of witness' testimony. Welch v. Sheley, 443 S.W.2d 110[4] (Mo.1969).

Where defendant had no duty to paint center stripe on highway detour and that issue was not submitted, court properly gave

withdrawal instruction where there was evidence of such failure. Gilmore v. Union Const. Co., 439 S.W.2d 763[12] (Mo.1969).

Withdrawal instruction held confusing and erroneous. State ex rel. State Hwy. Com'n v. Flick, 427 S.W.2d 469[3] (Mo.1968).

Giving or refusing MAI 30.01 [Now 34.02] withdrawing evidence of unrelated medical expenses is discretionary. Kasper v. Helfrich, 421 S.W.2d 66[16] (Mo.App.1967).

Defendant properly modified withdrawal instruction MAI 30.01 [Now 34.02] where it clarified plaintiff's verdict director by excluding consideration of a false issue. Temple v. Atchison, T. & S.F. Ry., 417 S.W.2d 97[1, 2, 4] (Mo.1967).

2. Harmless error

Instruction erroneously withdrawing an element of plaintiff's damage not prejudicial where jury found against plaintiff on the issue of liability; harmless error. Gardner v. McGee, 505 S.W.2d 452 (Mo.App.1974).

3. Workmen's Compensation

Instruction, that evidence of outcome of employee's worker's compensation claim was withdrawn from case, and jury was not to consider such evidence in arriving at verdict, was proper in workers' compensation retaliation action; allowing jury to consider administrative law judge's (ALJ's) finding that employee suffered from two work-related injuries, one of which was compensable, would likely have caused jury to confuse finding with actual ruling against employer. Wolfe v. Central Mine Equipment Co., 895 S.W.2d 83 (Mo.App. E.D.,1995).

Withdrawal instruction properly withdrew evidence of workmen's compensation benefits paid plaintiff by his employer. But error to add a paragraph that if plaintiff recovered from defendant he would have to repay his employer. Sampson v. Missouri Pacific R. Co., 560 S.W.2d 573[9–13] (Mo. banc 1978).

4. Automobile accidents

Defendant was not entitled to withdrawal instruction on issue of future medical expenses in personal injury action, in which doctor testified that he expected plaintiff's neck complaints to be permanent, and plaintiff testified, five years after accident, that he continued to occasionally take muscle relaxers to sleep. Stevens v. Craft, 956 S.W.2d 351 (Mo.App. S.D.1997).

Refusal to grant withdrawal instruction on issue of plaintiff's possible future surgery was not an abuse of discretion in automobile accident action in which there was evidence that plaintiff had been told he needed back surgery for pre-existing condition and that accident could have aggravated that condi-

tion; plaintiff did not mention such surgery in closing argument, there was nothing before jury concerning expenses for surgery of any kind, and there was no representation to jury that plaintiff's ruptured discs were attributable to accident or that any recommended surgery was intended to address injuries caused by accident. Stevens v. Craft, 956 S.W.2d 351 (Mo.App. S.D.1997).

34.03 [1969 New] Withdrawal Instructions—General Benefits—Eminent Domain

In determining the value of defendant's remaining property, you must not consider any general benefit which is conferred upon all property within usable range of (*here describe the improvement which is the subject matter of the action; e.g., the proposed highway, park, etc.*).

Notes on Use (1969 New)

This may be given as a separate instruction or as an addition to the general damage instruction, at the option of defendant. Evidence of general benefits should be excluded upon proper objection, but the withdrawal instruction should nevertheless be proper, because the jury would otherwise take them into consideration in determining fair market value.

If there is evidence of general detriments, they may be withdrawn in the same way.

If specific evidence of general benefits is improperly admitted, such evidence may be withdrawn by an instruction patterned after MAI 34.02. MAI 34.03 may be used in addition thereto.

While MAI 34.03 is called a "withdrawal" instruction, its use is not limited to withdrawing evidence which is accidently or improperly admitted. It is intended rather to clarify what the jury is to consider in assessing damages. Instructions patterned after MAI 34.02 are intended to withdraw a specific matter which might otherwise mislead the jury. MAI 34.03 may be given at the defendant's option while MAI 34.02 may be given only at the discretion of the trial judge.

Library References:

C.J.S. Eminent Domain § 308.
West's Key No. Digests, Eminent Domain ⊜222.

Notes of Decisions

In general 1
Mandatory 2

———

1. In general

Trial court's failure to give instruction requested by owner in partial condemnation proceeding precluding consideration of evidence of general benefit as offset against owner's damages was not prejudicial, and did not require reversal; evidence was presented of improvement in highest and best use of owner's land due to highway construction, which is quintessential example of "special benefit," as opposed to "general benefit." State ex rel. Missouri Highway & Transportation Commission v. Edelen, 872 S.W.2d 551 (Mo.App.1994).

In condemnation proceeding, any error in admitting evidence of general benefits was cured when MAI 34.03 was given; withdrawal and exclusion of erroneously admitted evidence leaves no ground for reversing judgment on account of such admission. State ex rel. Missouri Highway and Transp. Com'n v. Jim Lynch Toyota, Inc., 854 S.W.2d 490 (Mo.App.1993).

Landowners' testimony in condemnation proceeding that some damages were due to general traffic congestion on widened road was specific evidence of general damages that could be withdrawn by instruction. State ex rel. Missouri Hwy. and Transp. v. Mertz, 778 S.W.2d 366 (Mo.App.1989).

Permissible but not mandatory. Where condemnee objected to court's erroneous admission of evidence of general benefits, condemnee did not waive the error by failing to offer a withdrawal instruction. State ex rel. State Hwy. Com'n v. Johnson, 544 S.W.2d 276[2] (Mo.App.1976).

Even where there was no evidence of general benefits, giving MAI 34.03 was proper.

State ex rel. State Hwy. Com'n v. Sams, 484 S.W.2d 276[2] (Mo.1972).

Where defendant gave MAI 30.02 [Now 34.03] excluding consideration of general benefits to remaining tract, he cured error in admitting evidence of general benefits. State ex rel. State Hwy. Com'n v. Riss, 432 S.W.2d 193[12] (Mo.1968).

2. Mandatory

Trial court is required to give standard jury instruction preventing jury from considering evidence of general benefit as offset against owner's damage when requested by defendants, in partial condemnation proceeding, regardless of whether there is evidence of general benefit. State ex rel. Missouri Highway & Transportation Commission v. Edelen, 872 S.W.2d 551 (Mo.App.1994).

Error to refuse general benefit withdrawal instruction MAI 34.03 when requested by defendant whether or not there is evidence of general benefits. State ex rel. State Hwy. Com'n v. Southern Dev. Co., 509 S.W.2d 18[1, 2] (Mo.1974).

34.04 [1978 New] Withdrawal Instructions— F.E.L.A.—Assumption of the Risk

Plaintiff does not assume any of the risks of his employment. This matter is withdrawn from the case and you are not to consider such evidence in arriving at your verdict.

Notes on Use (1978 New)

This instruction may only be given if the false issue of assumption of the risk is injected in the case. See the General Comment at MAI 34.01.

Library References:

C.J.S. Trial § 305.
West's Key No. Digests, Trial ⚘203(4).

Notes of Decisions

1. In general

Trial court did not abuse its discretion in refusing to give railroad worker's proffered instruction that assumption of risk was not at issue in worker's suit under Federal Employ-ers' Liability Act against railroad, where issue of assumption of risk had not been raised by railroad. Rowe v. Norfolk & Western Ry. Co., 787 S.W.2d 751 (Mo.App.1990).

34.05 [1991 Revision] Withdrawal Instruction—Advance Payments, Undisputed Partial Settlements, or Collateral Source Payments

If the jury has knowledge, from the evidence or a trial incident, of an advance payment, a partial settlement, or a collateral source payment, then upon the request of any party the following addendum must be added to the appropriate damage instruction:

In determining the [total][1] amount of plaintiff's damages you are not to consider any evidence of prior payment [to] [on behalf of][2] plaintiff. The judge will consider any such payment and make an adjustment if required by law.

Notes on Use (1991 Revision)

1. Insert if the case is submitted under comparative fault.

2. Select the appropriate bracketed phrase; if both are appropriate, use both in the disjunctive.

When the fact or the amount of a partial settlement is in dispute, the addendum in MAI 7.02 is to be added to the damage instruction. If MAI 7.02 is used, MAI 34.05 is not to be used because both instructions contain similar withdrawal language.

Committee Comment (1983 New)

MAI 1.06 prohibits any instruction directing the jury to credit its verdict with the amount of any advance payment or partial settlement. If appropriate, such a credit will be allowed by the trial court. See the Committee Comment to MAI 1.06 for a discussion of this procedure. Thus, it is no longer necessary to admit evidence of a settlement payment or to allow counsel to advise the jury of a settlement in order to obtain credit for a prior payment.

Despite the fact that MAI 7.01 has been withdrawn, the jury may have knowledge of some prior payment. Such knowledge may be acquired from impeaching evidence, a nonresponsive answer, collateral source supposition, or inference from the disappearance of a settling party defendant from the scene during trial. Even though explanation thereof may be made by oral ruling of the court, the jury is likely to speculate about the effect of such payment on its award.

While MAI 34.05 is called a "withdrawal" instruction, its use is not limited to withdrawing evidence which is accidentally or improperly admitted. It is intended rather to clarify what the jury is to consider in assessing damages.

Library References:

C.J.S. Damages § 184.
West's Key No. Digests, Damages ⊙⟶214.

Notes of Decisions

1. In general

Motorist who was struck simultaneously by two automobiles, and who sued drivers of those other automobiles, settling with one for $25,000 prior to trial, was not prejudiced by trial court's failure to instruct jury that it could not consider $25,000 payment in assessing damages; jury rendered verdict in nonsettling defendant's favor, thus finding that plaintiff did not prove negligence or damages. Toppins v. Miller, 891 S.W.2d 473 (Mo.App. E.D.,1994).

Withdrawal instruction relating to payments to plaintiff was properly given by trial court where defense counsel injected collateral source payments of plaintiff's medical bills by insurance; withdrawal instruction did not improperly suggest to the jury that award would be reduced by the court by the amount of the payments. Wallace v. May, 822 S.W.2d 471 (Mo.App.1991).

35.00

ILLUSTRATIONS

Analysis of Instructions

ILLUSTRATIONS

Westlaw Electronic Research

See Westlaw Electronic Research Guide preceding the Table of Instructions.

35.00 [1998 Revision] Illustrations—General Comment

The Committee furnishes for your use illustrations prepared by the Committee in certain hypothetical cases using court-approved instructions. If any conflict exists between an instruction and an illustration, the court-approved instruction governs. *Northeast Mo. Elec. Power Co-op. v. Fulkerson,* 542 S.W.2d 26 (Mo.App.1976), and *State ex rel. State Highway Com'n v. Schwartz,* 526 S.W.2d 952 (Mo.App. 1975).

In referring to the illustrations, care should be used to be certain that the illustration and its instructions apply to the facts and legal theory of the case being submitted and that none of the instructions used in the illustration has been revised by the Committee. (Always check the most recent pocket part.)

In the illustrations in this edition of MAI, factual situations may differ from those used in illustrations in prior editions of MAI. The annotations to the prior illustrations will vary in applicability depending on the extent to which the former factual situation was carried over into the present illustration.

35.01 [1991 Withdrawn] Illustrations—Head–On Collision With Counterclaim

35.02 [1996 Revision] Illustrations—Apportionment of Fault—Defendant Adjudged at Fault in Prior Trial Claiming Apportionment in Separate Trial

Sam Sampson was a passenger in a Ford automobile being driven by his friend William White. Sampson was seriously injured when the Ford automobile collided with a Missouri Pacific train at a railroad grade crossing. In prior litigation, Sampson obtained a judgment for his personal injuries in the amount of $300,000 against Missouri Pacific.

In the present action, Missouri Pacific brings an independent action against William White seeking apportionment of fault of the damages awarded Sampson against Missouri Pacific.

Instruction No. 1
(Same as MAI 2.01)

Instruction No. 2
(See MAI 2.03 (1980 New))

As you remember, the court gave you a general instruction before the presentation of any evidence in this case. The court will not repeat that instruction at this time. However, that instruction and the additional instructions, to be given to you now, constitute the law of this case and each such instruction is equally binding upon you. You should consider each instruction in light of and in harmony with the other instructions, and you should apply the instructions as a whole to the evidence.

Instruction No. 3
(See MAI 11.02 II (1996 Revision))

The term "negligent" or "negligence" as used in these instructions means the failure to use that degree of care that a very careful person would use under the same or similar circumstances.

Instruction No. 4
(See MAI 3.01 (1998 Revision))

In these instructions, you are told that your verdict depends on whether or not you believe certain propositions

of fact submitted to you. The burden is upon the party who relies upon any such proposition to cause you to believe that such proposition is more likely to be true than not true. In determining whether or not you believe any proposition, you must consider only the evidence and the reasonable inferences derived from the evidence. If the evidence in the case does not cause you to believe a particular proposition submitted, then you cannot return a verdict requiring belief of that proposition.

Instruction No. 5
(See MAI 2.02 (1980 Revision))

In returning your verdict you will form beliefs as to the facts. The court does not mean to assume as true any fact referred to in these instructions but leaves it to you to determine what the facts are.

Instruction No. 6
(See MAI 2.04 (1981 Revision))

There are two claims submitted to you and each of them contains a separate verdict form. The verdict forms included in these instructions contain directions for completion and will allow you to return the permissible verdicts in this case. Nine or more of you must agree in order to return any verdict. A verdict must be signed by each juror who agrees to it.

* * * * * * *

Instruction No. 7
(See MAI 2.05 (1980 New))

Instructions 7 and 8 and general instructions 1 through 6 apply to the claim of plaintiff Missouri Pacific seeking an apportionment of fault. Use Verdict A to return your verdict on this claim.

Instruction No. 8
(See MAI 17.02 (1980 Revision), 17.03 (1965 New),
17.05 (1965 New), 19.01 (1986 Revision))

Your verdict must be for plaintiff Missouri Pacific if you believe:

First, either:

> defendant William White failed to keep a careful lookout, or

> defendant William White drove at an excessive speed, and

Second, defendant William White, in any one or more of the respects submitted in Paragraph First, was thereby negligent, and

Third, such negligence either directly caused or directly contributed to cause damage to Sam Sampson.

VERDICT A
(See MAI 36.16 (1979 New))

Note: Complete this form by writing in the name required by your verdict.

On your claim of plaintiff Missouri Pacific seeking an apportionment of fault, we, the undersigned jurors, find in favor of:

(Plaintiff Missouri Pacific)   or   (Defendant William White)

Note: All jurors who agree with the above findings must sign below:

_____   _____
_____   _____
_____   _____
_____   _____
_____   _____

*   *   *   *   *   *   *

Instruction No. 9
(See MAI 2.05 (1980 New))

Instructions 9 and 10 and general instructions 1 through 6 apply to the claim for assessment of the proportions of fault. Use Verdict B to return your verdict on this claim.

Instruction No. 10
(See MAI 4.14 (1979 New))

If your verdict is in favor of plaintiff Missouri Pacific and against defendant William White on the claim seeking apportionment of fault for the $300,000 damages awarded Sam Sampson in the other trial mentioned in the evidence, you must assess the proportion of the fault which each party listed in Verdict B has for such damage.

VERDICT B
(See MAI 36.15 (1979 New))

Note: Complete this form if fault is to be apportioned.

On the claim of plaintiff Missouri Pacific for assessment of the proportions of fault for Sam Sampson's damages assessed in the prior trial, we, the undersigned jurors, find:

Note: Complete by writing in the percentage of the relative fault for each party you believe to be at fault. You may not write in "zero" for plaintiff Missouri Pacific. The total of the percentage you assess must not exceed 100%.

Plaintiff Missouri Pacific is _____% at fault.

Defendant William White is _____% at fault.

Note: All jurors who agree with the above findings must sign below.

_____   _____
_____   _____
_____   _____
_____   _____
_____   _____
_____   _____

*   *   *   *   *   *   *

Committee Comment (1983 Revision)

Under the "packaging" concept certain instructions will be fastened together to form their respective packages. See MAI 2.00 General Comments. The asterisks through the Illustration designate the end of one package and the beginning of another.

In the prior trial, Missouri Pacific was found to be at fault for Sam Sampson's damages. The basis for that fault is not submitted by instruction for redetermination in the second trial. However, counsel may refer in statements or argument to any ground of Missouri Pacific's fault for Sam Sampson's damages which is supported by the evidence and which properly is before the jury in the second trial.

35.03 [1996 Revision] Illustrations—Head–On Collision—Suit by Passenger Against Other Driver—Third–Party Claim Against Driver of Passenger's Vehicle for Apportionment of Fault

A Buick driven by Prudence Driver and occupied by plaintiff-passenger, Easy Ryder, was struck head-on in its proper lane of travel by a Ford driven by defendant, Harold Careless, which crossed into the wrong lane. Ryder was injured and filed suit against Careless alone. Careless then filed a third-party claim against Driver seeking apportionment of fault for Ryder's damages.

Instruction No. 1
(Same as MAI 2.01)

Instruction No. 2
(See MAI 2.03 (1980 New))

As you remember, the court gave you a general instruction before the presentation of any evidence in this case. The court will not repeat that instruction at this time. However, that instruction and the additional instructions, to be given to you now, constitute the law of this case and each such instruction is equally binding upon you. You should consider each instruction in light of and in harmony with the other instructions, and you should apply the instructions as a whole to the evidence. The order in which the instructions are given is no indication of their relative importance. All of the instructions are in writing and will be available to you in the jury room.

Instruction No. 3
(See MAI 11.03 (1996 Revision))

The term "negligent" or "negligence" as used in these instructions means the failure to use the highest degree of care. The phrase "highest degree of care" means that degree of care that a very careful person would use under the same or similar circumstances.

606

Instruction No. 4
(See MAI 3.01 (1998 Revision))

In these instructions, you are told that your verdict depends on whether or not you believe certain propositions of fact submitted to you. The burden is upon the party who relies upon any such proposition to cause you to believe that such proposition is more likely to be true than not true. In determining whether or not you believe any proposition, you must consider only the evidence and the reasonable inferences derived from the evidence. If the evidence in the case does not cause you to believe a particular proposition submitted, then you cannot return a verdict requiring belief of that proposition.

Instruction No. 5
(See MAI 2.02 (1980 Revision))

In returning your verdicts you will form beliefs as to the facts. The court does not mean to assume as true any fact referred to in these instructions but leaves it to you to determine what the facts are.

Instruction No. 6
(See MAI 2.04 (1981 Revision))

There are three claims submitted to you and each of them contains a separate verdict form. The verdict forms included in these instructions contain directions for completion and will allow you to return the permissible verdicts in this case. Nine or more of you must agree in order to return any verdict. A verdict must be signed by each juror who agrees to it.

* * * * * * *

Instruction No. 7
(See MAI 2.05 (1980 New))

Instructions 7 through 9 and general instructions 1 through 6 apply to the claim of plaintiff Ryder for personal injuries against defendant Careless. Use Verdict A to return your verdict on this claim.

Instruction No. 8
(See MAI 17.01 (1980 Revision), 17.13 (1978
Revision), 19.01 (1986 Revision))

Your verdict must be for plaintiff Ryder if you believe:

First, defendant Careless' automobile was on the wrong
side of the road, and

Second, defendant Careless was thereby negligent, and

Third, such negligence directly caused or directly contributed to cause damage to plaintiff.

Instruction No. 9
(See MAI 4.01 (1980 Revision))

If you find in favor of plaintiff Ryder, then you must
award plaintiff such sum as you believe will fairly and justly
compensate plaintiff for any damages you believe he sustained and is reasonably certain to sustain in the future that
the collision directly caused or directly contributed to cause.

VERDICT A
(See MAI 36.01 (1980 Revision))

Note: Complete this form by writing in the name required
by your verdict.

On the claim of plaintiff Ryder for personal injuries
against defendant Careless, we, the undersigned jurors, find
in favor of:

_____

(Plaintiff Ryder)   or   (Defendant Careless)

Note: Complete the following paragraph only if the above
finding is in favor of plaintiff Ryder.

We, the undersigned jurors, assess the damages of plaintiff Ryder at $_____ (*stating the amount*).

Note: All jurors who agree to the above findings must sign
below.

_____   _____
_____   _____
_____   _____
_____   _____

_____   _____
_____   _____

*   *   *   *   *   *   *

Instruction No. 10
(See MAI 2.05 (1980 New))

Instructions 10 and 11 and general instructions 1 through 6 apply to the claim of defendant Careless against third-party defendant Driver seeking an apportionment of fault. Use Verdict B to return your verdict on the claim.

Instruction No. 11
(See MAI 17.02 (1980 Revision), 17.04 (1978 Revision), 17.05 (1965 New), 19.01 (1986 Revision))

Your verdict must be for defendant Careless if you believe:

First, either:

third-party defendant Driver failed to keep a careful lookout, or

third-party defendant Driver knew or by the use of the highest degree of care could have known that there was a reasonable likelihood of collision in time thereafter to have swerved but third-party defendant Driver failed to do so, and

Second, third-party defendant Driver, in any one or more of the respects submitted in Paragraph First, was thereby negligent, and

Third, such negligence directly caused or directly contributed to cause damage to plaintiff.

VERDICT B
(See MAI 36.16 (1979 New))

Note: Complete this form by writing in the name required by your verdict.

On the claim of defendant Careless against third-party defendant Driver seeking an apportionment of fault, we, the undersigned jurors, find in favor of:

_____

(Defendant Careless) or (Third–Party Defendant Driver)

Note: All jurors who agree with the above findings must sign below.

_____	_____
_____	_____
_____	_____
_____	_____

* * * * * * *

Instruction No. 12
(See MAI 2.05 (1980 New))

Instructions 12 and 13 and general instructions 1 through 6 apply to the claim for assessment of the proportions of fault. Use Verdict C to return your verdict on this claim.

Instruction No. 13
(See MAI 4.13 (1979 New))

If Verdict A is in favor of plaintiff Ryder and against defendant Careless and if Verdict B is in favor of defendant Careless and against third-party defendant Driver, you must assess the proportion of the fault which each party listed in Verdict C has for plaintiff's damages.

VERDICT C
(See MAI 36.15 (1979 New))

Note: Complete this form if fault is to be apportioned.

On the claim of defendant Careless for assessment of the proportions of fault for plaintiff's damage assessed in Verdict A, we, the undersigned jurors, find:

Note: Complete by writing in the percentage of the relative fault for each party you believe to be at fault. You may not write in "zero" for any party you have determined to be at fault under the other instructions in this case. The total of the percentages you assess must not exceed 100%.

Defendant Careless is _____% at fault.

Third–Party Defendant Driver is _____% at fault.

Note: All jurors who agree with the above findings must sign below.

_____   _____

_____   _____

_____   _____

_____   _____

_____   _____

*　　*　　*　　*　　*　　*　　*

Committee Comment (1979 New)

1. Under the "packaging concept," certain instructions will be fastened together to form the respective packages. See MAI 2.00 General Comment. The asterisks through the Illustrations designate the ending of a package and the beginning of another.

35.04 [1996 Revised] Illustrations—Comparative Fault—Right Angle Collision—Suit Against Driver and His Employer—Agency in Issue—Counterclaim for Personal Injury by Employee

Plaintiff, I.M. Hurt, was driving an automobile which collided with a truck owned by Beer Baron, Inc. and driven by its deliveryman-employee, Terry Trucker. The collision occurred at an uncontrolled intersection which Hurt entered from the right and Trucker from the left. Trucker testified that he got there first. Hurt has sued both defendants for personal injury and Trucker has counterclaimed for personal injury. Comparative fault is in issue as to both claims. There is a dispute as to whether Trucker was within the scope of employment.

Instruction No. 1
(Same as MAI 2.01)

Instruction No. 2
(See MAI 2.03 (1980 New))

As you remember, the court gave you a general instruction before the presentation of any evidence in this case. The court will not repeat that instruction at this time. However, that instruction and the additional instructions, to be given to you now, constitute the law of this case, and each such instruction is equally binding upon you. You should consider each instruction in light of and in harmony with the other instructions, and you should apply the instructions as a whole to the evidence. The order in which the instructions are given is no indication of their relative importance. All of the instructions are in writing and will be available to you in the jury room.

Instruction No. 3
(See MAI 2.02 (1980 Revision))

In returning your verdict, you will form beliefs as to the facts. The court does not mean to assume as true any fact referred to in these instructions but leaves it to you to determine what the facts are.

Instruction No. 4
(See MAI 3.01 (1998 Revision))

In these instructions, you are told that your verdict depends on whether or not you believe certain propositions of fact submitted to you. The burden is upon the party who relies upon any such proposition to cause you to believe that such proposition is more likely to be true than not true. In determining whether or not you believe any proposition, you must consider only the evidence and the reasonable inferences derived from the evidence. If the evidence in the case does not cause you to believe a particular proposition submitted, then you cannot return a verdict requiring belief of that proposition.

Instruction No. 5
(See MAI 2.04 (1981 Revision))

There are two claims submitted to you and each of them contains a separate verdict form. The verdict forms included in these instructions contain directions for completion and will allow you to return the permissible verdicts in this case. Nine or more of you must agree in order to return any verdict. A verdict must be signed by each juror who agrees to it.

Instruction No. 6
(See MAI 11.02 II (1996 Revision))

The term "negligent" or "negligence" as used in these instructions means the failure to use that degree of care that a very careful person would use under the same or similar circumstances.

Instruction No. 7
(See MAI 14.08 (1978 New))

The phrase "yield the right-of-way" as used in these instructions means that if both vehicles reach the intersection at approximately the same time, the driver on the left is required to yield but if both vehicles do not reach the intersection at approximately the same time, then a driver is required to yield to another vehicle which enters the intersection first.

*   *   *   *   *   *   *

Instruction No. 8
(See MAI 2.05 (1980 New))

Instructions 8 through 16 and general instructions 1 through 7 apply to the claim of I.M. Hurt for personal injury. Use Verdict A to return your verdict on this claim.

Instruction No. 9
(See MAI 13.05 (1990 Revision))

Acts were within the "scope and course of employment" as that phrase is used in these instructions if:

1. they were a part of the work defendant Trucker was employed to perform, and

2. they were done by defendant Trucker to serve the business of defendant Beer Baron, Inc.

Instruction No. 10
(See MAI 37.01 (1986 New), 17.02 (1980 Revision),
17.05 (1965 New), 17.08 (1965 New), 19.01 (1986
Revision) (First Option))

In Verdict A you must assess a percentage of fault to defendant Trucker, whether or not plaintiff Hurt was partly at fault, if you believe:

First, either:

> defendant Trucker failed to keep a careful lookout, or

> defendant Trucker failed to yield the right-of-way, and

Second, defendant Trucker, in any one or more of the respects submitted in paragraph First was thereby negligent, and

Third, such negligence directly caused or directly contributed to cause damage to plaintiff.

614

Instruction No. 11
(See MAI 37.04 (1986 New), 33.04(5) (1995 Revision))

In your verdict you must not assess a percentage of fault to defendant Trucker unless you believe defendant Trucker failed to keep a careful lookout or defendant Trucker failed to yield the right-of-way.

Instruction No. 12
(See MAI 37.01 (1986 New), 37.05(1) (1991 Revision))

In your verdict you must find defendant Beer Baron, Inc. responsible for any percentage of fault you may assess to defendant Trucker, whether or not plaintiff Hurt was partly at fault, if you believe defendant Trucker was operating defendant Beer Baron, Inc.'s truck within the scope and course of his employment by defendant Beer Baron, Inc. at the time of the collision.

Instruction No. 13
(See MAI 37.04 (1986 New), 33.04(5) (1995 Revision))

In your verdict you must not find defendant Beer Baron, Inc. responsible for any percentage of fault you may assess to defendant Trucker unless you believe defendant Trucker was operating defendant Beer Baron, Inc.'s truck within the scope and course of his employment by defendant Beer Baron, Inc. at the time of the collision.

Instruction No. 14
(See MAI 37.02 (1986 New), 17.02 (1980 Revision),
17.05 (1965 New), 17.08 (1965 New))

In Verdict A you must assess a percentage of fault to plaintiff Hurt, whether or not defendant Trucker was partly at fault, if you believe:

First, either:

> plaintiff Hurt failed to keep a careful lookout, or plaintiff Hurt failed to yield the right-of-way, and

Second, plaintiff Hurt, in any one or more of the respects submitted in paragraph First was thereby negligent, and

Third, such negligence directly caused or directly contributed to cause any damage plaintiff may have sustained.

Instruction No. 15
(See MAI 37.04 (1986 New), 33.04(5) (1995 Revision))

In your verdict you must not assess a percentage of fault to plaintiff unless you believe plaintiff failed to keep a careful lookout or plaintiff failed to yield the right-of-way.

Instruction No. 16
(See MAI 37.03 (1986 New))

If you assess a percentage of fault to defendant Trucker, then, disregarding any fault on the part of plaintiff, you must determine the total amount of plaintiff's damages to be such sum as will fairly and justly compensate plaintiff for any damages you believe he sustained and is reasonably certain to sustain in the future that the collision directly caused or directly contributed to cause. You must state such total amount of plaintiff's damages in Verdict A.

In determining the total amount of plaintiff's damages you must not reduce such damages by any percentage of fault you may assess to plaintiff. The judge will compute plaintiff's recovery by reducing the amount you find as plaintiff's total damages by any percentage of fault you assess to plaintiff.

VERDICT A
(See MAI 37.07 (1986 New), 37.05(1) (1991 Revision))

Note: Complete the following paragraph by writing the word(s) required by your verdict.

On the claim of plaintiff for personal injury against defendant Beer Baron, Inc. we, the undersigned jurors,

_____ find defendant Beer Baron, Inc. responsible
("do" or "do not")

for any percentage of fault assessed to defendant Trucker.

Note: Complete the following paragraph by filling in the blanks as required by your verdict. If you assess a percentage of fault to any of those listed below, write in a percentage not greater than 100%, otherwise write in "zero" next to that name. If you assess a percentage of fault to any of those listed below, the total of such percentages must be 100%.

On the claim of plaintiff I.M. Hurt for personal injury, we, the undersigned jurors, assess percentages of fault as follows:

Defendant Terry Trucker   _____%   (zero to 100%)
Plaintiff I.M. Hurt   _____%   (zero to 100%)
        Total   _____%   (zero OR 100%)

Note: Complete the following paragraph if you assessed a percentage of fault to defendant Trucker.

We, the undersigned jurors, find the total amount of plaintiff's damages disregarding any fault on the part of plaintiff to be $_____.

(stating the amount)

Note: The judge will reduce the total amount of plaintiff's damages by any percentage of fault you assess to plaintiff.

Note: All jurors who agree to the above must sign below:

_____   _____
_____   _____
_____   _____
_____   _____
_____   _____

*   *   *   *   *   *   *

Instruction No. 17
(See MAI 2.05 (1980 New))

Instructions 17 through 20 and general instructions 1 through 7 apply to the claim of Terry Trucker for personal injury. Use Verdict B to return your verdict on this claim.

617

Instruction No. 18
(See MAI 37.01 (1986 New), 17.02 (1980 Revision),
17.05 (1965 New), 17.08 (1965 New), 19.01 (1986
Revision) (First Option))

In Verdict B you must assess a percentage of fault to plaintiff Hurt, whether or not defendant Trucker was partly at fault, if you believe:

First, either:

> plaintiff Hurt failed to keep a careful lookout, or

> plaintiff Hurt failed to yield the right-of-way, and

Second, plaintiff Hurt, in any one or more of the respects submitted in paragraph First, was thereby negligent, and

Third, such negligence directly caused or directly contributed to cause damage to defendant Trucker.

(Converse Omitted)

Instruction No. 19
(See MAI 37.02 (1986 New), 32.01(2) (1991 Revision), 17.02
(1980 Revision), 17.05 (1965 New), 17.08 (1965 New))

In Verdict B you must assess a percentage of fault to defendant Trucker, whether or not plaintiff Hurt was partly at fault, if you believe:

First, either:

> defendant Trucker failed to keep a careful lookout, or

> defendant Trucker failed to yield the right-of-way, and

Second, defendant Trucker, in any one or more of the respects submitted in paragraph First, was thereby negligent, and

Third, such negligence directly caused or directly contributed to cause any damage defendant Trucker may have sustained.

(Converse Omitted)

Instruction No. 20
(See MAI 37.03 (1986 New))

If you assess a percentage of fault to plaintiff, then, disregarding any fault on the part of defendant Trucker, you must determine the total amount of defendant Trucker's damages to be such sum as will fairly and justly compensate defendant Trucker for any damages you believe he sustained and is reasonably certain to sustain in the future that the collision directly caused or directly contributed to cause. You must state such total amount of defendant Trucker's damages in Verdict B.

In determining the total amount of defendant Trucker's damages you must not reduce such damages by any percentage of fault you may assess to defendant Trucker. The judge will compute defendant's recovery by reducing the amount you find as defendant Trucker's total damages by any percentage of fault you assess to defendant Trucker.

VERDICT B
(See MAI 37.07 (1986 New))

Note: Complete the following paragraph by filling in the blanks as required by your verdict. If you assess a percentage of fault to any of those listed below, write in a percentage not greater than 100%, otherwise write in "zero" next to that name. If you assess a percentage of fault to any of those listed below, the total of such percentages must be 100%.

On the claim of defendant Terry Trucker for personal injury, we, the undersigned jurors, assess percentages of fault as follows:

Plaintiff I.M. Hurt	_____%	(zero to 100%)
Defendant Terry Trucker	_____%	(zero to 100%)
Total	_____%	(zero OR 100%)

Note: Complete the following paragraph if you assessed a percentage of fault to plaintiff Hurt.

We, the undersigned jurors, find the total amount of defendant Trucker's damages, disregarding any fault on the part of defendant Trucker, to be $_____.

(stating the amount)

Note: The judge will reduce the total amount of defendant Trucker's damages by any percentage of fault you assess to defendant Trucker.

Note: All jurors who agree to the above must sign below:

_____   _____

_____   _____

_____   _____

_____   _____

*   *   *   *   *   *   *

Committee Comment (1991 New)

This Illustration 35.04 demonstrates an appropriate comparative fault submission against the master and servant on respondeat superior where agency is in issue and the servant has counterclaimed. Instruction No. 12 and Verdict Form A in this illustration may not be used if separate theories of liability are submitted as to the master and the servant. See Committee Comment to MAI 37.05(1). Where the master is sued with the servant on respondeat superior and agency is not in issue, see MAI 37.05(2). Where only the master is sued under respondeat superior and agency is not in issue, see Committee Comment to MAI 37.05(2). For a non-comparative fault submission where agency is in issue, see MAI 18.01.

If the law compels assessment of the same percentages of fault to the parties on both the original claim and the counterclaim, the following sentence should be added to both verdict forms in this illustration as the last sentence in the initial note:

"If you find that plaintiff sustained damage in Verdict A and that defendant Trucker sustained damage in Verdict B, then the percentages of fault you assess to each party must be the same in both verdicts."

If the law compels the assessment of identical percentages of fault in other fact situations, a similar modification should be made.

Notes of Decisions

In general   1
Separate forms   2

---

1. In general

Where court gave verdict-directing instructions on both plaintiff's petition and defendant's counterclaim, it was not error to also instruct the jury it could return a verdict against both. Kirkwood Medical Supply Co. v. Ann Patterson Enterprises, Inc., 511 S.W.2d 433[3–5] (Mo.App.1974).

2. Separate forms

Where damages are proper on both petition and counterclaim, separate verdict forms should be submitted. Forsythe v. Starnes, 554 S.W.2d 100[2–3] (Mo.App. 1977).

35.05 [1996 Revision] Illustrations—Multiple Defendants—Damages and Apportionment of Fault Determined in Same Trial

Nancy Neighbor was a passenger in a Ford automobile being driven by her friend Harriet Host. This Ford was being driven on a through highway when it collided with a Chevrolet pickup driven by Fred Farmer. The pickup entered the through highway from an intersecting farm road. A stop sign faced Farmer.

Neighbor brought an action for her personal injuries against both Farmer and Host. Defendants filed cross-claims seeking apportionment of fault.

Instruction No. 1
(Same as MAI 2.01)

Instruction No. 2
(See MAI 2.03 (1980 New))

As you remember, the court gave you a general instruction before the presentation of any evidence in this case. The court will not repeat that instruction at this time. However, that instruction and the additional instructions, to be given to you now, constitute the law of this case and each such instruction is equally binding upon you. You should consider each instruction in light of and in harmony with the other instructions, and you should apply the instructions as a whole to the evidence. The order in which the instructions are given is no indication of their relative importance. All of the instructions are in writing and will be available to you in the jury room.

Instruction No. 3
(See MAI 11.03 (1996 Revision))

The term "negligent" or "negligence" as used in these instructions means the failure to use the highest degree of care. The phrase "highest degree of care" means that degree of care that a very careful person would use under the same or similar circumstances.

622

Instruction No. 4
(See MAI 14.05 (1978 Revision))

The phrase "yield the right-of-way" as used in these instructions means a driver is required to yield at the stop sign if the other vehicle is within the intersection or is so close to the intersection that it is an immediate hazard.

Instruction No. 5
(See MAI 3.01 (1998 Revision))

In these instructions, you are told that your verdict depends on whether or not you believe certain propositions of fact submitted to you. The burden is upon the party who relies upon any such proposition to cause you to believe that such proposition is more likely to be true than not true. In determining whether or not you believe any proposition, you must consider only the evidence and the reasonable inferences derived from the evidence. If the evidence in the case does not cause you to believe a particular proposition submitted, then you cannot return a verdict requiring belief of that proposition.

Instruction No. 6
(See MAI 2.02 (1980 Revision))

In returning your verdicts you will form beliefs as to the facts. The court does not mean to assume as true any fact referred to in these instructions but leaves it to you to determine what the facts are.

Instruction No. 7
(See MAI 2.04 (1981 Revision))

There are two claims submitted to you and each of them contains a separate verdict form. The verdict forms included in these instructions contain directions for completion and will allow you to return the permissible verdicts in this case. Nine or more of you must agree in order to return any verdict. A verdict must be signed by each juror who agrees to it.

*   *   *   *   *   *   *

Instruction No. 8
(See MAI 2.05 (1980 New))

Instructions 8 through 11 and general instructions 1 through 7 apply to the claim of plaintiff Nancy Neighbor for personal injury. Use Verdict A to return your verdict on this claim.

Instruction No. 9
(See MAI 17.02 (1980 Revision), 17.05 (1965 New),
17.08 (1965 New), 19.01 (1986 Revision))

Your verdict must be for plaintiff Nancy Neighbor and against defendant Fred Farmer if you believe:

First, either:

defendant Farmer failed to keep a careful lookout, or,

defendant Farmer failed to yield the right-of-way, and

Second, defendant Farmer, in any one or more of the respects submitted in Paragraph First, was thereby negligent, and

Third, such negligence either directly caused damage to plaintiff or combined with the acts of defendant Host to directly cause damage to plaintiff.

Instruction No. 10
(See MAI 17.01 (1980 Revision), 17.04 (1978
Revision), 19.01 (1986 Revision))

Your verdict must be for plaintiff Nancy Neighbor and against defendant Harriet Host if you believe:

First, defendant Host knew or by the use of the highest degree of care could have known that there was a reasonable likelihood of collision in time thereafter to have slackened her speed but defendant Host failed to do so, and

Second, defendant Host was thereby negligent, and

Third, such negligence either directly caused damage to plaintiff or combined with the acts of defendant Farmer to directly cause damage to plaintiff.

624

Instruction No. 11
(See MAI 4.01 (1980 Revision))

If you find in favor of plaintiff, then you must award the plaintiff such sum as you believe will fairly and justly compensate plaintiff for any damages you believe she sustained and is reasonably certain to sustain in the future that the collision directly caused or directly contributed to cause.

VERDICT A
(See MAI 36.01 (1980 Revision))

Note: Complete this form by writing in the name required by your verdict.

On the claim of plaintiff Nancy Neighbor for personal injuries against defendant Fred Farmer, we, the undersigned jurors, find in favor of:

_____

(Plaintiff Nancy Neighbor)   or   (Defendant Fred Farmer)

On the claim of plaintiff Nancy Neighbor for personal injuries against defendant Harriet Host, we, the undersigned jurors, find in favor of:

_____

(Plaintiff Nancy Neighbor)   or   (Defendant Harriet Host)

Note: Complete the following paragraph only if one or both of the above findings are in favor of plaintiff Nancy Neighbor.

We, the undersigned jurors, assess the damages of plaintiff Nancy Neighbor at $_____ (stating the amount).

Note: All jurors who agree to the above findings must sign below.

_____   _____
_____   _____
_____   _____
_____   _____
_____   _____

*   *   *   *   *   *   *

Instruction No. 12
(See MAI 2.05 (1980 New))

Instructions 12 and 13 and general instructions 1 through 7 apply to the claim for assessment of the proportions of fault. Use Verdict B to return your verdict on this claim.

Instruction No. 13
(See MAI 4.12 (1979 New))

If your verdict is in favor of plaintiff Neighbor and against both defendants on Verdict A, you must assess the proportion of the fault which each party listed in Verdict B has for plaintiff's damages.

VERDICT B
(See MAI 36.15 (1979 New))

Note: Complete this form if fault is to be apportioned.

On the claim between defendants for assessment of the proportions of fault for plaintiff's damage assessed in Verdict A, we, the undersigned jurors, find:

Note: Complete by writing in the percentage of the relative fault for each party you believe to be at fault. You may not write in "zero" for any party you have determined to be at fault under the other instructions in this case. The total of the percentages you assess must not exceed 100%.

Defendant Farmer is _____% at fault.

Defendant Host is _____% at fault.

Note: All jurors who agree with the above findings must sign below.

_____   _____
_____   _____
_____   _____
_____   _____
_____   _____

*   *   *   *   *   *   *

Committee Comment (1996 Revision)

Under the "packaging" concept certain instructions will be fastened together to form their respective packages. See MAI 2.00 General Comments. The asterisks through the Illustration designate the end of one package and the beginning of another. This illustration demonstrates a method of submitting the plaintiff's claim and the apportionment of fault issues in the same trial.

Notes of Decisions

----

1. In general

Where there was undisputed evidence of a wife's loss of consortium and jury found for injured husband but against wife, the verdict against her was void for inconsistency. Foster v. Rosetta, 443 S.W.2d 183[4] (Mo.1969).

2. Separate verdict directors

Plaintiff-husband and wife properly gave separate verdict directors since their damage submissions differed. Defendant erroneously gave one converse instruction to find for defendants unless plaintiffs were injured; separate converse instructions required since damages differed. Burrow v. Moyer, 519 S.W.2d 568[5–8] (Mo.App.1975).

Where plaintiffs husband and wife submitted separate verdict directors defendant was entitled to only one converse on plaintiffs' theory of recovery, and it was error to give defendant's two general converses (MAI 33.03) since that doubly conversed plaintiff's

theory of recovery. (Defendant could have given one converse on plaintiffs' theory of recovery and one converse on wife's separate damage element.) Wyatt v. Southwestern Bell Tel. Co., 514 S.W.2d 366[2–4] (Mo. App.1974).

When co-plaintiffs' measures of damage are different, each should submit a separate verdict-directing instruction. Watterson v. Portas, 466 S.W.2d 129[4] (Mo.App.1971).

3. Damages, multiple plaintiffs

Where multiple plaintiffs had separate verdict-directors, each was entitled to a separate damage instruction. Kennedy v. Tallent, 492 S.W.2d 33[4] (Mo.App.1973).

4. Variation

In consortium damage instruction use of "thereby" as in MAI 31.04 instead of "as the direct result of such injury" as in MAI's 35.05 and 35.06 not error. Penn v. Columbia Asphalt Co., 513 S.W.2d 679[19] (Mo.App. 1974).

627

35.06(1) [1991 Withdrawn] Illustrations—Husband and Wife Both Sue for Personal Injuries and Loss of Consortium

(This Illustration and the Committee Comment thereto are hereby withdrawn.)

35.06(2) [1991 Withdrawn] Illustrations—Husband Sues for Personal Injuries and Wife Sues for Loss of Consortium

(This Illustration and the Committee Comment thereto are hereby withdrawn.)

35.07 [1996 Revision] Illustrations—Bilateral Contract—Substantial Performance in Issue

Plaintiff Carl Carpenter agreed with defendant Henry Householder to furnish and install sixteen storm windows for $100.00 per unit. Plaintiff installed the sixteen windows, but defendant paid plaintiff only half the agreed amount, contending plaintiff had failed to make the windows airtight. Plaintiff sued for the balance.

Instruction No. 1
(Same as MAI 2.01)

Instruction No. 2
(See MAI 2.03 (1980 New))

As you remember, the court gave you a general instruction before the presentation of any evidence in this case. The court will not repeat that instruction at this time. However, that instruction and the additional instructions, to be given to you now, constitute the law of this case and each such instruction is equally binding upon you. You should consider each instruction in light of and in harmony with the other instructions, and you should apply the instructions as a whole to the evidence. The order in which the instructions are given is no indication of their relative importance. All of the instructions are in writing and will be available to you in the jury room.

Instruction No. 3
(See MAI 3.01 (1998 Revision))

In these instructions, you are told that your verdict depends on whether or not you believe certain propositions of fact submitted to you. The burden is upon the party who relies upon any such proposition to cause you to believe that such proposition is more likely to be true than not true. In determining whether or not you believe any proposition, you must consider only the evidence and the reasonable inferences derived from the evidence. If the evidence in the case does not cause you to believe a particular proposition submitted, then you cannot return a verdict requiring belief of that proposition.

Instruction No. 4
(See MAI 2.02 (1980 Revision))

In returning your verdict you will form beliefs as to the facts. The court does not mean to assume as true any fact referred to in these instructions but leaves it to you to determine what the facts are.

Instruction No. 5
(See MAI 2.04 (1981 Revision))

The verdict form included in these instructions contains directions for completion and will allow you to return the permissible verdict in this case. Nine or more of you must agree in order to return any verdict. A verdict must be signed by each juror who agrees to it.

Instruction No. 6
(See MAI 26.07 (1981 Revision))

Your verdict must be for plaintiff if you believe:

First, plaintiff and defendant entered into an agreement whereby plaintiff agreed to furnish and install 16 storm windows upon defendant's house and defendant agreed to pay plaintiff $100.00 per window, and

Second, plaintiff substantially performed such agreement in a workmanlike manner, and

Third, defendant failed to perform his agreement, and

Fourth, plaintiff was thereby damaged.

Instruction No. 7
(See MAI 33.04 (1995 Revision))

Your verdict must be for defendant unless you believe plaintiff substantially performed such agreement in a workmanlike manner.

Instruction No. 8
(See MAI 16.04 (1980 New))

The phrase "substantially performed" as used in these instructions means performance of all important parts of the contract with only slight variations.

Instruction No. 9
(See MAI 4.09 (1980 Revision))

If you find in favor of plaintiff then you must award plaintiff $800.00.

VERDICT A
(See MAI 36.01 (1980 Revision))

Note: Complete this form by writing in the name required by your verdict.

On the claim of plaintiff Carpenter against defendant Householder, we, the undersigned jurors, find in favor of:

_____

(Plaintiff Carpenter)   or   (Defendant Householder)

Note: Complete the following paragraph only if the above finding is in favor of plaintiff Carpenter.

We, the undersigned jurors, assess the damages of plaintiff Carpenter at $_____ (*stating the amount*).

Note: All jurors who agree to the above findings must sign below.

_____   _____
_____   _____
_____   _____
_____   _____
_____   _____

Committee Comment (1980 New)

In this Illustration, there is only one verdict form and, as a result, all instructions are included in one package. MAI 2.05 is not to be used when there is only one verdict form. See MAI 2.00.

35.08 [1996 Revision] Illustrations—Eminent Domain—All Property Taken

John and Mary Jones were the owners of Blackacre which was taken by the State on July 1, 1980. Commissioners were appointed and made their award of damages. Plaintiff and defendants filed timely exceptions to the Commissioners' award. The issue of damages was tried to a jury.

Instruction No. 1
(Same as MAI 2.01)

Note: In condemnation cases, the defendant is first in the order of proof and the references to plaintiff and defendants in MAI 2.01 will be reversed. See MAI 2.01 Notes on Use.

Instruction No. 2
(See MAI 2.03 (1980 New))

As you remember, the court gave you a general instruction before the presentation of any evidence in this case. The court will not repeat that instruction at this time. However, that instruction and the additional instructions, to be given to you now, constitute the law of this case and each such instruction is equally binding upon you. You should consider each instruction in light of and in harmony with the other instructions, and you should apply the instructions as a whole to the evidence. The order in which the instructions are given is no indication of their relative importance. All of the instructions are in writing and will be available to you in the jury room.

Instruction No. 3
(See MAI 2.02 (1980 Revision))

In returning your verdict you will form beliefs as to the facts. The court does not mean to assume as true any fact referred to in these instructions but leaves it to you to determine what the facts are.

Instruction No. 4
(See MAI 3.02 (1981 Revision))

The burden is on defendants to cause you to believe that they have sustained damage and the amount thereof. In determining the amount of your verdict, you must consider only the evidence and the reasonable inferences derived from the evidence. If you do not believe certain evidence, then you cannot consider that evidence in arriving at the amount of your verdict.

Instruction No. 5
(See MAI 2.04 (1981 Revision))

The verdict form included in these instructions contains directions for completion and will allow you to return the permissible verdict in this case. Nine or more of you must agree in order to return any verdict. A verdict must be signed by each juror who agrees to it.

Instruction No. 6
(See MAI 9.01 (1965 New))

You must award defendants such sum as you believe was the fair market value of defendants' property immediately before the taking on July 1, 1980.

Instruction No. 7
(See MAI 16.02 (1978 Revision))

The phrase "fair market value" as used in these instructions means the price which the property in question would bring when offered for sale by one willing but not obliged to sell it, and when bought by one willing or desirous to purchase it but who is not compelled to do so.

In determining fair market value you should take into consideration all the uses to which the property may best be applied or for which it is best adapted, under existing conditions and under conditions to be reasonably expected in the near future.

VERDICT A
(See MAI 36.01 (1980 Revision—Modified))

We, the undersigned jurors, assess the damages of defendants at $_____ (*stating the amount*).

Note: All jurors who agree to the above findings must sign below.

_____

_____

_____

_____

_____

_____

Committee Comment (1980 New)

In this Illustration, there is only one verdict form and, as a result, all instructions are included in one package. MAI 2.05 is not to be used when there is only one verdict form. See MAI 2.00.

Notes of Decisions

1. Comparable sales

In condemnation proceeding, trial court did not err in refusing instruction advising jury how to consider evidence of comparable worth, because MAI 2.01 was available to advise the jury how to consider evidence and illustrations in MAI 35.08 and MAI 35.09 do not include any additional instructions on comparable sales. City of Lake Ozark v. Campbell, 745 S.W.2d 799 [8] (Mo.App. 1988).

35.09 [1996 Revision] Illustrations—Eminent Domain—Part of Property Taken—Evidence of Damage to Remainder

Ajax Super Market, Inc., owned a four-acre tract of land adjacent to Highway 54. To enable it to widen the highway, the State condemned two acres of Ajax's land nearest the highway. The taking occurred on July 1, 1980. The two acres taken had been used as a parking lot. Defendant's store building is on the remaining two acres. The right of access was not disturbed. The State made no contention of special benefits. Commissioners were appointed and made their award of damages. The parties filed timely exceptions to the Commissioners' award and the case was tried to a jury. Defendant, Ajax Super Market, Inc., offered evidence of the value of the entire tract before the taking and of the value of the remainder after the taking. Defendant's witnesses took into account the severance damage to the two acres which remained after the taking because adequate parking was no longer available for super market purposes.

Instruction No. 1
(Same as MAI 2.01)

Note: In condemnation cases, the defendant is first in the order of proof and the references to plaintiff and defendant in MAI 2.01 will be reversed. See MAI 2.01 Notes on Use.

Instruction No. 2
(See MAI 2.03 (1980 New))

As you remember, the court gave you a general instruction before the presentation of any evidence in this case. The court will not repeat that instruction at this time. However, that instruction and the additional instructions, to be given to you now, constitute the law of this case and each such instruction is equally binding upon you. You should consider each instruction in light of and in harmony with the other instructions, and you should apply the instructions as a whole to the evidence. The order in which the instructions are given is no indication of their relative importance. All of the instructions are in writing and will be available to you in the jury room.

Instruction No. 3
(See MAI 2.02 (1980 Revision))

In returning your verdict you will form beliefs as to the facts. The court does not mean to assume as true any fact referred to in these instructions but leaves it to you to determine what the facts are.

Instruction No. 4
(See MAI 3.02 (1981 Revision))

The burden is on defendant to cause you to believe that it has sustained damage and the amount thereof. In determining the amount of your verdict, you must consider only the evidence and the reasonable inferences derived from the evidence. If you do not believe certain evidence, then you cannot consider that evidence in arriving at the amount of your verdict.

Instruction No. 5
(See MAI 2.04 (1981 Revision))

The verdict form included in these instructions contains directions for completion and will allow you to return the permissible verdict in this case. Nine or more of you must agree in order to return any verdict. A verdict must be signed by each juror who agrees to it.

Instruction No. 6
(See MAI 9.02 (1965 New))

You must award defendant such sum as you believe was the difference between the fair market value of defendant's whole property immediately before the taking on July 1, 1980, and the value of defendant's remaining property immediately after such taking, which difference in value is the direct result of the taking and of the uses which plaintiff has the right to make of the property taken.

Instruction No. 7
(See MAI 16.02 (1978 Revision))

The phrase "fair market value" as used in these instructions means the price which the property in question

636

would bring when offered for sale by one willing but not obliged to sell it, and when bought by one willing or desirous to purchase it but who is not compelled to do so.

In determining fair market value you should take into consideration all the uses to which the property may best be applied or for which it is best adapted, under existing conditions and under conditions to be reasonably expected in the near future.

VERDICT A
(See MAI 36.01 (1980 Revision—Modified))

We, the undersigned jurors, assess the damages of defendant at $_____ (*stating the amount*).

Note: All jurors who agree to the above findings must sign below.

_____   _____
_____   _____
_____   _____
_____   _____
_____   _____

Committee Comment (1983 Revision)

In this illustration, there is only one verdict form and, as a result, all instructions are included in one package. MAI 2.05 is not to be used when there is only one verdict form. See MAI 2.00.

When the condemning authority has evidence from which the jury can find that the property owner sustained no damage from the taking, MAI 31.05 must be used and the verdict form used in this Illustration should be modified to require a finding in favor of plaintiff or defendant.

35.10 [1996 Revision] Illustrations—Product Liability—Defective Ladder

Felix Fixit, an unmarried handyman, bought a wooden six-foot stepladder from Ladder Products Company which manufactured ladders and also maintained a retail outlet. Two weeks later, Felix was standing on the stepladder painting a ceiling in his family room when one of the brace legs at the rear of the ladder broke causing Felix to fall, head-first, into a stone fireplace and sustain injuries. He has sued Ladder Products under a theory of strict liability for product defect. Defendant Ladder Company relies upon contributory fault as an affirmative defense, since the date of injury was *prior to* the effective date of § 537.760, et seq., R.S.Mo.

The defect in the wooden leg at the place of the break was shown to have been a loose knot in the lumber from which the leg was fashioned.

Both the original receipt introduced by Fixit and the defendant's file copy show that the purchase price was thirty dollars and that Fixit had been given a six dollar, 20% discount.

Ladder Company's evidence indicated that Felix had selected the ladder from a number of ladders on display, had pointed out the knot to the salesman and requested and received a markdown in price because of the defect, stating that the knot would cause the leg to fail but that he would put a splice over the knot to strengthen the weak leg.

Felix denied any such occurrence and said he received the 20% discount because he qualified as a commercial contractor and had received a contractor's discount from Ladder Products. Although Ladder Products admitted it did give contractors a discount of 20%, it denied that Fixit was a commercial contractor or had received a contractor's discount.

Instruction No. 1
(Same as MAI 2.01)

Instruction No. 2
(See MAI 2.03 (1980 New))

As you remember, the court gave you a general instruction before the presentation of any evidence in this case. The court will not repeat that instruction at this time. However, that instruction and the additional instructions, to be given to you now, constitute the law of this case and each such instruction is equally binding upon you. You should consider each instruction in light of and in harmony with the other instructions, and you should apply the instructions as a whole to the evidence. The order in which the instructions are given is no indication of their relative importance. All of the instructions are in writing and will be available to you in the jury room.

Instruction No. 3
(See MAI 2.02 (1980 Revision))

In returning your verdict you will form beliefs as to the facts. The court does not mean to assume as true any fact referred to in these instructions but leaves it to you to determine what the facts are.

Instruction No. 4
(See MAI 3.01 (1998 Revision))

In these instructions, you are told that your verdict depends on whether or not you believe certain propositions of fact submitted to you. The burden is upon the party who relies upon any such proposition to cause you to believe that such proposition is more likely to be true than not true. In determining whether or not you believe any proposition, you must consider only the evidence and the reasonable inferences derived from the evidence. If the evidence in the case does not cause you to believe a particular proposition submitted, then you cannot return a verdict requiring belief of that proposition.

639

Instruction No. 5
(See MAI 2.04 (1981 Revision))

The verdict form included in these instructions contains directions for completion and will allow you to return the permissible verdict in this case. Nine or more of you must agree in order to return any verdict. A verdict must be signed by each juror who agrees to it.

Instruction No. 6
(See MAI 25.04 (1978 Revision))

Your verdict must be for plaintiff Felix Fixit if you believe:

First, defendant sold the ladder in the course of defendant's business, and

Second, the ladder was then in a defective condition unreasonably dangerous when put to a reasonably anticipated use, and

Third, the ladder was used in a manner reasonably anticipated, and

Fourth, plaintiff was damaged as a direct result of such defective condition as existed when the ladder was sold,

unless you believe plaintiff is not entitled to recover by reason of Instruction No. 7.

Instruction No. 7
(See MAI 32.23 (1978 Revision))

Your verdict must be for defendant Ladder Products if you believe:

First, when the ladder was used, plaintiff knew of the danger as submitted in Instruction Number 6 and appreciated the danger of its use, and

Second, plaintiff voluntarily and unreasonably exposed himself to such danger, and

Third, such conduct directly caused or directly contributed to cause any damage plaintiff may have sustained.

Instruction No. 8
(See MAI 4.01 (1980 Revision))

If you find in favor of plaintiff Felix Fixit, then you must award plaintiff such sum as you believe will fairly and justly compensate plaintiff for any damages you believe he sustained and is reasonably certain to sustain in the future as a direct result of the occurrence mentioned in evidence.

VERDICT A
(See MAI 36.01 (1980 Revision))

Note: Complete this form by writing in the name required by your verdict.

On the claim of plaintiff Felix Fixit for personal injuries, we, the undersigned jurors, find in favor of:

_____

(Plaintiff Fixit)   or   (Defendant Ladder Products Company)

Note: Complete the following paragraph only if the above finding is in favor of plaintiff Felix Fixit.

We, the undersigned jurors, assess the damages of plaintiff Felix Fixit at $_____ (*stating the amount*).

Note: All jurors who agree to the above findings must sign below.

_____   _____
_____   _____
_____   _____
_____   _____
_____   _____
_____   _____

Committee Comment (1991 Revision)

In this Illustration, there is only one verdict form submitted and, as a result, all instructions are included in one package. MAI 2.05 is not to be used when there is only one verdict form. See MAI 2.00.

Caution: This Illustration was drafted for use in cases in which the provisions of § 537.760, et seq., R.S.Mo. are *not* applicable.

**35.11   [1991 Withdrawn] Illustrations—Submission of
One Claim by Two Verdict Directors—Humanitarian and Primary Negligence**

35.12   [1996 Revision] Illustrations—Will Contest

Charlie Rich died on January 1, 1978, leaving an estate of $800,000. He was 84 at the time of his death. Rich was a widower who had lived with his adult daughter, Ima Rich, his only child. Ima had never married. She cared for her father during the 15 years following her mother's death. Charlie Rich died in the local hospital where he had been a patient for two months. Reverend Longwind of the Temple of Saints Church visited Charlie daily. Two days before his death Charlie made a will (the first he had ever made) leaving Ima $50,000 and the balance of his estate to the Temple of Saints Church. Attorney K.C. Mason, a respected practitioner, who had never represented Charlie previously, prepared the will. K.C. Mason and his secretary, Penny Writer, witnessed the will. The will was offered for probate and accepted. Ima filed a timely petition contesting the validity of the will based on undue influence.

Instruction No. 1
(Same as MAI 2.01)

Note: In will contest cases, MAI 2.01 must be modified as required by Notes on Use.

Instruction No. 2
(See MAI 2.03 (1980 New))

As you remember, the court gave you a general instruction before the presentation of any evidence in this case. The court will not repeat that instruction at this time. However, that instruction and the additional instructions, to be given to you now, constitute the law of this case and each such instruction is equally binding upon you. You should consider each instruction in light of and in harmony with the other instructions, and you should apply the instructions as a whole to the evidence. The order in which the instructions are given is no indication of their relative importance. All of the instructions are in writing and will be available to you in the jury room.

Instruction No. 3
(See MAI 2.02 (1980 Revision))

In returning your verdict you will form beliefs as to the facts. The court does not mean to assume as true any fact referred to in these instructions but leaves it to you to determine what the facts are.

Instruction No. 4
(See MAI 15.01 (1969 New))

The phrase "sound and disposing mind and memory" as used in these instructions means that when a person signed his will he:

First, was able to understand the ordinary affairs of life, and

Second, was able to understand the nature and extent of his property, and

Third, was able to know the persons who were the natural objects of his bounty, and

Fourth, could intelligently weigh and appreciate his natural obligations to those persons.

Instruction No. 5
(See MAI 15.03 (1995 Revision))

The phrase "undue influence" as used in these instructions means such influence as destroys the free choice of the person making the will.

Instruction No. 6
(See MAI 3.03 (1981 Revision))

The burden is upon defendant-proponent, to cause you to believe that the document dated December 29, 1977, is the last will and testament of Charlie Rich.

The burden is upon plaintiff-contestant, to cause you to believe her claim of undue influence as submitted in Instruction Number 9.

In determining whether or not you believe any proposition, you must consider only the evidence and the reasonable inferences derived from the evidence.

If the evidence in the case does not cause you to believe a particular proposition submitted, then you cannot return a verdict requiring belief of that proposition.

Instruction No. 7
(See MAI 2.04 (1981 Revision))

The verdict form included in these instructions contains directions for completion and will allow you to return the permissible verdict in this case. Nine or more of you must agree in order to return any verdict. A verdict must be signed by each juror who agrees to it.

Instruction No. 8
(See MAI 31.06 (1978 Revision))

Your verdict must be that the document in issue is the last will and testament of Charlie Rich if you believe:

First, the document was signed by Charlie Rich and declared by him to be his last will and testament, and

Second, that at the time of signing, Charlie Rich was of sound and disposing mind and memory, and

Third, that the document was attested by at least two competent witnesses, signing their names to the document in his presence and at his request,

unless you believe the document in issue is not the last will and testament of Charlie Rich by reason of Instruction Number 9.

Instruction No. 9
(See MAI 32.18 (1969 New))

Your verdict must be that the document in issue is not the last will and testament of Charlie Rich if you believe that Charlie Rich signed the document as a result of the undue influence of Reverend Longwind.

VERDICT A
(See MAI 36.17(A) (1995 New))

Note: Complete this form by inserting the words required by your verdict.

We, the undersigned jurors, find:

That the document in issue _____ (*here insert either "is" or "is not"*) the last will and testament of Charlie Rich.

Note: All jurors who agree to the above findings must sign below.

_____   _____
_____   _____
_____   _____
_____   _____
_____   _____

Committee Comment (1995 Revision)

In this illustration, there is only one verdict form submitted and, as a result, all instructions are included in one package. MAI 2.05 is not to be used when there is only one verdict form. See MAI 2.00.

Illustration 35.12 demonstrates the submission of a will contest action where the validity of the entire will is at issue. Section 473.081, RSMo, provides for probate of a portion of a will when only part of the will is challenged because of fraud, duress, undue influence, mistake, ignorance of the testator of its content, partial revocations or other cause. This illustration is not appropriate to submit a case involving a claim of partial invalidity under § 473.081. See MAI 31.21, 31.22 and 36.17(B).

35.13 [1985 Withdrawn] Illustrations—Head–On Collision With Counterclaim—Comparative Fault

[MAI Illustration 35.13 (published in Vols. 659–60 S.W.2d Missouri Cases, p. XXXIII, et seq.) containing the prior MAI Committee recommendation for submitting comparative fault is withdrawn.]

35.14 [1996 Revision] Illustrations—Comparative Fault—Head–On Collision—Two Defendants

Vehicles driven by defendant John Host, and defendant, Robert Hitter, had a head-on collision on a two-lane highway. Plaintiff Harry Hurt was a passenger in Host's auto. Plaintiff claims Host failed to keep a careful lookout. Plaintiff claims defendant Hitter was on the wrong side of the highway. Both defendants claim plaintiff was negligent in failing to warn Host. Plaintiff has received serious personal injuries.

Instruction Number 1
(Same as MAI 2.01)

Instruction Number 2
(See MAI 2.03 (1980 New))

As you remember, the court gave you a general instruction before the presentation of any evidence in this case. The court will not repeat that instruction at this time. However, that instruction and the additional instructions, to be given to you now, constitute the law of this case, and each such instruction is equally binding upon you. You should consider each instruction in light of and in harmony with the other instructions, and you should apply the instructions as a whole to the evidence. The order in which the instructions are given is no indication of their relative importance. All of the instructions are in writing and will be available to you in the jury room.

Instruction Number 3
(See MAI 2.02 (1980 Revision))

In returning your verdict, you will form beliefs as to the facts. The court does not mean to assume as true any fact referred to in these instructions but leaves it to you to determine what the facts are.

Instruction No. 4
(See MAI 3.01 (1998 Revision))

In these instructions, you are told that your verdict depends on whether or not you believe certain propositions

of fact submitted to you. The burden is upon the party who relies upon any such proposition to cause you to believe that such proposition is more likely to be true than not true. In determining whether or not you believe any proposition, you must consider only the evidence and the reasonable inferences derived from the evidence. If the evidence in the case does not cause you to believe a particular proposition submitted, then you cannot return a verdict requiring belief of that proposition.

Instruction Number 5
(See MAI 11.08 (1996 Revision))

The term "negligent" or "negligence" as applied to the driver of a motor vehicle means the failure to use that degree of care that a very careful person would use under the same or similar circumstances. The term "negligent" or "negligence" as applied to a passenger in a motor vehicle means the failure to use that degree of care that an ordinarily careful person would use under the same or similar circumstances.

Instruction Number 6
(See MAI 2.04 (1981 Revision))

The verdict form included in these instructions contains directions for completion and will allow you to return the permissible verdict in this case. Nine or more of you must agree in order to return any verdict. A verdict must be signed by each juror who agrees to it.

Instruction Number 7
(See MAI 37.01 (1986 New), 17.01 (1980 Revision),
17.13 (1978 Revision), 19.01 (1986 Revision) (First Option))

In your verdict you must assess a percentage of fault to defendant Hitter whether or not plaintiff was partly at fault if you believe:

First, defendant Hitter's automobile was on the wrong side of the road, and

Second, Defendant Hitter was thereby negligent, and

649

Third, such negligence directly caused or directly contributed to cause damage to plaintiff.

Instruction Number 8
(See MAI 37.04 (1986 New), 33.03(1) (1995 Revision))

In your verdict you must not assess a percentage of fault to defendant Hitter unless you believe defendant Hitter's automobile was on the wrong side of the road.

Instruction Number 9
(See MAI 37.01 (1986 New), 17.01 (1980 Revision),
17.05 (1965 New), 19.01 (1986 Revision) (First Option))

In your verdict you must assess a percentage of fault to defendant Host whether or not plaintiff was partly at fault if you believe:

First, defendant Host failed to keep a careful lookout, and

Second, defendant Host was thereby negligent, and

Third, such negligence directly caused or directly contributed to cause damage to plaintiff.

Instruction Number 10
(See MAI 37.04 (1986 New), 33.03(1) (1995 Revision))

In your verdict you must not assess a percentage of fault to defendant Host unless you believe defendant Host failed to keep a careful lookout.

Instruction Number 11
(See MAI 37.02 (1986 New), 32.02 (1991 Revision))

In your verdict you must assess a percentage of fault to plaintiff, whether or not either defendant was partly at fault, if you believe:

First, plaintiff knew he was in immediate danger, and

Second, plaintiff thereafter had time to warn defendant Host and failed to do so, and

Third, plaintiff was thereby negligent, and

Fourth, such negligence directly caused or directly contributed to cause any damage plaintiff may have sustained.

650

Instruction Number 12
(See MAI 37.04 (1986 New), 33.03(2) (1995 Revision))

In your verdict you must not assess a percentage of fault to plaintiff unless you believe plaintiff was negligent as submitted in Instruction Number 11.

Instruction Number 13
(See MAI 37.03 (1986 New))

If you assess a percentage of fault to any defendant, then, disregarding any fault on the part of plaintiff, you must determine the total amount of plaintiff's damages to be such sum as will fairly and justly compensate plaintiff for any damages you believe he sustained and is reasonably certain to sustain in the future that the collision directly caused or directly contributed to cause. You must state such total amount of plaintiff's damages in your verdict.

In determining the total amount of plaintiff's damages you must not reduce such damages by any percentage of fault you may assess to plaintiff. The judge will compute plaintiff's recovery by reducing the amount you find as plaintiff's total damages by any percentage of fault you assess to plaintiff.

VERDICT A
(MAI 37.07, modified)

Note: Complete the following paragraph by filling in the blanks as required by your verdict. If you assess a percentage of fault to any of those listed below, write in a percentage not greater than 100%, otherwise write in "zero" next to that name. If you assess a percentage of fault to any of those listed below, the total of such percentages must be 100%.

On the claim of plaintiff John Hurt for personal injury, we, the undersigned jurors, assess percentages of fault as follows:

Defendant Hitter	_____%	(zero to 100%)
Defendant Host	_____%	(zero to 100%)
Plaintiff Hurt	_____%	(zero to 100%)
TOTAL	_____%	(zero OR 100%)

Note: Complete the following paragraph if you assessed a percentage of fault to one or more defendants:

We, the undersigned jurors, find the total amount of plaintiff's damages disregarding any fault on the part of the plaintiff to be $_____ (stating the amount).

Note: The judge will reduce the total amount of plaintiff's damages by any percentage of fault you assess to plaintiff.

All jurors who agree to the above must sign below.

_____   _____

_____   _____

_____   _____

_____   _____

Committee Comment (1986 New)

Illustration 35.14 demonstrates the submission of comparative fault by one plaintiff against two defendants. This method of submission also should be used, with appropriate modifications, in other cases involving single or multiple plaintiffs or defendants. It may not be used where the defendant does not make a submissible case of comparative fault against the plaintiff.

Caution: The modification necessary to submit apportionment of fault among parties not sued by plaintiff depends upon substantive issues which may not yet be resolved. The Committee takes no position on unresolved substantive issues.

Gustafson v. Benda, 661 S.W.2d 11 (Mo. banc 1983) implies that cases following *Missouri Pacific Railroad v. Whitehead & Kales Co.,* 566 S.W.2d 466 (Mo. banc 1978) continue as authority under *Gustafson.* Case law indicates a separate action may be pursued for apportionment of fault. See: *Safeway Stores, Inc. v. City of Raytown,* 633 S.W.2d 727 (Mo. banc 1982); *Rowland v. Skaggs Companies, Inc.,* 666 S.W.2d 770 (Mo. banc 1984); *State ex rel. General Electric Co. v. Gaertner,* 666 S.W.2d 764 (Mo. banc 1984); MAI 35.03, MAI 36.15; MAI 36.16.

35.15 [1996 Revision] Illustrations—Negligence and Strict Liability Combined—Comparative Fault—Apportionment of Fault Among Defendants

Vehicles driven by defendant John Host, and defendant, Robert Hitter, had a head-on collision on a two-lane highway. Plaintiff Harry Hurt was a passenger in Host's auto. Plaintiff claims Host failed to keep a careful lookout. Plaintiff claims defendant Hitter was on the wrong side of the highway. *Plaintiff claims that Hitter's vehicle had defectively designed brakes that contributed to cause Hitter's vehicle to cross the center line. The vehicle was manufactured by defendant General Car Company. There is evidence that General had prior problems with "pulling" of certain models with the type of brakes on Hitter's vehicle.* All defendants claim plaintiff was negligent in failing to warn Host. Plaintiff has received serious personal injuries. *All defendants have filed crossclaims against each other seeking apportionment of fault.* The date of injury in this illustration was *prior to* the effective date of § 537.760, et seq., R.S.Mo.

GENERAL PACKAGE

Instruction Number 1
(Same as MAI 2.01)

Instruction Number 2
(See MAI 2.03 (1980 New))

As you remember, the court gave you a general instruction before the presentation of any evidence in this case. The court will not repeat that instruction at this time. However, that instruction and the additional instructions, to be given to you now, constitute the law of this case, and each such instruction is equally binding upon you. You should consider each instruction in light of and in harmony with the other instructions, and you should apply the instructions as a whole to the evidence. The order in which the instructions are given is no indication of their relative importance. All of the instructions are in writing and will be available to you in the jury room.

Instruction Number 3
(See MAI 2.02 (1980 Revision))

In returning your verdict, you will form beliefs as to the facts. The court does not mean to assume as true any fact referred to in these instructions but leaves it to you to determine what the facts are.

Instruction No. 4
(See MAI 3.01 (1998 Revision))

In these instructions, you are told that your verdict depends on whether or not you believe certain propositions of fact submitted to you. The burden is upon the party who relies upon any such proposition to cause you to believe that such proposition is more likely to be true than not true. In determining whether or not you believe any proposition, you must consider only the evidence and the reasonable inferences derived from the evidence. If the evidence in the case does not cause you to believe a particular proposition submitted, then you cannot return a verdict requiring belief of that proposition.

Instruction Number 5
(See MAI 11.08 (1996 Revision))

The term "negligent" or "negligence" as applied to the driver of a motor vehicle means the failure to use that degree of care that a very careful person would use under the same or similar circumstances. The term "negligent" or "negligence" as applied to a passenger in a motor vehicle means the failure to use that degree of care that an ordinarily careful person would use under the same or similar circumstances. *The term "negligent" or "negligence" as applied to an automobile manufacturer means the failure to use that degree of care that an ordinarily careful and prudent person would use under the same or similar circumstances.*[1]

1. The definition of "negligence" of an automobile manufacturer is used for illustrative purposes only. The Committee takes no position on whether that definition or a definition incorporating MAI 11.10 I or II is more appropriate under developing case law.

Instruction Number 6
(See MAI 2.04 (1981 Revision))

There are two claims submitted to you and each of them contains a separate verdict form. The verdict forms included in these instructions contain directions for completion and will allow you to return the permissible verdicts in this case. Nine or more of you must agree in order to return any verdict. A verdict must be signed by each juror who agrees to it.

*   *   *   *   *   *   *

PACKAGE ONE (PLAINTIFF'S CLAIM)

Instruction Number 7
(See MAI 2.05 (1980 New))

Instructions 7 through 13 and general instructions 1 through 6 apply to the claim of plaintiff Harry Hurt for personal injury [based on theories of product defect and negligence] [2]. *Use Verdict A to return your verdict on this claim.*

2. Bracketed matter in this instruction, patterned after MAI 2.05, may be added to introduce the concept of alternative theories on a single claim for personal injury but is not necessary.

Instruction Number 8
(See MAI 25.04 (1978 Revision), 19.01 (1986
Revision) (first option), modified)

In Verdict A, on plaintiff's claim for personal injury based on product defect, your verdict must be for plaintiff against defendant General Car Company if you believe:

First, defendant General Car Company manufactured the vehicle in the course of said defendant's business, and

Second, the vehicle was then in a defective condition unreasonably dangerous when put to a reasonably anticipated use, and

Third, the vehicle was used in a manner reasonably anticipated, and

Fourth, such defective condition as existed when the vehicle was manufactured directly caused or directly contributed to cause damage to plaintiff.

(Converse Omitted)

Instruction Number 9
(See MAI 25.09 (1990 New), 37.01 (1986 New), 19.01
(1986 Revision) (first option))

In Verdict A, on the claim of plaintiff for personal injury based on negligence, you must assess a percentage of fault to defendant General Car Company whether or not plaintiff was partly at fault if you believe:

First, defendant General Car Company manufactured the vehicle, and

Second, the vehicle had brakes with a propensity to pull to the left, and

Third, defendant failed to use ordinary care to manufacture the vehicle to be reasonably safe, and

Fourth, such failure directly caused or directly contributed to cause damage to plaintiff.

(Converse Omitted)

Instruction Number 10
(See MAI 37.01 (1986 New), 17.01 (1980 Revision),
17.13 (1978 Revision), 19.01 (1986 Revision)
(first option))

In Verdict A, on the claim of plaintiff for personal injury based on negligence, you must assess a percentage of fault to defendant Hitter whether or not plaintiff was partly at fault if you believe:

First, defendant Hitter's automobile was on the wrong side of the road, and

Second, defendant Hitter was thereby negligent, and

Third, such negligence directly caused or directly contributed to cause damage to plaintiff.

(Converse Omitted)

656

Instruction Number 11
(See MAI 37.01 (1986 New), 17.01 (1980 Revision),
17.05 (1965 New), 19.01 (1986 Revision) (first option),
modified)

In Verdict A, on the claim of plaintiff for personal injury based on negligence, you must assess a percentage of fault to defendant Host whether or not plaintiff was partly at fault if you believe:

First, defendant Host failed to keep a careful lookout, and

Second, defendant Host was thereby negligent, and

Third, such negligence directly caused or directly contributed to cause damage to plaintiff.

(Converse Omitted)

Instruction Number 12
(See MAI 37.02 (1986 New), 32.02 (1991 Revision),
modified)

In Verdict A, on the claim of plaintiff for personal injury based on negligence, you must assess a percentage of fault to plaintiff, whether or not any defendant was partly at fault, if you believe:

First, plaintiff knew he was in immediate danger, and

Second, plaintiff thereafter had time to warn defendant Host and failed to do so, and

Third, plaintiff was thereby negligent, and

Fourth, such negligence directly caused or directly contributed to cause any damage plaintiff may have sustained.

(Converse Omitted)

Instruction Number 13
(See MAI 37.03 (1986 New), modified)

In Verdict A, if you find in favor of plaintiff against defendant General Car Company on plaintiff's claim for personal injury based on product defect, or if you assess a percentage of fault to any defendant *on the claim of plaintiff*

for personal injury based on negligence, then, disregarding any fault on the part of plaintiff, you must determine the total amount of his damages to be such sum as will fairly and justly compensate him for any damages you believe he sustained and is reasonably certain to sustain in the future that the collision directly caused or directly contributed to cause. You must state such total amount of plaintiff's damages in Verdict A.

In determining the total amount of plaintiff's damages, you must not reduce such damages by any percentage of fault you may assess to plaintiff. The judge will compute any recovery *on plaintiff's claim for personal injury based on negligence* by reducing the amount you find as plaintiff's total damages by any percentage of fault you assess to plaintiff.

VERDICT A

(See MAI 36.01 (1980 Revision), 37.07 (1986 New), modified)

PART I

Note: Complete this form as required by your verdict.

On the claim of plaintiff Hurt for personal injury *based on product defect* against defendant General Car Company, we, the undersigned jurors, find in favor of:

(Plaintiff Hurt)	or	(Defendant General Car Company)

PART II

Note: Complete the following by filling in the blanks as required by your verdict *on the claim of plaintiff for personal injury based on negligence whether or not you found in favor of plaintiff on his claim for personal injury based on product defect.* If you assess a percentage of fault to any of those listed below, write in a percentage not greater than 100%. Otherwise, write in "zero" next to that name. If you assess a percentage of fault to any of those listed below, the total of such percentages must be 100%.

On the claim of plaintiff for personal injury *based on negligence,* we, the undersigned jurors, assess percentages of fault as follows:

Defendant General Car Company _____% (zero to 100%)
Defendant Hitter _____% (zero to 100%)
Defendant Host _____% (zero to 100%)
Plaintiff Hurt _____% (zero to 100%)
TOTAL _____% (zero OR 100%)

Part III

Note: Complete the following paragraph *if you find in favor of plaintiff on his claim for personal injury based on product defect or if you assessed a percentage of fault to any defendant* on plaintiff's claim for personal injury based on negligence.

We, the undersigned jurors, find the total amount of plaintiff's damages disregarding any fault on the part of plaintiff to be $_____.

(stating the amount)

Note: *The judge will compute any recovery on plaintiff's claim for personal injury based on negligence by reducing the amount you find as plaintiff's total damages by any percentage of fault you assess to plaintiff.*

Note: All jurors who agree to the above must sign below.

_____ _____
_____ _____
_____ _____
_____ _____

* * * * * * *

PACKAGE TWO (APPORTIONMENT AMONG DEFENDANTS)

Instruction Number 14
(See MAI 2.05 (1980 New))

Instructions 14 through 15 and general instructions 1 through 6 apply to the claim for apportionment of fault among defendants. Use Verdict B to return your verdict on this claim.

659

Instruction Number 15
(See MAI 4.12 (1979 New), modified)

If you find in favor of plaintiff and against defendant General Car Company on plaintiff's claim based on product defect and if you assess a percentage of fault to any other defendant in Verdict A,[3] you must assess the proportion of fault which each party listed in Verdict B has for plaintiff's total damage.

3. MAI 4.12 is modified since apportionment among defendants is handled by the findings on negligence in Verdict A if there is a finding for General Car Company on the strict liability claim. The jury need only address apportionment among the defendants if the verdict on "product defect" is for plaintiff and a percentage of fault is assessed in Verdict A to a defendant other than General Car Company.

VERDICT B
(See MAI 36.15 (1979 New),
modified)

Note: Complete this form if fault is to be apportioned among defendants.

On the claim among defendants for assessment of the proportions of fault for plaintiff's total[1] damages assessed in Verdict A, we, the undersigned jurors, find:

Note: Complete by writing in a percentage of the relative fault for each defendant you believe to be at fault. *If you believe a party named below is not at fault, write in "zero" for that percentage. You may not write in "zero" for General Car Company (if you found in favor of plaintiff on plaintiff's claim for personal injury based on product defect)[2] or for any defendant to whom you assessed a percentage of fault in Verdict A. (You should not complete this Verdict B if you found in favor of General Car Company on plaintiff's claim based on product defect.)[3] The total of the percentages you assess (in this Verdict B)[4] must not exceed 100%.*

Defendant General Car Company is _____% at fault.
Defendant Hitter is _____% at fault.

Defendant Host is _____% at fault.

Note: All jurors who agree with the above findings must sign below.

_____ _____
_____ _____
_____ _____
_____ _____
_____ _____

Committee Comment (1996 Revision)

MAI 35.15 demonstrates an appropriate submission of a strict liability claim with a negligence claim involving comparative fault along with crossclaims among defendants for apportionment of fault. In *Lippard v. Houdaille Industries, Inc.,* 715 S.W.2d 491 (Mo. banc 1986), the Supreme Court of Missouri held that comparative fault does not apply to plaintiff's claim based on strict liability in tort. This illustration may not be used where the comparative fault of the plaintiff is not in issue in the negligence claim.

Caution: The modification necessary to submit apportionment of fault among parties not sued by plaintiff depends on substantive issues which may not be resolved. The Committee takes no position on unresolved substantive issues.

Compare MAI 35.14 and Committee Comment. Italicized words and phrases in this illustration demonstrate the differences between the submission of the issues in this illustration and a simple comparative fault submission set forth in MAI 35.14.

CAUTION: This Illustration was drafted for use in cases in which the provisions of § 537.760, et seq., R.S.Mo., are *not* applicable. Changes in tort law effected by the provisions of House Bill 700, 84th General Assembly, 1st Regular Session (1987), applicable to the doctrines of comparative fault and strict liability apply only to causes of action accruing after July 1, 1987. § 537.760, et seq.

Notes of Decisions

1. In general

In a personal injury suit where the cause of action accrued in 1983, it was proper for the instruction not to submit strict liability under comparative fault, but to allow comparative fault to be assessed on the negligent failure to warn claim. Thus, 35.15 was appropriate for submitting strict liability and negligence claims in same suit. Johnson v. Hyster Co., 777 S.W.2d 281, 284–85 (Mo. App.1989).

661

35.16 [1996 Revision] Illustrations—Comparative Fault—Head–On Collision—Personal Injury and Loss of Consortium

Vehicles driven by plaintiff John Host and defendant Robert Hitter had a head-on collision on a two-lane highway. Plaintiffs claim defendant Hitter was on the wrong side of the highway. Plaintiff John Host received serious personal injuries. Plaintiff Mary Host has a consortium claim only and was not in the car. Defendant claims Host failed to keep a careful lookout.

Instruction Number 1
(Same as MAI 2.01)

Instruction Number 2
(See MAI 2.03 (1980 New))

As you remember, the court gave you a general instruction before the presentation of any evidence in this case. The court will not repeat that instruction at this time. However, that instruction and the additional instructions, to be given to you now, constitute the law of this case, and each such instruction is equally binding upon you. You should consider each instruction in light of and in harmony with the other instructions, and you should apply the instructions as a whole to the evidence. The order in which the instructions are given is no indication of their relative importance. All of the instructions are in writing and will be available to you in the jury room.

Instruction Number 3
(See MAI 2.02 (1980 Revision))

In returning your verdict, you will form beliefs as to the facts. The court does not mean to assume as true any fact referred to in these instructions but leaves it to you to determine what the facts are.

Instruction No. 4
(See MAI 3.01 (1998 Revision))

In these instructions, you are told that your verdict depends on whether or not you believe certain propositions

of fact submitted to you. The burden is upon the party who relies upon any such proposition to cause you to believe that such proposition is more likely to be true than not true. In determining whether or not you believe any proposition, you must consider only the evidence and the reasonable inferences derived from the evidence. If the evidence in the case does not cause you to believe a particular proposition submitted, then you cannot return a verdict requiring belief of that proposition.

Instruction Number 5
(See MAI 11.02 II (1996 Revision))

The term "negligent" or "negligence" as used in these instructions means the failure to use that degree of care that a very careful person would use under the same or similar circumstances.

Instruction Number 6
(See MAI 2.04 (1981 Revision))

The verdict form included in these instructions contains directions for completion and will allow you to return the permissible verdict in this case. Nine or more of you must agree in order to return any verdict. A verdict must be signed by each juror who agrees to it.

Instruction Number 7
(See MAI 37.01 (1986 New), 17.01 (1980 Revision),
17.13 (1978 Revision), 19.01 (1986 Revision)
(First Option))

In your verdict you must assess a percentage of fault to defendant Hitter, whether or not plaintiff John Host was partly at fault, if you believe:

First, defendant Hitter's automobile was on the wrong side of the road, and

Second, defendant Hitter was thereby negligent, and

Third, such negligence directly caused or directly contributed to cause damage to plaintiff John Host.

663

Instruction Number 8
(See MAI 37.04 (1986 New), 33.03(1) (1995 Revision))

In your verdict you must not assess a percentage of fault to defendant Hitter unless you believe defendant Hitter's automobile was on the wrong side of the road.

Instruction Number 9
(See MAI 37.02 (1986 New), 17.01 (1980 Revision),
17.05 (1965 New), 19.01 (1986 Revision)
(First Option))

In your verdict you must assess a percentage of fault to plaintiff John Host, whether or not defendant Hitter was partly at fault, if you believe:

First, plaintiff John Host failed to keep a careful lookout, and

Second, plaintiff John Host was thereby negligent, and

Third, such negligence directly caused or directly contributed to cause any damage plaintiff John Host may have sustained.

Instruction Number 10
(See MAI 37.04 (1986 New), 33.03(1) (1995 Revision))

In your verdict you must not assess a percentage of fault to plaintiff John Host unless you believe plaintiff John Host failed to keep a careful lookout.

Instruction Number 11
(See MAI 31.04 (1991 Revision))

If you assess a percentage of fault to defendant and if you believe that plaintiff Mary Host sustained damage as a direct result of injury to her husband John Host, then in your verdict you must find that plaintiff Mary Host did sustain such damage.

Instruction Number 12
(See MAI 33.03, Modified (1995 Revision))

Unless you believe plaintiff Mary Host sustained damage as a direct result of injury to her husband John Host, then in your verdict you must find that plaintiff Mary Host did not sustain such damage.

Instruction Number 13
(See MAI 37.08 (1991 New))

If you assess a percentage of fault to defendant, then, disregarding any fault on the part of plaintiff John Host, you must determine the total amount of plaintiff John Host's damages on his claim for personal injury. If you further find that plaintiff Mary Host did sustain damage as a direct result of injury to her husband, John Host, you must determine the total amount of Mary Host's damages on her claim for damages due to injury to her husband.

Total damages on each claim must be such sum as will fairly and justly compensate the plaintiff on that claim for any such damages you believe that plaintiff sustained and is reasonably certain to sustain in the future that the collision directly caused or directly contributed to cause. You must state separately in your verdict the total amount of each plaintiff's damages on each claim.

In determining the total amount of each plaintiff's damages you must not reduce such damages by any percentage of fault you may assess to plaintiff John Host. The judge will compute the recovery of each plaintiff under the law and the percentages of fault you assess.

Verdict
(See MAI 37.09 (1991 New))

Note: Complete the following paragraph by filling in the blanks as required by your verdict. If you assess a percentage of fault to any of those listed below, write in a percentage not greater than 100%, otherwise write in "zero" next to that name. If you assess a percentage of fault to any of those listed below, the total of such percentages must be 100%.

We, the undersigned jurors, assess percentages of fault as follows:

Defendant Hitter	_____%	(zero to 100%)
Plaintiff John Host	_____%	(zero to 100%)
TOTAL	_____%	(zero OR 100%)

665

Note: Complete the following paragraphs if you assessed a percentage of fault to defendant.

On the claim of plaintiff John Host for personal injury, we, the undersigned jurors, find the total amount of plaintiff John Host's damages, disregarding any fault on the part of plaintiff John Host, to be $_____ (stating the amount).

Note: Complete the following paragraph by writing the word(s) required by your verdict.

On the claim of plaintiff Mary Host for damages due to injury to her husband John Host, we, the undersigned jurors, find that plaintiff Mary Host _____,
("did" or "did not")

sustain damage as a direct result of injury to her husband, John Host.

Note: Compete the following paragraph only if the above finding is that Mary Host "did" sustain such damage.

We, the undersigned jurors, find the total amount of plaintiff Mary Host's damages due to injury to her husband, disregarding any fault on the part of plaintiff John Host, to be $_____ (stating the amount).

Note: The judge will compute the recovery of each plaintiff under the law and the percentages of fault you assess.

All jurors who agree to the above must sign below.

_____   _____
_____   _____
_____   _____
_____   _____

*   *   *   *   *   *   *

Committee Comment (1991 New)

In a case in which comparative fault is submissible, MAI 35.16 demonstrates an appropriate submission, in a single package, of a single injury claim along with a single, derivative consortium claim against one defendant. This illustration may be easily adapted for submission against additional defendants. This MAI 35.16 was drafted to comply with the mandate of *Johnson v. Hyster Co.*, 777 S.W.2d 281 (Mo.App. 1989), which held that the percentages of fault assessed on the claim of an injured plaintiff automatically apply to the consortium claim and that verdict forms that allow the jury to assess different percentages of fault on the consortium claim would be improper.

More complex comparative fault cases, such as a situation in which both husband and wife each have separate injury and consortium claims because they were hurt in the same accident, may more appropriately be packaged separately. This illustration should not be used where comparative fault is not in issue. See MAI 35.17 for a non-comparative fault submission of a simple case involving an injury claim and a consortium claim.

See the discussion of packaging in Chapter 2.00.

Caution: The modification necessary to submit apportionment of fault among parties not sued by plaintiff depends on substantive issues that may not be resolved. The Committee takes no position on unresolved substantive issues.

Compare MAI 35.14 and Committee Comment.

35.17 [1996 Revision] Illustrations—No Comparative Fault—Rear End Collision—Personal Injury and Loss of Consortium

A vehicle driven by plaintiff John Hurt was struck from the rear on a city street by a vehicle driven by defendant Robert Hitter. Plaintiff John Hurt received serious personal injuries. Plaintiff Mary Hurt has a consortium claim only and was not in the car. There is no submissible issue of fault on the part of plaintiff.

Instruction Number 1
(Same as MAI 2.01)

Instruction Number 2
(See MAI 2.03 (1980 New))

As you remember, the court gave you a general instruction before the presentation of any evidence in this case. The court will not repeat that instruction at this time. However, that instruction and the additional instructions, to be given to you now, constitute the law of this case, and each such instruction is equally binding upon you. You should consider each instruction in light of and in harmony with the other instructions, and you should apply the instructions as a whole to the evidence. The order in which the instructions are given is no indication of their relative importance. All of the instructions are in writing and will be available to you in the jury room.

Instruction Number 3
(See MAI 2.02 (1980 Revision))

In returning your verdict, you will form beliefs as to the facts. The court does not mean to assume as true any fact referred to in these instructions but leaves it to you to determine what the facts are.

Instruction No. 4
(See MAI 3.01 (1998 Revision))

In these instructions, you are told that your verdict depends on whether or not you believe certain propositions of fact submitted to you. The burden is upon the party who relies upon any such proposition to cause you to believe that such proposition is more likely to be true than not true. In determining whether or not you believe any proposition, you must consider only the evidence and the reasonable inferences derived from the evidence. If the evidence in the case does not cause you to believe a particular proposition submitted, then you cannot return a verdict requiring belief of that proposition.

Instruction Number 5
(See MAI 11.02 II (1996 Revision))

The term "negligent" or "negligence" as used in these instructions means the failure to use that degree of care that a very careful person would use under the same or similar circumstances.

Instruction Number 6
(See MAI 2.04 (1981 Revision))

The verdict form included in these instructions contains directions for completion and will allow you to return the permissible verdict in this case. Nine or more of you must agree in order to return any verdict. A verdict must be signed by each juror who agrees to it.

Instruction Number 7
(See MAI 17.01 (1980 Revision) and 17.16 (1973 Revision))

Your verdict must be for plaintiff John Hurt if you believe:

First, defendant's automobile came into collision with the rear of plaintiff's vehicle, and

Second, defendant Hitter was thereby negligent, and

Third, as a direct result of such negligence plaintiff John Hurt sustained damage.

(Converse Omitted)

Instruction Number 8
(MAI 31.04 (1991 Revision))

If you find in favor of plaintiff John Hurt on his claim for personal injuries and if you believe that plaintiff Mary

Hurt sustained damage as a direct result of injury to her husband John Hurt, then in your verdict you must find that plaintiff Mary Hurt did sustain such damage.

Instruction Number 9
(See MAI 33.03, Modified (1995 Revision))

Unless you believe plaintiff Mary Hurt sustained damage as a direct result of injury to her husband John Hurt, then in your verdict you must find that plaintiff Mary Hurt did not sustain such damage.

Instruction Number 10
(See MAI 4.18 (1991 New))

If you find in favor of plaintiff John Hurt, then you must award plaintiff John Hurt such sum as you believe will fairly and justly compensate plaintiff John Hurt for any damages you believe he sustained and is reasonably certain to sustain in the future as a direct result of the occurrence mentioned in the evidence.

If you further find that plaintiff Mary Hurt did sustain damage as a direct result of injury to her husband John Hurt, you must award plaintiff Mary Hurt such sum as you believe will fairly and justly compensate plaintiff Mary Hurt for any damages due to injury to her husband which you believe she sustained and is reasonably certain to sustain in the future as a direct result of the occurrence mentioned in the evidence.

Verdict
(See MAI 36.23 (1991 New))

Note: Complete this form by writing in the name(s) required by your verdict.

On the claim of plaintiff John Hurt for personal injuries against defendant Robert Hitter, we, the undersigned jurors, find in favor of:

(Plaintiff John Hurt)   or   (Defendant Robert Hitter)

Note: Complete the following paragraphs only if the above finding is in favor of plaintiff John Hurt.

We, the undersigned jurors, assess the damages of plaintiff John Hurt for his personal injuries at $_____ (stating the amount).

Note: Complete the following paragraph by writing in the word(s) required by your verdict.

On the claim of plaintiff Mary Hurt for damages due to injury to her husband John Hurt, we, the undersigned jurors, find that plaintiff Mary Hurt _____

("did" or "did not")

sustain damage as a direct result of injury to her husband John Hurt.

Note: Complete the following paragraph only if the above finding is that Mary Hurt "did" sustain such damage.

We, the undersigned jurors, assess the damages of plaintiff Mary Hurt due to injury to her husband at $_____ (stating the amount).

Note: All jurors who agree to the above findings must sign below.

_____   _____
_____   _____
_____   _____
_____   _____
_____   _____
_____   _____

Committee Comment (1991 New)

In a non-comparative fault situation, MAI 35.17 demonstrates an appropriate submission, in a single package, of a single injury claim along with a single derivative consortium claim against one defendant. This illustration may be easily adapted for submission against additional defendants. This MAI 35.17 was drafted to be consistent with the method of submitting loss of consortium in a comparative fault case as shown in MAI 35.16 and to avoid the duplication of the liability elements of the verdict director that was present under the old system of submitting loss of consortium.

More complex cases involving loss of consortium, such as a situation in which both husband and wife each have separate injury and consortium claims because they were hurt in the same accident, may more appropriately be packaged separately. This illustration should not be used where comparative fault is in issue. See MAI 35.16 for a comparative fault submission of a simple case involving an injury claim and a consortium claim.

See the discussion of packaging in Chapter 2.00.

Notes of Decisions

1. In general

The Missouri Supreme Court refused to recognize a cause of action for loss of parental consortium (consortium action by child due to injury to parent) or filial consortium (consortium action by sibling due to injury to another sibling). Powell v. American Motors Corp., 834 S.W.2d 184 (Mo. banc 1992).

35.18 [1996 Revision] Illustrations—Personal Injury and Consortium Claims—Action Against Health Care Provider—Comparative Fault

Dr. Edward Smith performed surgery on plaintiff John Jones. Plaintiff claims that Smith left a sponge in plaintiff's abdomen during the surgery. Smith claims that plaintiff failed to advise Smith of abdominal distention. Mary Jones has a claim for loss of consortium only and has presented no evidence or has chosen not to submit any elements of economic damage on her derivative claim. All parties agree that Jones would have had no residual problems from the surgery if the sponge had not been left in his abdomen.

Instruction No. 1
(Same as MAI 2.01)

Instruction No. 2
(See MAI 2.03 (1980 New))

As you remember, the court gave you a general instruction before the presentation of any evidence in this case. The court will not repeat that instruction at this time. However, that instruction and the additional instructions, to be given to you now, constitute the law of this case and each such instruction is equally binding upon you. You should consider each instruction in light of and in harmony with the other instructions, and you should apply the instructions as a whole to the evidence. The order in which the instructions are given is no indication of their relative importance. All of the instructions are in writing and will be available to you in the jury room.

Instruction No. 3
(See MAI 2.02 (1980 Revision))

In returning your verdict you will form beliefs as to the facts. The court does not mean to assume as true any fact referred to in these instructions but leaves it to you to determine what the facts are.

Instruction No. 4
(See MAI 3.01 (1998 Revision))

In these instructions, you are told that your verdict depends on whether or not you believe certain propositions of fact submitted to you. The burden is upon the party who relies upon any such proposition to cause you to believe that such proposition is more likely to be true than not true. In determining whether or not you believe any proposition, you must consider only the evidence and the reasonable inferences derived from the evidence. If the evidence in the case does not cause you to believe a particular proposition submitted, then you cannot return a verdict requiring belief of that proposition.

Instruction No. 5
(See MAI 11.06 (1990 Revision) (Modified))

The term "negligent" or "negligence" as used in these instructions with respect to a physician means the failure to use that degree of skill and learning ordinarily used under the same or similar circumstances by members of that physician's profession.

Instruction No. 6
(See MAI 11.07 (1996 Revision) (Modified))

The term "negligent" or "negligence" as used in these instructions with respect to a patient means the failure to use ordinary care. The phrase "ordinary care" means that degree of care that an ordinarily careful person would use under the same or similar circumstances.

Instruction No. 7
(See MAI 2.04 (1981 Revision))

The verdict form included in these instructions contains directions for completion and will allow you to return the permissible verdict in this case. Nine or more of you must agree in order to return any verdict. A verdict must be signed by each juror who agrees to it.

Instruction No. 8
(See MAI 21.01 (1988 Revision), MAI 37.01
(1986 New))

In your verdict you must assess a percentage of fault to defendant Smith, whether or not plaintiff John Jones was partly at fault, if you believe:

First, defendant Smith left a sponge in plaintiff's abdomen during surgery, and

Second, defendant was thereby negligent, and

Third, such negligence directly caused or directly contributed to cause damage to plaintiff.

(Converse Omitted)

Instruction No. 9
(See MAI 31.04 (1991 Revision))

If you assess a percentage of fault to defendant, and if you believe that plaintiff Mary Jones sustained damage as a direct result of injury to her husband, then in your verdict you must find that plaintiff Mary Jones did sustain such damage.

Instruction No. 10
(See MAI 37.02 (1986 New))

In your verdict you must assess a percentage of fault to plaintiff John Jones, whether or not defendant was partly at fault, if you believe:

First, plaintiff John Jones failed to advise Dr. Smith of abdominal distention, and

Second, plaintiff John Jones was thereby negligent, and

Third, such negligence of plaintiff John Jones directly caused or directly contributed to cause any damage plaintiff John Jones may have sustained.

(Converse Omitted)

Instruction No. 11
(See MAI 21.04 (1988 New), and 37.08 (1991 New) (Modified))

If you assess a percentage of fault to defendant, then, disregarding any fault on the part of plaintiff John Jones you must determine the total amount of plaintiff John Jones' damages on his claim for personal injury. If you further find that plaintiff Mary Jones did sustain damage as a direct result of injury to her husband, you must determine the total amount of her damages on her claim for damages due to injury to her husband.

Total damages on each claim must be such sum as will fairly and justly compensate the plaintiff on that claim for any such damages you believe that plaintiff sustained and is reasonably certain to sustain in the future that the medical treatment by the defendant directly caused or directly contributed to cause. You must state separately in your verdict the total amount of each plaintiff's damages on each claim, and you must itemize those total damages on each claim by the categories set forth in the verdict form.

In determining the total amount of each plaintiff's damages, you must not reduce such damages by any percentage of fault you may assess to plaintiff John Jones. The judge will compute the recovery of each plaintiff under the law and the percentages of fault you assess.

Instruction No. 12
(See MAI 21.05 (1988 New) (Modified))

In these instructions, you are told to itemize any damages you award by the categories set forth in the verdict form.

The phrase "past economic damages" means those damages incurred in the past for pecuniary harm such as medical expenses for necessary drugs, therapy, and for medical, surgical, nursing, x-ray, dental, custodial, and other health and rehabilitative services and for past lost earnings and for past lost earning capacity.

The phrase "past non-economic damages" means those damages arising in the past from non-pecuniary harm such as pain, suffering, mental anguish, inconvenience, physical impairment, disfigurement, loss of consortium, and loss of capacity to enjoy life.

The phrase "future medical damages" means those damages arising in the future for medical expenses such as necessary drugs, therapy, and medical, surgical, nursing, x-ray, dental, custodial, and other health and rehabilitative services.

The phrase "future economic damages" means those damages arising in the future from pecuniary harm such as lost earnings and lost earning capacity.

The phrase "future non-economic damages" means those damages arising in the future from non-pecuniary harm such as pain, suffering, mental anguish, inconvenience, physical impairment, disfigurement, loss of consortium, and loss of capacity to enjoy life.

VERDICT
(See MAI 36.22 (1988 New) and 37.09 (1991 New))

Note: Complete the following paragraph by filling in the blanks as required by your verdict. If you assess a percentage of fault to any of those listed below, write in a percentage not greater than 100%; otherwise write in "zero" next to that name. If you assess a percentage of fault to any of those listed below, the total of such percentages must be 100%.

We, the undersigned jurors, assess percentages of fault as follows:

Defendant Smith	_____%	(zero to 100%)
Plaintiff Jones	_____%	(zero to 100%)
TOTAL	_____%	(zero OR 100%)

Note: Complete the following paragraphs if you assessed a percentage of fault to defendant. Complete by writing in the amount of damages, if any, for each of the following itemized categories. If you do not find that a particular plaintiff was damaged in a particular category, write "none" in that category. The total damages for each plaintiff must equal the total of the itemized damage amounts you have assessed.

On the claim of plaintiff John Jones for personal injury, we, the undersigned jurors, find his total damages, disregarding any fault on the part of plaintiff John Jones, as follows:

For past economic damages including past
  medical damages $_____
For past non-economic damages $_____
For future medical damages $_____
For future economic damages excluding fu-
  ture medical damages $_____
For future non-economic damages $_____
           TOTAL DAMAGES $_____

Note: Complete the following paragraph by writing in the word(s) required by your verdict.

On the claim of plaintiff Mary Jones for damages due to injury to her husband, we, the undersigned jurors, find that plaintiff Mary Jones _____ sustain damage as
                                  ("did" or "did not")

a direct result of injury to her husband.

Note: Complete the following paragraph only if the above finding is that plaintiff Mary Jones "did" sustain such damage.

We, the undersigned jurors, find the total amount of plaintiff Mary Jones' damages due to injury to her husband, disregarding any fault on the part of plaintiff John Jones, as follows:

For past non-economic damages $_____
For future non-economic damages $_____
           TOTAL DAMAGES $_____

Note: The judge will compute the recovery of each plaintiff under the law and the percentages of fault you assess.

All jurors who agree to the above findings must sign below.

_____   _____
_____   _____
_____   _____
_____   _____
_____   _____

Committee Comment (1991 New)

This Illustration 35.18 demonstrates an appropriate comparative fault submission in an action against a health care provider where there is an injury claim along with a derivative consortium claim. This Illustration demonstrates an appropriate method for combining the elements of a submission peculiar to a claim against a health care provider under R.S.Mo., Sec. 538.205, et sequitur (see MAI Chapter 21 and verdict forms 36.20, 36.21, and 36.22), with the appropriate method for submission of a derivative claim such as loss of consortium (see MAI 21.07, 4.18, 37.08, and 37.09).

Instruction No. 12 and the Verdict Form in this Illustration have been tailored to the particular hypothetical fact situation described in this Illustration. If the actual facts in another case allow recovery of other elements of damage, appropriate modification of MAI 21.05 and the verdict form should be made if necessary. See MAI 21.07 for further guidance.

Notes of Decisions

1. In general

The Missouri Supreme Court refused to recognize a cause of action for loss of parental consortium (consortium action by child due to injury to parent) or filial consortium (consortium action by sibling due to injury to another sibling). Powell v. American Motors Corp., 834 S.W.2d 184 (Mo. banc 1992).

35.19 [1996 Revision] Illustrations—Punitive Damages—Bifurcated Trial Under § 510.263—No Comparative Fault—Two Defendants—Apportionment of Fault Between Defendants

Non-employee plaintiff Hurt was injured on a construction site (not a public highway) when Acme road grader backed over him. The road grader was manufactured by Acme without a back up warning device. At the time of the sale of the road grader Acme had notice of thirty incidents of individuals being backed over by this product. The claim against Acme is for design defect and for punitive damages.

Defendant Driver is sued for failure to keep a careful lookout for compensatory damages only. Driver and Acme have filed cross-claims against each other for apportionment of fault. There is no comparative fault. Acme has requested a bifurcated trial under § 510.263, RSMo.

Instruction Number 1
(Same as MAI 2.01)

Instruction Number 2
(See MAI 2.03 (1980 New))

As you remember, the court gave you a general instruction before the presentation of any evidence in this case. The court will not repeat that instruction at this time. However, that instruction and the additional instructions, to be given to you now, constitute the law of this case and each such instruction is equally binding upon you. You should consider each instruction in light of and in harmony with the other instructions, and you should apply the instructions as a whole to the evidence. The order in which the instructions are given is no indication of their relative importance. All of the instructions are in writing and will be available to you in the jury room.

Instruction Number 3
(See MAI 2.02 (1980 Revision))

In returning your verdicts you will form beliefs as to the facts. The court does not mean to assume as true any fact referred to in these instructions but leaves it to you to determine what the facts are.

Instruction No. 4
(See MAI 3.01 (1998 Revision))

In these instructions, you are told that your verdict depends on whether or not you believe certain propositions of fact submitted to you. The burden is upon plaintiff to cause you to believe that the evidence has clearly and convincingly established the propositions of fact required for the recovery of punitive damages. However, on all other propositions of fact, the burden is upon the party who relies upon any such proposition to cause you to believe that such proposition is more likely to be true than not true. In determining whether or not you believe any proposition, you must consider only the evidence and the reasonable inferences derived from the evidence. If the evidence in the case does not cause you to believe a particular proposition submitted, then you can not return a verdict requiring belief of that proposition.

Instruction Number 5
(See MAI 2.04 (1981 Revision))

There are two claims submitted to you and each of them contains a separate verdict form. The verdict forms included in these instructions contain directions for completion and will allow you to return the permissible verdicts in this case. Nine or more of you must agree in order to return any verdict. A verdict must be signed by each juror who agrees to it.

*   *   *   *   *   *   *

Instruction Number 6
(See MAI 2.05 (1980 New), Modified)

Instructions 6 through 14 and general instructions 1 through 5 apply to the claim of plaintiff Hurt for *compensatory damages* for personal injury *and to the determination of the liability of defendant Acme for punitive damages.* Use Verdict A to return your verdict on *these issues.*

Instruction Number 7
(See MAI 25.04 (1978 Revision), Modified, MAI 19.01 (1986 Revision))

On the claim of plaintiff Hurt for compensatory damages for personal injury against defendant Acme, your verdict must be for plaintiff Hurt if you believe [1]:

First, defendant Acme sold the road grader in the course of defendant's business, and

Second, the road grader was then in a defective condition unreasonably dangerous when put to a reasonably anticipated use, and

Third, the road grader was used in a manner reasonably anticipated, and

Fourth, such defective condition as existed when the road grader was sold directly caused or directly contributed to cause damage to plaintiff.

Instruction Number 8
(Converse Omitted)

Instruction Number 9
(See MAI 17.01 (1980 Revision), MAI 17.05 (1965 New), MAI 19.01 (1986 Revision))

On the claim of plaintiff Hurt for compensatory damages for personal injury against defendant Driver, your verdict must be for plaintiff Hurt if you believe [1]:

First, defendant Driver failed to keep a careful lookout, and

Second, defendant Driver was thereby negligent, and

Third, such negligence directly caused or directly contributed to cause damage to plaintiff Hurt.

Instruction Number 10
(Converse Omitted)

Instruction Number 11
(See MAI 11.07 (1996 Revision))

The term "negligent" or "negligence" as used in these instructions means the failure to use ordinary care. The phrase "ordinary care" means that degree of care that an ordinarily careful person would use under the same or similar circumstances.

Instruction Number 12
(See MAI 4.01 (1980 Revision), Modified)

If you find in favor of plaintiff and against one or more defendants, then you must award plaintiff such sum as you believe will fairly and justly compensate plaintiff for any damages you believe he sustained and is reasonably certain to sustain in the future that the occurrence mentioned in the evidence directly caused or directly contributed to cause.

Instruction Number 13
(See MAI 10.04 (1983 New), Modified)

If you find in favor of plaintiff Hurt and against defendant Acme under Instruction Number 7 [2], and if you believe that:

First, at the time defendant Acme sold the road grader, defendant knew of the defective condition and danger submitted in Instruction Number 7, and

Second, defendant Acme thereby showed complete indifference to or conscious disregard for the safety of others,

then, *in Verdict A, you may find that defendant Acme is liable for punitive damages.*

If you find that defendant Acme is liable for punitive damages in this stage of the trial, you will be given further instructions for assessing the amount of punitive damages in the second stage of the trial.

Instruction Number 14
(Converse Omitted, See MAI 33.16 (1991 New))[3]
Verdict A
(See MAI 36.11 (1980 Revision), Modified)[4]

Note: Complete this form as required by your verdict.

On the claim of plaintiff Hurt *for compensatory damages for personal injury* against defendant Acme, we, the undersigned jurors, find in favor of:

_____

Plaintiff Hurt   OR   Defendant Acme

On the claim of plaintiff Hurt *for compensatory damages for personal injury* against defendant Driver, we, the undersigned jurors, find in favor of:

_____

Plaintiff Hurt   OR   Defendant Driver

Note: Complete the following paragraph only if one or more of the above findings is in favor of plaintiff Hurt.

We, the undersigned jurors, assess the *compensatory* damages of plaintiff Hurt at $_____ (*stating the amount*).

Note: *If you found in favor of plaintiff Hurt and against defendant Acme, complete the following paragraph by writing in the word(s) required by your verdict.*

We, the undersigned jurors, find that defendant Acme _____ liable for punitive damages.
(*"is" or "is not"*)

Note: All jurors who agree to the above must sign below.

_____   _____

_____   _____

_____   _____

_____   _____

_____   _____

_____   _____

684

*   *   *   *   *   *   *

Instruction Number 15
(See MAI 2.05 (1980 New))

Instructions 15 through 16 and general instructions 1 through 5 apply to the claim between defendants for apportionment of fault. Use Verdict B to return your verdict on this claim.

Instruction Number 16
(See MAI 4.12 (1979 New), Modified)

If Verdict A is in favor of plaintiff Hurt and against both defendants, you must assess the proportion of fault which each defendant listed in Verdict B has for plaintiff's *compensatory* damages.

Verdict B
(See MAI 36.15 (1979 New), Modified)

Note: Complete this form if fault is to be apportioned.

On the claim between defendants for assessment of the proportions of fault for plaintiff Hurt's *compensatory* damages assessed in Verdict A, we, the undersigned jurors, find:

Note: Complete by writing in the percentage of the relative fault for each defendant you believe to be at fault. The total of the percentages you assess must not exceed 100%.
Defendant Acme is   _____% at fault.
Defendant Driver is   _____% at fault.

Note: All jurors who agree with the above findings must sign below.

_____   _____

_____   _____

_____   _____

_____   _____

* * * * * * *

Instruction Number 17 [5]
(See MAI 2.05 (1980 New), Modified)

Instructions 17 through 18 and *general instructions 1 through 5 apply to the determination of the amount of punitive damages to be assessed against defendant Acme. Use Verdict C to return your verdict as to the amount of punitive damages.* [6]

Instruction Number 18 [3]
(See MAI 10.04 (1983 New), Modified)

In addition to any *compensatory damages you assessed in Verdict A,* you may *assess* an additional amount as punitive damages in such sum as you believe will serve to punish defendant Acme *for the conduct for which you found that defendant Acme is liable for punitive damages* and *will serve* to deter defendant Acme and others from like conduct.

Verdict C
(Not in MAI)

Note: Complete this form as required by your verdict.
We, the undersigned jurors, assess punitive damages against defendant Acme at $_____ (stating the amount, or, if none, write the word "none").
Note: All jurors who agree to the above must sign below.

_____   _____
_____   _____
_____   _____
_____   _____
_____   _____

Notes on Use (1992 New)

This Illustration is intended to provide guidance for the submission of punitive damages in a bifurcated trial pursuant to § 510.263, RSMo, which was enacted as part of House Bill 700, 84th General Assembly, 1st Regular Session (1987), and applies only to causes of action accruing after July 1, 1987.

Italicized words and phrases in this Illustration demonstrate the modifications and additions to existing MAI instructions to accomplish bifurcation when required by § 510.263. Essentially, § 510.263 requires that, on request of any party, a civil action involving punitive damages shall be bifurcated. In the first phase, the jury is to determine: (1) liability for compensatory damages; (2) the amount of compensatory (or nominal) damages; and (3) liability for (but not the amount of) punitive damages. In the second stage of trial, the jury is to determine the amount of punitive damages.

This Illustration is not intended to take positions on the amount or type of proof necessary to support a punitive damage submission or the applicable legal standards for different torts that may support punitive damages. Case law must be consulted on such issues.

1. Comparative fault submissions under MAI 37.01 may also be modified in accordance with this Illustration for submission of punitive damages in such cases.

2. In a comparative fault case, the lead-in phrase "If you assess a percentage of fault to defendant Acme," should be substituted for the existing lead-in phrase in this Illustration.

In a comparative fault submission of punitive damages, the phrase "whether or not plaintiff was partly at fault" may be added after the phrase "then you may find defendant liable for punitive damages."

3. Defendant is entitled to a converse of a punitive damage instruction. See MAI 33.16. However, the converse for a punitive damage instruction modified for a bifurcated trial must also be modified. Counsel should consult MAI 33.01, General Comment, which advises that the pattern instruction for any converse is the *actual* instruction that is being conversed. The Committee takes no position as to whether defendant is entitled to a converse of Instruction Number 18 (on the amount of punitive damages) since the defendant may give a converse to Instruction Number 13 (on liability for punitive damages).

4. In a comparative fault case, MAI 37.07 may be modified in accordance with this Illustration to allow jury findings on punitive damage issues.

In any case involving multiple defendants against whom punitive damages are submissible, both the punitive damage instructions (Instruction Number 13 and Instruction Number 18 in this Illustration), and Verdicts A and C will need further modification. See the guidance provided in MAI 10.03 and add MAI 10.03 as the last paragraph to the equivalent of Instruction Number 18 in this Illustration.

5. The final package of instructions for the assessment of the amount of punitive damages will only be given to the jury if one or more of the defendants has been found liable for punitive damages in Verdict A. In the second stage of trial, the jury should be given only the general instructions (Instructions 1 through 5 in this Illustration), and the new instructions relating to the amount of punitive damages (Instructions 17 and 18 in this Illustration), and the verdict form as to the amount (Verdict C in this Illustration).

6. In the event multiple defendants have been found liable for punitive damages in the first phase of trial, Instruction Number 17 should be modified to identify those defendants.

Committee Comment (1992 New)

Under *Menaugh v. Resler Optometry, Inc.*, 799 S.W.2d 71 (Mo. banc 1990), the amount of punitive damages assessed against a defendant is *not* to be reduced by any percentage of fault assessed to plaintiff in a comparative fault case.

Caution: § 538.210.5, RSMo, provides that punitive damages may be assessed against a health care provider in actions accruing after February 3, 1986, only where the health care provider demonstrated willful, wanton, or malicious misconduct. The Committee takes no position on the constitutionality of Senate Bill 663, 1986 Mo. Laws 879.

The Committee takes no position on the constitutionality of House Bill 700, 84th General Assembly, 1st Regular Session (1987), of which § 510.263, RSMo, was a part.

The trial judge should exercise sound discretion in affording attorneys appropriate leeway during the various stages of trial to describe to the jury the proceedings contemplated by § 510.263, RSMo.

After the first stage of trial, there may be additional evidence in the second stage relating to the net worth of the defendants found liable for punitive damages. There may also be additional argument by counsel as to the amount (possibly "zero") to be assessed by the jury as punitive damages. The Committee takes no position as to whether additional evidence, other than net worth, may be admissible in the second stage of trial.

The method in this Illustration of splitting MAI 10.04 and modifying its component parts for submission of punitive damages in a bifurcated trial pursuant to § 510.263 may be utilized with any punitive damage instruction in Chapter 10.

The word "assess" is used in Instruction Number 18 rather than the phrase "award plaintiff" because the award of punitive damages may not inure entirely to the benefit of the plaintiff. Section 537.675, RSMo, provides a mechanism for the State of Missouri to obtain one-half of any final judgment awarding punitive damages. The Committee takes no position on the constitutionality of § 537.675 or whether the potential interest of the State of Missouri and the "Tort Victims Compensation Fund" created by § 537.675.1 may be argued to the jury.

35.20 [1998 New] Illustrations—Medical Malpractice—Minor Injured—Derivative Claim—No Comparative Fault

Megan Smith, a minor, sustained permanent injury during an operative procedure for which anesthetic was administered by Horace Jones, MD. It is alleged that defendant failed to adequately monitor vital signs and administered excessive anesthetic during surgery. In addition to the minor's claim for personal injury, John and Julie Smith, her parents, have joined the action with their derivative parental claim but have allowed their daughter to recover past and future medical expense in her claim.

Instruction Number 1
(Same as MAI 2.01)

Instruction Number 2
(See MAI 2.03 (1980 New))

As you remember, the court gave you a general instruction before the presentation of any evidence in this case. The court will not repeat that instruction at this time. However, that instruction and the additional instructions, to be given to you now, constitute the law of this case and each such instruction is equally binding upon you. You should consider each instruction in light of and in harmony with the other instructions, and you should apply the instructions as a whole to the evidence. The order in which the instructions are given is no indication of their relative importance. All of the instructions are in writing and will be available to you in the jury room.

Instruction Number 3
(See MAI 3.01 (1998 Revision))

In these instructions, you are told that your verdict depends on whether or not you believe certain propositions of fact submitted to you. The burden is upon the party who relies upon any such proposition to cause you to believe that such proposition is more likely to be true than not true. In determining whether or not you believe any proposition, you must consider only the evidence and the reasonable inference derived from the evidence. If the evidence in the case does not cause you to believe a particular proposition submitted, then you cannot return a verdict requiring belief of that proposition.

Instruction Number 4
(See MAI 2.02 (1980 Revision))

In returning your verdict you will form beliefs as to the facts. The court does not mean to assume as true any fact referred to in these instructions but leaves it to you to determine what the facts are.

Instruction Number 5
(See MAI 2.04 (1981 Revision))

The verdict form included in these instructions contains directions for completion and will allow you to return the permissible verdict in this case. Nine or more of you must agree in order to return any verdict. A verdict must be signed by each juror who agrees to it.

Instruction Number 6
(See MAI 11.06 (1990 Revision))

The term "negligent" or "negligence" as used in these instructions means the failure to use that degree of skill and learning ordinarily used under the same or similar circumstances by the members of defendant's profession.

Instruction Number 7
(See MAI 21.01 (1988 Revision), MAI 19.01 (1986 Revision))

Your verdict must be for plaintiff Megan Smith and against defendant Jones if you believe:

First, defendant Horace Jones, MD, either:

> administered excessive anesthetic to Megan Smith during induction of anesthesia, or

> failed to adequately monitor the vital signs of Megan Smith during induction of anesthesia, and

Second, Defendant, in any one or more of the respects submitted in paragraph First, was thereby negligent, and

Third, such negligence directly caused or directly contributed to cause damage to Megan Smith.

Instruction Number 8
(Converse Omitted)

Instruction Number 9
(See MAI 31.04 (1991 Revision))

If you find in favor of plaintiff Megan Smith on her claim for personal injuries, and if you believe that plaintiffs John and Julie Smith sustained damage as a direct result of injury to their child, then in your verdict you must find that plaintiffs John and Julie Smith did sustain such damage.

Instruction Number 10
(Converse Omitted)

Instruction Number 11
(See MAI 21.03 (1988 New), MAI 21.07 (1991 New), MAI 4.18 (1991 New))

If you find in favor of plaintiff Megan Smith, then you must award her such sum as you believe will fairly and justly compensate her for any damages you believe she sustained and is reasonably certain to sustain in the future that the occurrence mentioned in the evidence directly caused or directly contributed to cause.

If you further find that plaintiffs John and Julie Smith did sustain damage as a direct result of injury to their child, Megan Smith, you must award plaintiffs John and Julie Smith such sum as you believe will fairly and justly compensate them for any damages due to injury to their child which you believe they sustained and are reasonably certain to sustain in the future that the occurrence mentioned in the evidence directly caused or directly contributed to cause.

Any damages you award must be itemized by the categories set forth in the verdict form on each claim.

Instruction Number 12
(See MAI 21.05 (1988 New))

In these instructions, you are told to itemize any damages you award by the categories set forth in the verdict form.

The phrase "past economic damages" means those damages incurred in the past for pecuniary harm such as medical expenses for necessary drugs, therapy, and for medical, surgical, nursing, X-ray, dental, custodial, and other health and rehabilitative services and for past lost earnings and for past lost earning capacity.

The phrase "past non-economic damages" means those damages incurred in the past from non-pecuniary harm such as pain, suffering, mental anguish, inconvenience, physical impairment, disfigurement, and loss of capacity to enjoy life.

The phrase "future medical damages" means those damages arising in the future for medical expenses such as necessary drugs, therapy, and medical, surgical, nursing, X-ray, dental, custodial, and other health and rehabilitative services.

The phrase "future economic damages" means those damages arising in the future from pecuniary harm such as lost earnings and lost earning capacity.

The phrase "future non-economic damages" means those damages arising in the future from non-pecuniary harms such as pain, suffering, mental anguish, inconvenience, physical impairment, disfigurement, and loss of capacity to enjoy life.

Verdict

(See MAI 36.20 (1988 New), MAI 36.23 (1991 New))

Note: Complete this form by writing in the names required by your verdict.

On the claim of plaintiff Megan Smith for personal injuries against defendant Horace Jones, MD, we, the undersigned jurors find in favor of:

(Plaintiff Megan Smith)   or   (Defendant Horace Jones, MD)

Note: Complete the following only if the above finding is in favor of plaintiff Megan Smith. Complete by writing in the amount of damages, if any, for each of the following itemized categories. If you do not find that plaintiff has damages in a particular category, write "none" in that category. The total damages must equal the total of the itemized damage amounts you have assessed.

We, the undersigned jurors, assess the damages of plaintiff Megan Smith as follows:

> For past economic damages including past
>   medical damages $_____
>
> For past non-economic damages $_____
>
> For future medical damages $_____
>
> For future economic damages excluding
>   future medical damages $_____
>
> For future non-economic damages $_____
>
>   TOTAL DAMAGES $_____

Note: Complete the following paragraph by writing in the word(s) required by your verdict.

On the claim of plaintiffs John and Julie Smith for damages due to injury to their child, we, the undersigned jurors, find that plaintiffs John and Julie Smith _____ sustain damages as a direct result of injury to their child.

("did" or "did not")

Note: Complete the following paragraph only if the above finding is that plaintiffs John and Julie Smith "did" sustain such damage.

We, the undersigned jurors, assess the damages of plaintiffs John and Julie Smith due to injury to their child as follows:

> For past economic damages excluding past
>   medical damages $_____
>
> For future economic damages excluding
>   future medical damages $_____
>
>   TOTAL DAMAGES $_____

Note: All jurors who agree to the above findings must sign below.

_____   _____
_____   _____
_____   _____
_____   _____

Committee Comment (1998 New)

This Illustration 35.20 demonstrates an appropriate submission in an action against a health care provider where there is an injury claim along with a derivative claim but no claim of comparative fault. (For an illustration of a case with a claim for comparative fault, see Illustration 35.18). This Illustration demonstrates an appropriate method for combining the elements of a submission peculiar to a claim against a health care provider under sections 538.205 et seq., RSMo, (See MAI Chapter 21 and verdict forms, MAI 36.20 and MAI 36.21), with the appropriate method for submission of a derivative claim such as a parental claim (See MAI 21.03, 21.07 and 4.18.)

The verdict form in this Illustration has been tailored to the particular hypothetical fact situation described in this Illustration. The Notes on Use to MAI 21.05 allow appropriate modification of the elements of recoverable damages in one or more definitions; but, solely for the sake of simplicity, the Committee chose not to do so in this Illustration.

35.21 [2002 New] Illustrations—Health Care Providers—Settling Tortfeasor—Apportionment of Fault Under Section 538.230—<u>With</u> Comparative Fault

Dr. Edward Smith performed surgery on plaintiff John Jones. Plaintiff claims that Smith left a sponge in plaintiff's abdomen during surgery. Smith claims that plaintiff failed to advise Smith of abdominal distention. Plaintiff previously settled with Nurse Davis, a surgical nurse. Plaintiff obtained the settlement with Nurse Davis on the claim that the nurse failed to perform a sponge count. Defendant Smith now makes the same claim with respect to the sponge count by Nurse Davis. He seeks an apportionment of fault under section 538.230, RSMo, as to Nurse Davis as a "released party" and as to plaintiff Jones for his alleged comparative fault.

Instruction No. 1
(Same as MAI 2.01)

Instruction No. 2
(See MAI 2.03 (1980 New))

As you remember, the court gave you a general instruction before the presentation of any evidence in this case. The court will not repeat that instruction at this time. However, that instruction and the additional instructions, to be given to you now, constitute the law of this case, and each such instruction is equally binding upon you. You should consider each instruction in light of and in harmony with the other instructions, and you should apply the instructions as a whole to the evidence. The order in which the instructions are given is no indication of their relative importance. All of the instructions are in writing and will be available to you in the jury room.

Instruction No. 3
(See MAI 2.02 (1980 Revision))

In returning your verdict you will form beliefs as to the facts. The court does not mean to assume as true any fact referred to in these instructions but leaves it to you to determine what the facts are.

Instruction No. 4
(See MAI 3.01 (1998 Revision))

In these instructions, you are told that your verdict depends on whether or not you believe certain propositions of fact submitted to you. The burden is upon the party who relies upon any such proposition to cause you to believe that such proposition is more likely to be true than not true. In determining whether or not you believe any such proposition, you must consider only the evidence and the reasonable inferences derived from the evidence. If the evidence in the case does not cause you to believe a particular proposition submitted, then you cannot return a verdict requiring belief of that proposition.

Instruction No. 5
(See MAI 11.06 (1990 Revision) (Modified))

The term "negligent" or "negligence" as used in these instructions with respect to a physician or nurse means the failure to use that degree of skill and learning ordinarily used under the same or similar circumstances by members of those health care providers' respective professions.

Instruction No. 6
(See MAI 11.07 (1996 Revision) (Modified))

The term "negligent" or "negligence" as used in these instructions with respect to a patient means the failure to use ordinary care. The phrase "ordinary care" means that degree of care that an ordinarily careful person would use under the same or similar circumstances.

Instruction No. 7
(See MAI 2.04 (1981 Revision))

The verdict form included in these instructions contains directions for completion and will allow you to return the permissible verdict in this case. Nine or more of you must agree in order to return any verdict. A verdict must be signed by each juror who agrees to it.

Instruction No. 8
(See MAI 21.01 (1988 Revision), MAI 37.01 (1986 New), MAI 19.01 (1986 Revision))

In your verdict you must assess a percentage of fault to defendant Smith, whether or not plaintiff John Jones or Nurse Davis was partly at fault, if you believe:

First, defendant Smith left a sponge in plaintiff's abdomen during surgery, and

Second, defendant Smith was thereby negligent, and

Third, such negligence directly caused or directly contributed to cause damage to plaintiff.

Instruction No. 9
(Converse Omitted)

Instruction No. 10
(See MAI 21.01 (1988 Revision), MAI 37.01 (1986 New), MAI 19.01 (1986 Revision), (Modified))

If you assess a percentage of fault to Defendant Smith under Instruction No. 8, then you must assess a percentage of fault to Nurse Davis on Defendant Smith's claim that Nurse Davis is partly at fault if you believe:

First, Nurse Davis failed to perform a sponge count during surgery, and

Second, Nurse Davis was thereby negligent, and

Third, such negligence directly caused or directly contributed to cause damage to plaintiff.

(*Note: The burden of proof and the responsibility to tender this verdict director is on the party seeking an assessment of a percentage of fault to a released person.*)

Instruction No. 11
(Converse Omitted)

(*Note: Since Nurse Davis settled with plaintiff, and is not a
party to the lawsuit, plaintiff may submit a converse to
the defendant's tendered verdict directing instruction
regarding the negligence of the settling tortfeasor.*)

Instruction No. 12
(See MAI 37.02 (1986 New))

In your verdict you must assess a percentage of fault to
plaintiff John Jones, whether or not defendant Smith or
Nurse Davis was partly at fault, if you believe:

First, plaintiff John Jones failed to advise Dr. Smith of
abdominal distention, and

Second, plaintiff John Jones was thereby negligent, and

Third, such negligence of plaintiff John Jones directly
caused or directly contributed to cause any damage
plaintiff John Jones may have sustained.

Instruction No. 13
(Converse Omitted)

Instruction No. 14
(See MAI 21.04 (1988 New), Modified in accordance with
Carlson v. K–Mart, 979 S.W.2d 145 (Mo. banc 1998))

If you assess a percentage of fault to defendant Smith,
then, disregarding any fault on the part of plaintiff, you
must determine the total amount of plaintiff's damages to be
such sum as will fairly and justly compensate plaintiff for
any damages you believe he sustained and is reasonably
certain to sustain in the future that the sponge incident
directly caused or directly contributed to cause. You must
state such total amount of plaintiff's damages in your verdict, and you must itemize those total damages by the
categories set forth in the verdict form.

In determining the total amount of plaintiff's damages and in itemizing those total damages, you must not reduce such damages by any percentage of fault you may assess to plaintiff [or Nurse Davis]. The judge will compute plaintiff's recovery by reducing the amount you find as plaintiff's total damages by any percentage of fault you assess to plaintiff [or Nurse Davis (*see Note following Instruction No. 15*)].

Instruction No. 15
(See MAI 21.06 (1991 New))

Plaintiff's claim against Nurse Davis has been settled. In determining the total amount of plaintiff's damages and in assessing percentages of fault, you are not to consider such settlement. The total damages assessed by you on plaintiff's claim against the defendant Smith will be reduced by the judge by any percentage of fault you assess to Nurse Davis.

(*Note: This instruction, based on MAI 21.06, will be given only as a separate instruction if the jury has knowledge of the settlement from the evidence or a trial incident. If there is no such knowledge, the preceding damage instruction No. 14 should be modified by adding the phrase "or Nurse Davis" to the last two sentences.*)

Instruction No. 16
(See MAI 21.05 (1988 New))

In these instructions, you are told to itemize any damages you award by the categories set forth in the verdict form.

The phrase "past economic damages" means those damages incurred in the past for pecuniary harm such as medical expenses for necessary drugs, therapy, and for medical, surgical, nursing, x-ray, dental, custodial, and other health and rehabilitative services and for past lost earnings and for past lost earning capacity.

The phrase "past non-economic damages" means those damages arising in the past from non-pecuniary harm such as pain, suffering, mental anguish, inconvenience, physical impairment, disfigurement, and loss of capacity to enjoy life.

The phrase "future medical damages" means those damages arising in the future for medical expenses such as necessary drugs, therapy, and medical, surgical, nursing, x-ray, dental, custodial, and other health and rehabilitative services.

The phrase "future economic damages" means those damages arising in the future from pecuniary harm such as lost earnings and lost earning capacity.

The phrase "future non-economic damages" means those damages arising in the future from non-pecuniary harm such as pain, suffering, mental anguish, inconvenience, physical impairment, disfigurement, and loss of capacity to enjoy life.

VERDICT
(See MAI 36.22 (1988 New))

Note: Complete the following paragraph by filling in the blanks as required by your verdict. If you assess a percentage of fault to any of those listed below, write in a percentage not greater than 100%; otherwise write in "zero" next to that name. If you assess a percentage of fault to any of those listed below, the total of such percentages must be 100%.

On the claim of plaintiff John Jones for personal injury against defendant Smith, we, the undersigned jurors, assess percentages of fault as follows:

Defendant Smith	_____%	(zero to 100%)
Nurse Davis	_____%	(zero to 100%)
Plaintiff Jones	_____%	(zero to 100%)
TOTAL	_____%	(zero *or* 100%)

Note: Complete the following if you assessed a percentage of fault to defendant Smith. Complete by writing in the amount of damages, if any, for each of the following itemized categories. If you do not find that plaintiff has damages in a particular category, write "none" in that category. The total damages must equal the total of the itemized damage amounts you have assessed.

We, the undersigned jurors, disregarding any fault on the part of plaintiff or Nurse Davis, find the total damages of plaintiff Jones as follows:

For past economic damages including past
medical damages $_____

For past non-economic damages $_____

For future medical damages $_____

For future economic damages excluding
future medical damages $_____

For future non-economic damages $_____

TOTAL DAMAGES $_____

Note: The judge will compute the plaintiff's recovery under the law and the percentages of fault you assess.

Note: All jurors who agree to the above must sign below:

_____   _____
_____   _____
_____   _____
_____   _____

Committee Comment (2002 New)

Illustrations 35.21 and 35.22 demonstrate appropriate methods of submission of apportionment of fault under section 538.230, RSMo, in situations involving comparative fault of plaintiff (Illustration 35.21) and *no* comparative fault of plaintiff (Illustration 35.22). These illustrations are for use *only* in actions involving health care providers under sections 538.205, RSMo et seq. These illustrations are not to be used in other apportionment of fault cases. For claims submitting apportionment of fault under *Missouri Pacific R. Co. v. Whitehead & Kales Co.*, 566 S.W.2d 466 (Mo. banc 1978) (in cases not involving health care providers under sections 538.205 et seq.), see MAI 4.12, 4.13, 4.14, 36.14, and 36.15; and see Illustrations 35.02, 35.03, 35.05, 35.15, and 35.19.

In actions other than those against health care providers under sections 538.205, RSMo et seq., apportionment of fault issues among defendants or third party defendants have no direct relevance to liability and damage issues in plaintiff's claim in light of the doctrine of joint and several liability. See section 537.067, RSMo. Thus, traditional apportionment of fault issues under *Whitehead & Kales* should not be commingled with the instructions and verdict form pertinent to plaintiff's claim. In cases involving comparative fault of plaintiff, where all parties from whom apportionment is sought have been sued by plaintiff, all necessary percentages of fault of all parties on all issues (plaintiff's claim and apportionment claim) are determined in the verdict form in plaintiff's claim, and no separate package is necessary to submit apportionment issues.

However, the above discussion of the submission of apportionment issues under *Whitehead & Kales* is not applicable to actions involving health care providers under sections 538.205, RSMo et seq. By specific statutory directive in section 538.230, in actions against health care providers, "where fault is apportioned among the parties and persons released (pursuant to subsection 3 of section 538.230), the court, unless otherwise agreed by all the parties, shall instruct the jury to apportion fault among such persons and parties...." The findings of percentages of fault in such cases, unlike the traditional *Whitehead & Kales* cases, do affect the judgment on plaintiff's claim. Under subsections 2 and 3 of section 538.230, the jury verdict on plaintiff's claim is reduced by the percentage of fault assessed to a settling tortfeasor, and a non-settling tortfeasor is jointly and severally liable only for percentages of fault of other defendants whose apportioned percentage of fault is "equal to or less than such defendant." In light of this statutory interplay between "apportionment", fault of a "settling tortfeasor", and "joint and several liability" under section 538.230, the Committee believes it is most simple and efficient to submit all such issues in a single package (that submitting plaintiff's claim) whether or not the comparative fault of plaintiff is at issue, as demonstrated in these Illustrations 35.21 and 35.22.

35.22 [2002 New] Illustrations—Health Care Providers—Settling Tortfeasor—Apportionment of Fault Under Section 538.230—<u>No</u> Comparative Fault of Plaintiff

Dr. Edward Smith performed surgery on plaintiff John Jones. Plaintiff claims that Smith left a sponge in plaintiff's abdomen during surgery. Plaintiff previously settled with Nurse Davis, a surgical nurse. Plaintiff obtained the settlement with Nurse Davis on the claim that the nurse failed to perform a sponge count. Defendant Smith now makes the same claim with respect to the sponge count by Nurse Davis. He also seeks an apportionment of fault under section 538.230, RSMo, as to Nurse Davis as a "released party."

Instruction No. 1
(Same as MAI 2.01)

Instruction No. 2
(See MAI 2.03 (1980 New))

As you remember, the court gave you a general instruction before the presentation of any evidence in this case. The court will not repeat that instruction at this time. However, that instruction and the additional instructions, to be given to you now, constitute the law of this case, and each such instruction is equally binding upon you. You should consider each instruction in light of and in harmony with the other instructions, and you should apply the instructions as a whole to the evidence. The order in which the instructions are given is no indication of their relative importance. All of the instructions are in writing and will be available to you in the jury room.

Instruction No. 3
(See MAI 2.02 (1980 Revision))

In returning your verdict you will form beliefs as to the facts. The court does not mean to assume as true any fact referred to in these instructions but leaves it to you to determine what the facts are.

703

Instruction No. 4
(See MAI 3.01(1998 Revision))

In these instructions, you are told that your verdict depends on whether or not you believe certain propositions of fact submitted to you. The burden is upon the party who relies upon any such proposition to cause you to believe that such proposition is more likely to be true than not true. In determining whether or not you believe any such proposition, you must consider only the evidence and the reasonable inferences derived from the evidence. If the evidence in the case does not cause you to believe a particular proposition submitted, then you cannot return a verdict requiring belief of that proposition.

Instruction No. 5
(See MAI 11.06 (1990 Revision) (Modified))

The term "negligent" or "negligence" as used in these instructions with respect to a physician or nurse means the failure to use that degree of skill and learning ordinarily used under the same or similar circumstances by members of those health care providers' respective professions.

Instruction No. 6
(See MAI 2.04 (1981 Revision))

The verdict form included in these instructions contains directions for completion and will allow you to return the permissible verdict in this case. Nine or more of you must agree in order to return any verdict. A verdict must be signed by each juror who agrees to it.

Instruction No. 7
(See MAI 21.01(1988 Revision), MAI 37.01(1986 New), MAI 19.01 (1986 Revision))

In your verdict you must assess a percentage of fault to defendant Smith, whether or not Nurse Davis was partly at fault, if you believe:

First, defendant Smith left a sponge in plaintiff's abdomen during surgery, and

Second, defendant Smith was thereby negligent, and

Third, such negligence directly caused or directly contributed to cause damage to plaintiff.

Instruction No. 8
(Converse Omitted)

Instruction No. 9
(See MAI 21.01(1988 Revision), MAI 37.01(1986 New), MAI 19.01 (1986 Revision), (Modified))

If you assess a percentage of fault to Defendant Smith under Instruction No. 7, then you must assess a percentage of fault to Nurse Davis on Defendant Smith's claim that Nurse Davis is partly at fault, if you believe:

First, Nurse Davis failed to perform a sponge count during surgery, and

Second, Nurse Davis was thereby negligent, and

Third, such negligence directly caused or directly contributed to cause damage to plaintiff.

(*Note: The burden of proof and the responsibility to tender this verdict director is on the party seeking an assessment of a percentage of fault to a released person.*)

Instruction No. 10
(Converse Omitted)

(*Note: Since Nurse Davis settled with plaintiff, and is not a party to the lawsuit, plaintiff may submit a converse to the defendant's tendered verdict directing instruction regarding the negligence of the settling tortfeasor.*)

Instruction No, 11
(See MAI 21.04 (1988 New), Modified in accordance with *Carlson v. K–Mart,* 979 S.W.2d 145 (Mo. banc 1998))

If you assess a percentage of fault to defendant Smith, then, disregarding any fault on the part of Nurse Davis, you must determine the total amount of plaintiff's damages to be such sum as will fairly and justly compensate plaintiff for any damages you believe he sustained and is reasonably certain to sustain in the future that the sponge incident directly caused or directly contributed to cause. You must state such total amount of plaintiff's damages in your verdict, and you must itemize those total damages by the categories set forth in the verdict form.

In determining the total amount of plaintiff's damages and in itemizing those total damages, you must not reduce such damages by any percentage of fault you may assess to Nurse Davis. The judge will compute plaintiff's recovery by reducing the amount you find as plaintiff's total damages by any percentage of fault you assess to Nurse Davis.

Instruction No. 12
(See MAI 21.06 (1991 New))

Plaintiff's claim against Nurse Davis has been settled. In determining the total amount of plaintiff's damages and in assessing percentages of fault you are not to consider such settlement.

(*Note: This instruction, based on MAI 21.06, will be given only as a separate instruction if the jury has knowledge of the settlement from the evidence or a trial incident. The third sentence of MAI 21.06 has been deleted from this instruction to avoid repetition of information given to the jury in Instruction No. 11.*)

Instruction No. 13
(See MAI 21.05 (1988 New))

In these instructions, you are told to itemize any damages you award by the categories set forth in the verdict form.

The phrase "past economic damages" means those damages incurred in the past for pecuniary harm such as medical expenses for necessary drugs, therapy, and for medical, surgical, nursing, x-ray, dental, custodial, and other health and rehabilitative services and for past lost earnings and for past lost earning capacity.

The phrase "past non-economic damages" means those damages arising in the past from non-pecuniary harm such as pain, suffering, mental anguish, inconvenience, physical impairment, disfigurement, and loss of capacity to enjoy life.

The phrase "future medical damages" means those damages arising in the future for medical expenses such as necessary drugs, therapy, and medical, surgical, nursing, x-ray, dental, custodial, and other health and rehabilitative services.

The phrase "future economic damages" means those damages arising in the future from pecuniary harm such as lost earnings and lost earning capacity.

The phrase "future non-economic damages" means those damages arising in the future from pecuniary harm such as pain, suffering, mental anguish, inconvenience, physical impairment, disfigurement, and loss of capacity to enjoy life.

VERDICT
(See MAI 36.22 (1988 New))

Note: Complete the following paragraph by filling in the blanks as required by your verdict. If you assess a percentage of fault to any of those listed below, write in a percentage not greater than 100%: otherwise write in "zero" next to that name. If you assess a percentage of fault to any of those listed below, the total of such percentages must be 100%.

On the claim of plaintiff John Jones for personal injury, we, the undersigned jurors, assess percentages of fault as follows:

Defendant Smith	_____%	(zero to 100%)
Nurse Davis	_____%	(zero to 100%)
TOTAL	_____%	(zero *or* 100%)

Note: Complete the following if you assessed a percentage of fault to defendant Smith. Complete by writing in the amount of damages, if any, for each of the following itemized categories. If you do not find that plaintiff has damages in a particular category, write "none" in that category. The total damages must equal the total of the itemized damage amounts you have assessed.

We, the undersigned jurors, disregarding any fault on the part of Nurse Davis, find the total damages of plaintiff Jones as follows:

For past economic damages including past
   medical damages $_____

For past non-economic damages $_____

For future medical damages $_____

For future economic damages excluding
   future medical damages $_____

For future non-economic damages $_____

TOTAL DAMAGES $_____

Note: The judge will compute the plaintiff's recovery under
the law and the percentages of fault you assess.

_____   _____

_____   _____

_____   _____

_____   _____

_____   _____

Committee Comment (2002 New)

Illustrations 35.21 and 35.22 demonstrate appropriate methods of submission of apportionment of fault under section 538.230, RSMo, in situations involving comparative fault of plaintiff (Illustration 35.21) and *no* comparative fault of plaintiff (Illustration 35.22). These illustrations are for use *only* in actions involving health care providers under sections 538.205, RSMo et seq. These illustrations are not to be used in other apportionment of fault cases. For claims submitting apportionment of fault under *Missouri Pacific R.Co. v. Whitehead & Kales Co.*, 566 S.W.2d 466 (Mo. banc 1978) (in cases not involving health care providers under sections 538.205 et seq.), see MAI 4.12, 4.13, 4.14, 36.14, and 36.15; and see Illustrations 35.02, 35.03, 35.05, 35.15, and 35.19.

In actions other than those against health care providers under sections 538.205, RSMo et seq., apportionment of fault issues among defendants or third party defendants have no direct relevance to liability and damage issues in plaintiff's claim in light of the doctrine of joint and several liability. See section 537.067, RSMo. Thus, traditional apportionment of fault issues under *Whitehead & Kales* should not be commingled with the instructions and verdict form pertinent to plaintiff's claim. In cases involving comparative fault of plaintiff, where all parties from whom apportionment is sought have been sued by plaintiff, all necessary percentages of fault of all parties on all issues (plaintiff's claim and apportionment claim) are determined in the verdict form in plaintiff's claim and no separate package is necessary to submit apportionment issues.

However, the above discussion of the submission of apportionment issues under *Whitehead & Kales* is not applicable to actions involving health care providers under sections 538.205 et seq. By specific statutory directive in section 538.230, in actions against health care providers, "where fault is apportioned among the parties and persons released (pursuant to subsection 3 of section 538.230), the court, unless otherwise agreed by all the parties, shall instruct the jury to apportion fault among such persons and parties...." The findings of percentages of fault in such cases, unlike the traditional *Whitehead & Kales* cases, do affect the judgment on plaintiff's claim. Under subsections 2 and 3 of section 538.230, the jury verdict on plaintiff's claim is reduced by the percentage of fault assessed to a settling tortfeasor, and a non-settling tortfeasor is jointly and severally liable only for percentages of fault of other defendants whose apportioned percentage of fault is "equal to or less than such defendant." In light of this statutory interplay between "apportionment," fault of a "settling tortfeasor," and "joint and several liability" under section 538.230, the Committee believes it is most simple and efficient to submit all such issues in a single package (that submitting plaintiff's claim) whether or not the comparative fault of plaintiff is at issue, as demonstrated in these Illustrations 35.21 and 35.22.

36.00

FORMS OF VERDICT

Analysis of Instructions

FORMS OF VERDICT

Westlaw Electronic Research

See Westlaw Electronic Research Guide preceding the Table of Instructions.

712

36.01 [1980 Revision] Form of Verdict—Plaintiff vs. Defendant—Personal Injuries Only

VERDICT _____ [1]

Note: Complete this form by writing in the name required by your verdict.

On the claim of plaintiff (*state the name*) for personal injuries [2] against defendant (*state the name*), we, the undersigned jurors, find in favor of:

_____

| (Plaintiff (state the name)) | or | (Defendant (state the name)) |

Note: Complete the following paragraph only if the above finding is in favor of plaintiff (*state the name*).

We, the undersigned jurors, assess the damages of plaintiff (*state the name*) at $_____ (*stating the amount*).

Note: All jurors who agree to the above findings must sign below.

_____   _____
_____   _____
_____   _____
_____   _____
_____   _____

Notes on Use (1980 New)

1. Verdicts will be designated alphabetically (A, B, C, etc.).

2. The verdict form will contain a descriptive phrase describing and identifying the claim submitted by this particular package which will be the claim to which this verdict is applicable. The identifying phrase should be non-inflammatory and as neutral as possible and should avoid the assumption of disputed facts. See MAI 2.00 General Comment for a discussion and for examples of the appropriate identifying phrase.

Parenthetical directions to "(state the name)" in the above form are addressed to counsel. The appropriate party's name should be typed in the prepared verdict at those points. All other directions are for the jury and should be submitted to the jury as written.

A separate verdict form must be used for each "package" other than the package containing the general instructions. The verdict form will be the last instruction in each such package. See MAI 2.00 General Comment for an explanation of "packaging".

Verdict forms should not be read by the Court to the jury.

Library References:

> C.J.S. Trial § 541.
>
> West's Key No. Digests, Trial ☞352.1.

Notes of Decisions

Correcting verdict   1
Deviation   2
Multiple defendants   3

1. Correcting verdict

Where jury presented an ambiguously signed verdict the trial court properly told jury how verdict should be signed. This was not an improper oral instruction implicitly condemned by MAI 70.01. McWilliams v. Wright, 460 S.W.2d 699[2] (Mo.1970). Now see MAI 2.06.

2. Deviation

Addition of "and against the plaintiff" to defendant's form of verdict instruction erroneous, but harmless. Salsberry v. Archibald Plumbing & Heating Company, 587 S.W.2d 907[15] (Mo.App.1979).

3. Multiple defendants

Verdict forms patterned after MAI 36.01 were appropriate in action brought by accountants against clients to recover for accounting and tax services rendered where accountants' theory of quantum meruit required that the jury could not render a verdict against any less than all of the clients on any single count. Baron v. Lerman, 719 S.W.2d 72[6] (Mo.App.1986).

Where defendants were joint tortfeasors and there was not varying degrees of culpability, submission of separate verdict forms patterned after MAI 36.01 for each defendant rather than a single form patterned after MAI 36.12 was error since there can be "but one final judgment in the cause, and a judgment against joint tortfeasors must be for a single amount and cannot be split up." Chambers v. McNair, 692 S.W.2d 320[3] (Mo.App. 1985).

36.02 [1981 Revision] Form of Verdict—Plaintiff vs. Defendant—Personal Injuries and Property Damage

VERDICT _____ [1]

Note: Complete this form by writing in the name required by your verdict.

On the claim of plaintiff (*state the name*) against defendant (*state the name*) [2], we, the undersigned jurors, find in favor of:

_____

(Plaintiff (state the name))   or   (Defendant (state the name))

Note: Complete the following paragraph only if the above finding is in favor of plaintiff (*state the name*).

We, the undersigned jurors, assess the damages of plaintiff (*state the name*) as follows:

For personal injuries $_____ (*stating the amount or, if none, write the word, "none"*).

For property damage $_____ (*stating the amount or, if none, write the word, "none"*).

Note: All jurors who agree to the above findings must sign below.

_____   _____
_____   _____
_____   _____
_____   _____
_____   _____

Notes on Use (1980 New)

1. Verdicts will be designated alphabetically (A, B, C, etc.).

2. The verdict form will contain a descriptive phrase describing and identifying the claim submitted by this particular package which will be the claim to which this verdict is applicable. The identifying phrase should be non-inflammatory and as neutral as possible and should avoid the assumption of disputed facts. See MAI 2.00 General Comment for a discussion and for examples of the appropriate identifying phrase.

Parenthetical directions to "(state the name)" in the above form are addressed to counsel. The appropriate party's name should be typed in

715

the prepared verdict at those points. All other directions are for the jury and should be submitted to the jury as written.

A separate verdict form must be used for each "package" other than the package containing the general instructions. The verdict form will be the last instruction in each such package. See MAI 2.00 General Comment for an explanation of "packaging".

Verdict forms should not be read by the Court to the jury.

Library References:

C.J.S. Trial § 541.
West's Key No. Digests, Trial ☞352.1.

Notes of Decisions

1. In general

Failure of verdict to separate personal property from personal injury awards was error, but defective verdict was waived by defendant's silence. Cobb v. Cosby, 416 S.W.2d 222[4–7] (Mo.App.1967).

**36.03 [Withdrawn 1980] Forms of Verdict—Plaintiff
vs. Defendant—Personal Injuries and
Counterclaim for Personal Injuries**

**36.04 [Withdrawn 1980] Forms of Verdict—Plaintiff
vs. Defendant—Personal Injuries and
Property Damage and Counterclaim—Personal Injuries and Property Damage**

717

36.05 [1980 Revision] Form of Verdict—Plaintiff vs. Two Defendants

VERDICT _____ [1]

Note: Complete this form by writing in the name(s) required by your verdict.

On the claim of plaintiff (*state the name*) for personal injuries [2] against defendant (*state the name of one defendant*), we, the undersigned jurors, find in favor of:

_____

(Plaintiff (state the name))   or   (Defendant (state the name))

On the claim of plaintiff (*state the name*) for personal injuries [2] against defendant (*state the name of the other defendant*), we, the undersigned jurors, find in favor of:

_____

(Plaintiff (state the name))   or   (Defendant (state the name))

Note: Complete the following paragraph only if one or more of the above findings is in favor of plaintiff (*state the name*).

We, the undersigned jurors, assess the damages of plaintiff (*state the name*) for personal injuries at $_____ (*stating the amount*).

Note: All jurors who agree to the above findings must sign below.

_____   _____
_____   _____
_____   _____
_____   _____
_____   _____

Notes on Use (1996 Revision)

1. Verdicts will be designated alphabetically (A, B, C, etc.).

2. The verdict form will contain a descriptive phrase describing and identifying the claim submitted by this particular package which will be the claim to which this verdict is applicable. The identifying phrase should avoid the assumption of disputed facts. See MAI 2.00 General Comment, Section F for a discussion and for examples of the appropriate identifying phrase.

Parenthetical directions to "(state the name)" in the above form are addressed to counsel. The appropriate party's name should be typed in the prepared verdict at those points. All other directions are for the jury and should be submitted to the jury as written.

A separate verdict form must be used for each "package" other than the package containing the general instructions. The verdict form will be the last instruction in each such package. See MAI 2.00 General Comment for an explanation of "packaging".

Where the two defendants are master and servant, see MAI 18.01 for guidance in preparing the verdict form.

Verdict forms should not be read by the Court to the jury.

Library References:

C.J.S. Trial § 541.
West's Key No. Digests, Trial ☜352.1.

Notes of Decisions

In general   1
Master and servant   2

---

1. In general

In suit by injured union members against union local and its former president arising out of former president's assault of them following union election, trial court's error in refusing local union's request that jury be returned to their deliberations for correction of its verdict warranted reversal and remand for new trial on issue of compensatory damages only; though former president's acts of willfulness and local union's negligence were separate and independent, they were joint tort-feasors insofar as injuries caused were single and indivisible, and jury should have been given other forms of verdicts patterned after MAI Form of Verdict 36.05, which would have allowed single verdict and single amount of compensatory damages for each plaintiff. Fincher v. Murphy, 825 S.W.2d 890 (Mo.App.1992).

Verdict directing instruction and form of verdict instruction are read together. Colonial Construction Co. v. Sharp Indus. Inc., 421 S.W.2d 551[3] (Mo.App.1967).

Proper verdict form against all defendants (MAI 32.05 [Now 36.05]) where all or none, are liable. Dettler v. Santa Cruz, 403 S.W.2d 651[11] (Mo.App.1966).

2. Master and servant

Where plaintiff sued owner and operator of machinery for operator's negligence it was error to give a form of verdict instruction, MAI 36.05, authorizing a verdict against the owner and in favor of operator, and where jury returned such a verdict the plaintiff was entitled to a new trial. Lynch v. Hill, 443 S.W.2d 812[6, 8] (Mo.1969). Now see MAI 18.01 for guidance in preparing a verdict form in a master/servant case.

36.06 [1980 Revision] Form of Verdict—Crossclaim for Indemnity by Surety vs. Principal; by Employer vs. Employee

VERDICT _____ [1]

Note: Complete this form by writing in the name required by your verdict.

On the claim of defendant (*state the name*) for indemnity [2] from defendant (*state the name*), we, the undersigned jurors, find in favor of:

_____   _____
(Defendant (state the name))   or   (Defendant (state the name))

Note: All jurors who agree to the above finding must sign below.

_____   _____

_____   _____

_____   _____

_____   _____

Notes on Use (1980 New)

1. Verdicts will be designated alphabetically (A, B, C, etc.).

2. The verdict form will contain a descriptive phrase describing and identifying the claim submitted by this particular package which will be the claim to which this verdict is applicable. The identifying phrase should be non-inflammatory and as neutral as possible and should avoid the assumption of disputed facts. See MAI 2.00 General Comment for a discussion and for examples of the appropriate identifying phrase.

Parenthetical directions to "(state the name)" in the above form are addressed to counsel. The appropriate party's name should be typed in the prepared verdict at those points. All other directions are for the jury and should be submitted to the jury as written.

A separate verdict form must be used for each "package" other than the package containing the general instructions. The verdict form will be the last instruction in each such package. See MAI 2.00 General Comment for an explanation of "packaging".

Verdict forms should not be read by the Court to the jury.

Library References:

C.J.S. Trial § 541.
West's Key No. Digests, Trial ⚲352.1.

Notes of Decisions

1. In general

Form of verdict against all defendants was proper where they were joint guarantors and not severally liable. Linwood State Bank v. Lientz, 413 S.W.2d 248[12] (Mo.1967).

36.10 [1980 Revision] Form of Verdict—Plaintiff vs. Defendant Insurance Company—Interest— Vexatious Refusal Penalty—Attorney Fees

VERDICT _____ [1]

Note: Complete this form by writing in the name required by your verdict.

On the claim of plaintiff (*state the name*) for insurance benefits, interest, penalties and attorney fees [2] against defendant, we, the undersigned jurors, find in favor of:

_____

(Plaintiff (state the name))   or   (Defendant (state the name))

Note: Complete the following paragraph only if your verdict is in favor of plaintiff (*state the name*).

We, the undersigned jurors, assess the damages of plaintiff (*state the name*) as follows:

On the policy $_____ (*stating the amount*).

For interest $_____ (*stating the amount or, if none, write the word, "none"*).

For penalty $_____ (*stating the amount or, if none, write the word, "none"*).

For attorney fees $_____ (*stating the amount or, if none, write the word "none"*).

Note: All jurors who agree to the above findings must sign below.

_____   _____
_____   _____
_____   _____
_____   _____
_____   _____
_____   _____

Notes on Use (1980 New)

1. Verdicts will be designated alphabetically (A, B, C, etc.).

2. The verdict form will contain a descriptive phrase describing and identifying the claim submitted by this particular package which will be the claim to which this verdict is applicable. The identifying phrase should be non-inflammatory and as neutral as possible and should avoid the assumption of disputed facts. See MAI 2.00 General Comment for a discussion and for examples of the appropriate identifying phrase.

Parenthetical directions to "(state the name)" in the above form are addressed to counsel. The appropriate party's name should be typed in the prepared verdict at those points. All other directions are for the jury and should be submitted to the jury as written.

A separate verdict form must be used for each "package" other than the package containing the general instructions. The verdict form will be the last instruction in each such package. See MAI 2.00 General Comment for an explanation of "packaging".

Verdict forms should not be read by the Court to the jury.

Committee Comment (1996 New)

See MAI 10.08 for the damage instruction for submission of the issue of vexatious refusal to pay by an insurance company.

Library References:

C.J.S. Trial § 541.
West's Key No. Digests, Trial ☞352.1.

36.11 [1980 Revision] Form of Verdict—Plaintiff vs. Defendant—Actual and Punitive Damages

VERDICT _____ [1]

Note: Complete this form by writing in the name required by your verdict.

On the claim of plaintiff (*state the name*) for personal injuries [2] against defendant (*state the name*), we, the undersigned jurors, find in favor of:

_____

(Plaintiff (state the name))   or   (Defendant (state the name))

Note: Complete the following paragraph only if the above finding is in favor of plaintiff (*state the name*).

We, the undersigned jurors, assess the damages of plaintiff (*state the name*) as follows:

For actual damages $_____ (*stating the amount*).

For punitive damages $_____ (*state the amount or, if none, write the word, "none"*).

Note: All jurors who agree to the above findings must sign below.

_____   _____
_____   _____
_____   _____
_____   _____
_____   _____
_____   _____

Notes on Use (1980 New)

1. Verdicts will be designated alphabetically (A, B, C, etc.).

2. The verdict form will contain a descriptive phrase describing and identifying the claim submitted by this particular package which will be the claim to which this verdict is applicable. The identifying phrase should be non-inflammatory and as neutral as possible and should avoid the assumption of disputed facts. See MAI 2.00 General Comment for a discussion and for examples of the appropriate identifying phrase.

Parenthetical directions to "(state the name)" in the above form are addressed to counsel. The appropriate party's name should be typed in the prepared verdict at those points. All other directions are for the jury and should be submitted to the jury as written.

A separate verdict form must be used for each "package" other than the package containing the general instructions. The verdict form will be the last instruction in each such package. See MAI 2.00 General Comment for an explanation of "packaging".

Verdict forms should not be read by the Court to the jury.

Library References:

C.J.S. Trial § 541.
West's Key No. Digests, Trial ⊕352.1.

Notes of Decisions

In general   1
Harmless error   2

1. In general

Submission of verdict form amended by striking the reference to punitive damages, pursuant to agreement of the parties, waived any claim that form used was improper. Reece v. Missouri Delta Bank, 710 S.W.2d 21[3, 4] (Mo.App.1986).

Where plaintiff was entitled to actual damages as a matter of law, and to punitive damages at jury's discretion, it was not nec-essary to instruct on a verdict form to find for defendant. Hayden v. Grand River Mut. Tel. Corp., 440 S.W.2d 161[8] (Mo.App.1969).

2. Harmless error

Where multiple plaintiffs sued for actual and punitive damages they should have modified form of verdict MAI 36.11 instead of MAI 36.07, but error was harmless where counsel did not object to verdict forms prepared by court. Bower v. Hog Builders, Inc., 461 S.W.2d 784[8] (Mo.1970).

36.12 [1980 Revision] Form of Verdict—Plaintiff vs. Two Defendants—Actual and Punitive Damages

VERDICT _____ [1]

Note: Complete this form by writing in the names required by your verdict.

On the claim of plaintiff (*state the name*) for personal injuries [2] against defendant (*state the name of one defendant*), we, the undersigned jurors, find in favor of:

_____

(Plaintiff (state the name))   or   (Defendant (state the name))

On the claim of plaintiff (*state the name*) for personal injuries [2] against defendant (*state the name of the other defendant*), we, the undersigned jurors, find in favor of:

_____

(Plaintiff (state the name))   or   (Defendant (state the name))

Note: Complete the following paragraph only if one or more of the above findings is in favor of plaintiff (*state the name*).

We, the undersigned jurors, assess the damages of plaintiff (*state the name*) as follows:

For actual damages $_____ (*stating the amount*).

For punitive damages against defendant (*state the name*) [3] $_____ (*stating the amount or, if none, write the word, "none"*).

For punitive damages against defendant (*state the name*) [3] $_____ (*stating the amount or, if none, write the word, "none"*). [4]

Note: All jurors who agree to the above findings must sign below.

_____   _____
_____   _____
_____   _____
_____   _____
_____   _____

Notes on Use (1996 Revision)

1. Verdicts will be designated alphabetically (A, B, C, etc.).

2. The verdict form will contain a descriptive phrase describing and identifying the claim submitted by this particular package which will be the claim to which this verdict is applicable. The identifying phrase should be non-inflammatory and as neutral as possible and should avoid the assumption of disputed facts. See MAI 2.00 General Comment for a discussion and for examples of the appropriate identifying phrase.

Parenthetical directions to "(state the name)" in the above form are addressed to counsel. The appropriate party's name should be typed in the prepared verdict at those points. All other directions are for the jury and should be submitted to the jury as written.

A separate verdict form must be used for each "package" other than the package containing the general instructions. The verdict form will be the last instruction in each such package. See MAI 2.00 General Comment for an explanation of "packaging".

3. The names of the respective defendants will be filled in the punitive damage paragraphs when the instruction is prepared. Include a punitive damage paragraph for each defendant against whom punitive damages may properly be returned; if the jury finds no punitive damages against one or more defendants, they will so indicate by inserting "none" in the space for amount in the paragraph for each such defendant.

4. This form of punitive damage assessment is for use only where it is proper for the jury to return different amounts of punitive damage against the respective defendants by reason of evidence of different degrees of culpability or differences of wealth and ability to pay by the respective defendants. See *State ex rel. Hall v. Cook,* 400 S.W.2d 39 (Mo. banc 1966). See MAI 10.03. If the evidence does not support different amounts of punitive damages, modify the form of damage assessment as follows:

We, the undersigned jurors, assess the damages of plaintiff (state the name) as follows:

For actual damages $_____ (stating the amount).

For punitive damages $_____ (stating the amount or, if none, write the word, "none").

This form may be modified to apply to more than two defendants by repeating the first paragraph and the sentence with the blank for the amount of damages as many times as necessary.

Verdict forms should not be read by the Court to the jury.

Library References:

C.J.S. Trial § 541.
West's Key No. Digests, Trial ⊚352.1.

Notes of Decisions

1. In general

Where defendants were joint tortfeasors and there was not varying degrees of culpability, submission of separate verdict forms patterned after MAI 36.01 for each defendant rather than a single form patterned after MAI 36.12 was error since there can be "but one final judgment in the cause, and a judgment against joint tortfeasors must be for a single amount and cannot be split up." Chambers v. McNair, 692 S.W.2d 320[3] (Mo.App. 1985).

MAI 36.12 verdict form properly followed where jury awarded actual damages against four defendants and punitive damages against two of them. Tavernaro v. Dunn, 563 S.W.2d 114[6] (Mo.App.1978).

729

36.13 [1980 Revision] Form of Verdict—Uninsured Motor Vehicle—Both Individual Tort–Feasor and Insurance Carrier Sued

VERDICT _____ [1]

Note: Complete this form by writing in the names required by your verdict.

On the claim of plaintiff (*state the name*) for personal injuries [2] against defendant (*state the name of individual defendant*), we, the undersigned jurors, find in favor of:

_____

(Plaintiff (state the name))   or   (Defendant (state the name))

Note: Complete the following paragraphs only if the above finding is in favor of plaintiff (*state the name*).

We, the undersigned jurors, assess the damages of plaintiff (*state the name*) at $_____ (*stating the amount*).

On the claim of plaintiff (*state the name*) for personal injuries [2] against defendant (*state the name of insurer*), we, the undersigned jurors, find in favor of:

_____

(Plaintiff (state the name))   or   (Defendant (state the name))

Note: All jurors who agree to the above findings must sign below.

_____   _____
_____   _____
_____   _____
_____   _____
_____   _____

Notes on Use (1980 New)

1. Verdicts will be designated alphabetically (A, B, C, etc.).

2. The verdict form will contain a descriptive phrase describing and identifying the claim submitted by this particular package which will be the claim to which this verdict is applicable. The identifying phrase should be non-inflammatory and as neutral as possible and should avoid the assumption of disputed facts. See MAI 2.00 General Comment for a discussion and for examples of the appropriate identifying phrase.

Parenthetical directions to "(state the name)" in the above form are addressed to counsel. The appropriate party's name should be typed in the prepared verdict at those points. All other directions are for the jury and should be submitted to the jury as written.

A separate verdict form must be used for each "package" other than the package containing the general instructions. The verdict form will be the last instruction in each such package. See MAI 2.00 General Comment for an explanation of "packaging".

The jury verdict does not determine the amount of the judgment against the uninsured motorist insurance carrier. If the jury verdict is against both the uninsured motor vehicle operator and the insurance company, the court should enter a judgment against the operator in the amount of the jury verdict against him and enter a judgment against the insurance company in an amount in accordance with the policy limits and the verdict.

Verdict forms should not be read by the Court to the jury.

Committee Comment (1980 New)

The amount of the judgment against the uninsured motor vehicle operator defendant is determined by the jury verdict. The amount of the judgment against the defendant insurance company is a question of contract law to be decided by the court.

Library References:

C.J.S. Trial § 541.
West's Key No. Digests, Trial ⟐352.1.

36.14   [1980 Revision] Form of Verdict—Uninsured Motor Vehicle—Insurer Only Defendant

VERDICT _____[1]

Note: Complete this form by writing in the name required by your verdict.

On the claim of plaintiff (*state the name*) for personal injuries[2] against defendant (*state the name*), we, the undersigned jurors find in favor of:

_____

     (Plaintiff (state the name))   or   (Defendant (state the name))

Note: Complete the following paragraph only if the above finding is in favor of plaintiff (*state the name*).

We, the undersigned jurors, find plaintiff was damaged in the sum of $_____ (*stating the amount*).

Note: All jurors who agree to the above findings must sign below.

_____   _____

_____   _____

_____   _____

_____   _____

_____   _____

Notes on Use (1980 New)

1.   Verdicts will be designated alphabetically (A, B, C, etc.).

2.   The verdict form will contain a descriptive phrase describing and identifying the claim submitted by this particular package which will be the claim to which this verdict is applicable. The identifying phrase should be non-inflammatory and as neutral as possible and should avoid the assumption of disputed facts. See MAI 2.00 General Comment for a discussion and for examples of the appropriate identifying phrase.

Parenthetical directions to "(state the name)" in the above form are addressed to counsel. The appropriate party's name should be typed in the prepared verdict at those points. All other directions are for the jury and should be submitted to the jury as written.

A separate verdict form must be used for each "package" other than the package containing the general instructions. The verdict form will

732

be the last instruction in each such package. See MAI 2.00 General Comment for an explanation of "packaging".

This verdict form should be used only in uninsured motor vehicle cases where the insurance company is the only defendant and where MAI 4.11 is used.

Verdict forms should not be read by the Court to the jury.

Library References:

C.J.S. Trial § 541.
West's Key No. Digests, Trial ☞352.1.

36.15 [1979 New] Form of Verdict—Apportionment of Fault Among Defendants

VERDICT _____[1]

Note: Complete this form if fault is to be apportioned.

On the claim[s] (*here use descriptive phrase, i.e., of defendant Doe; between defendants; among defendants; between defendant Doe and third party defendant Roe, etc.*) for assessment of the proportions of fault for plaintiff's damage assessed in Verdict _____,[1, 2, 3] we, the undersigned jurors, find:

Note: Complete by writing in the percentage of the relative fault for each party you believe to be at fault. [If you believe a party named below is not at fault, write in "zero" for that percentage.][4] [You may not write in "zero" for _____.][5] The total of the percentages you assess must not exceed 100%.

(Party whose fault may be apportioned)[6] is _____% at fault.

(Party whose fault may be apportioned)[6] is _____% at fault.

(Party whose fault may be apportioned)[6] is _____% at fault.

Note: All jurors who agree with the above findings must sign below.

_____   _____
_____   _____
_____   _____
_____   _____
_____   _____

Notes on Use (1979 New)

1. Verdicts will be designated alphabetically (A, B, C, etc.).

2. Insert the letter designation of the verdict which assesses damage for which fault is to be apportioned by this verdict.

3. In a separate trial of apportionment issues the verdict assessing damages for the prevailing party in the former trial will not be before the jury. For the phrase "plaintiff's damage assessed in Verdict _____," use [claimant's damage assessed in the prior trial].

4. This bracketed sentence must be used in submissions wherein three or more parties are the targets of claims for apportionment of fault for one claimant's damage to avoid the mistaken belief by the jury that it must assign a percentage of fault to a party who has been found not to be at fault for the claimant's damage.

5. Use this sentence only if it is determined under the substantive law that the jury must find a certain party to be partially at fault. If apportionment is being tried in a separate trial, insert in the blank the name of any party found in the prior trial to have been at fault. If apportionment and liability to plaintiff are being tried in the same trial, insert in the blank the words "any party you have determined to be at fault under the other instructions in this case."

6. The names of the party or parties whom the evidence shows may be found by the jury to have been at fault for the claimant's damage must be inserted in the form of verdict by the preparer of the form.

If a master's liability is submitted only upon the acts of his servant and both are defendants, insert both their names on the same line in accordance with the directions to the jury to assess only the servant's fault as the fault of both.

A separate verdict form must be used for each "package" other than the package containing the general instructions. The verdict form will be the last form in each such package. See MAI 2.00 General Comment for an explanation of "packaging".

Regardless of how many claims for apportionment are pleaded between defendants (including third party defendants, etc.), only one verdict apportioning the fault for any one claimant's damage will be required.

Verdict forms should not be read by the Court to the jury.

Committee Comment (1996 Revision)

The requirement of Note on Use No. 6, above, that the preparer of the form of verdict must insert the names of the party or parties against whom an apportionment of fault may be made, forestalls any attempt on the part of the jury to assign a part of the fault to the original plaintiff. This requirement is a deviation from the other forms in MAI which require the jury to write in the names of parties and is intended to be so.

A jury finding of "zero %" is a verdict in favor of that party on the issue of apportionment of fault.

This instruction, Notes on Use, and Committee Comment were originally promulgated as recommended by the Committee, but were neither approved nor disapproved by the Supreme Court. The Supreme Court, with the publication of the Fifth Edition of MAI, approved the approach to "apportionment of fault" contemplated by MAI 4.12, 4.13, 4.14 and verdict forms 36.15 and 36.16.

Library References:

C.J.S. Trial § 541.
West's Key No. Digests, Trial ⊝352.1.

36.16 [1979 New] Form of Verdict—Verdict—Liability for Apportionment of Fault Against Party Not Claimed Against by Plaintiff

VERDICT _____[1]

Note: Complete this form by writing in the name(s) required by your verdict.

On the claim of [plaintiff] [third-party plaintiff] (*state the name*) seeking apportionment of fault against [defendant] [third-party defendant] (*state the name of one defendant*), we, the undersigned jurors, find in favor of:

_____ or _____

([Plaintiff] [Third-party Plain-   ([Defendant] [Third-party Defendant]
tiff] (state the name))   (state the name of one defendant))

On the claim [plaintiff] [third-party plaintiff] (*state the name*) for apportionment of fault against [defendant] [third-party defendant] (*state the name of the other defendant*), we, the undersigned jurors, find in favor of:

_____ or _____

([Plaintiff] [Third-party Plain-   ([Defendant] [Third-party Defendant]
tiff] (state the name))   (state the name of the other defendant))[2]

Note: All jurors who agree to the above findings must sign below.

_____ _____
_____ _____
_____ _____
_____ _____
_____ _____

Notes on Use (1996 Revision)

1. Verdicts will be designated alphabetically (A, B, C, etc.).

2. Include the appropriate number of descriptive paragraphs and findings to allow the jury to find for or against each party not claimed against by plaintiff and against whom apportionment of fault is sought.

This verdict form allows the jury to determine the liability of any party not claimed against by plaintiff. MAI 36.15 Verdict–Apportionment of Fault must also be used to allow the jury to return the appropriate percentages of fault.

Verdict forms should not be read by the Court to the jury.

This instruction, Notes on Use, and Committee Comment were originally promulgated as recommended by the Committee, but were neither approved nor disapproved by the Supreme Court. The Supreme Court, with the publication of the Fifth Edition of MAI, approved the approach to "apportionment of fault" contemplated by MAI 4.12, 4.13, 4.14 and verdict forms 36.15 and 36.16.

Library References:

C.J.S. Trial § 541.
West's Key No. Digests, Trial ⚖═352.1.

36.17 [Withdrawn 1995] Form of Verdict—Plaintiff vs. Defendant—Will Contest

(This verdict form and Notes on Use thereto are withdrawn. This verdict form has been replaced by MAI 36.17(A) relating to a will contest challenging a will in its entirety. See also MAI 36.17(B) relating to a challenge to only part of a will.)

36.17(A) [1995 New] Form of Verdict—Plaintiff vs. Defendant—Will Contest

VERDICT _____ [1]

NOTE: Complete this form by writing in the word(s) required by your verdict.

We, the undersigned jurors find:

That the document in issue [2] _____ (here insert either "is" or "is not") the last will and testament of (*insert name of decedent*).

NOTE: All jurors who agree to the above finding must sign below.

_____	_____
_____	_____
_____	_____
_____	_____
_____	_____
_____	_____

Notes on Use (1995 New)

1. Verdicts will be designated alphabetically (A, B, C, etc.).

2. If more than one document is in issue, modify the instruction to sufficiently identify each document; for example, "the document dated December 29, 1979."

This instruction is to be used in cases where the entire will is contested. For cases involving partial invalidity under § 473.081, RSMo, see MAI 36.17(B).

Library References:

C.J.S. Trial § 541.
West's Key No. Digests, Trial ⚎352.1.

36.17(B) [1995 New] Form of Verdict—Plaintiff vs. Defendant—Will Contest—Partial Invalidity

VERDICT _____ [1]

NOTE: Complete this form by writing in the word(s) required by your verdict.

We, the undersigned jurors find:

That the contested part of the will [2] _____ (here insert either "is" or "is not") a valid part of the last will and testament of (*insert name of decedent*).

NOTE: All jurors who agree to the above finding must sign below.

_____   _____
_____   _____
_____   _____
_____   _____
_____   _____

Notes on Use (1995 New)

1. Verdicts will be designated alphabetically (A, B, C, etc.).

2. If more than one part of the will is contested, modify the verdict form to sufficiently identify each part; for example, "providing $1,000,000 to the neighbor's cat."

This instruction is to be used in cases of partial invalidity under § 473.081, RSMo. For cases where the entire will is contested, see MAI 36.17(A).

Library References:

C.J.S. Trial § 541.
West's Key No. Digests, Trial ⊗352.1.

36.18 [1983 New] Form of Verdict—Commitment for Mental Illness

VERDICT _____ [1]

Note: Complete this form by filling in the word or words required by your verdict.

We, the undersigned jurors, find:

That respondent _____ (here insert either "should" or "should not") be detained for treatment.

Note: All jurors who agree to the above finding must sign below.

_____   _____
_____   _____
_____   _____
_____   _____
_____   _____

Notes on Use (1983 New)

1. Verdicts will be designated alphabetically (A, B, C, etc.).

Library References:

C.J.S. Trial § 541.
West's Key No. Digests, Trial ⟿352.1.

36.19 [1983 New] Form of Verdict—Plaintiff vs. Defendant—Disputed Partial Settlement

VERDICT _____[1]

Note: Complete this form by writing in the name required by your verdict.

On the claim of plaintiff (*state the name*) for personal injuries[2] against defendant (*state the name*), we, the undersigned jurors, find in favor of:

_____

(Plaintiff (state the name))　　　　or　　　　(Defendant (state the name))

Note: Complete the following paragraph only if the above finding is in favor of plaintiff (*state the name*).

We, the undersigned jurors, assess the damages of plaintiff (*state the name*) at $_____ (stating the amount) and further find that plaintiff previously has been paid $_____ (stating the amount or, if none, write the word "none") on plaintiff's claim.

Note: All jurors who agree to the above findings must sign below.

_____　　_____
_____　　_____
_____　　_____
_____　　_____
_____　　_____

Notes on Use (1983 New)

1. Verdicts will be designated alphabetically (A, B, C, etc.).

2. The verdict form will contain a descriptive phrase describing and identifying the claim submitted by this particular package which will be the claim to which this verdict is applicable. The identifying phrase should be noninflammatory and as neutral as possible and should avoid the assumption of disputed facts. See MAI 2.00 General Comment for a discussion and for examples of the appropriate identifying phrase.

Parenthetical directions to "(state the name)" in the above form are addressed to counsel. The appropriate party's name should be typed in the prepared verdict at those points. All other directions are for the jury and should be submitted to the jury as written.

A separate verdict form must be used for each "package" other than the package containing the general instructions. The verdict form will be the last instruction in each such package. See MAI 2.00 General Comment for an explanation of "packaging".

Verdict forms should not be read by the Court to the jury.

Verdict form MAI 36.19 is for use when the issue of a disputed partial settlement is submitted to the jury by MAI 7.02 and MAI 36.01 (Plaintiff vs. Defendant—Personal Injury Only) would otherwise be applicable. If a disputed settlement is submitted in a situation where another verdict form would otherwise be appropriate, modify MAI 36.19 by combining the language of MAI 36.19 concerning the jury's finding as to the settlement amount with the appropriate verdict form from Chapter 36.00.

Library References:

C.J.S. Trial § 541.
West's Key No. Digests, Trial ⊕352.1.

Notes of Decisions

1. In general

No prejudice resulted from omission of MAI 36.19 language in the verdict forms where jury obviously took into consideration the fact that plaintiffs had received a portion of their damages when they entered into prior settlement. M.P. Industries, Inc. v. Axelrod, 706 S.W.2d 589[4] (Mo.App.1986).

36.20 [1988 New] Form of Verdict—Actions Against Health Care Providers—Plaintiff vs. Single Defendant—No Comparative Fault

VERDICT _____[1]

Note: Complete this form by writing in the name required by your verdict.

On the claim of plaintiff (*state the name*) for personal injuries[2] against defendant (*state the name*), we, the undersigned jurors, find in favor of:

_____

(Plaintiff (*state the name*))   OR   (Defendant (*state the name*))

Note: Complete the following only if the above finding is in favor of plaintiff (*state the name*). Complete by writing in the amount of damages, if any, for each of the following itemized categories. If you do not find that plaintiff has damages in a particular category, write "none" in that category. The total damages must equal the total of the itemized damage amounts you have assessed.

We, the undersigned jurors, assess the damages of plaintiff (*state the name*) as follows:

For past economic damages including past
  medical damages[3,4] $_____
For past non-economic damages[3,4] $_____
For future medical damages[3,4] $_____
For future economic damages excluding future medical damages[3,4] $_____
For future non-economic damages[3,4] $_____
   TOTAL DAMAGES $_____

Note: All jurors who agree to the above must sign below:

_____   _____

_____   _____

_____   _____

_____   _____

_____   _____

Notes on Use (1988 New)

1. Verdicts will be designated alphabetically (A, B, C, etc.).

2. The verdict form will contain a descriptive phrase describing and identifying the claim submitted by this particular package, which will be the claim to which this verdict is applicable. The identifying phrase should be non-inflammatory and as neutral as possible and should avoid the assumption of disputed facts. See MAI 2.00 General Comment for a discussion and for examples of the appropriate identifying phrase.

3. Do not submit any category of damages that is not supported by the evidence.

4. The phrases describing the categories of damages must be defined. See definitions in MAI 21.05.

Parenthetical directions to "(*state the name*)" in the above form are addressed to counsel. The appropriate party's name should be typed in the prepared verdict at those points. All other directions are for the jury and should be submitted to the jury as written.

A separate verdict form must be used for each "package" other than the package containing the general instructions. The verdict form will be the last instruction in each such package. See MAI 2.00 General Comment for an explanation of "packaging."

Verdict forms should not be read by the Court to the jury.

Committee Comment (1988 New)

MAI 21.03 through MAI 21.07 and verdict forms 36.20 through 36.22 are applicable only to causes of action against health care providers accruing on or after February 3, 1986, and subject to the provisions of §§ 538.205 through 538.230, RSMo.

Library References:

C.J.S. Trial § 541.
West's Key No. Digests, Trial ⟜352.1.

Notes of Decisions

1. In general

MAI 21.03 and 36.20, which require itemization of damages in actions against "health care" providers, did not apply to amputee's professional negligence suit against orthotics and prosthetics laboratory, which was not licensed by any governmental body. Stalcup v. Orthotic & Prosthetic Lab, Inc., 989 S.W.2d 654 (Mo.App.1999).

36.21 [1988 New] Form of Verdict—Actions Against Health Care Providers—Plaintiff vs. Multiple Defendants—No Apportionment of Fault Among Defendants and No Comparative Fault

VERDICT _____ [1]

Note: Complete this form by writing in the name(s) required by your verdict.

On the claim of plaintiff (*state the name*) for personal injuries [2] against defendant (*state the name*), we, the undersigned jurors, find in favor of:

_____

(Plaintiff (*state the name*))　　　OR　　　(Defendant (*state the name*))

On the claim of plaintiff (*state the name*) for personal injuries [2] against defendant (*state the name*), we, the undersigned jurors, find in favor of:

_____

(Plaintiff (*state the name*))　　　OR　　　(Defendant (*state the name*))

Note: Complete thc following only if one or more of the above findings is in favor of plaintiff (*state the name*).

Complete by writing in the amount of damages, if any, for each of the following itemized categories. If you do not find that plaintiff has damages in a particular category, write "none" in that category. The total damages must equal the total of the itemized damage amounts you have assessed.

We, the undersigned jurors, assess the damages of plaintiff (*state the name*) as follows:

For past economic damages including past
　medical damages[3,4]　　　　　　　　　　　$_____
For past non-economic damages[3,4]　　　　　$_____
For future medical damages[3,4]　　　　　　　$_____
For future economic damages excluding fu-
　ture medical damages[3,4]　　　　　　　　$_____
For future non-economic damages[3,4]　　　　$_____
　TOTAL DAMAGES　　　　　　　　　　　　$_____

Note: All jurors who agree to the above must sign below:

_____   _____
_____   _____
_____   _____
_____   _____
_____   _____

Notes on Use (2002 Revision)

1. Verdicts will be designated alphabetically (A, B, C, etc.).

2. The verdict form will contain a descriptive phrase describing and identifying the claim submitted by this particular package, which will be the claim to which this verdict is applicable. The identifying phrase should be non-inflammatory and as neutral as possible and should avoid the assumption of disputed facts. See MAI 2.00 General Comment for a discussion and for examples of the appropriate identifying phrase.

3. Do not submit any category of damage that is not supported by the evidence.

4. The phrases describing the categories of damages must be defined. See definitions in MAI 21.05.

If fault is to be apportioned between two or more defendants in a case where no comparative fault is sought against the plaintiff, see Illustration 35.22 (and Committee Comment) which may be adapted for a case in which there are multiple defendants but no settling tortfeasor.

Parenthetical directions "(*state the name*)" in the above form are addressed to counsel. The appropriate party's name should be typed in the prepared verdict at those points. All other directions are for the jury and should be submitted to the jury as written.

A separate verdict form must be used for each "package" other than the package containing the general instructions. The verdict form will be the last instruction in each such package. See MAI 2.00 General Comment for an explanation of "packaging."

Verdict forms should not be read by the court to the jury.

Committee Comment (1988 New)

Under § 538.230.1, RSMo, there is no apportionment of fault among multiple defendants if all parties agree. If no defendant seeks apportionment, case law will determine whether the jury must nevertheless apportion fault among defendants.

MAI 21.03 through MAI 21.07 and verdict forms 36.20 through 36.22 are applicable only to causes of action against health care providers accruing on or after February 3, 1986, and subject to the provisions of §§ 538.205 through 538.230, RSMo.

Library References:

C.J.S. Trial § 541.
West's Key No. Digests, Trial ⊕352.1.

36.22 **[1988 New] Form of Verdict—Actions Against Health Care Providers—Plaintiff vs. Single or Multiple Defendants—Comparative Fault**

VERDICT _____ [1]

Note: Complete the following paragraph by filling in the blanks as required by your verdict. If you assess a percentage of fault to any of those listed below, write in a percentage not greater than 100%, otherwise write in "zero" next to that name. If you assess a percentage of fault to any of those listed below, the total of such percentages must be 100%.

On the claim of plaintiff (*state the name*) for personal injury,[2] we, the undersigned jurors, assess percentages of fault as follows:

Defendant[3] (*state the name*) _____% (zero to 100%)
Plaintiff (*state the name*) _____% (zero to 100%)
   TOTAL   _____% (zero <u>OR</u> 100%)

Note: Complete the following if you assessed a percentage of fault to (one or more) defendant(s). Complete by writing in the amount of damages, if any, for each of the following itemized categories. If you do not find that plaintiff has damages in a particular category, write "none" in that category. The total damages must equal the total of the itemized damage amounts you have assessed.

We, the undersigned jurors, disregarding any fault on the part of plaintiff, find the total damages of plaintiff (*state the name*) as follows:

For past economic damages including past
 medical damages[4,5] $_____
For past non-economic damages[4,5] $_____
For future medical damages[4,5] $_____
For future economic damages excluding fu-
 ture medical damages[4,5] $_____
For future non-economic damages[4,5] $_____
 TOTAL DAMAGES $_____

Note: The judge will reduce the total amount of plaintiff's damages by any percentage of fault you assess to plaintiff.

Note: All jurors who agree to the above must sign below:

_____   _____
_____   _____
_____   _____
_____   _____
_____   _____

Notes on Use (2002 Revision)

1.   Verdicts will be designated alphabetically (A, B, C, etc.).

2.   The verdict form will contain a descriptive phrase describing and identifying the claim submitted by this particular package, which will be the claim to which this verdict is applicable. The identifying phrase should be non-inflammatory and as neutral as possible and should avoid the assumption of disputed facts. See MAI 2.00 General Comment for a discussion and for examples of the appropriate identifying phrase.

3.   The names of those against whom fault may be assessed must be inserted in the verdict form by the preparer of the form.

Caution: Section 538.230.1, RSMo, provides for apportionment among the parties and persons released from liability pursuant to section 538.230.3, RSMo. Mere insertion of the name of the released person and a space for assessment of fault to that person is not sufficient and would constitute a roving commission to the jury if unaccompanied by an appropriate verdict directing instruction applicable to that released person. The burden of proof and the responsibility to tender such a verdict director is on the party seeking an assessment of a percentage of fault to a released person. See Illustration 35.21 (and Committee Comment) which may be adapted for a case in which there are multiple defendants but no settling tortfeasor.

4.   Do not submit any category of damage that is not supported by the evidence.

5.   The phrases describing the categories of damages must be defined. See definitions in MAI 21.05.

Parenthetical directions to "*(state the name)*" in the above form are addressed to counsel. The appropriate party's name should be typed in the prepared verdict at those points. All other directions are for the jury and should be submitted to the jury as written.

A separate verdict form must be used for each "package" other than the package containing the general instructions. The verdict form will be the last instruction in each such package. See MAI 2.00 General Comment for an explanation of "packaging".

Verdict forms should not be read by the court to the jury.

Committee Comment (1988 New)

MAI 21.03 through MAI 21.07 and verdict forms 36.20 through 36.22 are applicable only to causes of action against health care providers accruing on or after February 3, 1986 and subject to the provisions of §§ 538.205 through 538.230, RSMo.

Library References:

C.J.S. Trial § 541.
West's Key No. Digests, Trial ⚷352.1.

36.23 [1991 New] Form of Verdict—Combined Injury and Derivative Claims

VERDICT _____ [1]

Note: Complete this form by writing in the name(s) required by your verdict.

On the claim of plaintiff (*state name of plaintiff with primary claim*) for personal injuries against defendant (*state the name*), we, the undersigned jurors, find in favor of:

_____

(Plaintiff (*state name of plaintiff*   or   (Defendant (*state the name*))
with primary claim))

Note: Complete the following paragraphs only if [one or more of] [2] the above finding(s) is in favor of plaintiff (*state name of plaintiff with primary claim*).

We, the undersigned jurors, assess the damages of plaintiff (*state name of plaintiff with primary claim*) for personal injuries at $_____ (*stating the amount*).

Note: Complete the following paragraph by writing in the word(s) required by your verdict.

On the claim of plaintiff (*state name of plaintiff with derivative claim*) for damages due to injury to [his] [her] [husband] [wife] [child],[3] we, the undersigned jurors, find that plaintiff (*state name of plaintiff with derivative claim*)

_____ sustain damage as a direct result of injury

("did" or "did not")

to [his] [her] [husband] [wife] [child].[3]

Note: Complete the following paragraph only if the above finding is that plaintiff (*state name of plaintiff with derivative claim*) "did" sustain such damage.

We, the undersigned jurors, assess the damages of plaintiff (*state name of plaintiff with derivative claim*) due to injury to [his] [her] [husband] [wife] [child] [3] at $_____ (*stating the amount*).

753

Note: All jurors who agree to the above findings must sign below.

_____

_____

_____

_____

_____

Notes on Use (1991 New)

1.   Verdicts will be designated alphabetically (A, B, C, etc.).

2.   Insert if more than one defendant.

3.   Select the appropriate word(s).

Parenthetical directions to "(*state the name*)" in the above form are addressed to counsel. The appropriate party's name should be typed in the prepared verdict at those points. All other directions are for the jury and should be submitted to the jury as written.

A separate verdict form must be used for each "package" other than the package containing the general instructions. The verdict form will be the last instruction in each such package. See MAI 2.00 General Comment for an explanation of "packaging".

Verdict forms should not be read by the court to the jury.

Library References:

C.J.S. Trial § 541.

West's Key No. Digests, Trial ⚖️352.1.

36.24 [1995 Revision] Form of Verdict—Actions Against Health Care Providers—Lost Chance of Survival—No Comparative Fault

VERDICT _____ [1]

NOTE: Complete this form as required by your verdict.

On the claim of plaintiff (*state the name of plaintiff ad litem or personal representative*), for lost chance of [survival] [recovery] [2] against defendant (*state the name*), we, the undersigned jurors, find in favor of:

_____

(Plaintiff (*state the name*))   OR   (Defendant (*state the name*))

NOTE: Complete the following only if the above finding is in favor of plaintiff (*state the name*). Complete by writing in the amount, if any, for each of the following itemized categories of damages. If you do not find damages in a particular damage category, write "none" in that category. The total damages must equal the total of the itemized damage amounts you have determined.

We, the undersigned jurors, find the total damages as follows:

For past economic damages [3, 4]
including past medical damages $_____

For past non-economic damages [3, 4] $_____

For future economic damages [3, 4] $_____

For future non-economic damages [3, 4] $_____

    TOTAL DAMAGES $_____

We, the undersigned jurors, find that the chance of [survival] [recovery] [2] (*state the name of decedent*) lost was _____%.

NOTE: The judge will compute the final award by multiplying the total amount you determine as damages by the percentage you find as the lost chance of [survival] [recovery] [2].

755

NOTE: All jurors who agree to the above must sign below.

_____   _____

_____   _____

_____   _____

_____   _____

_____   _____

Notes on Use (1993 New)

1. Verdicts will be designated alphabetically (A, B, C, etc.).

2. The verdict form will contain a descriptive phrase describing and identifying the claim submitted by this particular package, which will be the claim to which this verdict is applicable. The identifying phrase should be noninflammatory and as neutral as possible and should avoid the assumption of disputed facts. See MAI 2.00 General Comment for a discussion and for examples of the appropriate identifying phrase. Select a term.

3. Do not submit any category of damages that is not supported by the evidence.

4. The phrases describing the categories of damages must be defined. See definitions in MAI 21.05.

Parenthetical directions to "(*state the name*)" in the above form are addressed to counsel. The appropriate party's name should be typed in the prepared verdict at those points. All other directions are for the jury and should be submitted to the jury as written.

A separate verdict form must be used for each "package" other than the package containing the general instructions. The verdict form will be the last instruction in each such package. See MAI 2.00 General Comment for an explanation of "packaging."

Verdict forms should not be read by the court to the jury.

Committee Comment (1995 Revision)

This verdict form applies to the cause of action for "lost chance of recovery (survival)" established in *Wollen v. DePaul Health Center*, 828 S.W.2d 681 (Mo. banc 1992). *Wollen* discussed the "lost chance of recovery" theory in the context of a survival action under § 537.020, RSMo, brought by a personal representative of an individual who died after losing a material chance of recovery from cancer.

Since this verdict form was drafted by the Committee for use in a "loss of a chance" case in which the patient died, the category of "future medical damages" has been deleted from the categories of itemized damages. Insertion of that category may be appropriate in a "lost chance" case based on "loss of a limb" discussed in *Wollen*.

See Committee Comment to MAI 21.08.

Library References:

C.J.S. Trial § 541.
West's Key No. Digests, Trial ⊕352.1.

36.25 [1995 Revision] Form of Verdict—Actions Against Health Care Providers—Lost Chance of Survival—Comparative Fault

VERDICT _____ [1]

NOTE: Complete the following paragraph by filling in the blanks as required by your verdict. If you assess a percentage of fault to any of those listed below, write in a percentage not greater than 100%; otherwise, write in "zero" next to that name. If you assess a percentage of fault to any of those listed below, the total of such percentages must be 100%.

On the claim of plaintiff (*state the name of plaintiff ad litem or personal representative*) for lost chance of [survival] [recovery] [2], we, the undersigned jurors, assess percentages of fault as follows:

Defendant [3] (*state the name*)   _____% (zero to 100%)
(*State name of Decedent*)   _____% (zero to 100%)
    TOTAL   _____% (zero *OR* 100%)

NOTE: Complete the following if you assessed a percentage of fault to (one or more) defendant(s). Complete by writing in the amount, if any, for each of the following itemized categories of damages. If you do not find damages in a particular category, write "none" in that category. The total damages must equal the total of the itemized damage amounts you have determined.

We, the undersigned jurors, disregarding any fault on the part of (*state name of decedent*), find the total damages as follows:

For past economic damages [4, 5]
including past medical damages $_____

For past non-economic damages [4, 5] $_____

For future economic damages [4, 5] $_____

For future non-economic damages [4, 5] $_____

    TOTAL DAMAGES $_____

We, the undersigned jurors, find that the chance of [recovery] [survival] [2] (*state the name of decedent*) lost was _____%.

NOTE: The judge will compute the final award by multiplying the amount you determine as total damages by the percentage you find as the lost chance of [recovery] [survival] [2] and making a reduction by any percentage of fault you assess to (*state name of decedent*).

NOTE: All jurors who agree to the above must sign below.

_____   _____

_____   _____

_____   _____

_____   _____

Notes on Use (2002 Revision)

1. Verdicts will be designated alphabetically (A, B, C, etc.).

2. The verdict form will contain a descriptive phrase describing and identifying the claim submitted by this particular package, which will be the claim to which this verdict is applicable. The identifying phrase should be non-inflammatory and as neutral as possible and should avoid the assumption of disputed facts. See MAI 2.00 General Comment for a discussion and for examples of the appropriate identifying phrase. Select a term.

3. The names of those against whom fault may be assessed must be inserted in the verdict form by the preparer of the form.

Caution: Section 538.230.1, RSMo, provides for apportionment among the parties and persons released from liability pursuant to section 538.230.3, RSMo. Mere insertion of the name of the released person and a space for assessment of fault to that person is not sufficient and would constitute a roving commission to the jury if unaccompanied by an appropriate verdict directing instruction applicable to that released person. The burden of proof and the responsibility to tender such a verdict director is on the party seeking an assessment of a percentage of fault to a released person. See Illustration 35.21 (and Committee Comment) which may be adapted for a case in which there are multiple defendants but no settling tortfeasor.

4. Do not submit any category of damage that is not supported by the evidence.

5. The phrases describing the categories of damages must be defined. See definitions in MAI 21.05.

Parenthetical directions to "*(state the name)*" in the above form are addressed to counsel. The appropriate party's name should be typed in the prepared verdict at those points. All other directions are for the jury and should be submitted to the jury as written.

A separate verdict form must be used for each "package" other than the package containing the general instructions. The verdict form will be the last instruction in each such package. See MAI 2.00 General Comment for an explanation of "packaging".

Verdict forms should not be read by the court to the jury.

Committee Comment (1995 Revision)

This verdict form applies to the cause of action for "lost chance of recovery (survival)" established in *Wollen v. DePaul Health Center,* 828 S.W.2d 681 (Mo. banc 1992). *Wollen* discussed the "lost chance of recovery" theory in the context of a survival action under § 537.020, RSMo, brought by a personal representative of an individual who died after losing a material chance of recovery from cancer.

Since this verdict form was drafted by the Committee for use in a "loss of a chance" case in which the patient died, the category of "future medical damages" has been deleted from the categories of itemized damages. Insertion of that category may be appropriate in a "lost chance" case based on "loss of a limb" discussed in *Wollen*.

See Committee Comment to MAI 21.08.

Library References:

C.J.S. Trial § 541.
West's Key No. Digests, Trial ☞352.1.

36.26 [1994 New] Form of Verdict—Actions Against Health Care Providers—Lost Chance of Recovery (Non–Death) Cases—No Comparative Fault

VERDICT _____ [1]

NOTE: Complete this form as required by your verdict.

On the claim of plaintiff (*state the name*), for lost chance of [survival] [recovery] [2] against defendant (*state the name*), we, the undersigned jurors, find in favor of:

_____

(Plaintiff (*state the name*))   OR   (Defendant (*state the name*))

NOTE: Complete the following only if the above finding is in favor of plaintiff (*state the name*). Complete by writing in the amount, if any, for each of the following itemized categories of damages. If you do not find damages in a particular damage category, write "none" in that category. The total damages must equal the total of the itemized damage amounts you have determined.

We, the undersigned jurors, find the total damages as follows:

For past economic damages [3, 4]
including past medical damages $_____
For past non-economic damages [3, 4] $_____
For future medical damages [3, 4] $_____
For future economic damages
excluding future medical damages [3, 4] $_____
For future non-economic damages [3, 4] $_____
TOTAL DAMAGES $_____

We, the undersigned jurors, find that the chance of [survival] [recovery] [2] (*state name of plaintiff*) lost was _____%.

NOTE: The judge will compute the final award by multiplying the total amount you determine as damages by the percentage you find as the lost chance of [survival] [recovery][2].

NOTE: All jurors who agree to the above must sign below.

_____	_____
_____	_____
_____	_____
_____	_____

Notes on Use (1994 New)

1. Verdicts will be designated alphabetically (A, B, C, etc.).

2. The verdict form will contain a descriptive phrase describing and identifying the claim submitted by this particular package, which will be the claim to which this verdict is applicable. The identifying phrase should be noninflammatory and as neutral as possible and should avoid the assumption of disputed facts. See MAI 2.00 General Comment for a discussion and for examples of the appropriate identifying phrase. Select a term.

3. Do not submit any category of damages that is not supported by the evidence.

4. The phrases describing the categories of damages must be defined. See definitions in MAI 21.05.

Parenthetical directions to "(*state the name*)" in the above form are addressed to counsel. The appropriate party's name should be typed in the prepared verdict at those points. All other directions are for the jury and should be submitted to the jury as written.

A separate verdict form must be used for each "package" other than the package containing the general instructions. The verdict form will be the last instruction in each such package. See MAI 2.00 General Comment for an explanation of "packaging."

Verdict forms should not be read by the court to the jury.

Library References:

C.J.S. Trial § 541.
West's Key No. Digests, Trial ☞352.1.

**36.27 [1994 New] Form of Verdict—Actions Against
Health Care Providers—Lost Chance of
Recovery (Non–Death) Cases—Compara-
tive Fault**

VERDICT _____ [1]

NOTE: Complete the following paragraph by filling in the
blanks as required by your verdict. If you assess a
percentage of fault to any of those listed below,
write in a percentage not greater than 100%; otherwise write in "zero" next to that name. If you
assess a percentage of fault to any of those listed
below, the total of such percentages must be 100%.

On the claim of plaintiff (*state the name*), for lost
chance of [survival] [recovery] [2], we, the undersigned jurors,
assess percentages of fault as follows:

Defendant [3] (*state the name*)   ____%   (zero to 100%)
Plaintiff (*state the name*)   ____%   (zero to 100%)
   TOTAL   ____%   (zero *OR* 100%)

NOTE: Complete the following if you assessed a percentage
of fault to (one or more) defendant(s). Complete by
writing in the amount, if any, for each of the
following itemized categories of damages. If you do
not find damages in a particular category, write
"none" in that category. The total damages must
equal the total of the itemized damage amounts you
have determined.

We, the undersigned jurors, disregarding any fault on
the part of (*state name of plaintiff*), find the total damages
as follows:

For past economic damages [4, 5]
   including past medical damages $_____
For past non-economic damages [4, 5] $_____
For future medical damages [4, 5] $_____
For future economic damages
   excluding future medical damages [4, 5] $_____
For future non-economic damages [4,5] $_____
   TOTAL DAMAGES $_____

763

We, the undersigned jurors, find that the chance of [recovery] [survival] [2] (*state name of plaintiff*) lost was _____%.

NOTE: The judge will compute the final award by multiplying the amount you determine as total damages by the percentage you find as the lost chance of [recovery] [survival] [2] and making a reduction by any percentage of fault you assess to (*state name of plaintiff*).

NOTE: All jurors who agree to the above must sign below.

_____   _____

_____   _____

_____   _____

_____   _____

_____   _____

Notes on Use (2002 Revision)

1. Verdicts will be designated alphabetically (A, B, C, etc.).

2. The verdict form will contain a descriptive phrase describing and identifying the claim submitted by this particular package, which will be the claim to which this verdict is applicable. The identifying phrase should be non-inflammatory and as neutral as possible and should avoid the assumption of disputed facts. See MAI 2.00 General Comment for a discussion and for examples of the appropriate identifying phrase. Select a term.

3. The names of those against whom fault may be assessed must be inserted in the verdict form by the preparer of the form.

Caution: Section 538.230.1, RSMo, provides for apportionment among the parties and persons released from liability pursuant to section 538.230.3, RSMo. Mere insertion of the name of the released person and a space for assessment of fault to that person is not sufficient and would constitute a roving commission to the jury if unaccompanied by an appropriate verdict directing instruction applicable to that released person. The burden of proof and the responsibility to tender such a verdict director is on the party seeking an assessment of a percentage of fault to a released person. See Illustration 35.21 (and Committee Comment) which may be adapted for a case in which there are multiple defendants but no settling tortfeasor.

4. Do not submit any category of damage that is not supported by the evidence.

5. The phrases describing the categories of damages must be defined. See definitions in MAI 21.05.

Parenthetical directions to "*(state the name)*" in the above form are addressed to counsel. The appropriate party's name should be typed in the prepared verdict at those points. All other directions are for the jury and should be submitted to the jury as written.

A separate verdict form must be used for each "package" other than the package containing the general instructions. The verdict form will be the last instruction in each such package. See MAI 2.00 General Comment for an explanation of "packaging".

Verdict forms should not be read by the court to the jury.

Library References:

C.J.S. Trial § 541.
West's Key No. Digests, Trial ⚬⇒352.1.

36.28 [1994 New] Form of Verdict—Paternity Actions

VERDICT

NOTE: Complete this form by writing in the word(s) required by your verdict.

We, the undersigned jurors, _____ find that

("do" or "do not")

(*state the name of the putative father*) is the natural father of (*state the name of the child*).

NOTE: All jurors who agree to the above finding must sign below.

_____   _____

_____   _____

_____   _____

_____   _____

_____   _____

Committee Comment (1998 Revision)

See Committee Comment to MAI 31.18.

MAI 3.08, MAI 31.18, MAI 31.19, MAI 31.20, and MAI 36.28 were drafted for civil paternity actions under sections 210.817 et seq., RSMo. Effective July 1, 1997, section 210.839.4 was amended to provide that no party in such a paternity action has a right to trial by jury. The Committee has chosen not to withdraw these instructions and the related verdict form in the event that they are instructive or perhaps useful in the future since the Supreme Court has held that the Parentage Act (sections 210.817 et seq.) is not the exclusive means to determine paternity. *Matter of Nocita*, 914 S.W.2d 358 (Mo. banc 1996).

Library References:

C.J.S. Trial § 541.
West's Key No. Digests, Trial ☞352.1.

37.00

COMPARATIVE FAULT

Analysis of Instructions

Westlaw Electronic Research

See Westlaw Electronic Research Guide preceding the Table of Instructions.

Library References:

C.J.S. Negligence § 299.
West's Key No. Digests, Negligence ⟸141(12).

37.01 [1986 New] Comparative Fault—Verdict Directing Modification

In a verdict directing instruction directing an assessment of fault in a comparative fault case, the initial phrase of plaintiff's verdict director should be modified as follows:

> In your verdict you must assess a percentage of fault to defendant [whether or not plaintiff was partly at fault] [1] if you believe:

For verdict directing modification in such an action involving multiple defendants, use the following initial phrase for plaintiff's verdict directors:

> In your verdict you must assess a percentage of fault to defendant (*state the name*) [whether or not plaintiff was partly at fault] [1] if you believe:

The remaining paragraphs of the verdict directing instruction would be derived from a verdict directing instruction where comparative fault is not submitted. Thus, if verdict directing instruction 17.01 were to be modified for a comparative fault case, it would read as follows:

> In your verdict you must assess a percentage of fault to defendant [whether or not plaintiff was partly at fault] [1] if you believe:

First, defendant violated the traffic signal, and

Second, defendant was thereby negligent,[2] and

Third, such negligence directly caused or directly contributed to cause damage to plaintiff.[3]

* [unless you believe you must not assess a percentage of fault to defendant by reason of Instruction Number _____ (*here insert number of complete affirmative defense instruction*)].

Notes on Use (1986 New)

1. The bracketed phrase may be used at plaintiff's option.

2. The terms "negligent" and "negligence" must be defined. See definitions in Chapter 11.00.

3. Paragraph Third of MAI 17.01 is shown here modified in accordance with the first alternate of MAI 19.01.

* Add only if complete affirmative defense is submitted. This bracketed material should not be used to submit comparative fault.

Committee Comment (1986 New)

This modification of traditional verdict directing instructions is for use in submitting comparative fault as adopted in *Gustafson v. Benda*, 661 S.W.2d 11 (Mo. banc 1983). The optional bracketed phrase in the opening sentence is intended to alleviate any doubt the jury may have about returning a verdict for plaintiff in a situation where plaintiff is partly at fault. For submission of a true affirmative defense in a comparative fault case, see MAI 37.06.

Library References:

C.J.S. Trial § 350–351.
West's Key No. Digests, Trial ⊕234(3, 4).

Notes of Decisions

In general   1
Rescue doctrine   2

_____

1. In general

Even if ski resort's comparative fault instruction was erroneous in minor skier's personal injury action, by stating skier could have been at fault if he left place of safety and moved into path of chair lift, instruction did not prejudice skier, since jury assessed no fault against resort. Ludwick ex rel. Ludwick v. Snow Creek, Inc., 37 S.W.3d 418 (Mo.App.2001).

Parties impliedly tried case under comparative fault principles, so that comparative fault instructions were properly given, where defendant initially introduced issue of comparative fault in its opening statement and reminded jurors in closing argument of plaintiff's actions, both parties elicited testimony from plaintiff about whether she was looking where she was going and whether she was paying attention, and such evidence constituted integral part of causation issue and was not relevant to other issues in case. Rudin v. Parkway School Dist., 30 S.W.3d 838 (Mo.App.2000).

Failure of trial court to modify phrase "as a direct result" in damage instruction, to conform to phrase "directly caused or directly contributed to cause" in verdict directing instruction, engendered confusion for jury and prejudiced plaintiff, entitling her to new trial on issue of damages in personal injury action arising from motor vehicle accident; evidence was presented that plaintiff experienced multiple possible causes for injuries to her body, i.e., automobile accident and prior and subsequent work-related injuries, and jury may have been confused as to how to award damages. Snelling v. Gress, 996 S.W.2d 538 (Mo.App.1999).

Any error in instructing the jury on plaintiff's comparative fault is harmless error if 100% of the fault is attributed to the complaining party. Inman v. Bi–State Development Agency, 849 S.W.2d 681 (Mo.App. 1993).

In suit by pedestrian to recover for injuries sustained as a result of being struck by motorist, trial court correctly instructed jury to determine the respective negligence of the pedestrian and the motorist and assess percentages of fault. Even if comparative fault instruction had been erroneous, pedestrian suffered no prejudice where jury found pedestrian 100% at fault for being struck by motorist. Biever v. Williams, 755 S.W.2d 291, 294 (Mo.App.1988).

In a suit by an invitee against a business for injuries sustained in a fall on the business premises, court erred in submitting verdict-directing instruction based on MAI 22.03, in that the second paragraph of the instruction submits issue of plaintiff's ordinary care in discovering an unsafe condition and thus is inimical to the concept of comparative fault. Cox v. J.C. Penney Co., 741 S.W.2d 28[3] (Mo. banc 1987).

Plaintiff cannot embrace the comparative fault doctrine in his verdict director and then repudiate it on appeal. Dodson By and Through Dodson v. Robertson, 710 S.W.2d 292[8] (Mo.App.1986).

In a negligence case, where there is evidence from which a jury could find that plaintiff's conduct was a contributing cause of his damages, unless the parties agree otherwise, the case should be submitted to the jury under the instructions and verdict forms approved for use in comparative fault cases regardless of whether the defendant submits an affirmative defense instruction or not.　Earll v. Consolidated Aluminum Corp., 714 S.W.2d 932[3] (Mo.App.1986).

Comparative fault does not apply in a strict products liability case, but the giving of MAI 32.23 is not precluded in the appropriate case.　Lippard v. Houdaille Industries, Inc., 715 S.W.2d 491[1–3] (Mo. banc 1986).　But now see § 537.765, et seq., RSMo.

2.　Rescue doctrine

In wrongful death action, comparative fault instruction submitted to the jury was erroneous, because it failed to differentiate the standards of care required in creating peril and in attempting rescue, and did not instruct jury that it could not assess comparative fault against rescuer-decedent unless his conduct in attempting rescue was rash or reckless.　Allison v. Sverdrup & Parcel and Assoc., Inc., 738 S.W.2d 440[12] (Mo.App. 1987).

37.02 [1986 New] Comparative Fault—Required Change of Former Contributory Negligence Instruction to Submit Plaintiff's Comparative Fault

In an instruction in a comparative fault case submitting fault on the part of plaintiff, the initial phrase of a defendant's instruction submitting fault on the part of plaintiff should be:

> In your verdict you must assess a percentage of fault to plaintiff [whether or not defendant was partly at fault] [1] if you believe:

The remaining paragraphs of defendant's instruction would be similar to the essential elements of those types of verdict directing instructions formerly used to submit contributory negligence as a complete defense. Thus, if partial fault of plaintiff is submitted to the jury based upon MAI 32.01(1), it would read as follows:

> In your verdict you must assess a percentage of fault to plaintiff [, whether or not defendant was partly at fault,] [1] if you believe:
>
> First, plaintiff drove at an excessive speed, and
>
> Second, plaintiff was thereby negligent,[2] and
>
> Third, such negligence [2] of plaintiff directly caused or directly contributed to cause any damage plaintiff may have sustained.

Notes on Use (1986 New)

1. The bracketed phrase may be used at defendant's option.

2. The terms "negligent" and "negligence" must be defined. See definitions in Chapter 11.00.

This sample instruction submits a single act of negligence. If more than one act is submitted in the disjunctive, see MAI 32.01(2). For other instructions on specifications of negligence which may be used in comparative fault submissions, see Chapter 17.00 and Chapter 32.00 to the extent allowed by substantive law.

Committee Comment (1996 New)

In Egelhoff v. Holt, 875 S.W.2d 543 (Mo. banc 1994); the Supreme Court held that under the Missouri pure comparative fault system, plaintiff's negligence is not compared with that of defendant A and then again with defendant B. Rather, it is compared with the cumulative fault of all defendants. Thus, under Egelhoff, only a single comparative fault instruction may be given against plaintiff where there are multiple defendants, even if the liability of those defendants is premised upon multiple theories (e.g.–strict liability and negligence).

Library References:

C.J.S. Trial § 350–351.
West's Key No. Digests, Trial ⚷234(3, 4).

Notes of Decisions

In general 1
Humanitarian doctrine 3
Mitigation 4
Multiple defendants 2

---

1. In general

Comparative fault instruction may be given in products liability case if there is sufficient evidence that plaintiff knowingly exposed himself to known danger. Watkins v. Toro Co., 901 S.W.2d 917 (Mo.App. E.D.1995).

Evidence in products liability action to recover for injuries sustained by user while operating commercial lawnmower did not warrant comparative fault instruction; user was injured when he slipped on loose grass clippings and his foot slid under mower, and he testified that he did not voluntarily put his foot into area of blade and that he did not knowingly or voluntarily put his foot where blade was rotating; moreover, there was no evidence that user misused mower. Watkins v. Toro Co., 901 S.W.2d 917 (Mo.App. E.D.1995).

Alleged error in product liability case that comparative fault instruction deviated from pattern instruction was harmless where jury determined that defendant was 0% at fault. Morrison v. Kubota Tractor Corp., 891 S.W.2d 422 (Mo.App. W.D.1994).

There is no requirement that plaintiff have actual knowledge of alleged defect in order to submit comparative fault of plaintiff in product liability case. Egelhoff v. Holt, 875 S.W.2d 543 (Mo. banc 1994).

In strict liability action for design defect of log splitter, evidence of plaintiff's voluntary exposure to known danger by reaching for log which was falling from log splitter, at which point his fingers were severed, supported submission of comparative fault instruction. Wilson v. Danuser Mach. Co., Inc., 874 S.W.2d 507 (Mo.App. S.D.1994).

Any error in giving comparative fault instruction in personal injury action which was not supported by the evidence and which omitted word "and" between first and second paragraphs, thereby deviating from MAI, was harmless, where 10 to 12 jurors assessed zero percent of fault to defendant and 100% of fault to plaintiff. Johnston v. Conger, 854 S.W.2d 480 (Mo.App.1993).

Evidence supported giving of instructions on comparative negligence of victim in automobile accident wrongful death case where there was evidence that victim had observed accident, left his car and walked across highway, going over median wall, and was standing in fast traffic lane when struck. Oldaker v. Peters, 817 S.W.2d 245 (Mo. banc 1991).

Comparative fault instruction in negligence suit by motorist injured in rear-end collision was supported by evidence that motorist stopped vehicle on highway to allow oncoming truck to pass through bridge, bridge was as wide as paved portion of highway, motorist did not pull off onto shoulder of road, did not engage emergency flashing lights, and road conditions were dark and wet. Tennison v. State Farm Mut. Auto Ins. Co., 834 S.W.2d 846 (Mo.App.1992).

Principle of comparative fault in failure of patient to follow physician instructions should also apply to failure to follow hospital nurse's instructions; however, hospital's requested instruction concerning patient's failure to turn over to allow nurse to check his condition and to check a heating pad was properly refused in action involving burns from the heating pad where hospital offered no evidence that patient could turn and it was not shown whether patient had already been burned by the heating pad by the time of the nurse's request. Hackathorn v. Lester E. Cox Medical Center, 824 S.W.2d 472 (Mo. App.1992).

In product liability case on behalf of injured worker due to alleged defect in press assembly, allegedly erroneous comparative fault instruction was held not to be prejudicial where the jury assessed zero percent fault to the manufacturer and zero percent fault to the plaintiff. Schaedler v. Rockwell Graphic Systems, Inc., 817 S.W.2d 499 (Mo. App.1991).

Conceded or undisputed conduct on the part of the plaintiff may be submitted as comparative fault. Court holds that comparative fault instruction in this case is not required to submit a hypothecation of actual or constructive knowledge on the part of the plaintiff of the danger. In this case, plaintiff was positioned on top of a railroad car in order to provide a repair estimate. Defendant's driver moved the railroad car with a tractor while the plaintiff was in that position. Comparative fault instruction submitted plaintiff's failure to wait to inspect the trailer until it had been parked and the tractor was removed or in failing to warn anyone operating the tractor that he was on top of the trailer. Lear v. Norfolk & Western Ry. Co., 815 S.W.2d 12 (Mo.App.1991).

It is permissible for a defendant to rely on multiple defense even though inconsistent. In this case, defendant denied that he was the operator of the motor vehicle in which decedent was a passenger and also submitted comparative negligence on the part of decedent while riding with him while defendant was drunk. Michael v. Kowalski, 813 S.W.2d 6 (Mo.App.1991).

Error in giving comparative fault instruction is harmless when jury apportions no percentage of fault to defendant. Vasseghi v. McNutt, 811 S.W.2d 453 (Mo.App.1991).

There was no prejudicial error in the trial court's use of a verdict directing instruction on comparative fault which stated at the bottom "submitted by defendant." Washburn v. Grundy Electric Cooperative, 804 S.W.2d 424 (Mo.App.1991).

Evidence in wrongful death case against electric utility supported an instruction calling for assessment of percentage of fault to decedent if decedent "failed to keep a careful lookout for electric lines" or "decedent caused or contributed to cause pool skimmer to come into contact with electrical line." Berra v. Union Electric Company, 803 S.W.2d 188 (Mo.App.1991).

In negligence action, trial court was not obligated to give jury instruction on comparative fault where defendant did not request such an instruction. Henderson v. Terminal R.R. Assoc. of St. Louis, 736 S.W.2d 594[1] (Mo.App.1987).

Error in giving a comparative fault instruction harmless where jury found no negligence on the part of defendant. Hyman v. Robinson, 713 S.W.2d 300[1, 2] (Mo.App. 1986).

In a negligence case, where there is evidence from which a jury could find that plaintiff's conduct was a contributing cause of his damages, unless the parties agree otherwise, the case should be submitted to the jury under the instructions and verdict forms approved for use in comparative fault cases regardless of whether the defendant submits an affirmative defense instruction or not. Earll v. Consolidated Aluminum Corp., 714 S.W.2d 932[3] (Mo.App.1986).

Comparative fault does not apply in a strict products liability case, but the giving of MAI 32.23 is not precluded in the appropriate case. Lippard v. Houdaille Industries, Inc., 715 S.W.2d 491[1–3] (Mo. banc 1986). See § 537.765, et seq., RSMo.

2. Multiple defendants

Where there were multiple defendants, it was error to submit more than one affirmative defense comparative fault instruction, but such error was not prejudicial where jury found that defendants were not guilty of any negligence that caused damage to plaintiff. Edwards v. Teeters, 781 S.W.2d 549, 550–51 (Mo.App.1989).

Damages instruction MAI 5.01, modified in accordance with MAI 37.03 to submit comparative fault, that permitted the jury to consider aggravating circumstances in assessing damages in wrongful death action is proper when the defendant could have reasonably been charged with knowledge of potentially dangerous situation but failed to act to prevent or reduce danger. Blum v. Airport Term. Serv., Inc., 762 S.W.2d 67, 72–73 (Mo.App.1988).

In case involving multiple defendants, only one affirmative defense comparative fault instruction should have been given, and the court erred when it gave two. Error, however, was not prejudicial since jury found one defendant free from fault and thus would not have had to consider the affirmative defense with respect to that defendant. Cornell v. Texaco, Inc., 712 S.W.2d 680[3] (Mo. banc 1986).

3. Humanitarian doctrine

Where comparative fault instruction was waived by defendant in negligence action, court properly submitted plaintiff's common law humanitarian negligence instruction (MAI 17.15) to jury, even though that doctrine has been replaced by comparative negligence. Henderson v. Terminal R.R. Assoc. of St. Louis, 736 S.W.2d 594[2] (Mo.App.1987).

4. Mitigation

Failure to mitigate damages is properly submitted as an element of plaintiff's fault. Love v. Park Lane Medical Center, 737 S.W.2d 720, 725 (Mo. banc 1987).

37.03   [1986 New] **Comparative Fault—Damages**

If you assess a percentage of fault to [any] [1] defendant, then, disregarding any fault on the part of plaintiff, you must determine the total amount of plaintiff's damages to be such sum as will fairly and justly compensate plaintiff for any damages you believe he sustained [and is reasonably certain to sustain in the future] [2] as a direct result of the occurrence [3] mentioned in the evidence. You must state such total amount of plaintiff's damages in your verdict.

In determining the total amount of plaintiff's damages you must not reduce such damages by any percentage of fault you may assess to plaintiff. The judge will compute plaintiff's recovery by reducing the amount you find as plaintiff's total damages by any percentage of fault you assess to plaintiff.

Notes on Use (2002 Revision)

1.   Insert if more than one defendant.

2.   This may be added if supported by the evidence.

3.   When the evidence discloses a compensable event and a non-compensable event, both of which are claimed to have caused damage, the term "occurrence" may need to be modified. See *Vest v. City National Bank & Trust Co.*, 470 S.W.2d 518 (Mo.1971). When the term "occurrence" is modified, substitute some descriptive phrase that specifically describes the compensable event.

The first example in Note 3 of MAI 4.01, ". . . as a direct result of the conduct of defendant as submitted in Instruction Number _____", is not appropriate in a comparative fault case because the jury is instructed to determine "total damages," which are obviously the direct result of the conduct of *both* the defendant *and* the plaintiff. The above-quoted example would inappropriately restrict the jury's assessment of damages to those damages solely caused by defendant's conduct.

In a simple comparative fault case, the first example in Note 3 of MAI 4.01, ". . . as a direct result of the automobile collision", may be an appropriate modification of the word "occurrence" if plaintiff sustained damage in an automobile collision but also had a non-compensable illness.

In a case such as *Carlson v. K–Mart Corp.*, 979 S.W.2d 145 (Mo. banc 1998), where MAI 19.01 is used in the verdict director, delete the entire phrase "as a direct result of the occurrence mentioned in the evidence" from this instruction and substitute the phrase "that (*describe the compensable event or conduct)* directly caused or directly contributed to cause."

In a more complex comparative fault case, it may be more appropriate to delete the entire phrase "... as a direct result of the occurrence mentioned in the evidence" and substitute the phrase "that the [fault]ᵃ [condition of the product]ᵇ [failure]ᶜ of the defendant directly caused or directly contributed to cause."

a. b. c. Select the appropriate term. If there is more than one defendant, or theory, more than one term may be appropriate.

a.   The term "fault" will generally be appropriate.

b.   The term "condition of the product" may be used in those cases involving product liability under MAI 25.04 and MAI 25.05.

c.   The term "failure" may be used in those cases involving submission under instructions such as MAI 22.02, MAI 22.03, MAI 22.05, MAI 22.07, and similar instructions in which the defendant's actionable conduct is described as a "failure" as opposed to "negligence."

Other modifications may also be appropriate. See MAI 4.01 for further discussion.

In a case in which mitigation of damages is properly submitted under MAI 32.29, this damage instruction should be modified with the bracketed sentence required by Note 4 of the Notes on Use to MAI 4.01.

Committee Comment (1986 New)

When appropriate, other damage instructions such as those applicable to wrongful death, etc., may be modified in the format of this instruction to submit comparative fault.

Library References:

C.J.S. Negligence § 871, 891, 900–901.
West's Key No. Digests, Negligence ⟐1746.

Notes of Decisions

1. In general

Failure of trial court to modify phrase "as a direct result" in damage instruction, to conform to phrase "directly caused or directly contributed to cause" in verdict directing instruction, engendered confusion for jury and prejudiced plaintiff, entitling her to new trial on issue of damages in personal injury action arising from motor vehicle accident; evidence was presented that plaintiff experienced multiple possible causes for injuries to her body, i.e., automobile accident and prior

and subsequent work-related injuries, and jury may have been confused as to how to award damages. Snelling v. Gress, 996 S.W.2d 538 (Mo.App.1999).

Defendant in comparative fault strict liability-failure to warn case was not entitled to jury instruction on present value of plaintiff's future economic loss, stating that future damages should be valued at their present worth; appropriate instruction on recovery of future damages was MAI 37.03, which was submitted. Cole v. Goodyear Tire & Rubber Co., 967 S.W.2d 176 (Mo.App.1998).

In comparative fault case, a determination of damages cannot survive independent of the accompanying determination of liability; where a finding on liability is reversed, the finding on damages must also be reversed. Barlett v. Kansas City So. Ry. Co., 854 S.W.2d 396 (Mo. banc 1993).

37.04 [1986 New] Comparative Fault—Converse Instructions—Plaintiff or Defendant

In a converse instruction using the "unless you believe" introduction in a comparative fault case, the initial phrase of the converse instructions should be modified as follows:

> In your verdict you must not assess a percentage of fault to [defendant] [plaintiff] [1] unless you believe . . .

The remainder of the converse instruction would then be derived from one or more of the substantive elements of the instruction being conversed under the rules governing converse instructions under MAI 33.01. Thus, if a converse derived from MAI 33.03(1) is used in a comparative fault case, it would read as follows:

> In your verdict you must not assess a percentage of fault to defendant unless you believe defendant violated the traffic signal.

Notes on Use (1986 New)

1. Under the system of pure comparative fault the plaintiff now is on precisely the same basis as is the defendant with respect to the use of converse instructions using the "unless you believe" introduction. Select the appropriate term. Both the plaintiff and the defendant are entitled to submit instructions conversing the instruction submitted by the opposing party on which an assessment of a percentage of fault may be made by the jury.

Library References:

C.J.S. Trial § 303.
West's Key No. Digests, Trial ☞203(3).

Notes of Decisions

1. In general

It was proper to modify MAI converse instruction so as to inform the jury that their verdict must not assess a percentage of fault to defendants, rather than instructing the jury that its verdict must be for the defendants, where the comparative fault verdict form did not permit the jury to find in favor of plaintiff or defendant but only to assess percentages of fault to one or the other or to both. McMullin v. Politte, 780 S.W.2d 94 (Mo.App. 1989).

37.05(1) [1991 Revision] Comparative Fault—Vicarious Liability—Agency in Issue

Servant Not Joined

Where defendant master or principal is sued without joinder of the alleged servant or agent in a comparative fault case and agency is at issue, the initial phrase of the verdict directing instruction against the master or principal should read as follows:

In your verdict you must assess a percentage of fault to defendant (*name of alleged master*), whether or not plaintiff was partly at fault, if you believe:

Thus, if the example in MAI 18.01 is used in such a comparative fault case, it would read as follows:

In your verdict you must assess a percentage of fault to defendant Ajax, whether or not plaintiff was partly at fault, if you believe:

First, driver Jones [was an employee of Ajax and] [1] was operating the Ajax Company motor vehicle within the scope and course of his employment by Ajax [at the time of the collision], [1] and

Second, Jones violated the traffic signal, and

Third, Jones was thereby negligent, [2] and

Fourth, such negligence [2] directly caused or directly contributed to cause damage to plaintiff. [3]

In assessing any such percentage of fault against Defendant Ajax, you must consider any fault of driver Jones as the fault of defendant Ajax.

Insert the master's name in the verdict form for apportionment of fault in such a case when the master is sued without joinder of the servant, agency is in issue, and the master's liability is submitted only on the basis of the servant's conduct. In this type of case there is no need for the verdict form to contain a separate space for the finding on the agency issue.

Both Master and Servant Joined

Where the master and servant are both joined as parties in a comparative fault case and agency is in issue, the

779

verdict directing instruction against the servant will be a typical verdict directing instruction such as MAI 37.01. Since the verdict directing instruction contains those elements relevant to the fault of the servant, the only remaining issue relating to the master will be the agency issue. Under these circumstances it is not necessary to repeat the elements relating to the servant's negligence in the verdict directing instruction against the master. Thus, the verdict directing instruction against the master would read as follows, utilizing MAI 18.01:

> In your verdict you must find defendant Ajax responsible for any percentage of fault you may assess to defendant Jones, whether or not plaintiff was partly at fault, if you believe driver Jones was operating the Ajax Company motor vehicle within the scope and course of his employment by Ajax.

In preparing the verdict form for apportionment of fault in such a case where the master's liability is submitted only on the servant's conduct, the servant is also joined, and agency is in issue, the following should be inserted as the first paragraph in the comparative fault verdict form:

Note: Complete the following paragraph by writing the word(s) required by your verdict.

> On the claim of plaintiff for personal injury against defendant (*name of master*), we, the undersigned jurors, _____ find (*name of master*) responsible
> ("do" or "do not")
>
> for any percentage of fault assessed to (*name of servant*).

In the remaining paragraphs of the comparative fault verdict form, only the name of the alleged servant will be listed in the space provided for assessment of percentages of fault. The master's liability for the percentage of fault assessed to the servant is then a matter of law based on the finding by the jury on the agency issue. See MAI 35.04.

Notes on Use (1986 New)

1.   Use bracketed terms if in issue.

2. Where the term "negligent" or "negligence" is used, it must be defined. See Chapter 11.00.

3. Paragraph Fourth of the example in MAI 18.01 is shown here modified in accordance with the first alternate of MAI 19.01.

Committee Comment (1996 Revision)

Where the liability of the master or principal is based on vicarious liability, only the conduct of the servant is to be considered in relation to the conduct of the plaintiff in assessing fault. See Note on Use No. 3, MAI 4.12; Note on Use No. 5 MAI 4.13 [1979 Committee Proposed]; and Note on Use No. 2 to MAI 4.14 [1979 Committee Proposed] for similar treatment of a vicarious liability situation in apportioning fault between defendants under Missouri Pacific R.R. Co. v. Whitehead & Kales Co., 566 S.W.2d 466 (Mo. banc 1978).

If a plaintiff seeks to recover in a comparative fault case from a master or principal based on both respondeat superior and also based upon the negligent acts of the master (i.e., based on the negligent driving of the employee and also based on the employer's negligence in furnishing a truck with defective brakes) then the jury should be asked to assess one percentage of fault based on the employee's driving, a different percentage of fault based on the employer's conduct in furnishing the truck with defective brakes and another percentage of fault based on the conduct of the plaintiff. In this instance the comparative fault verdict form would have a blank for the employee's percentage of fault (which is chargeable to both the employee and the employer); another blank for a percentage of fault for the employer's conduct as submitted in the verdict director submitting the employer's conduct in furnishing the truck with bad brakes (this fault is chargeable only to the master) and a blank for the percentage of fault assessed to plaintiff. However, in McHaffie v. Bunch, 891 S.W.2d 822 (Mo. banc 1995); the Supreme Court held that once an employer has admitted respondeat superior liability, it is improper to allow plaintiff to submit another theory of *imputed* liability against the employer (as distinguished from another theory of independent negligence).

Library References:

C.J.S. Trial § 350–351.
West's Key No. Digests, Trial ☞234(3, 4).

37.05(2) [1986 New] Comparative Fault—Vicarious Liability—Agency Not Disputed

Where the master or principal is sued with the servant or agent, and there is no issue of agency, a single verdict directing instruction may be directed against both the master and servant. An example follows:

> In your verdict you must assess a percentage of fault to defendants Ajax and Jones, whether or not plaintiff was partly at fault, if you believe:
>
> First, defendant Jones violated the traffic signal, and
>
> Second, defendant Jones was thereby negligent, and
>
> Third, such negligence directly caused or directly contributed to cause damage to plaintiff.
>
> In assessing any such percentage of fault against Ajax and Jones, you must consider them both as one party and assess only the fault of Jones as the fault of both.

In preparing the verdict form for apportionment in such a case where the master's liability is submitted only on his servant's conduct, and agency is not in dispute, insert the names of both master and servant on the same line in accordance with the direction to the jury to assess only the fault of the servant as the fault of both.

Committee Comment (1986 New)

Where the master is sued on a theory of vicarious liability for the fault of a servant, agency is not in dispute, and the servant is not joined as a party, the following example may be followed for submission of the case against the master:

> In your verdict you must assess a percentage of fault to defendant Ajax, whether or not plaintiff was partly at fault, if you believe:
>
> First, driver Jones violated the traffic signal, and
>
> Second, driver Jones was thereby negligent, and
>
> Third, such negligence directly caused or directly contributed to cause damage to plaintiff.
>
> In assessing any such percentage of fault against defendant Ajax, you must consider the fault of driver Jones as the fault of defendant Ajax.

In preparing the verdict form for apportionment in such a case where only the master is sued for vicarious liability, only the master's name should be inserted.

Library References:

C.J.S. Trial § 350–351.
West's Key No. Digests, Trial ⊚234(3, 4).

Notes of Decisions

In general 1
Assumption of facts 2

_____

1. In general

Instruction advising jury that conduct of agent served as basis for determination of any possible percentage of fault to be assessed against master is not needed in non-comparative fault negligent verdict director; jury is instructed that verdict for plaintiff and against defendant master must be returned if agent was negligent as submitted. Cline v. William H. Friedman & Associates, Inc., 882 S.W.2d 754[21] (Mo.App.1994).

2. Assumption of facts

Verdict-directing instruction must require jury to find all necessary elements of plain-

tiff's case, except for uncontroverted facts; it is reversible error for instruction to assume or ignore controverted fact. Cline v. William H. Friedman & Associates, Inc., 882 S.W.2d 754[22] (Mo.App.1994).

Verdict-directing instruction which stated that jury was required to consider fault of doctor as fault of his employer assumed as undisputed fact that fault was attributable to doctor and impermissibly assumed controverted fact in medical malpractice action. Cline v. William H. Friedman & Associates, Inc., 882 S.W.2d 754[23] (Mo.App 1994).

37.06 [1986 New] Comparative Fault—Complete Affirmative Defenses

Although fault is eliminated as a total, recovery-defeating defense by the doctrine of comparative fault, some other recovery-defeating affirmative defenses remain, e.g., a full release. When such an affirmative defense is submitted in a claim in which comparative fault must be apportioned, the initial phrase of the affirmative defense instruction should be modified as follows:

> In your verdict you must not assess a percentage of fault to defendant if you believe:

The remaining paragraphs of the affirmative defense instruction would be derived from an affirmative defense instruction where comparative fault is not submitted. Thus, if affirmative defense instruction MAI 32.21 were to be modified for use in a comparative fault case, it would read as follows:

> In your verdict you must not assess a percentage of fault to defendant if you believe:

First, plaintiff signed and delivered the release to defendant, and

Second, plaintiff was paid $_____ [1] for such release.

* [unless you find for plaintiff under Instruction Number _____ (*here insert number of plaintiff's instruction which hypothesizes that the release is not effective, such as MAI 32.22*)].

Notes on Use (1986 New)

1. If plaintiff's consideration was something other than money, modify Paragraph Second to describe the consideration received.

This instruction is to be given only when there is a disputed issue as to whether plaintiff gave a release. If the plaintiff disputes executing the release and claims in the alternative that if a release was given, it was obtained by fraud, then this instruction should be given along with the bracketed phrase shown. If the plaintiff admits he gave the release for consideration but claims that it was obtained by fraud, then neither this instruction nor MAI 32.22 should be given. The issues which would otherwise be given in MAI 32.22 should be added to plaintiff's verdict director. See Notes on Use, MAI 32.22.

* Add in the event plaintiff submits an avoidance of release.

Committee Comment (1986 New)

For financial responsibility releases, which release both the party giving the release and the party obtaining the release, see *Eberting v. Skinner,* 364 S.W.2d 829 (Mo.App.1963) and *Farmer v. Arnold,* 371 S.W.2d 265 (Mo.1963).

MAI 37.06 should be used only to submit affirmative defenses that constitute a complete bar to recovery. It should not be used to submit comparative fault.

Library References:

C.J.S. Negligence § 871, 891, 900–901.
West's Key No. Digests, Negligence ☞1746.

37.07 [1986 New] Comparative Fault—Form of Verdict—Plaintiff vs. Defendant

VERDICT _____ [1]

Note: Complete the following paragraph by filling in the blanks as required by your verdict. If you assess a percentage of fault to any of those listed below, write in a percentage not greater than 100%, otherwise write in "zero" next to that name. If you assess a percentage of fault to any of those listed below, the total of such percentages must be 100%.

On the claim of plaintiff (*state the name*) for personal injury,[2] we, the undersigned jurors, assess percentages of fault as follows:

Defendant[3]	(*state the name*)	_____%	(zero to 100%)
Plaintiff	(*state the name*)	_____%	(zero to 100%)
	TOTAL	_____%	(zero OR 100%)

Note: Complete the following paragraph if you assessed a percentage of fault to defendant:

We, the undersigned jurors, find the total amount of plaintiff's damages disregarding any fault on the part of plaintiff to be $_____ (*stating the amount*).

Note: The judge will reduce the total amount of plaintiff's damages by any percentage of fault you assess to plaintiff.

Note: All jurors who agree to the above must sign below.

_____   _____
_____   _____
_____   _____
_____   _____
_____   _____

Notes on Use (1986 New)

1. Verdicts will be designated alphabetically A, B, C, etc.

2. The verdict form will contain a descriptive phrase describing and identifying the claim submitted by this particular package which will

be the claim to which this verdict is applicable. The identifying phrase should be non-inflammatory and as neutral as possible and should avoid the assumption of disputed facts. See MAI 2.00 General Comment, Section F, for a discussion and for examples of the appropriate identifying phrase.

3. The names of those against whom fault may be assessed must be inserted in the form of verdict by the preparer of the form.

Caution: The modification necessary to submit apportionment of fault among parties not sued by plaintiff depends upon substantive issues which may not yet be resolved. The Committee takes no position on unresolved substantive issues.

Parenthetical directions to "(*state the name*)" in the above form are addressed to counsel. The appropriate party's name should be typed in the prepared verdict at those points. All other directions are for the jury and should be submitted to the jury as written.

A separate verdict form must be used for each "package" other than the package containing the general instructions. The verdict form will be the last document in each such package. See MAI 2.00 General Comment for an explanation of "packaging."

Verdict forms should not be read by the Court to the jury.

Committee Comment (1998 New)

In comparative fault cases, the jury assesses total damages disregarding any fault on the part of plaintiff and assesses percentages of fault to the parties. The trial judge uses these jury findings to compute the plaintiff's actual recovery by reducing the "total damages" by the percentage of fault assessed to plaintiff.

In MAI 37.07, the jury is reminded of these distinct functions by the language "The judge will reduce the total amount of plaintiff's damages ...." In MAI 37.09, slightly different language is used, i.e., "The judge will compute the recovery of each plaintiff ...." This difference in MAI 37.09 was deliberately adopted by the Committee to accommodate, without modification, more complex cases in which there might be more than one percentage of fault to consider in the computation (for instance, legally submissible fault on the part of both the primary and the derivative claimants). However, this difference was not intended to preclude argument by counsel with respect to the respective roles of the judge and jury, the method and manner of completing the verdict form, and the net effect (net recovery) of the jury findings. See "Why and How to Instruct a Jury", p. LXXVI, pointing out that a proper function of counsel in argument is to "flesh out" the instructions by explanation and illustration.

Library References:

C.J.S. Negligence § 871, 891, 900–901.
West's Key No. Digests, Negligence ⚷1746.

Notes of Decisions

1. In general

MAI 37.07 correctly states the law. Nagy v. Missouri Highway and Transportation Comm., 829 S.W.2d 648 (Mo.App.1992).

Father brought action for death of his minor daughter. Daughter was a passenger in a car operated by boyfriend of mother (ex-wife of father). Suit was also against driver of another vehicle. Counsel for driver of other vehicle repeatedly argued, during closing argument, that mother was negligent for allowing her daughter to ride with intoxicated boyfriend. Jury apportioned fault to boyfriend and mother. Held: Verdict form erroneously allowed assessment of percentage of fault to mother on an unpleaded theory. Bradley v. Waste Management of Missouri, Inc., 810 S.W.2d 525 (Mo.App.1991).

In a negligence case, where there is evidence from which a jury could find that plaintiff's conduct was a contributing cause of his damages, unless the parties agree otherwise, the case should be submitted to the jury under the instructions and verdict forms approved for use in comparative fault cases regardless of whether the defendant submits an affirmative defense instruction or not. Earll v. Consolidated Aluminum Corp., 714 S.W.2d 932[3] (Mo.App.1986).

Comparative fault does not apply in a strict products liability case, but the giving of MAI 32.23 is not precluded in the appropriate case. Lippard v. Houdaille Industries, Inc., 715 S.W.2d 491[1–3] (Mo. banc 1986). See § 537.765, et seq., RSMo.

37.08 [1991 New] Comparative Fault—Damages—Personal Injury and Loss of Consortium, Loss of Services or Medical Expenses—Spouse or Child Injured

If you assess a percentage of fault to [any] [1] defendant, then, disregarding any fault on the part of plaintiff (*name of plaintiff with primary claim*), you must determine the total amount of plaintiff (*name of plaintiff with primary claim*) damages on [his] [her] [2] claim for personal injury. If you further find that plaintiff (*name of plaintiff with derivative claim*) did sustain damage as a direct result of injury to [his] [her] [husband] [wife] [child],[2] you must determine the total amount of [his] [her] [2] damages on [his] [her] [2] claim for damages due to injury to [his] [her] [husband] [wife] [child].[2]

Total damages on each claim must be such sum as will fairly and justly compensate the plaintiff on that claim for any such damages you believe that plaintiff sustained [and is reasonably certain to sustain in the future] [3] as a direct result of the occurrence [4] mentioned in the evidence. You must state separately in your verdict the total amount of each plaintiff's damages on each claim.

In determining the total amount of each plaintiff's damages, you must not reduce such damages by any percentage of fault you may assess to plaintiff (*name of plaintiff with primary claim*). The judge will compute the recovery of each plaintiff under the law and the percentages of fault you assess.

Notes on Use (2002 Revision)

1. Insert if more than one defendant.
2. Select appropriate word(s).
3. This may be added if supported by the evidence.
4. When the evidence discloses a compensable event and a non-compensable event, both of which are claimed to have caused damage, the term "occurrence" may need to be modified. See *Vest v. City National Bank & Trust Co.,* 470 S.W.2d 518 (Mo.1971). When the term "occurrence" is modified, substitute some descriptive phrase that specifically describes the compensable event.

The first example in Note 3 of MAI 4.01, "... as a direct result of the conduct of defendant as submitted in Instruction Number _____", is not appropriate in a comparative fault case because the jury is instructed to determine "total damages," which are obviously the direct result of the conduct of *both* the defendant *and* the plaintiff. The above-quoted example would inappropriately restrict the jury's assessment of damages to those damages solely caused by defendant's conduct.

In a simple comparative fault case, the first example in Note 3 of MAI 4.01, ". . . as a direct result of the automobile collision", may be an appropriate modification of the word "occurrence" if plaintiff sustained damage in an automobile collision but also had a non-compensable illness.

In a case such as *Carlson v. K–Mart Corp.*, 979 S.W.2d 145 (Mo. banc 1998), where MAI 19.01 is used in the verdict director, delete the entire phrase "as a direct result of the occurrence mentioned in the evidence" from this instruction and substitute the phrase "that (*describe the compensable event or conduct*) directly caused or directly contributed to cause."

In a more complex comparative fault case, it may be more appropriate to delete the entire phrase ". . . as a direct result of the occurrence mentioned in the evidence" and substitute the phrase "that the [fault][a] [condition of the product][b] [failure][c] of the defendant directly caused or directly contributed to cause."

a. b. c. Select the appropriate term. If there is more than one defendant, or theory, more than one term may be appropriate.

a. The term "fault" will generally be appropriate.

b. The term "condition of the product" may be used in those cases involving product liability under MAI 25.04 and MAI 25.05.

c. The term "failure" may be used in those cases involving submission under instructions such as MAI 22.02, MAI 22.03, MAI 22.05, MAI 22.07, and similar instructions in which the defendant's actionable conduct is described as a "failure" as opposed to "negligence."

Other modifications may also be appropriate. See MAI 4.01 for further discussion. In a case in which mitigation of damages is properly submitted under MAI 32.29, this damage instruction should be modified with the bracketed sentence required by Note 4 of the Notes on Use to MAI 4.01. In a case involving combined primary and derivative claims, the law of Missouri has not yet developed to indicate whether mitigation of damages instructions may be given on both claims or only on the primary injury claim. The Committee takes no position on this issue.

Committee Comment (1991 New)

This is a damage instruction for both the primary and derivative claims in a comparative fault case involving both a personal injury claim and a derivative loss of consortium, loss of services or medical expense claim. See MAI 31.04 for the appropriate verdict directing instruction for the derivative claim and MAI 37.09 for the appropriate verdict form. See also MAI 35.16.

See MAI 4.18 for the damage instruction in a non-comparative fault case submitting both a primary claim and a derivative claim.

Library References:

C.J.S. Negligence § 871, 891, 900–901.
West's Key No. Digests, Negligence ⊕1746.

Notes of Decisions

1. In general

The Missouri Supreme Court refused to recognize a cause of action for loss of parental consortium (consortium action by child due to injury to parent) or filial consortium (consortium action by sibling due to injury to another sibling). Powell v. American Motors Corp., 834 S.W.2d 184 (Mo. banc 1992).

37.09 [1991 New] Comparative Fault—Form of Verdict—Combined Injury and Derivative Claims

VERDICT _____ [1]

Note: Complete the following paragraph by filling in the blanks as required by your verdict. If you assess a percentage of fault to any of those listed below, write in a percentage not greater than 100%; otherwise write in "zero" next to that name. If you assess a percentage of fault to any of those listed below, the total of such percentages must be 100%.

We, the undersigned jurors, assess percentages of fault as follows:

Defendant[2]   (*state the name*)   _____%   (zero to 100%)
Plaintiff[2]   (*state the name*)   _____%   (zero to 100%)
       TOTAL   _____%   (zero OR 100%)

Note: Complete the following paragraphs if you assessed a percentage of fault to [any][3] defendant.

On the claim of plaintiff (*state name of plaintiff with primary claim*) for personal injury, we, the undersigned jurors, find the total amount of plaintiff (*state name of plaintiff with primary claim*) damages, disregarding any fault on the part of plaintiff (*state name of plaintiff with primary claim*), to be $_____ (*stating the amount*).

Note: Complete the following paragraph by writing in the word(s) required by your verdict.

On the claim of plaintiff (*state name of plaintiff with derivative claim*) for damages due to injury to [his] [her] [husband] [wife] [child],[4] we, the undersigned jurors, find that plaintiff (*state name of plaintiff with derivative claim*) _____ sustain damage as a direct result of injury

("did" or "did not")

to [his] [her] [husband] [wife] [child].[4]

Note: Complete the following paragraph only if the above finding is that plaintiff (*state name of plaintiff with derivative claim*) "did" sustain such damage.

We, the undersigned jurors, find the total amount of plaintiff (*state name of plaintiff with derivative claim*) damages due to injury to [his] [her] [husband] [wife] [child],[4] disregarding any fault on the part of plaintiff (*state name of plaintiff with primary claim*), to be $_____ (*stating the amount*).

Note: The judge will compute the recovery of each plaintiff under the law and the percentages of fault you assess.

All jurors who agree to the above findings must sign below.

_____   _____
_____   _____
_____   _____
_____   _____

Notes on Use (1991 New)

1.   Verdicts will be designated alphabetically (A, B, C, etc.).

2.   The names of those against whom fault may be assessed must be inserted in the form of verdict by the preparer of the form.

3.   Insert if more than one defendant.

4.   Select appropriate word(s).

Caution: The modification necessary to submit apportionment of fault among parties not sued by plaintiff depends upon substantive issues that may not yet be resolved. The Committee takes no position on unresolved substantive issues.

Parenthetical directions to "(*state the name*)" in the above form are addressed to counsel. The appropriate party's name should be typed in the prepared verdict at those points. All other directions are for the jury and should be submitted to the jury as written.

A separate verdict form must be used for each "package" other than the package containing the general instructions. The verdict form will be the last document in each such package. See MAI 2.00 General Comment for an explanation of "packaging".

Committee Comment (1998 New)

In comparative fault cases, the jury assesses total damages disregarding any fault on the part of plaintiff and assesses percentages of fault to the parties. The trial judge uses these jury findings to compute the plaintiff's actual recovery by reducing the "total damages" by the percentage of fault assessed to plaintiff.

In MAI 37.07, the jury is reminded of these distinct functions by the language "The judge will reduce the total amount of plaintiff's damages ...." In MAI 37.09, slightly different language is used, i.e., "The judge will compute the recovery of each plaintiff ...." This difference in MAI 37.09 was deliberately adopted by the Committee to accommodate, without modification, more complex cases in which there might be more than one percentage of fault to consider in the computation (for instance, legally submissible fault on the part of both the primary and the derivative claimants). However, this difference was not intended to preclude argument by counsel with respect to the respective roles of the judge and jury, the method and manner of completing the verdict form, and the net effect (net recovery) of the jury findings. See "Why and How to Instruct a Jury", p. LXXVI, pointing out that a proper function of counsel in argument is to "flesh out" the instructions by explanation and illustration.

Library References:

C.J.S. Negligence § 871, 891, 900–901.
West's Key No. Digests, Negligence ☞1746.

TABLE OF EFFECTIVE DATES
OF MISSOURI APPROVED
JURY INSTRUCTIONS

The development of a good civil instruction system is a continually evolving process which arises both from the necessity to accommodate changes in the law and the improvements which can be obtained by revising existing instructions to meet unforeseen problems which inevitably surface as a particular instruction is put to use. The practicing bar and the judiciary are kept currently informed as to such changes in Instructions, Notes on Use and Committee Comments by the publication of current changes in the Missouri Bar Journal and ultimately in a pocket part or supplement to the bound volume.

MAI Sixth brings together a particularly large number of such changes because the Committee and the Court have been very active during the recent period in updating and improving the civil instruction system. The following table is included to provide a source of information of the effective date of all current versions of instructions as of the publication of MAI Sixth.

The date and designation "New" or "Revision" in the caption of each instruction indicates whether the current version of the instruction is as originally adopted or a revision and the year in which this version of the instruction first became effective. This designation is provided for use as part of the citation to the instruction (e.g., MAI 33.03 [1995 Revision]) so that reference to a particular instruction by citation, such as in a case opinion, will disclose the particular version of the instruction referred to. This becomes particularly significant when referring to an instruction which has had substantial revision at one time or another.

The designation CP means Committee Proposed and indicates that the instruction has not been adopted by the Court. The designation Withdrawn means the instruction is no longer approved for use by the Court. The Notes on Use and Committee Comment to such instructions have also been withdrawn.

	INSTRUCTION NO.	INSTRUCTION	NOTES ON USE	COMMITTEE COMMENT
I	Chapter 1.00—Excluded Areas			
	MAI 1.01	1965 New	—	1965 New
	MAI 1.02	1965 New	—	1996 Revision
	MAI 1.03	1965 New	—	1981 Revision
	MAI 1.04	1965 New	—	1965 New
	MAI 1.05	1965 New	—	1981 Revision
	MAI 1.06	1983 New	—	1983 New

TABLE OF EFFECTIVE DATES

	INSTRUCTION NO.	INSTRUCTION	NOTES ON USE	COMMITTEE COMMENT
II	Chapter 2.00—Explanatory			
	MAI 2.00	1996 Revision	—	—
	MAI 2.01	2002 Revision	1996 Revision	1996 Revision
	MAI 2.02	1980 Revision	1980 Revision	1980 Revision
	MAI 2.03	1980 New	1980 New	—
	MAI 2.04	1981 Revision	1980 New	—
	MAI 2.05	1980 New	1980 New	—
	MAI 2.06	1983 New	1989 Revision	—
III	Chapter 3.00—Burden of Proof			
	MAI 3.01	1998 Revision	1998 Revision	1981 Revision
	MAI 3.02	1981 Revision	1977 Revision	1969 New
	MAI 3.03	1981 Revision	1995 Revision	1995 New
	MAI 3.04	1981 Revision	—	1977 New
	MAI 3.05	1998 Revision	1989 Revision	1980 New
	MAI 3.06	1998 Revision	1989 Revision	1980 New
	MAI 3.07	1983 New	—	1983 New
	MAI 3.08	1998 Revision	1994 New	1998 Revision
IV	Chapter 4.00—Damages			
	MAI 4.01	2002 Revision	2002 Revision	2002 Revision
	MAI 4.02	1980 Revision	2002 Revision	1969 New
	MAI 4.03	1969 New	1981 Revision	1969 New
	MAI 4.04	1981 Revision	1981 Revision	1980 Revision
	MAI 4.05	1996 Revision	1996 New	—
	MAI 4.06	1996 Revision	1996 New	—
	MAI 4.07	1996 Revision	1996 New	1980 Revision
	MAI 4.08	1980 New	1980 New	—
	MAI 4.09	1980 Revision	1980 Revision	—
	MAI 4.10	1980 Revision	2002 Revision	—
	MAI 4.11	1980 Revision	2002 Revision	—
	MAI 4.12	1979 New	1979 New	1996 Revision
	MAI 4.13	1979 New	1979 New	1996 Revision
	MAI 4.14	1979 New	1979 New	1996 Revision
	MAI 4.15	1980 New	1980 New	1980 New
	MAI 4.16	1980 New	1996 Revision	—
	MAI 4.17	1980 New	1996 Revision	1980 New
	MAI 4.18	1991 New	2002 Revision	1991 New
V	Chapter 5.00—Wrongful Death			
	MAI 5.01	1996 Revision	1996 Revision	2002 Revision
	MAI 5.02	Withdrawn 1981	—	—
	MAI 5.03	Withdrawn 1981	—	—
	MAI 5.04	Withdrawn 1981	—	—
	MAI 5.05	Withdrawn 1981	—	—
	MAI 5.06	Withdrawn 1981	—	—
	MAI 5.07	Withdrawn 1981	—	—
	MAI 5.08	Withdrawn 1981	—	—
	MAI 5.09	Withdrawn 1981	—	—
VI	Chapter 6.00—Mitigation			
	MAI 6.01	1996 Revision	1965 New	2002 New

	INSTRUCTION NO.	INSTRUCTION	NOTES ON USE	COMMITTEE COMMENT
	MAI 6.02	1998 Revision	—	1996 New
VII	Chapter 7.00—Joint Tort Feasors			
	MAI 7.01	Withdrawn 1983	Withdrawn	1983 Revision
	MAI 7.02	1983 Revision	1983 Revision	1983 Revision
VIII	Chapter 8.00—F.E.L.A.			
	MAI 8.01	1996 Revision	1996 Revision	1991 Revision
	MAI 8.02	1996 Revision	1996 Revision	1996 Revision
IX	Chapter 9.00—Eminent Domain			
	MAI 9.01	1965 New	1981 Revision	1965 New
	MAI 9.02	1965 New	1981 Revision	1983 Revision
X	Chapter 10.00—Exemplary			
	MAI 10.01	1990 Revision	1998 Revision	1996 Revision
	MAI 10.02	1983 Revision	1998 Revision	1996 Revision
	MAI 10.03	1983 Revision	—	—
	MAI 10.04	1983 New	1998 Revision	1996 Revision
	MAI 10.05	1983 New	1998 Revision	1996 New
	MAI 10.06	1983 New	1998 Revision	1996 New
	MAI 10.07	1991 New	1998 Revision	1996 New
	MAI 10.08	1992 New	1992 New	1992 New
XI	Chapter 11.00—Definitions—Negligence			
	MAI 11.01	1996 Revision	1978 Revision	—
	MAI 11.02	1996 Revision	1996 Revision	—
	MAI 11.03	1996 Revision	1978 New	1978 New
	MAI 11.04	1996 Revision	1996 Revision	1996 Revision
	MAI 11.05	1996 Revision	1996 Revision	—
	MAI 11.06	1990 Revision	1990 Revision	1978 Revision
	MAI 11.07	1996 Revision	1978 New	1978 New
	MAI 11.08	1996 Revision	1978 New	—
	MAI 11.09	Withdrawn 1996	Withdrawn	Withdrawn
	MAI 11.10	1996 Revision	1988 New	1988 New
XII	Chapter 12.00—Uninsured Motor Vehicle			
	MAI 12.01	1988 Revision	1988 Revision	—
	MAI 12.02	1978 New	1978 New	—
XIII	Chapter 13.00—Agency			
	MAI 13.01	1996 Revision	—	—
	MAI 13.02	1978 Revision	1978 Revision	1965 New
	MAI 13.03	1990 Revision	1990 Revision	1965 New
	MAI 13.04	1990 Revision	1990 Revision	1965 New
	MAI 13.05	1990 Revision	1990 Revision	1965 New
	MAI 13.06	1990 Revision	1990 Revision	1965 New
	MAI 13.07(1)	1996 Revision	1986 New	1986 New
	MAI 13.07(2)	1996 Revision	1986 New	1986 New

TABLE OF EFFECTIVE DATES

TABLE OF EFFECTIVE DATES

INSTRUCTION NO.	INSTRUCTION	NOTES ON USE	COMMITTEE COMMENT
XIX	Chapter 19.00—Verdict Directing—Joint Tort–Feasors—Multiple Causes of Damage		
MAI 19.01	1986 Revision	1999 Revision	1995 New
XX	Chapter 20.00—Verdict Directing—Wrongful Death		
MAI 20.01	1981 Revision	1996 Revision	1981 Revision
MAI 20.02	1983 Revision	1996 Revision	1965 New
XXI	Chapter 21.00—Verdict Directing—Actions Against Health Care Providers		
MAI 21.01	1988 Revision	1990 Revision	2002 Revision
MAI 21.02	1988 New	1988 New	1988 New
MAI 21.03	1988 New	2002 Revision	1996 Revision
MAI 21.04	1988 New	2002 Revision	1996 Revision
MAI 21.05	1988 New	1991 Revision	1996 Revision
MAI 21.06	1991 New	—	2002 Revision
MAI 21.07	1991 New	—	—
MAI 21.08	1995 Revision	1993 New	2002 Revision
MAI 21.09	1996 Revision	1996 Revision	2002 Revision
MAI 21.10	1993 New	1993 New	1993 New
MAI 21.11	1996 Revision	1996 Revision	2002 Revision
MAI 21.12	1994 New	2002 Revision	2002 Revision
MAI 21.13	1994 New	1994 New	1994 New
MAI 21.14	1994 New	1994 New	1994 New
MAI 21.15	1994 New	2002 Revision	1994 New
XXII	Chapter 22.00—Verdict Directing—Owners and Occupiers of Land		
MAI 22.01	1996 Revision	1991 Revision	1995 Revision
MAI 22.02	1995 Revision	1991 Revision	1996 Revision
MAI 22.03	1995 Revision	1989 Revision	1996 Revision
MAI 22.04	Withdrawn 1993	Withdrawn	Withdrawn
MAI 22.05	1981 Revision	1996 Revision	1981 Revision
MAI 22.06	1969 New	1991 Revision	1991 Revision
MAI 22.07	1991 Revision	1991 Revision	1996 Revision
MAI 22.08	1978 New	1990 New	1996 Revision
MAI 22.09	1993 New	1993 New	1993 New
XXIII	Chapter 23.00—Verdict Directing—International Torts		
MAI 23.01	1981 Revision	1981 Revision	1981 Revision
MAI 23.02	1990 Revision	1990 Revision	1996 Revision
MAI 23.03	1965 New	1990 Revision	1996 Revision
MAI 23.04	1983 Revision	1980 Revision	1990 Revision
MAI 23.05	1996 Revision	1996 Revision	1996 Revision
MAI 23.06	Withdrawn 1980	—	—
MAI 23.06(1)	1980 New	1980 New	1980 New
MAI 23.06(2)	1980 New	1980 New	1990 Revision
MAI 23.07	2000 Revision	2000 Revision	1996 Revision
MAI 23.08	1990 Revision	1990 Revision	1990 Revision
MAI 23.09	Withdrawn 1980	—	—
MAI 23.10	Withdrawn 1980	—	—
MAI 23.10(1)	1980 New	1980 New	1995 Revision
MAI 23.10(2)	1980 New	1980 New	1995 Revision

INSTRUCTION NO.	INSTRUCTION	NOTES ON USE	COMMITTEE COMMENT
MAI 23.11	1981 Revision	1991 Revision	1991 Revision
MAI 23.12(1)	1989 New	1989 New	1989 New
MAI 23.12(2)	1989 New	1989 New	1989 New
MAI 23.13	2000 New	2000 New	2000 New

XXIV   Chapter 24.00—Verdict Directing—F.E.L.A.

MAI 24.01	1992 Revision	1992 Revision	1978 New
MAI 24.02	1981 Revision	1981 Revision	—
MAI 24.03	1981 Revision	1981 Revision	—

XXV   Chapter 25.00—Verdict Directing—Breach of Warranty and Product Liability

MAI 25.01	1981 Revision	1981 New	1965 New
MAI 25.02	1981 Revision	1981 New	1996 Revision
MAI 25.03	1980 Revision	1980 Revision	1980 Revision
MAI 25.04	1978 Revision	1991 Revision	1978 Revision
MAI 25.05	1978 New	1991 Revision	—
MAI 25.06	Withdrawn 1990	—	—
MAI 25.07	1991 Revision	1991 Revision	1991 Revision
MAI 25.08	1980 New	1991 Revision	1991 Revision
MAI 25.09	1990 New	1990 New	1990 New
MAI 25.10(A)	1990 New	1990 New	1995 New
MAI 25.10(B)	1995 Revision	1990 New	1995 Revision

XXVI   Chapter 26.00—Verdict Directing—Contract

MAI 26.01	1980 Revision	1980 Revision	—
MAI 26.02	1980 Revision	1980 Revision	—
MAI 26.03	1969 New	1969 New	—
MAI 26.04	1981 Revision	1981 Revision	—
MAI 26.05	1980 Revision	1980 Revision	1991 New
MAI 26.06	1981 Revision	1980 Revision	1973 New
MAI 26.07	1981 Revision	1980 New	1980 New

XXVII   Chapter 27.00—Verdict Directing—Ejectment

MAI 27.01	1981 Revision	1981 Revision	—
MAI 27.02	1981 Revision	1981 Revision	—
MAI 27.03	1978 New	1978 New	1978 New
MAI 27.04	1981 Revision	1981 Revision	1978 New

XXVIII   Chapter 28.00—Recovery for Services Furnished Decedent

MAI 28.00	1980 Revision	—	—
MAI 28.01	1969 New	1991 Revision	1969 New
MAI 28.02	1969 New	1969 New	1969 New
MAI 28.03	1969 New	1969 New	1969 New
MAI 28.04	1969 New	1969 New	1969 New

XXIX   Chapter 29.00—Verdict Directing—Real Estate Commissions

MAI 29.01	1978 Revision	1978 Revision	1996 Revision
MAI 29.02	1978 Revision	1978 Revision	1991 Revision
MAI 29.03	1978 Revision	1978 Revision	1978 Revision
MAI 29.04	1978 Revision	1978 Revision	1978 Revision
MAI 29.05	Withdrawn 1980	—	—

TABLE OF EFFECTIVE DATES

INSTRUCTION NO.	INSTRUCTION	NOTES ON USE	COMMITTEE COMMENT
XXX	Chapter 30.00—Verdict Directing—Third Party Plaintiff		
MAI 30.01	1969 New	1980 Revision	1969 New
MAI 30.02	1969 New	1969 New	1969 New
MAI 30.03	1969 New	1991 Revision	1969 New
XXXI	Chapter 31.00—Verdict Directing—Miscellaneous		
MAI 31.01	Withdrawn 1978	—	—
MAI 31.02(1)	1997 Revision	1997 Revision	1997 Revision
MAI 31.02(2)	1997 Revision	1997 Revision	1997 Revision
MAI 31.02(3)	1997 Revision	1997 Revision	1997 Revision
MAI 31.03	1981 Revision	1981 Revision	1996 Revision
MAI 31.04	1991 Revision	1991 New	1991 New
MAI 31.05	1981 Revision	1981 Revision	—
MAI 31.06	1978 Revision	1978 Revision	1995 Revision
MAI 31.07	1978 Revision	1996 Revision	—
MAI 31.08	1978 Revision	1978 Revision	—
MAI 31.09	1978 New	1978 New	—
MAI 31.10	1978 Revision	—	—
MAI 31.11	1996 Revision	1988 Revision	—
MAI 31.12	1978 New	1978 New	—
MAI 31.13	1996 Revision	1988 Revision	—
MAI 31.14	2000 Revision	2000 Revision	2000 New
MAI 31.15	1992 New	1992 New	1996 Revision
MAI 31.16	1995 Revision	1992 New	1995 Revision
MAI 31.17	1992 New	1992 New	1993 Revision
MAI 31.18	1994 New	—	1998 Revision
MAI 31.19	1994 New	1994 New	1998 Revision
MAI 31.20	1994 New	1994 New	1998 New
MAI 31.21	1995 New	1995 New	—
MAI 31.22	1995 New	1995 New	—
MAI 31.23	2000 New	2000 New	2000 New
XXXII	Chapter 32.00—Affirmative Defenses		
MAI 32.01	1991 New	—	—
MAI 32.01(1)	1991 Revision	1991 Revision	—
MAI 32.01(2)	1991 Revision	1991 Revision	—
MAI 32.01(3)	1991 Revision	1991 Revision	—
MAI 32.02	1991 Revision	1991 Revision	1969 New
MAI 32.03	1991 Revision	1991 Revision	1969 New
MAI 32.04	1991 Revision	1991 Revision	1969 New
MAI 32.05	1991 Revision	1991 Revision	—
MAI 32.06	1991 Revision	1991 Revision	1996 Revision
MAI 32.07	Withdrawn 1996	Withdrawn 1996	—
32.07(A)	1996 New	1996 New	1996 New
32.07(B)	1996 New	1996 New	1996 New
MAI 32.08	1969 New	—	1969 New
MAI 32.09	1969 New	1969 New	1969 New
MAI 32.10	1969 New	—	1969 New
MAI 32.11	1998 Revision	1981 Revision	1981 Revision
MAI 32.12	1969 New	—	1988 Revision
MAI 32.13	1978 Revision	1978 New	1978 Revision

	INSTRUCTION NO.	INSTRUCTION	NOTES ON USE	COMMITTEE COMMENT
	MAI 32.14	1969 New	—	1969 New
	MAI 32.15	1969 New	—	1969 New
	MAI 32.16	1969 New	1969 New	1969 New
	MAI 32.17	1995 Revision	1995 New	—
	MAI 32.18	1969 New	1995 Revision	—
	MAI 32.19	1981 Revision	1981 New	1981 Revision
	MAI 32.20	1981 Revision	1969 New	1969 New
	MAI 32.21	1978 Revision	1978 New	—
	MAI 32.22	1978 Revision	1978 Revision	1969 New
	MAI 32.23	1978 Revision	1978 Revision	1991 Revision
	MAI 32.24	1978 New	—	1978 New
	MAI 32.25	1981 New	1981 New	1981 New
	MAI 32.26	1990 New	1990 New	—
	MAI 32.27	1990 New	1990 New	—
	MAI 32.28	1995 Revision	1989 New	1995 Revision
	MAI 32.29	2002 New	2002 New	2002 New
XXXIII	Chapter 33.00—Converse Instructions			
	MAI 33.01	1996 Revision	—	—
	MAI 33.02	Withdrawn 1980	—	—
	MAI 33.03	1995 Revision	1995 Revision	—
	MAI 33.04	1995 Revision	1995 Revision	—
	MAI 33.05	Withdrawn 1988	—	—
	MAI 33.05(1)	1993 Revision	1996 Revision	1993 New
	MAI 33.05(2)	1988 New	1996 Revision	1988 New
	MAI 33.06	Withdrawn 1990	—	—
	MAI 33.07	Withdrawn 1980	—	—
	MAI 33.08	Withdrawn 1980	—	—
	MAI 33.09	Withdrawn 1980	—	—
	MAI 33.10	Withdrawn 1980	—	—
	MAI 33.11	Withdrawn 1980	—	—
	MAI 33.12	Withdrawn 1980	—	—
	MAI 33.13	Withdrawn 1980	—	—
	MAI 33.14	Withdrawn 1980	—	—
	MAI 33.15	1995 Revision	1996 Revision	—
	MAI 33.16	1991 New	1991 New	—
XXXIV	Chapter 34.00—Withdrawal Instructions			
	MAI 34.01	1978 Revision	—	—
	MAI 34.02	1978 Revision	1969 New	1969 New
	MAI 34.03	1969 New	1969 New	—
	MAI 34.04	1978 New	1978 New	—
	MAI 34.05	1991 Revision	1991 Revision	1983 New
XXXV	Chapter 35.00—Illustrations			
	MAI 35.00	1996 Revision	—	—
	MAI 35.01	Withdrawn 1991	—	—
	MAI 35.02 (No. 4)	1998 Revision	—	—
	MAI 35.02	1996 Revision	—	1983 Revision
	MAI 35.03 (No. 4)	1998 Revision	—	—
	MAI 35.03	1996 Revision	—	1979 New

INSTRUCTION NO.	INSTRUCTION	NOTES ON USE	COMMITTEE COMMENT
MAI 35.04 (No. 4)	1998 Revision	—	—
MAI 35.04	1996 Revision	—	1991 New
MAI 35.05 (No. 5)	1998 Revision	—	—
MAI 35.05	1996 Revision	—	1996 Revision
MAI 35.06(1)	Withdrawn 1991	—	—
MAI 35.06(2)	Withdrawn 1991	—	—
MAI 35.07 (No. 3)	1998 Revision	—	—
MAI 35.07	1996 Revision	—	1980 New
MAI 35.08	1996 Revision	—	1980 New
MAI 35.09	1996 Revision	—	1983 Revision
MAI 35.10 (No. 4)	1998 Revision	—	—
MAI 35.10	1996 Revision	—	1991 Revision
MAI 35.11	Withdrawn 1991	—	—
MAI 35.12	1996 Revision	—	1995 Revision
MAI 35.13	Withdrawn 1985	—	—
MAI 35.14 (No. 4)	1998 Revision	—	—
MAI 35.14	1996 Revision	—	1986 New
MAI 35.15 (No. 4)	1998 Revision	—	—
MAI 35.15	1996 Revision	—	1996 Revision
MAI 35.16 (No. 4)	1998 Revision	—	—
MAI 35.16	1996 Revision	—	1991 New
MAI 35.17 (No. 4)	1998 Revision	—	—
MAI 35.17	1996 Revision	—	1991 New
MAI 35.18 (No. 4)	1998 Revision	—	—
MAI 35.18	1996 Revision	—	1991 New
MAI 35.19 (No. 4)	1998 Revision	—	—
MAI 35.19	1996 Revision	1992 New	1992 New
MAI 35.20	1998 New	—	—
MAI 35.21	2002 New	—	2002 New
MAI 35.22	2002 New	—	2002 New

XXXVI Chapter 36.00—Forms of Verdict

INSTRUCTION NO.	INSTRUCTION	NOTES ON USE	COMMITTEE COMMENT
MAI 36.01	1980 Revision	1980 New	—
MAI 36.02	1981 Revision	1980 New	—
MAI 36.03	Withdrawn 1980	—	—
MAI 36.04	Withdrawn 1980	—	—
MAI 36.05	1980 Revision	1996 Revision	—
MAI 36.06	1980 Revision	1980 New	—
MAI 36.07	Withdrawn 1980	—	—
MAI 36.08	Withdrawn 1980	—	—
MAI 36.09	Withdrawn 1980	—	—
MAI 36.10	1980 Revision	1980 New	1996 New
MAI 36.11	1980 Revision	1980 New	—
MAI 36.12	1980 Revision	1996 Revision	—

TABLE OF EFFECTIVE DATES

INSTRUCTION NO.	INSTRUCTION	NOTES ON USE	COMMITTEE COMMENT
MAI 36.13	1980 Revision	1980 New	1980 New
MAI 36.14	1980 Revision	1980 New	—
MAI 36.15	1979 New	1979 New	1996 Revision
MAI 36.16	1979 New	1996 Revision	—
MAI 36.17	Withdrawn 1995	—	—
MAI 36.17(A)	1995 New	1995 New	—
MAI 36.17(B)	1995 New	1995 New	—
MAI 36.18	1983 New	1983 New	—
MAI 36.19	1983 New	1983 New	—
MAI 36.20	1988 New	1988 New	1988 New
MAI 36.21	1988 New	2002 Revision	1988 New
MAI 36.22	1988 New	2002 Revision	1988 New
MAI 36.23	1991 New	1991 New	—
MAI 36.24	1995 Revision	1993 New	1995 Revision
MAI 36.25	1995 Revision	2002 Revision	1995 Revision
MAI 36.26	1994 New	1994 New	—
MAI 36.27	1994 New	2002 Revision	—
MAI 36.28	1994 New	—	1998 Revision

XXXVII   Chapter 37.00—Comparative Fault

INSTRUCTION NO.	INSTRUCTION	NOTES ON USE	COMMITTEE COMMENT
MAI 37.01	1986 New	1986 New	1986 New
MAI 37.02	1986 New	1986 New	1996 New
MAI 37.03	1986 New	2002 Revision	1986 New
MAI 37.04	1986 New	1986 New	—
MAI 37.05(1)	1991 Revision	1986 New	1996 Revision
MAI 37.05(2)	1986 New	—	1986 New
MAI 37.06	1986 New	1986 New	1986 New
MAI 37.07	1986 New	1986 New	1998 New
MAI 37.08	1991 New	2002 Revision	1991 New
MAI 37.09	1991 New	1991 New	1998 New

TABLE OF STATUTES

TABLE OF STATUTES

TABLE OF RULES

TABLE OF CASES

TABLE OF CASES

810

TABLE OF CASES

TABLE OF CASES

813

TABLE OF CASES

TABLE OF CASES

TABLE OF CASES

TABLE OF CASES

821

TABLE OF CASES

TABLE OF CASES

TABLE OF CASES

TABLE OF CASES

TABLE OF CASES

TABLE OF CASES

828

TABLE OF CASES

829

TABLE OF CASES

TABLE OF CASES

TABLE OF CASES

TABLE OF CASES

TABLE OF CASES

INDEX

INDEX

INDEX

INDEX

INDEX

INDEX

INDEX

INDEX

INDEX

INDEX

INDEX

INDEMNITY OR INDEMNIFICATION
Forms of verdict, crossclaim for indemnity, 36.06

INDEPENDENT CONTRACTOR
Verdict directing, inherently dangerous activity, 31.15

INDIVIDUAL TORTFEASORS
Forms of verdict, uninsured motor vehicle, 36.13

INDUCEMENT
Intentional torts, inducement of apprehension, 23.03

INHERENTLY DANGEROUS ACTIVITY
Defined, 16.08
Verdict directing, 31.15

INSURANCE AND INSURANCE COMPANIES
Affirmative defenses
      Generally, 32.24
  Life Insurance, this index
Exemplary damages, insurance company's vexatious refusal to pay, 10.08
Forms of verdict
      Generally, 36.10
  Uninsured motor vehicle, 36.13
Life Insurance, this index
Motor vehicles. Uninsured Motor Vehicle, this index
Property insurance, 31.09
Uninsured Motor Vehicle, this index
Verdict directing
  Life insurance policy, 31.08
  Property insurance, 31.09

INTENT
Torts. Intentional Torts, this index

INTENTIONAL TORTS
Apprehension, inducement of, 23.03
Assault, 23.01
Battery, 23.02, 23.03
Contract, tortious interference with, 23.11
Conversion, 23.12(1), 23.12(2)
Criminal actions, malicious prosecution, 23.07
Discharge from employment, workers' compensation, 23.13
Discrimination in employment, workers' compensation, 23.13
Exemplary damages, 10.01
False imprisonment, 23.04
Fraudulent misrepresentations, 23.05
Inducement of apprehension, 23.03
Interference with contract, 23.11
Letters, service letters, 23.08
Libel or slander. Verdict directing, below
Malicious prosecution, 23.07
Per se libel or slander, 23.09, 23.10
Public figure, libel or slander, 23.06(1), 23.06(2), 23.10(1), 23.10(2)
Public official, libel or slander, 23.06(1), 23.06(2), 23.10(1), 23.10(2)
Retaliatory discharge, 23.13
Service letters, 23.08
Slander. Verdict directing, below
Surrender of possession failure, conversion, 23.12(2)
Verdict directing
  Apprehension, inducement of, 23.03
  Assault, 23.01
  Battery, 23.02, 23.03
  Contract, tortious interference with, 23.11
  Conversion, 23.12(1), 23.12(2)

INDEX

INDEX

856

INDEX

INDEX

INDEX

PERCENTAGES
Damages, broker's commission agreement, 4.05

PERFORMANCE
Definition of substantial performance, 16.04

PERSONAL INJURIES
Children and minors, medical malpractice illustrations, 35.20
Comparative Fault, this index
Damages
      Generally, 4.18
   Federal Employers' Liability Act, injury to employee, 8.02
Federal Employers' Liability Act, damages for injury to employee under, 8.02
Forms of verdict, 36.01-36.04
Head-on collision, 35.16
Health care provider, 35.18
Husband and Wife, this index
Illustrations
   Comparative fault, 35.04, 35.16-35.18
   Head-on collision, 35.16
   Health care provider, comparative fault, 35.18
   Husband and wife, personal injuries and loss of consortium, 35.06(1), 35.06(2)
   Medical malpractice, minor injured, 35.20
   Rear-end collision, 35.17
   Right angle collision, 35.04
Loss of consortium, 35.06(1), 35.06(2)
Medical malpractice, 35.20
Owners and Occupiers of Land, this index
Rear-end collision, 35.17
Right angle collision, 35.04
Verdict directing. Owners and Occupiers of Land, this index

PERSONAL PROPERTY
Damages, 4.01
Product liability, breach of warranty of title to personalty, 25.01

PHYSICAL FACTS
Exclusions, physical facts instructions, 1.05

PLACE OR LOCATION
Federal Employers' Liability Act, failure to provide safe place to work, 24.01

PREPAYMENT
Advancement or Prepayment, this index

PRIMARY NEGLIGENCE
Illustrations, 35.11

PRINCIPAL
Agency, this index

PRINCIPAL AND INTEREST
Forms of verdict, 36.09

PRIOR TRIAL
Illustrations, apportionment of fault, 35.02

PRIVATE NUISANCE
Owners and occupiers of land, 22.06

PRIVILEGES AND IMMUNITIES
Verdict directing, waiver of sovereign immunity, 31.16, 31.17

PRODUCT LIABILITY
Affirmative defenses, contributory fault, 32.23
Defective product, generally, 25.04
Design, negligent design, 25.09

INDEX

INDEX

INDEX

INDEX

INDEX

INDEX

INDEX